DICTIONARY OF NAUTICAL
WORDS AND TERMS

DICTIONARY

OF

NAUTICAL WORDS
AND TERMS

8000 Definitions in Navigation, Seamanship, Rigging, Meteorology,
Astronomy, Naval Architecture, Average, Ship Economics,
Hydrography, Cargo Stowage, Marine Engineering,
Ice Terminology, Buoyage, Yachting, etc.

BY

C. W. T. LAYTON, *F.R.A.S., M.R.I.N., Assoc.R.I.N.A.*

REVISED BY

PETER CLISSOLD

*Commander R.N.R. (Retd.), Master Mariner, Younger Brother
of Trinity House, Fellow of the Royal Institute of Navigation.*

GLASGOW
BROWN, SON & FERGUSON, LTD., NAUTICAL PUBLISHERS
4-10 DARNLEY STREET, G41 2SD

First Edition	–	1955
Reprinted –	–	1958
Second Edition	–	1967
Revised	–	1973
Reprinted –	–	1978
Revised	–	1982

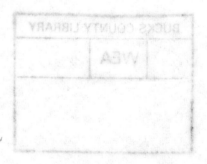

ISBN 0 85174 422 2 (Revised Second Edition)
ISBN 0 85174 296 3

© 1982 Brown, Son & Ferguson, Ltd., Glasgow, G41 2SD
Printed and Made in Great Britain

PREFACE

THIS book has been compiled to embody, in one volume, the words and terms that are, or have been, used by seamen in connection with their work. It deals with navigation, seamanship, rigging, meteorology, astronomy, naval architecture, average, ship economics, hydrography, cargo stowage, marine engineering, ice terminology, buoyage, yachting, and other nautical matters.

The number of entries is nearly 8000; as many of these entries bear more than one definition—some having as many as five—the total number of definitions given approximates 8600.

Every endeavour has been made to extend the scope of the book through as wide a range of subjects ancillary to nautical work as would be helpful and interesting to the professional mariner and to the enquiring layman. The book ranges through numerous aspects of nautical activity and through many centuries of navigation and seamanship.

For the shortcomings that may be found I offer my apologies to the reader.

C. W. T. LAYTON

DICTIONARY

OF

NAUTICAL WORDS

AND TERMS

(*) Indicates that the word or term is now obsolete or obsolescent.

A.1. Classification symbol denoting character of a vessel well constructed and efficiently equipped—letter referring to her construction, figure denoting equipment. A numeral, not exceeding 100, is usually prefixed to vessels built of iron or steel; some vessels built for special trades or purposes may not have the numeral. Roughly speaking, the numeral can be looked upon as a percentage of perfection.

A. When applied to a temperature, denotes that it has been measured from Absolute zero and is expressed in Centigrade or Celsius units.

Abaca. Philippine plant, of plantain genus, from which manilla hemp is made.

Aback. Said of a sail when the wind is on the fore side of it.

Abaft. On the after side of. Further towards the stern.

Abandonment. Surrender of an insured vessel and of all claims to ownership. Made by owners to underwriters when vessel is a constructive total loss and insurance is to be paid.

Abandonment of Voyage. Renunciation of, or withdrawal from, an intended voyage—whether done voluntarily or through force of circumstances.

Abandon Ship. Entirely to vacate a ship and to relinquish, or to repudiate, all duties towards her preservation. Done only when the carrying out of these duties is impossible, or when the destruction of the ship is imminent.

Abeam. Position or direction that lies at right angles to ship's fore and aft line.

Aberration. 'A wandering from the path.' In astronomy, is the difference between the true and apparent positions of a heavenly body when caused by Earth's movement in space: it is too small

1

to affect navigation. In meteorology, is the difference between directions of true and apparent winds that is caused by ship's movement when inclined to wind direction. In optics, is the deviation of light rays from a true focus.

Able Seaman. An experienced seaman competent to perform the usual and customary duties on deck. In sailing ships, had to be able to 'hand, reef and steer'. In Merchant Navy, has to have served satisfactorily on deck and pass an exam. In Royal Navy, has to have served a specified period at sea and satisfactorily completed certain courses of instruction.

Abnormal Refraction. Displacement of visible horizon and observed objects by an unusual amount. Objects that would, normally, be below horizon may be seen above it. Usual check is by 'Back Altitude'.

Aboard. On board. In, into or inside a vessel. Close alongside.

'Aboard Main Tack.' Order to haul main tack down to chess tree. Given when sailing close-hauled in a square-rigged ship.

Abordage.* The act of boarding and taking an enemy vessel.

About. Used, in conjunction with other word or words, with reference to changing from one tack to the other when under sail.

About Ship. To put a ship, under sail, on the opposite tack. 2. Order to crew to go to stations for tacking or wearing.

A-Box. Said of yards when those on one mast are braced in a direction opposite to that of yards on next mast.

'A' Bracket. Forging that carries after end of propeller shaft in twin-screw vessel. Upper arm is secured to shell plating or to a plate inside vessel, lower arm is secured to keel or to a steel casing on keel.

Abreast. Said of ships on parallel courses when abeam of each other. Objects inside a ship are abreast when they are in the same transverse line.

Abroad.* Said of a flag, or sail, when it is hoisted or extended.

Absence Without Leave. Remaining away from ship without permission, but not showing intention of deserting.

Absentee. One who fails to return to his ship, or place of duty, but who has not shown any intention to desert.

Absolute Force. In magnetism, is intensity of Earth's magnetism, or of a magnet's force, expressed in dynes.

Absolute Humidity. Weight of water held in a given volume of atmospheric air. Usually expressed in grammes per cubic metre.

Absolute Pressure. Pressure of a fluid measured above a perfect vaccum. In practical engineering, it is taken as steam pressure plus 15 lbs. Absolute pressure of condenser is taken to be—in barometric inches—half height of barometer minus vacuum reading.

Absolute Temperature. Temperature measured from an Absolute zero at which there is an entire absence of heat. Zero is equivalent to $-273 \cdot 1°C$ ($-459 \cdot 58°F$). Usually measured in Centigrade units.

Absolute Total Loss. Complete destruction, or removal, of ship or goods from hands of owners; or such a change in them that they cease to be what they were. Term is used, also, in assessment of loss of ship; absolute loss including loss of freight that ship was earning.

Absorption Coefficient. Amount of radiation absorbed by a given surface when expressed as a proportion of the radiation falling on it.

Absorptive Power. Rate at which radiant energy is absorbed at surface of a body. Varies with temperature and wavelength of the energy.

A-Burton. Stowage of casks, barrels, etc., so that they lie lengthwise athwartships.

Abyss. That volume of ocean lying below 300 fathoms from surface.

Abyssal. Pertaining to the abyss.

Acalephae. Class of sea creatures that sting if touched. Includes jellyfish and 'Portuguese man o' war'.

Acamar. Star θ Eridani. S.H.A. 316°; Dec. S 40°; Mag. 3·1.

Acceleration. A hastening or increase in rate of motion. In astronomy, is an apparent gaining of one heavenly body upon another when due to superior speed, a difference of direction, or both of these.

Acceleration of Fixed Stars. Progressive earliness of fixed star transits as compared with Sun's transits. Owing to Sun's eastward movement along Ecliptic, stars transit any meridian nearly four minutes earlier each day when referred to solar time.

Acceleration of Planetary Motion. Increase in a planet's angular velocity when travelling from aphelion to perihelion (in accordance with Kepler's second law).

Acceleration of Sidereal Time. Amount of sidereal time gained by a sidereal clock in any given interval of mean solar time.

Acceleration of Wind. Apparent increase in wind-force when due to ship approaching direction of wind.

Acceleration Tables. Give the amount by which any mean time value of an interval must be increased to give the sidereal time value.

Acceptance. A signing of a document as evidence of having read it, and of readiness to fulfil its requirements.

Accident Boat. Boat that is kept turned out and ready for instant manning and lowering in case of emergency.

Accident Report. Statement rendered to Department of T. & I. by Master when a British ship has been damaged, or when serious injury or death has been caused on board by any accident.

Accommodation. Spaces in ship set apart for messrooms, sleeping places, ablutions and recreation. Statutory allowance of floor space varies from 12 square feet and upwards for each person.

Accommodation Ladder. Sloping series of steps, usually of wood, fitted with handrails and extending from waterline to an entry into ship, to facilitate safe embarkation and disembarkation.

Account Position by.* 'Estimated Position.'

Account of Wages Book. Supplied by Shipping Office to Master when engaging crew. Accounts of each member of crew are kept in duplicate, one copy being given to man, and the other to Shipping Office, when paying off.

Accul.* Old name for an arm of the sea with no port or river.

Accumulated Rate. The daily rate of a chronometer multiplied by number of days since last comparison.

Accumulator. An electric storage battery.

Accumulator Capacity. Storage power of an accumulator; usually expressed in ampere-hours.

Accustomed Average. 'Average accustomed.'

Achernar. Star α Eridani. R.A. 01h 36m; Dec. S 57°; Mag. 0·6. S.H.A. 336°. Diameter is four times that of Sun, candlepower is 200 times greater. Distant 66 light years.

Achromatic Lens. Two or more lenses, in combination, that correct the chromatic aberration always present in single lens.

Acidity of Boiler Water. Is a result of impurities in it. Usually ascertained by use of litmus paper or methyl orange.

Acker. Alternative name for 'Eagre'.

Acker's Time Scale. First system of time allowances in yacht racing. Introduced, 1843, by G. Holland Acker. Based on length of course and tonnage.

Acker's Yacht Code. System of yacht signalling embodied in Acker's 'Universal Yacht Signals'.

Ackman.* One who steals from a ship in navigable waters. A fresh water pirate.

Acknowledgement. Formal admission that something has been received, or that some specified service has been rendered, or that certain liabilities have been incurred.

Aclinic Line. Magnetic equator. Line passing through all positions on Earth at which there is no magnetic dip.

A-Cockbill. State of an anchor when suspended from cathead by the cathead stopper only. State of a yard when one yard arm is topped by the lift, the other arm being boused down. This is done when using yard as a derrick; also done to prevent yard projecting over the side when vessel is berthed.

Acorn. Ornamental finish, resembling an acorn, at head of an upper wooden mast.

Acquittance. Formal and written discharge from a specified duty, liability or undertaking.

Acrab. Name sometimes given to star β Scorpii.

Acronical. Said of a heavenly body that rises at sunset and sets at sunrise.

Acrostolion.* Bow ornament, usually circular or spiral, carried by ancient warships.

Acrux. Star α Crucis. S.H.A. 174°; Dec. S 63°; Mag. 1·1.

Actinometer. Instrument for measuring intensity of Sun's rays, or of actinic rays.

Actinozoa. Class of sea creatures that includes jelly fish, sea anemones and the coral polyps responsible for coral reefs.

Action. Engagement or battle with hostile ships or forces.

Action Stations. Positions manned by personnel of a warship when battle is imminent.

Active Bond. A written undertaking to pay that commences to earn interest directly it is issued.

Act of God. Casualty due to extraordinary natural causes and circumstances, to which there was no human contribution, and which could not have been foreseen or averted by the exercise of any amount of reasonable intelligence or endeavour.

Actual Total Loss. 'Absolute Total Loss.'

Address Commission. Commission payable at discharging port.

Adhara. Star ε Canis Major. S.H.A. 256°; Dec. S 29°; Mag. 1·6.

Adiabatic. Applied to changes in temperature, pressure or volume of a fluid when occurring without heat being taken in or given up.

Adiabatic Lapse Rate. Falling rate of temperature of atmosphere by 5·4°F for each 1000 feet of height (0·98°C per 100 metres). Due to atmospheric expansion through reduced pressure.

Adie Barometer. Former name of a 'Kew Pattern' barometer.

Adjustment. Putting into correct relationship, or into proper place.

Adjustment of Average. *See* 'Average Adjustment'.

Adjustment of Instruments. Correct setting of those parts that have variable positions, or that have become displaced.

Adjustment of Magnetic Compass. Name loosely given to the compensation made at a magnetic compass.

Adjustments of Sextant. Comprise the setting of index and horizon mirrors so that they are perpendicular to plane of arc, setting the mirrors parallel when the index is at zero, setting line of collimation parallel to plane of arc.

Admiral. Naval officer competent to command a fleet of ships. In Elizabethan times denoted ship in which senior officer of a group of ships was borne. In the fishing fleet, may be applied to the senior skipper of a group of drifters working in company.

Admiral of the Blue.* Originally, admiral commanding rear division of a fleet. Later, a rear-admiral.

Admiral of the Fleet. Highest rank in Royal Navy. Distinguishing flag is Union Flag at mainmast head.

Admiral of the Red.* Senior admiral, commanding centre division of a fleet. Later, an admiral.

Admiral of the White.* Originally, admiral commanding van division of a fleet. Later, a vice-admiral.

Admiralty. Control of the seas. 2. The Lords Commissioners for executing the office of Lord High Admiral of Great Britain, etc. 3. The Board of Admiralty. 4. The buildings in which the offices of the Board of Admiralty are situated.

Admiralty Charts. Charts produced and issued by the Hydrographic Department of the Admiralty.

Admiralty Coefficients. Values used for comparing efficiency of hull forms. Based on displacement, speed, indicated horse power, and fuel consumption.

Admiralty Court. Usual name for the 'High Court of Admiralty' in which shipping cases are investigated and adjudicated upon.

Admiralty Flag. The proper flag of the Lord High Admiral of Great Britain, and of the Lords Commissioners for executing that office. Is a red flag with a horizontal yellow anchor.

Admiralty Hitch. Name sometimes given to a marline spike hitch.

Admiralty List of Lights, Fog Signals and Visual Time Signals. Nine volumes, arranged geographically, giving full particulars of navigational aids mentioned in title. Do not give particulars of buoyage.

Admiralty List of Radio Signals. Volumes published by Hydrographic Department of Admiralty. Give general regulations and signals for communicating with coast stations and services; give details of Radio Beacons, Time Signals, Ice and Navigational Warnings, etc.

Admiralty Method of Tidal Predictions. Method of finding tidal state at a required position by use of data in Admiralty Tide Tables and in conjunction with form H.D. 289.

Admiralty Pattern Anchor. Older type of anchor in which shank and arms are fixed and stock is at right angles to arms.

Admiralty Sailing Directions. Series of volumes, issed by Hydrographic Department of Admiralty, covering all navigable waters of the world. Give all possible information to the navigator concerning navigation in the waters they cover. Often called 'Pilots'.

Admiralty Tide Tables. Volumes giving daily predictions of times of high and low waters at principal ports and positions in the world, together with data and instructions for obtaining times and height of high and low water at ports for which predictions are not given.

Admiralty Warrant. Official authority from Admiralty to wear a blue ensign, a red ensign defaced or a yacht club burgee on a British vessel. Warrants are issued for other purposes.

Adrift. Unattached to the shore or ground and at the mercy of wind and tide. Colloquially used to mean missing from its place; absent from place of duty; broken away from fastening.

Adult. Passage rates in emigrant and passenger ships consider any person of 12 years of age, or over, to be an adult. Two persons less than 12 years of age count as an adult.

Ad Valorem. According to value. Used when goods referred to are assessed by their value, and not by weight or quantity.

Advance. Distance between position at which a vessel commences to alter course and the position at which she is on her new course. It is measured along a line parallel to original course.

Advance Freight. Proportion of contracted freight that may be paid on completion of loading, if mutually agreed. As freight is not due until cargo is delivered, this advance is debited with insurance and interest charges.

Advance Note. Issued, at Master's option, to a newly-engaged seaman. Authorises payment of a stated sum to the holder of the note after man has sailed in ship. Charged to a man's account. Rarely exceeds one month's wages.

Advection. In meteorology, denotes the horizontal transfer of heat by air currents.

Adventure. In insurance, is any undertaking that involves a risk or hazard.

Advertise. To announce or publish in such a manner that a matter should come to the notice of those concerned in normal circumstances.

Advice. Formal notification of information concerning a transaction.

Advice Boat.* Small vessel employed in distributing written or verbal orders and information to vessels of a fleet or squadron.

Aerial. Single wire, or system of wires, forming a radio antenna (U.S. 'antenna').

Aerolite. Meteorite that consists mainly of stone.

Aerology. Study of the atmosphere, particularly the upper reaches of it.

Affidavit. Solemn declaration made before a person legally authorised to administer an oath.

Affirmed. Ratified and confirmed.

Affreight.* To charter or hire a ship.

Affreightment. The chartering or hiring of a ship.

Afloat. Completely waterborne.

Afore.* Forward of; before.

Aft. Towards the stern; near the stern. Sometimes used as denoting officers' quarters. Applied to wind, means within four points from right aft.

After. Further aft; nearer the stern.

After date. In a financial document, means 'after date mentioned in document.'

Afterglow. Sunlight reflected from high clouds in west after Sun has set.

Afterguard. Originally, the hands who worked the after sails, and who were frequently berthed aft. Later, become synonymous with officers—for the same reason.

After Leech. Lee leech of a square sail when yard is braced round. Sometimes used, incorrectly, for leech of a trysail—to differentiate it from the luff (or 'fore leech').

After part. That part of a vessel, or of any space or fitting in a vessel, that is nearer the stern. 2. That part of a watch who work, or would have worked, the after sails.

After Peak. Enclosed space immediately forward of stern frame. Enclosed by a transverse bulkhead and side and bottom plating. Used as a ballast tank or store.

After Sight. In a financial document, means 'After payer has endorsed it as an acknowledgement of sighting it.'

After Swim. Submerged after part of hull that is shaped to give a lead in for water to propeller and rudder, and to give increased area of water plane with increased draught.

Aftmost. Furthest aft. Nearest the stern.

Against the Sun. Anti-clockwise circular motion. Left-handed ropes are coiled down in this way.

Agent. One who acts for another. In ship's business, is one who acts for one or more of the parties interested in the charter. The same agent may act on behalf of the shipowner and the charterer.

Age of Diurnal Inequality. Interval between instant of Moon's transit and the occurrence of maximum declinational effect in tide. By harmonic constants: Age of Diurnal Inequality= -0.91 $(K°-O°)$.

Age of Diurnal Tide. Interval between time of Moon's maximum declination and time of the following diurnal spring tide.

Age of Moon. Internal, in days and fractions, since Moon was new. Maximum value if about $29\frac{1}{2}$ days.

Age of Parallax Inequality. Interval between instant when Moon is in perigee and occurrence of maximum parallactic effect in tide. Usual value is between one and three days after.

Age of Phase Inequality. 'Age of Tide.'

Age of Semidiurnal Tide. Interval between syzygy and occurrence of spring semidiurnal tide.

Age of Tide. Interval between syzygy and the occurrence of the spring tide due to it. Value may be from more than 7 days after syzygy to nearly a day before it. Average age of British tide is about $1\frac{1}{2}$ days.

Ageton's Tables. H.O. 211 (U.S.A.) give, by inspection, azimuth and calculated altitude when latitude, hour angle, altitude and declination are known.

Agger. Name sometimes given to a 'double tide'.

Aggregate. Sand or other material mixed with cement when making concrete. For marine work sand is usual, and may be used in proportion of up to six times the amount of cement.

Aggregate Freight. Balance of freight due at port of delivery when all additions and deductions, for demurrage, advanced freight, etc., have been taken into account.

Aggregating Clause. Clause, in any agreement, that allows several items to be collected under one heading. One of the 'Institute' clauses.

Agonic Line. Line on Earth's surface that passes through all places where there is no magnetic variation of compass.

Agreement. Short name for 'Articles of Agreement' entered into by Master and crew of a vessel.

Aground. State of a vessel when she ceases to be completely water-borne and her weight is taken, partially or completely, by the ground.

Agulhas Current. Warm current flowing southward and westward from Mozambique Channel and Indian Ocean to SE Coast of Africa. Width is up to 50 miles; rate is occasionally nearly 4 knots.

A.H. Initials of 'Anno Hegirae' (the year of the Flight of Mahomet). Epoch of Mahommedan Calendar, A.D. 622.

Ahead. Direction in front of ship. Position in front of ship.

'Ahoy.' Seaman's call to attract attention. Said, on good authority, to be a Viking cry.

A-Hull. Said of a vessel riding out a gale broadside on, under bare poles and with helm lashed a-lee.

Air. Gaseous mixture that forms the atmosphere. Composed of, by volume, 78% nitrogen, 21% oxygen, and traces of neon, helium, krypton, hydrogen, zenon and ozone. Has low thermal conductivity.

Air Almanac. Ephemeris specially compiled for use in air navigation. Arranged in daily pages for ready reference and determination of Greenwich Hour Angles to nearest minute of arc.

Aircraft Carrier. Warship specially designed so that aircraft can take off and alight upon her.

Air Density. Weight of air of a given pressure and in a given volume at a given temperature. At temperature 273°A, pressure 1000mb, density is 0·001276 grammes per cubic centremetre.

Air Mass. Meteorological term for a mass of atmosphere that is bounded by fronts and differs from surrounding atmosphere.

Air Meter. Small portable anemometer, on windmill principle, for measuring wind-speed.

Air Pipe. Pipe that allows air to escape as a tank is filled. 2. Pipe through which air is pumped to a diver.

Air Pocket. Descending current of atmospheric air; such as those that develop on the lee side of steep cliffs.

Air-Speed Indicator. Portable instrument, with pitot head, used for measuring wind velocities between 10 and 70 knots.

Airt. Scottish word for a direction by compass.

Air Thermometer. Thermometer filled with dry air. Expansion and contraction of enclosed air, due to heat content, are measured by pressure required to keep the volume at a constant value. Pressure thus indicates temperature. Range is exceedingly large, readings to −300°F being obtainable.

Airy's Figure of Earth. Dimensions of Earth as computed by Sir George Airy (1801–1892), Astronomer Royal. Equatorial diameter 20,923,715 ft., polar diameter 20,853,810 ft., compression $\frac{1}{299\cdot3}$ Used in British Ordnance Survey.

Airy's Method of Great Circle Sailing. Used for finding position of mid-point in a great circle course between two places when rhumb line is laid off on a Mercator chart. Rhumb line is bisected and a perpendicular to it is extended towards or through Equator. Tables then give latitude in which the great circle course cuts the perpendicular.

Aitken's Nucleus Counter. Instrument for counting number of hygroscopic particles in a given volume of air, which is cooled adiabatically by expansion. Water droplets, each containing a nucleus, are deposited; these are counted with aid of a microscope.

Aker. Name given to a tidal bore sometimes met with in estuaries. Cognate with 'Eagre', 'Acker'.

Al. Arabic word meaning 'The'.

Alba.* Old name for a lighthouse or beacon.

Albacore. Small edible fish of mackerel family. Found near West Indies and in Pacific Ocean.

Albedo. Light reflecting power of Moon, planet or satellite. Value is expressed as a fraction that denotes proportion of light that is reflected. Term may be used in connection with radiations other than light.

Albert Medal. Established by Queen Victoria, in 1866, and awarded for saving life at sea. Later, extended to include saving life on land. Ribbon is blue for sea medals, red for land medals.

Albiero. Star β Cygni. S.H.A. 68°; Dec. N 28°; Mag. 3·2.

Alcor. Name of a small star close to Mizar in Ursa Major. Is often called 'the rider' (of one of the horses of Charles' Wain), or 'the Tester' (of eyesight).

Alcyone. Star α Tauri. S.H.A. 304°; Dec. N 24°; Mag. 3·0. Name is Greek for 'Kingfisher'. At one time was thought to be the central star of the Universe.

Aldebaran. Star Tauri. α R.A. 04h 33m; Dec. N 16°; Mag. 1·1. S.H.A. 292°. Diameter is 60 times that of Sun; distant 57 light years; temperature 3300°A. Is one of the Hyades. Name is Arabic for 'Eye of the Bull'.

Alderamin. Star α Cephei. S.H.A. 41°; Dec. N 62°; Mag. 2·6.

Aldis Signal Lamp. Electric flashing lamp for signalling. Beam is focussed on receiver, and cannot easily be seen by anyone on whom it is not trained or directed. Range exceeds 20 miles.

A-Lee. Towards, or on, that side of a ship that is further from the wind.

Aleutian Current. Ocean current setting S'ly through Aleutian Islands until it meets Alaskan Current, some of which it deflects into the North Pacific Drift.

Aleutian Lows. Meteorological depressions that frequently form over the Aleutian Islands.

Algae. Flowerless aquatic vegetation usually known as seaweed.

Algebar. Name sometimes given to constellation Orion, usually by poets. Means 'The strong and valiant one'.

Algeiba. Star γ Leonis. S.H.A. 206°; Dec. N 20°; Mag. 2·3.

Algenib. Star γ Pegasi. S.H.A. 357°; Dec. N 15°; Mag. 2·9.

Algol. Star β Persei and, also β Medusae. Is a binary star, one dark and one light, and varies between 3rd and 5th magnitudes in less than 3 days. S.H.A. 314°; Dec. N 41°. Name is Arabic for 'ghoul' or 'demon'. Was probably looked upon as the winking eye of a monster.

Alhena. Star γ Geminorum. S.H.A. 261°; Dec. N 16°; Mag. 1·9.

Alidade. Pivoted sight bar that moves over a graduated arc.

Alioth. Star ε Ursae Majoris. S.H.A. 167°; Dec. N 56°; Mag. 1·7.

Alkaid (Benetnasch). Star η Ursae Majoris. S.H.A. 154°; Dec. N 50°. Arabic for 'The Chief'.

All Aback. With the wind on fore side of the sails. Used colloquially to mean 'astounded' or 'flabbergasted'.

All Aboard. Order to embark.

All Hands. All the crew.

All in the Wind. With all sails shaking through wind being on their luffs. Normally occurs when ship passes through wind from one tack to the other, but can also be caused by bad steering when close hauled.

Allonge. Sheets attached to a Bill of Exchange for further endorsements when there is no more room on the Bill itself.

All other Perils. Phrase used in marine insurance policy to mean 'perils similar to those specifically mentioned'.

Allotment Note. Authority given by a seaman for the shipowner to pay part of the seamen's earnings to a near relative, or to a savings bank, nominated by the seaman. The amount to be paid and the intervals between payments are, within limits, at the discretion of the seaman.

Allowance. Short name for 'Fresh water allowance'. 2. Name often given to gratuity given to cargo trimmers and others by shipmaster.

All Standing. Applied to a sudden stopping of a ship when brought about without engines being eased or sail reduced. To turn in all standing is to lie down fully dressed.

All Told. All being counted.

Almak. Star γ Andromedae. S.H.A. 330°; Dec. N 42°; Mag. 2·2.

Almanac. Presentation of certain information day by day for a year.

Almucantars.* Circles parallel to horizon and passing through each degree of the vertical circles.

Almucantar's Staff.* Olden instrument, made of pear wood or boxwood with a 15° arc. Was used for measuring amplitude.

Al Na'ir. Star α Gruis. S.H.A. 29°; Dec. S 47°; Mag. 2.2.

Alnilam. Star ε Orionis. S.H.A. 276°; Dec. S 01°; Mag. 1·8.

Aloft. Has a variety of meanings. In the 18th century often meant above the mess deck. More usually means above the highest part of the upper deck; above the sheerpole; above the lower tops.

Alongside. Close beside a ship, wharf or jetty. In charter parties, means that ship is so close to wharf or lighter that cargo can be transferred from one to the other by tackles.

Aloof.* To windward.

Alow. Below; low down; not aloft.

Alow and Aloft. When applied to sails, means below and above the lower yards.

Alpha. α First letter of Greek alphabet. Commonly used as a symbol to denote a known quantity. Prefixed to name of a constellation, it denotes principal star in that constellation.

Alphard. Star α Hydrae. S.H.A. 219°; Dec. S 08°; Mag. 2·2. Also called 'Cor Hydrae'.

Alphecca. Star α Coronae Borealis. S.H.A. 127°; Dec. N 27°; Mag. 2·3.

Alpheratz. Star α Andromedae. S.H.A. 358°; Dec. N 29°; Mag. 2·1.

Alt. Abbreviation for 'Altitude'.

Altair. Star α Aquilæ. S.H.A. 63°; Dec. N 9°; Mag. 0·9. Diameter is about that of Sun; candlepower is nine times greater; temperature is 8600°A; distance is 16 light years.

Altar. Step in a dry dock, on which lower ends of shores rest.

Alt-Azimuth. Contraction of 'Altitude-azimuth', the two horizon co-ordinates for fixing position of a heavenly body.

Alt-Azimuth Instrument. One that measures altitude and azimuth simultaneously—such as a theodolite.

Alternating Current. Electric current with rapidly alternating positive and negative polarities.

Alternating Light. Navigational beacon light that changes colour in each period of its visibility.

Altimeter. Aneroid barometer graduated to show height instead of pressure.

Altitude. Angular distance of a heavenly body above the horizon. Linear distance above sea level or other datum.

Altitude a Double.* Obsolete term for a pair of altitudes taken to determine latitude.

Altitude Azimuth. Usually shortened to 'Alt-azimuth'. Applied to problems, methods, tables and instruments in which these two co-ordinates are inter-dependent.

Altitude Circle. Great circle of celestial sphere that passes through zenith and so cuts horizon at right angles. Also called 'Vertical Circle' or 'Circle of Altitude'.

Altitude of Heavenly Body. Intercepted arc of a vertical circle between horizon and the body. The altitude may be the 'observed', 'apparent' or 'true' according to the horizon from which it is measured, and the point at which the angle is situated.

Alto. Prefixed to name of cloud form, denotes that it is at high level.

Altocumulus. Cloud form consisting of flattened globular, small clouds in regular layers.

Altocumulus Castellatus. Altocumulus cloud form with top edge shaped somewhat like battlements.

Altostratus. Gauzelike cloud form, at high altidude, resembling mist or fog. Density varies, sometimes stars can be seen through it, at other times it may hide Moon or even Sun.

Alwaid. Star β Draconis.

Always Afloat. Charter party stipulation that a ship shall not be required to load, discharge or wait turn at a berth where she would take the ground at some state of the tide.

Amain.* Quickly and suddenly.

Amalfian Code. 'Amalphitan Code.'

Amalgam. Compound of mercury with another metal.

Amalgamated Trough. Metal trough into which mercury is put to form an artificial horizon. Inside of trough is amalgamated to prevent metallic action by the mercury.

Amalphitan Code. Collection of navigation laws codified at Amalfi in 11th century. Was generally accepted as authoritative for many years.

Amazon Current. Outflow of river Amazon, which is manifest for a very considerable distance north and east of river mouth.

Ambergris. Valuable and sweet-smelling substance ejected by the cachalot whale. May be found floating on sea in tropical latitudes.

'America.' Schooner yacht that won 'America's Cup', 22nd August, 1851, in race round Isle of Wight. Length 94 ft., tonnage 171. Built by G. & J. R. Speers, New York.

American Carriage of Goods by Sea Act, 1936. Legislation that affects all contracts of carriage by sea to or from ports in U.S.A.

American Grommet. Brass eyelet that is clinched into a sail, awning or other canvas article.

American Practical Navigator. Book on navigational methods, together with appropriate tables. Written by Nathaniel Bowditch, LL.D., in 1802. Has been revised and brought up to date frequently.

American Whipping. Similar to a common whipping except that the two ends of twine are brought out in middle of whipping and are finished off with a reef knot.

America's Cup. International yacht racing trophy. Given by Royal Yacht Squadron and won by yacht 'America' in 1851. Held by U.S.A. since then. Now held by New York Yacht Club as a challenge cup.

Amidships. Middle part of a ship, or a middle line in her—either fore and aft or athwartships.

'Amidships.' Order to helmsman to move wheel or tiller so that rudder is in ship's fore and aft line, and has no turning effect.

Ammiral.* 'Admiral.'

Amok. Homicidal frenzy that sometimes affects Malayans and other eastern peoples.

Ampere. Unit of electrical current. Amount passed by one volt through a resistance of one ohm. When passed through standard solution of silver nitrate deposits 0·001118 grame of silver per second.

Ampere's Rule. Expresses deflection of a magnetic needle when in field of an electrical current. Current flowing south to north above a magnetic needle will deflect red end westward; and eastward if flowing below needle.

Amphibia. Animals capable of living both under water and on land.

Amphidromic Point. Point at which cotidal lines meet, and at which there is no range of tide.

Amphidromic Region. Area around an amphidromic point, and in which there is no range of tide.

Amphidromic System. One in which cotidal lines meet at a point.

Amphitrite. In Greek mythology, was wife of Poseidon (Neptune).

Amplitude. The extent of any oscillation, swing or excursion.

Amplitude of Heavenly Body. Value of intercepted arc of horizon between the prime vertical and the vertical circle passing through the body when rising or setting. Measured, in degrees, from east or west point of horizon, and towards the nearer pole.

Amplitude of Tide. Distance between mean tide level and high or low water level of a tide or constituent tide.

Amuck. 'Amok.'

Anabatic Winds. Those winds that have an upward trend, such as daytime winds that pass upward from valleys.

Analysis. Separation into component elements, or into pre-determined groups or categories.

Anchor. Implement by which a ship becomes attached to the ground at sea bed, and so rendered stationary. Parts are: shank, arms, flukes, bill (or pea), stock, ring. They fall into three main groups: Admiralty Pattern, Close Stowing, Stockless. The Admiralty Pattern has a stock at right-angles to the arms which causes the anchor to lie so that one of the flukes will bite into the ground. The Close-stowing anchor has a stock in line with the arms, in the Danforth anchor the stock is attached at the same end of the stock as the arms. The Close-stowing and Stockless anchors have tripping palms which cause the flukes to bite into the ground. The Plough, or C.Q.R. anchor, has flukes shaped like a plough-share. Ship's equipment of anchors is laid down by law and is based, primarily, upon her length. The 'Anchors and Chain Cables Act' demands that exhaustive tests be made on ships' anchors. The 'Merchant Shipping Acts' require that every anchor shall be marked, in two places, with name or initials of maker, and shall carry a serial or progressive number.

Anchorage. An area in which the holding ground is good and suitable for ships to anchor. 2. A position in which ships are anchored. 3. The hold of an anchor in the ground. 4. Dues paid, in a port, for use of an anchorage ground.

Anchor Bed. Strongly-built fitting, on either side of forecastle in ships having stocked anchors, on which an anchor is stowed and secured.

Anchor Bell. Bell, in fore part of ship, rung during fog in accordance with Rule of 'Regulations for Preventing Collision at Sea'. Sometimes used for indicating to bridge the number of shackles of cable that are out.

Anchor Buoy. Small buoy, or block of wood, with its mooring rope made fast to crown of anchor. Used for indicating position of anchor when on the bottom.

Anchor Clinch. Alternative name for 'Inside Clinch'. Was often used when bending hemp cable to ring of anchor.

Anchor Flags. Small red, green and numeral flags used when anchoring or weighing. Red or green flag used on bridge to indicate which anchor is to be let go; numeral flag used forward to indicate to bridge the number of shackles out.

Anchor Ice. Ice, of any form, that is aground in the sea.

Anchor Lights. All round lights shown by vessel at anchor, in accordance with Rule of Collision Regulations.

Anchors and Chain Cables Acts. Statutory regulations concerning making, testing, marking and certifying of anchors, cables and connecting shackles used by seagoing vessels.

Anchor's Aweigh. (Away.) Report that anchor has been hove out of ground and is clear of it.

Anchor Shackle. Used in joining end of cable to anchor ring. Differs from joining shackle in being fitted with forelock for securing a protruding pin. Now obsolescent.

Anchor Stock.* Method of wooden shipbuilding in which butts of timbers were placed at middle of timbers above and below.

Anchor Watch. Officer and a few men of duty watch who remain on deck when ship is at anchor in an open roadstead.

Ancient.* Old name for 'Ensign'.

Andrew. Naval seaman's nickname for Royal Navy. *See* 'Andrew Miller'.

Andrew Miller. Naval nickname for the Royal Navy. Said to be name of a zealous press gang officer.

Andromeda. Constellation situated between R.A. 00h and 02h; Dec. 28° to 42° N. Contains three bright stars, Alpheratz, Mirach, Almak.

Anemogram. Record made by a recording anemometer.

Anemograph. Instrument for recording wind force and, sometimes, direction.

Anemometer. Instrument for measuring wind velocity or pressure.

Anemometry. Science dealing with measurement of wind pressures.

Anemoscope. Instrument for detecting wind and indicating its direction.

Aneroidograph. Aneroid barometer fitted with clockwork and a paper carrying a pen to give a continuous record of barometric pressures. Seamen usually call it a 'barograph', but this term included mercurial recording barometers.

Angle Bar. Rolled steel section of L shape.

Angle Iron. Iron or steel stiffener inserted in an angle.

Angle of Cut. The smaller angle at which a pair of position lines intersect on a chart.

Angle of Dip. *See* 'Dip'.

Angle of Incidence. Angle, at a point in a surface, between a perpendicular and a light ray coming to that point.

Angle of Position. In great circle sailing, is angle that great circle track makes with meridian at any given point. In celestial triangle, is angle at the heavenly body which is subtended by the colatitude.

Angle of Reflection. Angle, at reflecting surface, between a light ray and its reflected ray; its value is twice the angle of incidence.

Angle of Refraction. Angle that a refracted ray makes with the line of its original path.

Angle of the Vertical. Difference between the perpendicular at a place and the extended radius of Earth passing through the place. Arises through Earth being an oblate spheroid. It is, therefore, the difference between True and Reduced latitudes of the place. Value is maximum in Lat. 45° (about) and is minimum at Poles.

Angular Diameter. Diameter of an observed object when expressed as the angle it subtends at eye of an observer.

Angular Distance. Distance between two observed points when expressed as angle it subtends at eye of observer.

Angular Momentum. Product of mass, distances from centre and angular velocities of all particles in a rotating body. Also defined as moment of inertia multiplied by angular velocity. Often called 'Moment of moments'.

Angular Velocity. Rate of revolution when expressed as angle passed through in unit time.

Angulated Sails. Triangular sails in which upper cloths are parallel to leech, and lower cloths are parallel to foot. Cloths meet at a girth band that is perpendicular to luff.

Ankaa. Star α Phoenicis. S.H.A. 354°; Dec. S 43°; Mag. 2·4.

Annealing. Process by which metals, and other substances, are heated to an appropriate temperature and then allowed to cool very slowly; so that internal stresses are removed and resiliency and elasticity are restored or induced.

Annual Constituent (of tide). That part of a tidal undulation that varies with Earth's distance from Sun.

Annual Inequality. Variation in a tidal undulation that is more or less seasonal and periodic.

Annual Parallax. Apparent displacement of a heavenly body from its true position when caused by Earth's elliptical movement around Sun. Is negligible in stars.

Annular Eclipse. Moon's occultation of Sun when outside edge of Sun's disc is unocculted although centres of both bodies are in line. Due to Moon's diameter being less than diameter of Sun, through Moon being in or near apogee.

Anomalistic. Irregular: uneven. Applied to motions, intervals and values that are basically uniform but are made irregular through the action of one or more disturbing factors.

Anomalistic Month. Time taken by Moon to go from perigee to perigee. Interval is about 27·55455 days.

Anomalistic Period of Planet. Time taken by a planet to go from perihelion to perihelion. Interval is irregular through movement of perihelion point.

Anschutz Gyro Compass. German type in which three gyros revolve in air. Sensitive element floats in a mercury bath. Damping is effected by oil.

Answer the Helm. A ship is said to do this when she alters her direction in response to movements of tiller and rudder.

Antarctic. Region of Earth's surface south of latitude 66° 33′ S. Pertaining to this region.

Antarctic Circle. Region enclosed by parallel 66° 33′ S. Name is often given to the parallel itself.

Antares. Star α Scorpio. S.H.A. 113°; Dec. S 26°; Mag. 1·2. Diameter is 430 times that of Sun; temperature 3100°A. Name means 'rivalling Mars'—in the redness of its colour.

Antecians. People living in same latitude and longitude, but on opposite sides of Equator. They have same length of days, but at opposite times of the year.

Antedate. To date a document so that its effect counts as from a date previous to the date of signing.

Ante Meridiem. Between midnight and noon. Before midday (Latin).

Antenna. Arrangement of wires for sending or receiving radio waves.

Antenna Resistance. Sum of all leaks, resistances and abatements, in antenna, that reduce maximum current.

Anthelion. Faintly luminous disc seen in sky opposite Sun. Is due to reflection of Sun by ice particles in atmosphere.

Anticorrosive. Inimical to corrosion. Applied to paints, processes and preparations that are intended to prevent corrosion.

Anticyclone. Area of relatively high barometric pressure, around which wind circulation is clockwise in northern hemisphere, and anticlockwise in southern hemisphere. Generally associated with fine and settled weather. (Also called a High).

Anticyclonic Regions. Areas in about 30° N and 30° S latitudes; in which anticyclones are fairly prevalent and persistent.

Antifouling. Paints and preparations that attack and kill marine life that tries to attach itself to ship's underwater skin.

Antigropelos.* Waterproof leggings.

Antilogarithm. Natural number that is represented by a logarithm.

Antilunar Tide. Tidal undulation generated on side of Earth opposite to that on which tractive force of Moon is exerted.

Antipleon. Meteorological term for an area in which meteorological factors and conditions are below normal.

Antipodes. That area of Earth diametrically opposite to a given place; thus having the same latitude and longitude as the place, but of opposite names. Sometimes applied to New Zealand and, less correctly to Australia, as approximately fulfilling these conditions in regard to Great Britain.

Antiscorbutics. Medicinal substances that prevent or allay scurvy. Statutory antiscorbutics are lime, lemon and orange juices.

Anti-Solar Tide. Tidal undulation generated on side of Earth opposite to that on which tractive force of Sun is exerted.

Anti-Trades. High level winds that flow above and opposite to the trade winds. They are not surface winds, and so do not affect seamen directly: they do concern meteorologists.

Anvil Cloud. Cumulonimbus cloud with wedge-shaped projection of its upper edge. Fairly common in thunderstorms.

Apeak. Said of anchor when cable is taut and vertical. Said of yards when they are cockbilled in contrary directions.

A-Peek. Apeak.

Aphelion. That point, in orbit of planet or comet, that is farthest from Sun.

Aphraktos. Undeckted Grecian ship of classic times.

Aplanatic. In optics, means 'without aberration'. Used when spherical and chromatic aberrations have been eliminated.

Aplanatic Refraction. Refraction that has been corrected for spherical aberrations.

Apogean Range. Mean minimum range of an apogean tide; usually about 0·8 of mean tide.

Apogean Tide. Tidal undulation occurring about time of Moon being in apogee. Increase in Moon's distance from Earth reduces her gravitational and tractive efforts.

Apogee. Point in Moon's orbit that is farthest from Earth.

A-Port. To port; towards to the port side.

Apparel.* Removable fittings of a ship—such as sails, tackling, awnings, etc.—as distinguished from her permanent fittings.

Apparent. When applied to phenomena means 'as it appears to the human eye'; so disregarding aberration, speed of light, and other factors.

Apparent Altitude. Altitude of centre of a heavenly body when measured from sensible horizon.

Apparent Area. Term used in connection with Sun and Moon, whose areas appear to increase or decrease with variations in Earth's distance from them.

Apparent Declination. Declination of a heavenly body, as it appears to an observer, when displaced by the aberration of light.

Apparent Light. Navigational aid that appears to emit a light when it reflects or refracts a light more or less remote. Erected in a position where a light would be difficult to maintain.

Apparent Midnight. Instant when true Sun transits the inferior meridian of a place.

Apparent Motion. Movement of a heavenly body as seen from Earth. Due to Earth's diurnal rotation, annual revolution, periodic nutation and precession, apparent motions bear little resemblance to the true movements. 2. The movement on a relative radar display of the echo of another ship. It is her motion relative to own ship. ('Relative Movement,' 'Relative Course and Speed').

Apparent Noon. Instant when true Sun is on the meridian at a place.

Apparent Right Ascension. Right ascension of a heavenly body as it appears to an observer when displaced by the aberration of light.

Apparent Solar Day. Interval between successive transits of true Sun across any given meridian.

Apparent Solar Time. Time based on hour angle of true Sun. Differs from Mean Solar Time by the 'Equation of Time'. Rarely used in civil time reckoning, but frequently used in navigation.

Apparent Sun. The visible Sun, as distinguished from the fictitious 'mean' and 'dynamical' suns.

Apparent Time. Apparent solar time.

Apparent Time of Change Tide. Apparent time of high water at a place at full or new Moon.

Apparent Wind. Movement of air past an observer when arising from a true wind and motion of observer. May differ from true wind in direction, force, or both of these, according to observer's motion relative to wind direction.

Appleton Layer. Ionised layer of atmosphere about 150 miles above surface of Earth. Reflects short wave radio.

Apprentice. A minor who has been bound by indentures to serve a shipowner for a specified period—usually three or four years— in return for instruction in the duties of a deck officer, together with food, accommodation, and such money payments as may be agreed. Terms of apprenticeship are governed by Merchant Shipping Acts.

Approaching. Getting nearer. As far as the 'Collision Regulations' are concerned, a vessel under way but stopped, or hove to, or in irons, is considered to be approaching a vessel that is getting nearer.

Appulse.* Arrival of a heavenly body at a given meridian, or at conjunction with Sun or Moon.

Apron. Canvas protection in leadsman's chains. 2. Piece of timber, immediately abaft stem of a boat, that takes hooded ends of planks. 3. Curved piece of wood erected on fore end of keel of a wooden ship. 4. Projecting ledge of timber along bottom of entrance to a dock, against which the dock gates are closed.

Apse. Point, in orbit of a satellite body, at which the body is nearest to or farthest from the body around which it travels. It is perihelion or aphelion in case of a planet, perigee or apogee in case of Moon.

Aqualung. Apparatus consisting of bottles of compressed air, reducing valve, and face-mask which enables a swimmer to breathe under water.

Aquarius. Constellation lying, approximately, between R.A.s 21h and 23h. Has many discernible stars, but all are small: α Aquarii is Mag. 3·2. 2. Eleventh sign of Zodiac, extending from 300° to 330° celestial longitude. Sun is in this sign from January 20 to February 20. Name is Latin for 'Water Bearer'.

Aquila. Constellation lying between R.A.s 19h–20h. Dec. 0°–10° N. Contains important star Altair, α Aquilæ.

Arbalest.* Olden instrument for measuring star altitudes. Also called 'Jacob's Staff' or 'Cross Staff' (q.v.).

Arbitration. Judging of a matter under dispute by a person, or persons, mutually agreed upon by contending parties, and whose decision the contending parties agree to accept. Rules concerning arbitration are laid down in Arbitration Act, 1889.

Arc. Part of circumference of a circle. Of sextant, is that part on which the graduations are carried.

Arcform. Method of ship construction introduced by Isherwood. Sharp bilge of box form was done away with and replaced by an arc form from keel to deck line. To regain displacement lost through removing angle at bilge, beam in region of water line was increased. This results in a definite reduction of immersed midship girth and, due to easy sweep of bilge, improved water flow to propeller. Sea kindliness and economical consumption follow.

Arched. Hogged.

Archimedean Screw. Name given to screw propeller when first introduced.

Archimedes' Theorem. A body partially or wholly immersed in a fluid suffers an apparent loss of weight equal to weight of fluid displaced.

Arch Type. System of cargo ship construction developed by North-East coast shipbuilders. Outboard sides of holds were curved inward and upward towards hatchways, so that trimming of bulkhead cargoes was reduced.

Arc of Excess. That small portion of graduated arc of a sextant in which graduations from zero read in a direction opposite to that of the main graduations; thus allowing small angles below the horizontal to be measured.

Arc Proper. Arc of sextant graduated from 0° to 120° (about), and excluding the arc of excess.

Arctic. Pertaining to area of Earth's surface enclosed by parallel of latitude 66° 33' N.

Arctic Air. Atmospheric air that has come directly from north polar regions and arrives, eventually, as maritime polar air.

Arctic Circle. Parallel of 66° 33' N. Marks limit of Sun's visibility when in maximum southerly declination.

Arctic Current. Ocean current flowing from Davis Strait, along coasts of Labrador and Newfoundland, meeting Gulf Stream in latitude 41° to 42° N. It then turns eastward. From March onwards it brings down icebergs. Also known as 'Labrador Current', 'Davis Current'.

Arctic Sea Smoke. Fog on surface of sea when caused by cold air moving over warm water.

Arctic Zone. Area north of Arctic Circle.

Arctophylax. Old name for constellation Bootes. Name is sometimes given to star Arcturus. Is Greek for 'Bear Watcher'.

Arcturus. Star α Bootes. S.H.A. 147°; Dec. N 19°; Mag. 0·2. Diameter is 30 times that of Sun, candlepower is 100 times greater. Distant 41 light years; temperature 4100°A. Name is Greek for 'Bear Warden'.

Ardent. Said of a vessel under sail when she tends to run up quickly into the wind, and requires an unusual amount of weather helm.

Argentum. Skin layer of fishes. It makes them iridescent by reflecting light.

Argo. Southern constellation in about R.A. 6h to 11h; Dec. 37°–70° S. Named after mythological ship of Jason. Divided, by Herschel, into various parts: keel (carina), mast (malus), poop (puppis), sails (vela); stars being named by astronomers—but not seaman—after their part of ship. Canopus is principal star. γ Argus (Carinae) is a variable star, going from Mag. 1 to 7½ in 70 years.

Argon. Gas forming nearly 1 per cent of atmosphere.

Argonauts. Legendary companions of Jason, in ship 'Argo', when he sailed to regain the Golden Fleece. 2. Sea creature, with tentacles and a shell, often seen floating on surface of sea.

Argosy. Large Adriatic merchant ship of middle ages. Word is used, poetically, for freight-carrying ships in general. Is a corrupt form of Ragusa, the principal port from which the argosy sailed.

Argument. When using navigational, or other tables, is the known value, or values, with which the tables are entered.

Aries (The Ram). Constellation situated between R.A.s 01h 45m and 03h and Dec. 15° to 25° N. Has two navigational stars α (Hamel) and β Arietis. 2. First sign of Zodiac, extending from 0° to 30° celestial longitude. Sun is in this sign from March 21 to April 20 (about). Name is often used as a short form of 'First Point of Aries'.

Arisings. Old or damaged material that remains when repairs or refitting have been carried out.

Ark. Any enclosed vessel that will float. 2. Vessel, about the size of a medium liner, built by Noah. 3. Large boat formerly used on rivers of U.S.A. for transporting provisions.

Armada. A fleet of warships.

Armed Mast. A built mast.

Armed Merchant Cruiser. Ocean liner taken over by Admiralty, in time of war, armed with guns and other weapons, manned by naval officers and ratings and employed on active service.

Armilla.* Former astronomical and navigational instrument consisting of rings that represented great circles of the celestial sphere. When aligned and suspended from a point that represented the zenith it indicated position of Ecliptic or Equinoctial. Equinoctial armilla was used to determine arrival of Equinox; solstitial armilla measured Sun's altitude.

Armillary Sphere. Armilla having nine skeleton circles. Used for astronomical purposes from 3rd century B.C. until 18th century A.D.

Arming. Tallow or soap put in cavity at heel of a sounding lead or sinker to obtain a specimen of sea bed.

Arm of Anchor. That part of an anchor which extends from crown to fluke.

Armstrong's Patent. Humorous nickname for manually-worked machinery.

Arrest. Temporary detention and restraint of action when imposed by lawful authority.

Arse. Choke end of a common wood block.

Artemon. Small foresail of ancient Mediterranean vessels.

'Articles.' Short name for 'Regulations for Preventing Collisions at Sea',* or for the 'Articles of Agreement' between master and crew.

Articles of Agreement. Legal and binding agreement, entered into by master of ship and crew, concerning duties, conditions of service and remuneration. Terminates on fulfilment of embodied conditions or on a specified date. May terminate before time intended by mutual consent of master and seaman; by physical inability of seaman to continue service; by wreck or loss of ship.

Articles of War. Royal Navy code of discipline. Defines duties and embodies maximum punishments for stated offences.

Artificial Eye. Made in end of a rope by unlaying one strand, turning over the part from which strand has been taken, so that an eye is formed, and relaying single strand in opposite direction. Finished off by tucking ends.

Artificial Horizon. Perfectly horizontal reflecting surface used when obtaining altitudes where no horizon is available. Mercury is usual, but highly-polished surfaces, correctly levelled, may be used. Can be employed only when ashore. Bubble sextants are the usual alternatives for marine work.

Artificial Projection. Projection, of surface or sphere to a plane, in which fixed laws are evident but which entails distortion and alteration of perspective shape of area projected.

Ascending Node. Node in which Moon or planet passes to northward of Ecliptic.

Ascension. Formerly: was arc of Equinoctial intercepted between east point of horizon and First Point of Aries when a heavenly body was rising. Was qualified as 'right ascension' when referred to an observer at Equator, 'oblique ascension' when referred to an observer away from Equator. The latter term has lapsed.

Ascensional Difference. Difference between the right ascension and oblique ascension of a heavenly body.

Ascension Verse. French equivalent for the British 'Sidereal Hour Angle'.

Ascertained. As used in 'Collision Regulations', has been ruled as meaning 'determined distinctly and unequivocally'.

Ascians. People living in regions where, at some time, they have no shadow: thus living between tropics of Cancer and Capricorn.

Asdic. Device for detecting submerged submarines, and ascertaining their distance and direction, by making a sound signal in water and timing interval until return of echo. Name is taken from initials of 'Allied Submarine Devices Investigation Committee' of 1914–18 war. Now called Sonar.

Ash Breeze. No wind at all.

Ash Cat. Name given to steam ships, by sailing ship men, in early days of steam.

Ashore. On shore, on the land. Ship is ashore when aground on or near the shore.

'As long as the Maintop Bowline.' Said of a long-winded statement or yarn; this bowline being the longest in a ship.

Aspect. Old astronomical term for a planet's position relative to another planet. Five aspects were Conjunction, Sextile (60° different), Quartile (90° different), Trine (120° different), and Opposition. The first and last aspects still remain. 2. The nearer angle between another vessel's head and the line of sight. It is expressed in degrees (0° to 180°) and qualified red or green according to whether the port or starboard side of the other vessel is visible, e.g. Green 20.

Assigns. Those to whom certain rights, or property, have been allotted or transferred by signed document.

Assmann Psychrometer. Hygrometer with a clockwork fan that drives air at a constant rate past wet bulb. This causes exaggerated depression of wet bulb, so giving more precise values of humidity when referred to appropriate tables.

Assured. Those who have insured, or have been insured, against loss.

'A' Stars. Spectrum classification of stars in which hydrogen lines are very evident. Their light is white, and temperature is 10,000°A. Sirius and Vega are in this class.

Astatic. Arrangement of two or more magnetic needles on a single suspension so that there is no torque when in a magnetic field.

A-stay. Said of anchor cable when its line of lead approximates a continuation of line of fore stay. Also called 'short stay'.

Astern. Outside a ship and directly abaft her.

Asteroids. Large number of very small planetary bodies, the mean point of whose orbits lies between Mars and Jupiter at approximate distance (2·8 astronomical units) required by Bode's Law. Orbits of about 1200 have been observed; between 200 and 300 have been named; many have been observed for short periods only. Vesta is the only one discernible by the naked eye. The largest, Ceres, has a diameter of 480 miles; the majority are very much smaller.

Astigmatiser. Lens and mechanism, in a rangefinder, that causes a point of light to appear as a line of light; which can then be used to determine distance off.

Astres Fictifs. Name given to hypothetical bodies assumed to be responsible for component tides in harmonic analysis. More usually termed 'satellites' or 'constituents'. Fr. = 'False stars'.

Astrolabe. Probably oldest of navigational instruments. In its more advanced form consisted of a disc of metal, or wood, graduated in degrees and suspended from a ring representing the zenith. A movable bar, or alidade, pivoted at centre of dial, carried sight vanes that were aligned on observed body. Bar then indicated altitude. In all cases, vertical and horizontal planes were established by plumb line. 2. Optical instrument formerly used in surveying. Now superseded by theodolite.

Astro-Meteorology. Investigations into effects of Sun and Moon on weather.

Astro-Navigation. Conducting of a ship by observations of heavenly bodies, as distinguished from observations of terrestrial objects.

Astronomical Bearing. True bearing of a terrestrial object when derived from angle between a vertical circle passing through the object and another vertical circle passing through a heavenly body whose azimuth has been computed.

Astronomical Clock. Timepiece regulated to measure sidereal time.

Astronomical Cross Bearings. Crossed position lines obtained from observations of celestial bodies.

Astronomical Day. Interval between successive transits of mean Sun across a given meridian. Since 1924 it has coincided with the civil day: before then it commenced with Sun's superior transit and was, therefore, 12 hours slow on civil time.

Astronomical Position Line. Line of position obtained by observation of a heavenly body.

Astronomical Refraction. Difference between original direction of a ray of light, from a heavenly body, and its final direction when it reaches observer. Due to refractive effect of atmosphere.

Astronomical Tide. Alternative name for 'Equilibrium Tide'.

Astronomical Time. Time measured directly by hour angle of mean Sun: noon was thus 00 hours. Previous to January, 1925, this time was basic in navigation.

Astronomical Twilight. Interval between Sun's centre being 12° below horizon and 18° below it. Horizon is not distinct but vestiges of sunlight are refracted or reflected above it.

Astronomical Unit of Distance. Earth's mean distance from Sun (93,005,000 miles). Used for expressing planetary and inter-planetary distances.

Astronomics. The principles of nautical astronomy.

Astronomy. Combination of sciences dealing with nature, movements and appearances of heavenly bodies. Divided into various groups, each giving a prefix to the word; e.g. nautical, physical, descriptive, etc.

Astrophysics. Branch of astronomy that considers the physical and chemical properties of heavenly bodies, as distinct from the apparent motions, magnitudes and distribution.

Astroscope. Instrument for teaching and learning relative positions of heavenly bodies. Star globe is an example.

Asymptote. Line towards which a curve approaches but will never touch. Sometimes defined as a tangent to a curve with point of tangency at infinite distance.

Athwart. Across. Transversely.

Athwart Hawse. Position of one ship when she is ahead of, and at right angles to, the fore and aft line of a nearby ship.

Athwartships. Transversely across a ship. From one side to the other.

Atlantic Ocean. Expanse of sea between American continent and coasts of Europe and Africa. Bounded on north by lines made by parallel of latitude from Cape Farewell to Labrador, and by lines from Cape Nansen to Straumness (Iceland), from Gerspin to Fugloe and thence to Stadt. Bounded on south by line one mile south of Cape Horn to 40° S and 20° E. Divided into North and South Atlantic by parallel 4° 25′ N joining Cape Palmas, Liberia, and Cape Orange, Brazil.

Atmosphere. Gaseous envelope surrounding Earth. Consists of two layers; the lower, or troposphere, and the upper, or stratosphere. Weight of atmosphere on each square inch of Earth's surface is approx. $14\frac{1}{2}$ lb. at sea level.

Atmospheric Electricity. Positive potential in atmosphere that gives rise to electrical phenomena when coupled with negative potential on surface of Earth.

Atmospheric Pressure. Set up by weight of overlying air. At Earth's surface it is equivalent to about $14\frac{1}{2}$ lb. per sq. in. In meteorology, usually expressed in millibars.

Atmospherics. Crackling noises that interfere with radio reception.

Atmospheric Sounder. Instrument by which sea depth is measured by increased water pressure compressing air in a small bore tube that is carried down by lead or sinker.

Atmospheric Tides. Caused by attraction of atmosphere by Sun and Moon. Moon's atmospheric tide affects barometric pressure less than 0·1 mb. Sun's tide is swamped by changes due to this heating effect.

Atoll. Oval, or horseshoe shaped, coral reef bordering a lagoon.

Atria. Star α Triang. Australis. S.H.A. 109°; Dec. S 69°; Mag. 1·9.

A-Trip. Said of anchor immediately it is broken out of the ground. Topsails are a-trip when they are hoisted close up, or when just started from the cap preparatory to trimming.

At sight. Business term put in a financial document when payment is to be made on presentation to stated person or persons.

Attendance. Service rendered by being at a certain place at a certain time, even though further service was not required.

Attestation. Formal declaration that the statements in a document are affirmed by the persons or person signing it.

At the Dip. Position of a flag, pendant or hoist when it is not hauled close up but is a fathom or so short of being so. Answering pendant 'at the dip' means that signal is seen but not understood.

Atwood's Formula. For finding righting lever of ship-shaped bodies when heeled.

$$GZ = \frac{\text{Vol. of wedge displacement} \times h_1 h_2}{\text{Vol. of displacement}} - BG \sin \theta$$

Augmentation. Name applied to the optical illusion that makes Sun, Moon, planets and constellations appear to be larger when near horizon than they appear to be when at greater altitudes.

Augmentation of Moon's Horizontal Semi-diameter. Increase of Moon's semi-diameter as she rises above horizon, this increase being up to 18″ of arc greater in zenith than in horizon. Semi-diameter tabulated in Nautical Almanac is based on observer being at centre of Earth and, therefore, at centre of all rational horizons.

Augment of Resistance. Increase of resistance that accompanies increase of ship's speed. Due to increase in size of bow wave and decrease of pressure on stern through partial cavitation caused by propeller action and increased speed.

Aureole. Circle of light sometimes surrounding Sun or Moon, and bounded by rings of one or more colours.

Aurora. Name given to areas of faint luminosity in the night sky, more particularly to those in direction of north or south poles of Earth. Latin for 'Dawn'.

Aurora Australis. Southern 'Aurora Polaris'.

Aurora Borealis. Northern 'Aurora Polaris'.

Aurora Polaris. Tremulant light seen in night towards direction of north or south poles of Earth. Is electrical in origin and may take many forms—arcs, bands, coronæ, etc. Most frequently seen in latitudes 55°—75° N and 60°—90° S.

Auster. A hot south wind. Now only used poetically, but Sirocco was so called at one time.

Austral. Southern.

Australian Current. Branch of Equatorial Current, setting southwards along E coast of Australia as far as Sydney.

Australian Sea Carriage of Goods Act, 1914. Short Act, of ten clauses, governing shipment of goods from Australia, whether coastwise or abroad.

Autogenous Welding. Joining two pieces of metal by heating each of them and then welding them together without use of any other metal.

Autographic Instrument. Any instrument that makes a graphic record of its registrations. Barograph is an example.

Automatic Helmsman. Machine that is controlled by compass and controls steering engine. Automatically keeps ship's head on a pre-selected course.

Automatic Tide Gauge. Erection near shore of a tidal river, to indicate height of tide by a system of floats with a connected pointer that moves over a graduated board. By including a constant in the graduation the height of tide at a distant port can be indicated. 2. Tide gauge fitted with a timekeeping unit and a recording apparatus. Used for recording tidal effects over a fairly long period.

Autopilot/Automatic Pilot. Automatic Helmsman.

Autumnal Equinoctial Point. That point of intersection of Ecliptic and Equinoctial at which Sun passes from north to south declination.

Autumnal Equinox. That time when Sun passes from north to south declination (about Sept. 23) and length of day and night are equal in all latitudes.

Auxiliary Angle 'A'. Quantity necessary when 'clearing a Lunar'. Was usually obtained by inspection, but such tables are now unnecessary, and are not given. Value of angle was between 60° and 61°.

Auxiliary Boiler. Boiler in which steam is raised for working auxiliary machinery.

Auxiliary Machinery. All machinery, in a vessel, other than the main engines and their attachments.

Avast. Order to stop, or desist from, an action.

Average. Contribution to make good a maritime loss.

Average Accustomed. Usual small charges—dock dues, pilotage, etc., that normally fall on cargo. Formerly called 'Petty Average'.

Average Act. A general average act.

Average Adjuster. Skilled and competent person who computes the contributions due from various interests when making good a General Average loss.

Average Adjustment. Equitable sharing of the liability to make good a General Average loss. Based on the pecuniary value of the property each party had at stake.

Average Bond. Secured undertaking to satisfy a demand for a General Average contribution that is to be assessed. Given to ship by a consignee of cargo, or part cargo, when a General Average claim is pending.

Average Deposit. Money payment made to a ship, by a consignee of cargo, to cover a pending General Average claim.

Average Deposit Receipt. Receipt for a General Average Deposit.

Average Loss. 'General Average Loss.'

B

Average Statement. Document, drawn up by General Average adjuster, stating liabilities of the various interests concerned in making good a General Average loss.

Average Unless General. Denotes that insured goods are not covered by policy when subject to general average.

Awash. Water washing over.

A-Weather. To windward. Towards, or on, that side of ship on which wind blows.

Aweigh. Said of an anchor immediately it is broken out of the ground when cable is up and down.

A-Wheft. Said of a flag when stopped in middle to form a wheft.

Awning. Canvas spread above a deck to give protection from sun and rain.

Awning Curtain. Canvas screen coming downward from side of awning, and with lower edge stopped to eyeplates in deck.

Awning Deck. Light deck erected above upper deck, or main deck, as protection against sun and rain.

Awning Deck Vessel. First introduced for conveyance of natives between Eastern ports. Has large ventilation openings in top side plating. Has full scantlings to second deck; space between second and upper decks being in nature of a superstructure.

Awning Hitch. Name sometimes given to 'Roband hitch'; this being appropriate hitch for securing edge of awning to jackstay when spread.

Awning Shackle. Elongated D shackle having a roller fitted at about half length.

Axes. Plural of 'Axis'. Intersection of two axes in a plane, or three axes in space, define a point that is termed the 'origin'.

Axis. Axle, or hinge. In a plane figure is that straight line about which either part may rotate and generate the same solid. In a solid, is that line about which the solid is symmetrically disposed.

Axis of Earth. That diameter around which daily rotation takes place.

Axis of Great Circle. That diameter, of a sphere, that passes perpendicularly through a given great circle of the sphere.

Axis of Heavens. That diameter, of celestial sphere, around which the daily rotation of the heavens appear to be made. As this apparent rotation is due to Earth's rotation, axis of heavens usually coincides with Earth's axis prolonged indefinitely. Astronomical latitude and longitude assume an axis perpendicular to Ecliptic.

Axis of Small Circle. That diameter of a sphere that passes perpendicularly through a small circle of the sphere. It is, therefore, axis of a great circle parallel to the small circle.

Axis of Symmetry. Straight line that divides a plane figure into two similar parts.

'Aye, Aye, Sir.' Customary acknowledgement of an order. Means that the order is understood and will be carried out.

Azimuth. Intercepted arc of horizon between observer's meridian and a vertical circle passing through an observed object.

Azimuthal Projection. Alternative name for 'Zenithal' projection.

Altitude Azimuth Instrument. 'Alt-Azimuth Instrument.'

Azimuth Circle. Instrument similar to 'Azimuth Mirror', but is not pivoted at centre; an outer ring, encircling bowl, keeping it centred.

Azimuth Compass. Compass fitted to carry an instrument for taking azimuths at any altitude. Placed so that there is a minimum of obstructions to observations.

Azimuth Diagram. Engraved diagram by which azimuth can be graphically obtained by using declination, latitude and apparent time. Devised by Captain Weir, R.N.

Azimuth Mirror. Instrument for obtaining azimuth of observed objects by observing object's reflection in a mirror, or prism, pivoted in centre of glass over compass card. Preceded azimuth circle. Invented by Lord Kelvin.

Azimuth of Heavenly Body. Intercepted arc of horizon between meridian and vertical circle passing through body. Generally reckoned from elevated pole through 180° East or West.

Azimuth Prism. Alternative name for 'Azimuth Circle' or 'Azimuth Mirror'.

Azimuth Tables. Precomputed quantities that give azimuth corresponding to a given time, a given latitude and a known declination.

Azores Anticyclone. Atlantic part of a more or less permanent zone of anticyclonic weather that girdles Earth in 30° N approximately.

B

Babcock Erith Stoker. Mechanical apparatus for feeding boiler furnaces with coal, and so arranging it that efficient consumption and clean fires are maintained.

Babcock Johnson Boiler. Water tube boiler of fairly small dimensions and weight, but having very high efficiency.

Babcock Wilcox Boiler. Water tube boiler for main steam purposes. Working pressure up to 1400 lb. per sq. in.

Bac. Flat-bottomed boat, often with pram bow, used as a ferry.

Back. To back engines is to put them astern. To back an oar is to reverse the action of rowing and propel the boat astern. To back a sail is to haul its clew to windward. To back anchor is to lay another anchor ahead of it, and with a cable or hawser extending tautly between them. Wind is said to 'back' when it changes direction anti-clockwise.

Back Altitude. Measurement of greater arc of vertical circle passing through an observed body. Taken when horizon at foot of smaller arc cannot be distinguished.

Back and Fill. To fill sails and then back them, alternately. Done to keep vessel in a position for the time being.

Backboard. Board athwart after end of stern sheets of a rowing boat, for passengers to lean against.

Backbone. Fore and aft wire along middle of an awning.

Back Freight. Money payable to ship for carrying cargo back to port of shipment when it was impossible to discharge cargo at destination.

Back Letter. Name sometimes given to a 'Letter of indemnity'.

Back Pressure. In a steam cylinder, is pressure set up by steam on exhaust side of piston. In a pump, is resistance generated when discharge has to be forced.

Backrail. Name formerly given to 'Backboard'.

Back Rope. Small chain, or rope pendant, used for staying a dolphin striker.

Back Sailing. Hauling boom of mainsail, or mizen, to windward when a vessel loses way in going about. This forces her head on a new tack, and is a kind of box hauling.

Back Ship. To work ship astern with sails or engines.

Back Sight. Back altitude.

Backsplice. Method of finishing off end of a rope that is not required to reeve through a block. End is unlaid, 'crown' formed with the strands, ends tucked into rope below crown.

Backspring. Rope led aft, from forward in a ship, to a buoy, or bollard outside ship. Used for heaving ship astern, or for preventing her ranging ahead.

Backstaff. Forerunner of quadrant and sextant. Instrument devised by Captain Davis about 1590. Observer stood with his back to Sun and measured altitude by two concentric rings, one measuring 30°, the other 60°.

Backstays. Ropes led from a mast to a position abaft it. They support mast against forces acting in a forward direction.

Backstay Stool. Short timber in which lower ends of backstays are set up when no room has been allowed for them in the chains.

Backwash. Troubled water thrown astern of mechanically propelled vessels, especially paddle steamers.

Backwater. Area of a river that is sheltered from main stream and in which there is a very little lateral movement of the water. 2. To back an oar.

Baffle Plates. Iron or steel plates fitted in various parts of heating elements of a boiler to prevent radiation of heat, or to protect against corrosion by waste gases.

Bag Cargo. Cargo that is stowed in bags.

Baggage Room. Compartment, in a passenger ship, for storage of passengers' baggage that may be required during the voyage.

Baggala, Bagla. Two-masted dhow of about 200 tons. Used in Indian Ocean. Lateen rigged, mast raked forward; has high poop with windows, quarter galleries and lavish decoration.

Baggy Rinkle. Sennit used for chafing gear.

Bagpipe the Mizen.* To haul on weather mizen sheet until mizen boom is close to weather mizen shroud, and sail is aback.

Bag Reef. Fourth reef of a topsail.

Baguio, Bagiou. The term for a typhoon in the Philippine Islands.

Bailer. Baler.

Bail Out. To remove water from a boat.

Baily's Beads. Bead-like prominences apparently on limb of Moon during eclipse of Sun. Probably due to irradiation.

Baker Navigation Machine. Introduced to assist air navigation. Allows a transparent sheet, carrying curves of iso-azimuths to be adjusted over a chart. Invented by Cdr. T. Y. Baker, R.N.

Balaenidae. True, or 'right' whales. Have no teeth, but baleen (whale bone) instead. Have no dorsal fin. Greenland and Australian whales are examples.

Balaenoptera. Whales having soft dorsal fin and short baleen plates. Rorqual is an example.

Balanced Rudder. One in which rudder stock is not on leading edge of rudder, but an appropriate distance abaft it. Pressure on forward area or rudder nearly balances pressure on after area, thus reducing power necessary to turn rudder. Shearing stress on stock is increased, but torsional stress is decreased.

Balance Lug. Lugsail with foot laced to a boom that project forward of mast. Handy rig for small boats in fairly smooth waters, as boom remains on same side of mast on either tack.

Balances. Constellation of Libra. (Libra is Latin for Scales).

Balance Reef. Diagonal reef in spanker. Runs from peak earing to tack, so making sail triangular when reefed.

Balance Piston. 'Dummy Piston'.

Balancing. When applied to marine reciprocating marine engine, denotes the arranging of moving parts and adjustable weights so that engine runs smoothly and without undue vibration.

Balancing Band. Band and shackle, on shank of anchor, at such a position that anchor will lie horizontal when lifted by shackle of band. Not at centre of gravity of anchor, as allowance must be made for weight of attached cable.

Balandra. South American coasting vessel, of about 100 tons, having one mast. 2. One-masted vessel, fitted with outrigger, found in China Sea. Name is a form of 'Bilander'.

Balcony. Alternative name for stern gallery of olden ships.

Balc Yawl. Small Manx fishing vessel, with oars and lugsail, used in 'balc', or long line fishing.

Baldheaded Schooner. Schooner with no topsail on foremast.

Baldheader. Old nickname for a square rigged vessel that carried no sail above topgallant sails.

Bale. Package of cargo that is wrapped in canvas, hessian, etc. Also old name for bucket, whence 'baler'.

Bale Cargo. Cargo consisting entirely of bales.

Baleen. Whalebone obtained from mouth of true whale.

Baler. Small container for emptying a boat of water.

Bale Sling. Length of rope with its ends spliced together to form a loop strop.

Bale Space. Measurement of a hold based on volume calculated from distance from ceiling to lower edge of beams, distance between inner edges of opposite frames and length.

Ballace.* Old form of 'Ballast'.

Ballast. Heavy substances put into a vessel to improve stability or to increase submersion of propeller. 2. To take heavy items into a ship and so to dispose of them, that an increase in stability results.

Ballastage. Toll paid to harbour authority for permission to take ballast from the harbour or port.

Ballast Declaration. Short name for 'Masters Declaration and Stores Content for Vessels Outward in Ballast'. Is one of the documents rendered to Customs authorities when clearing outwards a vessel with no cargo.

Balsa. Extremely light wood from a South American tree. Specific gravity is about 1/7th that of water. 2. Small fishing raft used on coast of South America.

Balsa Raft. 'Copper Punt' used in Royal Navy when painting ship's side in the vicinity of waterline.

Baltic Sea. Expanse of water between Sweden and the mainland south of $59\frac{3}{4}°$ N, to about $12\frac{1}{2}°$ E, but excluding gulfs of Finland, Riga and Dantzig.

Balza. Alternative form of 'Balsa'.

Banca. Small dug-out canoe used for fishing in China Sea.

Bandrol. Small swallow-tailed flag, or pendant, flown at masthead as a wind vane or ornament.

Banjo Frame. Vertical frame holding the propeller of early screw-propelled steamers. When proceeding under sail only the banjo frame (and propeller) was hoisted up a well built through the counter until it was clear of the water, thus removing all propeller drag.

Bank. Area of sea bottom that rises rather considerably above surrounding ground.

Banker. Name given to cod fishing vessel on Grand Banks of Newfoundland.

Banking Oars. Properly means putting men to pull the oars, but rarely used in this sense. Generally used as meaning 'double banking'.

Bank of Oars. Series of manned oars on one side and at one level in a craft propelled by rowing.

Banner Cloud. Lenticular cloud that may appear to be 'flying' from top of a high mountain during strong breeze.

Banyan Day. Nowadays, a day on which discipline is relaxed and concessions are made. Originally, a day on which no meat ration was issued. How change of meaning came about is not clear.

Bar. Bank across entrance to a harbour, which acts as a partial breakwater but may cause confused sea with onshore winds. 2. Unit of barometric pressure; equals one megadyne per square centimetre. Equivalent to 29·53 inches of mercury, with temperature of 273°A in Lat. 45°.

Barbarising. Scrubbing a deck with cleansing powder and sand.

Barber-hauler. A line with a block on the end through which a jib sheet is rore, led down to the rail abreast the mast.

Barbette. Fixed armoured rampart around a warship's heavy guns; inside of which guns were trained, and over which they were fired. Superseded by turret mountings.

Barcarolle. Waterman's song that keeps time with oars. Originally a song of Venetian gondoliers.

Barcolongo. Spanish name for a long, narrow, undecked vessel that was propelled by oars and, or, sails.

Bareca. Original form of 'Breaker' and 'Barricoe'. Small keg used in a boat for holding drinking water or spirits.

Bare Poles. Masts when no sail is set.

Barge. Large flat-bottomed boat used for the conveyance of goods. Capacity from 50 to 1000 tons. 2. Flat-bottomed sailing craft, carrying about 100 tons, used in narrow seas and inland waters. 3. Fourteen oared, double banked boat used in Royal Navy.* 4. Power boat carried for exclusive use of flag officer in Royal Navy. 5. Pleasure boat, or boat of state, fitted for comfort and display.

Barge Pole. Long pole, sometimes fitted with hook, used as a boat-hook, bearing off spar, or quant.

Bark. Poetic word for a ship or boat. Barque.

Barkantine. Barquentine.

Bar Keel. Projecting keel that extends downwards outside plating.

Barnacle. Small marine animal in valved shell. Has legs like curled hair, and a stalk-like body. Attaches itself to underwater surface of hull, thus greatly increasing water friction.

Barnacle Paint.* Preparation formerly put on ships' bottoms in an endeavour to prevent attachment of barnacles and other marine life. Was forerunner of antifouling paints.

Barograph. Self-recording barometer, either mercurial or aneroid. That used at sea is, strictly speaking, an aneroidograph.

Barometer. Instrument for measuring pressure of atmosphere. For use at sea it can be either 'mercurial' or 'aneroid'.

Barometric Light. Luminous glow in vacuum of a barometer when mercury is agitated. Probably due to friction between mercury and glass, or to splashing of mercury, when these occur in a vacuum.

Barometric Tendency. Rate and direction in which barometric pressure changes. Is of utmost importance in weather prediction.

Barothermograph. Instrument that gives a graphical registration of both pressure and temperature.

Barque. Sailing vessel with three or more masts: fore and aft rigged on aftermast, squared rigged on all others.

Barquentine. Sailing vessel with three or more masts. Square rigged on foremast, fore and aft rigged on all others.

Barracuda. Edible but vicious pike-shaped fish that attacks fishing nets and bathers.

Barratry. Any wrongful act knowingly done by the master or crew of a vessel to the detriment of the owner of either ship or cargo; and which was done without knowledge or consent of owner or owners.

Barre.* Old name for tidal bore in river Seine.

Barrel. Wooden cask holding about 36 gallons.

Barrel of Capstan. Main member of capstan; circular in shape to allow hawsers to be passed around for heaving; fitted with poppets, in which capstan bars can be inserted; having pawls that take in a pawl ring around its lower edge.

Barricoe. Small cask often used in boats for storing drinking water. Also called 'breaker' or 'bareca'.

Barrier Ice. 'Shelf Ice.'

Barrow's Dip Circle. Instrument used in hydrographic surveying for measuring magnetic dip and total magnetic force at a place.

Bar Shoe. Suspended fitting, across stem of a ship, to take towing wires of a paravane.

Bar Taut. Said of a rope when it is under such tension that it is practically rigid.

Barysphere. Solid mass of iron, and other metals, assumed to exist inside Earth and under lithosphere.

Base. That solid ingredient in a paint that is responsible for its body.

Base Metals. Those that do not resist action of acids. All metals except those in gold, silver and platinum groups.

Basin. Artificially enclosed space of water in which ships are placed for loading, discharging or for repairs.

Basking Shark. Sometimes called 'Sunfish'. Lies motionless on sea surface for fairly long periods. Is about 36 feet long. Although a member of shark family, is not at all ferocious.

Bateau.* Name formerly given to a lightly-constructed boat that was relatively narrow for its length. Usually broad at middle length but narrowed quickly towards ends.

Bathometer. Instrument for measuring oceanic depths.

Bathyal Zone. Between 100 and 500 fathoms below sea surface. Bed is usually mud; perhaps containing organic oozes.

Bathybic. Existing in the depths of the sea.

Bathymetric. Pertaining to oceanic soundings.

Bathymetry. Measurement of deep sea soundings.

Bathysphere. Spherical diving chamber capable of withstanding oceanic pressures at great depths.

Batil. Two-masted sailing craft of China Seas. About 50 feet long and fitted with outrigger.

Batten. Long, narrow, thin strip of wood or metal used for different purposes, particularly for securing hatch tarpaulins. 2. Length of sawn timber from 2 to 4 inches thick and from 5 to 7 inches wide.

Batten Down. To securely cover a hatch with one or more tarpaulins that are secured by hatch battens and wedges.

Battened Sails. Sails stiffened with horizontal battens. The battens help to keep a taut sail when on a wind, and sail may be quickly struck in a squall. Though fairly common in the East they are not often seen in home waters.

Batten Observations. Method of determining amount of roll of a ship by having a sighting hole in centre line of ship, and a vertical graduated batten in same transverse line but near ship's side. Amount of roll is determined by noting where sea horizon cuts graduated batten.

Battery. A group of guns. All guns on one side of ship. 2. In electricity is two or more cells connected together, either in parallel or in series.

Battledore. Flat metal fitting put athwartships through cable bitts, and projecting on either side, to keep turns of cable from riding.

Battleship. Heavily armed and armoured warship in which a certain amount of speed is yielded to obtain maximum hitting power and protection. Displacement may approximate 50,000 tons.

Bauer Wach Turbine. Auxiliary turbine geared to propeller shaft and driven by exhaust steam from triple expansion main engines.

Baulk. Beam. Beam-shaped piece of timber.

Baulk Yawl. Balc yawl.

Bawley. Sailing boat used in lower reaches of Thames for shrimping or whitebait and sprat fishing. Usually cutter rigged with loose-footed mainsail.

Bawse.* Old name for a ship's boat. *See* 'Buss'.

Bay. Arm of sea extending into land and with a seaward width that is greater than amount it goes into the land. 2. Compartment, in hold or store, with entrance not less, in width, than depth of the compartment.

Bay Ice. Alternative name for 'Young Ice'.

Bayou. Long, narrow channel, often marshy, in Louisiana and nearby areas.

Beach. Sandy or shingle shore on which waves break. To beach a ship is to haul, or drive her ashore above high water line.

Beachcomber. Unemployed seaman who frequents the waterfront of ports abroad.

Beach Master. An officer whose duties are to supervise the landing of stores, and the disembarkation of men, on a beach.

Beacon. Erection on land, or in shoal waters, intended as a guide or warning to vessels navigating in sight of it. May be fitted with a light, or lights, or may emit a radio signal. Always carries some distinctive characteristic so that it may be identified.

Beak. Originally, a brass projection from prow of ancient ships, designed to pierce, or hold, an enemy vessel. Later, was a small deck forward of forecastle and supported by knees from stem and forward timbers.

Beak Head. Another name for 'Beak'.

Beam. Transverse member that goes between opposite frames, or ribs, to support ship's side against collapsing stresses, and to support a deck. As a dimension, is greatest width of a vessel. As a relative bearing, is a direction at right angles to ship's fore and aft line.

Beam (of Anchor). Old name for the shank.

Beam Clamp. Clamp fitted to grip bulb of a beam and provide an attachment for block of purchase.

Beam Ends. Vessel said to be 'on her beam ends' when she is lying over so much that her deck beams are nearly vertical.

Beam Fillings. Shifting boards fitted between beams of a hold to prevent movement of surface of a bulk grain cargo.

Beam Hooks. Strong and tested hooks used when lifting hatch beams.

Beam Knee. Member that connects a beam to the frame of a ship. Types in general use are bracket, slabbed, split, turned, welded knees.

Beam Sections. Those used in steel shipbuilding comprise angle, bulb angle, channel bar, T bar, T bar bulbed, built T, bulbed T (or Butterfly) and built girder.

Beam Trawl. Trawl in which mouth of purse is kept open by a beam. Usually fitted with iron trawl heads to keep trawl clear of ground.

Bear, Bears, Bearing. Words used to indicate a direction of an object; expressed as a compass direction, or as relative to ship's for and aft line.

Bear. Short name for constellation Ursa Major, the 'Great Bear'.

Bear. Heavy scrubber, weighing about 40 lb., used for cleaning decks. Paunch mat, loaded with holystones, used for same purpose.

Bear a Hand. To assist; to hasten; to work quickly.

Bear Away. To turn away from the wind by putting up the helm. To 'bear up'.

Bearding. Term used, in wood shipbuilding, for removing wood to modify a curve or line. Bearding of rudder is rounded fore edge that takes in a corresponding recess (also called a 'bearding') in stern post.

Bear Down. To approach: to move towards. To move tiller to leeward so that vessel's head comes to the wind.

Bearers. Short beams going across just above keelson of a wooden ship, or stern sheets of a boat. Also called 'Flat floor'.

Bearing. Direction in which an object, or position, lies from an observer. Usually defined by the angular measurement between a line from an observer's position and a datum line passing through that position. Can be a 'Relative', 'True', or 'Compass' bearing.

Bearing Plate. Graduated and ballasted plate by which relative bearings may be taken when it is inconvenient to use compass.

Bearings.* Widest part below plank sheer of wooden ship.

Bear Off. To thrust away; to hold off. Order given to bowman of boat when he is required to push boat's head away from jetty, gangway or other fixture at which boat is alongside. Order given, also, when it is required to thrust away, or hold off, an approaching object.

Bear Up. To put helm to windward, thus turning to leeward. Bear away.

Beating. Sailing close hauled to get to windward on alternate tacks.

Beaufort Notation. Code by which weather conditions may be tersely expressed by a combination of letters of alphabet.

Beaufort Wind Scale. Devised by Admiral Beaufort in 1808 to express wind force by use of numbers from 0 to 12. Revised in 1905 by Dr. G. C. Simpson. Further revised in 1926 to express wind speeds.

Beaufort Wind Force	Mean Wind Speed in Knots	Descriptive Term
0	0	Calm
1	2	Light air
2	5	Light breeze
3	9	Gentle breeze
4	13	Moderate breeze
5	19	Fresh breeze
6	24	Strong breeze
7	30	Near gale
8	37	Gale
9	44	Strong gale
10	52	Storm
11	60	Violent storm
12	—	Hurricane

Becalmed. Said of a sailing vessel when she is unable to make way owing to absence of wind.

Becket. Loop of rope, sennit or wire used for fastening, or for attachment.

Becket Bend. Name sometimes given to 'Sheet Bend'.

Becket Rowlock. Rope strop, around thole pin, to confine an oar when rowing.

Becueing. Sometimes called 'Scowing'. Dropping anchor with cable made fast to crown but stopped to ring with medium-strength lashing. In normal circumstances anchor will hold in usual way. Should anchor get foul, extra force used in weighing will break stop at ring, and anchor can then be weighed by crown.

Bed. That on which anything—anchor, engine, etc., rests. Formerly applied to the impression left in the ground by a vessel that has grounded.

Bed of Bowsprit. That part which rests on stem, or in bowsprit hole. Is greatest diameter of bowsprit; outer end diameter being 2/3rds, and inner end diameter being 5/6ths, that of bed.

Bed of Capstan. Trued and strengthened part of deck on which capstan is placed. Also applied to flat steel plate that carries pawl rack.

Bedplate. In general, any plate on which a fitting is bedded. Bedplate of main engines is of cast iron or mild steel. Carries crankshaft and bears engines. Rests on cast iron chocks and is through fastened to tank tops by holding down bolts.

Bees Block. Hardwood fitting at head of bowsprit for taking fore topmast stay and, in R.N., foretop bowline.

Bees of Bowsprit. Another name for 'Bees Blocks'.

Beetle. Heavy wooden mallet.

Before the Mast. Said of a man who goes to sea as a rating, and lives forward. Forward of a mast.

Before. On the forward side of.

Bel. Radio unit for measuring loss or gain in strength.

Belace.* Old form of 'Belay'.

Belage.* Old form of 'Belay'.

Belat. Strong N.N.W. offshore wind prevalent off south coast of Arabia during winter.

Belay. To make fast a rope by turning up with it around a cleat, belaying pin, bollard, etc. Often used by seamen in the sense of arresting, stopping or cancelling; e.g. 'Belay the last order'.

Belaying Pin. Pin-shaped pieces of wood or metal fitted in a socket and used for belaying ropes.

Belfry. Ornamental mounting for carrying ship's bell.

Belfast Bow. Name given to raked stem introduced by Harland & Wolff of Belfast. Allows larger forecastle deck without increasing waterline measurements; provides increased forward buoyancy when pitching.

Bell. Compulsory fitting in all seagoing ships. Must not be less than 12 in. diameter at mouth, and must be so placed that its sound is not obstructed. Frequent and rapid ringing of bell is required of an anchored vessel in fog. Ship's time is indicated by half-hourly striking of bell.

Bellatrix. Star γ Orionis. S.H.A. 279°; Dec. N6°; Mag. 1·7. Name is Latin for 'Warlike'. Astrologers maintained that star had a martial influence.

Bell Buoy. Buoy carrying bell often rung by action of waves, or wash of passing vessels.

Belleville Boiler. First large water tube boiler to be successful for marine purposes (1901).

Bell Rope. Small rope on tongue of bell for ringing it. 2. Rope on a pump handle to assist in turning it.

Belly. Rounded swell of sail caused by wind and stretching of the canvas.

Belly Band. Extra cloth of canvas in single topsail or course. Fitted below lowest reef points and in line with bowline bridle.

Belly Halyard. Gaff halyard leading through block at middle of gaff to give extra support.

Below. Below upper deck. Under hatches.

Beluga. Arctic whale that comes as far south as St. Lawrence river, and sometimes ascends it. Has no dorsal fin and is less than 20 feet in length.

Bembridge Type. Cutter-rigged yacht with jib and mainsail. Overall length about 20 ft., beam 6 ft.

Benches. Seats in after part of boat or in cockpit of a yacht. Often called 'Sheets'.

Bench Mark. Line cut in stone of a permanent erection to indicate a datum level or a distance from datum. British practice uses a line and an indicating small arrow; U.S.A. uses a 3½-in. disc of copper alloy.

Bend. An intertwining of a rope so that it is securely attached to another rope.

Bend Cable. To attach cable to an anchor.

Bending Moment. Force, or sum of forces, that bends or tends to bend any member out of its normal line.

Bending Shackle. Shackle that connects outboard end of cable to anchor.

Bends. Strongest and thickest side strakes of wooden ship. First bend is on water line, second and third bends immediately above it. They are responsible for girder strength of ship and form anchorages for beams, knees and foot hooks.

Bends. Name often given to 'Diver's Palsy' or 'Caisson Disease'.

Bend Sail. To attach a sail to its appropriate spar. Square sails are bent, by robands, to jackstays on yards. Fore and aft sails are usually laced to gaffs and booms, but may be seized to them.

Bend Test. Applied to rivets. Shank is bent and hammered through 180° while cold, and should show no sign of fracture.

Beneaped. State of a vessel when aground and unable to float at high water because rise of neaping tide is insufficient. Also said of vessel unable to leave harbour or dock for want of sufficient water due to the same cause.

Benetnasch. Star η Ursæ Majoris. S.H.A. 154°; Dec. N 50°; Mag. 1·9. Name is Arabic for 'Mourners'. The four stars of Ursa Major were anciently looked upon as a bier, and the three stars as mourners (benetnasch). Star is now known as Al Kaid, 'the chief (mourner').

Bengal Light. Old name for 'blue light' pyrotechnic signal.

Benguela Current. Inshore branch of Agulhas Current, setting N'ly from Cape of Good Hope and merging in Equatorial Current.

Bennis Stoker. Mechanical stoker for feeding furnaces of Scotch boilers.

Benson Steam Generator. High pressure boiler in which water is carried in tubes. Can raise steam from cold water in 20 minutes.

Bent Heads. Old name for ribs of boat.

Bentick. See 'Bentinck'.

Bentinck. Triangular course used as storm sail in American ships. Introduced by Captain Bentinck.

Bentinck Boom. Spar used for stretching foot of foresail in small square rigged vessels.

Bentinck Shroud. Shroud going from masthead to a spreader, or futtock stave, and thence to chains on opposite side of ship.

Bent Timbers. Ribs of a boat.

Berenice's Hair. See 'Coma Berenicis'.

Berg. Short form of 'Iceberg'.

Bergy Bits. Pieces of ice, about the size of a small house, that have broken off a glacier, or from hummocky ice.

Bermuda Rig. Yacht in which main feature is a triangular main sail with no gaff. Mast and head of sail are higher than with cutter rig, but centre of effort is somewhat lower. Owing to height of masthead it is usual to fit spreaders to shrouds.

Bernouilli's Equation. Relates to the motion of any particle of a frictionless fluid, and is considered in study of wave motion. When P is pressure, D density, G gravity, Z depth below a given horizontal plane, and Q resultant velocity, equation is then given as:—

$$\frac{P}{D} + \frac{Q}{2} = GZ + \text{constant.}$$

Berth. Place in which a vessel is moored or secured. Space around a vessel at anchor, and in which she will swing. An allotted accommodation in a ship. Employment aboard a ship. To berth a vessel is to place her in a desired or required position.

Berth and Space. Alternative form of 'Room and Space'.

Beset. Said of a vessel when she is entirely surrounded by ice.

Besselian Day Numbers. Quantities given in 'Nautical Almanac' for place of a star. They yield necessary corrections for long period precession, nutation and aberration.

Bessel's Figure of Earth. Equatorial diameter 6,377,397 miles; polar diameter 6,356,079 miles. Compression 1/299·2.

Best Bower. Name sometimes given to starboard bower anchor, which formerly was slightly larger than port (or 'small') bower.

Betelgeuse, -guese, -guex. Star α Orionis. S.H.A. 272°; Dec. N 7°; Mag. 2·1 to 2·6. An enormous star some 24,000,000 times size of Sun. Distant 190 light years. Candlepower 1200 times that of Sun. Temp. 2600°A.

Between Decks. Between lower and upper decks. In cargo vessels, is space in holds between lower hold and main deck. Also called 'Tween decks'.

Between Perpendiculars. Distance between fore side of stem and after side of stern post when measured along summer loadline.

Between Wind and Water. That area of a vessel's outer plating that lies between her waterline when upright and her waterline when heeled away from wind.

Bibbs.* Pieces of timber bolted to hounds of mast to secure trestle-trees. Hounds are sometimes called 'Bibbs'.

Bibis. Small one-masted vessel, fitted with outrigger, used for trading in China Sea.

Bible. Seaman's nickname for a large holystone.

Bidhook.* A small boathook.

Bight. Indentation in land, forming a gulf or bay. 2. Bent part of rope or hawser that forms a loop. 3. That part of slack rope, sail or canvas, that hangs down between the fastenings or attachments.

Big Topsail. Name given to a square topsail sometimes carried by cutter rigged yachts.

Bilander. Originally was a small coasting vessel (by land-er) of North Sea. Usually had two masts and carried about 100 tons. Name has spread all over the world, and is identical with French 'belandre' and Spanish and Portuguese 'balandra'.

Bilboes. Bar of steel, on which slide steel shackles for confining the ankles of unruly men.

Bilge. Originally 'bulge'. Rounded part of ship's underwater body where side curves round towards keel. 2. That part of a cask or barrel where circumference is greatest.

Bilge Blocks. Substantial blocks that support a vessel's bilge when in dry dock.

Bilge Boards. Planks that cover bilges and prevent cargo being damaged by bilge water, or affecting flow of water to pump.

Bilged. Said of a ship when she takes the ground so that her bilges leak.

Bilge Heels.* Old name for 'Bilge pieces'.

Bilge Keel. External keel placed along bilge of a steel ship. It assists in stiffening, protects plating from stresses when on ground, reduces rolling at sea. Similar keels are fitted to boats to reduce leeway, to protect bottom planking when on ground and to form hand grips in event of capsizing. All bilge keels cause a reduction in speed.

Bilge Keelson. Internal fitting going intercostally between floors, and along line of bilge, in vessels having no double bottom tanks. Margin plate of tanks fulfils this duty in modern ships.

Bilge Piece. Another name for 'Bilge Keel'; but sometimes used to denote 'Bilge Keelson'.

Bilge Planks. Doubling planks put in way of bilges of wooden ships, either externally or internally, to stiffen them.

Bilge Pump. Pump for drawing water from bilges. In modern ships this is operated by steam or electricity. In sailing ships it was worked by hand; in Scandinavian sailing ships it was compulsory to fit a windmill for working pumps.

Bilges. Spaces, between margin plates and ship's side, into which water drains, and from which it can be pumped.

Bilge Shore. Wooden shore put under bilge of a vessel when in dry dock, or during building.

Bilge Water Alarm. Old fitting that caused a clockwork bell to ring when there was excessive water in the bilges. Accumulated water raised a float that released an escapement on bell.

Bilgeway. Foundation of the cradle that supports a vessel on the sliding ways during building and launching.

Bill, of Anchor. Extreme and more or less pointed end of arm. Projects beyond fluke and assists anchor to bite into the ground.

Billage.* Old form of 'Bilge'.

Billboard. Inclined ledge, either of iron or sheathed with iron, that supported flukes of Admiralty pattern anchors when stowed.

Billet. Piece of steel, in an intermediate state, less than 36 inches sectional area.

Billet Head. Wooden post in bow of whaler, around which the harpoon line runs. 2. Decorative work on stem of a ship with no figure-head.

Bill of Adventure. Signed document issued by a person who states that the goods shipped by him belong to another person who stands by the risk or chance of the adventure. Also, signed document given by master or agent to one who ships goods at his own risk.

Bill of Entry. Document rendered by H.M. Customs by exporters or importers when shipping or unshipping goods. Gives nature, amount, and value of goods and declares port of origin, or destination.

Bill of Health. Medical certificate given to master by Health authorities at a port. States health conditions at that port and health conditions of ship's personnel. Can be 'Foul', 'Clean', or 'Suspected', according to whether infectious disease exists, does not exist, or may exist.

Bill of Lading. Receipt given by shipmaster, or other representative of owner, to shipper of cargo when received on board. Is not a contract of carriage but should epitomise the conditions under which the goods specified are carried.

Bill of Sight. Entry at Customs when, owing to insufficient knowledge of goods, a Bill of Entry cannot be made out. Goods are then landed, in presence of Customs Officers, and Bill of Entry prepared.

Bill of Store. Document authorising shipment of dutiable articles as ship's stores and free of duty.

Bill of Sufferance. Customs authority for a vessel to carry dutiable goods when trading in British waters.

Billow. Large, crested wave. Word is used more by poets than by seamen.

Billy Blue. Nickname given to Admiral Cornwallis (1744–1819) because he usually hoisted the 'blue peter' immediately after anchoring.

Billyboy. Small, bluff-bowed sailing vessel of Humber river.

Binary Star. One that appears to be a single star but is actually two stars revolving around a common centre of gravity. Sometimes one is dark star. In all cases the result is that apparent magnitude of star is a variable quantity.

Binnacle. Stand, of wood or metal, in which a compass is suspended and in which lighting and compensating units are carried. Top of binnacle protects compass from sea and weather and, also, reduces glare of lighting.

Binocle. Correct but never used name for binocular glass.

Binoculars. Common name for binocular, or 'two-eyed' glasses. A pair of small telescopes connected so that each eye looks through one of them. Those used by seamen are either 'Prismatic' or 'Galilean'.

Bipod Mast. Mast consisting of two members joined at the top, their bases seperated in athwartship direction, obviating the need for shrouds.

Bireme. Greek or Roman warship having two banks (or tiers) of oars on each side. Greek equivalent was 'Dieres'.

Birlin. Large boat, with six or eight oars, anciently used by chieftains of West Hebrides.

Bissextile. Name applied to a leap year, because it had 'two sixth' days before the calends of March (February 24) instead of an additional day at end of February.

Bite. Anchor is said to bite when it begins to hold in ground.

Bittacle.* Old name for binnacle. From Latin 'habitaculum' (lodging place), or from French 'boite d'aiguille' (box of the needle).

Bitt Compressor. Steel or iron lever with foot hinged near cable bitt, but with a sufficient clearance for cable to pass. By hauling on a tackle at head of compressor the cable is nipped against the bitt, and so held while turns are passed around bitt.

Bitter. Turn of cable passed around a riding bitt.

Bitter End. That part of a cable that is inboard of a riding bitt. It has been suggested that it should be 'better end'; the inboard part having had less wear than the outboard.

Bitt Head. Upper end of a vertical timber passing through two decks, and well secured at each. Generally used for stoppering, or turning up with, hemp cables.

Bitting Cable. Passing one or two turns of cable around a cable bitt.

Bitt Pin. Steel bar, circular in section, passed fore and aft, through a cable bitt. Together with battledore, which passes transversely, it prevents cable from coming off bitt.

Bitts. Vertical fittings of steel, iron or wood, securely fixed and adequately strengthened for taking ropes that are subject to heavy stresses; e.g. towing hawsers mooring ropes, etc. In sailing ships, they carried sheaves for topsails sheets and other ropes.

Bitt Stopper. Cable stopper that holds outboard cable while inboard part is being turned up around bitt.

Bitumastic Pains. Consist largely of pitch. They have an excellent body, no action on metals; are waterproof, elastic and durable.

Bitumen. Asphalt, tar, pitch and other non-mineral products of coal and coal residues. To a certain extent, may be product of wood distillation.

Blackbirder. Vessel employed in transport of negro slaves from Africa to America, or Pacific Islanders.

Black Book of Admiralty. Vellum folio containing ancient statutes of the Admiralty. Based largely on the 'Laws of Oleron', the existing folio was completed in Tudor times, but it contains matter that is certainly as old as 13th century.

Black Down. To paint standing rigging, starting aloft and working downwards.

Black Gang. Stokers, firemen and trimmers in a steamship.

Black Ice. Thin, dark-coloured-ice with no snow on it.

Black Strake. Strake below lower deck gun ports of old warships when they were painted in light colours. This strake was painted with tar and lamp black.

Black Stream. English form of 'Kuro Siwo'.

Blackwall Hitch. Manipulation of a rope for temporarily attaching it to a hook.

Blackwall Ratline. Length of rope seized to foremost shroud of lower rigging, and used to confine running gear.

Bladdy. Scottish word for squally weather accompanied by rain.

Blade. Of oar. Broad, flat part that is put vertically in water to form pivot of a lever. 2. Of turbine, small piece of steel, perpendicular to rotor drum, against which steam impinges. 3. Of propeller. One of projections from boss, and shaped as part of a screw thread.

Blake Stopper. Steel chain and slip, secured to anchor deck, for temporarily holding outboard cable. Proof strength is one-third that of cable.

Blanket. To take the wind from a vessel to leeward.

Blare. Paste made of tar and hair. Used for caulking seams of boats.

Blast Pipe. Steam pipe, with restricted aperture, fitted in funnel to induce or accelerate draught when necessary.

Blazer. This article of men's wear got its name from H.M.S.

Blazer. In 1845 her captain, J. W. Washington, dressed his ship's company in blue and white striped jerseys.

Bleed a Buoy. To make a hole in it and drain it of water.

Bleed the Monkey. Surreptitiously to remove spirit from a keg or cask by making a small hole and sucking through a straw.

Blind Bucklers. Hawse hole stoppers that completely close the holes; cable having been removed.

Blink. Pale yellow gleam in sky caused by light being reflected on cloud by ice. Rarely produced by bergs unless they are flat topped.

Blister. Compartment built on outside of ship's underwater body to minimise effect of torpedo on hull plating.

Blister Ship. Any ship fitted with blisters.

Blizzard. Strong wind accompanied with low temperature and snow.

Block. Grooved sheave working in a frame or shell. Used to alter direction of a rope or chain, or to gain a mechanical advantage by reeving a purchase. Types vary largely, to suit different purposes. They are classified by their special peculiarities. These are: number of sheaves, number of scores, nature of stropping, nature and size of shell, etc. Wooden types are: Common (taking a rope one-third their size), Clump (taking a rope half their size) and snatch blocks. Sailing vessels may carry Sister, Fiddle, Fly, Tye, Furniture and other blocks. Parts of block are: shell, sheave, strop, score, swallow, choke and pin. Loss of effort when using blocks is from one-tenth to one-eighth for each sheave used.

Blockade. War operation to prevent approach to, or departure from, an enemy's territory or coast, of all shipping and commerce.

Block and Block. 'Two blocks.'

Block Coefficient. Ratio that the immersed volume of a vessel bears to the product of her immersed length, breadth and draught. Also termed 'coefficient of fineness'.

Blood and Guts. Name sometimes given to Union Jack.

Blood Money. Bonus sometimes paid—usually to a keeper of a seaman's boarding house—for finding a seaman to fill a vacancy in crew.

Bloom. Piece of steel, in an intermediate state, having a sectional area of more than 36 inches. 2. An iridescent coating on iron or steel, usually known as 'Mill Scale'.

Blooper, Big Boy or Shooter. A very light large sail used in a yacht.

Blow. Gale of short duration. 2. Spouting of a whale.

Blubber. Thick coating of fat directly under skin of whales.

Blubber Guy. Strong triatic stay on old whalers. Tackles were made fast to it when removing blubber from whales alongside.

Blubber Spade. Spadelike knife, with staff handle, used for cutting blubber from whales.

Blue Back. Chart produced by private firm and mounted on stiff blue paper. Although based on Admiralty and other surveys they embody additions, omissions and alterations that are intended to be helpful to those for whom they are produced. Introduced by Imray, Laurie, Norie & Wilson, London.

Blue End. Of magnet is south-seeking end.

Blue Ensign. Blue flag with Union flag in upper canton. May be worn by merchant vessels, under warrant from Admiralty, when stated conditions have been fulfilled, and some yacht clubs.

Blue Funnel. Nickname given to line of ships owned by Alfred Holt & Co., of Liverpool, whose funnels are of this colour.

Blue Jacket. Seaman of Royal Navy. Often used to include other ratings who wear a somewhat similar uniform.

Blue Light. Pyrotechnic flare used as signal for pilot, and for some other purposes.

Blue Magnetism. Magnetism that is of same polarity as North Pole of Earth. It is, therefore, south seeking.

Bluenose. Name applied to a Nova Scotian vessel or seaman.

Blue Peter. 'P' flag of international Code of Signals. Hoisted singly, its significations is that vessel hoisting it is about to sail, and that all persons concerned are to repair on board.

Blue Pigeon. Name sometimes given to the hand lead. Name is also given to 'A Handy Book for Shipowners and Masters', on account of colour of its binding.

Blue Pole. That end of a magnet that has same polarity as Earth's north magnetic pole. It is usual to make an arbitary assumption that lines of magnetic force enter at blue pole.

Blue Squadron. Division of a fleet of warships. Was middle squadron of three, was commanded by a vice-admiral and flew a blue pendant. After 1653, was rear division, under a rear-admiral. Name was discontinued in 1864.

Bluff. Large, high, steep cliff that projects into the sea.

Bluff Bowed. Said of a vessel with broad bow and rather obtuse entry.

Bluff Headed. 'Bluff bowed.'

Blunt-Headed Cachalot. The sperm whale.

Board. Track of a sailing vessel between one tack and the next. 2. To go on or into a ship. 3. To forcibly enter a ship after beating down the defence. 4. Sometimes used as meaning the side of a ship.

Board and Board. Said of two ships that are close alongside each other. Sometimes used as meaning 'Tack and alternate tack'.

Board a Tack. To haul on a tack so that it is nearly two blocks.

Boarders. Men detailed for boarding an enemy vessel.

Boarding. Going on board a ship either peaceably or forcibly.

Boarding Nets. Rope netting formerly placed to deter boarders.

Boarding Pike. Spear, about 6 ft. long, formerly used both by boarders and defenders against boarders.

Board of Trade. Now the Department of Trade and Industry.

Board of Trade. Government department once responsible for, among other things, the examination of officers of Merchant Navy, and for issue of certificates of competency; for the survey of ships and other matters concerning shipping.

Board of Trade Enquiry. Investigation of accident or causalty connected with a British vessel.

Board of Trade Notices. Orders, instruction or advice given to seamen by the Board of Trade.

Board of Trade Returns. Periodical statistical information given by Board of Trade on matters connected with shipping.

Board of Trade Surveyor. Official who surveys and inspects ships and their equipment to ensure that all statutory requirements are fulfilled.

Boards. Sawn timber less than $2\frac{1}{2}$ in. thick and more than 4 in. wide.

Boat. Small craft not normally suitable for sea passages but useful in sheltered waters and for short passages. As far as Regulations for Preventing Collisions at Sea is concerned, a boat is a small non-seagoing vessel propelled exclusively by oars.

Boat Boom. Spar projecting from ship's side, when in harbour, and fitted with lizards and ladders for securing boats and for manning them.

Boat Drill. Statutory mustering at lifeboat stations so that all on board are fully aware of their duties and stations in the event of emergencies that require the use of boats.

Boat Flag. Small flag for use in a boat.

Boat Hook. Long wooden shaft with hook at one end. Used in a boat to extend reach of bowman or stern sheet man, and for fending off.

Boat Lead and Line. Small lead, about 7 lb., with five or six fathoms of small line attached. Marked in same manner as hand lead—but in feet instead of fathoms.

Boat Note. Receipt, given by Mate, for a parcel of cargo brought alongside in a boat, barge or lighter. Is acknowledgment that this has been put alongside.

Boat Oars. To place the oars fore and aft in boat after rowing.

Boat Pulling. Seaman's term for 'rowing'.

Boat Rope. Led from forward in a ship to a boat riding alongside, to hold it fore and aft against sea, wind and tide. Secured in sea boat to prevent boat broaching if foremost fall is released before after fall.

Boat's Badge. Distinctive badge or emblem on bows of naval boats, to distinguish boats of any one ship from similar boats of other ships.

Boat Skids. Transverse pieces of hard wood, on which a boat may rest when stowed inboard.

Boat's Recall. Signal flag, or flags, hoisted by a ship to recall a particular boat or boats.

Boatswain. The oldest rank of officer in shipping. Originally was the husband and master. In R.N. is a commissioned officer who, with other duties, is responsible for rigging of a ship and for the upkeep of it. In M.N., is a trustworthy and experienced petty officer who is foreman of the seamen.

Boatswain's Call. Small whistle, of unusual shape, that is used in R.N. to enjoin silence while an order is given; or to give an order. Has two notes, high and low, both of which can be 'trilled'. Most orders have a conventional 'call'. Parts are: Gun (pipe), Buoy (barrel or spherical chamber at end of gun), Orifice (hole in buoy), Keel (flat stiffener attached to gun and buoy), Shackle (ring in keel for attachment to chain).

Boatswain's Chair. Stave of cask, or other flat piece of wood, having hole at each end through which ends of a rope are passed and spliced. In upper bight of rope an eye, or thimble, is seized for attachment to halyard. Wood makes a seat when working aloft, man's weight being borne by rope sling.

Boatswain's Mate. Assistant to a boatswain. In R.N. is a petty officer whose duties are to repeat all orders and 'pipes', and to assist the officer of the watch.

Boatswain's Pipe. Name erroneously given to 'Boatswain's Call'.

Boatswain's Plait. Intertwining three strands of rope by using one as a heart and plaiting and hitching the other two around it.

Boatswain's Pride. Slight forward rake of a mast.

Bobstay. Rope or chain that stays a bowsprit downward. Lower end is secured to stem.

Bobstay Fall. Hauling part of bobstay purchase.

Bobstay Holes. Holes in stem to take lower end of bobstay.

Bobstay Purchase. Tackle in upper end of bobstay, for setting it up; fall leading inboard along bowsprit.

Bode's Law. Is not a law, but a remarkable coincidence. Writing 0, 3, 6, 12, and so on, and then adding 4 to each of the numbers we have a close approximation of relative distances planets are from Sun. Inserting a decimal point, we get approximate distances in 'astronomical units'. Neptune, however, does not conform.

Body Hoops. Bands around a built mast.

Body Plan. Drawing that shows end elevation of a vessel, either forward or aft, with water line, buttock lines, diagonals, etc.

Body Post. Forward part of stern frame, carrying end of tail shaft.

Boiler. Generator in which water is heated and converted into steam. Two main types used by ships are Scotch and water-tube boilers.

Boiler Mountings. Fittings on a boiler that are necessary for its efficient working. Include safety valve and its easing gear, water gauge, test cocks, pressure gauges, main and auxiliary stop valves, feed check valves, scum cock or valve, blow down valve, whistle valve, salinometer cock, etc.

Boiler Scale. Deposit that forms on inside of boiler, particularly on heating surfaces of furnaces and tubes. Its action is to obstruct transmission of heat to water, so causing a rise in fuel consumption, and to increase density of water. Scale is mainly sulphate of lime with smaller quantities of chalk and chloride of magnesia.

Bolide. Large meteor, particularly one that explodes.

Bolinder Engine. Two-stroke semi-Diesel type that requires a hot bulb to expedite vaporisation of fuel, but does not require air for fuel injection.

Bollard. Large and firmly secured post of circular section and used for securing hawsers, mooring ropes, etc. Often fitted in pairs on same base plate. Also, rotating post in bow of whale-boat. Used for taking a turn with harpoon line.

Bollard Timber. Alternative name for 'Knight head'.

Bollocks. Blocks in bunt of topsail yards of large ships. Topsail ties are rove through them to increase lifting power.

Bolometer. Instrument for measuring amount of radiant energy by measuring difference of resistance to electrical current when a fine wire is exposed to the radiation.

Bolsters. Shaped pieces of timber, sometimes canvas, placed in hawse pipe, on mast, or other position, to take chafe off a moving rope.

Bolt. Length of canvas as supplied. About 39 to 40 yards.

Boltrope. Special type of long thread rope sewn around edges of sail to strengthen it and to carry cringles and thimbles. Stitched on after side of square sails, and on port side of fore and aft sails.

Boltsprit.* Old name for 'Bowsprit'.

Bolt Strake. That timber of a wooden ship, through which the bolts fastening the beams were passed.

Bombard. Olden pieces of ordnance, of large calibre, that threw bombs up to about 300 lb.

Bomb Ketch. Small vessel with specially strengthened beams for carrying a bombardment mortar.

Bomb Vessel. Strongly-built vessel that carried a heavy gun for bombardment purposes.

Bonaventure Mizzen. The fourth mast carrying a lateen sail. (16th century).

Bonded Goods. Those held in a bonded warehouse pending payment of Customs charges.

Bonded Store. Bonded warehouse.

Bonded Warehouse. Building in which dutiable goods are stored until they are required, and duty is paid. Owner gives a bond to Customs authorities for payment of duty when goods are withdrawn.

Bond Note. Written authority to remove goods in bond from a bonded store; either for export or for transference to another store.

Bone. Foam at stem of a vessel underway. When this is unusually noticeable she is said to 'have a bone in her teeth'.

Bongrace.* Matting made of old rope and used for protecting outside of vessel when working amongst ice.

Bonito. Fish of mackerel family, found in Mediterranean. Is great enemy of flying fish.

Bonnet. Extension of a sail, that is laced along the foot of sail.

Booby Hatch. Sliding cover that has to be pushed away to allow passage to or from a store room, cabin of small craft, or crew's quarters.

Boom. Spar for extending foot of sail; usually for fore and aft sails—but studding sails were sheeted to booms. 2. Floating and moored obstruction placed across a navigable channel to prevent passage of enemy vessels, and to detain them while under fire. 3. A derrick boom. 4. Dhow largely used in Persian Gulf. Double ended, straight stem, steered by a yoke, plank bowsprit.

Boom Cradle. Block having a semi-circular recess for end of boom to rest in.

Boom Crutch. Vertical support for a boom when not in use.

Boom Foresail. Sail on after side of schooner's foremast, and having a gaff and boom. It is, actually, the foresail, but is given the name to differentiate it from the forestaysail—which is often called the 'foresail'.

Boom Guy. After guy of a spinaker or studdingsail boom.

Boom Irons. Flat, circular fittings at quarters and ends of yards of square rigged ships that carry studdingsail booms.

Boom Jigger. Tackle used for rigging out a studdingsail boom.

Boomkin. Small boom projecting from ship's side to give more spread to sail. Rigged forward, it takes fore tack; further aft, it takes standing part of main tack; right aft, takes tack of main trysail.

Booms. Spar deck between fore and main masts; on which spare booms, spars and boats are stowed.

Boom Square Sail. Name given to fore course in some old ships when foot of sail was extended on a boom—to facilitate getting it over fore stay when tacking.

Boom Stays. Attachments of boom to mast, together with fittings that keep heel of boom in its correct place.

Bootes. (Greek = Ploughman) Constellation in approx. R.A. 14 h; Dec. 20°N. Has one bright star, Arcturus.

Booti. Small coastal dhow of 20 to 40 tons. Has mat bulwarks. Undecked.

Bootlegging. Carrying intoxicating liquors up to, sometimes into, territorial waters of U.S.A. during period when prohibition was in force (1920–33).

Boot Top. Ship's side plating between light and load water lines.

Boot Topping. Paint or composition used for protection or preservation of boot top. In 18th century meant scraping ship's side in way of water line and then coating this area with a compound of resin, sulphur and tallow as a protection against worm and weed.

Bora. NE'ly winter wind in Adriatic Sea, often dangerous because it arrives without warning.

Bordage.* Planking on sides of wooden ship.

Borda's Circle. Repeating reflecting circle for measuring horizontal angles with great precision.

Bore. Steep tidal wave that develops in certain rivers and passes up in advance of normal tide undulation. Caused by narrowing of channel and decrease in depth. Occurs in Severn, Seine, Trent, Ganges and other rivers.

Boreas. Greek name for North wind.

Boring. Forcing a vessel through newly-formed ice.

Borrowing. Setting a course that may appear to be unsafe but will be safe through action of wind and/or current.

Bos'n. Boatswain.

Bosom Piece. Short length of angle iron inside a butted joint of angle iron. Usually extends for at least three rivets spaces on either side of butt.

Boson.* Old spelling of 'Boatswain'.

Boss (Propeller). That part in which blades are fixed, and through which the end of shaft passes.

Botter. Dutch coasting craft with one mast, jib and staysail and a mainsail with short gaff. Usually double ended and with lee boards.

Bottle Screw. Left hand and right hand threaded screws led into outer ends of a shroud or 'bottle'. Has largely superseded dead-eyes and lanyards for setting up rigging.

Bottom. Name sometimes given to hull of a ship.

Bottom Boards. Light boards fitted in bottom of boat to keep all weights off bottom planking, and on frames and timbers. Keep crew's feet dry if any water in boat.

Bottom End Bearing. Crank pin bearing, over which connecting rod of reciprocating engine is fitted.

Bottom Plating. That part of a ship's shell plating lying between the bilge and the keel plate.

Bottomry. Pledging a ship or the freight she earns to raise money necessary to complete voyage. Repayment is contingent on safe arrival of vessel. Name was given, originally, to 'Marine Insurance'.

Bottomry Bond. Legal document given to one who advanced money on bottomry. Guarantees repayment on safe arrival at destination.

Bouguer's Log. Invented by French scientist in 1747. Log ship consisted of a wood cone with a ballasting weight on a 50-ft. line, to prevent wind effect on cone.

Boulene.* Old spelling of 'Bowline'.

Boulter. Fishing line consisting of long pieces of tarred rope fitted with hooks at fathom intervals, and sinkers near each hook.

Bound. Proceeding in a specified direction, or to a specified place.

Bourdon Gauge. Instrument for measuring pressure of steam by means of a curved piece of flattened bronze tubing, the end of which is sealed. When steam is admitted at open end the tube tends to straighten, thus moving sealed end. Appropriate gearing causes amount of movement to indicate corresponding pressure.

Bouse. To heave, or haul, downwards on a rope. Originally, and strictly, heave meant an upward pull, haul meant a horizontal pull, bouse meant a downward pull: but these distinctions have not survived.

Bow. That part of a ship's side that extends aft and downwards from stem. 2. Direction between right ahead and 45° from it. 3. Bow of shackle is the rounded part opposite the jaw.

Bow Chaser. Gun mounted forward for firing at a pursued ship.

Bower Anchor. Principal anchor; carried forward and attached to a bower cable. Stowed in hawse pipe or on anchor bed.

Bower Cable. Cable attached to a bower anchor.

Bow Fast. Rope laid out from bow of vessel to a bollard or other fixure, on quay or wharf, for mooring.

Bowge.* Rope fastened to middle line of sail to make sail lie closer to wind.

Bowgrace.* **Bowgrass.*** 'Bongrace.'

Bowl. Hemispherical container of compass card.

Bowl.* Cylindrical fitting at mast head for lookout man to stand in.

Bowline. Rope leading from deck to leeches of topsails and courses when on a wind; weather bowlines being hauled taut to stop leeches from shivering. 2. Secure and quickly made loop that was put in end of bowline for attachment to bridle, and in bridles for attachment to bowline cringles. This very useful loop is used for numerous purposes in everyday work, and is particularly valuable for giving security to a man working with insecure foothold, or over the side.

Bowline Bridle. Rope stretched between two bowline cringles in leech of a square sail. Bowline rides on this bridle.

Bowline Cringles. Cringles fitted into leeches of square sail to take ends of bowline bridle. They had no thimble.

Bowline on a Bight. Bowline made with rope doubled and so made that two loops are formed. Gives increased safety to man working aloft or over side, one loop being under his arms, man sitting in other loop.

Bow Locker. Compartment just abaft stem. Usually contains boatswain's gear that is in frequent use.

Bowman. In a pulling boat, is man who pulls a bow oar. In all boats he is responsible for working forward boat hook and for such other duties necessary at the bows.

Bow Oar. Foremost oar in a pulling boat. The bowman.

Bow Painter. Boat's painter.

Bow Rudder. Additional rudder fitted at stem of certain vessels, ferries, etc., that work in restricted waters in which there is not always room to turn round.

'Bows.' Order given in a pulling boat when approaching ship's gangway or landing place. Bowman boats his oar and stands by with boat hook.

Bowse. To pull downward on a rope or fall.

Bowse Down. To bouse.

Bow Shackle. Harp shackle.

Bow Sheets. Flooring in fore part of boat. Head sheets.

Bowsprit. Spar projecting over stem, on which it rests. Outer end is stayed down to stem by bobstay; inner end is secured by gammoning. In sailing ships is often prolonged with a jib boom and flying jib boom.

Bowsprit Cap. Vertical fitting at forward end of bowsprit to take heel of jib boom, jib boom footropes, heel chain and heel ropes of jib boom.

Bowsprit Collars. Strops or bands round bowsprit to take bobstay, bobstay shrouds and stays.

Bowsprit Shrouds. Ropes or chains extending from outer end of bowsprit to ship's bows on either side. Give lateral support to bowsprit.

Bow Stopper. Short length of strong cable-laid rope with stopper knot in foremost end. Formerly used for holding hemp cables— to which it was lashed—while bitting or unbitting. Name is now given, by Merchant Navy, to a cable controller.

Bow Thruster. A controlable pitch propeller placed in an athwart-ship tunnel in the fore part of a ship open to the sea, which gives a transverse thrust to assist a ship when berthing or manoeuvring at slow speed.

Box Hauling. Wearing a sailing ship on her heel. Only done when there is no room to wear and ship misses stays while trying to tack. Headsails are thrown aback, and helm put down as ship gathers sternway.

Boxing the Compass. Reciting the points, or quarter points, of the compass in correct order, and starting at any named point.

Box Off. To pay off ship's head from wind by flattening in head sails and bracing head yards close up. Done when ship has been brought too close to wind by bad steering, or if wind has shifted ahead.

Box Ventilator. Temporary wooden ventilator inserted in cargo, particularly grain, to ensure through ventilation. Usually square in section. Longitudinal sides may be solid planking or skeleton battens, depending on nature of cargo.

Boxwood Scale. Specially graduated scale for converting measurement of unchanged coating of a Kelvin sounding tube into fathoms of depth.

Boyer. Flemish sloop having superstructure, or 'castle' at each end. Used for buoy laying.

Boyle's Law. The volume of a perfect gas, at constant temperature, varies inversely as the pressure on it. This law is fundamental in engineering and other branches, and is the fundamental principle of the Kelvin, and similar, sounders.

Brace. Rope or tackle by which a yard is adjusted in the horizontal plane.

Brace.* Arm of the sea. Mandeville calls St. George's Channel 'Brace of Seynt George.'

Brace Aback. To adjust a yard so that wind comes on fore side of sail.

Brace In. To adjust a yard by bracing so that it becomes more athwartships.

Brace of Shakes. Very short interval of time. (Etymology very dubious.)

Brace Pendant. Pendant, from yard arm, through which a brace is rove.

Braces. Gudgeons of a rudder.

Brace To. Adjust a yard so that sail becomes a little aback. Done when tacking or wearing.

Brace Up. To adjust a yard so that it becomes less athwartships.

Bracket.* Carriage of a ship's gun.

Bracket Frame. Floor or frame in which frame and reverse frame are stiffened by plates (brackets) that may be watertight, or may have lightening holes.

Bracket Knee. More or less triangular plate secured to beam and frame to unite them, and to preserve the angle.

Bracketless System. Introduced by Sir Joseph Isherwood to dispense with brackets at end of longitudinal and bulkhead stiffeners. Loss is made good by increasing scantlings of girders.

Bracket Plate. Iron or steel plate secured with its plane perpendicular to another plate which it supports and stiffens.

Brackets. Ornamental work. *See* 'Hair Bracket', 'Console Bracket'.

Bragozzi. Small fishing vessels of the Adriatic.

Brahmin Knot. Triangle knot.

Brailed Up. Said of spanker, gaffsail or trysail when it is gathered into mast by hauling on brails.

Brails. Ropes used for gathering a spanker, trysail or gaffsail into mast. Led through block on one side of mast, round sail and through block on other side of mast; being seized, at bight, on leech of sail.

Brake.* Name given to handle of ship's bilge pump.

Brash. Ice broken into pieces, about 6 ft. in diameter and projecting very little above sea level.

Bratsera. Ubiquitous trader in the Aegean Sea carrying 50 to 150 tons of cargo. Originally a two-masted lugger.

Brave West Winds. Prevalent west winds in temperate latitudes.

Brazil Current. Southern branch of Equatorial Current. Sets S'ly from off Cape San Roque to approximately latitude of River Plate; there merging into 'Southern Ocean Drift'.

Breach. Said of waves that break over a vessel.

Breadth. Of a flag, is measure of its vertical side. Also used to denote number of widths of bunting used; width of bunting being 18 inches, a five breadth flag would measure 7 ft. 6 in. vertically.

Breadth Line. Longitudinal line of a ship, following the upper ends of timbers of frames.

Break. Of forecastle or poop, is the midship end of the raised deck. A wave is said to break when it curls over and foams.

'Breakage.' Ship's immunity from this damage exists only when it is not due to any fault of ship.

Break Bulk. To commence to discharge cargo.

Breaker. Small cask used for bringing off water in boats. Also used for carrying provisions in a boat. Anglicised form of Spanish 'Bareca'. 2. Wave with broken or breaking crest.

Break Ground. To heave anchor out of ground. Term had a special meaning when sailing on Sunday was considered unlucky. If possible, ship broke ground on Saturday, moved a few yards and then re-anchored: voyage could then be considered as starting on Saturday. This subterfuge was known as 'Breaking ground'.

Breaking (a Flag). Hoisting a flag that has been rolled up and secured by a bow knot in its halliard, and then freeing the flag by jerking on its downhaul. It is conventionally wrong to break a ship's national ensign.

Break Sheer. Said of a vessel at anchor when, due to action of wind or tide, she brings wind or tide on the opposite bow.

Breakwater. Construction, usually of masonry, erected on seabed and extending above sea level. Intended to protect a harbour, anchorage or other area from effect of sea waves. Word is used, also, to denote any structure that defends against a free flow of water.

Breaming. Removing fouling from a ship's bottom by burning.

Breast. Mooring line leading approximately perpendicular to ship's fore and aft line. To breast a sea is to point a ship's bows in the direction from which the sea comes.

Breast Anchor. Anchor laid out from forward or aft, in direction at right angles to ship's fore and aft line.

Breast Backstay. Royal or topgallant mast backstay that was set up, on either side, with tackles that could be slacked off when yard was braced sharp. Often called 'shifting backstay'.

Breast Band. Name sometimes given to breast rope of leadsman's chains.

Breast Casket.* Old form of 'Breast Gasket'.

Breast Fast. Mooring rope that leads at right angles, approximately, to ship's fore and aft line.

Breast Gasket. One of the gaskets used for securing bunt of sail.

Breast Hooks. Horizontal plates in fore end of vessel. Are secured to ends of stringers, and thus hold two sides together and preserve the bow form. In wooden vessels, are horizontal knees fulfilling the same functions.

Breast Knees. 'Breast Hooks.'

Breast Off. To move a vessel away from a wharf or jetty by forcing her sideways from it, either by warps or bearing off spars.

Breast Plate. Horizontal plate that connects the upward extensions of the side plating at the stem.

Breast Rail. Upper rail at fore end of poop.

Breast Rope. Mooring rope, leading from bow or quarter, at about right angles to ship's fore and aft line. 2. Sennit band at top of apron of leadsman's chains, against which leadsman leans when

heaving lead. 3. Formerly, ropes attaching parrels to yards, and
so confining yards to mast.

Breastwork. Stanchions and rails at fore end of poop and after
end of forecastle in old ships; and, athwart upper deck of ships
with no poop—to indicate forward limit of quarter deck.

Breech. Outside angle of a knee timber. 2. The rear end of a gun.

Breeches Buoy. Life-buoy fitted with canvas breeches on inner
circumference and used, with rocket apparatus, for hauling
ashore people in a vessel wrecked near the shore.

Breechings. Back ropes or backstays. 2. Ropes by which guns
were hauled out before firing and which limited their recoil
on firing.

Breeze. Wind of moderate strength. Usually convectional.

Brereton's Log Scale. For timber measurement. Gives actual or
solid contents of a log in 'board feet'. Is based on mean
diameter of log. Invented by Bernard Brereton of Seattle,
Washington.

Brewerton's Course Recorder. *See* 'Course Recorder'.

Brickfielder. Hot N'ly wind in Australia during summer.

Bridge. Superstructure, on upper deck, having a clear view forward
and on either side, and from which a ship is conned and navigated. 2. In boiler furnace, is an arch of firebricks built at
combustion chamber end of furnace.

Bridle. In general, any fairly short length of rope secured at both
ends. In particular, length of rope used as 'bowline bridle'.

Bridle Cable. Length of cable led from ship to middle of another
length of cable that is anchored at each end.

Bridle Part. That part of cable that extends from hawse pipe to
anchor when anchor is stowed outboard.

Bridle Port.* Port, in bow, in which a bow chaser gun was mounted
but which was used, also, for a bow fast or mooring bridle.

Brig. Vessel with two masts and square rigged on both of them.

Brigantine. Originally, a ship of brigands, or pirates. Up to end
of 19th century was a two-masted vessel square rigged on foremast and main topmast, but with fore and aft mainsail. Latterly,
a two-masted vessel with foremast square rigged, and mainmast
fore and aft rigged.

Brig Mast.* Mast fitted with a topgallant mast.

Briming. Fisherman's name for phosphorescence of sea.

Brine. Non-freezing liquid made by dissolving calcium chloride in
water—40 oz. per gallon—for refrigerating purposes.

Bring To. Stop way of ship. Bring ship's head to wind. Bring
ship to an anchor.

Bring Up. To bring ship's head to the wind. To come to anchor.

Bristol Fashion. Good and seamanlike appearance. Precisely
correct.

British Corporation. Former classification society that was founded
to classify ships built on lines that Lloyd's would not accept. Is
an 'Assigning Authority' for granting load line certificates.

British Ship. Vessel owned by a British subject, or by a corporation established in, and subject to, some part of the Empire; and whose owner or owners have their principal place of business in the British Empire.

British Summer Time. Greenwich Mean Time plus one hour.

British Thermal Unit. Amount of heat necessary to raise temperature of one pound of fresh water from 62°F to 63°F. Equals 252 calories.

Broach. To turn a ship to windward.* 2. To pilfer or steal cargo. 3. To make a hole in a cask or barrel, generally with unlawful intent.

Broach To. Said of a ship under sail when she turns toward wind while running free, possibly putting all sails aback.

Broad Fourteens. Sea area off N.E. coast of Holland, having an almost uniform depth of about fourteen fathoms.

Broad on the Bow. Bearing of an object when 45° or more from right ahead, but before the beam.

Broad Pennant. Swallow tailed, tapering burgee, white with a red St. George's cross, flown by a British warship carrying a Commodore or the senior officer of a squadron when not of flag rank. May have a red ball in inner upper canton.

Broadside. Side of a ship as distinguished from bows and stern. 2. Salvo from all guns on one side of a warship.

Broken Backed. Said of a vessel excessively hogged.

Broken Stowage. Space, amongst the cargo in a hold, that it is impossible to fill on account of it being too small to take a unit of the cargo loaded.

Broker. An intermediary between two principals. Insurance broker arranges insurance between a shipowner and underwriter. Ship-broker acts between shipowner and shipper or charterer.

Brokerage. Fee charged by a broker for his services.

Broom at Masthead. Traditional sign that a vessel is for sale. Rarely seen nowadays.

Brought by the Lee. Said of a vessel when running under sail and wind comes on the other quarter.

Brought To. Said of a rope or cable when it is brought to a capstan, windlass or a winch, and turns are taken for heaving.

Brought Up. Said of a ship when she rides to her anchor after dropping it. Also said when a vessel is under sail and the wind suddenly comes ahead and stops her way.

Brought up all standing. Said of a vessel under way when her sails are put aback by a sudden shifting of the wind. Used colloquially to mean 'astounded' or 'flabbergasted'.

Brow. Substantial gangway used to connect ship with shore when in a dock or alongside a wharf.

Brown Boveri Turbine. Low-pressure exhaust turbine geared to propeller shaft of reciprocating engine. Reverses when going astern, and is then fed with live steam.

Brown Curtis Turbine. Impulse turbine of Curtis type and compounded for velocity.

Brown Gyro Compass. British made gyro compass with several novel features. *See* 'Gyro Compass'.

B.S.T. British Summer Time.

B.T.H. Curtis Turbine. Steam turbine (British Thomson-Houston) in which kinetic energy in first wheel is abstracted in two or more stages, and part of turbine is compounded for velocity and pressure.

Bubble Sextant. Sextant fitted with an attachment carrying a very sensitive bubble that indicates the horizontal. By use of this instrument sights can be taken when horizon is indistinct or invisible.

Buccaneer. Literally means 'a smoker of meat or fish'. Name was given to privateers who traded with the New World, in defiance of Spain, between about 1524 and 1700.

Bucklers. Shaped blocks of wood inserted in hawse holes to prevent the entry of sea.

Bucko. A bullying and tyrannical officer.

Budgee Jack. Flag worn at spritsail topmast by British privateers of 17th and early 18th centuries. Consisted of Union flag with red border on outer and lower sides.

Budget. Flat vertical plate under after swim of Thames dumb barges: practically a fixed rudder.

Buffer. Spring unit inserted in rudder chains to absorb sudden shocks. 2. R.N. nickname for a Chief Boatswain's Mate.

Bugalet.* Small coasting craft of Brittany. Had a very short foremast with two jibs and a taller mainmast with two square sails.

Buggalow. East Indian coasting vessel having one mast and lateen sail. Has navigated from Gulf of Cutch since time of Alexander the Great.

Builders' Measurement. Tonnage rating resulting from:

$$\frac{\text{Length} - 0.6 \text{ Breadth} \times (\text{Breadth} \times \frac{1}{2} \text{ Breadth})}{94}$$

Was legal measurement for merchant ships from 1773 to 1835; and for yachts until 1873.

Building Slip. Sloping erection, in shipbuilder's yard, on which ships are built.

Built Block. Wood pulley block with shell made of more than one piece of wood. Also called 'Made block'.

Built Mast. Mast made from more than one tree or timber.

Bulb and Plate Keel. Vertical plate with additional weight distributed along lower edge. Gives additional stability to broad, shallow draught sailing craft.

Bulb Angle. Angle bar having one edge bulbed.

Bulb Lead Keel. Forerunner of 'Bulb and Plate' keel. Introduced by Bentall in 1880.

Bulge. Former name for 'Bilge'. Now alternative name for 'Blister'. The latter is a cellular compartment built on outside of bilge. Introduced during 1914–18 war to take impact of torpedo, and so preserve hull plating.

Bulgeway. Bilgeway.

Bulk.* Old name for hull of a ship. 'Bulkhead' is a reminder.

Bulk Cargo. Cargo such as grain, coal, iron ore, etc., that is loaded in bulk and not in packages or containers.

Bulkhead. Transverse, or fore and aft, vertical partition in a vessel to divide interior into compartments. Not necessarily watertight. Increases rigidity of structure, localises effects of fire and, when watertight, localises inflow of water.

Bulk Oil. Oil cargo when carried in tanks instead of casks, drums, etc.

Bull Bars. Galvanised iron bars between beams of holds in ships carrying carcases of meat.

Bull Dog Grip. U-shaped steel of circular section with a movable bridge that forms a clamp. Two wires being inside U, and clamp screwed up, the wires are incapable of independent movement.

Bulling. Putting water into empty cask or barrel to prevent it drying and becoming leaky. Colloquially used to signify diluting.

Bullivant's Wire Nippers. Steel appliances for securely holding a wire when under stress. There are two types, fixed and portable. In either type an increase of stress results in an increase of clamping effect.

Bull Ring. Transverse circular steel ring at stem head. Fairleader for head ropes and tow rope. Also called 'Panama Lead'.

Bull Rope. Rope leading downward from bowsprit to a buoy, to keep latter away from ship's bows or stem. Name is generally given to any rope leading steeply downward from forward. 2. Length of rope used for hauling items of cargo under square of hatch for hoisting. 3. Rope used for topping a derrick so that standing topping lift can be shackled to deck.

Bull's Eye. Solid, round wooden block with groove around circumference and three or four holes pierced transversely. Lower end of rigging is seized in around groove; lanyard is rove through holes to make a purchase for setting up the rigging. 2. A more or less circular patch of blue sky very often observable over centre of a revolving storm.

Bull's Eye Cringle. Bull's eye with one large hole in centre; sometimes used in tack or leech of sail.

Bull's Nose. Masonry; with rounded front on outward side, between dock entrances.

Bullwanger. Small strop on yard arm through which a lashing is rove to keep head cringle of a sail in place.

Bulwarks. Plating or wooden erections around outboard edge of upper deck to protect deck from entry of sea.

Bumboat. Shore boat that comes alongside ships in harbour with provisions for retail sale.

Bumping. Name given to the intermittent touching of the ground by a vessel in shoal water.

Bumpkins. Small booms projecting on either side of bows, to which the fore tacks are hauled down.

Bunder Boat. Surf boat of Malabar Coast.

C

Bung. Plug that closes the hole in bilge of a cask, keg, barrel, etc.
Bung Up and Bilge Free. Correct stowage of casks, barrels, etc., especially those containing liquids. It precludes leakage and ensures the head timbers of the cask being vertical. Bilge is kept free by support under quarters.
Bunk. Built in bed, or one of a series of beds, on board a ship.
Bunker Clause. Inserted in a charter party to define the terms on which the charterer takes over the bunkers at the commencement of a time charter, and the ship owner at the conclusion of the time charter.
Bunkers. Compartments in which coal is carried. Name is also given to the fuel (oil or coal) used for ship's propelling and auxiliary machinery.
Bunt. Middle portion of a square sail.
Bunting. Thin, woollen material used for making flags, ensigns, etc.
Buntline. Line for hauling up middle of foot of a square sail when furling it.
Buntline Cloth. Additional cloth stitched to a square sail in way of buntlines. Keeps chafe of buntlines off sail.
Buntline Hitch. Made by passing buntline through its cringle and then clove hitching it around its own part, with final hitch next to the cringle.
Buoy. Floating object that is used to mark a position. 2. Object with a large reserve buoyancy that allows it to support a required load. 3. To buoy a position is to mark it with a buoy.
Buoyage. The act of placing buoys. 2. Establishment of buoys and buoyage systems. Applied collectively to buoys placed or established.
Buoyancy. Difference between weight of an immersed, or partly immersed, object and the upward pressure of the liquid in which it is. If the weight be lighter the buoyancy will be 'positive'; if it be heavier the buoyancy will be 'negative'. Also defined as the vertical component of the water pressures acting on an immersed or partly immersed body.
Buoyancy Aid. A lifejacket which has less than the officially required buoyancy or does not keep the wearer face-up when floating.
Buoyant Jacket. A lifejacket or Buoyancy Aid.
Buoyancy Tank. Tank fitted in lifeboat to give one cubic foot of positive buoyancy for each person boat is certified to carry. Made of brass, copper, muntz or yellow metal, weighing at least 18 oz. per square foot.
Buoy Rope. Rope connecting a buoy with its moorings, or with the sunken object that it marks. Particularly applied to rope connecting anchor and anchor buoy.
Buoy Rope Knot. Very similar to a stopper knot. It was put in end of hemp cable when used for mooring to a buoy. Purpose was to prevent end of rope slipping through seizing by which it was secured.
Burden. Carrying capacity of a vessel expressed in tons. In M.S.A. means 'Net registered tonnage'.

Burdwood's Tables. Tables computed by Commander John Burdwood, R.N., to give Sun's true azimuth at intervals of 4 mins. when observed between Lats. 30° and 60°. Later extended by Commander J. E. Davis and P. L. Davis of Nautical Almanac Office, to include Lats. 0° to 30°.

Bureau Veritas. International body that supervises building of ships and other maritime matters. An 'Assigning authority' for Load Line.

Burgee. Rectangular flag with a swallow tail fly. 2. Triangular flag of a yacht club.

Burgoo. Seaman's name for oatmeal porridge. First mentioned in Edward Coxere's 'Adventures by Sea' (1656).

Burlap. Coarse cloth made from jute and other fibre. Used for protecting cargo.

Burr Pump.* Old type of bilge pump, in which a leather cup was lowered down a wooden shaft. When lifting, side of cup fitted side of shaft and brought up all water above cup.

Burthen.* 'Burden.'

Burton. Tackle made with single and double block. Standing part is spliced round neck of single block strop. Differs from a luff tackle in that strop of single block has a longer throat.

Burton's Tables. Volume of navigational tables with 5-figure logarithm values. Led the way in giving comprehensive nautical quantities with minimum number of pages.

Burt's Bag and Nipper. Ingenious apparatus that was one of the first attempts to give reliable soundings while under way. Lead line was rove through nipper on an inflatable bag that remained on surface—vertically above lead—as long as it was slacked out. When line was hauled in, nipper on bag gripped lead line, thus indicating depth.

Buscarle.* Man in command of 'Buss'.

Bush. Lining inserted in machinery and in sheaves of blocks to reduce friction and take wear that would otherwise come on member around which a particular item revolves.

Buss. Formerly, a cargo vessel with large stowage space, in the 16th century up to about 100 tons. Later, the name was given to a fore and aft rigged fishing vessel, with main and mizen masts and bowsprit, used in herring fishing. The name is very old.

Butt. Joining of timber or plates in which the ends are flush and in close contact. 2. Cask containing liquid, the quantity varying with the nature of the liquid. With beer, is 108 gallons and wine is 117 gallons.

Butter Battens. Special small-sized dunnage wood used when stowing butter or eggs.

Butterfly Block. Small snatch block, of clump type, with hemp strop and tail. Formerly used for hauling in deep sea lead line.

Butterly Bulb. Rolled steel of bulb T section.

Butt Joint. Joining of two plates, or timbers, in which their ends are flush and in close contact. Can be strapped or welded.

Buttock. Overhanging and rounded-in part of a vessel's stern. It commences aft and terminates, on either side, where it merges into the run.

Buttock Lines. Curves derived from a series of longitudinal sections of the hull of a vessel by vertical planes parallel to keel and at uniform intervals from it. They thus indicate the transverse form at any given thwartship position.

Butt Sling. Length of rope with eye splice in one end and whipping on other end.

Butt Strap. Piece of metal covering a butted joint. Riveted to each of the butted plates to regain strength lost by the butting.

Butt Weld. The joining of two members by putting their edges closely in contact and welding along the seam.

Buys-Ballot's Law. Originally stated that if observer's back is to a wind in Northern hemisphere then barometric pressure will be lower on his left hand than on his right; this rule being reversed in Southern hemisphere. Modern convention assumes man faces direction of wind, thus reading 'higher' for 'lower' in original rule.

By. Used with other words, in sailing, to mean close to the wind.

By and Large. Sailing with wind before the beam—and sailing with wind abaft the beam. 2. A nautical way of saying, 'Taking the rough with the smooth' or 'striking a mean'.

By Points. Those points of the compass that contain the word 'by'.

By the Board. Overboard and by the ship's side.

'By the Deep.' Erroneous report sometimes made by leadsman when depth is judged to be an exact number of fathoms not marked on line, Should be 'Deep'.

By the Head. Said of a vessel when her draught forward exceeds her draught aft.

'By the Mark.' Prefix to a leadsman's report of depth when the mark on a vertical lead line is at water level; this report being free from estimation.

By the Run. To let go a rope and let it run without hindrance.

By the Stern. Said of a vessel when her draught aft exceeds her draught forward.

By the Wind. Said of a vessel sailing close hauled.

C

c. 'Mainly cloudy, (not less than three-quarters covered)'. (Beaufort Weather Notation).

Cab. Name given to screened shelter at wing of a navigating bridge.

Caban.* Cabane.* Old spelling of 'Cabin'.

Cabin. Small compartment in a ship set apart for use of an officer, passenger or other person.

Cabin Boy. Junior rating whose duty is to attend on officers of a ship. Title is obsolescent. At one time he was a protege in the retinue of an admiral; as such he was the forerunner of the midshipman.

Cabin Passenger. Person who has paid at least £25 for his passage (or £3 25p for every 1000 miles), has at least 36 clear square feet of space for his exclusive use and has a signed contract ticket.

Cable. Nautical unit of distance, having a standard value of 1/10th of a nautical mile (608 ft.). For practical purposes a value of 200 yards is commonly used. 2. Rope of more than 10 inches in circumference and made of three right-handed ropes laid up left handed. These were used for attachment to anchor before chain cable was manufactured, and were up to 36 inches, or more, in circumference. 3. Wrought iron chain used for attachment of ship to her anchor. Made in lengths of 12½ fathoms (R.N.) or 15 fathoms in Merchant Navy: these lengths are called 'shackles'. 4. Wire carrying an electric current. 5. Telegraphic message from overseas.

Cable Bends.* Two small ropes used for lashing end of hemp cable to its own part after it had been bent to anchor ring.

Cable Certificate. Signed document stating strength of cable supplied to a ship.

Cable Clench. Strong steel forging fitted at bottom of cable locker for securing inboard end of cable. Is securely attached to ship's structure, vertically below navel pipe, and is tested to 20 per cent above proof strength of cable.

Cable Flags. Small numeral flags that may be used forward, when working cable, to indicate to bridge the number of shackles of cable that are out.

Cable Holder. Horizontal drum having sprockets to take link of cable. Is frictionally connected to spindle geared to capstan engine. Each cable has its own holder, thus allowing for independent veering or heaving.

Cable Hook. 'Chain Hook.' 'Devil's Claw.'

Cable Jack. Long steel lever fitted with a fulcrum. Used for slightly-lifting cable when a slip has to be passed under it.

Cable Laid. Said of ropes made by laying up three ropes so that they make one large rope.

Cable Locker. Compartment in which cable is stowed and the inboard end secured.

Cable Nipper. Short length of small rope, sennit or selvagee that was used for temporarily lashing a messenger to a cable when heaving in. Alternatively, an iron nipper, consisting of two shaped bars, hinged at one end, were used with chain cables and a chain messenger.

Cable Party. Part of a watch, or specially selected men, detailed to work cable.

Cable Shackle. Special shackle used for joining lengths of cable. Pin is flush with sides of shackle and is secured by a metal or wood pin passing through lug and pin.

Cable Ships. Vessels specially fitted for laying and repairing submarine telegraph cables. They have a large vertical sheave at stem head.

Cable Stopper.* Short length of very strong rope, securely attached to deck, with stopper knot at outboard end. Cable was lashed to it while inboard part was passed around the riding bitts.

Cablet.* Hemp cable not exceeding 10 inches in circumference. Like cables, it was 101 fathoms in length.

Cable Tier.* Special platform built right forward, between decks and used for flaking rope cable clear for running out.

Cable Tire.* The coils of a rope cable.

Caboose. Old name for cook's galley. At one time was applied to the funnel casing. Now applied to any small enclosed space.

Caburns.* Small spunyarn line used for serving rope cables to prevent chafe. Also used for seizings.

Cachalot. Sperm whale. Length up to 70 feet. Lives in 'schools'; one school of females, or cows, and another of immature bulls.

Cage Mast. Lattice mast of steel tubes formed into a criss-cross spiral, held at intervals by horizontal rings. Fitted to U.S. battleships of early twentieth century.

Cagework.* Name once given to the uppermost decorative work on the hull of a ship.

Caique. Light craft of Bosphorus, propelled by oars or sail. Elsewhere in the Mediterranean a two-masted cargo-carrying vessel.

Caisson. Steel floating structure that can be flooded and sunk to close entrance to a dry dock. In engineering, is a watertight casing in which men can work under water.

Caisson Disease. Diver's palsy, or bends. Paralysis caused by the formation of air bubbles in blood of a diver coming to surface too quickly after working at considerable depth, or under unusual air pressure. If bubble reaches the heart, the man dies at once: if it forms on brain or spinal cord there is paralysis of legs.

Calcareous. Word used to denote quality of bottom when of limestone. Fragments of shell, coral and minute skeletons may often be seen.

Calcium Light. Cylinder containing phosphide of calcium, which ignites when in contact with water. Is attached to a life buoy so that its position can be known when put overboard in the dark.

Calendar. Presentation of civil time in days, weeks, months and years.

Calendar Line. Alternative name for 'Date Line'.

Calendar Month. Interval between any given date and 00 hrs. of the same date in the following month.

Calibration. Determination of error, if any, between the value indicated by an instrument and the actual value that it should indicate.

California Current. Name used in U.S.A. for 'Mexico Current.'

Caliper. Pair of bowed legs, working on a common pivot, used for measuring internal or external diameters of circular items. Size of chain cable is measured with it.

Calk.* Old astrological word for the calculating of a horoscope. 2. Old spelling of 'Caulk'.

Call. Small whistle, of a special type, used by boatswains' mates—occasionally by a commissioned boatswain—in Royal Navy when passing orders or piping the side.

Call Boy. Junior rating in Royal Navy whose duty is to repeat all orders piped by boatswain's mate.

Callipers. Calipers.

Callippic Cycle. Period of 27,759 days, or 940 lunations, being approximately 76 years. New and full Moons occur on same day and date—within about 6 hours. Calculated by Callippus (Greek), about 350 B.C., as an improvement on Metonic Cycle.

Call Sign. Group of Morse signs allotted to a ship, or shore station, for identification purposes.

Calm. Absence of wind. No agitation of sea surface.

Calorie. Amount of heat necessary to raise temperature of one gramme of pure water through one degree Centigrade.

Calorific Value. Number of heat units obtained by complete combustion of unit amount of fuel. Generally expressed as number of British Thermal Units (B.T.U.) per lb. of fuel.

Calorimeter. Apparatus for determining specific heat of a substance by finding how much heat is lost or gained when its temperature is changed in standardised circumstances.

Calving. Breaking away of a mass of ice from a glacier or iceberg.

Cam. Projection on wheel or curved plate when shaped to give an alternating or eccentric movement to another member that is in contact.

Camber. Arched form of a deck or beam to shed the water. Standard camber for weather decks is 1/50th of vessel's breadth. 2. Recess, in masonry of a dock entrance, for a sliding caisson to enter when entrance is opened. 3. Small tidal dock, originally for discharge of timber, now used for loading or discharging and for embarkation and disembarkation from small boats.

Camber Keel. Keel so shaped that its depth increases as it approaches the forward and after ends.

Camel. Hollow vessel of iron, steel or wood, that is filled with water and sunk under a vessel. When water is pumped out the buoyancy of camel lifts ship. Usually employed in pairs. Very valuable aid to salvage operations. At one time were usual means of lifting a vessel over a bar or sandbank. Were used in Rotterdam in 1690.

Cam Shaft. Shaft carrying a cam.

Cam Wheel. Wheel eccentrically mounted to transmit an alternating movement.

Canadian Water Carriage of Goods by Sea Act, 1910. Relates to carriage of goods by sea from Canadian ports to places outside Canada.

Canal. An artificial waterway used for the passage of ships or boats.

Canals of Mars. Name given to lines of dark spots on surface of Mars. Suggestions has been made that they are irrigation canals, but this is not now accepted.

Can Buoy. Buoy with flat top above water. Said to be corruption of 'cone buoy'. Often conical under water, with mooring chain attached to apex of cone.

Cancelling Clause. Inserted in a charter party, or other document, to entitle one party to withdraw from the contract if specified conditions are not observed.

Cancelling Date. In a charter party, is latest date at which a chartered ship must be ready to commence to fulfil terms of the charter.

Cancer. Latin for 'crab'. Constellation situated about R.A. 9 h and Dec. $10°-13°$N. Has no star brighter than Mag. 4. 2. Fourth sign of Zodiac, extending from $90°$ to $120°$ celestial longitude. Sun is in this sign from June 21 to July 22 (abt.).

Candela. International unit of luminous intensity since 1948. 1 candela $=0.98$ candles.

Cane Fender. Large bundles of canes bound together and used to protect ship's side from chafing when alongside wharf, quay or another vessel. Hazel rod fenders are frequently called by this name.

Canes Venateci. 'Hunting dogs.' Constellation between Bootes and Ursa Major. Brightest star is Cor Caroli, Mag. 3.

Can Hooks. Two flat hooks running freely on a wire or chain sling. Hooks are put under chime of casks, weight is taken on chain sling or wire. Weight of lift prevents unhooking.

Canicula. Latin for 'Dog Star'. Alternative name for Sirius. Name is sometimes given to constellation 'Canis Major'.

Canis Major. Latin for 'Greater Dog'. Constellation S.E. of Orion. Brightest star is Sirius Mag. -1.6.

Canis Minor. Latin for 'Lesser Dog'. Constellation E. of Orion. Brightest star is Procyon, Mag. 0.5.

Canoe. Narrow-beamed craft propelled by paddles. Vary widely in construction from primitive dug-out to the Eskimo kayak and oomiak.

Canera.* Type of ship formerly used in Black Sea.

Canoe Rig. The sail arrangement of a canoe. There is no fixed type, but sails are arranged to keep centre of effort as low as possible. To avoid moving about in these tender craft much ingenuity is needed in arrangements for trimming, reefing and furling sail.

Canopus. Star α Argus. S.H.A. 264°; Dec. 53° S; Mag. —0·9. Diameter is 180 times that of Sun; candlepower is 180 times greater; distant 650 light years. Named after Egyptian god of water, or the city of same name.

Canopy. Canvas cover on metal frames. Placed over a hatch or companionway, and in other places.

Cant. Corner or angle. One of segments forming a side piece in head of cask. 2. To tilt in the vertical plane, or to incline in horizontal plane. 3. Cut made between neck and fins of whale so that a hook can be attached for canting. 4. To roll-over a whale when flensing.

Cant Blocks. Purchase blocks used when canting whales.

Cant Falls. Purchases used to sling a whale alongside.

Cant Frames. Short frames that support the overhanging counter of a vessel with an elliptical stern.

Cant Hook. Lever with hook in lifting end. Used for lifting heavy weights.

Cantick Quoin. Triangular piece of wood used to prevent rolling of a cask.

Cantilever Beam. Girder with one end unsupported, and depending on its girder strength to bear stresses on unsupported end.

Cantline. Groove between strands of a rope. 2. Groove between casks or bags when stowed in rows.

Canton. Square division of a flag at its corner or corners.

Cant Piece. 'Cant timber.' Also, piece of timber put along edge or a side fish to strengthen it.

Cant Purchase. Flensing purchase extending from mainmast head to a cut in a whale.

Cant Ribbon. That part of a gilded or painted moulding, along a ship's side, that sweeps upward towards stem or stern.

Cant Spar. Pole or hand mast that is suitable for making a small mast or spar.

Cant Timber Abaft. Projection of after cant timber, which formed a chock on which spanker boom rested when not in use.

Cant Timbers. Timbers, at extreme ends of a vessel, that are not perpendicular to keel; those forward leaning slightly aft, those aft leaning slightly forward.

Canvas. Material made from flax, jute, cotton or hemp. Supplied in bolts of approximately 40 yards. Usually 24 in. wide, but up to 72 in. in some materials. Graded in numbers from 0 to 7, 0 being the heaviest.

Cap. Fitting over the head of a mast, and in which a mast above can be moved or confined.

Capabar (re).* Old name for misappropriation of Government stores.

Capacity Plan. Plan and/or sectional elevation of a vessel showing capacities of all holds, bunkers, tanks, and other relevant compartments.

Cap a Rope. To cover the end with tarred canvas, or hessian, and then whip it.

Cape. A projection of land into the sea.

Cape Horn Fever. Feigned illness of an incompetent seaman in cold and stormy weather.

Capella. Star α Aurigae. S.H.A. 282°; Dec. N 46°; Mag. 0·2. Diameter is 12 times that of Sun; candlepower is 150 times greater; distant 47 light years; temp. 5500°A. Is a double star, the one seen being Capella A. Name is Latin for 'Little Goat'.

Cape Stiff. Seaman's nickname for 'Cape Horn'.

Capful of Wind. Passing wind of no great strength.

Caph. Star β Cassiopeiae. S.H.A. 359°; Dec. N 59°; Mag. 2½.

Cappanus. Sea worm that attacks ship's wooden bottoms and attaches itself to them.

Capricornus. (Lat. = Goat) Constellation situated between R.A.s 20 h 15 m and 21 h 45 m and Dec. 12°—27° S. Has no star brighter than Mag. 3. Tenth sign of Zodiac extending from 270° to 300° celestial longitude. Sun is in this sign from Dec. 22 to Jan. 21 (about).

Capshore. Small spar supporting overhanging part of mast cap; heel being secured in a shoe on foremost crosstree.

Capsize. To overturn or upset. Said to be derived from words meaning 'to move a barrel by turning it on head and bilge alternatively'.

Capsize (a Coil). To turn over a coil of rope so that working end is on deck.

Capstan. Vertical barrel, working on a vertical spindle that is used for heaving on ropes and chain cable. May be operated by hand or by steam, electric or hydraulic engine. Top of barrel has square sockets in which capstan bars may be shipped when working by hand. Lower edge of barrel carries pawls which work in a pawl rack on deck, and prevent capstan walking back.

Capstan Bar. Stout wooden bar, often with an iron shoe, fitting into sockets of capstan when working capstan by hand. Outer end may be notched to take a 'Capstan swifter'.

Capstan Bar Pin. Strong pin passing through head of capstan and end of a shipped capstan bar. Prevents capstan bar becoming unshipped.

Capstan Swifter. Rope having a cut splice in middle and a thimble in one end. Cut splice is passed over top of notch of capstan bar, swifter is back hitched over end of the other bars and swifter is then set up to its opposite part. This results in bars being firmly secured with an upward cant.

Captain. Rank in R.N. between Commander and Commodore. In Merchant Navy is a courtesy title for a master mariner in command of a ship. R.N. has a custom of calling certain petty officers, who are in charge of certain parts of the ship, 'captain' of that part of ship. There are 'captains of the hold', 'the forecastle', etc.

Captain of Top. Petty officer who is responsible to Commander for upkeep of a certain part of the ship, and for the hands allotted to that part.

Capture. Forcible taking of a vessel as prize, or reprisal, in time of war.

Caput Draconis. 'Head of the dragon.' Name sometimes given to star α Draconis.

Carack/Carrack. Large 15th-century ship with high bow and stern castles.

Caravel. Spanish and Portuguese sailing vessel of Moorish origin. Was broad beamed with fore and after castles. Usually square rigged forward, lateen rigged on after masts. Both Columbus and Magellan used them. Name was given also to a small herring fishery boat of France.

Carbon Fibre. An immensely strong costly material of high tensile strength.

Cardinal Points. Of compass: North, South, East, West. Named after cardinal points of horizon. 2. Of horizon: points in which horizon is cut by meridian and prime vertical. 3. Of Ecliptic: points in which Ecliptic is cut by secondary circles passing through the equinoctial and solstitial points. These are: First Points of Aries, Cancer, Libra and Capricorn.

Careen. To list a vessel so that a large part of her bottom is above water. Formerly done to remove weed and marine growth, to examine the bottom, to repair it and to put on preservative or anti-fouling. Still done with small craft.

Cargazon.* Old name for 'Bill of Lading'.

Cargo. Goods or merchandise loaded into a ship for carriage.

Cargo Book. Book kept by master of a coasting vessel. Gives full particulars of all cargo carried, name of consignee and name of consignor—if known.

Cargo Battens. Wood battens, portable or fixed, in hold of a cargo vessel to keep cargo away from ship's side and to allow necessary through ventilation.

Cargo Net. Large square net, of wire or rope, used when making up a hoist of small packages for loading or discharging.

Cargo Plan. Diagrammatic outline of a vessel, either vertically or horizontally, in which holds and cargo spaces are exaggerated, and machinery and accommodation spaces are diminished. Used for readily indicating positions of different cargoes, parcels and consignments.

Cargo Port. Watertight door in ship's side. Used for passing cargo inboard and outboard in certain types of ship.

Caribbean Sea. Area between Central American continent and Yucatan Strait, the Greater Antilles and a line, on eastward of Lesser Antilles, that ends at Baja Point, Venezuela.

Carlins (-ings). Fore and aft members that support the ends of beams that have been cut to form a hatchway or other opening. 2. Wooden sections, about 5 in. by 5 in., lying fore and aft below beams and carrying ledges on which decks of wooden ships are laid.

Carmilhan. Phantom ship of the Baltic. Somewhat similar to the 'Flying Dutchman'.

Carney. Seaman's term for hypocrisy. Said to be the name of a notorious master who was bland ashore but a fiend afloat.

Carpenter. Commissioned officer in R.N., petty officer in Merchant Navy, who is responsible for minor repairs and all woodwork in a ship.

Carpenter's Stopper. Portable fitting for holding a wire under stress. Consists of a clamp—secured to any fixture by chains—and a shaped wedge that fits rope. Any surging of rope causes wedge to move further into clamp, and so increase nip.

Carriage of Goods by Sea Act, 1924. Relates to carriage of goods from ports in Great Britain and Northern Ireland. Applies only while goods are in carrying vessel. Deck cargoes are outside the Act.

Carrick Bend. Method of joining ends of two ropes by turning the end of one rope over its own part and then passing the end of the other rope through the bight thus formed, over the cross in the first rope and then back through the loop on that side that is opposite to the one on which the first end is lying.

Carrick Bitts. Strong timbers in which a windlass is mounted.

Carrier. Owner or charterer who enters into a contract of carriage with a shipper. 2. Ship carrying cargo. 3. An aircraft carrier.

Carronade. Gun throwing a medium weight shot 600 yards with fairly high velocity. First made at Carron in 1779. Compared with cannon, shorter range but heavier shot.

Carry Away. To break, part or fracture.

Carry On. To continue sailing under the same canvas despite the worsening of the wind.

Cartel Ship. Unarmed ship used for exchanging prisoners of war during hostilities. Also applied to an armed ship carrying emissaries for negotiating terms under a flag of truce.

Cartographer. Person employed in compiling or drawing charts.

Cartography. The drawing or compiling of charts.

Carvel. Short form of 'caravel'.

Carvel Built. System of building wooden craft in which the side planking goes fore and aft, with the longitudinal edges butting and flush.

Carvel Joint. Flush or butting joint.

Carving Note. Form filled in by owner of a ship under construction. States particulars of tonnage, construction, name, port of registry, etc. When signed by surveyor, becomes authority for relevant particulars to be 'carved' in main beam of vessel.

Case. Name given to inner planking of a diagonally-built boat, to differentiate it from the outer planking, or 'skin'.

Casing. Short form of 'Funnel casing'.

Cask. Barrel for containing either solids or liquids.

Cassini's Projection. Used in British ordnance survey maps. Graticule is built in relation to a point in a central meridian.

Cassiopeia. Constellation on opposite side of North Pole to Ursa Major. In Greek mythology, was wife of Cepheus and mother of Andromeda.

Cast. To sheer a vessel in a desired direction. 2. To take a sounding with lead and line.

Cast a Traverse. To reduce, arithmetically, a number of courses steered to a resultant distance and direction made good.

Cast Away. Said of a vessel that has been deliberately wrecked. Said of a man who has been shipwrecked.

Casting. Turning a vessel's head in a desired direction, before weighing anchor or slipping a buoy, by action of propeller, sail, rudder, wind or tide.

Casting Off. Letting go the ropes and hawsers that attach a vessel to a wharf quay, etc.

Castor. Star α Geminorum. S.H.A. 247°; Dec. N 32°; Mag. 1·6. When observed by a telescope is seen to consist of three pairs of twin stars.

Castor and Pollox. Name given to two corposants when seen at the same time.

Casuarinas. Trees having no leaves but with short, ribbed sheaths. Observable in Indian Archipelago and Australia.

Casualty. Any accident to a ship or man that involves damage or death.

Cat. Purchase or rope by which an anchor is lifted to billboard after weighing. 2. Former sailing vessel having three masts, no beakhead, narrow stern, projecting quarters and high waist. Carried about 800 tons. (This may have been Dick Whittington's 'cat').

Catabatic. *See* 'Katabatic'.

Catadioptric Lens. Arrangement of lenses so that a light is both reflected and refracted in a desired direction. Suggested by Alan Stevenson in 1834. Used in many lighthouses.

Catamaran. Small craft whose stability is obtained by having a log parallel to its fore and aft line and maintained at proper distance by projections from main craft. Common in Indian Sea and other tropical and sub-tropical waters. 2. A flat wooden float used in docks as fender, and for painting ship's side. 3. A yacht with twin hulls.

Cat Back. Small rope attached to back of hook of cat purchase. Used for placing cat hook into ring, or balancing band, of anchor when anchor is awash.

Cat Block. Lower block of a cat purchase; carries the cat hook.

Cat Boat. Small boat with single gaff sail and mast set right forward.

Catch.* Old form of 'Ketch'.

Catch a Crab. To put blade of oar in water so that it is inclined from horizontal, and forward edge is lower than after edge. Way of boat causes blade to be pushed downward and aft, thus jamming it in rowlock.

Catch a Turn. Take a temporary turn with a rope.

Catching up Rope. Light rope secured to a buoy to hold vessel while stronger moorings are attached.

Catch Ratline. Ratline of greater strength than the majority. Was placed at regular intervals, usually every fifth ratline.

Cat Davit. Strong davit for lifting anchor from water line to bill-board when weighing anchor.

Catenary. Originally, length of chain put in middle of a tow rope to damp sudden stresses. Now applied to any weight put in a hawser for same purpose. 2. Curve formed by a chain hanging from two fixed points.

Cat Fall. Rope rove in a cat purchase.

Cat Harp- (ings)-(ins)-(ens). Ropes bent to foremast shroud of futtock rigging to bowse it aft when sailing close hauled. 2. Name given to iron leg confining upper ends of standing rigging to mast. Ropes bowsing in the lower ends of the port futtock shrouds to the lower ends of the starboard futtock shrouds.

Catharpin Swifter. Foremost shroud of futtock rigging.

Cat Heads. Strong timbers projecting from either side of bows of olden ships. Fitted with sheaves for reeving cat purchase.

Cathead Stopper. Chain or rope that holds ring of anchor when stowed on billboard.

Cathode Ray Tube. A type of electronic valve with a screen which glows brightly where it is struck by a stream of electrons released when an echo is received. This type, used in a radar set, is known as a Plan Position Indicator.

Cat Holes.* Two small holes, for mooring ropes, in sterns of olden ships.

Cat Hook. Strong hook in end of cat pendant for lifting anchor to billboard when catting.

Catoptric. Name given to lights intensified by means of mirrors.

Cat Pendant. Wire rope rove through block on cat davit to lift anchor when catting it.

Cat Purchase. Tackle by which anchor is lifted from water level and placed on billboard.

Cat Rig. Modern version: schooner or ketch rig with no head sails, with unstayed masts, wish-bone booms and wrap-round sails.

Cat Rope. 'Cat Back.'

Cat's Eye. 'Cat Hole.'

Catspaw. Manipulation of a bight of rope so that two small loops are made for taking hook of a tackle. 2. Ripple made on calm water by a passing light air.

Cat's Skin. Light, warm wind on surface of sea.

Cat Tackle. 'Cat Purchase.'

Catting. Lifting the flukes of a weighed anchor on to billboard or anchor bed. Hoisting the anchor from the water to the cathead.

Catting Link. Special link, with broad palm, used in catting anchor.

Catting Shackle. Special screw shackle used when catting anchor.

Cattle Door. Large door in vicinity of bridge or 'tween deck super-structure. Used when loading or discharging cattle on the hoof.

Cattlemen. Men carried to attend cattle when carried on the hoof.

Catug. A catamaran tug locked onto the stern of a barge, the centrebody of the tug riding on the stern of the barge.

Catwalk. A narrow and unfenced gangway.

Caulk. To make a joint watertight. 2. To press oakum, or other

fibre, in a seam between planking preparatory to 'paying'.
3. To expand the overlapping edge of a riveted iron or steel plate
so that it prevents water seeping through the joint.

Caulker. One who caulks seams.

Caulking Iron. Tool used for pressing down caulking in a seam
preparatory to paying.

Caulking Mallet. Wooden mallet used for applying force to caulking iron.

Causa Proxima. Latin for 'Proximate Cause'.

Ceiling. Wooden covering over tank tops in bottom of a hold.
Formerly, was that portion of a ship's side inboard and between
deck beams and limber strake. This meaning is still retained
in 'spar ceiling'.

Celestial. Pertaining to the sky, or celestial concave.

Celestial Concave. The heavens. The celestial sphere.

Celestial Equator. Great circle of celestial sphere that is 90° from
celestial poles. Is plane of Earth's equator carried to celestial
concave. Usually called the Equinoctial.

Celestial Horizon. 'Rational horizon.'

Celestial Latitude. Angular distance above or below plane of
Ecliptic. Measured on a circle of celestial longitude and prefixed
with plus sign if north of Ecliptic, minus sign if south of it. Not
usually considered in navigation.

Celestial Longitude. Angular distance along Ecliptic from First
Point of Aries, measured in direction of Sun's apparent path and
expressed in arc 0° to 360°. Not usually considered in navigation.

Celestial Meridian. Great circle of celestial sphere that is a
secondary circle to Equinoctial. Declination is measured on it.

Celestial Poles. Those points in celestial concave that are in the
zenith at north and south poles of Earth.

Celestial Sphere. General name for the heavens, or sky. Heavenly
bodies are assumed to be on the interior surface of a hollow
sphere. Name is sometimes given to a globe showing places of
stars on its outer surface. It is preferable to call this a 'star globe'.

Cellular System. Ship construction in which double bottom is
divided into small spaces by erection of intercostal longitudinals
between floors.

Celox. Fast, single-banked vessel of Rhodes in classic times.

Celonavigation. Name suggested by Harbord *(Glossary of Navigation)* to denote navigational workings requiring observations of
celestial bodies. Astro-navigation.

Celsius. (Centigrade) Graduation of thermometer scale in which
the freezing temperature is 0°C and boiling point 100°C.

Cement. Calcined chalk and clay in powder form. Mixed with
water and an aggregate (sand, etc.). Is alkaline, so neutralising
acids. Used in ships as protection against abrasion, corrosion,
percussion, to give addtional strength and for stopping leaks.

Cement Box. Portland cement and aggregate inserted between
wooden shuttering and a leaking plate, or seam, to stop the leak.

Centaur(us). Bright constellation in southern sky. Indicated by a line drawn through Arcturus and Spica. Has two navigational stars, α and β. Approx. R.A. 14 h; Dec. 60°S.

Centering Error. Sextant error due to centre of pivot not being at exact centre of arc. Error varies with altitude.

Centigrade Scale. Graduation of thermometer in which freezing point of water is 0° and boiling point is 100°. Is a modification of Celsius scale, and was introduced by Christin, of Lyons, in 1743.

Central Eclipse. Eclipse in which centres of the two heavenly bodies are exactly in line to an observer at a specified place.

Central Latitude. Angle at centre of Earth between plane of Equator and a line projected through observer. As Earth is not a true sphere this angle will differ from angle formed by downward projection of observer's vertical—which is the 'normal' latitude.

Central Projection (of sphere). Projection of surface of sphere to a tangent plane by lines from centre of sphere.

Central Sun. Point in the heavens about which the universe may be considered to turn. At one time was considered to be in constellation of Taurus.

Centre Board. Name often given to a 'drop keel'.

Centre-Castle. The raised part of a ship's hull amidships.

Centre of Buoyancy. That point in a floating body, at which the total moments of buoyancy in any one direction are balanced by equivalent moments of buoyancy in the opposite direction.

Centre of Cavity. 'Centre of displacement.'

Centre of Displacement. That point, in a floating body, which is the geometrical centre of the immersed portion.

Centre of Effort. That point, in a sail, at which all wind force may be assumed to act. Theoretically, it would be the geometrical centre of sail area. In practice, it will be somewhat away from the theoretical point, due to sail not presenting a perfectly flat surface to wind, and not being at a uniform angle to wind in all parts.

Centre of Flotation. Geometrical centre of immersed volume of a floating body.

Centre of Gravity. That point, in any body, at which the moments of gravitational force in any one direction are balanced by the moments of gravitational force in the opposite direction.

Centre of Gyration. That distance along a radius of a revolving body at which the mass may be considered to act. With disc of uniform density and thickness the centre of gyration is 0·707 of radius from centre of rotation.

Centre of Immersion. 'Centre of displacement'.

Centre of Lateral Resistance. Point, in lee side of underwater body of a vessel, at which the forces resisting leeway are equal in any two opposite directions in the fore and aft line.

Centre of Oscillation. That point, in a pendulum, at which total of moments of forces on upper side are equal to moments on lower side.

Centre of Percussion. That point, in a striking mass, at which the whole force of the blow would cause no jar. In case of a bar of uniform density, revolving around one end, would be ⅔rds distant from centre of revolution.

Centre through Plate. Continuous girder going fore and aft along centre of bottom of a steel ship. Floors are attached to it on opposite sides.

Centrifugal Pump. Pump in which liquid is withdrawn by giving it a high rotational speed and allowing it to escape tangentially. Suction is provided by a partial vacuum caused by escaping liquid.

Cepheids. Short period variable stars whose magnitudes vary in the course of a few days. Rigel, Canopus, Antares are examples.

Cepheid Variables. 'Cepheids.' Particularly notable in constellation Cepheus.

Cepheus. Northern constellation situated between Cassiopeia and Andromeda. In Greek mythology, Cepheus was father of Andromeda and husband of Cassiopeia.

Ceres. First of the asteroids to be discovered.

Certificated Cook. Ship's cook who holds a certificate granted by D.T.I. or an approved cookery school. Ships of 1000 tons gross and upward must carry a certificated cook.

Certificated Lifeboatman. Seaman, who has passed through a course in work connected with ship's lifeboats, and has received a certificate of efficiency.

Certificated Officer. Officer holding a Certificate of Competency issued by the Department of Trade and Industry.

Certificate of Clearance. Issued to master of emigrant ship, by emigration officer, when the latter is satisfied that ship is sea worthy, in safe trim, fit for intended voyage, that steerage passengers and crew are fit in health, that master's bond has been fully executed.

Certificate of Competency. Certificate issued by D.T.I. to a seaman or officer who has passed an examination in a specified grade, and has been found fit to perform the duties of the grade.

Certificate of Freeboard. International certificate, issued by an 'Assigning Authority', detailing minimum permissible freeboards in stated areas at specified seasons. Often called 'Load Line Certificate'.

Certificate of Grain. 'Grain Certificate.'

Certificate of Pratique. Certificate issued by medical officer of port to an arrived ship when he is satisfied that health of crew is satisfactory. Prerequisite to 'Entry Inwards'.

Certificate of Registry. A vessel's identity certificate. Issued by the Government of a country, through assigning authorities, after vessel has been surveyed. Gives relevant particulars, rig, dimensions, tonnage, machinery, etc., and name/s of owner/s. Master's name is endorsed on it at each change of appointment.

Certificate of Seaworthiness. Certificate granted by a surveyor, or Court of Survey, when the seaworthiness of the vessel may be open to question, and after she had been examined and found seaworthy.

Cetacea. Members of whale family, including dolphins and porpoises. They have warm blood and suckle their young. Some have vestiges of legs.

Cetology. The study of cetacea.

Cetus. (Lat.=Whale.) Largest constellation in sky. Situated S of Aries. Has 97 discernible stars. two being of 2nd mag., eight of 3rd mag. and nine of 4th mag.

Chain. Name often given to chain cable.

Chafe. To wear away through friction.

Chaffer. Said of a jib sail when it shivers in the wind.

Chafing Board. Piece of wood used to protect against chafing.

Chafing Cheeks. Wooden blocks without sheaves sometimes used in running rigging of lightly rigged, small sailing craft.

Chafing Gear. Paunch matting, sennit, strands, battens, etc., put on mast yard, standing rigging, etc., to protect against damage from chafe.

Chafing Mat. Any mat used as chafing gear, but particularly to paunch and thrum mats put on yards to protect them from chafe by backstays.

Chain Boat. Boat used, in harbour, for recovering chain cable and anchors when slipped or parted.

Chain Bolt. Iron bolt used when fastening chain plates and ends of deadeye chains to side of a wooden vessel.

Chain Cable. Anchor cable when made of wrought iron.

Chain Ferry. A ferry which proceeds by hauling itself along a chain laid across a river or channel.

Chain Gantline. Any gantline made of chain, particularly that rove through block at top of funnel.

Chain Hook. Iron hook, with **T** handle, used when working cable. 2. Strong, two-pronged hook used for temporarily holding cable, inboard end being secured to deck, 'Devil's Claw'.

Chain Knot. Succession of loops in rope, each loop being passed through previous loop.

Chain Lifter.* Former name for sprocket ring of capstan.

Chain Locker. Cable locker.

Chain Pipe. Strengthened hole in cable deck, and through which cable passes to locker.

Chain Plait. 'Drummer's Plait.'

Chain Plates. Plates on ship's side to take lower ends of links o bars passing upwards to the chains. These plates take stress off shrouds, while chains give spread to the shrouds.

Chains. Projecting ledge on outside of vessel, abaft a mast, to which lower rigging is set up and given increased spread. Name is also given to a platform for taking soundings with hand lead: this was formerly done from the main chains.

Chain Shot. Two cannon-balls joined by a length of chain and fired simultaneously. Used for destroying masts, spars and rigging. Invented by Admiral De Witt, 1666.

Chain Slings. In general, any slings made of chain. Applied to the slings of a yard when made of chain instead of rope.

Chain Splice. Method of splicing rope to link of chain. One strand is unlaid and two strands passed through link; one of these two strands is laid up in space of strand taken out, and is half knotted to that strand. Other strand is tucked as usual.

Chain Stopper. Length of chain, about a fathom, used for holding a wire under stress while the wire is manipulated.

Chain Top.* Additional sling (of chain) put on lower yards of warships before going into action.

Chain Towing. Method used, by ferry craft, to pass between the two terminals by hauling on a chain lying on the bottom and secured at each end.

Chain Well.* Former name for a chain locker.

Chamber of Shipping of U.K. Body formed to promote and protect the interests of British shipowners. Received Royal Charter, 1922.

Change of Moon. Instant when centres of Sun and Moon are on same celestial meridian, and a new lunation commences.

Change of Trim. Alteration in the difference between the forward and after draughts of a floating ship.

Change the Mizzen. To brace the crossjack yard so that the mizzen course is on a tack different from the remaining sails.

Change Tide. Tide occurring at change of Moon, and, therefore, nearly a spring tide.

Channel. Narrow arm of sea between two land areas. 2. Deepest part of a body of water, and through which main current flows. 3. Longitudinal hollow or cavity. 4. Flat projection from side of a ship to give spread to rigging (usually called 'chains'). 5. Standard rolled steel section in form of three sides of a rectangle.

Channel Bar. Rolled steel section having three sides of a rectangle.

Channel Bolt. Long bolt that passes through chains, or channels and side planking of a wooden ship; so clamping the chains to the side.

Channel Money. Advance payment of money due to a seaman 48 hours before being paid off. Is £2, or one-quarter of wages due, whichever is the lesser.

Channel Pilot. Pilot engaged in conducting ships in English Channel, or other specified channel. 2. A book of sailing directions for navigation of the English Channel.

Channel Plates. 'Chain Plates.'

Channel Wale. That strake of side planking, of wooden ship, that carries a chain plate.

Chanty. Nautical song of merchant seamen. Used to co-ordinate effort when hauling on a rope, or heaving at capstan or windlass.

Chapelling. Putting a close-hauled vessel's head through the wind without bracing head yards. May be deliberate, or through negligence of helmsman. Word is sometimes applied to wearing in same circumstances, but this is a later application of the word.

Characteristic. Of a logarithm, is the whole number of the Log, as distinguished from its mantissa. 2. Of a navigational light, is its colour, phase and period.

Charges Clause. Inserted in Charter Party to denote who shall pay harbour and dock dues, wharfage, pilotage, towage, etc.

Charles's Law. States that volume of a gas, at constant pressure and at temperature 0°C increases by $\frac{1}{273}$rd for each degree rise in temperature.

Charles's Wain. 'Churl's wain,' or 'waggon'. Old name for 'Ursa Major'.

Charley Moore. The embodiment of fair dealing. (R.N.)

Charley Noble. R.N. nickname for a galley funnel.

Chart. Representation of part of ocean or sea for use in navigation. Gives depth of water, nature of bottom, configuration and characteristics of coast, with positions and brief particulars of navigational aids. 2. Diagram showing certain facts in graphical or tabular form. 3.* Old name for mariner's compass.

Chart Abbreviations. Standardised abbreviations used in charts. The more important are generally shown under chart title, but all those used in British Admiralty charts are given on a special chart.

Chart Border. Graduated lines, at border of chart, for determining latitude and longitude of a position, and for measuring distances.

Chart Compass. Compass rose engraved on chart, to determine courses and bearings. Usually has an outer graduation 0°–360°, and inner graduation in quadrantal form. Inner compass gives variation, for a given epoch, and the secular change.

Chart Datum. Sea level used in connection with soundings on a chart. In British charts, is a level below which the tide very rarely falls.

Chart Distortion. Differentiated into distortion in and distortion of charts. Distortion in a chart is an unavoidable extension of charted area due to impossibility of accurately reproducing a spherical surface on a plane surface. It is adjusted by extending the units of measurement, latitude or longitude, to correspond with the extension of the area. Distortion of a chart is a possible stretching or contraction that may occur after printing, and so cause a slight relative displacement of a charted positions. In modern charts this distortion is rarely enough to affect navigation, but if the chart be large it may affect very precise surveying.

Charterer. One who enters into a contract with a shipowner for the hire of a vessel, or for the carriage of goods by sea.

Charter Party. Document by which a shipowner leases his ship to some person or persons, or by which he agrees to carry goods or perform other services. It states the conditions, terms and exceptions that are to prevail in the contract.

Chart Plate. Plate, usually of zinc or copper, on which a chart is engraved for printing. The exact size of this plate is given, in inches, in border of chart. This allows for checking the chart for distortion.

Charybdis. Name of one of the whirlpools, or garofali, in Straits of Messina.

Chasse Marees. Bluff-bowed French luggers formerly used for fishing, and in short voyage trades. Had up to three masts and often carried topsails.

Chatham Chest. Fund for support of disabled and superannuated seamen of R.N. Founded in reign of Queen Elizabeth, on a voluntary basis which, later, became compulsory. Abolished during reign of William IV.

Chebacco Boat.* Sailing craft formerly used in Newfoundland fisheries. Had high, narrow stern. Named after a small river in Massachusetts.

Check. To ease a rope a little, and then belay it.

Checking. Slacking a rope smartly, carefully and in small amounts.

Check Stopper. Length of small chain with one end made fast to a ring bolt, or other annular opening, then around a wire and back through the ring bolt. By hauling on free end of chain the speed of a moving wire can be checked and regulated.

Cheek Block. Sheave on side of a spar, etc., and having a half shell on outer side.

Cheeks. Brackets below head of mast and at sides of it. Support crosstrees and mast above. 2. Knee pieces either side of stem. 3. Sides of a wooden (pulley) block. 4. Old name for a Royal Marine.

'Cheerily.' Injunction to perform an action smartly and with a will.

Cheese Cutter. Form of drop keel for small craft. Has a projecting upper part that is supported in housing when keel is down. 2. A peak cap.

Cheesing down. Coiling a rope ornamentally with each flake flat, or almost flat, on deck; usually in a circular or figure-of-eight pattern.

Chequered. Said of a flag or pendant made up of small squares of two different colours; and of a buoy or beacon painted in squares of two different colours.

Chernikeef Log. Submerged log that projects through bottom of ship. Carries an 'impeller' that turns as vessel moves through the water. Directly records distance run and, with electrical attachment, can indicate speed.

Cherub Log. Towed log consisting of a towed rotator, non-kinkable log line and an inboard registering unit. Measures distance directly, and can be used for speeds up to 12 knots.

Chess Tree. Oak block secured to ship's side abaft fore chains. Used for boarding main tack, or as lead for fore sheet.

Chest Rope. Long boat rope led from forward to a gangway into ship.

Chetwynd Compass. Liquid type compass for use in quick-turning craft. Drag of liquid on rim of card was reduced by making card much smaller than containing bowl.

Chevils. Small pieces of timber, inside a ship, to which tacks and sheets can be secured.

Chief Buffer. Nickname for a chief boatswain's mate in R.N. He is senior chief petty officer of upper deck, and so acts as buffer between the hands and the Commander.

Child Fender. Roller fender for wharf or quay. Consists of a central shaft, free to rotate, around which are large diameter rubber tyres filled with cork.

Chiliad. 18th-century name for logarithmic tables. Means '1000'.

Chime. Projection of staves beyond head of a cask, barrel, etc.

Chime Hoop. Hoop that protects chime of a cask, barrel, etc.

Chimes. Intersection of the lines forming sides and bottom of a flat-bottomed boat. 'Chine.'

Chinckle. Small bight in a rope or line. Often called 'half crown'.

Chine. Former name for chime of a cask. 2. Gap in landward side of a cliff. 3.* That part of a deck waterway that is left above deck level, so that spirketting may be caulked. 4. 'Chimes.'

Chinese Windlass. Machine, by which purchase is gained by heaving one part of a rope, on a drum, and veering the other part on a drum of smaller diameter—a block being in bight of rope between the two drums. This principle is adopted in the 'differential' block.

Chinse. To fill a seam or crack by inserting oakum.

Chinsing Iron. Steel or wrought iron tool used for inserting oakum in a seam in planking, etc. Has a curved lower edge scored with a groove. Upper extension of handle has a wide, circular, convex head for applying power with a mallet.

Chip Log. Quadrantal piece of flat wood, weighted on curved rim, attached to log line for finding speed of a vessel. Often called 'ship' log, or log 'ship'.

Chippy Chap. Nickname for ship's carpenter, or one of his crew.

Chips. Nickname for a ship's carpenter.

Chocks. Shaped pieces of wood on which various items rest and are secured. Of capstan, are wooden blocks, at top and bottom of drum, that house wooden whelps.

Chock a Block. Said of a purchase when two blocks are close together, and further hauling is impossible. Also called 'Two blocks'.

Choke a Luff. To prevent a tackle walking back by passing a bight of the fall between a sheave and the rope rove through it, and on that side of sheave where rope would go into block if walking back.

Cholera. Infectious disease of Eastern origin. Marked by diarrhoea, cramp, vomiting and drying of tissues.

Chop Mark. Merchant's mark on goods. Indicates grade and other particulars.

Chops of the Channel. Sea area immediately to westward of English Channel. First known use of this name was in 1748.

Chromatic Aberration. Deviation of light rays after passing through curved lens. Results in coloured fringes around observed objects, caused by unequal refraction of lenses breaking up light into its constituent colours.

Chromosphere. Incandescent gaseous envelope surrounding Sun.

Chronograph. A watch combined with a stop-watch mechanism.

Chronometer. Very accurately constructed timepiece with a balance wheel of a form that precludes error through change of temperature. Balance wheel is affected by mainspring for only a very small period of its oscillation. Invented by John Harrison about 1728.

Chronometer Journal. Book for recording comparisons of chronometers carried in a ship. Shows their error on time signal, and on each other. Daily rates, also, are deduced and entered.

Chronometer Watch. Small timepiece made on chronometer principle and used for taking times on deck.

Chronometric Difference. Difference of longitude between two places when expressed as the difference of their local mean times.

Chuch. Name sometimes given to a fairlead.

Chutes. Inclined troughs, down which coal, ashes and fluid substances can slide. 2. Vertical canvas tubes used for ventilating. Often spelt 'shoots'.

Circle. Plane figure bounded by a line that, at all points, is equidistant from a point termed the 'centre'. Can be considered as the section of a sphere by a plane. Word is frequently applied to its circumference, as in 'position circle'.

Circle of Altitude. Great circle of celestial sphere, secondary to horizon, on which altitudes are measured.

Circle of Azimuth. Great circle of celestial sphere passing through zenith; so passing through all points having the same azimuth.

Circle of Curvature. Circle whose curvature is the same as that of a curve under consideration.

Circle of Declination. Great circle of celestial sphere that is perpendicular to Equinoctial. So called because declination is measured along it. Not to be confused with 'Parallel of Declination'.

Circle of Equal Altitude. Circle, on surface of Earth, passing through all positions at which the body has the same altitude. It is a great circle when body is in horizon, decreasing to a point when body is in the zenith.

Circle of Excursion. Small circle, parallel to Ecliptic, marking the maximum celestial latitude of a planetary body.

Circle of Illumination. Great circle, on surface of Earth, that divides day from night.

Circle of Latitude. Alternative name for a circle of celestial longitude. So named because latitude is measured on it.

Circle of Longitude. Great circle of celestial sphere, secondary to Ecliptic, passing through all points having the same celestial longitude.

Circle of Perpetual Apparition. Parallel of declination, above which all the diurnal circles are entirely above horizon.

Circle of Perpetual Occultation. Parallel of declination, below which all the diurnal circles are entirely below horizon.

Circle of Position. Small circle on surface of Earth, and on the circumference of which an observation shows observer to be.

Circle of Right Ascension. Great circle of celestial sphere, passing through all points having the same right ascension.

Circle of Sphere. Formed by intersection of a sphere by a plane. May be 'great circles' or 'small circles', depending on whether the plane does, or does not, pass through centre of sphere.

Circle of Tangency. 'Tangent Circle'.

Circuit. Series of connected conductors that form a path for an electric current.

Circular Note. Letter of credit addressed to financial firms in other countries. Authorises them to make payment to person named.

Circular Parts. 'Napier's Circular Parts.'

Circular Sailing.* Former name for 'Great circle sailing'.

Circular Storm.* Former name for a cyclonic storm.

Circulating Pump. Centrifugal, or double-acting pump, that draws water from sea and delivers it at external surfaces of condenser tubes, so condensing exhaust steam from engines.

Circulation. Process by which water in a boiler is moved so that the whole mass is of uniform temperature. Partly done by convection, but hastened by pump and special fittings.

Circummeridian. About or near the meridian.

Circumnavigate. To sail completely around. Sometimes especially applied to sailing around Earth.

Circumnavigator's Day. The day 'lost' or 'gained' by the navigator when date is altered on crossing the Date Line on W'ly or E'ly course (respectively).

Circumpolar. Term applied to a heavenly body that makes a diurnal revolution around pole of heavens without passing below horizon.

Cirrocumulus. An intermediate form of cloud often called 'Mackerel sky'. Formed by small, rounded masses of cloud.

Cirrostratus. High, tenuous cloud of uniform density. Often precedes a depression.

Cirrus. Feathery, fibrous, detached clouds, white in colour, that are formed by ice crystals at heights of five to seven miles.

Cirrus Nothus. 'False Cirrus.'

Cistern. The mercury container of a barometer. Pressure of atmosphere in cistern forces mercury up the glass tube that has been exhausted of air.

Civil Day. Period from midnight to midnight in the mean time standard at a given place.

Civil Twilight. Interval between Sun's upper limb being in horizon, and his centre being 6° below it.

Civil Year. The year in common use. Is the Tropical year adapted for civil purposes. Has 365 days for three years and 366 in fourth with slight adjustment at ends of centuries.

Clack Valve. Hinged valve that opens by suction and closes by gravity.

Clamp. Formerly, strong plank supporting deck beams at ship's side. 2. Cleat, on after end of a boom, to take reef pendants. 3. Half round, hinged fitting for securing heads of derrick booms, etc.

Clamp Nails. Strong nails with large, round head. Used for fastening clamps to sides of wooden vessels.

Clap On. To apply extra power, either by increasing purchases used, or by putting on additional men. 2. To set more sail.

Clapper. Tongue of a bell. 2. Chafing piece in jaws of a gaff.

Clarke's Figure of Earth. Measurement of Earth's polar and equatorial diameters and factors of compression made by Clarke in 1858–66–80. Equatorial diameter 20,926,348 ft., polar diameter 20,855,233 ft., compression 1/294·3. These values are still used in many modern charts.

Clark Russell's Log. Early type of towed log in which speed of ship was indicated by amount of compression in a spring.

Clasp Hook.* Former name for 'Clip hook'.

Classification of Stars. Astronomers group stars according to spectra and temperature. Seven principal groups are O, B, A, F, K, G, M. The temperature of O stars is about 50,000°C. M stars do not exceed 3000°C. This classification is not usually considered by seamen, but is to be found in the unabridged Nautical Almanac.

Classification Societies. Organisations established for the purpose of obtaining an accurate classification of merchant shipping, for maintaining a standard of seaworthiness and safety, and for making the obtained information available for shipowners, merchants, underwriters and others concerned. The principal are Lloyd's Register of Shipping (founded 1760) and an international Bureau Veritas. They are, also, 'assigning Authorities' for granting Load Line Certificates under the 'Safety and Load Lines Conventions Act, 1932.'

Claw Off. To beat to windward of a lee shore or danger.

Cleading. Any covering used to protect or to prevent the radiation or conduction of heat.

Clean. Said of a Bill of Lading, or other document or receipt, when it contains no restrictive endorsement. Ship is said to be clean when her Bill of Health is satisfactory. Said of a ship's underwater surface when it is free from weed or other fouling.

Clean Lines. Said of a vessel having fine entrance and lines.

Clear Anchor. Said of a weighed anchor when it comes in sight and is seen to be clear of turns of cable.

Clear a Lunar. To deduce Moon's true distance, from a heavenly body, from her apparent distance. Short form of 'Clearing a Lunar Distance'.

Clearance. Act of clearing a vessel through a Customs House by the fulfilment of required duties. 2. Certificates given by Customs authorities when a vessel has been satisfactorily cleared. 3. The amount of free space between two nearly adjacent surfaces or points.

Clearance Inward. Customs procedure of an arrived vessel. Jerquing Note is delivered to master when cargo has been discharged and Customs authorities are satisfied that all requirements have been met.

Clearance Label. 'Cocket Card.' Attached to a Victualling Bill and stamped by Customs authorities as evidence that all requirements have been satisfactorily met by an outward bound vessel.

Clearance Outwards. The obtaining of a Victualling Bill and clearance by the master of an outward bound ship. The issue of these is an official permission to sail.

Clear a Ship. To enter a vessel 'Inwards' or 'Outwards' at Custom House.

Clearer. Tool on which hemp for sailmaker's twine is finished.

Clear for Action. To remove all obstacles and unnecessary fittings in way of a gun, or in path of its projectile, and all furnishing that may hinder the fighting of the ship, or are liable to cause fire.

Clear for Running. Said of ropes coiled down so that the end of rope is underneath, and rope can run freely and uninterruptedly.

Clear Hawse. Said of cables when each leads clear to its anchor, and there is no cross or turn in them.

Clear Hawse Slip. Special slip, on cable deck, for holding inboard end of foul cable while clearing it of turns.

Clearing Bearing. Clearing line that is projected through one particular bearing only.

Clearing Line. Straight line, on chart, that marks boundary between a safe and a dangerous area; or that passes clear of a navigational danger. Sectors of lighthouse lights are usually bounded by them.

Clearing Mark. Conspicuous object which, with another object, gives a clearing line.

Clearing the Distance. Converting the observed angular distance of a star from Moon to its true angular distance.

Clear the Land. To attain such distance from the coast as to be out of danger from outlying obstructions and shoals, and from risk of being carried on to them by currents or wind.

Cleat. Metal or wood fitting having two projecting horns and fastened securely at the middle. Used for securing or controlling ropes.

Clench Built. 'Clinker built.'

Clench Bolt. Bolt whose end is beaten out over a washer after passing through the items it clenches.

Clenched. Old form of 'Clinched'.

Clencher. 'clincher.'

Clencher Build. 'Clincher build.'

Clench Nail. Nail whose tapered end is beaten out, over a roove, after being passed through the items it fastens.

Clew. Lower corner of a square sail, lower after corner of fore and aft sail. Has thimble for taking sheet and other tackle.

Clew Garnet. Tackle attached to clew of a course for hauling clew to yard when furling.

Clewline. Rope for hauling up clew of an upper square sail when furling.

Clew to Earing. Said of a sail when clew has been hoisted to earing by clewline or clew garnet.

Clew Up. To haul clew to earing when furling a square sail.

Climatic Zones. Eight zones of climate into which Earth's surface can be divided. They comprise one of Tropical Rain; two of Steppe and Desert; two of Temperate Rain; in Northern hemisphere; one Boreal, with large annual range of temperature; two Polar caps of snow.

Clinch. To fasten two overlapping strakes by a fastening through the overlap. 2. Half hitch stopped to its own part. 3. To chinse. 4. Old name for attachment of inboard end of rope cable to ship.

Clincher Build. Method of building wooden craft so that each strake of side planking overlaps strake below it, and is clinched to it along the doubling.

Clinching Iron. Tool used when clinching nail over a washer.

Clinker. Fused ash, and other incombustible substances, that form when coal is burned in a furnace.

Clinker Build. 'Clincher build.'

Clinker Pieces. Small doubling patches at peak and clew of gaff sails.

Clinometer. Instrument used for measuring the heel or inclination of a vessel.

Clip. Jaw end of a boom or gaff. 2. Inglefield clip.

Clip Hooks. Two flat hooks, on one ring or thimble, that hook in opposite directions and overlap.

Clipper. Name applied to fast sailing ships, particularly—at first—to the sharp-lined, raking schooners of U.S.A. Hall mark of a clipper is generally taken to be a fine entrance with concave bow. First vessel of the type was 'Scottish Maid', a schooner built by Alexander Hall & Co., of Aberdeen, in 1839.

Clipper Bow. Name applied to a bow in which stem curves forward as it rises above waterline.

Clipper Built. Said of a sailing vessel having fine lines and raked masts.

Clock Calm. Absolutely calm weather with a perfectly smooth sea.

Clock Stars. Stars whose right ascensions and declinations are very accurately known, so that they can be used for determining time. (Astronomers do not use Sun for this purpose.)

Close Aboard. Close alongside. Very near.

Close Butt. Joint, in wooden shipbuilding, that is so close that caulking is not necessary.

Closed Stokehold. Stokehold that can be made airtight, and so allow air pressure to be increased for more efficient combustion of fuel.

Closed Traverse. *See* 'Traverse'.

Close Fights. Barriers and obstructions erected to prevent capture of ship by boarding. In some cases, but not in R.N., were strong bulkheads erected on upper deck, behind which ship's company could retreat when boarded; so commanding upper deck with musket fire through loopholes in the bulkhead.

Close Harbour.* Old name for a harbour made by engineering skill and excavation; to distinguish it from a natural harbour.

Close Hauled. Said of a sailing vessel when she has the wind before the beam. In some cases is applied to a vessel sailing as close to wind as possible. Collision Regulations assume a vessel to be 'Close hauled' when wind is between her closest point of sailing and one point free of it.

Close Jammed. So close hauled that any movement nearer the wind would put sails aback.

Close Lined. Said of a vessel when ceiling on sides of hold is so close that there is no air space between the planks.

Close Pack. Mass of ice-floes, mostly in contact, that impede or stop navigation.

Close Quarters. In close proximity. Yard arm to yard arm. 2. Close fights. 3. Close fights fitted in slave ships to prevent uprising of slaves.

Close Reefed. Said of sails that have been reefed as much as possible.

Close Stowing Anchor. Any anchor having its stock in line with arms.

Close the Land. To approach the land from seaward.

Close Winded. Said of any vessel that can sail close to wind.

Cloth. Piece of canvas forming part of a sail.

Clothe. To fit a vessel with her running rigging and sails.

Clothed. Said of a mast when all sail is set on it. Sometimes used as meaning that the foot of a lower sail is so close to deck that no wind can pass beneath it.

Cloud. Water vapour condensed into minute particles and suspended in higher reaches of atmosphere.

Cloudburst. Name often given to very heavy rain.

Clove Hitch. Manipulation of rope end for attaching it to a bar, taut wire, etc. End is passed round, then over its own part, then round again—in same direction—and brought up under its own part.

Clove Hook.* Clip Hook.

Club. Spar at foot of jib, or other triangular sail. 2. Group of shipowners forming a mutual insurance society. *See* 'Small Damage Club'.

Clubbing. Dropping down with tide or current, with anchor at short stay, and sheering vessel as necessary with rudder. Usually termed 'dredging'.

Club Hauling. Method of putting a sailing vessel about when on a lee shore and there is no room to tack or box haul. Necessitates use of, and loss of, an anchor, a length of cable and a spring from lee quarter to anchor. As vessel comes head to wind, and loses way, anchor is let go, yards are braced to new tack and cable is slipped. Spring is slipped as soon as after sails are filled.

Clue.* Old form of 'Clew'.

Clump Block. Thick wooden block built to take a rope whose circumference is half the length of the block.

Clump Cathead. Small projection from ship's side just abaft hawse pipe. Used for suspending an anchor when cable is disconnected and used for mooring to a buoy.

Clutter. Confused, unwanted echoes on a radar display from, e.g. waves or rain.

Clyde Lug. Standing lug with high peak, mast stepped well forward, sheet travelling on a horse mounted on transom.

Co. Prefix meaning 'Complement of'.

Co$_2$. Symbol for 'Carbon dioxide' or carbonic acid gas.

Coach.* Old name for a poop.

Coach Horses.* Old name for the 15 picked men who formerly manned the captain's barge in the Royal Navy.

Coach Whip. Commissioning pendant at masthead of one of H.M. ships.

Coach Whipping. Covering made by small line and used for ornamental purposes, or as a protection against chafing. Three or four lengths are passed over and under other lengths, of the same number, so that a close diaper pattern is made.

Coadherent.* Old name for a bilge keel.

Coak. Bush of a sheave.

Coaking. Joining timbers by scarphing, in which one timber has a projection and the other timber has a recess into which the projection is fitted.

Coal Bunker. Compartment in which coal for ship's consumption is kept.

Coal Consumption. Amount of coal, in tons, consumed in a given time, for a given distance, or for a time given speed in knots. Consumption in a given time varies as cube of speed; consumption per knot varies as square of speed; consumption over any distance varies as square of speed × distance. All the above are approximate.

'Coal Sack.' Area in the Galactic (Milky Way), and in vicinity of α Centauri, where no star whatever is visible to the naked eye. The area is about 8° in length and 5° in breadth.

Coaling Stations. Ports and places where coal suitable for marine boilers may be had by ships.

Coamings. Vertical erections around hatches, and other openings in a deck, to prevent water passing to the opening.

Coast. That part of any country or land that is washed by the sea. 2. To sail along a coast, or to follow the coastline.

Coaster. Vessel trading along the coast of a country.

Coastguard. Force of men, who are stationed around coast of British Isles for the suppression of smuggling and for watching of coast for vessels in distress. First established 1817; transferred to R.N. in 1831; retransferred to H.M. Customs in 1920; now under Department of Trade and Industry.

Coastline. That line in which sea meets the border of a country; more specifically at low water.

Cob. Harbour protected by a stone breakwater.

Cobalt. Hard, white metal used in high carbon steels for permanent magnets. Is feebly magnetic.

Cobbing.* Old maritime punishment in which a man was struck on the breech with flat pieces of wood or ropes' ends.

Cobble.* Original form of 'Coble'.

Coble. Boat with flat floor, square stern and deep rudder. About 20 feet long. Pulls three pairs of oars and has a mast with lugsail. Once in daily use on North-East Coast.

Coboose. Old form of 'Caboose'.

Cochrane Boiler. Small vertical boiler sometimes installed in ships for port use. Has combustion chamber and smoke tubes. Working pressure is about 120 lb. per sq. in.

Cock. Valve in which flow of a fluid is controlled by a rotatable plug which has a perforation that can be masked by turning. 2. Old name for a yawl. 3. Old name for a 'Cog' (boat).

Cockbill. To top a yard by one lift. 2. To suspend an anchor by ring stopper.

Cock Boat.* Small, light boat used in sheltered waters.

Cocked Hat. Former full dress headgear of an officer of the R.N. 2. Triangle, on chart, formed by three position lines that do not cross at one point.

Cocket. Seal of H.M. Customs. Name is given, also, to 'Clearance Label', and to an Entry officer in a Custom House.

Cocket Card. 'Clearance Label.'

Cockpit. Compartment, usually on orlop deck, in old men of war. Was the messroom for midshipmen and junior officers. In action, was used as a dressing station for wounded. 2. A sunken part, or well, in a deck in which, in a yacht, the helmsman sits to steer.

Cockroach. Dark-brown insect, of beetle family, often found in ships.

Cockscombing. Decorative covering of a small spar or rope. Made by attaching several small lines and half hitching them, successively, around object to be covered. Number of lines used should be odd. Half hitches are made to right and left alternately.

Cockswain.* Original form of 'Coxswain'.

Cod Line. Small line made of Italian hemp, and supplied in hanks of 20 fathoms. Originally, was a fishing line, with a size between mackerel and dolphin lines.

Cod of Track. Most westerly point in track of a revolving storm. Storm centre turns toward pole, and then eastward.

Cod's Head and Mackerel Tail. Nickname given to ships built with bluff bows and a long and tapering run.

Coefficient. Numerical constant used as a multiplier of a varying quantity.

Coefficient of Fineness. Decimal fraction by which the volume of a rectangular block must be multiplied to obtain displacement of a floating vessel whose underwater body has the same maximum length, breadth and depth. Also known as 'Block coefficient'.

Coefficient of Waterplane Area. Area of waterplane, at a given draught, expressed as a fraction of the area of a circumscribing rectangle. Value, for ship shaped bodies, usually varies between 0·7 and 0·85.

Cofferdam. Space between two bulkheads, or walls, that receives and retains any liquid that has leaked through one wall.

Coffin Ships. Vessels unseaworthy through defect in building, fitting or loading. Were unduly prevalent before legislation enforced loading limits and other safety measures.

Coffin Stern. Name given to stern plating that is vertical, flat and V-shaped.

Cog. The dominant type of vessel of the period 1200 to 1400. Flat bottomed, clinker built at first, but later carvel built, high sides, straight sloping stern and stern posts with stern rudder. Single mast and square sail.*

Coggle.* Old name for a small cog, or boat.

Coil. Quantity of rope when made up in circular form. Length may be 113 or 120 fathoms, more or less, according to type. To coil a rope is to lay it in coil.

Coir. Fibrous outer covering of the coconut.

Coir Hawser. Hawser made of coir fibre. About two-thirds the weight and one-quarter the strength of hemp hawser of same size. As it floats on water it is useful for warping.

Col. Saddle-shaped area between two anticyclones and two depressions when they are arranged so that a line joining the two depressions crosses a line joining the two anticyclones. Through this area there is an air-flow from anticyclones to depressions.

Co-latitude. Complement of any given latitude. Value of intercepted arc of a meridian between elevated pole and observer's zenith.

Cold Front. Line in which cold air inserts itself beneath a mass of warm air.

Cold Sector. That part of a depression in which cold air is in contact with surface of Earth. Varies from 75% to total according to age of depression.

Cold Wall. Longitudinal area of cold air. 2. Line of demarcation separating the Gulf Stream from the Labrador current.

Cold Wave. Fall of temperature that follows the passing of cold front of a depression.

*Words may change their meaning with time. By 1600 **cog** had become **cock** or **cock-boat**, a ship's boat propelled by oars and sail; **hulk** became a ship without masts; **barge** became a flat-bottomed cargo boat, or the admiral's boat in a flagship.

Collapsible Boat. Boat with wood or metal framing and fabric skin, so arranged that boat can be folded up for close stowage.

Collar. Name given to eye formed in bight of a rope that is used as a pair of shrouds. Passed over a mast head when rigging.

Collar Beam.* Beam on which stanchions of beak head bulkhead rested.

Collar Knot. 'Granny' knot in middle parts of two ropes that are to make two pairs of shrouds when jury rigging. Knot is opened out and dropped over mast head.

Collier. Vessel specially fitted for carrying coal.

Collimation. Correct alignment of the optical parts of an instrument.

Collimation Error. Of a sextant, is an error due to optical axis of telescope not being parallel to plane of sextant arc.

Colling & Pinkney's Topsail.* Was carried on a rolling spar on fore side of topsail yard. Could be furled, or reduced in area, by ropes working on principle of a roller blind.

Collin's Rule. For determining the positive buoyancy of a cask or barrel in lbs. Usually expressed as $5C^2L-W$; C being mean circumference, L being distance between headings and along curve; W being weight in lbs. All dimensions in feet.

Collision. The striking together of two bodies in motion. Sometimes used to denote a moving vessel striking a stationary object. In the 'Memorandum' of a marine insurance policy it is limited to collision with another vessel, but not with permanently stationary objects. Does not include striking pier heads, wharves, piers, derelicts, floating wreckage, trawl net or a wreck that could not be salved. Does include collision with light-vessel, anchor cable, or a wreck that could be salved.

Collision Bulkhead. Unpierced bulkhead extending to upper deck. Placed about 0·05 of vessel's length from stem. Limits entry of sea in event of head-on collision.

Collision Clause. 'Running Down Clause.'

Collision Mat. Thrum mat, about 10–12-ft. square, which can be hauled under ship's bottom to cover collision damage resulting in a leak. Kept in place by lowering line, bottom line and two fore and aft ropes.

Collision Regulations. Name given by Merchant Shipping Act, 1894, to the articles of the 'Rule of the Road' at sea.

Colour Blindness. Inability to distinguish between different colours, through defective eyesight.

Colours. Ship's national ensign.

Colt. Knotted rope's end used for minor punishment.

Columba (Noachi). (Noah's) Dove. Constellation SW of Canis Major. Has one navigational star, Phact. S.H.A. 275°; Dec. 34°S; Mag. 2·8.

Column. Line of two or more ships sailing in formation. 2. A derrick post.

Colure. Great circle passing through poles of Equinoctial. Generally restricted to the great circles passing through Equinoctial and Solstitial points.

Comb. Small piece of timber for carrying fore tack block. Was usually under lower part of beak head.

Comb Cleat. Small fitting having holes through which ropes may be rove to prevent fouling of one rope by another.

Combined Altitude. Two altitudes of one heavenly body, or altitudes of two different bodies, when taken to solve one problem.

Combings. 'Coamings.'

Combustion. Burning, the act of burning, the state of being burnt. Is a chemical action accompanied by heat and, usually, by light.

Come Home. Sometimes said of an anchor when it drags along bottom. More correctly said of an anchor when it comes towards ship when heaving on cable, instead of ship moving towards anchor.

Come To. Injunction, to helmsman of sailing ship, to come nearer to wind.

Come to Anchor. To drop an anchor and ride by it.

Come Up. Order to those hauling on a rope to cease hauling and light the rope in opposite direction, so that it can be belayed.

Coming up Tack. That tack on which a sailing vessel rides out a cyclonic storm. Is the tack on which she will be brought to windward of her course by changes in wind direction.

Commander. Naval officer next in rank below Captain. Master of a Merchant Navy vessel. 2. Large wooden mallet used in rigging work.

Commanding Officer. Of a ship, is the senior officer aboard at the time.

Commercial Code. Signalling code formerly used in merchant ships. Based on Marryat's Code. Superseded by 'International Code'.

Commission. Document issued by sovereign of a state and authorising a person to hold office and rank. 2. To take a naval ship out on service. 3. Document authorising an officer to take a naval ship on service. 4. Period a naval ship is on service. 5. Money paid to a factor or agent for services rendered: generally calculated as a percentage of subject matter concerned.

Commissioning Pendant. Narrow white pendant with St. George's Cross in red at inner end. Flown by all H.M. ships in commission, excepting flagships and ships wearing a Commodore's broad pendant.

Commodore. Naval officer senior to Captain but junior to Rear-Admiral. 2. Officer commanding a convoy. 3. Courtesy title given to senior officer of two or more warships or to the senior Master of a shipping company. 4. Senior member of a yacht club who has been elected to the position of highest rank in the club.

Commodore's Burgee. Tapered white burgee with red St. George's Cross. Is flown by vessels carrying a Commodore (First Class).

D

Commodore (Second Class) has same burgee, but with red
torteau in upper inner canton. A commodore of a convoy's
burgee is white with a blue St. George's Cross.

Common Bend. Name sometimes given to a single sheet bend
when not rove through a thimble.

Common Bill. Name sometimes given to a Promissory Note.

Common Carrier. One who contracts to carry any goods offered
subject only to the statutory exceptions of fire, restraint of
princes and act of God.

Common Law. Unwritten laws that, by long usage, have been
accepted as having the same authority as statutes.

Common Pilotage. Name formerly given to that branch of navigation that deals with the conducting of a ship by methods that
do not involve celestial observations and calculations. Now
termed 'Pilotage'.

Common Whipping. Binding on end of rope, made by passing
turns of twine from an inch or two from end and towards end.
Finished off by passing end of twine under last few turns.

Commutator. Drum of insulated copper discs on shaft of dynamo.
Used for converting alternating current to direct current. 2.
Switch for reversing direction of current.

Companion. Hood, or covering, over a ladder leading from one
deck to another.

Companion Ladder. Steps going from one deck to another below
or above; particularly from poop or raised quarter deck to main
deck.

Companion Stairs. Companion ladder when consisting of stairs.

Companion Way. Stairs or ladder leading to cabin.

Company Flag. Flag bearing special device of a shipowning
company.

Comparison of Chronometers. Comparing the time shown by
chronometer with time indicated by time signal, or by another
chronometer, and recording any difference observed.

Compartment. Any one of the spaces into which a ship is divided
by watertight bulkheads and doors.

Compass. Instrument for ascertaining direction, relative to the
meridian, by means of magnetic needles, directional gyroscope,
or alignment on a known bearing; the last being known as a
'dumb' compass.

Compass Bearing. Direction of an observed point or object as
indicated by compass.

Compass Box. Case or box in which a compass is kept.

Compass Card. Graduated card, with its directive needles and cap,
that is the essential part of a compass. Graduations may be in
points, points and quarter-point, degrees measured clockwise
from north, or quadrantly, e.g. NE, 045°, N45°E.

Compass Correction. As applied to a compass bearing, is the
amount to be applied to the bearing to reduce it to a magnetic
bearing, or to a true bearing. In former case it would be the
Deviation; in latter case it would be a combination of Deviation

and Variation—known as 'Total Error'. The name of the correction will be opposite to that of the error.

Compass Course. Angle between North-South line of a magnetic compass and ship's fore and aft line.

Compass Error. Angle that North-South line of compass makes with true meridian at a position. Is of same value as the 'Correction' but opposite in name.

Compass Float. Buoyant element incorporated in card of liquid compass to reduce friction between cap and pivot.

Compass Needles. Magnetised steel needles, of high retentivity, that tend to keep North-South line of compass card in magnetic meridian.

Compass Pivot. Column, in centre of compass bowl, having a needle point—usually of iridium—on which a jewelled cap, in centre of compass card, rests and is free to move.

Compass Rose. Graduated circles, on a chart, that indicate direction of true and magnetic North, and angular values from these points.

Compass Timber. Timber that is naturally bent, and is suitable for securing deck beams to frames, etc., in wooden vessels.

Compeared. Word used in Protests and other legal documents. Signifies that one person was in the presence of another.

Compensation. In ship construction, is a restoration of strength lost by a member or members being pierced or otherwise weakened. 2. Recompense for a loss sustained. 3. Magnetic adjustment of mariner's compass.

Complement. Quantity necessary to complete a given value. 2. Correct number of men required for manning a ship.

Complete Superstructure Vessel. One of relatively small tonnage, but large-carrying capacity, resulting from having additional space not having permanent means of closing openings in deck.

Complimentary Ensign. Flag of the country whose territorial waters a ship is entering. Usually hoisted at foremast head of merchant vessel as an act of courtesy and starboard spreader of a yacht.

Component. (Of tide.) That part of a tidal undulation that is due to an actual tide raising body, or ascribed to an hypothetical harmonic constituent.

Composite. Applied to vessels built with iron framing and wood sides.

Composite Build. Composite construction.

Composite Policy. Policy of marine insurance that is subscribed by more than one company.

Composite Sailing. Method of sailing in which part of the track is a great circle, and part is along a parallel of latitude.

Composite Track. Track of vessel when 'composite sailing'.

Compound Engine. Steam engine with high- and low-pressure cylinders through which steam passes, thus making use of expansive property of steam.

Compression of (Earth's Axis). Difference between equatorial and polar diameters (or radii) of Earth, when expressed as a fraction of the equatorial value: this is 1/297.

Compulsory Pilotage. Pilotage that is compulsory, in a given area, for all vessels other than those exempt by statute.

Compressor. Strong steel lever that is pivoted on under side of cable can be nipped between compressor and navel pipe—or bitts—and so held temporarily. Ring compressor is one in which pivoted end is formed into ring of same size as navel pipe.

Con. To guide or direct a ship by giving orders to helmsman.

Concealment. Deliberately, or negligently, withholding from an insurer relevant information that he would normally be unable to obtain.

Conchoidal Fracture. Rupture of metal in which fractured surface has a shell-like appearance.

Concluding Line. Small line rove through small holes in treads of a wooden jumping ladder. Used for contracting treads into small space.

Condensation. Formation of liquid by cooling of a vapour.

Condenser. Chamber in which exhaust steam is led to outside surface of a number of pipes, through which sea water is circulated, so causing steam to condense into water.

Condenser Tudes. Usually about ½-in. diameter and made of brass or aluminium bronze. Due to expansion stresses, they are liable to leak at ends.

Conder. One who cons. More particularly, a masthead man who sights and gives notice of shoals of fish.

Conduction. Transference of heat through a stationary medium.

Conductivity. Capacity to transmit electricity or heat.

Conjunction. Position of heavenly bodies when they have same right ascension, or celestial longitude. Minor planets have two conjunctions with Sun in each revolution of orbit.

Conn. Position from which a ship is conned (U.S.A.).

Conning. Directing the course of a ship.

Connaissance de Temps. The French nautical almanac.

Connecting Links. Split links of C shape. Used for joining two ends of chain, or for temporarily replacing a fractured link.

Connecting Rod. Mild steel forging connecting end of piston rod and crank pin of reciprocating engine.

Connecting Shackle. 'Joining Shackle' of chain cable.

Conning Tower. Armoured citadel in a warship, from which ship is conned in action. 2. Tower on upper deck of a submarine from which the vessel is conned while on the surface.

Consignee. One to whom goods are sent.

Consignment. That which is consigned or transferred to another. The act of forwarding goods to another.

Consignor. Person who consigns.

Consol. A long-range aid to navigation in which a radion station transmits a pattern of dots and dashes. A ship may receive these signals with an ordinary radio receiver and thus obtain a bearing of the consol station.

Console Bracket. Light ornamental work at fore end of quarter gallery of olden ships.

Constant. Factor that is invariable in a variable quantity or value. A 'Tidal Constant'.

Constant Bearing. Bearing that does not change although ship is moving. If another vessel be crossing on a constant bearing it must be assumed that a risk of collision exists.

Constellation. Arbitrary grouping of stars according to a fancied, or obvious, resemblance to a figure or shape. Used as aid to star identification.

Constituent. Specific part of tide. Also applied to fictitious body responsible for the part.

Construction Policy. Contract of insurance covering risks while a vessel is being built. Stamped as a 'voyage' policy. Often issued for a vessel in dry dock.

Constructive Total Loss. Said of a ship or goods when so damaged or situated that cost of salvage and repair would exceed their value when salvaged.

Consul. Agent of a foreign state who resides in a country, as an accredited agent, to promote the mercantile interests of his state and the interests of its subjects when visiting, or resident in, the country to which he is accredited.

Consulages. Consular fees and charges.

Consular Fees. Moneys payable to a consul for services rendered in his consular capacity.

Consular Flag. Proper flag of a consul. British flag is blue ensign with Royal Arms in centre of fly. Is one of the flags authorised to be displayed afloat.

Consular Invoice. Invoice, attested by consul, that is required to accompany certain goods shipped to foreign countries. Nature, quality and quantity must be specified.

Container. Large, strong case of standard size which is 'stuffed' with merchandize for export and 'stripped' or unloaded at its final destination.

Container Ship. Merchant ship built to carry large containers of standard size packed with cargo.

Contamination. Tainting or pillution of a substance through contact with, or near approach to, another substance.

Continuation Clause. Special contract that is inserted in a time policy of marine insurance. Undertakes that if vessel has not completed voyage when time policy expires she will be held covered at a pro rata premium until arrival, and for up to 30 days after.

Contents Bill. Customs document describing goods and stores shipped, and number of crew and passengers.

Contline. Angular space between strands of a rope. Space between casks, barrels, etc., when stowed alongside each other, bilge to bilge.

Contraband. Prohibited, illegal. Applied to goods forbidden to be imported or exported.

Contraction of Moon's Semidiameter. Apparent difference in angular values of Moon's horizontal and vertical diameters when near horizon. Due to unequal refraction. Was of importance when measuring lunar distances.

Contract Ticket. Document by which a shipowner contracts to carry a passenger other than a steerage passenger. Minimum value £25, or £3 25s. for every 1000 miles of voyage.

Contra Propeller. Propeller-like fitting on fore side of rudder post and close to ship's propeller. It redirects the flow of water from ship's propeller, so giving a 'ahead' reaction. 'Star' type had six blades originally; this has been reduced to two blades erected vertically.

Contributory Negligence. Neglect which, though not being directly responsible for an accident, is one of the factors that made it possible.

Controller. Cast iron fitting, just abaft hawse pipe on cable deck, over which the cable can run freely. Has a bed that can be lowered, so causing outboard end of link to be brought up against a shaped portion that holds cable from further running out.

Controlling Depth. Minimum depth of water in an anchorage or channel.

Convection. Mode by which heat is propagated through a fluid. Heated mass rises and unheated mass descends to source of heat.

Convectional Rain. Rain caused by surface layers of atmosphere expanding and rising, so giving place to cooler and denser air. When rising air is charged with moisture, precipitation occurs.

Conventional Signs and Abbreviations. The accepted and established symbols and abbreviations used in a chart.

Convergence. Term used in meteorology to define a condition when more air flows into an area than out of it. This causes air to rise and results in formation of clouds and, possibly, precipitation of rain.

Convergency. Tendency to meet at a point. Particularly applied to meridians and their inclination towards each other as they approach the pole.

Conversion. The changing of a vessel's class by alterations, reductions or additions.

Convex Iron. Rolled steel or iron having one surface flat and the other a raised arc of a circle.

Convoy. Group of merchant vessels escorted by warship or warships.

Copernican Hypothesis. The view held by Copernicus regarding the solar system. He called it an 'hypothesis' to avoid antagonising the Pope of Rome.

Copernican System. Placed Sun in centre and relegated Earth and planets to subordinate positions. Considered Earth and planets to be joined to Sun by bars. Until Kepler and Newton proved the falsity of this latter assumption the view of Copernicus was generally accepted.

Copernican Theory. Later name for 'Copernican hypothesis'.

Coping. Former name for the turning of ends of iron lodging knees so that they hooked into beams, thus easing strains on bolts when vessel rolled.

Copper. Soft and ductile metal that forms base for brass or bronze. Is good conductor of heat and electricity. As it slowly exfoliates in sea water, it prevents accumulation of fouling when used as sheathing on underwater body of a ship.

Copper Bottomed. Said of a vessel whose bottom is sheathed with copper plates as protection against worm and fouling. First used 1761; retained fairly largely until about 1910. Still has limited use.

Copper Fastened. Applied to a vessel in which fastenings of timbers are made of copper, and not iron.

Copper Punt. Light raft on two hollow wooden floats. Used in R.N. when cleaning or painting boot top or lower area of ship's side. Was used, originally, for cleaning copper sheathing when vessel was careened.

Coral. Carbonate of lime that is formed by skeletons of polypes or zoophytes.

Coracle. Boat comprised of wickerwork base covered with skins or oiled fabric. Dates from very early times and still to be seen in Wales and Ireland.

Coral Reef. Reef that largely consists of coral. Most important runs parallel to N.E. Coast of Australia, being about 1000 miles long and having a 350-mile length with no gap. Also found in Solomon Islands, New Hebrides and other places.

Co-range Lines. Lines, on a chart, connecting positions having the same range of tide.

Cor Caroli. Star 12 Canum Venaticorum. S.H.A. 166°; Dec. N39°; Mag. 2·9. Name means 'Heart of Charles', being given, by Halley, in memory of Charles I.

Cord. Unit of measurement for small pieces of wood. Contains 128 cu. ft. ($4' \times 4' \times 8'$).

Cordage. Collective name for all fibre ropes and lines.

Cordonazo. Violent cyclonic storm off Pacific coasts of Central America and Mexico.

Cord Wood. Small lengths of branches, about a foot long. 2. Wood piled up for measurement into cords.

Core. Central heart in a four-stranded rope.

Cor Hydræ. 'Heart of the Hydra.' The star 'Alphard'.

Cork Fender. Canvas bag containing cork shreds and covered with coir sennit or matting.

Corkscrew Rule. Variation of 'Ampere's Rule' proposed by Maxwell. Imagines a corkscrew point moving in direction of current. Then, direction of turning force—to left below, to right above—will indicate deflection of red end of magnetic needle by current below or above it.

Cor Leonis. 'Lion's Heart.' Name given to star Regulus.

Cormorant. Sea bird found in both hemispheres. Nearly 2½ ft. long. Common cormorant is greenish-black on head, rump and lower parts; whitish collar under throat, brownish back and wings. Used by Chinese for catching fish.

Corocore. Vessel of Eastern Archipelago. Formerly used by pirates. Had one mast, carried crew of up to 60, sometimes pulled two tiers of oars. Up to 60 ft. long.

Corona. Luminous appearance, millions of miles in width, observable around Sun when totally eclipsed. 2. Luminous circle sometimes observable around Sun or Moon. Has reddish band at outer edge. Due to diffraction of light by suspended water particles in air.

Corona Australis. Southern constellation near Centaurus. 'Southern Crown.'

Corona Borealis. Constellation between Bootes and Hercules. 'Northern Crown.'

Corporation Flag. One of the flags of Trinity House.

Corposant. Electric luminosity that sometimes appears at end of mast or yard, or on rigging, during an electrical storm.

Corrected Establishment. Mean value of time interval, at a given place, between transit of Moon and appearance of high water.

Correcting Magnets. 'Corrector Magnets.'

Correction of Chart. Incorporation, in a chart, of new information issued by a hydrographer, or other authority.

Corrector Magnets. Permanent magnets placed in binnacle of magnetic compass to compensate for deviation and heeling errors.

Corrosion. The breaking down of a metal when due to electro-chemical action.

Corrugated Furnace. Boiler furnace enclosed in a circular tube that is corrugated to increase heating surface.

Corsair. Pirate. A pirate vessel.

Cor Serpentis. 'Heart of the Serpent.' Star α Serpentis. Mag. 2·8; S.H.A. 124°; Dec. 7°N.

Corvette. Formerly, flush-decked sailing vessel carrying one tier of 18 to 31 guns. Ranked next below a frigate. Latterly, name has been given to small vessels for escort, patrol and convoy duties in time of war.

Corvus. Small constellation S.E. of Spica. Four of its stars form 'Spica's Spanker'.

Cosmical. Said of a heavenly body that rises and sets with Sun.

Cost, Insurance and Freight. Merchant's quotation of a price that includes purchase of goods, cost of insurance and cost of freight to destination.

Cotidal. Said of places having tidal undulations at same time.

Cotidal Lines. Lines on a chart, connecting positions having the same lunitidal interval.

Cotton Rope. Often used in yachts on account of its clean appearance. Very flexible when dry but becomes hard when wet. Tensile strength is less than that of manilla.

Coulomb. Unit of electrical quantity. Amount carried by one amp. in one second.

Counter (Engine). Small mechanism attached to an engine to count and indicate number of revolutions made.

Counter. Sloping and curved underside of after part of hull abaft sternpost and above waterline.

Counter Brace. To brace fore and main yards in opposite directions.

Counter Current. Ocean current that flows in the direction opposite, approximately, to that of main current. Equatorial counter currents are continuations of main currents after they have recurved.

Countermart. To resist attack of an enemy.

Counter Rails. Ornamental moulding across square sterns of olden ships.

Counter Sea. Sea running in direction opposite to prevailing wind.

Counter Stays. Projecting timbers that support an overhanging stern.

Counter Trades. Winds on polar side of trade wind, but blowing in an opposite direction.

Coup d' Assurance. Firing of a gun by a warship when she shows her national ensign to vessel she is chasing.

Coup de Semonce. Firing of a shot across the bows of a vessel chased by a warship.

Coupee. Flag having vertical stripes.

Couple. Two equal forces that are parallel to each other but working in opposite directions—so generating a turning movement.

Courge. Small wickerwork basket towed astern of a shrimper. Prawns and shrimps are kept alive in it.

Course. Direction steered by a vessel. Angle that ship's fore and aft line makes with a meridian, or with north-south line of a compass. May be true, Magnetic, Compass or Gyro course. 2. Sail bent to lower yard of a sailing ship.

Course Error. Error of indication, by a gyro compass, on any particular course.

Course Recorder. Mechanical aid to pilotage. A 'plotter' is moved, electrically, over a chart; being controlled in speed and direction by electric log and gyro repeater. Recorder thus indicates ship's charted position at any moment.

Courtesy Flag. 'Complimentary Ensign.'

Court of Survey. Composed of a judge and nautical assessors. Has powers to order survey of a vessel, to detain or to release her, to order repairs or alterations to be made, to order a certificate of seaworthiness to be given.

Covering Note. Document in which each underwriter states his acceptance of a proportion of a marine risk by stating the amount and then initialing it. Is evidence of insurance pending issue of policy.

Cove. Small creek, inlet or bay sheltered from wind. 2. Arched moulding at foot of taffrail.

Covering Board. Plank that overlaps seam between planking of side of a wooden ship and the outboard deck plank.

Covering Strap. Doubling piece covering butt of ship's side plating, and to which the butted plates are riveted.

Cowl. Metal fitting for collecting and directing an air-stream to a particular space.

Cowner.* Old corruption of ship's 'counter'.

Coxcomb. 'Cockscomb.'

Coxswain. Person who steers a boat and is in charge of crew.

Crab. Winch whose axis lies in a fore and aft line. Originally a portable hand winch used in sailing ships for hauling on topsail halyards, fore and main sheets, and for working cargo.

Crachin. Northerly wind bringing drizzle and mist, occurring between January and April in the China Sea.

Crackerhash. 'Crackerjack.'

Crackerjack. Hash made of preserved meat, broken biscuit and any other available ingredient.

Crack On. To carry sail to full limit of strength of masts, yards and tackles.

Cradle. Framework of iron or wood, resting on launching ways, that supports a ship under construction for about three-quarters of her length. Slides down the ways when ship is launched. 2. Padded box in which horses, etc, are hoisted aboard. 3. Railed stage used for painting ship's side, or for repairs, when ship is in dry dock.

Craft. Vessel or vessels of practically any size or type.

Cran. Fish measure equivalent to $37\frac{1}{2}$ gallons, or 420 lb. of herrings.

Cranage. Money paid for use of cranes. 2. Outfit of cranes in a port.

Crance Iron. Iron rigging band at extremity of jib boom or bowsprit. Sometimes applied to any boom iron.

Crane. Machine for hoisting or lowering heavy weights. Name is also given to a projecting bracket, or pillar with curved arms, used for supporting booms or spars.

Crank. Said of a vessel with small stability, whether due to build or to stowage of cargo. 2.*Iron braces that supported lanterns at quarters of poop.

Cranse Iron. 'Crance Iron.'

Crayer. Three-masted, square-rigged merchant vessel of Tudor times.

Creek. Inlet on sea coast. Short arm of a river. 2. Seaside town that is not of sufficient importance to be a Customs station.

Creep. To search for a sunken object by towing a grapnel along bottom. 2. Gradual and steady deformation of a metal fitting when under stress.

Creeper. 'Grapnel.'

Crepuscular Rays. Coloured rays radiating from the Sun when it is below visible horizon but above crepusculum. Results in alternate dark and light rays being visible across sky. Caused by light being broken up by clouds or intervening mountains.

Crepusculum. Twilight circle. Small circle parallel to horizon and about 18° below it.

Crescent. Moon's shape from new moon until first quarter.

Crevasse. Crack in an ice sheet.

Crew. Personnel, other than Master, who serve on board a vessel. In some cases a differentiation between officers and ratings is made; but officers are 'crew' in a legal sense.

Crew Gangways. Elevated gangways provided for crew in tankers. Extend from poop to bridge and from bridge to forecastle.

Crew List. Nominal list of crew, their ages, birthplaces, nationality and rating, together with other particulars. Delivered to Superintendent of a Mercantile Marine Office after arrival in U.K. and prior to paying off; also, when required in a foreign port, delivered to Port Authority.

Crimp. Person who decoys a seaman from his ship and gains money by robbing him and, or, forcing him on board another vessel in want of men.

Cringle. Rope loop, with or without a thimble, worked into bolt-rope of a sail. See 'Bowline Bridle'.

Crinolines.* Small lines put on a purchase block and held in hand to steady a lifted weight.

Critical Angle. Least angle of incidence at which a light is reflected.

Critical Pressure. Of steam, is that pressure (3200 lb. per sq. in.) at which it has no latent heat and its density is that of water.

Critical Speed. Of turbine, is that rate of revolution that is almost similar to vibration rate of turbine shaft.

Critical Temperature. Maximum temperature at which a given gas can be liquefied by pressure. CO_2 is 88°F; Ammonia 256°F.

Cro'jack, Cro'jick. Abbreviations of 'Crossjack'.

Cromster. Old name for 'Hoy'.

Cross (in Cable). Exists when cables of a ship moored with two anchors lead on bow opposite to that of their respective hawse hole. Will occur when ship swings through 180° after anchoring.

Cross Bar.* Round iron bar bent to Z shape and used for turning shank of anchor when stowing.

Cross Beam. Heavy piece of timber fitted athwart a pair of wooden riding bitts.

Cross Bearings. Bearings of two or more charted objects that are taken simultaneously and laid off on chart to fix ship's position.

Cross Channel Packet. Vessel carrying mails between southern England and coast of France.

Cross Chocks. Filling pieces put at foot of timbers at ends of wood-built ship.

Cross Curves. Diagrammatic curves, based on displacement and righting moment, that indicate stability at any displacement.

Crossed Observations. Sights taken with Borda's repeating reflecting circle: first observations being taken with instrument in direct position, second observation with instrument reversed. This eliminates index error if mean is taken.

Cross Grip. Steel clamp for gripping two crossing wires or hawsers.

Crosshead. Lower, or outer, end of a piston rod. Carries the guide shoes and top end pin of connecting rod.

Crossing. Applied to a vessel that is on such a course that she will pass ahead of another vessel. Sometimes limited to a vessel that is entitled to cross ahead of another.

Crossing Rules. Those articles of the 'Collision Regulations' that refer to crossing vessels.

Crossing the Line. Crossing the Equator.

Cross Jack. Pronounced 'Crojjik'. Lower yard on a mizen mast. Name is sometimes given to yard in which square sail of a cutter is bent.

Cross Pawl. Temporary horizontal timber holding frames of a wooden vessel in position during building.

Cross Piece. Bar of timber connecting heads of bitts. 2. Bar athwart knight heads, and carrying pins for belaying ropes. 3. Flooring piece resting on keel between half floors.

Cross Pointing. Name sometimes given to 'Coach Whipping'.

Cross Sea. Confused sea caused by two seas that run in different directions.

Cross Seizing. Round seizing that is finished off by dipping the end between upper and lower turns and expending it around standing part of a shroud.

Cross Spale, Cross Spall. Cross pawl.

Cross Staff. Olden navigating instrument. Consisted of a long batten with graduated surface. Along the batten were three sliding transoms of different length. An observed celestial body was 'touched' by one of the transoms, and the position of the transom in the graduations indicated the natural co-tangent of the half arc.

Cross Timber. Floor timber, of a frame, with its middle on the keel.

Cross Tired. Having tire plates, extending from mast to ship's sides, on underside of deck; so preventing mast wedges distorting deck planking.

Cross Trees. Thwartship timbers, on a mast, to increase spread of shrouds and form support for tops.

Cross Wind. Wind blowing across course of a vessel, or across direction of sea.

Cross Wires. Wires or etched lines, at right angles, in object glass of an astronomical telescope or sighting telescope.

Crotch. Shaped timber resting on keel in forward and after ends of a wooden vessel. 2. Forked post for supporting a boom or horizontal spar.

Crow. Iron lever with a wedge end that is forked.

Crowd. Colloquial term for 'crew'.

Crowd On. To carry a press of sail.

Crowfoot. Number of small lines radiating from a euphroe or eye.

Crowfeet.* Crowfoot.

Crown (of Anchor). That part, directly beneath shank, where arms go in opposite directions.

Crown. Of a block, is the head.

Crown Knot. Made by unlaying end of rope, turning down one strand so that a bight is formed; passing second strand over bight of first strand; passing third strand over end of second strand and through bight of first strand; then working strands until tight down.

Crown Plait. Made with alternate crown and diamond knots.

Crow's Nest. Protected look-out position near mast head.

Croziers.* Constellation Crux Australis, or 'Southern Cross'.

Cruise. Voyage made in varying directions. To sail in various directions for pleasure, in search, or for exercise.

Cruiser. Warship in which armour and armament are reduced to gain speed and sea endurance, so that it can be employed in search and scouting duties; but sufficiently armed and armoured that it can take its place in a battle line.

Cruiser Arc Lamp. Arc flashing lamp of about 900 c.p. Shutter is made up of numerous pivoted slats that turn their edges to light simultaneously.

Cruiser Stern. Stern having additional floors abaft transom so that a fuller form is obtained down to water line and above rudder.

Cruising. Sailing in different directions for the purpose of search, or for visiting different places.

Crupper Chain. Chain that secures heel of jib boom to bowsprit, and prevents it rising.

Crustacea. Aquatic creatures having bony casing, ten or more joined limbs and two pairs of antennae. Lobsters and crabs are examples; but there are 8000 species.

Crutch. Horizontal plate that supports side plating at fore or after end of vessel. 2. Knee timber securing cant timbers abaft. 3. Crotch. 4. Swivelled metal fitting in which oar rests when rowing.

Crux. Small but important southern constellation. Brightest star is α Crucis. S.H.A. 174; Dec. 63°S; Mag. 1·1.

Cu. Abbreviation for 'Cumulus'.

Cuckold's Knot (Neck). Used for securing ropes to a spar. Something like clove hitch but both ends come out in same direction.

Cuddy. Cabin in fore part of a boat or small craft.

Culage. Laying up of a vessel, in dock, for repairs.

Culmination. Coming to the meridian. Point at which altitude of a heavenly body has its greatest or least altitude; the former being the upper culmination, the latter the lower culmination.

Culverin.* Sixteenth century cannon. From 10 to 12 ft. long and 5½-in. calibre. Threw 18-lb. shot about two miles. Name means 'Serpent'.

Cumulonimbus. Heavy mass of cloud rising to considerable height. Sometimes anvil-shaped at top. Associated with rain, hail, lightning and thunder.

Cumulostratus. 'Stratocumulus' cloud.

Cumulus. Dense cloud form with firm, rounded edges and horizontal base. Only moderate elevation.

Cunningham Patent Topsail. Topsail fitted to a yard that could roll up the sail to a close reef.

Cupola Ship. Early type of turret warship. Characteristic features were very small freeboard and heavy gun mounted in turret. American 'Monitor' was first one built, but idea was introduced by Captain Cooper Coles, R.N., some years before.

Curragh. Wooden-framed boat with skin or canvas covering.

Current. Horizontal movement of a stream of water through ocean or sea. Primarily due to wind action, but also to differences in specific gravities of water. Direction is more or less constant, but deviations occur. Seasonal variations are usual. Due to Earth's rotation, currents trend away from path of generating wind; to right in N. hemisphere, to left in S. 2. Flow of negatively-charged electrons along a conductor, due to difference of potential.

Current Chart. Chart in which direction and extent of ocean currents are delineated, and approximate rates noted, for information of navigators.

Current Log. Instrument for measuring rate of a current.

Current Meter. Instrument for measuring rate and direction of a current of water.

Current Sailing. Determination of position in which set and drift of currents experienced are treated as a course and distance run.

Curtis Turbine. Impulse turbine that is compounded for pressure and velocity. Essentials are retained in Brown Curtis turbine.

Cushioning. Bringing to rest the reciprocating parts of an engine by leaving a little steam on exhaust side of piston. This steam acts as a cushion and prevents shock on crank pin.

Cusp. Point, or horn, of crescent Moon or other phasing body.

Customary Dispatch. Usual and accustomed speed.

Custom House. Office where vessels are entered and cleared, and where duty or customs charges are paid.

Custom of Port. Usual and established methods prevailing in a port.

Customs. Duties imposed by law on merchandise exported or imported. 2. Common abbreviation for Custom House officers, or Custom House.

Customs Debenture. Authorisation for return of money paid as duty when goods on which duty was paid are re-exported.

Customs Declaration. Report, signed by a sender, giving description of parcels exported from United Kingdom.

Customs Entry. Written declaration—by exporter, importer or shipper—of nature, value and weight of goods exported or imported.

Cust's Station Pointer. Rectangular sheet of transparent xylonite with edges graduated in degrees and half degrees. Observed angles are drawn, in pencil, on under side.

Cut a Feather. Said, in 16th century, of a vessel when she foamed through the water with a breaking wave at the stem.

Cut and Run. To cut hemp cable and run from an anchorage.

Cut (a Sail). To loose gaskets and let sail fall.

Cutlass. Short, heavy sword used in hand-to-hand fighting at sea.

Cut Splice. Made by splicing one rope to another at a little distance from end of each, so leaving a small length where ropes lie side by side.

Cutter. Sailing vessel with one mast, bowsprit and fore and aft sails. Carries mainsail, fore staysail and jib. 2. Twelve oared rowing and sailing boat of R.N. 3. Revenue vessel, generally steam-propelled, that superseded previous revenue cutters. 4. Boat that follows racing boats, carrying trainers and coaches.

Cutter Stay Fashion. Method of setting up lower rigging. End of lanyard has knot in end, and is then rove through upper and lower deadeyes. Normally, standing end of lanyard was made fast away from deadeye. Name is also applied to a deadeye held in a running eye, or clinch, at end of shroud.

Cutting. Said of high-water levels that decrease as tide changes from spring to neap.

Cutting Down Line. Curved line on sheer plan. Passes through lowest point of inner surface of each of the frames.

Cutting Out. Capturing an enemy vessel in a port of her own country and taking her away.

Cuttle, Captain. Generous, simple and delightful shipmaster in Dickens' 'Dombey and Son.' His motto was, 'When found, make a note of.'

Cutwater. Forward edge of stem.

Cycle. Period in which a series of events will occur, after which they will repeat themselves.

Cyclone. Rotary storm in tropical latitudes. An area of low barometric pressure, though these are usually called in temperate latitudes 'Depressions' or 'Lows'.

Cyclonic Rain. Rainfall associated with cyclones. Caused by elevation of an air mass that moves over a denser air mass of different temperature.

Cyclostrophic. Name applied to that component which causes a gradient wind to move outwards from its axis of rotation due to curvature of path.

Cygnus. (Swan.) Constellation between Lyra and Pegasus. Principal star is Deneb.

Cylinder. Of engine, is a tubular chamber in which piston moves reciprocally.

Cylindrical Projection. Projection of surface of sphere to inside surface of a cylinder that touches sphere on one line. Projection is by straight lines from centre of sphere. Mercator's Projection is not of this type, though it may resemble it.

Cynosure. Constellation Ursa Major. Name was given to Polaris. As it is Greek for 'dog's tail', it is obvious that the constellation was looked upon as resembling a dog.

D

Dabchick. Diving bird. Particularly applied to the Little Grebe, which is frequently seen near coast.

Dagger. Piece of timber used to support poppets of bilgeways during launching of a vessel.

Dagger Keel. Deep and narrow drop-keel.

Dagger Knees. Knees placed obliquely, instead of vertically, to give as much-uninterrupted stowage space as possible.

Dagger Piece. Name applied to any oblique member in a vessel's framing.

Dagger Plank. Plank uniting poppets and stepping up pieces of a launching cradle.

Daltonism. Inability of eye to distinguish between red and green colours. A form of colour blindness.

Dalton's Law. In a mixture of gases each gas exerts its own pressure independently of the others, the pressure of the mixture being the sum total of the constituent pressures.

Damp. To damp fires is to reduce the air supply so that combustion goes on very slowly. 2. To damp a gyro is to constrain its movements to a limited amount.

Damp Air. Atmospheric air when its water content is about 85% of maximum.

Dan Buoy. Pole or spar with ballasting weight at one end and buoyant unit at middle. Mooring rope, with weighted mooring, is attached to middle. Used by trawlers, surveying vessels, minesweepers and others as a temporary sea mark.

Dandy. Sloop or cutter with a jiggermast right aft, on which a small lugsail is set.

Dandyfunk. Kind of pudding made from crushed ship's biscuits.

Dandy Note. 'Pricking Note.'

Danger Angle. Vertical or horizontal sextant angle which, when used in conjunction with charted objects, will indicate when a vessel is approaching a position of danger.

Dangerous Goods. Commodities that seriously endanger the safety of a vessel in which they are carried. M.S.A. specifically mentions aquafortis, vitriol, naphtha, benzine, gunpowder, lucifer matches, nitroglycerine, petroleum and explosives.

Dangerous Quadrant. That half of front of a cyclonic storm that is on the side towards which recurvature is to be expected.

Danube Tonnage Rules. Special tonnage rules applied to vessels when navigating river Danube.

Dash. The longer flash or sign in Morse signalling. Is three times the length of the 'dot'.

Date Line. Line on which time zones -12 hours and $+12$ hours meet. The time is the same on either side, but the dates are one day different; 180°E being a day in advance of 180°W. This line is mainly, but not entirely, on the 180th meridian; varying between 170°E and 172½°W, to avoid having different dates in a group of islands, or same area of land.

Datum. Given level, or other value, to which varying values are referred.

Davis Current. Alternative name for Labrador Current.

Davis Quadrant.* The 'Backstaff' of Captain Davis, which was the usual navigating instrument from 1590 to latter half of 18th century.

Davit. Iron or steel (formerly wood) fitting projecting over ship's side for attachment of tackle for hoisting and lowering boat, accommodation ladder, anchor, stores, etc. Sometimes fitted at hatch.

Davy Jones. Evil spirit of the sea, who lies in wait for seamen. Said to be a corruption of 'Duffy Jones'; 'duffy' being a negro word for 'ghost', and 'Jones' being a corruption of 'Jonah'.

Davy Jones Locker. The bottom of the sea, where Davy Jones holds drowned seamen and foundered ships.

Day. Period of time based on Earth's revolution on its axis. Its duration is based on successive transits of a point of definition at a given place. This point is, in most civilised countries, based on the mean Sun for civil time, and First Point of Aries for sidereal time.

Day Mark. Shape hoisted, in daytime, by vessels in specified circumstances, and in accordance with international rules. 2. Distinguishing characteristic of a light vessel. 3. Navigational beacon that is not observable at night.

Days of Grace. Time allowed, beyond a time and date specified during which no action will be taken for non-fulfilment of a contract. In the case of money bills the usual period is three days.

Day's Work. At one time called 'Day's works'. Practical methods of deducing ship's noon position, usually by dead reckoning, and computing course and distance made good and course to be steered.

Dead Beat Compass. Magnetic compass in which swing due to quick alterations of course, or liveliness of vessel, is greatly reduced both in time and amplitude. Has short but very strong needles, and comparatively large bowl.

Dead Calm. Perfectly smooth sea and no wind whatever.

Dead Door. Sliding wooden shutter for blanking square window of a cabin.

Deadeye. Hard wooden block, pierced with holes, fitted in lower end of shroud to take lanyard for setting up.

Dead Flat. Midship frame of a vessel where breadth is greatest.

Dead Freight. Money paid to ship for failure to provide a full cargo promised.

Dead Head. Solid piece of wood used as anchor buoy.

Dead Horse. Performance of work that has already been paid for.

Dead Lights. Plates fitted over portholes to protect them or to prevent lights inside the ship from showing outboard.

Dead Man. Rope's end, or small piece of yarn or line, when left hanging untidily. 2. Counterbalancing weight that assists guy of derrick.

Dead Men's Eyes.* Early name for 'Deadeye'.

Dead Neap. Lowest possible high water of a tide.

Dead on End. Said of wind when exactly ahead; and of another vessel when her fore and aft line coincides with observer's line of sight.

Dead Reckoning. Calculation of a ship's position by consideration of distance logged, courses steered and estimated leeway. Sometimes said to be corruption of 'deduced reckoning'; but this is very debatable.

Dead Rising. Those parts of a vessel's floor, throughout her length, where floor timbers meet lower futtocks.

Dead Ropes. All ropes, or running rigging, that are not led through a block or sheave.

Dead Slow. Minimum speed that will give steerage way.

Dead Water. Eddy water immediately astern of a sailing vessel or boat.

Deadweight. Total weight, in tons, of cargo, stores and fuel carried by a vessel at her maximum permitted draught.

Deadweight Cargo. Cargo whose specific gravity is such that a vessel loading it will go down to her marks.

Deadweight Scale. Table, or graph, showing total weight of fuel, stores and cargo, and corresponding mean draught of vessel.

Deadweight Tonnage. Deadweight expressed in tons avoirdupois.

Dead Wind. Wind directly contrary to ship's course.

Deadwood. Flat, vertical surfaces at junction of stem or stern post with keel. Has no buoyant effect.

Dead Work.* Old name for 'Freeboard'.

Deals. Planks, particularly of fir, 7 to 11 in. in width and 2 to 4 in. thick.

Decca Navigator. A radio aid for fixing positions up to at least 300 miles from the transmitter. A master transmitter ashore controls a chain of other transmitters, designated Slaves. All transmit signals continuously. A ship provided with a special receiver can receive these signals, the phase-difference between them being measured by Decometers. The numbers indicated on the Decometers refer to coloured lattice lines printed on special charts. The ship's position is where the numbered lines cross each other.

Deck. Horizontal flooring, or plating, above bottom of vessel. May be continuous or partial.

Deck Beam. Thwartship member that supports a deck and preserves form of a vessel.

Deck Bridge.* Former name for a navigating bridge.

Deck Cargo. Cargo that must be carried on deck. 2. Cargo that is customarily carried on deck. 3. Cargo actually carried on deck.

Deck Hand. Seaman, other than officer, who serves on deck. Man of 17 years of age, or over, with at least one year's sea service.

Deck Head. Underside of a deck.

Deck Hook. Thwartship frame across apron, to strengthen bow and support fore end of deck.

Deck Light. Strong glass bull's eye fitted in a deck to light a compartment below. 2. A permanent light fitted on a deck.

Deck Line. Horizontal mark, cut in plating of side and painted in a distinct colour, that indicates position of freeboard deck.

Deck Load. Deck cargo.

Deck Log. Log book kept by officer of watch and entered with events, changes of course, weather, log readings, work done and other items occurring during the watch. In harbour, is kept by duty officer.

Deck Nail. Large nail, of diamond section, used for securing deck plank to beam of a wooden ship.

Deck Officer. In general, an officer whose duties are connected with the deck department. Sometimes applied to the duty officer of the deck or watch.

Deck Passage. Voyage of a passenger for whom no accommodation is available. Confined to short voyages and trades, such as the carrying of pilgrims.

Deck Pipe. Navel pipe, through which chain cable passes to chain locker.

Deck Sheet. Studdingsail sheet that leads directly from sail to deck.

Deck Stopper. Formerly, length of very strong rope to which cable could be lashed; one end of a stopper being secured to deck. Name is sometimes given to any fitting on deck for holding cable for a short time.

Deck Transom.* Formerly, a horizontal timber under counter of a ship.

Deck Watch. Watch that is used for timing sights taken on deck. Is compared with chronometer before and after sights are taken, so avoiding disturbance of chronometer.

Declaration of London, 1909. Rules and regulations framed by an International Naval Conference, but not formally ratified.

Declaration of Paris, 1856. Abolished privateering; declared that neutral flag covers enemy goods, but not contraband of war; neutral goods, other than contraband, not liable to capture; blockade must be effective to be legal.

Declination. Angular distance, of a heavenly body, north or south of Equinoctial. 2. Former name for variation of compass.

Declination Circle. Great circle, of celestial concave, that is perpendicular to Equinoctial. Also called hour circle, of circle of Right Ascension.

Declination Inequalities. Variations in heights or intervals of high and low waters of tides when due to variations in declination of Sun and Moon.

Deep. Navigable channel bounded by shoal water. 2. Applied to frames and stringers that have been widened, by extending plate between angle bars, to give additional strength.

'Deep.' Leadsman's call before naming a sounding in fathoms that is not marked in lead line.

Deep Sea Lead. 28-lb. lead used for taking soundings by hand in deep water.

Deep Sea Leadline. One-inch cable laid rope, 100 fathoms long, used with deep sea lead. Marked as hand leadline to 20 fathoms, then every 5 fathoms.

Deep Sea Sounding. Ascertaining sea depths beyond reach of hand lead. Also applied to a sounding exceeding 100 fathoms.

Deep Tank. Ballast tank extending from 'tween deck to bottom of ship, and from shipside to shipside. Has centre fore and aft bulkhead, with valve between compartments. May be utilised for cargo.

Deep Waist. Upper deck in a ship with high forecastle and poop.

Deep Waisted. Said of a ship having a deep waist.

Deface.* To strip a wooden ship of her planking and leave the ribs bare.

Deflector. Instrument invented by Lord Kelvin for measuring directive force of a compass mounted in a steel or iron ship. Measurements are made with ship's head on four cardinal points.

Degaussing. Neutralising magnetic effect of steel or iron vessel by encircling her with wires carrying electric current. Used as protection against magnetic mines.

Degree. Originally, arc of Ecliptic travelled by Sun in one day. Now, angle subtended by 1/360th of circumference of a circle.

Degree of Dependence. Measure of probable error in an observation or assessment.

Dekad. Meteorological name for a period of ten days.

Delambre's Analogies. Formulae for solving spherical triangles in terms of those used for solving plane triangles.

De Laval Turbine. Uncompounded turbine that is used for driving pumps and dynamos.

Delta. Triangular area of sediment in mouth of a river, so giving river more than one discharging channel.

Delta Metal. Alloy of copper, zinc and iron. Much used for engineering purposes.

Demi-Culverin. Naval gun of Tudor times. Threw ball of 9–10 lb.

Demise. Temporary transfer of a vessel to another party under such terms and conditions that the owner ceases to have any control over her for the period of the charter.

Demurrage. Money paid to shipowner, by charterer, when his ship is detained beyond the lay days mentioned in charter party.

Deneb Adige. Star α Cygni. Usually called 'Deneb'. S.H.A. 50°; Dec. 45°N.

Deneb Aleet. Old name for star Denebola.

Denebola. Star β Leonis. S.H.A. 183°; Dec. 15°; Mag. 2·2.

Density. Weight per unit volume, e.g. weight in oz. per cub. ft. Relative Density=Specific Gravity=Ratio of unit volume of water compared with weight of same volume of fresh water. 2. Density of sea water is about 1026, but varies between 1000 and 1038 (Port Sudan) in ports. 3. Density of boiler water is expressed in $\frac{1}{32}$nds of increase in weight, $\frac{3}{32}$nds being upper limit tolerated. Due, principally, to sulphate of lime in suspension.

Departure. The distance made good due East or West when sailing on any course.

Departure Course. Course made good from a point of reference at which a voyage, or stage of voyage, commenced.

Departure Distance. Distance of a ship from a point of reference at which a voyage, or stage of a voyage, commenced.

Deposition. Statement made on oath or affirmation.

Deposit Receipt. Acknowledgement of receipt of a sum of money, from a receiver of cargo, when a general average contribution is likely to be claimed.

Depression. Of horizon, is angular distance of visible horizon, or shore horizon, below sensible horizon. Usually termed 'Dip'. 2. Atmospheric mass in which barometric pressure is lower than that of surrounding atmosphere.

Depression of Wet Bulb. Amount, in degrees, that registration of wet bulb thermometer is less than that of dry bulb. Occasionally there may be a negative depression when temperature is falling quickly. Depression is usually zero in fog or wet mist.

Depth. Of boat, is vertical distance from level of gunwale to keel. 2. Of flag, measure of its vertical length. More usually termed its 'breadth'. 3. Of hold, is vertical distance from underside of beam to top of keelson. 4. Of sea, is distance, in fathoms or feet, from level of low water spring tide to sea bed. 5. Of sail, is vertical distance from head to foot of square sail; length of leech of a fore and aft sail.

Depth Charge. Canister of explosive detonated at a required depth by a hydrostatic valve. Used against submerged submarines.

Depth Finder. Lead having a vane attachment that measures depth on the same principle that a towed log measures horizontal distance. *See* 'Harpoon Depth Finder'.

Deratisation. Extermination of all rats aboard a vessel.

Derelict. Floating vessel that has been totally abandoned.

Derrick. Boom or spar used for hoisting or lowering weights. Made of wood or steel, controlled by guys, supported by topping lift, and pivoted at lower end.

Derrick Post. Stump mast used for taking topping lift of a swinging derrick.

Descending Latitude. Decreasing celestial latitude of Moon or planet.

Descending Node. That point in Ecliptic at which Moon passes to South (minus) celestial latitude.

Deserter. One who leaves, or remains away from, his ship without permission and shows no intention of eventual return.

Desertion. Leaving, or remaining away from, a ship without permission and showing no intention of eventually returning.

Despatch. Quickness in performance. 2. To send away.

Despatch Money. Agreed amount paid by shipowner to receiver of cargo when cargo is discharged in less time than that contracted.

Destination. Port to which a vessel is bound, or at which cargo is to be delivered.

Destitute Foreign Seamen. In M.S.A. is applied to certain Asiatics, Africans, South Sea Islanders and foreign seamen of countries who have no Consul in the United Kingdom.

Destroyer. 'Torpedo Boat Destroyer.' Fast, unarmoured, warship armed with torpedoes and guns, capable of attacking large warships with her torpedoes and submarines with depth-charges.

De-Superheater. Appliance for removing excess heat from superheated steam that is to be used for auxiliary machinery. Generally effected by an automatically controlled system of water spraying.

Detention. The holding of a vessel in a port—without resorting to seizure, arrest or capture—by a sovereign power or competent authority.

Determination. Exact ascertainment of position, amount, or other required information.

Deviation. Applied to a voyage, is an unjustified and unnecessary departure from normal course or customary route; delay in sailing, tardiness on voyage, arrival at port other than that intended, or any divergence that makes the voyage other than that intended.

Deviation (or Compass). Angle that compass needle makes with the magnetic meridian at a place when due to attracting forces in ship or cargo.

Devil. Deck seam between ship's side and outboard line of planking.

Devil Fish. Large fish of ray family. Has enormous head, and is 3 to 5 ft. in length.

Devil's Claw. Two-pronged hook, or claw, that drops over side of link of cable. Attached to deck and used for holding cable temporarily.

'Devil to pay and no pitch hot.' Refers to 'devil' deck seam. Means a difficult job to be done and no preparation made.

De Vries-Smitt Tide Gauge. Submerged tide gauge used by Netherlands Hydrographic Office. Records variations of water pressure due to change in height of water level; gauge being at constant distance from bottom.

Dew. Particles of water deposited by atmosphere when in contact with a surface whose temperature is below that of dew point.

Dew Point. Lowest temperature to which air can be cooled without condensation of its water vapour. Should temperature fall below this point fog or mist may form.

D.F. Bearing. Position line obtained from a directional radio beam.

Dghaisa. Open boat with greatly extended stem and stern posts. Peculiar to Malta. Two oars are pushed.

Dhow. Arab sailing vessel of about 150–200 tons. Has one mast and very large lateen sail.

Diacoustics 113 Dip

Diacoustics. Science of direct sound.

Diagonal. Any knee, plank, brace, etc., that is placed diagonally. 2. Line cutting a body plan in an oblique direction.

Diagonal Built. Said of wooden boats and vessels in which side planking is made up of two layers at an angle of 45° with keel, upper layer crossing lower layer in opposite directions.

Diamagnetic. Name given to substance whose magnetic permeability is less than unity. 2. A substance which, when magnetised, lies across lines of magnetic force.

Diametral Plane. Great circle of a sphere.

Diamond Knot. Fancy bend in two ropes' ends made by interlacing them. Similar to 'Carrick Bend'. 2. Knot formed in a rope, somewhat similar to single 'Turk's Head'.

Diaphone. Sonic fog-signalling apparatus that gives a high note that descends to a low note of great carrying power. Fitted in light vessels.

Diatomic Ooze. Yellowish-brown ooze containing the algæ 'bacillareophyta'. Found at depths from 600 to 2000 fathoms.

Dicrotum.* Boat propelled by two oars.

Dielectric. Insulating material that prevents conduction of electricity but allows induction. Used in electrical condensers.

Diesel Engine. Oil engine in which ignition of fuel is caused by compression. Cycle comprises air compression, fuel injection, ignition, and scavenging. Cycle may be completed in two or four strokes.

Difference of Latitude. Angular value of arc of meridian intercepted between parallels of latitude passing through two different positions.

Difference of Longitude. Angle at pole, or intercepted arc of Equator, between two meridians.

Differences (Tidal). Amounts that heights or times of high and low water at a given place differ from the corresponding heights and times at a port of reference.

Differential Block. Wheel with two sets of sprockets around its circumference, one set being on a smaller diameter than the other, and so having less sprockets. Endless chain is laid in each wheel, each having hanging bight. Weight is lifted in bight of larger wheel, power is applied to bight of lower. Difference in number of sprockets is measure of lift.

Dikrotos.* Ancient Greek vessel similar to bireme.

Dingbat. Slang term for a small swab made of rope and used for drying decks.

Dinghy. Small boat, about 10–14 ft. long, pulling two oars and fitted with mast and one or two sails.

Dioptric. Applied to lenses and lights when concentration of light rays is obtained by refraction.

Dip. Angular amount that visible horizon is below horizontal plane due to height of observer's eye. 2. Angle that a freely-suspended magnet makes with horizontal plane when aligned with lines of magnetic force. 3. To lower a flag a small distance, either as salute or signal. 4. To commence to descend in altitude. 5. To pass a rope, end of spar or other article down and under an obstruction. 6. Amount of submergence of a paddle wheel.

Diphda. Star β Ceti. S.H.A. 350°; Dec. S18°; Mag. 2·2.

Dipper. Ladle used for baling a boat. 2. Name is common in U.S.A., and in Britain, for constellation Ursa Major.

Dipping a Light. Sailing away from a navigational beacon light and so causing it to dip below horizon.

Dipping Colours—Ensign. Lowering national colours as a salute.

Dipping Lug. Lugsail that has to be lowered a little, when going about, so that throat of sail and end of yard can be dipped round mast.

Dipping Needle. Magnetic needle on horizontal axis; used when measuring inclination of Earth's magnetic force.

Dipsy. Name sometimes given to deep sea lead. 2. Float on fishing line.

Direct Current. Electrical current flowing in one direction.

Directing Force. That component, of magnetism of a compass needle, that directs the needle into the magnetic meridian.

Direction. Of wind, is compass point from which it blows. Of current, is direction towards which it sets.

Direction Finder. Instrument for finding the bearing of a transmitting radio station or radio beacon.

Directive Force. 'Directing Force.'

Direct Motion. Movement in space that is in direction of Earth's rotation and Sun's apparent motion in heavens. All planets have direct motion. Applied to movement of planet when its right ascension increases.

Direct Tide. Undulation of tide that synchronises with Moon's transit at a place.

Dirk. Short sword forming part of R.N. midshipman's uniform. Also, colloquial name for a seaman's knife.

Disbursement. The paying of money. Sum of money paid out.

Disbursements. Sums of money paid out of a fund credited or allotted.

Disc. Circular face of a solar system body.

Discharge. To put cargo out of a ship and obtain freedom of responsibility for it. 2. To pay off a man, or crew, and relinquish all claims for service.

Discharge Book. Continuous record of a seaman's service at sea. Issued by D.T.I. and held by man except when actually serving in ship. Contains names and particulars of ships served in, rating, reports on character and ability. Held in custody of master while serving in ship.

Discipline. Due and honest rendering of service and obedience. Equitable co-ordination of duties and responsibilities for the common benefit. Maintenance of proper subordination.

Disembark. To come out of a ship. To put out of ship and put ashore.

Disengaging Gear. Applied to fittings, to boat and falls, that release a boat from her falls simultaneously and rapidly.

Dismast. Carry away, or remove, the mast or masts of a vessel.

Dispatch. 'Despatch.'

Dispatch Money. 'Despatch Money.'

Dispatch Note. 'Despatch Note.'

Displacement. Amount of water displaced by a floating vessel in a given condition. May be expressed in tons, or volume in cubic feet; tons being weight of vessel and contents, volume being that of immersed part of vessel.

Display. Visual presentation of recevied radar signals. *Relative Display.* The observer's position remains stationary and the movement of targets (coastline, ships, etc.) is thus relative to the observer. *Stabilised Display* in which the heading marker and bearings of targets are stabilised by a transmitting compass. *True-motion Display.* The observer's position moves across the display in accordance with his ship's course and speed. Movements of targets are thus in their proper direction and at their proper speed.

Disrating. Degrading from one rank or rating to a lower. Withdrawal of a rating given to a man.

Distance. Length in a particular direction of course. Length of shortest track between two places. Length of customary track between two places. Time difference between two given meridians. Angular value, at a given point, between two other points.

Distance of Visible Horizon. Varies with height of observer's eye. Can be found, in miles, from product of square root of height of eye, in feet, and constant factor of 1·15.

Distance Recorder. In general, any log or log mechanism that records distance. In particular, *see* 'Forbes Distance Recorder'.

Distant Signals. System of shapes used between ships when far apart in daytime, and colours of flags were indistinguishable. With development of brilliant Morse lamps and radio the system became unnecessary.

Distiller. Combined condenser and aerator used when converting steam to drinking water.

Distortion of Charts. *See* 'Chart Distortion.'

Distraint. Legal seizure of ship or goods in satisfaction of a debt.

Distress. In a state of danger and in need of assistance. Also alternative name for 'Distraint'.

Distressed Seaman. Seaman, who, through no fault of his own but through some event in his employment, is in need of assistance, to maintain himself and to return home or to a proper return port.

Distress Signals. Customary and statutory indications that a vessel, or her personnel, are in danger and in need of assistance.

Ditch. Colloquial name for the sea. To ditch is to throw overboard.

Ditcher. Name given to a small light draught vessel that can navigate narrow, shallow channels.

Ditty Bag. Small canvas bag in which a seaman keeps his small stores and impedimenta.

Ditty Box. Small wooden box, with lock and key, in which seamen of R.N. keep sentimental valuables, stationery and sundry small stores.

Diurnal. Daily. Occurring once a day.

Diurnal Aberration. Apparent error in position of heavenly body due to light rays from the body being received by an observer who is being moved by Earth's diurnal rotation.

Diurnal Arc. Apparent arc made in the sky, by a heavenly body, when due to Earth's diurnal rotation.

Diurnal Circle. Circle in celestial concave in which a heavenly body, when viewed from Earth, seems to move.

Diurnal Components. Those tidal components whose maxmium values are attained once a day approximately.

Diurnal Inequality of Tides. Difference, in time or height, between two successive semidiurnal tides when a diurnal factor has affected one tide differently from the other.

Diurnal Liberation. Parallactic effect due to Earth's rotational movement, in which we see a little around western side of Moon when she is rising, and a little around eastern side when she is setting.

Diurnal Motion. Measure of arc through which a solar system body moves in celestial concave during a day. Also applied to apparent movement of heavenly bodies when due to Earth's rotation on axis.

Diurnal Parallax. Difference between position of heavenly body, when viewed from a point on surface of Earth, and its position when viewed from centre of Earth. Difference varies throughout day.

Diurnal Tide. Tide that has one high water and one low water in a tidal day.

Diurnal Variation of Barometer. Small rise of barometric pressure between 4 a.m. and 10 a.m., then fall until 4 p.m., followed by rise till 10 p.m. and fall to 4 a.m.

Diver. One who goes under water. Particularly applied to man who goes under water in a special dress in which he can be supplied with air. 2. Long-necked bird that dives into ocean in search of fish.

Diver's Palsy. 'Caisson Disease.'

Dividers. Instrument for measuring distance on a chart with two legs connected at one end by a movable joint.

Divisions. Daily morning muster of ship's company in R.N. Men muster by divisions and proceed to prayers. Introduced by Kempenfeldt, 1780.

Dock. Artifical excavation or construction in which ships can be placed for loading, unloading, fitting out, or repairing. Principal types are wet, dry and floating docks.

Dock Dues. Money paid for use of a dock and its equipment.

Docket. Label or document giving particulars of goods to which it refers.

Docking. Placing of a vessel in dock. 2. Overhaul of a vessel in dock.

Docking Bridge. Small thwartship bridge on poop, to give clear view to officer in charge aft when docking a ship.

Docking Keel. Name sometimes given to bilge keel.

Docking Stresses. Particular stresses set up in a ship in dry dock. Due to lack of water support. Most important are compressive stresses on bottom, shearing stresses in decks, tensile stresses at upper edges of floors.

Dockmaster. Official in charge of a dock.

Dock Pass. Receipt for dock dues paid, and authorisation for ship to leave dock and proceed to sea. Authorisation for a person to leave or enter a dock area.

Docks Regulations. Rules and regulations governing ships when in a dock.

Docks Regulations, 1934. S.R.O. 279. Those sections of the Factory Act that apply to the loading, unloading, handling and moving of goods in a ship or dock, or on wharf or quay.

Dock Rent. Charges made for storage of goods in a dock warehouse.

Dock Warrant. Receipt given by dock warehouseman for goods deposited with him.

Dockyard. Enclosed space containing docks, storehouses and workshops, and having facilities for the fitting, refitting and repair of ships.

Doctor. Usual nickname for a ship's cook.

Dodger. Small piece of canvas spread as wind screen for man on watch.

Dog. Short form of 'Dog Watch', or of 'Dog shore'. 2. Meteor when seen low in horizon at dawn or sunset. 3. Short iron bar fitted with teeth at one end and ring at other end. Used as a lever, with tackle hooked in ring.

Dogger. Dutch fishing vessel, with two masts, employed on Dogger Bank.

Dogging. Passing twine or small rope rightly around another rope.

Dog's Lug. Projection of boltrope of sail, between earing cringle and reef cringle, when sail is reefed.

Dog Star. Sirius, α Canis Majoris.

Dog Vane. Small piece of bunting stopped to shroud, when under sail, to indicate wind direction to helmsman.

Dog Watch. One of the two-hour watches between 4 p.m. and 8 p.m., introduced to effect changes in watches kept on consecutive days.

Doldrums. Comparatively windless zone, along Equator, that separates the prevailing winds of north and south latitudes.

Dolphin. Mammalian marine creature that frequently sports around ships' bows at sea. 2. Iron or wood structure, in harbours, for mooring of ships. 3. Moored spar to which a ship can be moored. 4. Plaited cordage formerly put around mast, immediately below jaws, to support yard if lifts were shot away.

Dolphin Striker. Spar vertically below end of bowsprit to give downward lead to martingales of jib boom and flying jib boom.

Dominical Letter. Letter that Sundays will have in a given year when January 1 is A and days are successively lettered from A to G.

Donkey. Short form of 'Donkey Boiler', 'Donkey Engine' or 'Donkeyman'.

Donkey Boiler. Small boiler, often vertical, used for generating steam for winches and other machinery used in harbour.

Donkey Engine. Small steam winch used in sailing ships to reduce number of men required when weighing anchor, pumping, or working cargo.

Donkeyman. Rating who tends a donkey boiler, or engine, and assists in engine-room.

Donkey's Breakfast. Merchant seaman's name for his bed or mattress.

Donkey Topsail. 'Jack Topsail.'

Dory. Flat-bottomed boat with sharp ends, and sides sloping upward and outward. 2. Edible fish sometimes found in British waters. Has spiny rays along back and on lower side.

Dot. Short flash in Morse signalling. One-third length of 'dash'.

Double. To alter course round a point of land.

Double Altitude. Two altitudes of one heavenly body, with an elapsed interval; or approximately simultaneous altitudes of two bodies. Taken to obtain position lines.

Double Bank. To put two men to pull one oar.

Double Banked. Said of a boat in which two oars are pulled on one thwart. Said of an oar pulled by two men.

Double Block. Pulley block having two sheaves on the same pin.

Double Bottom. Space between inner and outer bottom plating of hull.

Double Chronometer. Name given to the finding of a ship's position by Sumner's Method, and using two heavenly bodies sufficiently distant from the meridian.

Double Clewed Jib. Four-sided jib with two clews. Introduced by Sopwith in 'Endeavour', 1934, to take place of jib and jib top sail.

Double Compound Engine. Reciprocating engine consisting of two engines having h.p. and l.p. cylinders.

Double Luff. Purchase having two double blocks with standing part of rope made fast at head of one block.

Double Summer Time. See 'Summer Time'.

Double Tide. Occurrence of two high waters in one semidiurnal period. Noticeable at Portland, Southampton and other places.

Double Topsail. Two topsails, without reefs, that take the place of a large topsail that can be reefed. Sail area is reduced by furling upper topsail.

Double Up. (Moorings.) To duplicate all mooring ropes.

Double Whip. *See* 'Whip'.

Doubling Angle on Bow. Method of finding distance from a fixed point, or object, by measuring distance run from a point where its angle on bow has certain value, to another point where the angle on bow of same object, is double the value of the first. Distance run between bearings will be equal to distance of observed object at second bearing if course steered and distance run through water are made good over the ground. Correction must be made for any leeway, or set and drift of tidal current.

Doubling. Sailing round a point of land. 2. Extra strip of canvas stitched to sail for strengthening. 3. Turned in edge of sail that takes boltrope. 4. Piece of timber on after side of wooden bitts. 5. Additional timber fastened to outer skin of vessel when working amongst floating ice. 6. Generally applied to any lap of plate, planking or canvas.

Doublings. Those parts of a built mast where the upper end of one mast lies abaft the lower part of a mast extending above it.

Douglas Protractor. Square, transparent, protractor with a graticule of squares, and degrees marked on the edges.

Douglas Sea and Swell Scale. International scale for recording state of sea by a figure between 0 and 9; and swell by figures between 00 and 99, upper and lower figures inclusive.

Douse. To lower quickly and suddenly. To extinguish a light by dousing an extinguisher. To take in a sail. 'Douse the glin': Put out the light.

Dousing Chocks. Pieces of wood laid across apron of wooden ship, and extended to knight heads.

Dow. 'Dhow.'

Dowel. Small circular piece of wood let into deck plank to cover countersunk head of fastening bolt.

Dowelling. Joining wood spars by making shaped projections, on one of the parts, fit into corresponding cut-out portions in the other part.

Down. Said of a tiller when it is put to leeward while sailing.

Downhaul. Rope rove for hauling down purposes. Especially applied to rope by which jib, staysail, jaw of gaff, or flag are hauled down.

Downton Pump. Double-acting pump in which piston is solid, and valves are so placed as to be easily accessible for clearing. Used for pumping bilges, or for sea suction.

Dowse. 'Douse.'

Drabler. Strip of canvas laced to bonnet of square sail to increase its area.

Draco. Winding constellation between Lyra and Ursa Minor.

Draft. Old name for a chart. 2. Document authorising one party to draw on the funds of another. 3. Draught.

Drag. To draw an anchor along the bottom. 2. Difference between propeller speed and ship's speed through water when ship is going faster than propeller's speed. 3. Alternative name for 'Drogue'.

Drag Anchor. Old name for 'Drogue' or 'Sea Anchor'.

Drag Net. Net dragged along the bottom by fishing vessel.

Dragon. 1. Norse Longship of about 900 A.D. of largest size. The biggest had a keel 148 ft. long and rowed 68 oars. Named from its figurehead. 2. Northern constellation 'Draco'.

Drag Sheet. Sail laced to a spar that is weighed at foot, and used as a drogue.

Draught. Depth in water at which a ship floats.

Draught Indicator. Instrument fitted inside a ship to indicate draught at which she is floating.

Draught Gauge. Instrument that indicates a ship's draught.

Draught Marks. Figures cut into stem and sternpost and painted. Used for ascertaining draught at any moment and for finding trim.

Draughts.* Old name for charts or plans.

Draw. To submerge hull a specified distance. To require a stated depth of water to be afloat. 2. Sail is said to draw when filled with wind and straining at sheets and attachments to ship. 3. To draw a jib is to shift it to leeward when aback. 4. To draw a splice is to withdraw the spliced strands.

Drawback. Money paid back. More especially applied to refund of import duties when goods are re-exported; and to remission of excise duties on goods of home manufacture, when consigned to a port abroad.

Drawee. Firm or persons responsible for redeeming a bill of exchange or money order.

Dredge. Drag net drawn along sea bed when fishing. 2. Apparatus for bringing up a sample of the sea bed when surveying. 3. Bucket of a dredger.

Dredger. Vessel fitted with an endless chain of bucket dredges that bring up the bottom ground when deepening a channel or area.

Dredging. Manoeuvring a vessel in a tideway by dragging an anchor on bottom and using difference in speed, between rate of current and speed over ground, for steerage purposes.

Dressing Line. Line to which flags are stopped when preparing to dress ship.

Dress Ship. To pay compliment or respect by hoisting flags at mastheads, bow and stern. To dress ship overall is to hoist ensigns at mastheads and a continuous line of flags from stem to fore masthead, between mastheads and from after masthead to stern.

Driers. Pastes or liquids mixed with oil paints to accelerate the solidifying of the oil.

Drift. Name given to ocean current that is generated and maintained by a more or less constant wind. 2. To be carried along by a current. 3. Distance a current flows in a given time.

4. Tapered steel tool of circular section. Used for fairing rivet holes.

Drift Anchor. Sea anchor. Drogue.

Drift Angle. Difference between course steered and course made good when due to action of current.

Drifter. Fishing boat that streams very long buoyed nets, and rides to the leeward end of them.

Drift Ice. Ice in an area containing several small pieces of floating ice, but with total water area exceeding total area of ice.

Drift Lead. Hand lead dropped on bottom, and with end of line made fast inboard, to indicate if an anchored vessel commences to drag anchor.

Drift Net. Fishing net about 120 ft. long by 20 ft. deep. Buoyed with cork along head. Several of these are joined to form a very long net; so that nets may extend a considerable distance to windward of the drifter to which they are attached.

Drift Piece. Upright or curved timber connecting plank sheer with gunwale of wooden ship.

Drifts. In sheer draught, are where rails are cut, and ended with scroll iron.

Drift Sail. Sail used as a drogue.

Drive. To carry too much sail. To run before a gale.

Driver. Alternative name for a spanker. 2. Foremost spur in bilgeways of a vessel on the stocks. Heel is fayed to foreside of foremost shore.

Driver Boom. Spanker boom.

Driver Spanker. Sail that is also called 'Driver' and 'Spanker'.

Drizzle. Precipitation of very small rain drops.

Drogner. Sailing boat that both caught and cured herrings. Also, West Indian boat used for cargo carrying. Has light mast and lateen sails.

Drogue. Drag anchor. Sea anchor. 2. Square piece of wood attached to harpoon line of whaler, to check speed of whale.

Dromon. A light, swift sailing vessel. At one time the name was given to any sailing vessel.

Dromoscopic Card. Compass card having two graduations, the outer giving true bearings, the inner one giving magnetic bearings. Could be used only in one locality, and for a limited time.

Drop. The depth of a sail measured on its middle line. 2. Machine for lowering a coal waggon from a staith to a position just above hatch of a ship. Used to avoid breakage of coal while loading.

Drop Anchor. To let go anchor.

Drop Astern. To fall astern.

Drop Keel. Metal plate keel that can be withdrawn into a water-tight box over a slot in bottom of boat. When boat is heeled and trimmed by the stern a capsizing moment is generated. Has obvious merits when working in shoal water, or beaching

Drum Head. Head of a capstan.

Drummer's Plait. Simple plait made by passing bight of rope through each preceding loop.

Dry Card Compass. Mariner's compass having no liquid in bowl.

Dry Compass. Dry card compass.

Dry Dock. Excavated dock, fitted with watertight entrance, from which water can be pumped to allow work to be done on underwater portion of a docked ship. Floating dry docks are usually called 'floating docks'.

Drying Features. Underwater obstructions that appear as tide recedes, but are covered as tide rises.

Drying Height. Height that a drying feature is above level of chart datum.

D shacke. Shackle having its sides parallel to one another.

Dub. To shape a smooth and even surface on a spar or timber.

Dubhe. Star α Ursa Majoris. S.H.A. 195°; Dec. N62°; Mag. 2·0.

Du Boulay Roller Jib. Works on principle of roller blind. Luff of sail is attached to hollow spar through which passes fore stay. Bottom of spar carries a grooved wheel to which furling-reefing line is attached. Hauling on this line furls, or reduces area of, sail. Invented by Captain E. du Boulay.

Duck. Flax fabric that is lighter and finer than canvas. 2. To dip into the sea.

Ducking (a Sail). Tricing, or clearing it, so that helmsman's view is not obstructed.

Duck Lamp. Small oil container with an inclined spout that holds wick. Burns colza oil.

Duct Keel. Twin centre girders with space between them. Increases longitudinal strength and allows bilge and ballast piping to lie in the space and be easily accessible.

Dumb Barge. Barge with no sail, engine or rudder and unable to move except by towing or, to a limited degree, by sweeps.

Dumb Compass. Compass card that has no needle, but is adjustable by hand. A pelorus.

Dummy Gantline. Rope rove through a block to act as a reeving line for a gantline.

Dumb Lighter. Lighter with neither means of propulsion nor rudder.

Dummy Piston. Disc on shaft of a reaction turbine. Steam impinges on this disc, so reducing end thrust.

Dumb Fastening. Short screw fastening that holds a strake until a through fastening is passed.

Dune. A low sand hill.

Dungiyan. One-masted Arabian sailing vessel.

Dunnage. Any material, permanent or temporary, that is used to ensure good stowage, and protect cargo during carriage.

Dunstos Rudder Brake. Fitting for preventing sudden snatches on rudder chains during heavy weather. Thwartship wire, with ends secured on either side of ship, passes around a sheave on tiller. At normal speed of rudder, the sheave 'rolls' along wire; with sudden stresses, wire temporarily grips sheave, so absorbing stress that would, otherwise, come on engine and steering chains.

Duration of Tide. Time interval between occurrence of low water and the following high water, or between high water and following low water.

Dutchman's Log. Piece of wood thrown overboard, well forward and used for ascertaining speed of ship by timing its passage between two marks, of known distance apart, on ship.

Duty. Service or work that should rightly be rendered. 2. Tax or custom charge imposed by a government on goods imported, exported or consumed.

Duty Free. Exempted from customs duty.

Dwarf Star. One of small mass and low candle power, but of enormously high density. Dwarf star companion of Procyon weighs about 250 tons per cubic inch.

Dygogram. Geometrical construction representing the direction and amount of each force acting on a magnetic compass.

Dynamical Mean Sun. Imaginary body moving along Ecliptic and travelling from perigee to perigee at a constant speed and in the same time as that taken by true Sun. Not considered in navigation.

Dynamical Stability. Of a ship, is amount of work necessary to heel the vessel through a given angle.

Dynamo. Machine that converts mechanical energy into direct electric current. Effected by revolution of an armature in a magnetic field.

Dyne. C.G.S. unit of force, representing amount necessary to produce or accelerate, velocity of one gramme mass by one centimetre per second.

Dysa, Dyso, Diso. 'Dghaisa.'

E

E

'E.' Time value that represents the westerly hour angle of a heavenly body from the point of definition of mean time. Local mean time added to 'E' is hour angle of body concerned.

Eager, Eagre. Large and disturbed tidal undulation passing up an inlet or river.

Earing. Length of rope spliced in a cringle of sail, or awning, for fastening.

Earth. Third planet of solar system. Distance from Sun varies between 94·5 and 91·4 million miles. Rotates on axis in 23 h 56 m 04 s mean solar time. Revolves round Sun in 365·2422 mean solar days. Is an oblate spheroid with polar diameter of 7899·7 miles; equatorial diameter 7926·5 miles.

Earth Light. Sunlight reflected to Moon by Earth when Moon's age is either small or fairly large.

Earth Shine. 'Earth Light.'

Ease. To reduce strain on a rope by slightly slackening it. 2. To reduce the amount of helm carried. 3. To reduce speed of engines. 4. To loosen a fitting that is too tight.

East. That cardinal point of horizon lying in direction of sunrise, and in which the prime vertical cuts equinoctial.

Easting. Departure made by a vessel on an easterly course.

Easy. Order given when rowing and a reduction of speed is desired. Oars are pulled but with reduced effort. Also given when any reduction of effort is required.

Easy Trimmer. Coal-carrying vessel having large hatches, no 'tween decks and no obstructions in holds. Trimming of cargo is not required until hatches are nearly filled.

Ebb. Vertical falling of water level due to tidal force.

Ebb Stream. Horizontal movement of water due to fall of tidal height.

Ebb Tide. Tide that is falling from high water to low water.

Eccentric. Any circle or sheave revolving on an axis not in its centre.

Eccentricity (of Orbit). Distance of focus from centre of ellipse of a planetary path.

Echelon. Formation of a line of ships in which each ship is on the quarter of ship ahead: thus allowing all guns to be used ahead, astern or on the beam.

Echo. Reflected sound. Travels at same speed, whatever its wavelength. In radar (2) the radio energy returned to the aerial as a result or reflection or scattering from an object. 3. The representation of (2) on a radar display. *False echo*, one whose position on the display does not indicate the correct range and/or bearing of the target.

Echo Box. A type of Performance Monitor which shows the performance of a radar set.

Echometer. Echo sounder produced by Marconi Sounding Device Co., Ltd.

Echo Sounder. Electrically operated instrument that emits a sound from vessel's submerged surface and then measures time interval until return to echo—which is recorded. Graduated scale converts interval to depth indication. May be of 'Sonic' or of 'Supersonic' type.

Echo Sounding. Ascertainment of depth of water by use of an echo sounder.

Eclipsareon. Instruction apparatus for explaining the occurrence of eclipses.

Eclipse. Cessation of light due to passing into a shadow. Applied to darkening of Moon's disc when she passes into shadow cast by Earth. Also applied to occultation of Sun by Moon. Strictly speaking, the latter is a misnomer, but is universally sanctioned by long-established usage.

Eclipsing Binaries. Twin stars that revolve around a common centre and thus alternately occult each other, as viewed from Earth. Due to their great distance from us they appear as one star of varying magnitude. Algol is a well-known example.

Ecliptic. Great circle of celestial sphere in which Earth revolves around Sun. So named because Moon must be in it, or near it for an eclipse to occur.

Eddy. Wind or water moving in a curved or circular direction. 2. Current of water running in a direction contrary to that of a tidal stream.

Efficiency. Term that denotes amount of energy delivered as a percentage of that put in. Boiler efficiency is about 65–70%; mechanical efficiency of an engine is about 90%. Steam efficiency of engine is 20–30%. Propeller efficiency is about 60%.

Efficient Deck Hand. Seaman over the age of 19 who has passed an examination entitling him to rank as a competent seaman.

Eft Castel.* Old name for after castle or poop.

Eft Schip.* 'Eft castel.'

Ekeing. Additional piece of wood used for making good a deficiency in length of a supporting member of a wooden ship. 2. Carved work at after end of quarter gallery.

Ekman Current Meter. Mechanism that is lowered into water for measuring translation of water forming a current. Result is a distance, which can be converted to rate by comparing it with time submerged. Kept in line with current by a vane. Measures speeds up to $3\frac{1}{2}$ knots. With reversing currents, reverse of direction of instrument results in a separate counting of revolutions of meter; this being effected by a compass unit.

Ekman Theory of Drift. Proposes that drift of sea at surface, in Northern hemisphere, is inclined 45° to right of wind direction; and average of all values, from surface to bottom, is 90° from wind direction.

Elastic Coupling. Coupling in which springs are incorporated to deaden excessive shocks put on mechanism. 2. Connection in a machine in which a certain amount of change in alignment is allowed for.

Elastic Limit. Maximum value in tons per square inch of sectional area of a metal member, that can be applied to the member without causing permanent deformation.

Elastic Propeller. Experimental propeller having blades of elastic steel. As pressure increases, blades approach a disc-like form.

Elbow. Half turn of one cable around the other when riding at open hawse. Results from swinging twice in the same direction at turn of tide. 2. Alternative name for 'Knee.'

Elder Brethren. Masters of Trinity House, London.

Electric Circuit. Conductor along which an electric current is confined.

Electric Current. Passage of negatively-charged electrons along a conductor.

Electric Fish. Fish that gives a galvanic shock when touched. Silurus and torpedo fish are examples.

Electricity. Energy that is possibly due to movement in atoms. Manifests its existence in production of light, heat, decomposition, and in formation of a magnetic field.

Electric Log. Log that is electrically connected to register distance, and/or speed, at a position remote from the log. Name was originally given to a log that had a wire in the logline so that registration unit could be started or stopped at a precise instant.

Electric Propulsion. Ship propulsion by propellers driven by electricity generated in a ship.

Electric Psychrometer. Hygrometer of Assmann type but with electrically-driven fan.

Electric Superheater. Electrically-heated element interposed between H.P. and I.P. engine to reheat exhaust steam from H.P. cylinder.

Electric Welding. Uniting of two pieces of metal, by fusion, with an electric arc.

Electrode. Conductor by which electricity is passed to a liquid or gas.

Electro Magnet. Core of iron or steel, surrounded by a coil, and becoming magnetised when electric current passes through coil.

Elephanta. Electrical storm accompanying the break of the Indian rainy season and commencement of Madras monsoon.

Elevated Pole. That pole of Earth, or heavens, that has same name as observer's latitude, and is, therefore, above his horizon.

Elevation. Height above a given plane. May be expressed in lineal measurement, or as an angle. Formerly used as meaning 'altitude'.

Elliot's Eye.* Splice formerly made in rope cable. One strand was unlaid into three smaller ropes: two of these ropes were long-spliced together, the third was eye-spliced. Thimble was then fitted into the two eyes thus formed; the whole being finished off with a seizing and keckling.

Ellipse. Plane figure bounded by a curve around two points (foci) of such form that the sum of length of two lines drawn from any point in curve to the two foci will be equal to length of major axis. Ellipse is important in that its perimeter is the curve in which any satellite heavenly body goes around its primary.

Elliptical Constituents. Those increases and decreases in tidal heights and intervals that are due to elliptical curve of Moon's orbit around Earth.

Ellipticity. Alternative name for 'Compression of Earth's axis'.

Elmo's Fire. Corposant. 'St. Elmo's Fire.'

Elnath. Star β Tauri. S.H.A. 279°; Dec. N29°; Mag. 1·8.

Elongation. Distance of Moon, or planet, from Sun, when measured in celestial longitude. Elongation of metal is increase in length when due to tensile stresses; also applied to the maximum amount that it will increase without fracture.

Elphinstone's Speed Indicator. Instrument used in conjunction with Forbe's log to convert distance recordings into speed indications.

Eltanin. Star γ Draconis. S.H.A. 91°; Dec. N51°; Mag. 2·4.

Embargo. Governmental restraint on the sailing of a ship from a port, or the shipment of specified cargoes.

Embarkation. The going on board, or putting on board a vessel.

Embrail. To brail up, or brail in, a sail.

Emersion. End of an occulation when occulted body emerges from behind the occulting body.

Emigrant. Person who goes from one country to settle in another. In law, is a steerage passenger.

Emigrant Ship. One carrying emigrants. In law, is one carrying more than 50 steerage passengers, or one statute adult for every 20 tons (33 tons in sailing ship) of registered tonnage.

Enavigate.* To sail out.

Encumbered Vessel. One so employed that full movement under sail, engines or steering gear is not to be expected.

End for End. Reversal of a rope, spar, etc., so that one end occupies the position previously held by the other.

End On. Said of a vessel when her fore and aft line coincides with observer's line of sight. More specifically applied to an approaching vessel whose fore and aft line is in line with fore and aft line of observer's vessel.

End on Rule. Rule of International Rules for Preventing Collision at Sea. So called because it deals with steam vessels approaching end on.

Endorsement. Writing on back of document as a ratification, approval, acknowledgement or sanction.

End Plates. Flat plates forming ends of a cylindrical boiler.

End Ring. Band fitted at end of a spar to prevent splitting.

End Seizing. 'Flat Seizing.'

Endurance. Number of miles a vessel can travel at a given speed, or horse power, before exhausting her fuel.

Engagement. Act of hiring or employing.

Engineer. Officer who is in charge of engines for the time being. Certificated officer competent to take charge of engines and to effect repairs and adjustments.

Engine-Room. Space in which main engines are situated, controlled and attended.

Engine Seat. Strengthened floors, plates and other members, in which bedplate and main engines rest.

English Quadrant. 'Backstaff,' or 'Davis Quadrant'.

English Sennit. Made with any number of parts, each of which is laid alternately over and under the other parts.

Enif. Star ε Pegasi. S.H.A. 34°; Dec. S10°; Mag. 2·5.

Enquette du Pavillon. Demand, made by warship, for a vessel to show her national ensign.

Ensign. National flag or banner; more especially when national ensign is in upper inner canton and remainder is of one colour.

Entering In. Reporting arrival of a ship to Customs authorities, by Master.

Entering Out. Report made to Customs authorities before taking cargo into a ship.

Entering Port. 'Entry Port'. In some countries special ports are nominated at which vessels must first call before other harbours may be visited. Vessels must also call at the Entry Port before finally leaving the country.

Entrance. Form of fore part of vessel's hull below water line.

Entropy. Heat energy that is not convertible to work.

Entry. Opening, in ship's side, by which one enters. 2. Entrance.

Epact. Difference in days and parts of a day, between 12 lunations and a solar year. Value is 10 days 15 hours. Epact for the year is Moon's age at 00 hrs. on January 1. Epact for the month is Moon's age at 00 hrs. on first day of month, assuming Epact of year to be 00 hrs.

Ephemerides Nautiques. Abridgment of 'Connaissance des Temps' made for use of seamen. It is thus the French equivalent to the British 'Nautical Almanac.'

Ephemeris. Almanac giving positions of heavenly bodies at intervals not exceeding one day.

Epicycle. Circle whose centre is situated in circumference of another circle.

Epoch. A particular moment of time from which other times are reckoned. In tides, it may be used to define the instant when an harmonic constituent transits a meridian. In U.S.A. practice it is used to denote the interval between the transit of a tidal constituent and the occurrence of its maximim effect.

Epoch of Chronometer. Elapsed interval from the last comparison. Generally expressed in days and fraction of a day.

Epotides.* Blocks of wood on either side of stem of a galley.

Equal Altitudes. Two observations of the same body, one on either side of meridian, when used for finding longitude.

Equation 129 **Eyebrow**

Equation. Two quantities, or groups of quantities, that are equal algebraically or arithmetically. Also, a constant to be applied to one value to obtain a required value.

Equation of Equal Altitudes. Method of finding time of meridian transit of a heavenly body by timing an altitude on one side of meridian and then noting instant when altitude is the same on other side of meridian. Ignoring change in declination, mean of times will be time of meridian transit.

Equation of Light. Time taken by light of Sun to reach Earth. Value is 08 m 20 sec.

Equation of Time. Difference between mean time and apparent time; between hour angles of mean and true suns; between right ascensions of mean and true suns. Varies between $16\frac{3}{4}$ minutes minus to apparent time, and $14\frac{1}{2}$ minutes plus to it. Is zero about April 15, June 15, September 1 and December 24.

Equator. That great circle, of terrestrial sphere, whose axis and poles are the rotational axis and poles of earth. Latitude is measured north and south from it.

Equatorial Air. Name sometimes given to 'Tropical Air'.

Equatorial Counter Current. Ocean current setting E'ly through Doldrums between N and S Equatorial Currents.

Exmeridian Altitude. Altitude of a heavenly body taken when near to meridian but not on it. Used for finding latitude.

Expansion. Increase in volume due to application of energy or force, or to release of compression.

Expansion Joint. Joint across the top decks of a large passenger ship to allow for the working of that part of the ship in a seaway.

Expansion Trunk. Compartment in oil-carrying vessel. Carries a reserve supply of oil for compensating changes in volume of cargo due to changes of temperature.

Expiration Clause. Alternative name for 'Continuation Clause'.

Explosives. Defined by statute as including gunpowder, nitro-glycerine, gun cotton, blasting powder, fulminate of any metal, coloured fibres and every other substance made to produce a practical effect by explosion, or a pyrotechnic effect.

Express Warranties. Detailed and explicit warranties included in, or written upon, a policy of marine insurance or some other document incorporated by reference into the policy.

Extending/Extension of Protest. Amplifying/amplification of a protest previously noted in common form. Must be done within six months of noting.

Extra Flexible Steel Wire Rope. Has 24 wires, around a fibre heart, in each of its six strands.

Extra Zodiacal Planet, Planet whose orbit extends beyond zodiacal belt. An asteroid.

Eye. Loop of eye splice, particularly one in stays and shrouds.

Eyebolt. Circular loop of metal secured for taking hook of shackle of purchase, or rigging.

Eyebrow. Semicircular guttering above a circular port or a scuttle.

Eyelet/Hole. Small hole in canvas to take a lacing or lanyard. May be stitched or grommeted.

Eyelet Punch. Specially shaped tool used, with block, when clinching brass grommets to an eyelet.

Eye of Anchor. Circular hole, at upper end of shank, to take ring or shackle pin.

Eye of Storm. Central area of calm in a tropical cyclone.

Eye of Wind. Direction from which wind blows. Point directly to windward.

Eyepiece. Small lens of telescope, through which observer looks.

Eyes of Her. Extreme forward end of a vessel. Hawse holes for cable. Chinese vessels have eye painted each side of stem on outboard side.

Eye Splice. The tucking of strands of a rope into the same rope after its end has been turned back to make a loop.

F

Face Piece. Timber on fore part of knee of head to allow for shortening of bolts and for simplifying fitting of main piece.

Factor of Safety. Number that represents breaking strength as compared with safe working load. In propeller shafts it is about 6; in shell plating 4½; in piston rods 12.

Factory and Workshops Act, 1901. Main Act under which 'Docks Regulations' derive their authority.

Faculae. Unusually bright patches sometimes observable near Sun's limb.

Fading. Falling off in strength of a radio signal. Due to variations in atmospheric path.

Fag (Fagg) End. Unlaid end of a rope. 2. Old name for a young and inexperienced seaman, to whom odd jobs were given.

Fag Out. To unlay end of a rope.

Fahrenheit Scale. Calibration of thermometer by G. O. Fahrenheit. Range between freezing and boiling points of water is divided into 180 degrees. Zero is temperature of a mixture of snow and salt. Boiling point of water is 212°; freezing point 32°. Having a zero well below freezing point of water, the general readings of air temperature are positive.

Faik.* 'Fake'.

Failure to Join. Non-compliance with undertaking to rejoin ship at a specified time. Used as denoting such non-compliance when reason for not rejoining is unknown.

Fair. To adjust to proper shape or size.

Fair Curve. Line drawn through certain parts of ship for which special delineation is desired.

Fairing. Checking and correcting a ship's plans before commencing construction.

Fair in Place. To fair a fitting or member without removing it.

Fairlead, Fairleader. Fixture that ensures a rope leading in a desired direction. May be of any shape or material. Special fairleads are fitted at bows and sterns of ships for taking mooring ropes. Pierced lengths of wood are used in sailing craft to separate falls of running rigging.

Fair On. Fair in place.

Fairway. Navigable water in a channel, harbour or river.

Fair Weather. Adjective applied to a person or fitting that is satisfactory in fair weather, but disappointing in adverse circumstances.

Fair Wind. Wind that is not before the beam and not directly aft.

Fake. One circle of a coil of rope. To coil or arrange a rope ornamentally with each fake flat, or almost flat, on the deck, usually in a circle or figure-of-eight pattern. Sometimes called 'cheesing down'.

Falcate. Said of Moon when in first or fourth quarter. Sickle-shaped.

Falconet.* Old ordnance firing a shot of 1¼ to 2 lb. Length 6 ft.; weight 4 cwt.

Fall. Hauling part of a purchase or tackle. Rope by which a boat is hoisted.

Fall Away. To be blown to leeward. Can be said of a vessel with relation to a fixed object, or to ship's head with relation to her projected course.

Fall Astern. To get astern of another vessel by reduction of speed.

Fall Aboard. To come in contact with another vessel, more or less broadside on, through action of wind or tide.

Fall Block Hook. Former fitting for releasing a ship's boat in a seaway. Pendant from davit head released hook from slings when boat was at a predetermined distance below davits.

Fall Cloud. Low-lying stratus cloud.

Fall Down. To move down a river or estuary by drifting with stream or current.

Fall Foul Of. To come in contact with another vessel and become foul of her rigging or cable.

Fall Home, Falling Home. Said of ship's sides when they slope upward and inward.

Falling Off. Movement of ship's head to leeward of course.

Falling Star. Meteorite that has become incandescent through friction with Earth's atmosphere.

Falling Time. Of barometer, is time taken by mercury of an inclined barometer to fall to proper level when placed vertically. Is an indication of sensitivity of instrument.

Fall In With. To sight or closely approach another vessel at sea.

'Fall Not Off.' Injunction to helmsman of sailing ship not to allow vessel's head to fall to leeward.

Fall Off. Movement to leeward of ship's head.

Fall Out. Said of ship's sides when breadth increases as sides go upward.

Fall Wind.* Sudden gust.

False Cirrus. Cirriform cloud extending above cumulonimbus.

False Colours. National flag shown by a vessel when it is other than the ensign she is entitled to wear.

False Fire.* Old name for blue pyrotechnic light.

False Keel. Additional keel fitted to main keel to protect it in event of vessel taking the ground.

False Keelson. Additional keelson fitted above main keelson.

False Points.* Name sometimes given to 'three-letter' points of mariner's compass.

False Rail. Additional piece of timber attached to head rail, or main rail, for strengthening or facing purposes.

False Stem. Tapered cutwater clamped to stem of wooden vessel.

Family Head.* Olden name for vessel's stern when decorated with several full-length figures.

False Sternpost. Timber attached to after side of wooden sternpost.

Fanal. The lamp, and its mechanism, in a lighthouse.

Fancy Line. Downhaul runner at throat of a gaff. 2. Line for hauling on a lee toppinglift.

Fang. Valve of a pump box. 2. To prime a pump.

Fanion. Small marking flag used when surveying.

Fanny Adams. Name given to tinned mutton in R.N. First issued in 1867. A child of this name, 9 years old, was murdered about the same time.

Fantod. A nervour and irresolute person.

Farcost.* A ship or boat. A voyage.

Fardage. Dunnage used with bulk cargo.

Farewell Buoy. Buoy at seaward end of channel leading from a port.

Fash. An irregular seam.

Fashion Pieces. Outer cant frames.

Fashion Plate. Ship side plate at end of well deck. Usually has an end that is swept in a curve.

Fast. Hawser by which a vessel is secured. Said of a vessel when she is secured by fasts.

Fast Ice. Ice extending seaward from land to which it is attached.

Father of Lloyds. Name given to Julius Angerstein, 1735–1823.

Father of Navigation. Dom Henrique, better known as Prince Henry the Navigator. 1394–1460.

Fathom. Six feet (1·83 metres); length covered by a man's outstretched arms. Fathom of wood is a cubical volume $6' \times 6' \times 6' = 216$ cu. ft.

Fathometer. Echo-sounder made by Submarine Signal Co. of Boston, U.S.A.

Fathom Lines. Lines drawn on chart to limit areas having depths of 1, 3, 6, 10, 30, and 100 fathoms.

Fathom Wood. Second-hand wood sold in cubic fathom lots.

Fatigue. Deterioration in strength of a metal due to stress, variations in temperature, vibration and other factors.

Faying. Uniting or joining closely. Joining edges of plates or planks to make a flat surface.

Faying Surface. That surface of a fitting, or member, by which it is joined to another faying surface.

Feather (an Oar). To put the blade of oar horizontal, when taken from water at end of stroke, and keep it so during its movement forward.

Feather Edged. Said of a plank that is thicker along one edge than along the other edge.

Feathering Float. Paddle board of a feathering paddle wheel.

Feathering Paddle Wheel. Wheel having a subsidiary gearing so that paddles are mechanically governed and enter water vertically, remain vertical while submerged, and so propel vessel directly forward or astern.

Feathering Propeller, Screw. Propeller having gearing that can cause blades to be turned fore and aft when vessel is under sail alone.

Feather Spray. Foaming water that rises upward immediately before stem of any craft being propelled through water.

Feed. Water pumped into boiler to maintain water level. 2. Oil fed to sprayers of oil-burning furnace.

Feeder. Temporary wooden trunkway fitted in hatch of a vessel carrying grain in bulk. Contains between 2 per cent and 6 per cent of hold capacity, and feeds the hold as grain settles. 2. Usual name for 'oil feeder'.

Feed Heating. Increasing temperature of boiler feed water, or fuel oil, immediately before feeding.

Feed Tank. Any tank that feeds a service. Particularly, tank that contains feed water for boilers.

Feeler. Small implement used when sounding with deep-sea apparatus. Consists of stout wire, mounted in a wood handle, with extremity of wire bent at right angle to remainder. Laid on wire, when sounding, to detect momentary slacking of wire when sinker reaches the bottom.

Felucca. Undecked boat of Mediterranean. Has long beak, lateen sails and may pull up to 12 oars a side.

Fend. To protect. To bear off. To insert a fender.

Fender. Any material or fitting used for protecting a floating object from damage by chafing or collision.

Fender Bolt. Bolt having a large, rounded and projecting head. Used, formerly, on outside planking of wooden vessels to protect from chafing.

Ferro-Cement. Method of constructing vessels with steel re-enforced concrete.

Ferry. Boat or vessel plying across a narrow piece of water. Also used as a verb.

Fetch. Of wind, is distance from starting point to observer, and measured along the water troubled by it. In sailing, is to reach or attain. To fetch a pump is to prime it by putting water inside pump and above plunger.

Fetch Away. To break adrift.

Fid. Strong wood or metal pin passing horizontally through heel of an upper mast and resting on trestle tree of mast below. 2. Large and conical piece of wood used for opening strands of large rope. Often has broad base so that it can stand vertically when rope is worked over its point.

Fiddle Block. Block having one shell but appearing to be two blocks end to end. Each part has its own sheave, but strop passes around both parts. Has all advantages of a double block with additional advantages that it is narrower, and block has no tendency to topple.

Fiddle Head. Ornamental carving on stem of a vessel when it remotely resembles a fiddle.

Fiddles. Wooden fittings clamped to meal tables in heavy weather. They limit movement of dishes, plates, glasses, etc.

Fiddley, Fidley. Stokehold casing and funnel casing.

Fid Hammer. Hammer with one end elongated and tapered. Used when knocking out a fid. Tapered end makes an emergency fid.

Fiducial Points. Those indications, in the graduation of a scale, that were carefully and precisely ascertained; and were not deduced from other indications in the scale.

Fiducial Temperature. That temperature at which the reading of a mercurial barometer requires no correction for expansion of mercury.

Field Ice. Ice pack whose limits cannot be seen from ship.

Field Magnet. Permanent magnet of a dynamo. Establishes a magnetic field in which armature rotates.

Field of View. Area that can be seen when looking through an optical instrument.

Fife Rail. Horizontal rail, or timber, in which are a series of belaying pins.

Fifteen-Metre Type. First international type of yacht (1911). Length overall, 76 ft.; L.W.L., 49 ft.; Beam, 13·8 ft.; Sail area 4450 sq. ft.; Reg. tonnage, 27·5; T.M. tonnage, 50; Freeboard, 3·7 ft.

Fifty-Gun Ship. Man of war intermediate between frigate and ship of the line.

Figsies. Elizabethan spelling of 'Fizgigs'.

Figure Head. Carved figure on stem and immediately below bowsprit.

Figure of Eight. Knot put in end of rope or fall to prevent it unreeving through a block or sheave.

Filibuster. Originally, a buccaneer. Now applied to any lawless adventurer.

Fill (a Sail). To trim a sail so that wind acts on it.

Filler, Filling. Piece put into a made mast to complete its shape.

Filling. Name was formerly given to a composition sheathing— placed between frames of a wooden vessel to close seams and exclude vermin.

Fine Lines. Said of a ship that has a fine entrance and less than average beam.

Fire Appliances. Usual name for fire-fighting appliances.

Fire Booms. Booms rigged out from ship's side and carrying a rope secured at head of each boom. Used for keeping off fire ships and other hostile craft.

Firefoam. Preparation for extinguishing oil fires by spreading foam over oil surface, and smothering the ignited layer.

Fire Ship. Comparatively worthless vessel loaded with combustibles and allowed to drift amongst fleet of enemy ships at anchor; fire ship being ignited just before contact.

Firing Point. That temperature at which a given liquid gives off vapour in sufficient quantity for the surface layer to ignite when vapour is ignited by flash.

First Mate. Deck officer next in rank below Master. Officer holding a First Mate's Certificate of Competency.

First Meridian. Prime meridian. Meridian from which longitude is reckoned. By general consent the meridian of Greenwich has been adopted.

First of Exchange. Stamped and No. 1 bill of exchange when more than one copy make a set.

First Point of Aries. That point in which Equinoctial and Ecliptic intersect and Sun passes from south to north declination. It was, originally, in constellation Aries but, due to precession of Equinoxes, is now in sign of Pisces. Sun enters Aries on March 21 (about).

First Point of Cancer. That point in Ecliptic which is farthest removed from Equinoctial in a northerly direction; Sun reaches this point about June 21. Owing to precession of equinoxes this point is now in Gemini.

First Point of Capricorn. That point in Ecliptic that is farthest removed from Equinoctial in a southerly direction. Sun reaches this point about December 21. Owing to precession of equinoxes this point is now in Sagittarius.

First Point of Libra. That point in which Equinoctial and Ecliptic intersect and Sun passes from north to south declination. It was, originally, in constellation Libra but, due to precession of Equinoxes, is now in Virgo.

First Rate. Old classification for war vessels carrying 100 or more guns.

'First Turn of the Screw (propellers) Pays all Debts.' Seaman's remark when leaving a port at which he owes money.

Fish. To fish a spar is to strengthen it, when fractured or weakened, by lashing or fastening another piece to it. To fish an anchor, when weighed, is to lift the arms so that anchor lies horizontally on anchor bed or billboard.

Fish Block. Lower block of a fish tackle.

Fish Bolt. Used for replacing a missing rivet in ship's plating. May be drawn through hole by line led through hole and floated to surface. Alternative type has spring fins in extremity of bolt; these open out when clear of hole and allow washer and nut to be screwed up.

Fish Davit. Davit taking upper block of fish tackle.

Fisherman's Bend. Useful bend for securing a rope to a ring. Made by taking end twice through ring and then over standing part and between ring and turn put round it. Additional half hitch round standing part is optional, and rarely necessary.

Fishery Cruiser. Armed vessel whose duties are to preserve order on the fishing grounds, to maintain rights of fishing vessels and to prevent smuggling and unlawful practices.

Fishes. Pieces of timber lashed to a yard or mast to strengthen it.

Fish Eye. Name sometimes given to streamlined connecting piece in Walker's log line.

Fish Fall. Fall of a fish tackle.

Fish Front. Rounded timber on fore side of a made mast.

Fishing Boat. Any fishing vessel other than those engaged in seal, whale, walrus, or Newfoundland cod fisheries—but including Canadian and Newfoundland cod fishing vessels, and Scottish vessels whaling off Scottish coasts.

Fishing Boat's Register. Certificate of registry of a fishing boat.
Fishing Lights. Statutory lights required to be shown by a vessel engaged in fishing.
Fish Plate. Name given to boundary iron on outboard side of a superstructure deck.
Fish Sides. Convex timbers on sides of a made mast.
Fish Tackle. Small tackle at head of fish davit. Used for lifting flukes of anchor to billboard or anchor bed.
Fish Tail. Name sometimes given to rotator of patent log.
Fitting Out. Supplying and fitting hull of a vessel with all the additional fixtures, rigging and attachments it requires.
Fitzroy Beacon. Type of dan buoy used by surveying ships. Is somewhat similar to Ormonde beacon, but is floated by two 25-gallon oil drums and has a heel weight of $1\frac{1}{2}$ cwt.
Five Eight Rule. Used for finding area of a plane surface having one curved side. From base line, perpendiculars are drawn to ends of curve, a third perpendicular being drawn at mid length of base. Area of either space is found by adding five times length of end ordinate to eight times length of middle ordinate, subtracting length of third ordinate, and multiplying result by $\frac{1}{12}$th of common interval.
Fix. Position of ship when found by intersection of two or more position lines.
Fixed Laydays. Laydays that are specified by number, and not derivable by calculation, rate of working, etc.
Fixed Light. Applied to a navigational aid that shows a continuous light, without eclipse or occulation.
Fixed Signs.* Four signs in which weather was supposed to be less variable than usual when Sun was in them. They were Taurus, Leo, Scorpio, Aquarius.
Fixed Stars. Name that distinguishes stars from planets. More particular, to distinguish stars that have no proper motion from those that have.
Fizgig. Steel or iron implement with two or more barbed prongs. When attached to a shaft carrying a line, is used for spearing fish. Neptune's trident is a form of fizgig.
Fjord. A deep, narrow and winding gulf.
Flag. Any colours or signal bunting other than pendants, but including burgees and triangular flags.
Flag Lieutenant. Lieutenant in R.N. who is on staff of, and personally attends, a flag officer.
Flag of Convenience. A foreign flag under which a ship is registered to avoid taxation etc, at home.
Flag Officer. Naval officer entitled to fly the flag of his rank. Includes Rear-Admiral, Vice-Admiral, Admiral, Admiral of the Fleet, and Chief officer of a yacht club.
Flag Ship. Warship carrying an admiral in command of a squadron or fleet.
Flake. To coil a rope so that each coil, on two opposite sides, lies on deck alongside previous coil; so allowing rope to run freely.

Flaking a Mainsail. Lowering a gaff mainsail and disposing of it in bights on either side of boom.

Flam.* Former name for flare of ship's bows.

Flamming Tackle. Purchase used for hauling an anchor to ship's side when stowed vertically outside a flared bow. Was manned between decks; and outboard end of purchase was passed through a 'flamming port'.

Flange Bows. Flared bows.

Flare. Upward and outward sweep of a ship's bows. 2. Large, bright but unsteady light that dies down after a time.

Flashing. Applied to a light that suddenly appears, shows for a short interval and then ceases. A recurring light that shows for a period that is shorter than the interval between its appearances. 2. Morse signalling with a lantern or other light.

Flashing Lamp Lantern. One that has mechanism for quickly showing a light and quickly obscuring it, so that Morse signals may be made.

Flashing Light. Navigational aid that shows a light for a period that is less than its period of eclipse.

Flash Point. That temperature to which a combustible liquid must be heated for it to give off a vapour that will momentarily flash in presence of a naked light.

Flat. Expanse of low-lying ground over which tide flows. 2. A flat-bottomed craft. 3. A flat floor. 4. Working space below decks in a warship.

Flat Aback. Said of a ship, or sail, when wind is on fore side of sail and is pressing it back.

Flat Aft. Said of a fore and aft sail when sheet is hauled to fullest extent.

Flat-Bottomed. Said of a craft whose bottom has no curvature.

Flat Floor. Girder or timber going athwart bottom of a vessel and having no upward curvatures of outboard ends.

Flat In. To haul aft the sheet of a fore and aft sail to fullest extent.

'Flat Iron.' Shallow draught war vessel specially designed for river and coastal work. Had abnormal beam and bulged sides. Correct name was 'River gunboat'. 2. Steam vessel designed for carrying coal cargoes to berths above bridges of Thames. Has very low superstructure; masts and funnel are hinged for lowering.

Flat Plate Keel. Shaped plating running along centre line outside ship's bottom, being strengthened by an internal vertical girder.

Flat Seam. Made in canvas by overlapping edges and stitching edge of each cloth to standing part of other cloth.

Flat Seizing. Used for binding two parts of rope together with small line, spunyard or wire. Eye is made in small line and line is passed round parts of rope and through its own eye. Taut turns are then passed, being finished by a clove hitch between the two parts of rope and round all turns of seizing.

Flat Sennit. Usual name for 'English Sennit'.

Flatten. To flat in a sail.

Flaw. A gust of wind.

Flax Rope. Made of Irish flax, and has a breaking strain more than twice that of manilla hemp rope of same size.

Fleet. Number of ships under one command or ownership. 2. To overhaul a tackle and shift moving block to a position further away. 3. Area in which a man, or party, of men can work without shifting. 4. Flat land covered by water.

Fleet Auxiliary. Vessel, other than a warship, attending a fleet for repair service, bunkering, hospital service or other duties.

Fleeting. Shifting the moving block of a tackle from one place of attachment to another place farther along. Moving a man, or men, from one area of work to area next to it.

Fleet Policy. Contract of marine insurance that covers all vessels under one ownership.

Flemish Coil. Successive ovals, or circles, of rope so arranged that each coil lies closely alongside the previous coil, end being in centre.

Flemish Eye. Made in end of a rope by unlaying the rope to a distance marked by a whipping, and unlaying strands. Using a round bar, one yarn is brought up on either side and half knotted together, the ends lying along rope. When all yarns are hitched, the eye so formed is served or marled. Ends of yarns are tapered and served.

Flemish Horse. Foot rope on yard, from yard arm to band of slings, or to strop of brace block.

Flense. To remove the blubber and cut up a whale or seal.

Fleur de Lys. Used for indicating North point of compass card. First introduced in 1302, by Flavio Gioja, as a compliment to the king of Naples, who was of French descent.

Flexible Steel Wire Rope. Has 6 strands around central fibre heart. Each strand has 12 wires around fibre heart. Breaking stress is approximately equal to tons denoted by twice the square of circumference in inches.

Flinders Bar. Sections of cylindrically-shaped soft iron that are mounted vertically on fore, or after, side of binnacle to compensate for vertical-induced magnetism of ship. Named after Captain Matthew Flinders, R.N.

Float. To be waterborne. 2. Abbreviation of 'paddle float' or 'float board'. 3. Name of a file having cuts in one direction— not cross cut. 4. Buoyant ball or cylinder operating a valve or cock.

Float Board. One of the boards on a paddle-wheel.

Floating Anchor. 'Sea anchor,' 'Drogue'.

Floating Battery. Heavily armed, shallow draught warship, formerly used for harbour defence.

Floating Clause. Clause inserted in a charter party to stipulate that vessel shall always lie afloat.

Floating Dock. Buoyant dock that can be flooded so that keel, blocks are below level of keel of vessel to be docked; and pumped out so that docked vessel is lifted entirely above water level.

Floating Harbour. Expanse of water protected by buoyant breakwaters.

Floating Policy. One made in general terms and for an overall sum of money. Generally taken out by shipper when goods are to be carried in more than one ship. As each ship loads, the value of cargo is declared, and is deducted from overall sum to be covered.

Floating Power of Spars, etc. Positive buoyancy of a spar, or other floating body, expressed as a weight that can be carried by it, or suspended from it.

Floating Trot. Line of baited hooks made fast, at each end, to the mooring rope of a buoy.

Floe. Area of floating ice, up to 3 ft. thick, that has broken off a sheet.

Floe Berg. Heavily-hummocked ice from a pressure ridge. Is usually separated from floes. Built up by rafting and freezing.

Flood Anchor. That anchor by which a ship rides at flood tide.

Flooding. Deliberately admitting water into a hold or compartment for the purpose of extinguishing a fire, or for improving stability.

Flood Stream. Horizontal movement of water that is causing a tidal rise.

Flood Tide. Rising of water level due to tide.

Floor Boards. Planking laid on floors of wooden vessels.

Floor Head. Upper end of a floor timber.

Floor Hollow. Concave form of upper edge of a floor.

Floor Riband. Longitudinal strip that supports floors below heads.

Floors. Transverse members, erected vertically, that connect lower ends of frames on opposite sides of vessel.

Floor Timber. That part of the floor, in a wood built ship, that crosses the keel beneath the keelson.

Flota.* Spanish fleet that formerly sailed every year to Cadiz to transport cargo from Spanish South America.

Flotilla. Fleet of small vessels.

Flotilla Leader. Comparatively large, high-speed vessel that leads, and has charge of, a destroyer flotilla.

Flotsam, Flotson. Goods and fittings that remain floating after a wreck.

Flowing Sheet. Sheet that is eased off and is controlling a well-filled sail of a vessel running free.

Flowing Tide. A flood stream.

Fluid Compass. Liquid compass.

Fluke. Flattened triangular extremity of arm of an anchor.

Fluky. Said of wind when it is of no great force and varies in strength and direction.

Flurry. Sudden gust of wind. 2. Passing rain storm. 3. Agitated water caused by death throes of a harpooned whale.

Flush Deck. Upper deck that extends the whole length of vessel that has no poop or topgallant forecastle.

Flute. Boat with flat floors, rounded stern and broad beam.

Fluted Shackle. Has a grooved pin and a corresponding groove in lug. When these grooves are aligned a locking-pin is inserted.

Fly. Lengthwise expanse of a flag. 2. Old name for a compass card.

Fly Block. Double or single block used as upper purchase block of topsail halliards.

Fly Boat. Fast boat used for passenger and cargo traffic in fairly sheltered waters.

Flying Bridge. Light fore and aft bridge above main deck.

Flying Dutchman. Phantom vessel, commanded by Vanderdecken, said to be met with off Cape of Good Hope. Was sighted and and reported by H.M.S. 'Bacchante' at 4 a.m., 11th July, 1881.

Flying Jib. Sail set on outer fore topgallant stay (or flying jib stay). Foremost of fore and aft sails.

Flying Jib Boom. Either the outer length of jib boom, or a separate boom extending forward of it.

Flying Kites. Fine weather upper sails.

Flying Light. Said of a vessel when in ballast and her draught marks are well above water line.

Flying Moor. Alternative name for 'Running Moor'.

Flying Pier. Light and temporary pier erected for embarkation or disembarkation.

Flying Skysail. Skysail with yard attached to sail and sent aloft on truck halliards; clews being stopped to royal yard. Was the earliest form of skysail.

Fly to. To come to the wind quickly while under sail.

Foam. Whitish froth that appears when water is agitated. It is generated more quickly in salt water than in fresh, consisting of a mass of bubbles containing air.

Fog. Impaired visibility near sea level caused by small particles of moisture suspended in air. Is usually a cloud at sea level, but may be due to smoke when in vicinity of land. A combination of smoke and fog is particularly dense. Meteorologists consider fog to exist when visibility is less than half a mile; seamen make this limit one mile.

Fog Bank. Low-lying dense fog.

Fog Bell. Bell rung by anchored vessel in fog, in accordance with international regulations. Sometimes applied to a bell rung in fog by a lighthouse, or at a pier end. Occasionally applied to bell on a moored buoy.

Fog Bow. White 'rainbow' sometimes seen opposite to Sun during fog.

Fog Horizon. Near horizon as observed in foggy weather.

Fohn. A warm dry wind blowing down the leeward slopes of a mountain range.

Following Sea. Sea that runs, approximately, in direction of ship's course.

Fomalhaut. Star α Piscis Australis. S.H.A. 16°; Dec. 230°; Mag. 1·3. Name is Arabic for 'Mouth of the big fish'.

Food Scale. Statutory scale of food for seamen. Laid down by Merchant Shipping Act and Order in Council.

Foot (of Sail). Lower edge of sail.
Foot Brail. Lowest brail on a spanker.
Foot Hook. Original form of 'Futtock'.
Footing Down. Method of getting a rope as taut as possible. Man stands midway along it so that his weight causes a small bight to be formed. As he takes his weight off it the small amount of slack rope is gathered in and rope is turned up.
Foot Outhaul. Tackle for hauling out foot of spanker.
Footrope. Rope stretched under a yard or jib boom for men to work on when handling sail. Sometimes called a 'horse'. Also, the boltrope along foot of a sail.
Footrope Knot. Diamond knot worked round a rope by using the four ends of two pieces of small line passed through the rope.
Foot Waling.* Former name for the 'ceiling'.
Foraminifera (ous). Very small and elementary type of marine life that lives in a shell. 'Foraminiferous' is adjective used when describing ooze, or other sample of sea bed, that contains foraminifera.
Forbes' Distance Recorder. Attachment used with Forbes' log to record the distance run.
Forbes' Log. Consists, basically, of a manganese bronze tube that can be protruded through bottom of ship at a position near her turning point. Bottom of tube carries a vane that rotates as ship moves through water, sending an electric signal every 0·01 of a mile travelled. These signals operate the 'Distance Recorder' and Elphinstone's Speed Indicator.
Force of Wind. Velocity, or momentum, of wind expressed by a figure in the Beaufort Scale. Seldom exceeds 20 lb. per sq. ft.
Forced Draught. Air supply, to a furnace, that has been increased beyond normal by subjecting it to pressure, by increasing its speed, or by expediting the removal of exhaust gases.
Forced Points. Alternative name for 'By points' of compass.
Fore. In or towards the forward part of a ship.
Fore and Aft. Leading or lying in the same direction as the length of a ship. 2. Embracing the whole length of a ship.
Fore and Aft Schooner. Vessel having fore and aft sails only. Used for differentiating such a vessel from a topsail schooner.
Fore Bitters. Songs sung on forecastle during dog watches. (R.N.)
Fore Cabin. Passenger accommodation that is inferior to saloon.
Forecastle. In Royal Navy is the upper deck from right forward to some line, usually the screen bulkhead, abaft the cable holders. In Merchant Navy is the crew's quarters, even when these are aft. In flush-decked sailing ships it extended from forward to the main tack block.
Forecastle Head. Merchant Navy name for topgallant forecastle.
Fore Course. Sail bent to fore lower yard.
Forefoot. Lower extremity of stem, usually curved, where it joins keel. Generally regarded as part of keel, the stem being said to rest upon it.

Fore Ganger. Short piece of rope, grafted on harpoon, and to which harpoon line is bent.

Fore Halliard. Halyard. Rope by which a foresail is hoisted.

Fore Hold. Foremost hold in a cargo vessel.

Fore Hood. A foremost plank in side of a wooden vessel.

Fore Hook. A breast hook.

Foreign Agreement. Articles of agreement, between Master and crew, entered into when a vessel is going outside Home Trade limits. Signed, by all parties concerned, in presence of superintendent of a Shipping Office.

Foreign Going Ship. Ship trading to ports outside British Isles and other than ports between Elbe and Brest inclusive.

Foreland. Land projecting some distance seaward.

Forelock. Flat piece of metal that is passed through protruding end of shackle pin to prevent its accidental withdrawal. Lower end is split so that it can be splayed.

Forelock Hook. Winch in ropemaking tackle block. Used for twisting yarns into strands.

Foremast. Forward mast in a vessel having two or more masts.

Fore Peak. Space between fore collision bulkhead and stem plating.

Fore Rake. That part of a vessel forward of a vertical line passing through fore end of keel.

Fore Reach. To continue making headway while going about under sail. Sometimes used as meaning to overtake, or shoot ahead

Fore Runner. Name sometimes given to bunting that marks end of stray line in line of a log ship.

Foresail. In a vessel having two sails, is the foremost sail. In fore and aft vessels having two or more masts it is the foremost gaff sail. In square-rigged vessels it is the fore course.

Fore Sheet. Rope or tackle by which clew of foresail is controlled and adjusted to wind.

Fore Ship.* Former name for bows, or forecastle.

Foreshore. Land that lies between high and low water marks on a beach. 2. Inclined surface on seaward side of a breakwater.

Fore Shroud. Standing rigging that supports and stays a foremast in a thwartship direction.

Forestaff.* Cross Staff used when facing an observed object.

Forestay. Stay of foremast, extending from head of mast to a position forward of it.

Fore Stem.* Former name for the stem of a vessel.

Fore Top. Platform, at head of foremast, to give spread to fore topmast rigging.

Foretopman. Man whose station is in fore top, or at fore topmast, when working aloft. In R.N. the name is still used to denote a man belonging to one of the four quarters into which a watch is divided.

Fore Topmast. Mast next above fore lower mast.

Forge. To force. Sometimes applied to forcing a vessel over a shoal.

Forge Ahead. To go ahead by extra effort.

Forge Over. To force a vessel over a shoal.

Forge Test. Applied to rivets. Head is heated and then hammered until diameter is 2½ times that of shank. There must be no cracking around edge.

Fork Beam. Half beam supporting a deck in way of a hatch.

Forming. Shaping a beam, frame, or other member, to exact form required.

'Forties.' Fishing ground off S.W. coast of Norway. Has an almost uniform depth of 40 fathoms.

'Forty Thieves.' Forty line of battle ships built, by contract, for Admiralty during Napoleonic wars. They were, more or less, failures.

Forward. Towards or at the bows. Fore part of a vessel.

Fothering. Closing small leaks in a vessel's underwater body by drawing a sail, filled with oakum, underneath her.

Fottinger Clutch. Hydraulic clutch in gearing of Bauer Wach turbine to propeller shaft. Used for smoothing out variations in torque.

Foul. To entangle, obstruct, or collide with.

Foul Anchor. Anchor when foul of its own cable. Sometimes said when anchor is foul of an obstruction on bottom.

Foul Berth. Anchorage in which there is not room to swing at change of tide.

Foul Ground. Sea bottom in which sunken wrecks or other obstructions may cause anchor to become foul.

Foul Hawse. Having two cables out and one across, or foul of, the other.

Foul Water. Area of water containing menaces to navigation.

'Foulweather Jack.' Name given to Admiral Sir John Norris (1660–1748) and Vice-Admiral Hon. John Byron (1723–86) both of whom were singularly unfortunate in the weather their ships experienced.

Foul Wind. Wind blowing from direction a vessel wishes to sail, or in a direction that may set her into danger.

Founder. To fill with water and sink.

Fourcant. Four-stranded rope.

Four Cycle. Applied to oil engines in which the operations of charging, compression, ignition and scavenging are done in four piston strokes.

Four-Point Bearing. Direction of an observed terrestrial object when bearing is 45° from ship's course. Distance to position when object is abeam is equal to distance off when abeam.

Four S's. Four matters to have in mind before sailing. They are, steering gear, side-lights, side ports, stowaways.

Fox. Made by laying up three or more yarns and smoothing them down.

Foxon's Log. Early 19th century towed spiral log made of wood.

Foy Boat. Used in Tyne and other N.E. coast ports. About 15 ft. long, 4 ft. 6 in. beam. Pulls two oars and has a lugsail. Attended mooring of ships.

Fracto. Term used in meteorology. Means 'broken'.

Fracto Nimbus. Small and irregular pieces of nimbus cloud, generally known as 'Scud'.

Frame. Steel or iron member that extends vertically from outer end of floor to outer end of beam.

Frame Spacing. Fore and aft distances between successive frames.

Frame Timbers. Parts that make up a wooden frame.

Framing. System of frames, floors and intercostals to which outside plating of a ship is attached.

Franchise. In marine insurance is the maximum amount, usually 3 per cent. if insured value, that cannot be claimed under a policy when a loss is incurred.

Frap. To bind tightly by passing a rope around and heaving it taut. 2. To close the seams of a leaking wooden vessel by passing ropes under bottom and hauling them taut on deck, or across the deck.

Frazil. Small, cake-shaped pieces of ice floating down rivers. Name is given, also, to newly-formed ice sheet off coast of Labrador.

Free. Said of a vessel under sail when she has wind abaft the beam. 2. Legally, used as indicating that no responsibility attaches to a named party in specified circumstances.

Free Alongside Ship. Stipulation that no charge or responsibility falls on ship or owner of cargo until goods for shipment are alongside ship in which they are to be loaded.

Freeboard. Height that outboard edge of deck is above water-level. Specifically, distance that statutory deck line is above water-level.

Freeboard Certificate. Load line certificate, issued by an assigning authority acting on behalf of Government, stating the statutory freeboards of a vessel in specified areas and seasons.

Free In and Out. Stipulation that carrying vessel is not to bear any expense incidental to loading and discharging.

Freeing Port. Opening in bulwarks, allowing water shipped on deck to flow overside.

Freeing Scuttle. Non-return flap that allows water to drain from deck to sea, but prevents sea entering.

Free of Address. Stipulation that specified charges shall not be made against a ship at port to which she is bound.

Free of Average. Inserted in policy of insurance to relieve insurers of liability for payment of specified losses.

Free of Capture and Seizure. Included in a policy of insurance to relieve insurers of liability for loss sustained by attack, capture or seizure made by a belligerent or enemy.

Free of Damage Absolutely. Inserted in policy of insurance to relieve insurers of liability for damage incurred. Policy would cover total loss, general average charges, salvage charges, three-fourths of 'Running Down' charges.

Free of Expense. Stipulation that loading and discharging of cargo shall not entail expense to ship.

Free on Board. Stipulation that no expense shall fall on ship for the putting of cargo on board.

Free Overside. Stipulation that no expense shall fall on ship after cargo is put over the side.

Free Puff. Yachting term for a gust of wind that requires weather helm to be applied, and causes yacht to sail closer to windward.

Free Ship, Free Goods. Proposition that, in time of war, enemy goods, other than contraband, carried in a neutral vessel are not subject to capture.

F Region. 'Appleton Layer.'

Freight. Freightage. Goods loaded for transport in a vessel. 2. Money paid for carriage of goods by sea. In marine insurance, includes value of service in carrying goods of owner. Does not include passage money.

Freightage. Freight. Payment for carriage of goods by sea.

Freighter. Sea-going vessel carrying cargo. 2. One who ships cargo into a vessel.

Freight/ing. Load/ing a ship with cargo.

French Bowline. Similar to bowline except that two bights are made, instead of one, before finishing off.

French Fake. 'Flemish Coil.'

French Sennit. Made with an odd number of strands, passing outside strand over other strands to centre, and working from each side alternately.

French Shroud Knot. Joining of two 3-stranded ropes by marrying them and making wall knot on one side and a crown on the other side.

Fresh Breeze. Wind of Force 5 in Beaufort Scale. Speed 17–21 knots.

Freshen Ballast. To turn over shingle or stone ballast.

Freshen the Nip. To veer or haul on a rope, slightly, so that a part subject to nip or chafe is moved away and a fresh part takes its place.

Fresh Water Allowance. Amount that a load line may be submerged when loading in water of less density than that of salt water.

Frigate. Originally, a Mediterranean vessel propelled by oars and sails. Later, name was given to a square-rigged warship having two gun decks and mounting 30 to 50 guns. They were used as scouts or cruisers and had a raised forecastle and quarter deck. Later still, they were flush-decked and mounted 28 to 44 guns; being rated as intermediate between a ship of the line and a corvette. With the coming of iron and steel ships they were displaced by cruisers, and the name lapsed. In the war of 1939–45 the name was reintroduced and given to small ships used for escort and patrol duties.

Frigate Built. Term applied to vessel having a raised forecastle and quarter-deck.

Frigatoon. Venetian vessel having a square stern, main and mizen mast but no foremast.

Frictional Current. Water dragged along by a vessel when due to friction with her underwater surface. Reduces effectiveness of rudder.

Frictional Wake. Effect of frictional current as manifested at rudder; pressure of water being reduced on fore side of rudder when angled.

Frigid Zone. Area of Earth's surface around N or S geographical pole, and bounded by Arctic or Antarctic Circle.

Front. Used in meteorology to denote a line of demarcation between warm and cold air masses.

Frontogenesis. Birth of development of a meteorological front.

Frontolysis. The fading away, or disappearance, of a meteorological front.

Frost. Atmospheric state in which water freezes.

Frost Smoke. Congealed fog that forms over Arctic waters.

Frustration. Circumstance or event that is outside control of contracting parties and prevents fulfilment of contract.

Frustration Clauses. Included in a war-time policy of insurance not containing the 'Free of Capture' clause. Relieves insurers of liability to make good a depreciation of freight, or cargo, caused by frustration of voyage through restraint of princes.

Fuel Coefficient. Ratio between fuel consumed and effective work done. The Admiralty coefficient for ship propulsion is based on:
$$\frac{D^{\frac{2}{3}} . V^3}{\text{Fuel consumed in 24-hr. (in tons)}}$$
D being displacement in tons, V being speed in knots.

Fuel Consumption. Amount of fuel used in (*a*) going a given distance, or (*b*) one hour at a given speed: (*a*) varies as square of speed, (*b*) varies as cube of speed. These are approximate values.

Fuel Oils. Viscous oils, of petroleum group, used in marine boilers. S.G. 0·9 to 0·96; flash point 150°F to 180°F.

Full. Said of sail when full of wind.

Full and By. Sailing close-hauled with all sails drawing.

Full Due. Used as indicating finality or permanency; e.g. 'Belay for a full due.'

Fullering. Closing edge of lapped plate by forcing down its lower edge of lap with a fullering tool and hammer.

Full Moon. Phase of Moon when in opposition, and her disc is entirely illuminated.

Full Rigged. Said of a vessel carrying a full suit of square sails, to topgallants or above, on all of her three or more masts.

Full Scantling. Applied to a vessel with flush main deck—but may have raised forecastle, bridge deck and poop and having such constructive strength that allows her to have minimum freeboard.

Fulmar. Small sea bird met with off St. Kilda island and in Arctic Ocean.

Fumigation. Destruction of vermin, insects or bacteria by application of fumes, gases or vapours.

Fundamental Formula. Equation cos a = cos b × cos c+ cos A × sin b × sin c. Used in navigational problems to connect latitude, altitude, declination and hour angle.

Funnel. Tubular erection over boilers to carry away products of combustion. 2. Copper sheathing around head of topgallant masthead. Used for making a smooth surface for eyes of rigging to rest on, and so preventing chafe.

Funnel Cloud. Upper and visible part of water vapour arising from sea to form a waterspout.

Funnel Draught. Natural draught caused by convection and by top of funnel being considerably higher than furnaces.

Funnel Net. Fishing net in form of a tapering tube.

Funnel Temperature. Temperature of exhaust gases in funnel. Usually between 600° and 700°F.

Furling. Gathering in a sail, or awning, and confining it with stops.

Furling in a Body. Harbour stowing of a sail. Sail is gathered in towards bunt and there arranged in smooth and neat stowage, the yard being clearly defined.

Furling Lines. Name sometimes given to gaskets.

Furnace. That part of a boiler in which fuel is burnt. Can be internal or external.

Furniture. The essential fittings of a ship, such as masts, davits, derricks, winches, etc.

Furring. Double planking along a ship's side in way of her waterline to improve her stability in 16th and 17th centuries.

Futtock. One of the pieces of timber forming a rib of a wood-built vessel.

Futtock Hoop. Iron band, near head of lowermast, that takes lower ends of futtock rigging.

Futtock Plank. Ceiling plank next to keelson.

Futtock Plate. Iron plate, at edge of lower top, to which deadeyes of topmast rigging are secured. Upper ends of futtock shrouds are attached to its lower edge.

Futtock Shrouds. Short lengths of rope, wire or chain connecting futtock plate and lower ends of topmast rigging to futtock hoop.

Futtock Staff/Stave. Length of rope, or band of wood or iron, to which the lower ends of catharpins are secured.

Futtock Timbers. Middle futtocks in the built rib of a wooden vessel. Situated between upper and lower futtocks.

G

Gacrux. Star γ Crucis. S.H.A. 173°; Dec. S57°; Mag. 1·6.

Gaff. Spar, having jaw that fits round mast, and to which the head of a gaff sail or trysail is attached and extended.

Gaff Topsail. Small triangular sail having its foot extended along gaff, and its luff along mast.

Gage.* Old name for a vessel's draught in water. Also, her position relative to wind and another vessel.

Galactic. Pertaining to the Galaxy or 'Milky Way'.

Galaxy. The 'Milky Way'.

Gale. A strong wind. Formerly applied to any fresh wind; now usually denotes wind of force 8 and above.

Gale Warning. Notice of an impending gale. May be given by radio, visual signal, telegram, or other means.

Galilean Glasses. Optical aid consisting of two tubes, each with a double concave eyepiece and double convex object glass.

Galiot.* Galley with one mast and 16 rowing benches. Most popular vessel of ancient times.

Gallant. Former name for 'topgallant'.

Galleass/Galliass. Former warship having three masts, three tiers of guns and 32 rowing benches.

Galleon. Large 16th-century sailing vessel used, principally, in trade with South American colonies.

Gallery. Projecting walk, or balcony, at stern or quarters of old sailing ships.

Galley. Compartment in which cooking and other food preparation is done in ships. 2.* Single-banked pulling and sailing boat reserved for captain's use in R.N. 3. Craft of varying sizes, at different times built for pulling oars, though fitted for sailing when conditions were favourable. 4. Open boat formerly used by Customs officers and Thames police.

Gallery Built. Name given to a flush-decked sailing vessel.

Galley Foist.* State barge used on ceremonial occasions.

Galliot. Bluff-bowed, two-masted trading vessel formerly used by Dutch. Usually rigged as a topsail schooner.

Gallivat.* Swift sailing craft of about 70 tons, formerly used on Malabar coast. Had two masts, lateen sails and was armed with small swivel guns.

Gallows. Horseshoe-shaped girder, hinged on deck of trawler. Carries block through which trawl warp is led. 2. Support for a boom when sail is lowered and furled.

Gallows Bitts. Vertical framework fitted on deck to take stowage of spare spars and timbers.

Gallows Stanchions. 'Gallows Bitts.'

Gallows Top. Cross timbers at upper end of gallows bitts.

Galton's Sun Signal. 'Heliostat.'

Gam. Visit between whalemen when on whaling ground.

Gambling Policy. Uncomplimentary, and usually unjustified, name for a policy issued without proof of interest having been given.

Gammon. To lash heel of bowsprit in place.

Gammon (Gammoning) Iron. Iron band clamping bowsprit to stem.

Gammoning Hole. Hole, near or in stem, through which turns of gammoning are passed.

Gammon Plate. Iron plate, bolted to stem head, carrying a ring through which gammoning is passed.

Gammon Shackle. Ring, on gammon plate, to which gammoning is secured.

Gangboard. Plank bridge from quay or wharf to ship. Usually fenced.

Gang Casks. Small casks used for bringing off water from shore to ship.

Ganger. Cable between hawse pipe and a sheet anchor that is stowed on an anchor bed.

Gangway. Entrance into a ship at head of accommodation ladder. Steel or wooden bridge connecting ship with shore, or with another vessel. 2. A clear path along which men can walk.

Gannet. Sea bird of which the principal type is the 'Solan Goose'.

Gantline. A line rove through a block near the masthead used to hoist anything aloft.

Garland. Rope or selvagee circle, carrying additional strops, placed round head of mast when taking it in and stepping it. Temporary stays, shrouds and guys are made fast to the strops. 2. Rope put round mast, under eyes of rigging, to protect mast and rigging from chafe. 3. Rope grommet put under round shot to prevent rolling. 4. Mesh bag for holding vegetables, mess cleaning gear, etc. 5. Circle of evergreens hoisted at triatic stay on wedding day of an officer of the ship. 6. Wreath of green leaves surrounding shield in centre of Union flag flown by military officers commanding a station, diplomatic servants and Governors or High Commissioners of British colonies.

Garnet. Purchase, on main stay, for hoisting purposes. Also, applied to other purchases, such as 'clew garnet'.

Garofali. Whirlpools in straits of Messina.

Gas Buoy. Navigational buoy carrying a light.

Gas-Freeing. Removing pockets of gas from compartments of an oil-carrying vessel after cargo has been discharged.

Gasket. Length of sennit fitted for securing sail when furling. 2. Grommet or packing in a gland or pipe joint.

Gat. Navigable waterway between shoals.

Gather Way. To start to move through water with increasing speed.

Gaussian Logarithms. Tabulated values that facilitate the subtraction or addition of quantities when expressed in logarithmic form.

Gaussin Error. Temporary compass error when changing course. Due to time lag in adjustment of sub-permanent magnetism to ship's new heading.

Gear. Rigging, tackle, fittings, implements, equipment, tools or essential parts.

Geared Turbine. Turbine in which high rotor speed is reduced, before reaching propeller, by reduction gearing; thus allowing turbine to run at high speed and propeller at a lower but more effective speed; so reducing cavitation at propeller.

Gearing. Arrangement of pinions or wheels by which motion may be transmitted, or speed reduced to give more power, or power reduced to give increased speed.

Gelves. Oriental sailing craft of 16th century. Had one or two masts.

Gemini (The Twins). Constellation situated between R.A.'s 05 h 40 m and 07 h 40 m (about) and Declination 12° to 32°N. Has three navigational stars. Castor (α), Pollux (β), Alhena (γ). Also, third sign of Zodiac, extending from 60° to 90° celestial longitude. Sun is in this sign from May 21 to June 21 (about).

Gemma. Star α Coronae Borealis.

General Average. General indemnity made by all interests concerned—and in proportion to the financial value of property each had at stake—for a maritime loss deliberately but reasonably incurred for the safety of the remaining property when in peril.

General Average Act. Voluntary and extraordinary action reasonably taken for preserving property in peril.

General Average Expenditure. Extraordinary expenditure voluntarily and reasonably incurred for preserving property in peril.

General Average Loss. Loss that is due to a general average act or expenditure.

General Average Sacrifice. Deliberate and extraordinary sacrifice reasonably made for preservation of property in peril.

General Cargo. Cargo made up of different commodities.

General Equation. Alternative name for 'Fundamental Formula'.

General Purpose Rating. A rating who signs-on to work on deck or in the engineroom as required.

General Service Pump. Steam pump that can be used for several purposes. Can feed donkey boiler, provide deck salt water service, supply fresh water to drinking tanks. Cannot pump bilges.

General Transire. Transire issued by H.M. Customs to vessels on regular voyages between U.K. ports. Holds good for a stated period.

Genoa Jib. Large jib used in yachts. Sheets home well abaft mast. Very effective in light winds; dispenses with spinnaker when running.

Geocentric Latitude. Angle at centre of Earth between plane of Equator and a radius of Earth going to any position on surface.

Geocentric Longitude. Angular value at centre of Earth, of arc of Ecliptic intersected between First Point of Aries and a secondary circle passing through a heavenly body. Measured eastwards.

Geocentric Parallax. 'Diurnal Parrallax'.

Geographical Latitude. Angle between plane of Equator and a perpendicular passing downward from a given point on Earth's surface. Owing to Earth's spheroidal shape, this angle will not be at centre of Earth unless latitude is 0° or 90°.

Geographical Mile. Length of one minute of arc of Equator. Value is 6087·2 feet.

Geographical Position of Heavenly Body. Latitude and longitude of a point on Earth's surface at which a given heavenly body would be in the zenith.

Geo-Navigation. Term proposed, by J. B. Harbord, for methods of conducting a ship, or fixing her position, by geographical observations.

Geordie. Nickname given to brigs formerly used in Tyne coal trade.

Geostrophic. Meteorological term for Earth's rotational effect on wind. Deflection of wind caused by this is termed the 'geostrophic component'.

German Eye Splice. Made in a rope by tucking first strand with lay, second strand tucked under same strand, but against the lay, third strand tucked as usual.

Gib. Projecting arm of a crane; a jib. 2. Forelock of a shackle. 3. Wedge-shaped piece of metal used for transmitting thrust to a collar, or inclined surface.

Gibbous. Applied to Moon's phase after her second quarter and when her disc is more than a semi-circle but less than a circle. Also applied to inferior planets and Mars, who take this form at times.

Gienah. Star γ Corvi. S.H.A. 177°; Dec. S17°; Mag. 2·8.

Gift Rope. Rope leading from forward to an accommodation ladder, for use of boats. 2. Additional line given to a boat when towed.

Gig. Single-banked rowing boat pulling four, five or six oars and about 25 to 30 feet long.

Gilliwatte. Name given to Captain's boat in 17th century.

Gimbals. Two rings, pivoted at right angles to each other, which keep a compass or chronometer in horizontal plane in all circumstances.

Gimletting. Turning an anchor by moving stock through a circle, with shank as axis.

Gin. Hoisting apparatus consisting of a barrel mounted in bearings and turned by a crank.

Gin Block. Name given to metal pulley blocks, particularly those with skeleton frames.

Gingerbread. Decorated scroll work, usually gilded, around stern and quarters of olden ships.

Gin Tackle. Purchase made by reeving rope through double and treble blocks.

Gipsy. The sprocketted cable holder of a windlass.

Girder. Strong beam of H section used for keelson and other members requiring considerable strength. Generally built by riveting two channel bars back to back, or by riveting angle bars along both edges and on both sides of a strong plate.

Girder Strength. Resistance offered by any member, or construction, to deformation of its longitudinal axis.

Girding. Binding. Passing frapping lines. *See* 'Furring'.

Girdle. A binding passed round an object.

Girt. Said of a vessel having two cables out and so taut that she cannot swing. 2. The condition of a tug when her towrope leads abeam or before the beam and the stress on it causes danger of capsizing.

Girth Band. Strengthened strip stitched from clew to luff of jib or staysail.

Girtline. Name sometimes given to 'Gantline'.

Give Way. Order given to boat's crew to commence rowing. If already rowing, is an order to put extra weight on oars.

Glacial. Applied to deposits, sands and gravels that are out-wash of glacier sheets.

Glass. Name commonly given to a barometer. 2. German name for a telescope, which was, formerly, called a 'perspective glass'. 3. Sand glass for measuring intervals of time. Two of these were used with the 'ship log'; one measuring 14 seconds, the short glass; the other, the long glass, measuring 28 seconds. Before the introduction of clocks, the watches on board were regulated by sand glasses taking half an hour to empty; the bell being struck each time the glass was turned. Intervals of time at sea were measured in 'glasses' up to end of 18th century.

Glasses. Binoculars.

Glazed Frost. Rain that freezes when surface temperature is below freezing point.

Globigerina Ooze. Chalky, light-coloured mud found at about 3000 fathoms in Atlantic Ocean. Mainly composed of decomposed shells of globigerina and other crustacea and molluscs.

Globular Sailing.* Old name for 'Spherical Sailing'.

Gloomy. Applied to weather that is dark, lowering and dismal.

Glory Hole. Any small enclosed space in which unwanted items are stowed when clearing up decks.

Glut. Doubling piece at centre of head of a square sail. Has a hole into which is passed becket of bunt jigger.

G.M.T. Greenwich Mean Time.

Gnomon. Perpendicular rod, or pillar, formerly used for measuring altitude.

Gnomonic Chart. Chart constructed by gnomonic projection. All British Admiralty charts on scale of 1/50,000 or smaller are gnomonic. Charts of polar area are nearly always gnomonic.

Gnomonic Projection. Projection of Earth's surface on a plane that is tangent to surface at a given spot, and by lines from centre of Earth. Advantages are (1) So long as area is small there is no appreciable distortion: (2) projection of great circles are straight lines: (3) there is little distortion in polar regions. Its disadvantage is that scale is not constant; areas away from point of tangency are distorted.

Go About. To go from one tack to the other, when under sail, by putting ship's head through the wind.

Go Ahead. To move forward through the water. 2. To take station ahead of another vessel.

Goal Poster. Nickname given to a vessel having a rectangular girder structure athwart upper deck to support derricks. Stump mast is usually stepped in middle line of transverse girder.

Go Astern. To reverse engines so that vessel moves stern first. To move through water stern first. To take station astern of another vessel.

Gob Line. Back rope of a martingale. 2. A length of rope used in a tug to bowse in the towrope. Gog Rope.

Go by the Board. Said of a mast that breaks close to the deck.

Godfray's Azimuth Diagram. Devised by Hugh Godfray to facilitate the finding of true azimuth from latitude in, apparent time, and declination of observed heavenly body.

Godown. Oriental name for a storehouse or warehouse.

Going Free. Sailing with wind abaft the beam.

Going Large. Sailing with wind abaft the beam.

Golden Number. Every 19 years Moon goes through her changes on different dates, and then repeats them on these dates; this is called the 'Lunar Cycle' and was adopted in 433 B.C. The Golden Number of any year is the number it is in the Lunar Cycle. To find it: Add 1 to the year A.D. and divide by 19. The remainder, up to and including 19, is the Golden Number.

Gold Slide. Adjustable attachment to a mercurial barometer for giving resultant of corrections for index error, height of instrument above sea level, variation in gravity due to latitude, temperature. Correction is read from a scale alongside a small thermometer, and is noted before reading barometer. Invented by Col. E. Gold, D.S.O., F.R.S.

Gondola. Venetian boat rowed with one oar. Has a cabin amidships and an extended and ornamental stem piece.

Gondolo. Ship's Longboat of the 16th century.

Gonies. Albatrosses.

Goods. Articles that are bought and sold.

Goole Fender. Fender placed across stem of vessels moving in Goole docks to prevent damage to low dock sills.

Gooseneck. Projecting iron fitting with ring or band at its outer extremity. Used for studdingsail yards and similar purposes. 2. Iron that connects end of a spar or boom with its pivot.

Goosewing. Course or topsail with weather clew hauled out, lee clew hauled up and buntlines taut. 2. A studding sail. 3. Wing and wing.

Gopher Wood. Timber used for building Noah's ark. Probably cypress wood.

Gore. 'Goring Cloth.'

Gore Strake. Strake that tapers to a point before reaching stern.

Gorge. Aperture, in a wood block, through which rope is rove. More usually called 'swallow'.

Goring. Said of a sail that increases in width downwards.

Goring Cloth. Side cloth of a topsail. Has oblique edge, at side, to increase width of foot.

Gottlieb's Log. Submerged log fitted near keel in early 19th century. Way of ship caused a wheel to turn, and so actuate registering mechanism inside ship.

Grab. Steel bucket consisting of two hinged parts which are open when lowered but closed when weight is taken for hoisting. Used when discharging, or loading, fluid cargoes such as shingle, coal, grain, etc.

Grab Lines. Becketted line around outside of a lifeboat. Fitted for men in water to grasp them.

Grab Rail. Protruding rail around sides of a deck house. Fitted for grasping in heavy weather.

Grab Ratline. Taut wire stretched just above rim of lower tops. Placed to assist men going aloft by futtock rigging.

Gradient. Rise or fall of barometric pressure as related to distance. Said to be 'steep' when pressure changes quickly with change of position; 'low' when it changes slowly.

Gradient Wind. Air movement due to a barometric gradient.

Graduated Meridian. Meridian, on a Mercator chart, graduated for the measurement of distance. Is generally in chart border, but may be a central meridian.

Graduated Parallel. Parallel of latitude, on a Mercator chart, graduated for measuring Mercatorial distance and determining longitude. Usually in upper and lower borders, but may be along a central parallel.

Graduations. Series of marks, or lines, for facilitating measurements.

Graft. Decorative finish to an eye splice in rope. A certain number of yarns from ends of tucked strands are left out, the other yarns being tapered and marled to rope. Over the marled yarns the other yarns are woven—the yarns forming the warp, sailmaker's twine being used for weft.

Grafting. Making a graft around a rope.

Grain. Defined as 'any corn, rice, paddy, pulse, seeds, nuts, or nut kernels'. 2. The water ahead of a ship, and through which she will pass. Opposite of 'Wake'.

Grain Laden. Technically, applied to a vessel carrying an amount of grain equivalent in weight to two-thirds of her registered tonnage; or bulk equal to 100 cubic feet for each registered ton.

Grain Certificate. Document giving particulars of a vessel loading grain, her draught and freeboard when loaded, quantity and kind of grain, method of stowing and measures taken to prevent shifting.

Grains. Harpoon with four barbs and 5-ft. wooden handle.

Grain Space. Internal volume of all holds in a ship. Measured from tank top to underside of deck, and from ship's side to ship's side in holds.

F

Grampus. Large mammal, of the porpoise family, about 20 feet long. Met with in North Atlantic ocean.

Grampussing. Old-time punishment for a man found asleep on watch. His arms were triced up by rope and two buckets of water were poured down his sleeves.

Granny. An incorrectly-made reef knot.

Grape Shot. Cannon balls with diameter rather less than half the calibre of the gun firing them.

Grapnel. Iron shank with ring at one end and four curved arms, or claws, at other end. Used for hooking a submerged cable or wire. Formerly used for making attachment to a vessel so that she could be boarded. 2. Rope attached to a boat's anchor for riding by.

Grappling Iron. Grapnel when used for laying hold of a ship, or other floating body.

Grass Line. Coir hawser.

Graticule. From same root as 'Grating'. Network made on chart by lines of latitude and longitude.

Grating. Open work covering for a hatch or compartment requiring ventilation. 2. Open framing of crossed slats, with square open spaces, used in stern sheets of boats. 3. Bars or perforated covering across an opening.

Grave. To clean a vessel's bottom by burning off the fouling.

Graveyard Watch. The middle watch, midnight to 4 a.m.

Graving Dock. A dry dock. Originally, a dock in which a vessel's bottom was cleaned by burning off the fouling.

Graving Piece. Small piece of wood let into a plank having a small defect.

Greaser. Engine-room rating whose duty is to attend to lubrication. 2. Old-time nickname for the Mate.

Great Circle. Circle of sphere whose plane passes through centre of sphere. All great circles of a sphere have a common centre, and each great circle bisects all other great circles.

Great Circle Sailing. The sailing of a ship between two positions when her course is along a great circle of Earth. Her head is continuously kept pointing to her destination by frequent adjustments of course—except when sailing along Equator or a meridian.

Great Circle Track. Arc of great circle, on surface of Earth, between two given positions. Is line of shortest distance between these positions.

Greave. To 'Grave'.

Grecian Splice. Neat and strong splice often used for splicing standing rigging that had parted. Each end is unlaid to a whipping. Heart yarns of each end are laid up into three small strands, and spliced. Remainder of yarns are laid up into foxes and cross pointed over splice.

Greek Fire. 'Wildfire.'

Green Flash. Momentary flash of green light occasionally seen in horizon just after sunset, or before sunrise, in clear atmosphere. Due to refraction of Sun's light.

Green Sea. Sea that sweeps over a vessel without breaking.

Greenwich Date. Time and date at Greenwich corresponding to an instant of time at another position.

Greenwich Hour Angle. Intercepted arc of Equinoctial between hour circle at Greenwich and hour circle at a given place, measured westerly.

Greenwich Mean Time. Time based on hour angle of point of definition of mean time as measured at Greenwich.

Greenwich Meridian. Adopted as the prime, or International, meridian, largely because its antimeridian—the Date Line—passes through no important land masses.

Gregale. N.E. gale in vicinity of Malta during winter. Name is also given to similar wind in Tyrrhenian Sea and off S. Coast of France.

Gregorian Calendar. Reformed calendar introduced by Pope Gregory XIII in 1582. Previous (Julian) calendar assumed year to be 365¼ days, which was 0·0065 of a day in excess. Gregorian calendar will be in error by one day in A.D. 5442.

Gridiron. Horizontal, grated framework on to which a small vessel can be hauled for examination and repair of bottom; grating being hauled up inclined ways until clear of water.

Gripe. The forward deadwood. Flat surface in way of forefoot of a sailing vessel. Designed to make her more sensitive to helm, particularly when wearing, and to reduce leeway. 2. Sennit strips by which a boat is prevented from swinging when suspended from davits at sea. Also, length of wire or chain having a claw that fits over gunwale of boat and prevents movement in the crutches when stowed inboard. 3. Resistance set up by gripe of forefoot, causing vessel to lie closer to wind.

Griping. Coming too close to wind when under sail.

Grog. Mixture of rum and water. Named after Admiral Vernon, who first issued watered rum. He was in the habit of wearing grogram breeches, and was nicknamed 'Old Grog'.

Grommet. Ring made of rope strand laid up around its own part.

Grooving. In a steel plate, is the formation of a narrow groove by corrosion.

Gross Pressure. Total pressure as differentiated from pressure that ignores atmospheric pressure. Steam gauges of boilers indicate pressure in excess of atmospheric pressure.

Gross Tonnage. Measurement of total internal volume of a vessel and includes all under deck tonnage and all enclosed spaces above tonnage deck; 100 cubic feet of space being considered as one ton.

Groundage. Money paid by a vessel for occupying space in a port.

Grounding. Bringing vessel's keel into contact with the bottom so that she ceases to be completely waterborne.

Grounding Clause. Inserted in a policy of marine insurance to exclude the taking of the ground, in certain rivers and harbours, from consideration as a stranding.

Ground Futtock. Floor timber lying on keel and bolted to keelson.

Ground Hold.* Old name for 'Ground Tackle'.

Ground Log. Log that measures vessel's speed over the ground. Has a lead, or other weight, and a marked log line.

Ground Rope. Roping along bottom of a trawl net.

Ground Swell. Swell not caused by wind prevailing at the place.

Ground Tackle. Ship's outfit of anchors and cables—particularly that part that is in use.

Ground Tier. Lowest tier of cargo in a hold.

Ground Ways. Launching ways down which the cradle slides.

Growing. Increasing of size of a wood-built vessel after launching.

Growler. Small iceberg that has broken away from a larger berg.

Grown Spar. Wooden spar made from one tree, as distinguished from a made spar.

Grus. Constellation in about R.A. 22 h; Dec. 47°S. Has one navigational star.

Guard Boat. Ship's boat, in R.N., carrying the officer of the guard.

Guard Rails. Permanent rails, or iron stanchions, with wire or chain rove, fitted on outboard edge of a weather deck or superstructure.

Guards, The. Stars γ and β of Ursae Minoris, the Little Bear.

Guard Ship. Warship formerly anchored in a port to act as a receiving ship, to control movements afloat, and to maintain order.

Gudgeon. Fixture, on sternpost, in which pintle of a rudder is hinged. Formerly, a cut away part of carrick bitts that carried a metal bush in which spindle end of windlass worked. In engineering, a gudgeon is often a pin.

Guess Rope. 'Guess Warp.'

Guess Warp. Rope with one end made fast at a distant point and the other end kept handy in ship so that a boat can be hauled along it by her crew. Standing end may be at a point well forward in ship, at a lower boom or at ring of a laid out kedge anchor.

Guess Warp Boom. Boom guyed out well forward in a ship to keep guess warp clear of ship's side, and give good length for boat to ride by.

Guest Warp. 'Guest Warp'.

Guiana Current. Westerly current about 50 miles off N Coasts of Brazil and Guiana. About 200 miles wide.

Guides. Iron castings guiding crosshead of piston of a reciprocating engine. Ahead guide is larger than astern guide and usually has a water service for cooling purposes.

Guinea Current. Easterly current running between Cape Roxo and Bight of Biafra. Rate sometimes exceeds three knots.

Gulf Stream. That part of Equatorial Current that has passed through Gulf of Mexico and has been deflected by land. Flows north and east to about Cape Hatteras, where it meets Arctic Current. It is a warm current and its contact with Arctic Current causes fogs in that area. Although warm current continues towards British Isles and Norway, modern practice considers Gulf Stream as ending southward of Newfoundland, the continuing current then being called the 'North Atlantic Drift'.

Gulf Weed. Weed found floating in an area of about a quarter of a million square miles of Gulf Stream between 19°W and 47°W and 20° to 45°N. Some of it is occasionally carried to British Isles.

Gull. Sea bird that feeds on fish and breeds on rocky headlands. There are about 20 different types and, in common speech, the name includes skua, tern, petrel and others.

Gunboat. Small warship with relatively large gun power. Primarily, though not exclusively, intended for service in rivers and shallow waters.

Gunner. Commissioned officer in R.N. Responsible for ammunition and gunnery stores. Has other duties in connection with armament, and is assistant to gunnery officer.

Gun Room. Nowadays, mess of R.N. officers of subordinate rank—sub-lieutenants, midshipmen, cadets. Originally, was Gunner's store room, and messing place of Gunner and his subordinates.

Gun Running. Illicitly carrying arms into a country.

Gun Tackle. Purchase by which a gun was hauled out after recoil due to firing. Consists of two single blocks with hook in each.

Gunter's Scale. Large, flat boxwood board having scales of equal parts on one side and logarithmic scales on other side. Required values were found by use of dividers or a ruler. Invented by Edmund Gunter (1581–1636) and in use for more than 200 years.

Gunwale. Side timber, or wale, covering the timber heads, and to which the breechings of upper deck guns were secured. 2. The upper strake of a boat's planking, particularly its upper edge, is now called the gunwale; as, also, is the upper edge of bulwarks.

Gunwale Bar. Angle bar connecting deck stringer plate to frames.

Gusset Plate. Plating that is attached by angle irons to knit together two members of a ship's structure.

Gust. Short period increase in strength of wind.

Gutter Bar. Inboard angle bar of a waterway at side of deck.

Gutter Ledge. Fore and aft beam in middle fore and aft line of a hatch covered with arched hatch covers—which it supports at their middle and highest part.

Guy. Rope or tackle by which a boom or derrick is controlled laterally.

Gyassa. Egyptian boat used on Nile for transport of cargo. Has two masts, lateen sails and can carry up to about 200 tons.

Gybe. To shift over the boom of a fore and aft sail, without brailing, while sailing free or running.

Gyn. 'Gin.'

Gyration. Movement, round an axis, that is accompanied by generation of centrifugal and centripetal forces.

Gyro Compass. Gyroscope so mounted, ballasted and fitted that the diurnal revolution of Earth is made to constrain the North-South line of compass to seek the meridian, and remain in it. Speed of gyro varies with different makes: Anshutz being 20,000, Brown 14,000, Sperry 6000, Arma-Brown 11,800, revolutions per minute. Weights of rotors are respectively, 5 lb., 4½ lb., 52 lb. and ½ lb. Corrections have to be made for latitude and speed of ship; some corrections are made by hand, others are automatically adjusted by the compass. Gyro compasses are ineffective in latitudes higher than about 75°.

Gyropilot. Gyro-controlled automatic steering device.

Gyro Repeater. Electrically-operated dial that is graduated as a compass and kept in step with master gyro compass; so indicating position of gyro compass at stations remote from it.

Gyroscope. Rapidly-rotating wheel so mounted that it has three degrees of freedom: 1, freedom to rotate on its own axis; 2, freedom from constraint about its horizontal axis; 3, freedom from restraint about its vertical axis. These allow the rotating body to keep its direction in space unless otherwise disturbed.

Gyrostat. Rapidly rotating wheel that is constrained about either its vertical or its horizontal axis. It thus has two degrees, only, of freedom.

H

Haar. Local name for a wet sea fog off E Coast of Scotland.

Hack Watch. Small timekeeper that is set to chronometer time and used on deck for timing astronomical sights.

Hadar. Star β Centauri. S.H.A. 150°; Dec. S60°; Mag. 0·9.

Hadley's Quadrant. First English quadrant devised for measuring altitudes. Invented by John Hadley, 1730.

Hague Convention, 1899. International convention that gave immunity to hospital ships in time of war, and formulated rules for the settlement of international disputes.

Hague Rules, 1921. Enunciated certain rules and conditions regarding the carriage of goods by sea; most of these rules being incorporated in the 'Carriage of Goods by Sea Act, 1924'.

Hail. Precipitation of small pieces of ice, or small balls of packed snow, from cumulonimbus cloud. 2. To call to a distance by word of mouth.

Hailstone. A single ball of hail.

Hair Bracket.* Moulding immediately abaft a figurehead.

Hale.* Old English form of 'Haul'.

Half Beam. Beam that is cut to form a hatchway, or to give clearance.

Half Breadth Plan. Plan of a ship from centre line to ship's side on one side. Shows buttock lines, bow lines and water lines at different draughts.

Half Breadth Staff. Wooden rod marked to show half lengths of ship's beams. Used for measuring the beams.

Half Cardinal. Name applied to a point of compass halfway between two cardinal points.

Half Crown. Small circular bight in a rope.

Half Deck. Non-continuous deck extending from right forward to about half length of a boat. 2. Covered part of upper deck that is under a poop and contains accommodation for officers, apprentices or crew. 3. In R.N. is that part of lower deck that is aft, and in which is accommodation for officers. 4. Non-continuous deck extending from mainmast to right aft above main deck. 5. Quarters of cadets or apprentices in a merchant ship.

Half Decked. Said of a vessel with an upper deck that is not continuous.

Half Ebb. Said of a tide when halfway from high water to low water.

Half Flood. Said of a tide that is halfway from low water to high water.

Half Floor. Frame timber going from keel to the heel of second futtock.

Half Hitch. Made by passing end of rope round its own part and through the bight formed.

Half Mast. Position of an ensign or flag when partially hauled down as sign of mourning.

Half Minute Glass. Sand glass that takes half a minute to run down. Used when timing a ship log and line.

Half Moon. Phase of moon when at first and third quarters; and half of disc being illuminated.

Half Poop. Low poop about 4 ft. in height.

Half Port. One of two ports, each having a semicircular piece cut away so that they could be closed around a protruding gun.

Half Round Strip. Rolled steel or iron bar having a semicircular section.

Half Sea.* Old name for 'mid channel'.

Half Tide Rock. Rock that is covered between half flood and half ebb of tide.

Half Timber. Short futtock in those parts of a wooden ship where the bottom is inclined, not flat.

Halliards. Ropes by which sails, yards, flags, gaffs, etc., are hoisted.

Halo. Circle of light around a luminous body. Particularly applied to such a circle around Sun or Moon when due to refraction caused by ice crystals in atmosphere.

Halshed Chain. Chain sling or strop in which one end of chain is rove through an open link in other end.

Halyards. 'Halliards.'

Hamal. Star α Arietis. S.H.A. 329°; Dec. N23°; Mag. 2·2.

Hambro Line. Hard laid, three yarn small stuff, generally tarred. Used for lashings, seizings and for lacings of sails of small craft.

Hammock. Rectangle of special type canvas that contains the naval seaman's bed.

Hammock Clews. Twelve lengths of nettle stuff, middled and seized in the bight, which are attached to ends of a naval seaman's hammock so that it can be extended between hooks in beams.

Hammock Cloth. Canvas cover over hammock nettings.

Hammock Hooks. Small hooks screwed into beams of warships for the slinging of hammocks.

Hammock Lashing. Length of small rope with which a naval rating's hammock is lashed up, with seven turns, when not in use.

Hammock Netting. Small compartment, in a warship, for stowage of hammocks. Formerly, were two rows of netting above bulwarks. Hammocks were stowed between them to form protection against small arms fire and splinters when in action.

Hand. Any one member of a crew.

Hand the Log. To haul inboard the logline and rotator.

Hand a Sail. To furl a sail.

Hand Gear. Alternative means by which a machine, usually actuated by power, is actuated by hand.

Hand Lead. Sounding lead, weighing between 10 and 14 lb., by which sea soundings may be taken by one man in depths not exceeding 20 fathoms (about).

Handling Ship. Manoeuvring and controlling a vessel by engines, or sails, and helm movements.

Hand Log. Name sometimes given to common log and log line, to differentiate is from mechanical logs.

Hand Mast. Mast made from one timber, so distinguishing it from a built mast.

Hand over Hand. To haul on a rope by putting one hand before the other on the rope, alternately; so keeping a continuous movement instead of a succession of pulls.

Hands. Persons employed to man and work a ship.

Hand Organ. Large holystone fitted with beckets and lines; dragged by two men when cleaning decks.

Handsail. Small sail managed and controlled by hand.

Handsomely. Slowly and carefully. Keeping a rope or fall well in hand.

Hand Spar. Straight piece of timber of circular section. Usually a trimmed trunk of a tall tree.

Handspike. Short wooden lever, often shod with iron.

Hand Steering Gear. Wheel, and its connections to rudder, when operated entirely by hand.

Hand Taut. Said of a rope when it is hauled as taut as possible by hand. Said of a rope under similar tension even when not hauled taut by hand.

Hand Tight. 'Hand taut.'

Handy Billy. Small and light purchase used for hauling ropes taut and for miscellaneous jobs of a light nature. Has one single and one double block.

Hang. Of a timber, is its downward droop. Vessel is said to hang in the wind if her head comes to it and she does not fall off. To hang a rudder is to suspend it by its pintles and braces.

Hanger. A cutlass; so called because it hangs from a belt at waist.

Hanging Bracket. Bracket with its horizontal edge facing downwards, so that attachment is made underneath.

Hanging Compass. Compass having its binnacle overhead and its graduated card facing downwards.

Hanging Knee. Vertical knee or bracket attached to underside of a deck or beam.

Hang Judas. Said of a rope when not properly secured; and of any stop, yarn or small line that hangs down freely.

Hank. Skein of sailmaker's twine, spunyard or small line. 2. One of the metal rings, or ash wood hoops, used for confining luff of staysail to a stay.

Hank for Hank. Said of two sailing vessels when tacking or wearing at the same time. Colloquially used to denote a fair exchange, or equal terms.

Harbour. Port or haven in which a vessel may lie in good safety.

Harbourage. Shelter or refuge.

Harbour Gaskets. Special gaskets for giving a smart and neat appearance to furled sails when in harbour.

Harbour Launch. Small vessel used for conveyance of harbour officials.

Harbour Log. Log book giving details of ship's work done while in harbour, together with usual log entries in harbour.

Harbour Master. Official having superintendence over a harbour; and who is responsible that harbour regulations are complied with.

Harbour Reach. That part of a river that leads to a harbour.

Harbour Watch. Part of duty watch that remain on board to take any action required on a ship in harbour.

Hard. Boat landing place at which a muddy bottom has been covered with gravel or shingle. 2. Applied to helm orders, means 'to the fullest extent'.

Hard Chine. If a vessel's sides meet her bottom at an angle, instead of being rounded, she is said to be hard-chined.

Hard Iron. Iron, or ferrous alloy, that is slow to receive magnetism, but retains it when received.

Hard Laid. Said of a yarn or rope that has been tightly laid up.

Hard Tack. Nickname for ship's biscuits.

Hard Up in a Clinch. Seaman's expression that means being in a critical and difficult position.

Harfield's Compensating Gear. Steering gear in which an eccentrically-mounted pinion actuates a toothed rack shaped to conform to eccentricity of pinion. At small angles of helm the long radius of pinion gives quick movement: at large angles of helm the small radius of pinion gives decreased speed but increased power.

Harmattan. Dry and cool NE wind over NW Africa.

Harmonic Analysis. The separation of component tides of an undulation and the determination of their individual values and incidence. These values are considered as being due to action of hypothetical tide-raising bodies.

Harmonic Constants. Angular values of hypothetical tide raising bodies at given times and places, together with the amplitudes of waves they generate, and the height of mean sea level, at a place, as related to chart datum.

Harmonic Method of Tidal Prediction. Based on Harmonic Analysis. Assumes that tides are the results of tractive forces of several hypothetical tide-raising bodies, each moving at its proper speed and having an unvarying tractive effort. By tabulating the angular positions of these bodies, at a given epoch, and their tide-raising power, the determination of tidal effect at a place can be derived arithmetically or mechanically.

Harness. Belt and straps fitted with a clip-hook by which the wearer can secure himself to guardrail or rigging in bad weather.

Harness Cask. Wooden tub, with cover, in which salt meat was kept on board in former years. 'Harness' has an oblique reference to salt 'horse'.

Harness Tub. 'Harness cask.'

Harpings. Forward planking of a wooden vessel's sides. Is more substantial than remainder of planking.

Harpoon. Barbed weapon mounted on a shaft and used in whaling.

Harpoon Depth Finder. Sounding lead carrying a rotator, so measuring vertical distance to bottom in same way as towed log measures horizontal distance. A clamp on rotator is lifted as lead sinks, but drops as lead rises when hauled up—so retaining registration on dial. Now nearly obsolete, but was remarkably accurate.

Harpoon Log. Early form of towed log with registering mechanism in towed unit. This unit was in two parts; one part rotated, the other part carried the registration mechanism.

Harp Shackle. Shackle in which bow is wider than distance between lugs.

Harriet Lane. Name formerly given to tinned mutton. A woman of this name was murdered in 1874.

Harroway Dixon Type. Early type of steamers in which upper parts of framing incline inwards for about one-quarter of breadth, so forming a centre trunk. Outer plating was carried straight up, so making a space in which water ballast could be placed. Vessels of this type were practically self trimming when carrying bulk cargoes.

Harter Act. Passed by Congress of U.S.A., 13th Feb., 1893. Makes it illegal for any ship trading to or from U.S.A. to contract out of responsibility to be seaworthy in all respects and to carry cargo with due diligence and care. Failure to provide a seaworthy vessel entails fine, and loss of rights to cargo's share of General Average contribution.

Hartford Shackle. Special shackle for connecting a mooring wire to ring of a buoy. Wire is shackled to lug at bow of shackle. Pin of shackle has an extended bar at end. When pin is inserted, it is turned through 90° and bar lies alongside shackle; a hinged loop, on side of shackle, drops over it and prevents it turning and unlocking.

Harvest Moon. Full Moon occurring about autumnal equinox. As angle between Moon's orbit and ecliptic is very small, Moon rises at same time for several days. Can occur only when Moon's ascending node is in Aries, every $18\frac{1}{2}$ years (about): 1969 was last occurrence. During the Harvest Moon the moon rises as the sun sets and sets as the sun rises.

Hatch. Opening in deck that gives access to hold or space below.

Hatch Bar. Steel or iron bar that secures hatch covers.

Hatch Beam. Removable section of a beam, on which hatch covers are laid. When removed, access to hold is given; when shipped, transverse strength is restored.

Hatch Boat. Half decked fishing boat with hatch through which fish are passed.

Hatch Coaming. Raised wall of steel, or other material, around a hatch. Raises hatch covers above level of deck and carries fittings for securing hatch covers.

Hatch Feeder. Vertical wooden erection between an upper deck hatchway and hatch of a lower hold. Erected when carrying bulk grain. Grain in feeder keeps lower hold full as grain settles down.

Hatch Money. Gratuity formerly given to a shipmaster on right discharge of cargo.

Hatch Rest Section. Specially designed rolled steel section for fitting to coamings of hatches. Has a flat side for attachment to coaming, a shoulder for supporting ends of hatch covers, and a stopping edge to retain covers in position.

Hatchway. Hatch leading to another deck and provided with stairs or a ladder. Sometimes used as meaning 'Hatch'.

Hatchway Screens. Canvas screens around a hatchway. Formerly, heavy woollen screens around hatchways of warships during action.

Haul. To pull; to drag along. 2. To open seams in planking of ship's side through excessive strain on rigging. 3. In rope-making, is a bundle of 300 to 400 yarns when ready for tarring.

Haul About.* Old method of making a cable laid rope from a long hawser laid rope. One end is turned back, at one-third of length, and laid up around centre part. Other end is then turned back and laid up, around previous parts.

Hauling Line. Transporting wire, or rope, used for warping or hauling a vessel in a dock or harbour.

'Haul of Haul.' Order given in a sailing vessel before going about. Yards are braced as sharply as possible, buntlines are hauled taut, halliards are sweated up.

Haul Round. When said of wind, means 'to veer'.

Haul the Wind. To come closer to the wind by bracing in the yards.

Hausing In.* Former name for 'Fall home'.

Hawker.* Olden sailing vessel. Sloop rigged with long, narrow stern.

Hawse. Angle between a forward extension of a ship's fore and aft line and a line between stem and anchor. With two anchors down, is angle at stem between lines going to each anchor. Vessel with two anchors down was said to be 'Riding a hawse'.

Hawse Block. Wooden chock shaped to fit a hawse pipe, and to prevent entry of water when at sea. A hawse plug.

Hawse Bolster. Planking immediately above or below hawse hole of a wooden ship. Name is sometimes applied to 'Hawse Block'.

Hawse Fallen. Said of a pitching vessel when she puts her hawse holes under water.

Hawse Holes. Holes cut in bows of ship, on either side of stem, and through which cable passes from ship to anchors.

Hawse Hook. Breast hook above upper deck.

Hawse Piece. Cant frame next to knight heads in wooden vessel. It forms a solid mass of wood around hawse hole. Name is sometimes given to the wale in which hawse holes are made.

Hawse Pipe. Tube that connects hawse hole with cable deck or forecastle, and through which cable goes from ship to anchor.

Hawse Plug. 'Hawse Block.'

Hawser. Flexible steel wire rope, or fibre rope, used for hauling, warping or mooring.

Hawser Laid. Said of rope in which yarns are spun right handed, laid up into strands left handed, strands laid up right handed.

Hawse Timber. Vertical bow timber in which hawse holes are cut.
Haze. Atmospheric state in which visibility is reduced to about one mile.
Hazel Rod Fender. Large and long bundle of hazel rods bound with wire and used as fender in docks, alongside ships and hulks, etc.
Hazing. Giving a man a dog's life by continual work, persistent grumbling and petty tyranny.
H Bar. Rolled steel section of H shape.
Head (of Sail). In four-sided sails is the upper edge; in triangular sails is the upper corner.
Head Board. Extreme forward bulwark. 2. Small piece of wood inserted in upper corner of flag to ensure that the flag is close up to the truck when hoisted.
Head Fast. Mooring rope leading forward from fore end of a vessel.
Headings. Timbers forming the head of a wooden cask, barrel, etc.
Head Knee. Timber fayed sideways to stem of wooden vessel.
Head Ledge. Thwartship coaming of a hatchway.
Head Line. Transporting wire that is run from bow of a vessel to a position ahead when warping. 2. Lacing that attaches head of sail to a gaff or yard.
Head Netting. Ornamental meshwork bulwarks formerly fitted in many ships.
Head Rope. Hawser leading forward from bows of a ship to a point outside the ship. May be used for warping or mooring.
Heads. Latrines in a warship. Formerly situated between knight heads.
Head Sails. All sails that are set forward of foremast.
Head Sea. Sea in which waves run directly against heading of a ship.
Head Sheets. Sheets of head sails. 2. Flooring in fore part of a boat; bow sheets.
Head Timber. Cant timber in fore part of wooden ship, to support gratings.
Headway. Forward movement of a ship through the water.
Head Wind. Wind blowing from a point right ahead of a ship.
Heart. Inner part of a shroud laid rope. 2. Fibre in strand of flexible wire rope. 3. Triangular deadeye.
Heart Thimble. Grooved metal protector put in eye of a rope. One end semicircular, and tapering to a point.
Heart Yarns. Inside yarns of a strand of rope.
Heave. To lift; to haul strongly; to haul in cable; to lift an anchor; to rise up; to throw—as in heaving a lead.
Heave Ahead. To haul a ship or boat ahead on a warp or cable.
Heave and Hold. Order to haul strongly and not to surrender any gain.
Heave and Rally. Injunction to heave forcefully and cheerily.
Heave and Set. Said of motion of a vessel at anchor when set lifts her and she falls back quickly.

Heave and Up Pawl. Capstan order to heave enough for a capstan pawl to be lifted. Is also a caution that capstan can walk back.

Heave Astern. Haul a vessel astern by a warp or sternfast.

Heave Down. To careen a ship by putting tackles from lower mast heads to a sheer hulk—or other arranged attachments—and then hauling on falls of tackles.

Heave in Sight. To come up over the horizon. Loosely used as meaning coming into sight.

Heave in Stays. To bring a ship to the wind when tacking.

Heavenly Body. Name that includes star or solar system body.

Heaver. Short wooden lever tapered at both ends.

Heave Short. Heave in cable until it is at short stay.

Heave the Lead. To swing and heave the lead so that it falls into the water some distance ahead of the leadsman.

Heave To. To bring ship's head near to wind and to remain stopped in that position by trimming yards, or working engines, as may be necessary.

Heaving. Being lifted up by a wave or sea. 2. Hauling heavily on a rope or hawser.

Heaving Alongside. Hauling a vessel alongside by means of ropes or hawsers.

Heaving Line. Small line that is thrown so that one end reaches a position outside ship, and allows connection to be established.

Heaving the Log. Throwing a ship log into the water so that speed of ship may be ascertained.

Heaving To. *See* 'Heave to'.

Heavieside-Kennelly Layer. Ionized layer, in upper atmosphere, that reflects radio waves.

Heavy Derrick. Strong derrick specially provided for lifting very heavy weights. Usually has a special heel fitting that takes in corresponding socket fitted on deck, the deck being suitably supported underneath.

Heavy Floe. Piece of floating ice more than three feet thick.

Hedgehog. Squid. Limbo. Multi-barrelled mortars firing a pattern of depth charges. Anti-submarine weapons.

Heel. To list as a result of wind pressure, or of a shift of weight. 2. Junction of stern post and keel. 3. The lower end of a mast that is fitted in a step. 4. Inboard end of a bowsprit or jib boom.

Heel Chain. Chain that prevents heel of jib boom coming inboard.

Heeling Error. Compass error due to ship not being upright, so causing an unsymmetrical disposal of iron around a compass.

Heeling Experiment. Deliberate listing of a vessel to ascertain her righting moment.

Heel Knee. Knee connecting keel and sternpost.

Heel Over. To list or incline transversely.

Heel Post. Vertical member supporting after end of propeller shaft.

Heel Rope. Rope by which a bowsprit or jib boom is hauled out. 2. Rope that hauls out and secures a studdingsail boom.

Height. Of a flag, is its vertical dimension. Sometimes used as meaning its breadth.

Height.* Elizabethan term for 'Latitude'.

Height of Tide. Distance that water level is above chart datum when due to tidal effect.

Height of Wave. Vertical distance from trough to crest expressed in feet. May, rarely, exceed 70 feet.

Height Staff. Graduated rod used for measuring heights during the building of a vessel.

Heliacal Rising. The rising of a star or planet during morning twilight.

Heliocentric. Having Sun as a centre.

Heliometer. Instrument for finding solar time and latitude, when appropriately set, at noon.

Heliostat. Instrument used in hydrographic surveying for reflecting Sun's rays at one observation station to another at distances up 40 miles or so. Used when direct observations and identification of the station are not possible. 'Heliograph.'

Helm. Tiller by which a rudder is controlled. Also applied to the machinery by which a rudder is controlled, and to the duty of controlling it.

Helmet. Brass cover over a compass carried in a binnacle. Usually carries the lighting arrangements.

Helm Indicator. Pointer geared to steering wheel and moving over a graduated arc to indicate amount of helm being used, and angular position of rudder.

Helm Orders. Orders given to a helmsman.

Helm Port. Opening through which a rudder stock passes into a ship.

Helm Port Transom. Wooden stiffener in way of a helm port.

'Helm's Alee.' Report made when under sail and going about. Warns personnel concerned that vessel is coming up to the wind.

Helm Signal. Sound signal, or visual signal, made to another vessel in sight when altering course under helm.

Helmsman. Person steering a vessel.

Helmstock.* Old name for a 'Tiller'.

Hemp. Vegetable fibre, largely from India, from which rope is made.

Hencoop. Enclosed framework in which fowl were formerly carried by sea-going ships.

Hercules. Northern constellation situated south of Draco and Hydra.

Hermaphrodite Brig. Former name for a brigantine. Brig rigged on foremast, schooner rigged on mainmast.

Herring Buss.* Sailing drifter of 10 to 15 tons.

Herring Gull. Sometimes called 'Silvery Gull'. Common British species.

Hesperus. Name given to planet Venus when an evening star. Greek for 'Western'.

High. Alternative name for an anticyclone. A gyro compass is said to be 'high' when its indication, in arc, is higher than it should be.

High and Dry. State of a grounded vessel when sea level is below her keel as tide ebbs.

High Charged.* Said of a vessel with lofty superstructure.

High Court of Admiralty. British court of law in which a judge—assisted by Trinity Masters, who act as assessors and nautical advisers—deals with matters concerning ships and shipping in navigable waters.

High Frequency. Electrical frequency exceeding 15,000 per second.

High-Pressure Boiler. Water tube boiler generating steam at pressures between 400 and 650 lb. per sq. in.

High Seas. Oceans and extra-territorial areas of seas conected with oceans.

High Tide. The high water of any tidal undulation.

High Water. Highest level reached by any particular tidal undulation.

High-Water Mark. Permanent mark that indicates a high-water datum. That in London was established by Act of Parliament in 1800, and is cut into Hermitage entrance to London Docks. Is 12·53 feet above mean sea level at Liverpool.

High Wooded. Said of a boat with high freeboard.

Hill & Clarke's Lowering Apparatus. One of the earliest type of boat releasing gear (1880). Immediately both ends of boat were waterborne the falls became disconnected from boat.

Hire and Payment Clause. Inserted in a time charter to specify amount of money to be paid, and when payment is to be made.

Hitch. Manipulation of end of a rope by which it becomes attached to any object other than another rope's end.

Hoar Frost. Small particles of ice formed by small drops of water being deposited on a surface whose temperature is below that of freezing point.

Hog. Stiff brush used for scrubbing ship's bottom. Old sail, filled with holystones, etc., used for same purpose when at sea. 2. To clean bottom of a ship by scraping or scrubbing. 3. To droop at fore and after ends through structural weakness or bad disposition of cargo. Can occur when vessel is excessively supported amidships and not fully supported at ends.

Hog Chain.* Iron chain tautly stretched between stem and stern posts. Formerly fitted in some ships to prevent hogging.

Hog Frame. Strong fore and aft frame built to prevent hogging.

Hogging. Cleaning ship's bottom. 2. Drooping of a vessel at fore and after ends and arching at middle part. Also applied to any structural member that droops at ends.

Hogging Strain. Excessive stress that causes a vessel or member to hog.

Hog Piece. Timber going from forward to after deadwood, in a wooden boat, to increase girder strength and so resist hogging stresses. Is attached to top of keel, and garboard strake is attached to hog piece.

Hogshead. Cask holding about 52½ gallons, but may vary with different liquids.

Hoist. To lift. Amount of goods lifted at one time. 2. Group of flags forming a signal or part of a signal. 3. The perpendicular extent or measurement of a flag. 4. Extent to which a yard or sail can be hoisted.

Hold. Interior space in which cargo is carried in a vessel. One of the divisions into which the interior space is divided.

Hold a Luff. To keep close to the wind when under sail.

Hold Beam. Thwartship beam supporting a deck covering a hold. Name is sometimes given to a 'Hatch Beam'.

Holding Ground. Bottom of sea when its nature is such that an anchor will grip with a reasonable amount of security.

Holding On. Continuing on a course.

Hold Pillars. Vertical members extending from floor to beam in a hold. Support deck and help to resist racking stresses.

Hold Stringers. Horizontal strength members going fore and aft alongsides of hold.

Hold Water. To retard or stop fore and aft motion of a rowed boat by putting blades of oars vertically in water, with looms at right angles to fore and aft line, and maintaining them in this position.

Holidays. Days on which it is customary not to work in a given port or country. 2. Spaces carelessly left when painting or cleaning an area.

Hollow Sea.* Swell that is not due to a prevailing wind.

Holme's Compass. Magnetic compass designed to control and operate a number of repeaters at remote positions.

Holme's Light. Calcium phosphide light that ignites on contact with water, giving off both smoke and flame. Attached to life buoys to make them more conspicuous when in the water.

Holophonal. Term applied to a light when its rays are reflected or refracted into a beam.

Holystone. Small piece of soft white sandstone used for cleaning wooden decks by abrasion. To clean with holystones.

Home. In place. Close down.

Home Trade. Seaborne trade between British and Irish ports and ports in Europe between Elbe and Brest inclusive.

Home Trade Agreement. Contract between master and crew of vessel in the Home Trade. In force for six months from date of opening. Wages are usually on a weekly basis; crew usually find their own provisions; short notice of termination, on either side, is fairly general.

Home Trade Limits. Coasts of Great Britain, Northern Ireland, Eire and Channel Islands and coast of Europe from Elbe to Brest, both inclusive.

Homeward Bound. Said of a vessel when she is bound for a port in her own country. 2. Colloquial term for any work, particularly sewing of canvas, when it is done hurriedly and carelessly.

Honda Steels. Steel alloys having exceptional magnetic retentivity. They contain cobalt, nickel and aluminium.

Honour Policy. Policy of marine insurance in which the good faith of the insurer is assumed by the underwriter without documentary or other evidence. Policy automatically lapses, against insurer, if good faith is lacking.

Hood. Covering for a hatch or companionway. 2. Cover of a compass mounted in a binnacle.

Hooded, Hooding, Ends. Those ends of planking, of a boat or wood-built vessel, that are fitted into rabbeting on stern and stem posts.

Hook. Transverse connecting piece in fore end of a boat or ship. Name is often given to such fitting in other parts of a vessel.

Hook and Butt. Joint in planking that is made by scarphing or lapping.

Hook Block. Sheaved block that is fitted with a hook for making attachment.

Hook Bolt. Bolt with hooked end for attachment purposes.

Hooker. Colloquial name for a ship. Corrupt form of 'Hawker'.

Hook's Law. Generally defined as 'For elastic strains, strain is proportional to stress.' Strain equals stress multiplied by a constant that varies with the material under consideration.

Hook Rope. About 10 to 12 fathoms of rope having a hook on one end. Used in working cable, or for general purposes.

Hoops. Wooden rings by which a luff of a fore and aft sail is confined to a mast.

Hope. A small inlet or haven.

Hopper. Usual name for a 'Hopper barge'; sometimes for a 'Hopper dredger'.

Hopper Barge. Barge having flap doors in bottom and buoyancy spaces at ends. Receives dredged material from a dredger, and is then towed to a dumping ground.

Hopper Dredger. Dredger having a compartment with flap doors in the bottom. Dredged material is placed in this compartment for subsequent release.

Horary Circle. 'Hour Circle.'

Horizon. Line along which sky and surface of Earth appear to meet.

Horizon Glass. Of sextant, is a fixed glass through which horizon is sighted. Half of glass is a reflector in which reflected image of an observed body is sighted and brought down to horizon.

Horizontal. Pertaining to the horizon. Perpendicular to vertical.

Horizontal Danger Angle. Danger angle when measured between two objects in the same horizontal plane.

Horizontal Parallax. Value of parallax of a heavenly body when in observer's horizon. It is then greatest.

Horn Book. Volume giving elementary principles and methods.

Horn Bowsprit. 'Spike Bowsprit.'

Horne.* 17th century name for constellation Ursa Major.

Hornpipe. Originally, a Welsh musical instrument. Later, a dance performed to hornpipe music. Now, one of the dances of nautical origin.

Horns. Name sometimes given to jaws of a gaff, or arms of a cleat.

Horn Timber. Strong timber sloping up and aft from keel of a wooden vessel to form the backbone of the counter.

Horse. Beam or bar along which the sheet of a fore and aft sail travels. 2. Foot rope beneath a yard. 3. Ridge rope from knight heads to bowsprit cap, for safety of men working along bowsprit. 4. Breast rope, in chains, for safety of man heaving the lead. 5. Wooden frame on which men sat when woolding mast. 6. Shoal across line of tide and over which a tidal current flows without breaking, but with a slight rise of level.

Horse Iron. Large caulking iron used when horsing.

Horse Knot. Alternative name for 'Footrope Knot'.

Horse Latitudes. Calm area between trade wind belt and 'Westerlies' in Atlantic Ocean. Approximately 30° to 35°N.

Horse Marine. Unhandy seaman.

Horse Packet. Team boat at Yarmouth in early 19th century. Worked by four horses.

Horse Power. Unit of work equivalent to lifting power of 33,000-foot pounds per minute.

Horseshoe Clamp. Iron fastening between fore foot and gripe.

Horseshoe Rack. Curved rack, abaft mainmast, carrying ninepin blocks through which running gear of light sails was led to belaying pins.

Horseshoe Splice. Made in end of a single topmast shroud or backstay. End is turned down and a short length of rope is put across bight and spliced into each part. Sometimes used in jib guys.

Horsing. Caulking the seams in ship side planking.

Horsing Iron. Large caulking iron used when horsing.

Horsing Mallet. Heavy wooden mallet used when horsing.

Horsing Up. Final caulking of ship's side planking.

Hose Coupling. Metal fitting, in end of hose, by which one length of hose is connected to another.

Host Men. Fraternity, at Newcastle-upon-Tyne, who were responsible for the carriage of north country coal.

Hot Bulb Engine. Internal combustion engine in which ignition of fuel is assisted by having a hot bulb head in compression-combustion space.

Hot Well. Chamber in which exhaust steam from engines is stored after condensation.

Hounds. Timbers secured on either side of a mast to form rests for crosstrees and upper eyes of rigging. Also, step on mast, made by reducing its diameter, when used for same purpose.

Hounds Band. Iron or steel band secured near head of mast to take upper eyes of shrouds and stays.

Hour. Twenty-fourth part of a day. Interval in which the hour angle of a heavenly body changes 15° in respect to the hour circle of an observer. Arc of 15° of Equinoctial.

Hour Angle. Angle, at elevated pole, between meridian of observer and meridian passing through a heavenly body. Conventionally reckoned westward from observer, but can be expressed as an easterly value.

Hour Circle. Great circle, secondary to Equinoctial, passing through points having the same Right Ascension and, therefore, the same hour circle.

House. To put into a position of increased safety. To lower an upper mast until its head is in line with head of mast below. To run back a gun and secure it.

House Flag. Private and acknowledged flag of a ship's owner or owners.

Houseline. Soft-laid three-yarn stuff used for general purposes. May be tarred or untarred.

Housing (of Bowsprit). Inboard part from bed, or wedges, to the heel.

Hove. Heaved.

Hoveller. Person who assists in saving life or property from a vessel wrecked near the coast. Often applied to a small boat that lies in narrow waters ready to wait on a vessel, if required. Possibly a corruption of 'hoverer'.

Hovercraft ('Cushioncraft'). A vessel which can support herself a short distance above the surface of the water or land by exerting a downward pressure of air.

Hove To. Lying nearly head to wind and stopped, and maintaining this position by trimming sail or working engines.

Howden-Johnson Boiler. Cylindrical boiler of Scottish type but having external tubes that pass through combustion chamber and connect water below furnaces with upper volume of water. Superheater is mounted above front ends of return tubes. Efficiency is a little less than 0·9.

Howl.* To scarph foothooks into the ground timbers of a vessel.

'How's Her Head?' 'What is the direction of ship's head at this moment?'

Hoy. Small, one-masted sailing vessel used for short voyages or for carrying passengers or goods to or from ships.

Hug. To keep close to.

Hulk. Hull of a vessel not fit for sea service. Sailing vessel without masts. 2. In 13th to 15th centuries a vessel larger than the earlier cog. Hulc/hourque.

Hull. Body of a ship, and excluding interior fittings.

Hull Down. Said of a distant ship when her hull is below horizon and her masts and upper works are visible.

Hulling. Floating, but at mercy of wind and sea. 2. Piercing the hull with a projectile. 3. Taking in sail during a calm.

Humber Keel. Flat-sided, round-ended, flat-bottomed vessel used in Humber and other Yorkshire waterways. Has one mast amidships, square mainsail and a topsail. Mainsail can be single or double reefed to yard.

Humidity. Moistness of atmosphere due to its water-vapour content.

Humidity-Mixing Ratio. Relative weights of water and vapour forming damp air. Expressed as number of grams of water-vapour combined with a kilogram of dry air.

Humpbacked Whale. Rather short whale having flippers of a length up to one-third length of body. Occasionally seen in British waters.

Hunter's Moon. Full moon following Harvest Moon. Characteristics are somewhat similar to those of Harvest Moon, but less marked.

Hunting Gear. Mechanism by which a differential motion is produced so that the final movement of some part is the result of two movements having opposite effects. Used in steering engine mechanisms to stop the engine when rudder has been turned through an angle that corresponds with angle indicated at wheel.

Hunting Tooth. Tooth, in a wheel actuated by a pinion, that is in excess of a multiple of the number of teeth in the pinion. It ensures that any tooth in pinion will not mesh continually into same teeth of wheel.

Hurricane. Violent cyclonic storm, especially around Cape Verde Islands, Atlantic seaboard of U.S.A., West Indies and Gulf of Mexico. Any wind of Force 12 on the Beaufort Scale.

Hurricane Deck. A superstructure deck. Formerly, a deck reserved for use of officer of watch, or commander.

Hurricane Lamp. More or less stormproof oil lantern used for general purposes of illumination about decks and open spaces.

Husband.* Owner's representative who formerly went with ship to take charge of stores, arrange for repairs and transact ship's business. In Plantagenet times he was the sailing master.

Hyades. Cluster of five (formerly seven) stars in the head of Taurus.

Hydra. 'Water Snake.' Long constellation extending south of Cancer, Leo and Virgo. Principal star is Alphard—Cor Hydrae.

Hydraulic Jack. Machine by which heavy weights may be lifted by pumping small quantities of water underneath a ram.

Hydrofoil. A fast vessel which, when at speed, lifts her hull clear of the surface of the water, supporting herself upon foils, or wings, which project beneath her bottom.

Hydrogap Rudder. Rudder so mounted that a gap, between its leading edge and sternpost, is formed when rudder is angled. This allows water to flow from pressure side of rudder to suction side when angled.

Hydrograph. A recording hygrometer.

Hydrographer. One who surveys oceans, seas and inland waters for the purpose of navigation and commerce; and who produces charts and sailing directions to impart the information obtained.

Hydrographer of the Navy. A senior officer—usually a flag officer—of the Royal Navy who is responsible for British hydrographic work. First to be appointed was Alexander Dalrymple, 1795. First R.N. officer was Captain Thomas Hurd, 1808.

Hydrographical Abbreviations. Standard abbreviations used in charts and hydrographic notices.

Hydrographic Department. Branch of Admiralty, founded in 1795, to 'select and compile such information as might appear to be requisite for the purpose of improving navigation'. Is responsible for all hydrographic work and for the publication of requisite information regarding surveys, tidal data, chart preparation, etc.

Hydrographic Office. Branch of U.S. Navy corresponding to British Hydrographic Department.

Hydrography. The science and practice of surveying oceans and seas, the charting of coasts, the collection of information relating to navigation, the production of charts and sailing directions, the investigation of tides, and the placing of the ascertained facts at the disposal of navigators and others concerned.

Hydrometer. Instrument for measuring the density of liquids. Usually consists of a ballasted float carrying a scale that indicates density as related to fresh water. This zero is 1000; the density of sea water is about 1026, but varies, in different ports and areas, between 1000 and about 1040.

Hydrophone. Instrument for collecting sound transmitted by water.

Hydrostatic. Pertaining to the principles of equilibrium of fluids.

Hygrometer. Dry and wet bulb thermometers mounted alongside each other so that depression of wet bulb can be ascertained and humidity of atmosphere deduced. Special hygrometers are used by engineers for determing the dryness fraction of steam.

Hygroscopic. Capable of abstracting moisture from the atmosphere.

Hyperacme Block. Heavy lift purchase consisting of upper sheave having a toothed disc, into which a worm engages, and a sprocket wheel of smaller diameter. Length of chain is secured to framework, passes through a single shave hook block and then into sprockets on upper shave. Worm is actuated by endless chain going over sprocket wheel secured at end of worm shaft.

Hyperbola. A curve, any point upon which has the same difference of distances between two fixed points, called loci: e.g. point X, 10 units from one locus and 8 from the other: difference 2; point Y, 13 from one locus and 11 from the other: difference 2.

Hyperbolic Navigation. Finding a Position Line or Position Lines corresponding to a hyperbola or hyperbolae associated with a chain of two or more radio stations.

Hysteresis. The lagging behind of a certain amount of magnetism when an object has been temporarily magnetised and the magnetising agent has been withdrawn.

I

I Bar. Flat rolled steel section with small flat flange across longitudinal edges.
Ice. Water that has congealed due to lack of heat. Fresh water freezes at 0°C; salt water at about −3°C. Eleven cubic feet of ice represent 10 cubic feet of water. Owing to heat absorbed by melting ice, the meteorological aspect of ice is important.
Ice Anchor. Single fluke with shank. Put in hole or crack in ice for mooring purposes.
Ice Beam. Baulk of timber fitted to bow of ship, for fending off ice.
Iceberg. Great mass of floating ice that has broken off a glacier and been carried seaward. Waterplane area may be more than five square miles; underwater depth up to 300 fathoms. Movement may be with prevalent wind or current, but may be due to deep current. Generally advisable to pass to windward of it.
Ice Blink. *See* 'Blink.'
Icebound. Said of a ship when she cannot move because of surrounding ice. Said of a port when it is inaccessible because of ice.
Ice Breaker. Steam vessel with bow specially shaped to tread down and break sheet ice, and make a navigable lane. 2. Sloping piles on upstream side of a pier to deflect or break up floating ice.
Ice Clause. Inserted in marine contracts, when appropriate, to cover cases in which a ship or port may be ice bound.
Ice Fender. 'Ice Beam.'
Icelandic Lows. Meteorological depressions that frequently form over Iceland.
Ice Lead. Navigable lane of water through ice.
Ice Master. One who takes charge of navigation of a whaler when in ice.
Ice Patrol. Ships and personnel employed in watching for ice, and derelicts, in North Atlantic Ocean. Established by International Safety Convention, 1929. Maintained by contributions of maritime nations interested.
Ice Report. Radio report, to shore stations and near-by ships, made by master of any vessel sighting ice. Penalty for not reporting is £50.
Idler. Member of a crew who works all day but does not keep night watches; e.g. carpenter, sailmaker. Termed 'dayman' in R.N.
'If Sufficient Water.' Clause inserted in a charter party to qualify the obligation to discharge in a named dock, or berth, if there be not sufficient depth of water when the order to berth is given.
Ignition Point. Minimum temperature at which a substance will ignite and burn. Is always higher than 'Flash point'.
Ignition Temperature. Temperature to which a substance must be raised for it to burn.
Ikara. An anti-submarine missile delivering a homing torpedo.
Immersion. The sinking of a substance into a fluid.

Immigration Regulations. Laws and rules regulating the entry of aliens into a country.

Impedance. Circuit resistance to an alternating current when caused by self-inductance, circuit capacity and ohmic resistance.

Implied Warranties. Assurances that are not made specifically by an insurer but are implied by his application for insurance. These are, that the ship is seaworthy; that the venture is lawful; that the venture will be carried out in a lawful manner.

Import. To bring into a country, from abroad.

Imports. Goods brought into a country from another country.

Impulse. Force applied to cause movement.

In Ballast. Said of a vessel when she is not carrying cargo.

Inboard. Inside a ship. That end, or part, of anything that is nearer to the ship's fore and aft line than is the other end or part.

'Inchmaree' Clause. Clause, in a policy of marine insurance to cover damage or loss to ship when caused by latent defect not discoverable by due diligence.

Inch Trim Moment. Moment of force required to change trim of vessel by one inch. Formula is:—

$$\text{I.T.M.} = \frac{30 \times (\text{T.P.I.})^2}{\text{Moulded breadth (in feet)}}$$

Inclination. Leaning. The mutual leaning of two planes, or lines, towards each other. The angular intersection of two planes or lines.

Inclination of Ecliptic. Angular intersection of plane at Equinoctial by plane of Ecliptic. Value is 23° 27'.

Inclination of Needle. Angle of magnetic dip. Angle that a magnetic needle will make with the sensible horizon when freely suspended in the vertical plane.

Inclination of Orbit. Angular intersection of Ecliptic by the orbital plane of a heavenly body.

Inclination of Ship. Angle of list, or thwartship deviation from the vertical, of a line perpendicular to the deck of a vessel.

Inclining Experiment. 'Heeling experiment.'

Increment. Quantity, usually variable, that is added to an independent variable in an invariable expression. When very small it is termed a 'differential'.

Indenture. Sealed and binding agreement entered into by two parties. Particularly applied to agreement between ship owner or master, and parent and guardian of a minor apprenticed to sea service.

Independent Piece. Beak-shaped projection from a vessel's stem under the bowsprit.

Index. That which points out, or indicates. Of a logarithm, is the integral number that precedes the mantissa.

Index Bar. Radial arm moving over a sextant, and carrying index glass and vernier.

Index Correction. Quantity to be applied to an incorrect indication to convert it to a correct value.

Index Error. Difference between a true value and a value indicated.

Index Glass. Pivoted mirror on index bar of sextant.

Index Mirror. Alternative name for an index glass.

Indiaman. Name formerly given to any large ship regularly trading to India.

Indian Spring Low Water. Datum used in Indian tides. Is below sea level by an amount made up by sum of amplitudes of M_2, S_2, K_1, O_1. First used by Prof. G. H. Darwin.

Indicated Horse Power. Measurement of power developed in cylinder of a reciprocating engine as deduced from an indicator diagram.

Indicator. Any instrument that indicates mechanically. Especially applied to instrument that graphically indicates work done by steam while in a cylinder of a reciprocating engine.

Indicator Diagram. Graph of work done by steam while in a cylinder. Produced by mechanism incorporated in an 'Indicator'.

Indorsement. Endorsement. That which is written on the back of a document.

Induced Current. Current developed in a conductor that is near another conductor carrying an alternating or fluctuating current. 2. Current passing through a conductor that is in the field of moving magnet.

Induced Draught. Artificial draught through a furnace caused by expediting exhaust of funnel gases; so causing a partial vacuum on escape end of furnace and stimulating flow of air to furnace.

Induced Magnetism. Magnetism, of a ferrous substance, due to proximity of a magnet or magnetic field.

Induction. Generation of an effect by the action of a distant cause.

Indulgence Passenger. Person given a passage in one of H.M. ships; usually on compassionate grounds.

Inertial Navigation. A highly-refined system of Dead Reckoning navigation. Accelerometers, or doppler techniques, and a computer measure the distance travelled from the original departure position.

Inferior Conjunction. Conjunction of Moon or planet occurring between Earth and Sun.

Inferior Meridian. That meridian 180° distant from a given meridian.

Inferior Planet. Either Venus or Mercury, whose orbits around Sun lie inside orbit of Earth.

In Haul. Any rope acting in a direction opposite to that of an outhaul. Particularly applied to rope or purchase by which a jib boom, studdingsail yard, or other spar, is hauled inboard.

Inherent Vice. Inseparable property of a substance whereby it damages or destroys itself.

In Irons. Said of a sailing vessel when she is close to the wind and will not fall off on either tack.

Initial Condensation. Conversion of a certain amount of steam into water as it enters a cylinder. Due to temperature of cylinder being less than temperature of steam.

Initial Stability. Resistance offered by a vessel, when floating upright, to forces tending to list her.

Injection. Forcing of fuel into cylinder of a compression ignition oil engine. Forcing of feed water into a boiler.

Innavigable. Not navigable by ships.

Inner Bottom. Plating laid on top of floors. Upper plating of double bottom tanks. Deck resting on upper sides of floor timbers.

Inner Post. Timber secured to fore side of stern post to take seatings of transom.

Inner Turns. Those turns, of earing of a square sail, that confine the sail against the yard.

Inshore. Near to the shore. On the shoreward side.

Inside Clinch. Name given to end of rope that is formed into a loop by taking a round turn on standing part with end on inside of loop.

Insolation. Sun's radiation as received at surface of Earth.

Inspection. Visual examination. 2. Entering a table with known data and abstracting a tabulated resultant.

Instantaneous Triangle.* Astronomical (PZX) triangle.

In Stays. The position of a sailing vessel when she is going from one tack to the other, head to wind.

Institute Clauses. Standard forms of clauses that may be inserted in a policy of marine insurance to limit it, or to extend its scope. Framed and sanctioned by the Institute of London underwriters. They cover practically all contingencies and requirements.

Institute of London Underwriters. Organisation of firms and persons undertaking marine insurance. Founded 1884.

Instrumental Error. Error in a measured quantity when due to defect or limitation in the measuring instrument.

Insulating Coat. Coating of paint, or other substance, to protect a plate or fitting from deterioration by a subsequent coating. Particularly applied to bitumastic coat between ship's bottom plating and a corrosive anti-fouling paint.

Insulation. Prevention of leakage from, or into, a body or substance.

Insurable Interest. Such interest in a ship or voyage that failure of ship to carry out voyage as intended would entail financial loss.

Insurable Value. Sum of money for which insurable items may lawfully and reasonably be insured. In case of goods carried by sea it is made up of invoiced cost of goods, cost of freight, cost of insurance, profit. Profit usually assessed as 10 per cent of other costs.

Insurance Broker. Person who acts as intermediary between those requiring insurance and those willing to insure; more especially those who place marine risks with underwriters.

Insurance Clubs. 'Mutual Indemnity Associations.' 'Small Damage Clubs.'

Insurance Policy. Signed contract of an insurer to make good a loss against which insurance has been effected.

Insurer/s. Person/s who have contracted to make good a maritime loss.

Intake. Specific amount taken into ship as cargo.

Intake Measurement. Actual measurement, by weight or volume, of cargo taken into a vessel.

Intercalary Day. 29th February. Inserted every fourth year, with exceptions, to keep the Civil year in step with the Tropical year.

Intercardinal Points. Those points halfway between the cardinal points of a compass.

Intercept Method. Alternative name for 'Marc St. Hilaire Method'.

Intercostal. Between the ribs. Applied to structures or members between the floors or frames of a vessel.

Intercostal Centre Keelson. Internal keel that is stopped at each floor but extends the full length along centre line of the keel.

Intercostal Plates. Lengths of plating that go fore and aft between frames.

Interest Policy. Contract of insurance covering some special interest or parcel of cargo. Also applied to valid policies to distinguish them from 'Honour' or 'No interest' policies.

Interior Planets. Inferior planets. Those whose orbits lie within that of Earth.

Intermittent Light. Former name for a flashing or an occulting light. Any light that does not show continuously.

Internal Combustion Engine. Engine that operates through fuel being consumed in itself.

International Code. System of flag and Morse signals that superseded the 'Commercial Code'. Last revised 1969.

International Convention. Meeting of representatives of maritime nations to formulate rules concerning shipping.

International Load Line Ship. Any vessel of 150 tons (gross), or over, that carries cargo or passengers, and thus comes under the International Load Line Rules.

International Nautical Mile. Unit adopted by the International Hydrographic Bureau and having a value of 1852 metres. This length—6076 ft. 2 in.—is equivalent to one minute of latitude in Lat. $44\frac{1}{2}°$.

International Rating Rules. Rules for measurement of yachts of $14\frac{1}{2}$ metres (L.W.L. $47\frac{1}{2}$ ft.) and under. Adopted in Europe, 1933.

Interpolation. Determination of value of a quantity intermediate between two quantities whose values are given.

Interrupted Quick Flashing. Name given to a quick flashing light that is eclipsed at regular intervals.

Interval. Time value of difference between any two epochs. Distance between any two points. Arithmetical value of difference between any two given arithmetical quantities.

Intrinsic Energy. Of steam, is the amount of heat energy available for work at the point of application.

Inversion. Used in meteorology to denote that temperature increases with height above surface of Earth. In tides, is a rise in water level with a rise in barometric pressure.

Inverted Tide. Occurrence of low water at the same time as Moon's transit at the place.

Invoice. Document sent by shipper to Customs authorities. States nature, quantity and value of goods shipped.

Inwale. Name sometimes given to the internal fore and aft stiffener running along inboard side of upper strake of a boat. More usually called 'gunwale'.

Inward Clearing Bill. Document issued by Customs authorities when ship has been searched for unentered goods, stores checked and formalities complied with.

Iridium. Extremely hard metal used for compass pivots.

Irish Pendant. Nickname for a rope end, or yarn stop, blowing about in a wind. More correctly, is any flag, pendant or ensign with a frayed fly.

Ironbound. Said of shore having rocky cliffs and no safe landing place.

Ironclad. Early name for warships whose wooden sides were sheathed with iron. Name persisted after hulls were entirely of steel.

Iron Wire Rope. Non-flexible rope made of small iron wires and no hearts. Used for standing rigging and other purposes in which extension due to stress cannot be tolerated.

Irradiation. Apparent increase in size of a heavenly body caused by the brightness of its light.

Isaz. Short name for a line of iso-azimuth.

Isallobar. Line, on a meteorological chart, passing through all positions at which pressure changes were similar during a given period.

Isallobaric Wind. Wind component that is due to changing pressure gradients.

Isentropic. Adiabatic.

Isherwood System. Shipbuilding method in which continuous longitudinal framing is the dominant feature.

Iso. Prefix meaning 'equal'.

Iso-Azimuth. Equal, or similar, in azimuth.

Isobar. Line, on a meteorological chart, passing through all places having the same barometric pressure.

Isobath. Line, on a chart, passing through points having the same depth.

Isoclinic Line. Line passing through all positions on Earth that have the same value of magnetic dip.

Isodynamic Line. Line passing through all places on Earth having the same value of magnetic force.

Isogonal, Isogonic, Line. Line drawn through all positions on Earth having the same magnetic variation.

Isohel. Line, on meteorological chart, passing through all places having the same period of sunshine.

Isohyet. Line, on meteorological chart, passing through all places having the same amount of rainfall.

Isoneph. Line, on a meteorological chart, passing through all positions having the same amount of cloud.

Isotherm. Line, on a meteorological chart, passing through all positions having the same temperature.

Isothermal Expansion. Expansion of gas, or steam, without an accompanying reduction of temperature. This necessitates an intake of heat during expansion.

Isothermal Line. An isotherm.

I.T.B. Integrated Tug Barge. A barge pushed by a tug joined to it.

Ivory's Rule. Method of solving the 'latitude of double altitude' problem; the PZX triangle being divided into right-angled spherical triangles.

J

Jack. Union flag. 2. Crosstrees. 3. Instrument or machine for lifting heavy weights. 4. Colloquial name for a seaman.

Jackass Rig. Name applied to a four-masted sailing vessel that is square rigged on fore and main masts, and fore and aft rigged on the two after masts.

Jack Block. Large wooden block used when hoisting or lowering a topgallant mast.

Jack Crosstrees. Iron crosstrees on a tall topgallant mast.

Jacket. Doubling piece on outside planking of a wooden vessel. 2. Casing on a pipe or funnel where it passes through a deck. 3. Space between inner and outer walls of a steam cylinder. Steam is supplied to this space to reduce initial condensation.

Jack in the Basket. Pole with basket, or basket-shaped, topmark. Used for marking a shoal or sandbank.

Jack Knife. Knife with a folding blade. Invented by Jacques de Liege in late 16th century.

Jack Ladder. Ladder with wooden rungs, or treads, and rope sides.

Jack Nastyface. Nickname for an unpopular seaman. Originally, *nom de plume* of a seaman who wrote a pamphlet about conditions in Royal Navy in early years of 19th century.

Jack Pin. Belaying pin.

Jack Screw. Large screw purchase used for lifting heavy weights, or for screwing, compressing or forcing. May be used for stowing cotton and similar cargoes.

Jackstaff. Small staff erected at stem head, or bowsprit cap, for flying a jack or other flag.

Jackstay. Iron rod, wooden batten, or taut wire on upper side of a yard, and to which the head of a square sail is bent. 2. Taut ropes that are stretched for a specific purpose; such as those extended between heads of davits; from head of davit to water line; between stanchions to take lacings of awings.

Jack Tar. Former nickname for a seaman, now used by landsmen only. When used by seamen is a term of mild contempt for a man whose nautical knowledge is less than his knowledge of nautical terms.

Jackyard Topsail. Yacht sail, with a wooden spar along foot, that is set above the mainsail and extends beyond it.

Jacob's Ladder. Jack ladder, particularly one going up a royal mast, or from a boat to a swinging boom.

Jacob's Staff. Nickname given to 'Cross staff'.

Jag Up. To stop up old rope in 5-fathom bights.

Jansen Clause. Included in a policy of marine insurance to relieve insurers of liability for losses less than 3 per cent of insured value. Also called 'Franchise Clause'.

Japan Stream. Alternative name for 'Kuro Siwo'.

Jason Clause. Usually inserted in maritime contracts that are subject to Harter Act. As a separate contract, it allows the owner of a technically 'unseaworthy' vessel to claim cargo's contribution to General Average when he has exercised due diligence in making his ship seaworthy in all respects, and the 'unseaworthiness' was such that it could not have been avoided or discovered by any reasonable amount of forethought or care.

Jaunty. R.N. nickname for a master-at-arms. Corruption of 'gendarme'.

Jaw. Forked end of a gaff or boom. 2. Space between lugs of a shackle. 3. Distance along a rope from any one strand to the next appearance of the same strand in a straight line along the rope.

Jaw Rope. Rope by which jaw of a gaff is confined to mast. A parrel.

Jears, Jeers. Tackles at bunt of lower yard, and by which it is hoisted or lowered.

Jehazi. Undecked coastal dhow of about 20 to 40 tons. Usually has matting bulwarks.

Jergue. Old form of 'Jerque'.

Jerking Note. 'Jerquing Note.'

Jerque. Search of a vessel, by Customs authorities, for unentered goods.

Jerquing Note. Certificate given by Customs searcher when ship has been searched and no unentered goods are on board.

Jet Foil. Hydrofoil propelled by waterjets situated in the foils upon which the vessel rides when at speed.

Jetsam. Goods that have been cast out of a ship and have sunk.

Jettison. Deliberate throwing overboard of goods or fittings for the preservation of a ship in peril.

Jetty. Wharf, or other similar construction, that projects into the sea or harbour.

Jewel Block. Wood block, at yard arm, that takes a studdingsail halyard.

Jew's Harp Shackle. Special bow shackle that formerly connected cable to anchor.

Jib. Triangular fore and aft sail set on a forward stay.

Jib Boom. Boom projecting forward from bowsprit, on which it is housed.

Jib Downhaul. Rope by which a jib is hauled down and inboard along jib boom.

Jibe. 'Gybe.'

Jib Frame. Vertical frame at side of a marine reciprocating engine.

Jib Guys. Rope stays leading inboard and downward from end of jib boom.

Jib Halyard. Rope by which head of a jib sail is hoisted.

Jib Headed. Said of any sail resembling a jib in shape.

Jib Inhaul. Alternative name for 'Jib downhaul'.

Jib Iron. Iron hoop that travels along jib boom and carries tack of a jib (sail).

Jib of Jibs. Outermost jibsail when three or more are carried.
Jib Outhaul. Rope by which a jib tack is hauled out to jib boom when setting jibsail.
Jib Sheet. Rope by which clew of a jib is controlled.
Jib Stay. Stay to which luff of a jib is confined.
Jigger. General purpose tackle consisting of single and double blocks, with standing part spliced to arse of single block. 2. After trysail of a four-masted barquentine. 3. After mast of a four-masted vessel.
Jimmy Bungs. Nickname for a ship's cooper.
Jimmy Duck's. Nickname for a ship's poulterer.
Jimmy Green. Square sail set beneath bowsprit in later clipper ships.
Jockeying. Manoeuvring a yacht, in vicinity of starting line, with a view to getting a favourable position and a flying start.
Joggled Frame. Steel or iron frame having alternate raised and recessed portions—on outer edge—that are of same dimensions as depth and thickness of ship's side plating. Allows plating to rest closely on frame and lap over plates above and below, without joggling plate edges.
Joggled Plate. Ship side plating so shaped that longitudinal edge of plate curves and overlaps plate next above or below it; the rest of the plate resting closely on the frame.
Joggled Timber. Frame, of a wooden vessel, so shaped that an attached strake has a clincher appearance, although there is no overlap or doubling.
Joggle Shackle. Elongated and slightly bent shackle that can confine a link of chain cable. Has a quick-release pin.
John Dory. Dory, the fish.
Joining Shackle. Flush shackle joining two lengths of cable.
Jolly. Nickname for a Royal Marine.
Jolly Boat. General purpose boat of a ship. In R.N. was usually a 28-ft. double-banked boat pulling ten oars.
Jolly Jumper. Square sail set above a 'moonraker'. Was rarely carried.
Jolly Roger. Skull and crossbones flag of a pirate.
Jonah, Jonas. Person whose presence on board is coincident with misfortune.
Joule's Equivalent of Heat. Expresses the relationship between heat energy and mechanical work as 778-foot pounds; being equal to heat required to raise one pound of water through one degree Fahrenheit. The British Thermal Unit assumes 762-foot pounds.
Journal. Old name for a log book. 2. Book entered with day by day recordings.
Judas. Said of any yarn or rope end that hangs down and is at the mercy of the wind.
Julian Calendar. Devised by Sosigenes and inaugurated by Julius Caesar. Assumes a year to be exactly $365\frac{1}{4}$ days. Commonly used until 1582.

Julian Day. Figure that denotes the serial number of a day as reckoned from an epoch in 4713 B.C. The day begins at noon, G.M.T. Used by astronomers to avoid calculations for intercalary days, and for other factors. Introduced in 16th century by Joseph Scaliger, who named it after his father, Julius.

Jumbo Derrick. Heavy-lift derrick. Used when discharging very heavy items of cargo.

Jumper. Alternative name for a 'Jolly Jumper'. 2. Blouse-like upper garment of R.N. seaman. 3. Man who discharges cargo by jumping.

Jumper Guys. Additional guys for supporting jib boom.

Jumper Stay. Triatic stay. So called because used when jumping cargo. 2. Stays on a yacht's mast which are angled forward by spreaders, or jumper struts, to give support fore and aft as well as athwartships.

Jumping. Discharging cargo, in small craft, by reeving a whip through a block on triatic stay, and then lifting cargo by holding the fall and jumping off a specially-built platform.

Jumping Ladder. Light rope ladder used for manning a lifeboat, or for men working over the side.

Jump Ship. To desert a ship, or improperly leave her.

Jumpsurgee Strop. Exceedingly strong rope strop for a block. Made by taking enough rope to go three times round block and once round thimble. Each end is unlaid until there is enough unlaid rope to encircle block and thimble. Ends are then married and strands unlaid. Yarns are then made into nettles and grafted along unlaid rope.

Junk. Old and unserviceable rope used for making fenders, mats, swabs, oakum, etc. Originally was bulrush, from which the first ropes were made. 2. Large sailing vessel of China, Japan and Malaya. Sails are battened, balanced-lug sails. Mast usually in one piece. Rudder is suspended.

Junk Ring. Cast iron ring on upper part of piston. Is removable so that packing ring can be renewed when worn. Name is a relic of days when packing was of rope.

Jupiter. Largest of the planets, being 1300 times larger than Earth and 317 times heavier. Has at least nine satellites. Orbit lies between Mars and Saturn. Distance from Sun, 478,000,000 miles.

Jury Knot. Three bights of a rope so interlaced that when knot is shipped over head of a jury mast all parts encircle the mast and there is a bight on either side, a bight forward, and two ends aft. Fore stay and shrouds were attached to bights, the two ends being backstays.

Jury Mast. Temporary mast erected in place of a mast that has carried away.

Jury Mast Knot. Shamrock knot. Centre shipped over jury mast head; the other three loops forming attachments for stay and breast backstays.

G

Jury Mat. Mat made by making bights in a length of rope, and then interweaving with bights and ends.

Jury Rig. Temporary and makeshift rig in place of rigging carried away or lost.

Jury Rudder. Makeshift rudder constructed in ship when proper rudder has been lost or damaged.

Jury Steering Gear. Alternative steering gear for controlling rudder when usual steering gear cannot be operated.

K

Kamal. Mediaeval Arabian instrument for observing the altitude of a star. A small tablet of wood was attached to a knotted string. The tablet was held so that its lower edge was in line with the horizon and the star rested on the upper edge. The distance was measured by holding the string in the teeth, the number of knots left hanging gave a measure of the latitude.

Kamchatka Current. Branch of Kuro Siwo about 200 miles wide. Sets NE-ward from 40°N, 150°E to 51°N at about ¼ knot. Between 51°N and 60°N it is hardly noticeable, but then passes W of St. Matthew Island and E of St. Lawrence Island to American coast, Behring Strait, and Arctic Ocean. Its temperature off U.S.A. coast is about 15° F higher than water off coast of Asia.

Kappa. Harmonic tidal value, in degrees of arc, representing lag of phase of a tidal constituent as compared with phase of the corresponding equilibrium constituent.

Kaskazi. Arabic name for NE monsoon on east coast of Africa.

Katabatic. Term applied to winds that flow from elevated land to lower land. Caused by greater rapidity of heat radiation in the higher land. Also applied to any downward movement of air when due to convection.

Kataphraktos. Decked Greek vessel of classic times.

Kaupskip. Beamy sailing coaster of Norway and Baltic Sea, c. 900 A.D.

Kaus. SE wind prevailing in Persian Gulf between December and April.

Kaus Australis. Star ε Sagittarii, S.H.A. 85°; Dec. S34°; Mag. 2.

Kayak. Eskimo boat constructed of sealskins stretched over light wooden framing.

Keckling. Winding small rope around a cable or hawser to prevent damage by chafing. 2. The rope with which a cable is keckled.

Kedge Anchor. Small anchor used for kedging.

Kedging. Moving a vessel by laying out a small anchor and then heaving her to it.

Keel. Principal member of a ship's construction. Lies fore and aft along centre line of bottom. May be an external or an internal construction. 2. Craft formerly used on River Tyne for carrying cargo, particularly coal. Propelled by three sweeps or, when possible, by a square sail. Usual capacity about 20 tons. *See* 'Humber Keel'.

Keelage. Money paid by a vessel for occupying space in a harbour. Also the right to exact keelage from vessels.

Keel Band. Metal strip going up fore side of a boat's stem from just abaft forefoot. Also called a 'stem band'.

Keel Blocks. Strong and adjustable erections along centre line of bottom of dry dock, or building slip, on which keel of a vessel rests and so allows workmen to pass underneath the vessel.

Keeler. Man employed on a keel (craft). 2. Shallow tub that holds material for caulking seams in a vessel.

Keel Hauling. Olden punishment in which an offender was lowered from one yard arm and hauled under the keel by another halliard from the opposite yard arm.

Keelson. Internal keel fitted immediately above the main keel.

Keel Staple. Large copper staple fastening false keel to main keel in wooden ship.

Keep Her Away. Injunction to helmsman to keep ship's head from coming too close to wind.

Keep Her So. Order to helmsman to keep ship's head on her heading when the order was given.

Keep the Luff. Order to helmsman to keep ship's head closely to the wind.

Kelp. Large seaweed.

Kelpie. Fabulous spirit, generally in the form of horse, supposed to haunt ferries and fords.

Kelter. Good order and readiness.

Kelvin. Unit of absolute temperature, freezing point of water 273K, boiling point of water 373K. The length of each unit being the same as on the Celsius scale.

Kelvin Deflector. *See* 'Deflector'.

Kelvin Sounding Machine. Apparatus by which a sinker can be dropped to sea bottom at end of a wire, taking with it a glass tube sealed at upper end. Inside of tube is coated with a chromate preparation which, as water is forced into tube, changes into a chloride through action of salt in the water. When sinker is hauled up, the line of demarcation between chromate and chloride is a measure of water pressure at seabed. This pressure is an indication of depth.

Kelvin Tide-Prediction Machine. Apparatus by which tidal states and times, at any given place, can be determined mechanically when the machine has been set to conform with the harmonic tidal constants at the place.

Kelway Electric Log. Early type of submerged log. Rotator under bottom of ship sent electric impulses to an inboard indicator.

Kempstock. Old name for a capstan.

Kennet. Old name for a large cleat.

Kenne. 'Kenning.'

Kennelly-Heaviside Layer. Atmospheric layer in stratosphere. Reflects radio waves at night.

Kenning. Sixteenth-century sterm for a sea distance at which high land could be observed from a ship. Varied between 14 and 22 miles according to average atmospheric conditions in a given area.

Kentledge. Permanent pig iron ballast specially shaped and placed along each side of keelson. Name is sometimes given to any iron ballast.

Kepler's Laws of Planetary Motion. 1. Every planet moves in an ellipse having Sun at one of its foci. 2. Radius vector of any planet sweeps through equal areas in equal times. 3. Squares of periodic times of planets are proportional to cubes of their mean distances from Sun.

Ketch. Sailing vessel having fore and aft rig on each of two masts. Mainmast carries foresails, jib, mainsail. Mizen carries mizensail. Mizenmast is stepped about one-fifth of length of ship from aft.

Kevel. Large bitt, or cleat, used for belaying large-sized ropes. 2. Palm of an anchor.

Kevel Head. Projection of rib timber above gunwale when shaped for use as a kevel.

Kevler. A costly material with high impact resistance.

Kew Pattern Barometer. Mercury barometer specially designed for use at sea. Is mounted in gimbals and has a constricted tube to minimise 'pumping' in a seaway.

Key. A reef or low island.

Key of Keelson. Fictitious article for which greenhorns at sea are sometimes sent.

Kicking Strap. A tackle placed between boom and deck to prevent the boom rising.

Kid. Small, shallow wooden tub, usually circular in shape.

Killer Whale. Savage and bloodthirsty whale of dolphin family. They haunt sealing-grounds and kill and devour sperm whales.

Killick. Nautical name for an anchor. Originally, was a stone used as an anchor.

Kinetic Energy. Energy due to motion.

King Post. Alternative name for a 'Samson Post'.

King's Harbour Master. Officer of R.N. appointed as harbour master in a dockyard port under Dockyard Port Regulations, 1865.

King's or Queen's Hard Bargain. R.N. term for an inefficient rating.

King's Letter Boys. Certain boys who went to sea in R.N., between 1676 and 1728, under a scheme introduced by Charles II.

King Spoke. Marked 'midship' spoke of a steering-wheel. Acts as an indicator to helmsman.

King's or Queen's Regulations and Admiralty Instructions. Rules, regulations and orders by which the Royal Navy is regulated and governed.

Kink. Short bend in a rope, due to twist or turns, that prevents free running. Causes severe strain if under tension.

Kippage. Former name for the equipment (equipage) of a vessel, and included the personnel.

Kisbie Lifebuoy. Annular life-buoy made of cork, covered with canvas and fitted with rope beckets.

Kit. Seaman's outfit of clothes. 2. A set of tools.

Kit-bag. Canvas bag in which a seaman's clothes are stowed.

Kites. Fine-weather sails set above royals.

Knarr. Scandinavian large open boat used chiefly in coastwise trading in and around 10th century.

Knee. Wood grown, or shaped, to a right-angled form. Used for connecting and supporting two members perpendicular to one another. 2. Steel or iron plates, roughly triangular, used for above purpose.

Knee Timber. Wooden knee.

Knight Heads. Heads of two strong timbers, usually of oak, that came up on either side of stem and on either side of bowsprit, which they supported. Also called 'Bollard Timbers'.

Knittles. 'Nettles.'

Knot. Nautical unit of velocity representing a speed of 6080 ft. per hour, 101·3 ft. per minute, 1·69 ft. per second. Nearly equal to ·5 metres per second. One metre per second=1·944 knots. Is the only unit of velocity in existence. Name is derived from the knots in the common log line. 2. Manipulation of a rope so that a knob is formed in it. The exception to this is a reef knot, which is made with two ropes and is, properly, a 'bend'.

Knots per Hour. An expression never used by careful seamen, being tautological and illogical.

Knuckle. Outer side of a sharp bend in a jetty or breakwater. An acute angle in certain wooden timbers of a vessel.

Knuckle Timber. One of the top timbers, of angular form, in fore body of a wooden ship, where there is a sharp change in form of the body.

Koff. Former two-masted Dutch sailing vessel having spritsail on each mast.

Kraken. Fabulous sea monster supposed to have been seen off coasts of America and Norway. Sometimes mistaken for an island.

Krang. Carcase of a whale after all blubber has been removed.

Krennels. Small cringles for bowline bridles, on a square sail.

Kudastre. Two-masted sailing craft of China Seas. About 50 ft. in length; fitted with outrigger.

Kuro Siwo. Ocean current running ENE-ward from SE coast of Japan towards American coast. Rate and direction vary with prevailing winds.

Kuzi. Arabic name for SW monsoon on E coast of Africa.

Kynaston's Apparatus. Early form (1880) of quick-release gear for boats lowered in a seaway. Principle was pretty much the same as that of the Robinson release gear.

L

Label Clause. Inserted in policies of marine insurance covering bottled goods. Excludes claims for damaged or discoloured labels.

Labile. Term applied to atmosphere when lapse rate exceeds adiabatic lapse rate.

Labour. As applied to ship, is to roll and pitch heavily and slowly.

Labrador Current. Alternative name for 'Arctic Current'.

Labyrinth Packing. Invented by Sir Charles Parsons. Escape of steam is throttled by successive glands, each having less clearance than the preceding gland.

Laced Mainsail. Mainsail that is laced to main boom. First used in British waters by 'America' in 1851

Lacing. Running line by which a sail is laced to a gaff or boom, or to another sail. 2. Line by which a boat's canvas cover, or other canvas gear, is secured in place. 3. *Name formerly given to a support immediately abaft a figurehead.

Lade. Old form of 'Load'. 2. Deepest part of an estuary when caused by outflow of main stream.

Laden in Bulk. Said of a vessel carrying a bulk cargo in all holds.

Ladies' Ladder. Name applied to ratlines of rigging when they are closely spaced.

Lading. That which is loaded into a ship. The act of loading.

Lady of the Gunroom. Originally, a night watchman in the gunroom. Later, a marine responsible for care and cleanliness of gunroom.

Lady's Hole. Small compartment in which gunroom stores were kept.

Lag. Interval between cause and effect. Time taken by a registering instrument to adjust itself to a change in the value it is registering. A slowness in following up.

Lagan. Jettisoned goods that sink and are buoyed for subsequent recovery.

Lagging. Non-conducting coating of a boiler, cylinder, or other container in which transfer of heat must be prevented. 2. A falling behind; being late in occurrence or arrival. 3. Lagging of tide is an increase in the time interval between successive high waters. Roughly speaking, it occurs as tide increases from neap to springs.

Lagoon. Sheet of water connected with sea but nearly surrounded by land.

Lagoon Reef. Atoll surrounding a lagoon.

Laid Up in Ordinary. Said of a warship when paid off and under charge of master attendant of a dockyard.

Lambda. Greek letter (λ). Used as a symbol to denote the directive force of a magnetic needle, in a given position, as a proportion of the directive force it would have if entirely free to respond to terrestrial magnetism alone.

Lamp Trimmer. Rating responsible for the trimming and care of oil and candle-lighting arrangements.

Lanby. Large Automated Navigation Buoy. Increasingly used in place of a lightvessel.

Land Blink. Gloomy-yellow light over distant ice-covered land.

Land Breeze. Wind blowing seaward from land after sunset. Due to land temperature of atmosphere being below that of sea atmosphere. Sometimes applied to any off-shore wind.

Landfall. Land first sighted when approaching from seaward.

Landfast Ice. Ice that is fast to the land.

Landing. Overlap of strakes or plating.

Landing Account. Statement of goods landed at dock or wharf, and of charges for warehousing and storing.

Landing Craft. Vessel built for the purpose of landing men or materials on a beach. Very shallow draft forward, with bow door, and with engines aft.

Landing Order. Document authorising transference of goods from ship to shore.

Landing Strake. Second line of planking below gunwale.

Landlubber. Seaman's derogatory name for a landsman, or incompetent seaman.

Landmark. Shore object, sometimes especially erected, that assists seamen in identifying their position when in sight of it.

Lands. Overlaps in planking of a clincher-built boat.

Land Waiter. Customs officer attending a vessel that is discharging a cargo liable to duty.

Land Wind. An offshore wind.

Lane. Narrow waterway through ice.

Langrage. Former missile used for destroying rigging of enemy ships. Was a bundle of scrap iron, bolts, etc., and was fired from a gun.

Language Test. Examination of a seaman, engaged at a port within Home Trade limits, to ascertain that he has sufficient knowledge of English to understand all orders he may be given.

Lantern. Casing, with transparent sides, in which a light is carried.

Lanyard. Rope or cord used for securing or attaching.

Lap. Overlap of edge of one plate along the edge of another. 2. The cutting off of steam supply to a piston before end of stroke.

Lapse Rate. Amount by which temperature of atmosphere alters with increase of height. Usually about 0·6°C per 100 metres. Is positive if decreasing with height, negative if increasing.

Lapstrake. Alternative name for 'Clincher' build of boats.

Larboard. Opposite to starboard. Formerly in general use, but supplanted by 'Port' to avoid possible confusion due to similarity in sound.

Larbowlines. Nickname for men in port (larboard) watch.

Large. Said of a vessel sailing with wind abaft the beam but not right aft.

Laridae. One of the gull families. Are swimmers with slender beaks, lateral nostrils, long wing span. Hind toe is a spur, and is not connected to outer toes. Plumage is usually white with a certain amount of grey.

Larinae. True gulls. Somewhat similar to Laridae, but beak is wider and stouter. Wings are long and pointed; feet are very powerful.

Lascar. Native of east India employed as a seaman.

Lascar Agreement. Special and approved form of agreement under which lascars are engaged, carried and discharged by ships.

LASH (Lighter Aboard Ship). A ship specially constructed to carry loaded lighters or barges. These are floated on board in one port and floated out at the discharging port ready to be towed away.

Lashing. Rope used for securing anything in place, or for binding two objects together.

Lask. To sail large, with wind about four points abaft beam.

Laskets. Beckets along edge of a bonnet or drabbler, Used for attaching these sails to the sail above.

Lastage. Cargo, ballast, or anything loaded in a ship. 2. Toll or other duty levied on a cargo ship.

Latch. Lasket. 2. Cord clamping inboard end of a mackerel line.

Latchings. Laskets.

Lateen Rig. Sailing rig embodying a lateen sail.

Lateen Sail. Triangular sail with a vertical leech and inclined luff. Is laced to a yard and suspended at about mid-distance along yard.

Lateen Yard. Long yard to which luff of a lateen sail is laced.

Latent Heat. Amount of heat absorbed and retained by a substance, or body, when changing from a solid to a liquid; or from a liquid to a gas.

Lateral Resistance. Resistance to sideway movement set up by underwater body of a vessel.

Latitude. Angular distance from Equator. Measured by arc of meridian intercepted by Equator and parallel of latitude passing through a given point. *See* 'Celestial Latitude'.

Lattern Sail. 'Lateen Sail.'

Launch. To move a vessel into water so that she becomes waterborne. 2. To move a longitudinal object in the direction of its length. 3. Large open or half-decked boat, particularly a large diagonally-built rowing- and sailing-boat used in R.N.

Launching Ways. Large, rectangular timbers, or plating, down which slides the cradle supporting a newly-built vessel.

Laws of Oleron. Early shipping laws—about 13th century—brought into England by Richard I. They form the basis of most European laws regarding shipping.

Laws of Storms. Fundamental facts about the formation and phases of cyclonic storms.

Lay. Of rope is direction—right or left—that the strands trend when viewed along the rope. 2. Tension put into rope when laying it up. *See* 'Hard Laid', 'Soft Laid'.

Lay Aboard. To come alongside.

Lay a Hold. To put down the helm and come close to the wind.

Lay Along. To list; to lean over.

Lay Days. Days allowed by charter party for loading and/or discharging cargo.

Lay In. Order given to men on foot ropes of a yard when they are to come in to the mast.

Laying Hook. One of the hooks in a rope-making machine. End of strand is attached to it when laying up the rope.

Laying on Oars. Holding oars at right angles to fore and aft line of boat with blades horizontal and parallel to surface of water. Is used also as a sarcastic term for idling, or not pulling one's weight.

Laying Up Returns. Return of part of premium paid when an insured vessel has been laid up for 30 (sometimes 15) consecutive days.

Lay Out. Order to men at mast to extend themselves at intervals along a yard. 2. To keep a vessel at a certain place until a specified time has elapsed.

Lay the Course. To keep a ship's head on a required course.

Lay the Land. To cause the land to sink below horizon by sailing away from it.

Lay Up. To put torsion in yarns and strands so that they form rope or cordage. 2. To take a ship out of service and moor her in a dock or harbour.

Lazarette, Lazaretto. Storeroom containing provisions of a ship. 2. Ship or building in which persons in quarantine are segregated.

Lazy Guy. Guy that consists of a single rope and is used for moving or temporarily securing, a boom or derrick when little weight is involved.

Lazy Painter. Additional painter that is of smaller size than proper painter. Used when mooring for a short time and no great strain is anticipated.

Leach. Leech of a sail.

Lead (Leed). Direction in which a rope goes, or is guided, by blocks, sheaves, fairleads, cleats, etc. 2. Open-water channel between ice-sheets. 3. Arrangement of a slide valve so that some steam is admitted to exhaust side of piston a little before end of stroke. This cushions end of stroke, and ensures adequate steam for the commencement of return stroke. 4. Setting of crank of one engine a certain distance in advance of another.

Lead (Led). Shaped mass of lead—weighing 10–14 lb.—used with a marked line when ascertaining depth of water or nature of sea bottom.

Lead Ballast. Used in sailing yachts to keep centre of gravity as low as necessary. Previous to 1846, iron ballast was used. After 1876, the lead was put into the keel.

Leading Block. Block used for altering the direction of a rope led through it.

Leading Lights. Two or more lights that identify a leading line when they are in transit.

Leading Line. Line passing through two or more clearly-defined charted objects, and along which a vessel can approach safely.

Leading Marks. Objects that identify a leading line when in transit.

Leading Part. That part of a tackle fall passing through the blocks. It is, therefore, all the rope that passes between the blocks except that part that is the standing part at the time.

Leading Wind. Any wind that is abaft the beam.

Lead Line. Special line used with hand lead. Usually about 30 fathoms of 1½-inch untarred hemp. Marked with leather at 2 and 3 fathoms, white bunting at 5 and 15, red bunting at 7 and 17, blue bunting at 13, leather with circular hole at 10, two knots at 20 fathoms. If marked in metres: 1 & 11m—1 strip of leather; 2 & 12m—2 strips of leather; 3 & 13m—blue bunting; 4 & 14m—green and white bunting; 5 & 15m—white bunting; 6 & 16m—green bunting; 7 & 17m—red bunting; 8 & 18m—yellow bunting; 9 & 19m—red and white bunting; 10m—leather with a hole in it; 20m—leather with a hole in it and 2 strips of leather. *See* 'Deep Sea Lead Line'.

Lead Mine. Nickname given to 'plank on edge' type of yacht, on account of the heavy lead keel necessary for stability.

Leadsman. Seaman engaged in taking soundings with hand lead and line.

League. Measure of distance three miles in length. One-twentieth of a degree of latitude.

Leakage. That which has escaped by leaking. 2. Allowance made for loss due to leaking of contents of casks, barrels, etc.

Leak Stopper. Device for stopping a small leak, particularly when due to loss of a rivet, by passing the stopper through the hole and clamping it to ship's plating by nut or screw. End passed outboard has a hinged bar that drops athwart hole, when passed through, so anchoring outboard end on ship's plating.

Ledge. Ridge of rock, or shelf-like projection of rock, below water. 2. Additional support, for decks, that goes athwartships between beams.

Lee. Area sheltered from the wind. Pertaining to that quarter towards which the wind is blowing.

Lee Board. Vertical wooden board, pivoted in forward edge, attached to side of flat-bottomed sailing craft and lowered into water to reduce leeway.

Lee Bowing. Yacht racing manoeuvre when on a wind. Giving way yacht goes about on lee bow of another, thus giving a back wind to the other.

Leech. Side edge of a square sail, after edge of a fore and aft sail.

Leech-line. Halliard passing downwards from block at yard arm to leech of a square sail. Used for lifting sail when reefing or furling it.

Leech Rope. Boltrope on side of a square sail.

Lee Fange. Thwartship iron rail along which a sheet block of a fore and aft sail can move when tacking. 2. Rope going from deck and through cringle of a sail so that sail can be hauled in when lacing or unlacing a bonnet.

Lee Gauge. Position to leeward, as relative to another vessel.

Lee Helm. Tiller to leeward to keep vessel's head up to wind.

Lee Helmsman. Assistant helmsman, when required, in a sailing ship: the proper helmsman being at weather side of wheel.

'Lee-ho.' A warning that the helm has been put down and that the vessel is coming up into the wind in order to go about.

Lee Lurch. Heavy roll to leeward with a beam wind.

Lee Shore. Shore that is to leeward of a vessel.

Lee Side. That side of a ship, or object, that is sheltered from the wind.

Lee Tide. Tidal flow that goes in same direction as prevailing wind.

Leeward. The area on the lee side of an observer, or named object.

Leewardly. Said of a vessel that makes excessive leeway.

Leeway. Distance a vessel is forced to leeward of her course by action of wind. 2. Angle between ship's projected course and her track through the water.

Left-Handed. Said of ropes in which the strands trend to the left as they go away from an observer.

Leg. One part of a rope that is seized on the bight. 2. One tack when beating to windward under sail.

Legal Day. For payment of seamen, begins and ends at 00 hours.

Legal Wharf. Wharf legalised by Act of Parliament, or approved by commission from Court of Exchequer.

Leg of Mutton Sail. Triangular mainsail used in boats and yachts. Lateen sail.

Legs. Strong pieces of timber placed vertically at the sides of a vessel to keep her upright when she takes the ground on a falling tide.

Lembus. Light, fast war vessel of the Romans.

Lend a Hand. To assist.

Length. Fore and aft dimension of a ship. Length between perpendiculars is measured from fore side of stem to after side of sternpost on summer load water line.

Length of Wave. Usually measured as the distance between two successive crests, which is also the distance between lowest point of two successive troughs. Expressed in feet.

Lenticular. Cloud form in which upper and lower edges are convex, thus resembling a lens, or a lentil seed.

Leo (Lat.=Lion). Constellation situated between R.A.s 09 h 20 m and 11 h 50 m; Dec. 0° to 38°N. Has several bright stars: Regulus, or Cor Leonis, Denebola, Algeiba, Zosma. 2. Fifth sign of Zodiac, extending from 120° to 150° celestial longitude. Sun is in this sign from July 22 to August 23, about.

Leonid Meteors. Meteoric shower visible in Leo about middle of November. Due to break up of a comet.

Let Draw. Order given when it is required that weather fore sheet of head sail of a craft tacking shall be released, so that sail can be controlled by lee sheet.

Let Go. Of an anchor. To let it drop in the water.

Let Fall. Order given when a square sail, that has been loosed, is to be dropped so that it can be sheeted home.

Let Fly. Order to release sheets fully. Given as a salute, or in a heavy gust of wind, or other emergency.

Letter of Credit. Document, addressed to certain bankers, or firms, and authorising them to allow stated persons or person to draw money, up to a specified amount, against the credit of the bank or firm issuing the letter.

Letter of Hypothecation. Written authority given to a lender of money and empowering him to sell goods, purchased with money advanced by him, if the undertaking to replay him be not fulfilled.

Letter of Indemnity. Document given by one person to another whereby the person issuing the letter renounces any claim he may have in specified circumstances.

Letters of Marque and Countermarque. Written authority, from a sovereign state, to attack enemy ships in retaliation for a loss suffered, and to resist attack from enemy ships.

Letters of Mart and Countermart. 'Letters of Marque and Countermarque.'

Levanter. Easterly wind in Straits of Gibraltar during March, and from July to October.

Leveche. Hot S'ly wind on SE coast of Spain. Precedes a depression and is often accompanied by dust.

Level Lines. Lines representing boundaries of horizontal sections of a ship made by planes parallel to keel.

Leviathan. Biblical name for a marine monster. Name has been given to the Egyptian crocodile, to a large Mediterranean cetacean, and to a sea serpent.

Liberty Man. R.N. seaman when on leave.

Liberty to Call. Inserted in charter party, or other document, when a vessel has permission to call at intermediate port or ports in circumstances specified.

Libra. (Lat.=Balances, Scales.) Constellation between R.A.s 14 h 55 m and 15 h 45 m; Dec. 9°S to 25°S. Has two bright stars: Kiffa Australis and Zubenelg. 2. Sixth sign of Zodiac, extending from 180° to 210° celestial longitude. Sun is in this sign from September 23 till October 23.

Liberation. A slight nodding of Moon's axis, together with a slight variation in her revolution, which result in her showing a little more than the area we see normally; 41 per cent being visible at all times, 59 per cent being visible at one time or another.

Liberation in Latitude. Due to Moon's axis being inclined to Equinoctial her north pole is inclined towards Earth at one point in her orbit, and away from it at the opposite orbital point.

Liberation in Longitude. Moon shows one hemisphere only towards Earth, but as her speed in orbit is not uniform she shows a little of the other hemisphere when her angular velocity around Earth is greater or less than her rotational speed.

Liburnian. Roman warship with a ram of 1st century. Name derived from the Liburnians of Dalmatia.

Licensed Pilot. Pilot duly licensed by the pilotage authority of a port or district.

Lie. To remain in a particular place or position.

Lie Along. To heel over because of wind.

Lie Along the Land. To sail parallel to the coast.

Lie By. To remain nearly alongside another vessel.

Lien. Legal right to retain possession of another person's goods until certain claims have been satisfied.

Lie Over. To heel over.

Lie To. To stop a ship and lie with wind nearly ahead.

Lifebelt. Buoyant belt or jacket worn to support a person when in water. Statutory requirements are that it shall be capable of supporting 16½ lb. of iron in fresh water for 24 hours.

Lifeboat Certificate. Issue by Board of Trade to a seaman who has passed an examination proving his competence to man and handle a lifeboat of a seagoing ship.

Lifeboats. Boats compulsorily carried in a ship for preservation of crew and passengers in the event of foundering or wreck. 2. Specially designed, self-righting, and unsinkable boat that is maintained on coasts of maritime nations for rescue of persons from vessels wrecked in its vicinity.

Lifeboatman. One who mans a shore-based lifeboat. 2. 'Certificated Lifeboatman.'

'Lifeboat Service.' Saving, or attempted saving, of vessels, or of life and property, on board vessels wrecked, aground, sunk, or in danger of being wrecked, sunk, or grounded.

Lifebuoy. Specially designed portable float for throwing overboard to sustain a person in the water until he can be taken into a boat or ship. Standard requirements are that it must be capable of floating 32 lb. of iron, in fresh water, for 24 hours.

Lifejacket. A jacket made buoyant by 35 oz. of kapok or other equally buoyant material, or by being inflated by air, and constructed so that an unconscious wearer will float with his face above water. *See* Buoyancy Aid.

Lifeline. Rope rigged or attached for purposes of security or rescue. 2. Line attached to a man working overside, and attended by a man inboard. 3. Rope from head of davit to a boat in the water and alongside, for security of men in boat during hoisting and lowering. 4. Line stretched horizontally between mast and lift of yard when manning yards. 5. Line stretched along deck in heavy weather. 6. Line attached to a buoy floated down to a man in the water.

Life-Saving Apparatus. Gear placed at certain positions ashore for rescue of personnel shipwrecked in the vicinity. Includes rockets and lines, lifelines, breeches buoy, 'triangle' (tripod), hawsers, whips, small gear, and a vehicle for transporting these to a position near to wreck.

Life-Saving Appliances. All boats, rafts, buoys, jackets, line-throwing apparatus, and other appliances and stores carried for life-saving purposes.

Life-Saving Rocket. Pyrotechnic missile fired from shore to pass over a stranded vessel and carry a line for establishing communication between ship and shore.

Lifting Gear. Derrick and cranes, with all their furniture and attachments, used when lifting and lowering weights.

Lifting Screws. Screw propellers that were formerly carried in ships carrying sails and engines. When under sail alone, propeller was lifted, by tackles, into a specially-built recess in counter—the rail end shaft being withdrawn. See Banjo Frame.

Lifts. Ropes from mast to arms of a yard, and used for supporting, canting, and squaring the yard.

Ligan. 'Lagan.'

Light. Opening in deck or sides of a vessel for admitting light. 2. Established navigational beacon light. 3. State of a vessel when without cargo, or when not submerged to her load line. 4. To assist in carrying a fall or rope in a desired direction. 'Light to!'

Light Airs. Intermittent wind that does not exceed three knots.

Light Along. To lift or carry a rope in the direction that it lies.

Light Bill. Receipt for light dues paid.

Light Boat. Unattended vessel moored in a fixed position to emit a light as a navigational aid or warning.

Light Breeze. Wind with velocity between four and six knots. Force 2 Beaufort Scale.

Light Draught. State of a vessel when her submerged volume is least. Technically, her draught when she has no cargo but her bunkers are full, stores complete, and boilers filled to working level.

Light Dues. Money chargeable on a vessel as part payment of cost of maintaining lighthouses, light vessels, and similar navigational aids.

Lightening Hole. Opening in a member, or fitting, when arising from removal of unnecessary material to reduce weight.

Lighter. Craft of barge type and without means of propulsion. Used for transport of goods to and from ships. Formerly used for taking goods out of a vessel to lighten her, and so allow her to cross a bar.

Lighterage. Loading or unloading of a lighter. 2. Carriage of goods in a lighter. 3. Charge made for loading or unloading into a lighter.

Light Hand. Youthful but smart seaman.

Light-Handed. When applied to crew, means 'Short-handed'.

Lightning. Brilliant and momentary light due to discharge of atmospheric electricity from cloud to earth, or from cloud to cloud.

Lightning Conductor. Protective strip of copper, led from masthead to sea, for carrying away atmospheric electrical discharges. Essential in wooden vessels and in vessels with wooden topmasts.

Light Port. Scuttle or porthole fitted with glass.

Light Sector. That part of a circle in which a certain phase of a navigational beacon light is observable.

Lightship. Vessel, having its own means of propulsion, moored in a particular position and exhibiting a light and daymark to mark a navigational danger and to be a navigational aid.

Light Ship. Cargo vessel when not carrying cargo.

Lightvessel. Similar to a lightship, but having no means of propulsion.

Light Year. One of the units of astronomical distance. Distance that light travels in one year. Value is 5,878,310,400,000 miles.

Ligsam. Old name for 'Lagan'.

Limb. Edge of disc of a heavenly body, particularly Sun or Moon. 2. Graduated arc of sextant or quadrant.

Limber Boards. Removable boards forming covers of limbers.

Limber Chain. Long length of chain rove through limber holes for clearing them.

Limber Holes. Holes in floor timbers, or tank side-brackets, through which bilge water flows to pump suction.

Limber Rope. Rope rove through limber holes for clearing them.

Limbers. Channel formed by tank side-plating and skin of ship, into which any water in hold will run. In wooden ships, was a channel alongside keelson on either side; floor timbers being pierced on either side.

Limber Strake. Strake next to keelson in a wood-built ship.

Lime Juice. Antiscorbutic carried in British ships and issued when on salt provisions, or risk of scurvy exists.

Lime Juicer. Nickname given to British ships by U.S. seamen, when British law first required lime juice should be carried and issued. Was used by British seamen as a nickname for a foreign-going vessel.

Limitation Clause. Sometimes inserted in a bill of lading to fix an upper limit to amount claimable for loss of an item of cargo.

Limitation of Liability. The limiting of the amount that can be claimed from a shipowner for loss of goods and/or life when due to a casualty to ship that was not due to fault or privity of shipowner. Amount is limited to £15 per ton for loss of life and goods, £8 per ton if no loss of life. Tonnage is based on registered tonnage plus engine-room space. 2. Liability of a British pilotage authority for damage done through fault or default of a licensed pilot is limited to £100 multiplied by the number of pilots holding licences from the authority.

Line. A light rope or hawser. Small rope used for a specific purpose. 2. Equator. 3. Number of ships in such formation that a straight line passes through them. 4. Delineation of ship form in a vertical or horizontal direction.

Line Fisher. Fishing vessel using line or lines.

Line of Battle Ship. Name formerly given to a heavily-armed warship fit to take a place in a line of battle.

Line of Bearing. Straight line through a ship or drawn on a chart, passing through positions at which an observed object would have the same bearing, either by compass or relatively.

Line of Collimation. That line, in an optical instrument, that passes through centre of object glass and cross wires.

Line of No Dip. Alternative name for magnetic equator. 'Aclinic Line.'

Line of Position. Position line. Line, on a chart, drawn through all positions at which ship may be situated. May be a line of bearing, or arc of a circle of equal altitude.

Line of Soundings. Series of soundings, with course and distances sailed between them, laid off to scale of chart in an endeavour to ascertain ship's position. 2. Series of soundings made along a line, and at stated intervals, when surveying.

Liner. Vessel sailing regularly between specified ports. 2. Former name for a line of battle ship. 3. A line fishing vessel. 4. Packing piece placed between parts to adjust them. 5. Thin metallic sleeve in a cylinder, which is renewed when worn.

Line Squall. Squall that travels along a line, but has no great breadth—probably a mile or so.

Line-Throwing Appliances. Guns, rockets, and lines used by ships to establish communication when necessary. Lines are usually 120 fathoms in length; rocket can carry line 200 yards in calm weather.

Link Block. Metal block at end of slide-valve spindle. Carries slippers in which radius link moves when reversing engine.

Linking Up. Movement of link reversing gear so that slide-valve cuts off earlier than normal.

Link Motion. Valve gear for reversing a reciprocating engine, and for regulating cut off of steam to cylinder. Consists of two rods, radial link, and two eccentric sheaves. Invented by George Stephenson.

Link Worming. Worming of hemp cables with small chain, to reduce chafe.

Lipper. Small sea that rises just above bows or gunwale.

Liquid Compass. Magnetic compass mounted in a bowl filled with a liquid having a very low freezing point. Weight on pivot is reduced, and card is steadier in lively vessels when in a seaway.

Liquid Fuel. 'Oil Fuel.'

List. Transverse inclination of a vessel.

Listing. The operation by which a vessel is inclined transversely. 2. Inclining transversely.

Little One Bell. R.N. name for one stroke on ship's bell after changing a night watch. Is a signal for the watch to muster and be checked.

Littoral. Sea area between a coast and the 100-fathom line.

Liverpool Hook. Hook, in end of cargo runner, having bill of hook curved inward, and a downward inclined projection above the bill. Inward curving prevents accidental unhooking; inclined projection prevents hook lifting underside of beam.

Liverpool Pantiles. Nickname for ships' biscuit.

Lizard. Rope or wire pendant with a round thimble at unattached end. Used as a fairleader, or for the attachment of a boat's painter.

Lloyd's. An international insurance market and world centre for shipping intelligence which originated in the 17th-century coffee house of Edward Lloyd in London. Incorporated by Act of Parliament in 1871, Lloyd's was originally concerned exclusively with marine insurance but nowadays individual underwriters accept almost every type of risk in the huge Underwriting Room in Lloyd's New Building, Lime Street, London, with annual premiums totalling over £360m. Insurances are placed through the 220 firms of Lloyd's brokers. The Corporation of Lloyd's does not itself transact business but provides the premises and many other services. Lloyd's Agents throughout the world, channel information to the Corporation of Lloyd's and these reports are published in many forms, including *Lloyd's List* (Lloyd's own, and London's oldest daily newspaper) and *Lloyd's Shipping Index* (a daily publication which lists the movements of some 16,000 ocean-going merchant vessels).

Lloyd's Agents. Representatives whose duties are to protect underwriters from fraud, negligence, needless expense, or mismanagement in the treatment of insured property that is in peril. They have a wealth of local and technical knowledge which they place at a Master's disposal; but they do not interfere with the Master, or relieve him of his responsibilities.

Lloyd's Bond. Stereotyped form of Average Bond approved and issued by Lloyds.

'Lloyd's List.' Daily paper reporting movements of ships, rates of exchange, and other information of value to those interested in shipping matters.

Lloyd's Numerals. Numerical code by which appropriate scantlings of a proposed vessel can be derived from intended dimensions.

Lloyd's Policy. First printed 1779, and has remained the standard form since that date. All marine policies are based upon it.

Lloyd's Register of Shipping. The oldest and largest ship classification society, established in 1760. An independent authority which publishes technical rules for the construction and maintenance of ships. Employs 1300 exclusive surveyors stationed all round the world and classifies nearly 40 per cent of the world's merchant tonnage. Authorised to assign freeboards on behalf of some 50 governments and also carries out other statutory surveys in accordance with the International Convention for the Safety of Life at Sea. The Register Book, published annually with monthly supplements, describes every known merchant ship in the world of 100 tons gross and above.

Lloyd's Signal Stations. Established and maintained all over the world for transmitting and receiving maritime information in one universal code.

Load. To put cargo into a vessel. 2. 'Load' of timber is a measurement of 50 cu. ft. of undressed wood, 40 cu. ft. of dressed wood.

Load Draught. Vertical distance from lowest part of keel to load water line.

Loading Port Survey. Inspection of a ship, particularly one loading refrigerated cargo of meat, before loading.

Load Lines. Marks cut into ship's side plating and painted. They indicate maximum draughts to which vessel may be loaded in specified circumstances.

Load Star. Star used as a guide when steering. 2. Pole Star.

Load Stone. Magnetic oxide of iron, which is a natural magnet.

Load Waterline. Former name for 'Load Line'.

Loblolly Boy.* Former name for an assistant to ship's surgeon. His duties included mixing ointments and medicines.

Lobscouse. Nautical stew made with preserved meat and vegetables.

Local Attraction. Former name for deviation of compass. Now confined to deviation due to magnetic attraction outside ship.

Local Load Line. Load line assigned to a vessel not trading outside the country of the assigning authority.

Local Load Line Ships. Those vessels to which a Local Load Line Certificate can be given. Must be less than 150 tons gross if carrying goods or passengers.

Local Marine Boards. Bodies introduced in British ports to ensure the fulfilment of requirements of Merchant Shipping Act, 1895. Were responsible for Mercantile Marine Officers' Examinations for certificates of competency, etc. Most of their functions have been taken over by the Department of Trade and Industry.

Local Time. Time kept in a particular port or country.

Lock. Artificial enclosure of water in which a vessel can be floated from one level to another.

Locker. Chest, box, cupboard or compartment in which gear may be stowed. Can usually be locked, but chain locker is one exception.

Lock Gates. Pair of massive hinged doors at each end of a lock.

Locking Bars. Iron strips lying athwart a covered hatch. Can be padlocked to coamings when required.

Locking Pintle. One of pintles of a hinged rudder. Has a collar on protruding lower end, to prevent accidental unshipment of rudder.

Lode Star. 'Load Star.'

Lode Stone. 'Load Stone.'

Lodging Knee. Knee fastened in horizontal plane with its head, or platform, secured to side of beam.

Loft Template Method. System of shipbuilding in which certain parts of shell plating are marked off and punched from data obtained from scrieve board body plan.

Log. Instrument or apparatus for ascertaining ship's speed through water and/or distance run. 2. Log book. 3. Abbreviation for 'Logarithm'.

Logarithm. Exponent of the power to which a fixed number called the 'base', must be raised to produce a given number. Base of common logarithm is 10. Fractional part of the exponent is termed 'mantissa'.

Log Board. Hinged pair of boards on which log readings, alterations of course, and other happenings, were entered in chalk during the watch. Superseded by 'Deck', 'Scrap', or 'Rough' Log.

Log Book. Book in which events connected with the ship are entered. Several may be kept, the principal being Official Log, Deck Log, Mate's Log, Engine-room Log, Wireless Log.

Log Chip. Segmental piece of wood, ballasted along curved edge, attached to log line to keep it stretched when measuring ship's speed through water.

Log Error. Difference between indication of a mechanical log and the actual distance travelled through the water. Always expressed as a percentage of the log indication.

Loggerhead. Bollard, in a whale boat, for snubbing harpoon line. 2. Spherical piece of iron on long handle. Heated and used for melting pitch.

Logging. Entering in a log book. 2. Punishment entailing the entry of man's name, offence and punishment in the official log book.

Log Glass. Sand glass measuring interval of about half or quarter minute; 14 seconds and 28 seconds being common. Used for timing the line run out when heaving the log.

Log Line. Line attached to a log when streamed. Line used with towed log is non-kinkable and braided. Line used with ship log is small and specially made so that it will not stretch unduly.

Log Line Splice. Splice put in olden log line. End of one part was spliced some little distance along other part; end of other part being laid around first part and then spliced. Sometimes called a 'Water Splice'.

Log Oil. Specially-prepared oil for lubricating mechanical logs.

Log Reel. Reel having extensions to the axle on which it turns, these extensions being used as handles when streaming the log.

Log Ship. 'Log Chip.'

Log Slate. Slate used for same purpose as 'Log Board'.

London Conference Rules of Affreightment, 1893. Six rules that can be inserted in contracts of affreightment to clarify shipowner's responsibilities and immunities.

Longboat. Formerly, longest and largest boat carried by a merchant ship. Length between 32 and 40 ft., beam 8 to 10 ft., carvelbuilt and flat floored.

Long Gasket. Length of small rope used at sea for securing a sail to yard when furled.

Long Glass. Sand glass used with ship log for speeds up to five knots. Runs down in 28 or 30 seconds. 2. A telescope.

Longitude. Intercepted arc of Equator, or angle at Pole, between the prime meridian and the meridian passing through a named position.

Longitude Star. Star whose position has been accurately determined and tabulated, so that it can be used for ascertaining longitude.

Longitudinal. Pertaining to longitude, or length. Applied to any fore and aft member of a ship's structure.

Longitudinal Bulkhead. Bulkhead going fore and aft in a vessel.

Longitudinal Framing. Framing, of a vessel's hull, that goes fore and aft instead of transversely.

Longitudinal Stress. Stress that tends to deform the longitudinal form of a vessel or member.

Long Jaw. Said of a rope when the cantlines of strands lie at an angle that is appreciably less than 45° from the run of the rope.

Long Period Species. Tidal species that occur at intervals greatly exceeding a tidal day. The most common are those with 14 days and 19-year periods.

Long Period Variable. Star whose magnitude varies during a period between 50 days and two years or more. Majority have a period of about 300 days. Mira, in constellation Cetus, varies between magnitudes 3·5 and 9·0 in 350 days.

Longship. Norse warship c. 900 A.D. Rowed 40 to 50 oars and had one mast and square sail.

Longshore Man. Labourer on a wharf or dock side.

Long Splice. Splice that joins two ropes and can reeve through a block. Strand of each rope displaces a strand in the other, for a distance equal to about six times size of rope; end is then tucked. Remaining strand of each rope is half knotted to opposite strand.

Long Stay. Said of a cable of anchored vessel when amount of cable out is more than four times depth of water.

Long Tackle Block. Two sheaves, one above the other, in a long shell. Diameter of upper sheave is one-and-a-half times that of lower sheave. Used with a single block to form a purchase.

Long Timber. Single timber rising from cant timbers to top of second futtock.

Long Waisted. Said of a vessel having a long waist between poop and topgallant forecastle.

Loof.* That part of a ship that lies between the stem and the part of ship's side that is parallel to keel. Sometimes called 'bluff' of the bows.

Look Out. Man posted to keep a continuous look out, and to report anything sighted. 2. The duty performed by a look out man.

Loom. To appear in sight. 2. The reflection of a light in the sky when the light itself is hidden below the horizon. 3. Indistinct but enlarged appearance due to mist. 4. The end part of an oar forming a hand-grip when feathering and rowing. Sometimes defined as all that part of the oar that is inside the rowlock.

Looming. Appearing unusually large due to mist or fog.

Loop of Retrogression. Apparent loop in path of planet, occurring when motion changes from direct to retrograde, or vice versa as viewed from Earth.

Loose. To let go the ropes confining a furled sail.

Loose-footed. Said of a mainsail that is hauled out on a boom, but not laced to it. Also applied to a gaffsail or trysail that has no boom.

Lop. Small but quick-running sea.

Loran. A Long Range Aid to Navigation. A master and slave stations transmit synchronised signals which can be received by a special receiver on board ship. Since radio signals travel at a known speed, the difference in time at which the signals arrive at the ship can be converted into distance. Signals from two pairs of Loran stations can thus fix the position of a ship at ranges up to, and sometimes over, 6000 M.

Lorcha. Sailing craft of China Sea. European type of hull, Chinese mast and rigging, 60 to 80 ft. long.

L'Ordannance de la Marine. Important codification of law and practice of marine insurance compiled under supervision of M. Colbert in 1681. Still forms basis of modern procedure.

Lost Day. Day ignored when crossing Date Line from west longitude to east longitude.

Lost or Not Lost. Clause in a marine insurance policy covering interests insured after ship has sailed. Average is then payable even if ship was lost when policy was taken out, provided insurer was unaware of the loss.

Low. Area of low barometric pressure. Cyclonic depression. 2. Said of gyro compass when its indications are lower than they should be.

Lower Anchor. Stern anchor of a vessel moored in a river with head up river.

Lower and Dip. Order given when going about under sail in a boat with dipping lug. Sail is lowered a little, fore end of yard is dipped round mast to new lee side; tack is unhooked, passed abaft mast and rehooked; sail rehoisted.

Lower Boom. Originally, lower studdingsail boom. Now: boom projecting from ship's side when in harbour. Fitted with lizards and ladders for securing and manning boats.

Lower Deck. Deck next below middle deck in three-decked ship; next below main deck in frigate; next below upper deck in corvette. In R.N. term is used to denote all ratings, as differentiated from officers.

Lowerer. Man stationed to lower a boat at davits.

Lower Mast. Principal mast, carrying other masts fitted above it.

Lower Transit. Passage of a heavenly body across inferior meridian of an observer.

Low Water. Lowest level reached by a particular tide.

Low-Water Mark. Line along a coast, or beach, to which the sea recedes at low water of tide.

Lowitz Arc. Inverted arc between mock suns, and touching halo at upper edge and, sometimes, in vicinity of horizon.

Loxodrome. Curve, or surface of a sphere, cutting all secondary great circles of the sphere at a constant angle. Curve will continually approach a pole of sphere, but will not reach it in a finite distance.

Loxodromic Curve. Loxodrome. Rhumb line on surface of Earth.

Lubber. A clumsy and unskilled man.

Lubberland. Imaginary place of bliss where even lubbers are not a nuisance.

Lubber Line. Vertical line on fore side of inside of compass bowl, and in fore and aft line of ship. Compass reading in line with it is the direction of ship's head.

Lubber's Hole. Trap-door in flooring of top of a mast, and just above lower rigging. Forms an entry into top as alternative to going by futtock rigging.

Lubber's Point. Short projection aft from inside of compass bowl and in fore and aft line of ship. Has same purpose as 'Lubber Line'.

Lucas Sounding Machine. Special type of machine made for measuring depths up to 6000 fathoms. Modern type has motor for heaving up.

Luff. Weather edge of a fore and aft sail. 2. Weather side of any vessel: opposite to 'Lee'. 3. Coming closer to wind. 4. Broadest part of ship's bows. 5. A luff tackle.

Luff Hooks. Leech line leading from mainsail or foresail to chess trees. Has a hook in each end.

Luffing Puff. 'Free Puff.'

Luffing Rule. Yacht racing rule that allows a yacht that is being overtaken on her weather side to haul to windward until her stem is pointing abaft main shrouds of overtaking yacht.

Luff Purchase. 'Double Luff.'

Luff Tackle. Purchase consisting of single and double blocks. Standing part is spliced round neck of strop of single block, so allowing purchase to be hauled 'two blocks'.

Luff upon Luff. Purchase obtained by hooking block of one luff tackle to fall of another, so gaining power of 9 or 16.

Lug. Lugsail. 2. Extremity of shackle through which pin is passed.

Lugger. Vessel having one or two masts and a lugsail on each. May carry two or three jibs.

Lugsail. Four-sided sail on a yard slung at a point one-third of length of yard from forward. May be 'balanced', 'dipping' or 'standing'.

Lull. Temporary cessation of wind-force.

Lumper. Man employed in unloading ships in harbour, or in taking a ship from one port to another. Paid a 'lump' sum for services.

Lump Sum Charter. Hire of a ship for a stated period and for a stated sum of money.

Lump Sum Freight. Agreed sum to be paid for carriage of cargo, on discharge, whether part of cargo has been lost or not.

Lunar. Pertaining to Moon. Particularly applied to method of determining longitude by measurements of Moon's distance from other heavenly bodies.

Lunar Cycle. Period of 19 years, after which full and new Moons will occur on same day of same months. Also known as 'Cycle of Meton' or 'Metonic Cycle'.

Lunar Day. Interval between successive transits of Moon over any given meridian. Mean value is 24 h 54 m mean solar time.

Lunar Distance. Angular distance of Moon from one of 14 heavenly bodies formerly tabulated in Nautical Almanac. These bodies were Sun, four planets and nine selected stars.

Lunar Method. Determination of longitude by lunar distances.

Lunar Month. Interval between successive conjunctions of Moon and Sun. Mean value is 29 days 12 hours 44·05 minutes.

Lunar Observation. Altitude of Moon when taken for determining position.

Lunar Tables. Logarithmic tables for correcting apparent distance of Moon from a heavenly body for refraction and parallax.

Lunation. Period taken by Moon to go through all her phases. Mean value is 29 days 12hrs. 44 mins. 2·87 secs. 'Lunar Month.'

Lunisolar Constituent. Used in harmonic analysis of tides to represent the effect of variations in relative distance and declination of Sun and Moon.

Lunitidal Interval. Mean time interval between Moon's transit at a place and occurrence of next high water following.

Luper. Swivel hook used for twisting strands together when rope making.

Lurch. Sudden and long roll of a ship in a seaway.

Lustrum. Five-year period used when considering meteorological information extending over a considerable time.

Lutine Bell. Bell of H.M.S. *Lutine*, formerly French *La Lutine*. Vessel was wrecked near Terschelling in 1799 while carrying £1,400,000 in gold. Bell was recovered in 1859 and is now at Lloyd's in London. It is mounted inside Rostrum and is rung when news important to members is to be announced. It weighs 106 lb.

Lying To. Said of a vessel when stopped and lying near the wind in heavy weather.

Lyra. Constellation south of Draco and Cygnus. Has one navigational star, Vega.

M

Mackerel Sky. Cloud form in which cirrocumulus and alto-cumulus are arranged in bands in a blue sky.

Mac Ships. Merchant vessels converted into aircraft carriers during 1939–45 war. Name derived from initials of 'Merchant Aircraft Carrier'.

Made Bill. Bill of exchange drawn and endorsed in United Kingdom and payable abroad. Specifies name of person entitled to payment.

Made Block. Built block. Shell is made up of parts.

Made Eye. 'Flemish Eye.'

Made Mast. Built mast, as differentiated from mast made from a single tree.

Madrepore. A genus of coral.

Maestro. NW wind in Adriatic and Ionian seas and off coasts of Sardinia and Corsica.

Magazine. Compartment or structure in which explosives are kept. Name is given also to a warehouse.

Magellanic Clouds. Three masses of whitish nebulae near south pole of celestial concave.

Magnet. Body or substance having the property of attracting iron and steel. Usually iron or steel, but may be cobalt or nickel. Can have natural magnetism or electrically-induced magnetism.

Magnetic Amplitude. Angle of bearing measured from east or west point of a compass whose needle lies in magnetic meridian.

Magnetic Azimuth. Angle east or west of magnetic meridian and expressed in degrees.

Magnetic Bearing. Bearing of an object when referred to a compass whose needle lies in magnetic meridian.

Magnetic Compass. Compass whose directional property is due to its needles seeking the magnetic meridian.

Magnetic Compensation. Introduction of soft iron or magnets in the vicinity of a compass so that magnetic effects of iron or steel in ship or cargo can be neutralised or reduced.

Magnetic Dip. Vertical angle that a freely-balanced magnetic needle would make with the horizontal plane at a given place.

Magnetic Equator. Line, on surface of Earth, passing through all positions at which there is no dip of a freely-suspended magnetic needle. It forms a dividing line between Earth's red and blue magnetisms.

Magnetic Field. Area, around a magnet, in which its magnetism is manifest.

Magnetic Meridian. Line of magnetic force, between North and South magnetic poles, in which a freely-pivoted magnetic needle would lie if all disturbing forces were removed.

Magnetic Needle. Thin strip, needle, ring or cylinder of magnetised steel so pivoted that it is free to respond to Earth's magnetic field and seek and lie in the magnetic meridian.

Magnetic Poles. Of Earth: areas in high latitudes North and South at which a freely-suspended magnetic needle would remain vertical. One area is near Hudson Bay, the other in South Victoria Land. Each area is about 50 square miles in extent. 2. Of magnet: are those points, near its ends, at which its magnetic force is at a maximum.

Magnetic Storm. Disturbance of Earth's magnetic field lasting for a period that may be measured in hours or days. Is world wide in effect and possibly due to sunspots.

Magnetic Variation. Horizontal angle, at a given place, between the magnetic and geographic meridians. Is the angle that a freely suspended and undisturbed magnetic needle would make with the geographic meridian at the place.

Magnetic Zenith. That point in the heavens indicated by a line passing upwards through a freely-suspended magnetic needle.

Magnetism. Property which can be imparted to certain substances, so causing them to attract or repel other magnetised substances and to exert a force on conductors of electrical current in their vicinity. Ferrous metals, cobalt and nickel can receive magnetism. 2. The attractive or repulsive property of a magnet.

Magnetometer. Instrument for measuring intensity of Earth's magnetic force at any place.

Magneto-Striction. Contraction of a magnetic metal when subjected to magnetism. Particularly noticeable in nickel; this property being utilised in supersonic sounding apparatus.

Magnet Steels. Steels capable of being permanently magnetised. Usually alloyed with cobalt or tungsten.

Magnetron. The transmitter of a radar set.

Magnitude of Star. Its comparative brightness, as compared with other stars. May be 'relative Magnitude' or 'Absolute Magnitude'.

Mohammedan Calendar. Dates from flight of Mohammed from Mecca to Medina, July 16, 622 A.D. Has 12 lunar months of 29 or 30 days alternately. In every 30-year period there are 11 years of 354 days and 19 years of 355 days.

Maiden Voyage. First voyage made by a new ship after all trials have been carried out and she has been taken into service.

Maierform, Maier Form. Hull design that allows displaced water to flow aft by shortest route, reduces wave making to a minimum and keeps wetted area to small proportions. Forward and after deadwoods are largely removed. Pitching is reduced and directional stability is good.

Mail. Letters, posted papers and parcels shipped for conveyance. 2. Interwoven metal rings fastened to a stout backing material and used for smoothing the surface of newly-made ropes.

Mail Boat. Vessel carrying mails.

Mail Pendant. 'Royal Mail Pendant.'

Mail Room. Compartment in which mail is carried in a ship.

Mail Steamer. Steamer carrying mail.

Main. Ocean, or open sea. 2. Principal. 3. Main mast. 4. Mainsail.

Main and Foresail Rig. Has a fore staysail and a fore and aft mainsail that is loose-footed or stretched along a boom.

Main and Mizen Rig. Small boat rig having two masts, each carrying a four-sided fore and aft sail, main being larger than mizen.

Main Boom. Spar to which foot of a fore and aft mainsail is extended.

Main Breadth. Greatest distance between any two opposite frames.

Main Course. Sail attached to main yard of a square-rigged vessel.

Main Deck. Principal deck. Next below upper deck in five-deck ships.

Main Halyard. Rope by which a mainsail is hoisted.

Main Hatch. Principal hatch, usually the largest.

Main Hold. Space entered through main hatch. Principal hold.

Mainmast. Principal mast. Second mast in vessels having two or more masts, except when second mast is smaller—in which case forward mast is mainmast, after mast is mizen.

Main Pendants. Two short pieces of strong rope having thimbles in lower ends. Secured under upper ends of shrouds of main-mast to take hooks or shackles of main tackles.

Main Piece. Of rudder, is the vertical piece to which the steering-gear is attached. Of a wooden ship, is a piece stepped into stem head and notched for heel of bobstay piece.

Main Post. 'Stern Post.'

Main Rigging. Shrouds and ratlines on main lower mast.

Mainsail, Main Sail. Principal sail. In fore- and aft-rigged ships is sail on after side of mainmast; in square-rigged vessel is sail bent to main yard.

'Mainsail Haul.' Order given when tacking a square-rigged vessel. As ship's head comes to wind the main yard and all after yards are braced for new tack—yards on foremast are then aback to assist ship's head to pay off.

Main Tack. Rope or purchase by which weather clew of mainsail is hauled out and down.

Main Tackle. Purchase attached to main pendant when setting up main stays.

Main Top. Platform at head of mainmast. 2. Division of the watch in R.N.

Main Yard. Lower yard of a mainmast.

Make and Mend. Afternoon watch allotted to R.N. seaman for making and mending clothes. Afternoon watch in which no work is done.

Make Sail. To set sail, or to increase the sail already set.

Make the Land. Steer towards land so as to bring it into sight.

Make Water. To take in water through a leak.

Making. Said of tide when it is increasing from neap to spring tide.

Making Her Number. Said of a vessel when indicating her name by signal.

Making Iron. Rather large caulking iron used for final hardening up of oakum when caulking a seam.

Making Way. Moving ahead or astern through the water. *See* Under Way.

Malinger. To feign illness to avoid work.

Mallet. Small maul.

Mallock's Rolling Indicator. Instrument for indicating amplitude of roll of a vessel. Consists of a circular box in which a paddle-wheel is mounted in jewelled bearings and immersed in liquid, on a vertical bulkhead. As ship rolls, paddle-wheel maintains an attached and graduated scale in true horizontal. A vertical line on glass face of box indicates amount of roll.

Malone CO₂ Indicator. Instrument that measures CO_2 content of air, as a percentage, by automatically weighing unit volume of air against unit volume of air mixed with CO_2.

Mammatocumulus. Cumulus cloud with udder-shaped projections downward from lower edge.

Mammatus. Udder-shaped cloud form.

Man. To provide with men, or manpower.

Managing Owner. Shipowner who actively controls the commercial affairs of his ship or ships.

Manavalins. Seaman's word for 'odds and ends'.

Manganese. Black oxide of manganese sometimes found on sea-bed when sounding.

Manger. Space, on cable deck, between hawse pipes and thwart-ship breakwater in vessel where cable deck is below forecastle deck.

Mangrove. Tropical tree, or shrub, that covers large areas of coast in tropics. Seed germinates on trees and send roots down to the water. Wood is straight-grained, elastic and hard; often used for boat and shipbuilding.

Manhelper. Paint brush fastened to a long wooden pole.

Man-Harness Hitch. Put in a rope when dragging or towing by manpower. Large 'half crown' is made in rope and laid across it; bight on one side of rope is taken under the rope and through the other bight.

Manhole. Perforation in a boiler shell, tank top or other enclosed space, to allow a man to enter. As this usually demands the smallest possible removal of metal, the opening is approximately the shape of a man's transverse section, this shape allowing the covering piece to be inserted from outside.

Manifest. Document given to Master when cargo is shipped. Contains particulars of cargo, shipper's name, marks and numbers, quantities, where loaded, Master's name, ship's name, tonnage and port of registry.

Manifold. Group of valves for pump suctions and deliveries. Small compartment in which such valves are placed.

Manilla Hemp. Product of a species of banana, principally from Philippine Islands.

Manilla Rope. Made from manilla hemp. Contains natural oil, so does not need tarring. Is about three-quarter weight of hemp rope of same size, and has a higher breaking point.

Manning Scale. Statutory scale (1936) specifying minimum number of efficient deck hands to be carried in steamships of stated tonnages.

Manoeuvre. Regulated change of direction, position or speed to attain a desired end. 2. To change direction, position or speed for a specific purpose.

Man-of-War. A warship.

Manometer. Instrument that measures pressure and elastic properties of gases. Barometer and steam gauges are examples.

'Man Overboard.' Call and report given when a person has been seen to fall into the sea from a vessel.

Manropes. Protective ropes at side of a ladder or inclined wooden steps. Short ropes, used when embarking or disembarking from, or into, boats from lower platform of accommodation ladder; ropes being attached to stanchions on the platform.

Manrope Knot. Made in end of manrope to form standing part at eye of stanchion on platform of accommodation ladder, or at a hatchway. Is a wall knot with crown above and all parts followed round once.

Man Ship. Naval ceremony indicating compliment and, formerly, peaceful intentions. Crew are spaced at regular intervals along sides of upper decks. 2. To provide a crew for a vessel.

Man Yards. Ceremonial disposition of crew of sailing ship. Men are placed at intervals on all yards, standing on the yards and being steadied by jackstays stretched from mast to lift of yard. Discontinued by R.N. in 1902, by order of King Edward VII.

Marconi Rig. Nickname for 'Bermuda Rig'.

Marcq St. Hilaire Method. Procedure for finding ship's position line from an observation of a heavenly body and the calculation of the altitude and azimuth it would have if ship were at estimated position. The difference between the calculated altitude (or zenith distance) and observed altitude (or zenith distance) is the error in locus of assumed position line. The position line is moved towards or away from the geographical position of the observed body according to the amount the two altitudes (or zenith distances) differ.

Mareel. Shetland name for phosphorescence of the sea.

Maregraph Plongeur. Instrument for measuring changes in sea level by automatically recording changes in pressure at sea bottom. Two Bourdon tubes are open to pressure and mechanism records the resultant movements of their free ends.

Mare's Tails. Tufted cirrus clouds.

Margin of Safety Line. Line drawn parallel to bulkhead deck at side line, and three inches below the upper surface of that deck at sides.

Margin Plate. Plating forming side of double-bottom ballast tank.

Marina. A yacht harbour which usually provides fuel, fresh water and other facilities besides moorings, for yachts.

Marine. Pertaining to the sea. 2. A Royal Marine.

Marine Barometer. Mercurial, Kew-pattern barometer mounted in gimbals.

Marine Engine. In general, is any engine designed for propulsion of ships. More especially applied to compound, triple-expansion and a quadruple-expansion engines that are fitted with a condenser.

Marine Glue. Usually a compound of crude rubber, oil and shellac. Used for paying deck seams, closing small leaks, and other purposes.

Marine Growth. Marine vegetation and fauna that attach to the underwater body of floating craft.

Marine Insurance. Insurance against losses occurring at sea, or in sea-going ships, or in relation to a marine adventure.

Marine Insurance Act, 1906. First codification of rules governing marine insurance. Before this date marine insurance was governed, largely by precedent.

Marine Insurance Corporations. Companies who insure against marine risks and are corporately liable for payment. Insurance made by Lloyd's is paid individually by all underwriters who subscribe to the contract.

Mariner. In general, a person employed in a sea-going vessel. In some cases, applied to a seaman who works on deck.

Mariner's Compass. Compass used for directing course of a ship. The card, or 'fly', is mounted in a ballasted bowl fitted with a lubber line or pointer that coincides with ship's fore and aft line; the compass graduation coinciding with this indicates direction of ship's head. Usually mounted in a binnacle containing lighting arrangements, corrector magnets and soft-iron compensations.

Mariner's Splice. Long splice put in cable-laid rope. Made in same manner as long splice with the addition that the three small ropes forming the strand are unlaid into 'readies', and are also spliced.

Marine Society. Instituted 1756; incorporated 1772. Principal objects are to train and fit out poor boys of good character for the sea services, and to ensure a steady stream of lads of good character and physique into the Royal and Merchant Navies.

Marine Store. Warehouse or shop in which rope, canvas and other ships' stores are bought and sold.

Marine Store Dealer. Person who buys and sells marine stores. His business is controlled, in part, by Merchant Shipping Act, 1894, Sections 538–542.

Marine Surveyor. One who surveys ships to ascertain if all statutory and appropriate measures have been taken for the good order and safety of ships, cargoes and personnel. 2. One who surveys seas, and waters connected with them.

'Marine Surveyor.' Early 19th-century spiral-towed log. Invented by Henry de Saumarez, of Guernsey.

Maritime. Pertaining to the sea, to navigation, to shipping and to shipping commerce. 2. Bordering on the sea.

Maritime Air. Air-mass that has travelled over the sea for a considerable distance.

Maritime Conventions Act, 1911. Modifies Merchant Shipping Acts of 1897 and 1906 relative to collisions due to infringement of Collision Regulations. Failure to go to assistance of a vessel in distress is made a misdemeanour.

Maritime Courts. Those courts of law that deal with shipping matters: Court of Admiralty, Court of Appeal, Judicial Committee of Privy Council, are the British Maritime Courts.

Maritime Interest. Interest chargeable on a bottomry bond.

Maritime Law. Law as relating to shipping, seamen, navigation and harbours.

Maritime Lien. Legal right of Master and seamen to have a ship held as security for wages unpaid. Takes precedence over any other lien on ship.

Maritime Polar Air. Air stream, from high latitudes, that has passed over an appreciable expanse of sea before reaching observer.

Mark. One of the marked fathoms in a lead line. 2. Beacon or erection, marking a navigational danger or a position of navigational interest.

Marl(ing). To bind or frap with small line in such a manner that each turn is an overhand knot.

Marline. Superior kind of spunyard laid up left-handed.

Marline Hitch. Half hitch made by passing end over and under, so that an overhand knot is formed.

Marline Spike. Tapered and pointed iron pin used for opening up a rope when splicing. Has a perforation at larger end to take a lanyard.

Maroon. To put a man ashore, forcibly, on desolate land. Formerly done as a punishment, or as a criminal act. 2. Pyrotechnic signal exploding with a loud report.

Marry. To interlace the strands of two ropes preparatory to splicing. 2. To put two ropes together, side by side, so that they can be hauled upon simultaneously.

Marryat's Code. 'Code of signals for the Merchant Service', compiled by Captain Frederick Marryat, R.N., 1817.

Marry the Gunner's Daughter. Old Navy nickname for a flogging, particularly when across a gun.

Mars. Fourth planet from Sun and, therefore, next outside Earth. Diameter is about half that of Earth. Has two satellites, Deimos and Phobos. Named after Roman god of war, on account of its ruddy colour.

Marsden Square. Area of Earth's surface bounded by meridians 10° apart and parallels of latitude 10° apart, so forming 100 squares. Used for identifying position of a meteorological report, first figure denoting latitude, second figure denoting longitude.

Mart. To traffic. 'Mart' is often corrupted to 'Marque'.

Martelli's Tables. 'Short, Easy and Improved Method of Finding Apparent Time at Ship.' G. F. Martelli has not been identified. The tables give quite trustworthy results, but the tabulated quantities have been so disguised that the underlying principle has been obscured. Basic formula is:

$$\operatorname{Cosec}^2 \frac{t}{2} = \cos L, \cos D \div \frac{\cos (L \sim D) - \sin A}{2}$$

Martinet. 'Martnet.'

Martingale. Stay leading downward to prevent upward movement of a jib boom or flying jib boom.

Martnet. Leechline for tricing up a square sail when furling.

Mascaret. Local name for tidal bore in Seine and Garonne rivers.

Mast. Vertical wooden pole—made of single tree or lengths of wood or a tube of steel or metal, erected more or less vertically on centre-line of a ship or boat. Its purpose may be to carry sail and necessary spars, to carry derricks, to give necessary height to a navigation light, look-out position, signal yard, control position, radio aerial or signal lamp. Tall masts are usually made up of three or four masts, one above the other. From the deck, they are named lower mast, topmast, topgallant mast, royal mast —the last two usually being one piece.

Mast Bands. Iron bands clamped round a mast to take upper eyes of rigging, belaying pins, etc.

Mast Carlings. Fore and aft timbers—or girders—on underside of deck and on either side of mast. Also called 'mast partners'.

Mast Clamp. Semi-circular band for securing lower part of a boat's mast to thwart of a boat.

Mast Coat. Conical-shaped canvas covering over wooden mast wedges. Painted to protect wedges from water; which would cause wedges to set up exceptional stresses, and to rot.

Master. Merchant Navy officer in command of ship. Name was given, formerly, to the navigating officer of H.M. ships.

Master-at-Arms. Senior chief petty officer of regulating staff in H.M. ships. Formerly, senior rating in merchant ship whose duty was to see that passengers maintained good order and, especially, committed no offence likely to cause fire.

Master Attendant. Officer of Royal Dockyard next in rank below Superintendent.

Master Compass. Principal gyro compass controlling the repeaters.

Master Gunner. Formerly, officer-in-charge of gunnery equipment of a vessel of R.N. Now, superseded by gunnery lieutenant, senior commissioned gunner or commissioned gunner.

Master Mariner. Officer of the Merchant Navy holding a certificate entitling him to command a vessel.

Master of Trinity House. Senior of the Elder Brethren of Trinity House—who are known as 'Trinity Masters'.

Master's Bond. Bond for £2000–£5000 if owner or charterer are resident abroad—required by Crown before granting outward clearance of an emigrant ship.

Master's Declaration. Short name for 'Master's Declaration and Stores Content for Vessels Outward in Ballast', which is signed by Master when clearing outwards in ballast.

Mast Head. That part of mast between truck and upper eyes of rigging.

Masthead Angle. Angle, at observer's eye, between truck of a vessel's mast and the waterline vertically beneath it. By means of tables—or by trigonometry—this can give ship's distance off when height of eye and height of masthead are known.

Masthead Battens. Vertical strips of wood or metal placed on lower masthead to protect mast from chafe of wire rigging, and to protect eyes of lower rigging from chafe by masthead hoops.

Masthead Light. White, screened light required to be carried on fore or mainmast of a vessel propelled by engines.

Mast Hole. Circular hole in deck through which a mast passes.

Mast Hoop. Circular ring, of metal or wood, that encircles a mast and is free to move up and down it. Often fitted in luffs of gaff sails.

Mast House. Long shed in which masts are built.

Masting. Erecting masts in a vessel.

Masting Sheers. Tall sheer legs used for stepping a mast, or for removing it from a vessel. Erected near edge of a fitting-out berth, with line of splay parallel to edge of berth. Heels are hinged so that sheers can be inclined until head is over centre-line of vessel.

Mast Knife. Clasp-knife with 9- to 12-inch blade, used for scraping wooden mast.

Mast Lining. Doubling piece of canvas on after side of a topsail. Takes the chafe against topmast and cap.

Mastless. Having no mast.

Mast Prop. Long spar formerly used to strut a mast when vessel was careened.

Mast Rope. Rope by which an upper mast is hoisted. A 'Heel Rope.'

Mast Scraper. Triangular scraper used on wooden masts. Edges are concave to fit round of mast. Bevel is away from handle.

Mast Step. Socket into which heel of a mast is stepped. Strengthened fitting to which heel of mast is secured.

Mast Tackle. Purchase for hoisting or lowering a mast. 2. Heavy-lift tackle depending from a mast.

Mast Trunk. Casing into which mast of a small vessel may be stepped.

Mat. Woven strands of rope, or thrummed yarns on canvas, used as protection against chafing, or for controlling a small leak.

Mate. An officer assistant to Master. A 'Chief Officer'. From time immemorial he has been responsible for stowage and care of cargo and organisation of work of seamen, in addition to navigating duties.

Matelot. French for 'Sailor'. In common use on lower deck of R.N.

H

Mate's Log. Book kept by Mate, and recording work done by crew and, with particular emphasis, all matters concerning stowage, carriage, ventilation and discharge of cargo.

Mate's Receipt. Document signed by Mate when goods for carriage are received into ship's charge.

Matthew Walker. Knot put in end of rope. Made by unlaying end of rope, making a bight of one strand, passing second strand over bight of first, passing third over bight of second and through bight of first.

Matting Sword. Length of thin wood used for beating in the wheft of a woven, or 'sword', mat.

Maul. Heavy hammer of iron or wood.

Mayday. (French 'm'aidez', 'Help me'.) The international spoken radiotelephony signal of distress.

Maximum Altitude. Greatest angular distance above horizon.

Maxwell's Rule. 'Corkscrew Rule.'

McIntyre System. Double-bottom construction involving the cutting of frames and reverse frames and the fitting of a continuous water-tight angle bar to take lower edge of tank margin plate.

McIntyre Tank. Water-ballast tank seated on top of ordinary floors. Preceded double-bottom tank.

Meade Great Circle Diagram. Graticule for solving great circle sailing problems from projection of course on a Mercator chart.

Mean Draught. Half sum of forward and after draughts of a vessel. It differs slightly from draught at half length.

Mean High Water. Mean of all high waters at a place when observed during a lunation of 29 days.

Mean High-Water Springs. Mean height of spring high waters at a place when deduced from an adequate number of observations.

Mean Latitude. That latitude whose numerical value is half the sum of a latitude left and a latitude reached.

Mean Low Water. Mean of all low waters at a place when observed during a lunation of 29 days.

Mean Low-Water Springs. Mean height of spring low waters at a place when deduced from an adequate number of observations.

Mean Noon. Instant in which Mean Sun is on meridian of a place.

Mean Place of Star. That position on the celestial concave at which a star would appear to be if viewed from Sun. It is expressed in declination north or south of Equinoctial and sidereal time angle from First Point of Aries on January 1 of current year.

Mean Sea Level. Level that sea would maintain if no tidal effect were manifested and average meteorological conditions prevailed. For hydrographic and surveying purposes the level is derived from very prolonged and careful observations at an appropriate position—Newlyn, Cornwall, being selected for British standard level.

Mean Solar Day. Interval between successive transits of Mean Sun across a given meridian. Its length is the mean length of all apparent solar days in a year.

Mean Solar Year. Average time taken by Sun to go round Ecliptic or, to be precise, for Earth to go round Sun. Due to slight irregularities in the movement of First Point of Aries the time varies slightly and irregularly. Mean value, when taken over about 100 years, gives 365 days. 5 hrs. 48 mins. 48 secs. (approx.).
Mean Sun. Fictitious body that travels along Equinoctial at a constant speed, and in the same time that true Sun takes to travel round Ecliptic at a variable speed.
Mean Tide Level. Average tidal height above chart datum. Found by evaluating half sum of Mean High Water and Mean Low Water at a given place. Name is sometimes applied to mean level of a tide.
Mean Time. Time regulated by Mean Sun.
Measured Distance. Accurately measured distance used for determining speeds of ships. Most of the so-called 'measured miles' are measured distances, and require adjustment when calculating speeds in knots.
Measured Mile. Measured distance of 6080 ft. *See* 'Measured Distance'.
Measurement Goods. Cargo in which freight is based on the amount of space goods occupy in the ship carrying them.
Measurement of Ships. Determination of a ship's displacement. Gross, Net and Under-Deck Tonnages, Draught, Freeboard, Length and Breadth.
Mechanical Advantage. Ratio between force applied and weight lifted when using a purchase or other machine.
Mechanical Integrator. Instrument used for finding a vessel's displacement and moments of displacement by moving a pointer along line of sections of body plan; this movement actuating registering mechanism.
Mechanical Navigation.* Former name for ship handling and manoeuvring.
Mechanical Stoker. Machine that feeds furnaces of a coal-fired vessel.
Median. Middle quantity of a series of values; not necessarily the mean value. 2. Line, from angle of a triangle, bisecting opposite side.
Medusa. Umbrella-shaped jelly-fish with several long and hairlike tentacles.
'Meet Her.' Order to helmsman when helm is righted during a turn and he is required to check swing of ship's head.
Mega. Prefix meaning 'Great' or 'Million'.
Megadyne. Million dynes. Pressure of one megadyne per square centimetre is equivalent to 1000 millibars.
Mend. To put additional service on a rope. 2. To loose a sail and refurl it.
Meniscus. Curved upper surface of liquid in a tube, particularly mercury in a barometer. Curve can be concave or convex. 2. Concave-convex lens.
Menkalin. Star β Aurigae, S.H.A. 271°; Dec. N45°; Mag. 2·1.

Menkar. Star α Ceti. S.H.A. 315°; Dec. N4°; Mag. 2·8.

Menkent. Star θ Centauri. S.H.A. 149°; Dec. S36°; Mag. 2·3.

Merak. Star β Ursae Majoris. S.H.A. 195°; Dec. N57°, Mag. 2·4.

Mercantile Marine. Merchant shipping, including personnel. Merchant Navy. Merchant Service.

Mercantile Marine Fund. Fund into which various fees and charges were paid, and from which salaries and expenses were recovered. Abolished 1898.

Mercantile Marine Office. Established and controlled by Merchant Shipping Acts for giving effect to the Acts as regards employment and discharge of personnel, keeping registers of men and their characters, facilitating apprenticeship to the sea service and other matters of like nature.

Mercantile Marine Superintendent. Officer in charge of a Mercantile Marine Office.

Mercantile Marine Uniform. Standard uniform for officers of British Merchant Navy in accordance with Orders in Council of 1918 and 1921. Penalty for unauthorised wearing is up to £5; for wearing it in such a manner as to bring it into contempt, £10 or up to one month's imprisonment with or without hard labour.

Mercator Chart. Projection of Earth's surface in which all meridians are made parallel and the latitude scale is increased in the same ratio as the expansion of the longitude scale in the area. All straight lines are rhumb lines. Distances are measured by minutes of latitude in area considered. Distortion in high latitudes is very great.

Mercatorial Bearing. Bearing of a given position as deduced from a rhumb line passing through the position and position of observer. Differs from great circle bearing by half the convergency between meridian of observer and meridian passing through the given point.

Mercator Sailing. Method by which problems of sailing on spherical surface of Earth can be solved by plane trigonometry. Its fundamental equation is: Difference of Longitude = Meridional Difference of Latitude × Tangent of Course. It requires that difference of latitude shall be converted into the invariable units of the longitude scale; this being done by tables of 'Meridional Parts'. Disadvantages of this sailing are that: (1) Course is a loxodrome, and not a great circle; (2) Method cannot be used in high latitudes except for very short distances.

Mercator's Projection. Delineation of Earth's surface on a chart or map in accordance with the principles used in making a Mercator chart.

Merchant Captain. Captain of a merchant vessel. Captain in the Merchant Navy.

Merchant Navy. Ships and personnel of the British Mercantile Marine.

Merchant Seaman. Seaman employed in a merchant vessel.

Merchant Service. 'Merchant Navy.'

Merchant Shipping Acts. Acts of Parliament governing the building, manning, employment, fitting-out, seaworthiness, registration, management, governance, etc., of British ships. Embrace numerous Acts, from 1882 onwards, the principal being those of 1894, 1906, and 1932.

Mercurial Barometer. Barometer that indicates atmospheric pressure by height of a balancing column of mercury—as distinguished from an aneroid barometer.

Mercury. White metal with melting point of −38·5°C. Specific gravity about 13·55. Used in thermometers and barometers for registration purposes, and in some gyro compasses as a ballistic pendulum.

Mercury. Innermost of the planets. Greatest angular distance from Sun is about 29°. Very rarely observable, and then only near sunrise or sunset. Nautical almanac then gives a warning that its appearance may cause it to be mistaken for a star or another planet.

Mercury Ballistic. Pots of mercury, one on either side of a Sperry Gyro Compass. These have a connecting tube through which mercury flows when compass tilts and tends to wander out of meridian. Extra weight on one side causes gyro to precess into meridian and regain horizontal position.

Mercury Trough. Receptacle in which mercury is placed to form an artificial horizon when taking celestial observations ashore. Has a glass roof to ensure unruffled surface of mercury.

Meridian. Semi-circle of terrestrial sphere passing between the poles. All positions on this line have noon at the same instant, and the same longitude.

Meridian Altitude. Value of intercepted arc of observer's meridian, between horizon and a celestial body on the meridian of observer—thus having its greatest altitude.

Meridian Distance. Distance between any two meridians expressed as the difference in their respective local times.

Meridian Line. Line connecting North and South points of observer's sensible horizon.

Meridian Passage. Transit of heavenly body across a given meridian.

Meridian Transit. 'Meridian Passage.'

Meridian Zenith Distance. Arc of meridian intercepted between the zenith and a heavenly body in the meridian.

Meridional. Pertaining to the meridian. Sometimes has the meaning 'facing the direction of the noon Sun'.

Meridional Difference of Latitude. Difference of Latitude expressed in meridional parts of Mercator projection.

Meridional Distance. Old name for 'departure' between two places on different meridians.

Meridional Parts. Length of any part of an extended meridian of a Mercator chart when expressed in units that are the length of a minute of longitude.

Meridional Projection. Projection of a sphere to a plane that is parallel to the meridian, or coincident with it.

Mermaid. Fabulous creature having upper part of a woman and lower part of a fish. Dugong is an animal somewhat of this type.

Merman. Masculine counterpart of a 'Mermaid'.

Mesh Stick. Flat, wooden slat used when net making. Width of slat forms mesh and regulates its size.

Mess. Group of persons who feed at the same table. The space table, and utensils allocated to a group of persons.

Mess Deck. Deck on which the feeding places and tables of a ship's company are situated.

Messenger. Endless chain, or rope, passing round barrel of capstan and through block, or blocks, some distance away—thus moving as capstan is turned. Formerly used when cable was stowed some distance away from capstan. Slack cable was attached to messenger by short rope 'nippers', which were cast off as cable came to locker. 2. Endless chain, passing over sprocket-wheels, used for increasing power of a windlass by connecting it with a winch. 3. A light rope used to haul in a heavier one.

Mess Kit. Utensils supplied to a mess for eating, drinking and cooking.

Mess Traps. R.N. name for 'Mess Kit'.

Metacentre. Theoretical point considered in questions of ship stability. When a floating vessel is upright and afloat in water the upward force of buoyancy is equal to the downward force of gravity, and a vertical line through centre of buoyancy will pass through centre of gravity. When vessel is heeled by extraneous forces, centre of buoyancy will shift to low side. Where the vertical line, passing through the new centre of buoyancy, cuts the former vertical line is termed the 'metacentre'. This point is more or less static for angles of heel up to about 15°. Similarly, we can consider a metacentre in a fore and aft plane. We thus have a longitudinal and a transverse metacentre, their positions changing with draught and inclination of vessel.

Metacentric Height. Distance that metacentre is above centre of gravity in a ship.

Metallic Barometer. Name formerly given to an aneroid barometer.

Metalling Clause. Inserted in policy of insurance to exclude loss of metal sheathing due to action of water.

Metal Mike. Seaman's name for 'Automatic Helmsman'.

Meteorological Wind Scale. Development of Beaufort Wind Scale, and relating wind-force to wind-speed. Introduced 1926.

Meteorology. Science concerned with study of Earth's atmosphere, its phenomena and variations.

Meteors. Fragments of solid matter in space that meet Earth's atmosphere. Friction with atmosphere heats them to incandescent point. Altitude of incandescence is probably less than 120 miles. Size of fragments is usually between that of a pea and that of a grain of sand. Occasionally, fragments of considerable size reach Earth's surface.

Meteor Shower. Succession of meteors observable when Earth's atmosphere passes through a ring of meteors.

Mete Stick. Horizontal batten extending from a vertical timber. Formerly used for levelling ballast, or for measuring height in a hold.

Metonic Cycle. Period of 19 years in which 12 years consisted of 12 lunar months, and 7 years of 13 lunar months. Dates of new Moon were practically invariable, the error being one day in 237 years.

Mexican/Mexico Current. Cold current that sets SE'ly down west coast of Mexico and eventually merging in the NE Trade Drift.

Miaplacidus. Star β Carinae. S.H.A. 222°; Dec. S70°; Mag. 1·8.

Michell Thrust. Thrust block in which the thrust is taken, primarily, on segments that can cant slightly away from collars on shaft. In the space thus formed is oil, so that frictional resistance and wear are reduced to a minimum.

Micrometer Screw. Screw for making very small adjustments with a large movement. In measuring instruments it permits very accurate measurements to be recorded.

Microsecond. One millionth (0·000,001) of second of time.

Middle Deck. Second deck below upper deck in a three-decker (which had five decks).

Middle Ground. Shoal area between two navigational channels.

Middle Latitude. That latitude in which the length of a parallel intercepted between two meridians is equal to the departure made when sailing between the two meridians on a rhumb. Owing to spheroidal shape of Earth, middle latitude differs from mean latitude, but can be derived from mean latitude by Workman's Table.

Middle-Latitude Sailing. Method of solving certain navigational problems when sailing between two points in different latitudes and longitudes. The length of intercepted arc of parallel midway between the two latitudes is taken to be equal to the departure made, and is found by formula Dep. = D. Long. × Cos Mid. Lat. The method is said to have been introduced by Ralph Handson, a mathematician, in 1614.

Middle Passage. Area of Atlantic Ocean between West Indies and U.S.A. Is an old 'Slave Trade' name.

Middle Topsail. Deeply-roached topsail formerly set at heel of topmast in some schooners and sloops.

Middy. Colloquial name for a 'Midshipman'.

Midland Sea. Mediterranean Sea.

Mid Main. Said of a position far out at sea. Sometimes used to denote a position halfway between an observer and his horizon.

Midship. Situated in or near the middle line—transversely or longitudinally—of a vessel.

Midship Beam. Longest beam in midship body of a vessel.

Midship Bend. Largest of the transverse sections of a vessel.

Midship Body. That part of hull of a ship in which there is little change in transverse shape.

Midship Frame. Largest transverse frame of a ship.
Midshipman. Young subordinate officer in R.N. Intermediate between cadet and sub-lieutenant.
Midshipman's Hitch. Alternative but little-used name for a 'Marlinespike Hitch'.
Midshipmen's Nuts. Broken ship biscuit.
Midships. Commonly used form of 'Amidships'.
Mid Stream. Middle line of a stream or current.
Mile. Unit of geographical distance. Has various values and names, those that concern seamen being Statute, Nautical, Standard Nautical, International Nautical and Geographical miles. Each of these will be found under its prefix.
Milky Way. Unsymmetrical and irregular belt of luminosity extending round the heavens. Is an immense congregation of stars in shape of a lens—roughly. Diameter is about 150,000 light years, Earth being about 40,000 light years from centre.
Millibar. Unit of barometrical pressure. 1/1000th of a 'Bar'.
Minelayer. Vessel specially fitted for carrying mines and laying them at sea.
Minesweeper. Vessel specially fitted for sweeping up enemy-laid mines and for destroying them.
Minimum Altitude. Altitude of an observed object at the instant its altitude ceases to decrease.
Minion. Small gun that threw a ball less than 4 lb.
Ministry of Agriculture and Fisheries. Government department that regulates the sea fishing fleets and the carriage of live stock from British ports.
Minor Planet. One of the asteroids.
Minute. Interval of time equivalent to $\frac{1}{60}$ of an hour. 2. $\frac{1}{60}$ of a degree of arc.
Minute Gun. Firing of a gun, at intervals of about one minute, as a signal of distress.
Mirage. Optical effect, caused by unusual atmospheric refraction, by which distant objects appear to be nearer, or in remarkable positions.
Mirfax. An apparatus for transmitting and receiving weather-charts by radio.
Missing. Said of a vessel when no news has been heard of her and it is feared, but not proved, that she has been lost.
Missing Stays. Failing to go from one tack to the other when attempting to go about close-hauled.
Mist. Thin fog that reduces visibility to less than two miles. Meteorologists have a visibility limit of one mile, but the usual practice of seamen is to assume mist to be present when ships and ships' lights are not visible at two miles.
Mistral. Strong NW to North wind that is met with in Gulf of Lions and Gulf of Genoa.
Mitchboard. Wooden stanchion, with curved socket, for taking weight of a boom when not in use.

Mixed Policy. Marine insurance policy covering two or more different kinds of risk, such as 'sea' and 'land' risks; or a 'Voyage' risk with a 'time' element incorporated. A 'mixed' policy, covering a voyage and a period of time exceeding 30 days, is not uncommon.

Mixed Tide. Tidal undulation in which both semi-diurnal and diurnal constituents are definitely manifested.

Mizen, Mizzen. Fore and aft sail, with gaff and boom, set on after side of mizen mast. Small sail, set on small mast, right aft in a boat having a mainmast.

Mizen, Mizzen Mast. Third mast from forward in a vessel having three or more masts.

Mizzle. Combination of drizzle and thick mist. 'Scotch mist'.

Moderate Speed. In fog, is such a speed that all way can be taken off the vessel before she has travelled a distance equal to half the range of visibility.

Modulator. A device for generating a succession of short pulses of energy which cause a radar transmitter valve to oscillate during each pulse.

Molgogger. A folding or removable fairlead fitted to the bulwarks of a tug.

Moment of Change Trim. Weight and leverage necessary to change trim of a vessel by one inch.

Monitor. War vessel in which speed and other considerations have been sacrificed to obtain maximum gun power and armour protection.

Monkey Block. Large iron-bound block bolted to a wooden chock on deck of a sailing vessel. 2. Block fastened on topsail yard as a fairleader for buntlines.

Monkey Boat. Long, narrow canal boat. 2. Small boat used in a dock.

Monkey Chains. Small rigging chains abaft main chains. Royal and topgallant backstays are set up in them.

Monkey Face. Shamrock-shaped connecting piece of a mooring swivel.

Monkey Fist. Knot sometimes put in end of heaving line to increase its carrying power. Three round bights are made in end, leaving enough end to cross first turns with three round turns, and then a further three turns going over second turns and under first turns.

Monkey Gaff. Gaff hoisted above a spanker gaff.

Monkey Island. Screened navigating and compass position on top of a wheel house or chart house.

Monkey Jacket. Uniform jacket as distinguished from frock coat.

Monkey Lever. Iron lever operating tumblers that release securing chains of an anchor stowed on an anchor bed.

Monkey Poop. Low poop. Sometimes applied to a deck above an after cabin.

Monkey Rail. Light rail on and above a quarter rail.

Monkey Seam. Flat seam put in centre of sail when making it. Made by overlapping selvages of two cloths, and then tabling them.

Monkey Tail. Rope attached to end of a lever so that extra hands can heave on it.

Monkey Topsail. Sail that was used in instructional ships for teaching young seamen to hand, reef, furl and loose a topsail; to lay out on a yard; to bend and unbend a sail; to pass an earring. The yard was crossed a small distance above the deck; the names of the various parts of the sail were painted on it.

Monsoon. Persistent wind that blows from one direction in summer, and from an approximately opposite direction in winter. Speaking generally, they come from seaward in summer, and from landward in winter. They are well developed in E and S Asia, and may be noticed in China Sea, Indian Ocean and off African coast. The West African monsoon prevails from S to SW throughout the year.

Month. Period of time based on Moon's revolution around Earth. It has various values, depending on the epoch used. The Anomalistic, Nodical, Periodic, Sidereal, Synodical and Tropical months are dealt with under their prefixes.

Moon. Secondary planet that is a satellite of Earth. Distance from Earth varies between 225,463 miles at perigee to 252,710 miles at apogee. Diameter 2160 miles. Plane of orbit is slightly more than 5° from plane of Ecliptic. Declination varies between $18\frac{1}{2}°$ and $28\frac{1}{2}°$ when maximum in a lunation. Moon's gravitational effect on Earth has important effects in tidal phenomena.

Moon Culminating Star. Star sufficiently near Moon, both in R.A. and Declination, that observations could be taken of it to determine difference of longitude.

Moon in Distance. Term denoting that angular distance of Moon from another heavenly body allowed measurement of lunar observations.

Moonraker. Sail that was sometimes carried above skysail in square-rigged ships during fine weather and light airs.

Moonsail. Alternative name for 'Moonraker'.

Moonsheered. Said of a vessel whose upper deck has exaggerated sheer forward and aft.

Moor. To secure a ship in position by two or more anchors and cables. 2. To attach a vessel to a buoy, or buoys. 3. To secure a vessel by attaching ropes to positions ashore.

Mooring Buoy. Buoy, carrying a large ring or shackle, securely moored so that a vessel can be attached to it and ride in safety.

Mooring Swivel. Strong swivel piece for insertion in cables of a vessel riding by two anchors in a tideway. Each end of swivel is connected to a strong trefoil member that is pierced with three holes, one of which is for its connection to swivel, the other two being for inboard or outboard connections of ship's cables. Use of swivel necessitates disconnection of each of ship's cables, and a reconnection to the swivel.

Moral Hazard. Term used in marine insurance to denote possible risk of dishonesty in an assured person or his representatives.

Morning Watch. Division of nautical day from 4 a.m. to 8 a.m.

Moro Vinta. Vessel of China Seas. About 40 ft. long. Has tripod mast, lugsail and outrigger.

Morse Code. Alphabet and numbers used in signalling. Each letter or figure is represented by a long sign, a short sign or a combination of them. May be transmitted by light, sound or graphically. Invented by Professor Morse of Massachusetts.

Mortar. Short ordnance used for firing projectiles at short ranges. Angle of elevation was constant, about 45°, range being increased or decreased by increase or decrease of propelling charge. Now used only for line-throwing purposes.

Mortar Vessel. Small, broad beam vessel in which a mortar was mounted for bombardment purposes. Bomb Ketch.

Mortgage. The granting of a ship as security for money advanced. Any mortgage of a ship must be registered with Registrar at ship's port of registry. Mortgage can be raised by the owner only.

Mortice Block. Clump block.

Moseley's Formula. Equation by which the dynamical stability of a vessel may be ascertained from inclining experiments.

Mother Cary's Chickens. Stormy petrels.

Motor Ship/Vessel. Vessel propelled by internal combustion engines.

Mould. Pattern or template from which a member of ship's structure is shaped.

Moulded Depth. Vertical depth, measured amidships, between the horizontal plane passing through ship's keel and a parallel plane passing through top of freeboard deck beams at sides.

Moulding. Correctly forming the depth and outline of a vessel's frames or timbers when building.

Mould Loft. Large covered space, in shipbuilding yard, where moulds, or templates, are made for the various members to be erected.

Mount Misery. Colloquial name for an unprotected or unsheltered upper bridge.

Mouse, Mousing. To pass turns of yarn, or small line, across open part of hook to prevent accidental unhooking. Formerly: a knot worked in eye of stay to take chafe against the mast.

Mousing Hook. 'Self-mousing hook.'

Mudhole. Small door, in lower part of boiler shell, through which sediment may be withdrawn when not under steam.

Mudian. Bermuda-rigged boat.

Muffle (Oars). To put soft material around loom of oar, where it rests in crutch or rowlock, to deaden sound when rowing.

Mulct. To fine, or impose a penalty.

Multihull. A vessel which has more than one hull, e.g. a catamaran or trimaran.

Mumbleby. Devonshire name for a fishing boat rather smaller than a trawler.

Mumford Boiler. Water-tube boiler somewhat similar to Thorny-croft type, but having tubes more curved. Practically obsolete.

Munnions. Decorative work separating windows in sterns of old ships.

Munro Wind-Speed Recorder. Instrument that points a pressure head into the wind and, by means of measuring elements and a clockwork attachment, gives an anemogram.

Mush Ice. Broken ice in pieces up to 6 ft. across.

Mushroom Anchor. Umbrella-shaped anchor. Invented 1809 by Hemman of Chatham.

Mushroom Head. Domed top of a ventilator.

Mussel Bow. Name given to yachts that were cut away at fore-foot, thus having a broad shallow part forward.

Muster. To assemble at a specified place.

Mutatis Mutandis. Latin term used in Lloyd's Salvage Agreement, and other documents. Means, 'after making the needful changes.'

Mutiny. Revolt from, or forcible resistance to, duly constituted authority.

Mutual Indemnity Insurance Association. Group of shipowners, and others, who combine to carry those risks excluded from policies of marine insurance. They are conducted on a non-profit-making basis, and mutually subscribe to make good an uninsured loss sustained by a member. 'Small Damage Club.'

Muzzler. Very strong head-wind.

Mystery Tables. Name given to Martelli's 'Tables for Finding Apparent Time at Ship' on account of the obscuration of their basic formulae.

N

Nacodah. Master of an Arab dhow ('Nakhoda').

Nadir. Point in heavens diametrically opposite zenith.

Nail Sick. Minor leaks caused by erosion of nails in a wooden hull.

Name of Ship. That name appearing in her certificate of registry. Is cut or punched in her bow and stern.

Nanoplankton. Minute sea creatures and plant that float in clusters on surface of sea.

Napier's Curve, Diagram. Curved line drawn on a specially designed diagram and passing through a limited number of points on which deviation of compass has been ascertained. This facilitates the determination of deviations on points for which no observation has been made.

Napier's Rules of Circular Parts. Diagrammatic arrangement of five parts, or their complements, of a right-angled or quadrantal spherical triangle, the right angle or 90° side being disregarded, in five sections of a circle. If these be put in the rotation of their occurrence, an unknown part can be found from the other parts; the rule being that sine of middle part equals product of tangents of adjacent parts, or product of cosines of opposite parts.

Narrow Channel Rule. Rule of Collision Regulations. Requires a vessel navigating a narrow channel to keep to that side of mid-channel that is on her starboard hand.

Narrows. Areas where navigable waters become narrow due to shoals or adjacent land.

Narrow Seas. Seas as distinguished from oceans. Seas having no great breadth. At one time, was especially applied to English Channel.

Narrow Waters. Areas in which navigable waters become narrow due to shoals or land.

Narwhal. Member of the whale family. Male has left tusk developed into a spiral horn, 6 to 10 ft. long, right tusk being rudimentary. Were formerly met with around 80°N, and hunted for their excellent oil.

Natural Draught. Furnace draught arising from height of funnel above that of furnace, and from temperature of furnace gases.

Natural Projection. One in which lines of sight are directly projected to a plane. Used when distinguishing this projection from an artificial projection.

Natural Scale. One in which the delineation of a charted area is directly proportional to the area charted.

Nau. *See* 'Nef'

Naufrage.* Shipwreck.

Naufragate.* To shipwreck. To wreck a ship.

Naulage.* Freight, passage money or ferry charge.

Naumachy. Naval battle, sea fight. Representation of a sea fight.

Nauropometer. Instrument for measuring inclination or heel of a ship.

Nauscopy. Art of discovering the approach of a distant ship to the land.

Nausea. Sea sickness. Originally meant 'ship sickness'.

Naut. Depth unit of 1000 fathoms. Used only in cable laying work.

Nautical. Pertaining to ships, seamen or navigation.

Nautical Almanac. Annual volume, published by the Admiralty, giving astronomical information essential to navigation. First issued 1767.

Nautical Astronomy. Astronomy as applied to navigation.

Nautical Day. Day, formerly used at sea, commencing with Sun's noon transit. Abolished in Merchant Navy, January 1, 1925, but abolished in Royal Navy several years before.

Nautical Distance. Length of rhumb line intercepted by two positions.

Nautical Dromometer. Early 19th century towed log invented by Benjamin Martin.

Nautical Mile. Length of arc of 1' of meridian in latitude of position of measurement. Value varies between 6046·4 ft. in Equator and 6107·8 ft. at Poles. A standard of 6080 ft. (1853·18 m), correct for Lat. 48°, is used in log registrations and practical navigation. The International Nautical Mile=1852 metres, correct for Lat. 44½°. Sea Mile.

Nautical School. Educational establishment in which navigation, seamanship and other subjects connected with shipping are taught.

Nautical Tables. Book containing tabulated data—arithmetical, geometrical, astronomical and geographical—for use in navigation.

Nautical Twilight. Interval between Sun being 6° below visible horizon and 12° below it. Horizon is sufficiently distinct for sextant use, and bright stars are observable.

Nautilus Propeller. Water jet discharged astern from a submerged orifice for propelling purposes in a boat. Is uneconomical in use but is retained in some lifeboats where risk of propeller being fouled is likely to arise.

Nautophone. Electrically-operated instrument that sounds a high note as a fog signal.

Naval. Pertaining to ships, or to a navy.

Naval Architecture. Science and practice concerned with design, building and fitting of ships, and with the investigation of the forces acting upon them in a seaway, and in specific circumstances.

Naval Cadet. Student for officer rank in Royal Navy.

Naval Court. Consists of three to five officers of R.N., consular officers, or masters of British ships. Convened abroad only by an officer commanding H.M. ship or by Consul, when necessary to investigate charges against master, officer or seaman of a British ship; when a British ship is lost or abandoned; when interests of owner make it advisable.

Naval Crown. Device showing stern and square sail of a ship, alternately, on a fillet or circle.

Naval Discipline Act. Act of Parliament governing the conduct of men and officers of Royal Navy. First introduced 1661.

Naval Lines. Lines going across a reefing topsail, from leech to leech, on after side, to secure reef line. Secured to upper eyelet holes of reef cringles.

Naval Officer. Commissioned or subordinate officer in Royal Navy, or in a foreign navy.

Navel Futtock. Ground futtock in midship timber of a wooden ship.

Navel Hood.* Timber immediately above hawse pipe of wooden ship.

Navel Pipe. Large tube through which cable goes from deck above locker to cable deck.

Navicert. Certificate of Destination for Specified Cargoes, issued by governments in wartime.

Navigability. Of a vessel, capability of being controlled and steered. Of a water area, capability of beign navigated.

Navigable. Capable of being safely navigated.

Navigable Semicircle. That half of a cyclonic depression in which there is no risk of encountering the vortex. Is left-hand semicircle in N Latitudes and right-hand semicircle in S latitudes.

Navigate. To direct and control a ship. To pass from one place to another by ship.

Navigation. Art and science of conducting a ship from one place to another. Sometimes used in a limited sense to restrict it to conducting by celestial observations and methods. 2. Canal made for passage of ships, barges and boats.

Navigational Planets. Four planets—Venus, Mars, Saturn, Jupiter —whose positions are precisely tabulated, in Nautical Almanac, for navigational purposes.

Navigational Stars. Selected bright stars whose positions are precisely tabulated in Nautical Almanac for navigational purposes.

Navigation Laws. Laws passed, at different times, to regulate, restrict or encourage shipping and shipborne trade. First English code is of time of Richard I. *See* 'Laws of Oleron.'

Navigation Lights. Those lights compulsorily shown by vessels at sea, in accordance with international rules.

Navigator. Person skilled in the art and practice of navigation. A person in charge of navigation of a ship. Specialised officer appointed to a ship for navigation duties. Name was given, formerly, to a man employed in digging canals (navigations), hence 'navvy'. 'Navigator shovel' is a relic of latter use of name.

Navigator's Yeoman. Rating, trained in chart correction, who works under orders of navigating officer of H.M. ship.

Navis Aperta. Undecked Roman ship.

Navis Tecta. Decked Roman ship.

Navivium.* Early type of submerged log on paddle-wheel principle. Way of ship acted on lower half of paddle, causing it to rotate and actuate inboard-registering gear. Early 19th century.

Navy. The shipping of a country when considered collectively. The war vessels of a country when considered collectively. The personnel of a navy when considered collectively.

Neap. Applied to the tides of small amplitude occurring about the time of Moon being in quadrature.

Neaped. Said of vessel when she grounds at high water when tides are decreasing from spring to neap. Also applied to a vessel unable to leave a tidal harbour through decrease of high-water height of tide.

Neap Tide. Tidal undulation that has the highest low water, and the lowest high water, in the series. Occurs about time of quadrature of Sun and Moon.

Necklace. Open link chain secured around wooden mast of a sailing ship to take lower eyes of futtock rigging.

Needle. Magnetised bar that provides directional property of a magnetic compass.

Nef, Nau. Term for a ship in about 17th century, from Latin 'Naris'=ship.

Negative. Opposite of 'positive'. 2. Annul, or cancel, a signal or order.

Negative Slip. Term used when vessel's progress through the water is greater than that due to propulsive action of propeller. May be due to indraught of a following wake.

Negligence Clause. Inserted in a contract to relieve one of the contracting parties from responsibility for loss due to negligence of a third party who may, or may not be, a servant of the contracting party.

Nelson Room. Room at Lloyd's, in London, containing several valuable and important mementoes of Admiral Lord Nelson.

Nemedri. 'North European and Mediterranean Routeing Instructions.' Contain routeing instructions to enable vessels to avoid passing through mined areas.

Nephoscope. Instrument used for determining direction and speed of clouds.

Neptune. God of the sea in Roman mythology. Son of Saturn. 2. Eighth planet from Sun. Discovered by Adams (England) and Leverrier (France) at about the same time. Has one satellite. Orbital period, 164·79 years.

Neptune Log. Towed log of Cherub type, but constructed to register speeds of 18 knots and upwards.

Nereids. Nymphs of the sea, daughters of Nereus and Doris. 2. Sea centipedes.

Ness. Projection of land into sea; headland; cape.

Nets. Fishing-nets. Torpedo-nets.

Nettles. Halves of two yarns twisted together to make another yarn. 2. Lengths of nettle stuff used for attaching clews to hammocks.

Nettle Stuff. Superior type of spunyarn consisting of either two or three yarns laid up together. Used for gaskets and similar fittings, and for hammock clews in R.N.

Nett Tonnage. Ship measurement derived from gross tonnage by deducting spaces allowed for crew and propelling power; 100 ft. of space being reckoned as one ton.

Neutral Axis. That line, in a girder or other member under stress, separating the tensile and compressive components of the stress.

Neutral Equilibrium. As applied to ship, is that state of flotation in which she will have neither righting nor capsizing moment if moved. In mechanics, is that equilibrium that does not alter with displacement of the body.

Newel. Vertical timber to take tenons of rails going from breastwork to gangway.

New Moon. That phase of Moon when she is in conjunction with Sun and reflects no light towards Earth.

New Style. Used when indicating dates reckoned by Gregorian Calendar that was introduced into England, September, 1792, but was not adopted universally.

Nickey. Large Manx fishing boat similar to a Cornish lugger used in 19th century.

Night Glasses. Binoculars with large light-gathering power, but with small magnification—about 2½ diameters.

Nimbostratus. Cloud form characterised by uniform grey, low-lying sheet. Usually coincident with steady rain or snow.

Nimbus. Rain- or snow-cloud. Usually of grey colour, and combining stratus, cumulus, and cirrus.

Ninepin Blocks. Rack containing nine sheaves, through which running rigging is rove. 2. Blocks with upward projections from top and bottom of metal stropping. Fitted between two horizontal metal rails into which projections fitted and allowed sheave to swivel. Placed in vicinity of mast.

Nineteen-Metre Type. First international type of yacht (1911). Length overall 95 ft., L.W.L. 62·3 ft. Beam 17 ft. Sail area 6850 sq. ft. Reg. tonnage 60. T.M. tonnage 100. Freeboard 4 ft. 6 in.

Nineteen-Yearly Period. As 18·61 years is the period in which Moon's nodes make a circuit of Ecliptic, it follows that heights and times of tidal undulations repeat, approximately, in this period.

Nine-Thread Stuff. One-inch cordage having nine threads in each strand.

Nip. Short turn in a rope. 2. To secure a rope by seizing, frapping or racking. 3. To confine by clamping. To Freshen the Nip is to move a rope slightly so that a different part bears upon a fairlead or sheave.

Nipa Palms. Creeping plants found in tidal estuaries of Ganges and other East Indian rivers. Frequently impede navigation.

Nipped. Said of a vessel when pressed by ice on both sides.

Nipper. To nip a rope or cable. 2. Person who nips or nippers. 3. Length of rope by which hemp cables were attached to messenger. 4. 'Bullivant's Nipper.'

Noah's Ark. Vessel, mentioned in Bible and in Chaldean history, in which Noah rode out a flood. Dimensions were (about): length, 450 ft.; breadth, 75 ft.; depth, 45 ft. Built of cypress wood and had three decks.

Nobby. Manx fishing boat, dandy rigged, named from its first builder, Clarke of Peel.

Nock. Forward upper corner of four-sides fore and aft sail. Also spelt 'knock'. More usually 'Throat'.

Noctilucent Clouds. Luminous cirriform clouds, travelling at high speed, occasionally seen about midnight after summer solstice.

Nocturlabium.* The 'Nocturnal' instrument.

Nocturnal. Pertaining to night. 2. Early 16th-century instrument used for determining latitude by observations of Polaris. Had a base plate, graduated for time and date, on which was a disc graduated in arc. When inner disc was set to time and date the instrument was suspended vertically and a pointer, pivoted at centre of disc, was sighted on Polaris. Pointer then indicated altitude of Pole. Invented 1520.

Nocturnal Arc. Arc above horizon described by a heavenly body during hours of darkness.

Nocturnal Radiation. Outgoing radiation of heat from Earth to space during hours of night.

Nodes. Those points in Ecliptic where orbit of Moon or planet cut it. Termed 'ascending' node if body crosses in N'ly direction, and 'descending' if in S'ly direction.

Nodical Month. Interval between successive passages of Moon through the same node. Value is 27 d 05 h 05·6 m.

Nog. Treenail in heel of a shore supporting a ship on the slip.

Nogging. Driving treenails in heel of shore.

'No Higher.' Injunction to helmsman, when under sail, not to come closer to the wind.

Nolloth's Ship Clinometer. Hinged instrument with one arm clamped athwartships, in ship's horizontal plane, and one arm pivoted. By sighting horizon along movable arm the angle of roll can be read on a graduated arc.

Non-Harmonic. When applied to tidal data and methods, denotes those values and methods based upon, or derived from, observation and experience, and not from harmonic analysis or methods.

Non-toppling Block. Ballasted pulley-block used in lower end of a purchase to ensure that purchase can be rounded up without block capsizing.

Noon. That instant when true or mean Sun is on the meridian of a place. Named 'apparent' or 'mean', according to the Sun considered.

Norfolk Wherry. Large flat-bottomed craft with mast stepped well forward. Carries a large, loose-footed gaff sail abaft mast. Met with on Norfolk Broads and in the vicinity.

Normal Centre (of Earth). That point, in Earth's axis, at which a vertical line passing through an observer would meet the axis.

Normal Latitude. Angle between plane of Equator and a vertical line passing downwards through an observer.

Normand's Formula. Introduced by M. Normand, in 1882, to calculate 'Inch Trim Moment' from area of waterplane, length of load waterline, beam and volume of displacement.

Norman Heads. Shaped extremities of cross piece of wooden bitts. Used for taking turns with ropes.

Normans. Short lengths of shaped timber put into sprockets of capstan to take turn of a rope that has been led to capstan for heaving. 2. U-shape irons put over whelps of capstan to prevent riding turns in hemp cable.

Norte. Cold N'ly wind in Gulf of Mexico.

North. Cardinal point of the compass. The direction of that pole of Earth at which an observer would note that direction of Earth's rotation was towards his left hand.

North Easter. Gale blowing from a NE'ly point.

North East Monsoon Current. Ocean current caused by NE monsoon in Arabian Sea. Sets S along Malabar coast and then SW'ly to African coast, where it meets a northerly stream from Zanzibar. Then sets E'ly across Indian Ocean.

North East Passage. Navigable waterway, between Atlantic and Pacific Oceans, that passes along north coast of Europe. Discovered by Nordenskiold in 1878-9.

Northern Signs. Signs of Zodiac north of Equinoctial. They are those from Aries to Virgo, both inclusive.

Northern Waggoner.* Old name for constellation Ursa Major.

North Following. In or towards the N to E quadrant of the compass. Formerly used in connection with a pair of observed stars that had not reached the meridian.

Northing. Distance, or latitude, made good in a N'ly direction.

North Pole. Northern extremity of Earth's axis of rotation. North pole of Equator, or Equinoctial.

North Preceding.* In or towards the N to W quadrant of compass. Formerly used in connection with a pair of observed stars that had crossed the meridian north of observer.

North Star. Star Polaris α Ursae Minoris.

Notary Public. Public official who is authorised to take statements on oath, and who keeps a record of all statements so made.

'Nothing Off.' Injunction to helmsman to keep ship's head close to wind, and not let it fall to leeward.

Notice of Abandonment. Formal surrender, by owner, to underwriters of policy on an insured ship that is a constructive total loss. Is a prerequisite to payment of insurance.

Notice of Readiness. Written notice, given by Master or agent of an arrived ship, stating ship's readiness to load and approximate amount of cargo required. Delivered to shipper or his agent.

Notice to Mariners. Periodical, or casual, notices issued by Hydrographic Department, or other authority, regarding changes in lights, buoys, and other navigational aids; alterations in charted information; menaces to navigation and other matters of importance and urgency to shipping and navigation.

Noting a Bill. The recording, by a notary public, that a Bill of Exchange has been presented but not accepted.

Noting Protest. Making a statement under oath in the presence of a notary public, and before the full implication of the matter protested is known. By reserving the right to 'extend', the Protest can be amplified as relevant information becomes available.

Not Under Command. Said of a vessel when, through some accident, she is not fully under control while under way.

Ntepe Dhows. Remarkable craft once built at port of Lamu. They had no stem or sternposts and planking was sewn together with coir twine. They were remarkably weatherly and fast—but very wet.

Nuclear Power. Power derived from nuclear fision which generates heat used to produce steam. Chief advantages are that large quantities of bunkers need not be carried and (for submarines) no fresh air is consumed.

Number. Flag hoist that indicates a vessel's name.

Nunatak. Isolated rocky peak rising from a sheet of inland ice.

Nun Buoy. Buoy having the shape of two cones, base to base.

Nut (of Anchor). Key piece, on stock, that fits in slot in shank and prevents stock from turning.

Nutation. A 'nodding' of Earth's axis during a period of 18 years 220 days. Caused by variation in the Lunisolar gravitational pull on Earth's equatorial bulge—the variation being due to Moon's maximum declination varying between 18° 18′ and 28° 36′ in the period. Pole of Equinoctial describes a small ellipse about its mean place. The value of nutation is $18\frac{1}{2}''$ of arc, that is $9\frac{1}{4}''$ above or below its mean value.

O

Oakum. Rope that has been unlaid and the yarns teased out. Used for caulking seams, filling fenders, and other purposes.

Oar. Rowing implement made of wood and consisting of a blade, a long shaft and a loom that forms a hand-grip. Blade may be flat or curved.

Oar Lock. 'Rowlock.'

Oar Propeller. Machine for propelling a boat by actuating an oar in the manner adopted when sculling with oar over stern.

Oar Swivel. Name once given to a 'crutch'.

Object Glass. That lens, in a telescope or binocular, at which light rays from an object enter the instrument.

Oblate Spheroid. Solid produced by semi-rotation of an ellipse about its minor axis. Sometimes applied to a spheroid that rotates on its minor axis—as do Earth and planets.

Oblique Sailing. Sailing obliquely to the meridian, so that latitude and longitude are changing.

Oblique Sphere. Terrestrial sphere as it appears to an observer who is not at Equator or a pole. Apparent movement of all heavenly bodies are along circles oblique to horizon.

Obliquity of Ecliptic. Angle between plane of Equinoctial and plane of Ecliptic.

Observation. Measurement of altitude and bearing of a heavenly body. 2. Measurement of tidal phenomena.

Observed Altitude. Sextant altitude of a heavenly body when corrected for index error.

Observed Distance. Angular distance between two heavenly bodies when corrected for index error of sextant.

Obstruction. In a chart, signifies something below chart datum that is a possible menace to navigation.

Occlude. To enclose; to shut up.

Occlusion. Line, on a meteorological chart, indicating the meeting of cold and warm fronts. Also the interposition of the cold front between the surface and the warm air mass under which it has intruded.

Occultation. Obscuration of a heavenly body by a nearer body passing between it and an observer. 2. The hiding of a light by the interposition of a screen.

Occulting. Said of light when its period of visibility is not less than its period of occultation.

Ocean. Originally a great river that was supposed to encircle the habitable world. Now applied to the great seas that extend between the continents.

Ocean Greyhound. A fast passenger liner.

Ocean Plait. An under and over plaiting of a single rope that is often used for making mats.

Oceanus. In ancient mythology was the god of the river Oceanus. He and his wife, Tethys, were parents of all rivers, and of 3000 nymphs (Oceanides).

Octant. Reflecting instrument with arc of 45°, and graduated to 90°.

Oertz Rudder. Streamlined rudder designed to reduce eddy currents from propeller streams and to eliminate dead water.

Off and Fair. Order to take off a damaged member of a vessel, to restore it to its proper shape and condition, and to replace it in position.

Off and On. Said of a sailing along a coast when progress is made by alternately standing in towards the land and standing off it.

Officer of the Watch. Officer in charge of a watch for the time being.

Official Log. Book in form approved by Dept. of T. & I. issued to Master of a British ship when engaging crew. Is entered with information required by Merchant Shipping Acts concerning such matters as draught of water on sailing, any casualty affecting the vessel, marriages, births, or deaths occurring on board, disciplinary action taken against offenders, particulars regarding boat and other drills, deck cargo carried, etc. At end of voyage is delivered to Superintendent of Marine Mercantile Office.

Offing. Sea area lying between visible horizon and a line midway between horizon and observer on the shore. To keep an offing is to keep a safe distance away from the coast.

Off the Wind. Sailing with wind abaft the beam. Sometimes used to mean being further from wind than justifiable while sailing close-hauled. Said of cowl ventilator when back to wind.

Ohm. Unit of electrical resistance. Equivalent to force of one ampere of current at a pressure of one volt. Standardised as resistance set up in a column of mercury, of uniform diameter, with temperature of 0°C, mass of 14·4521 grammes, length of 106·3 centimetres.

Ohm's Law. Links up relationship between electrical current, voltage, and resistance by formula $E=CR$ when E is voltage, C is current in amperes, and R is resistance in ohms.

Oil Bag. Canvas bag containing oakum, or waste, saturated with oil. Veered, when required, for modifying storm waves.

Oil Fuel. Petroleum residue used in furnaces for raising steam in boilers. Flashpoint must be at least 150°F for marine purposes. Heat value is about 1·3 that of same weight of coal—but about 1·6 bulk for bulk.

Oiling. Taking in oil fuel. Lubricating machinery.

Oilskins. Waterproof clothing made of calico and soaked with linseed oil, or covered with a bitumastic preparation.

Oil Tanker. Vessel specially constructed and fitted for carrying oil in bulk.

Okta. Unit equalling in area to ⅛ of sky, used in specifying cloud amount.

Old Dreadnought. Nickname given to Admiral Boscawen on account of his valorous conduct in H.M.S. *Dreadnought*.

Old Grog. Nickname given to Admiral Edward Vernon, 1684–1757, who wore a grogram coat in bad weather. He was the first to dilute seamen's rum.

Old Horse. Salt beef.

Old Ice. Ice that was not melted during previous summer.

Old Man. Colloquial name for the commander of a merchant vessel.

Oleron. Island at mouth of river Charente, France. Gave its name to the famous maritime 'Laws of Oleron'.

Ombrometer. A rain gauge.

Omega. A global position-fixing system using Very Low Frequencies and comparing phases of signals (as in Decca) received from earth-based transmitters by reflection from satellites in fixed orbits.

On a Bowline. Said of a vessel when sailing close-hauled with bowlines taut.

One for Coming Up. Final pull on a rope to obtain rather more than is required, and so allow for slight loss when turning up.

On the Wind. Close-hauled.

Oomiaks. Sealskin canoes used by Eskimo.

Ooze. Deep-sea deposit composed of very fine grains of foraminifera, shell, diatoms, and other substances.

Opening a Transit. Moving to one side of a transit line so that there is an angle between the objects previously in transit.

Open Bearings. Two bearings of the same object, one taken before running a known distance and the other after running it. Used in common pilotage for finding ship's position at second bearing.

Open Boat. An undecked boat.

Open Cover. Development of 'Floating Policy'. Has no limit to value that may be shipped. Premiums not payable until closings are made and policies are issued.

Open Hawse. Said of cables when riding by two cables, one on each bow, and each cable leads directly to its anchor.

Open Hawse to the Gale. Said of a vessel when moored open hawse with the wind right ahead.

Open Link. The unstudded link in each end of a shackle of cable.

Open Pack. Pack-ice in which there are some navigable lanes of water.

Open Policy. 'Floating Policy.'

Open Roadstead. Roadstead that has good anchorage ground but is not sheltered from winds.

Open Sea. The sea when observer is in such a position that there is an uninterrupted sea horizon. 2. Sea in which there is no shoal water. 3. Sea outside territorial limits.

Open Water. Unobstructed water. 2. Navigable waterway through ice.

Opposed Cylinder Engine. Internal combustion engine having cylinders on opposite sides of each crank. Impulses are applied at twice the usual rate.

Opposed Piston Engine. Internal combustion engine having two pistons in each cylinder. Charging, compression and ignition take place between the pistons, each of which operates its own connecting rod.

Opposition. Relative positions of two heavenly bodies, particularly solar system bodies, when their celestial longitudes differ by 180°, or their R.A.'s differ by 12 hours.

Optional Pilotage. Pilotage service that is available but is not compulsory for specified vessels.

Orbit. Path of planet around Sun, or of a satellite around its primary.

Ordinary.* Formerly, 'in ordinary' denoted H.M. ships that were not in commission but had care and maintenance crews on board.

Ordinary Seaman. Seaman aged 18, or more, who has not qualified to be rated able seaman.

Ordnance Datum. Level to which heights and depths are referred in English surveying. Formerly, the level was a rather inaccurate approximation of mean sea-level at Liverpool. Is now mean sea level at Newlyn, Cornwall.

Orient. The Far East. East point. To define a direction by its relation to the east point of compass—a relic of the days when the east point of compass was the prime cardinal point, and was marked by a fleur-de-lys.

Original Bill. The first of a set of bills of exchange to be presented. Prior to presentation, No. 1 is the original bill.

Orion. One of the most notable constellations. Lies between R.A.'s 5 h and 6 h and Dec. N10° to S10°. Name is that of a mythical giant hunter who was supposed to be the son of a peasant. Other myths make him a prince of Tanagra. As Lecky says, 'Orion moves in the highest stellar society,' being surrounded by important constellations and stars.

Orionids. Meteor shower through which Earth passes in autumn, and which appears to radiate from constellation Orion.

Orlop Beams. Beams supporting an orlop deck.

Orlop Deck. Was the lowest deck in a line of battleship, being a platform laid over timbers of the hold.

Ormonde Beacon. Dan buoy used by surveying ships. Buoyancy is supplied by three 25-gallon oil-drums. Is ballasted with a 3-cwt. sinker, its bamboo mast carries a flag, 16 ft. by 10 ft.

Orographic. Pertaining to mountains.

Orographic Rain. Deposit of rain by a saturated air-stream coming into contact with rising land.

Oropesa Sweep. Towed wire used for sweeping sea bottom when surveying for shoals, or locating wrecks. Consists of two kite 'otters', one at each end of a 450-ft. sweep wire, and a third otter—close astern—to keep both sweep wires down.

Orrery. Machine that illustrates the relative movements of the solar system bodies.

Orthodromics. Science and methods of great circle sailing.

Orthodromy. Art of sailing on a great circle.

Orthographic Projection. Projection of surface of a sphere to a plane perpendicular to line of sight, all lines of sight being considered as parallel.

Osculating. Said of two arcs, or circles, when in contact but not intersecting.

Osmosis. Water penetrating the gel coat of Glass Reinforced Plastic and travelling along the fibres of glass.

Otter. Plane surface towed forward of its middle length so that it will incline and dive. Used in fishing, mine-sweeping or surveying.

Outboard. Suspended or projecting outside a vessel. At or towards the side of a ship.

Outboard Motor. Portable motor attached to the stern of a boat with a vertical shaft driving an immersed propeller.

Outer Turns. Turns of a seizing, or whipping, that override the inner turns. 2. Those turns of an earing that tend to stretch a sail.

Outhaul. Any rope or purchase used for hauling outward. Specifically applied to clew of a gaff sail, and to outboard whip of union purchase.

Outlying. At a distance from the shore, or from a given position.

Outpoint. To sail closer to the wind than does a rival vessel.

Outport. Customs term for any U.K. port other than London.

Outrigger. Spreader set up to windward of crosstrees or tops to give more spread to breast backstay. 2. Projecting bracket for carrying rowlock in a small skiff or racing boat. 3. Boat fitted with outriggers.

Outsail. To sail faster than another ship, and leave her astern.

Outside Clinch. Turn of end of rope round its own part and with the end of rope outside the bight thus formed.

Outward Bound. Said of a vessel leaving a port in her own country. Said, relatively, of any vessel going to sea, even if homeward bound.

Outward Clearance. Formalities and procedure for obtaining 'Clearance Outwards'.

Overboard. Over and outside the sides of a ship.

Overcast. State of sky when it is 4/5, or more, covered with cloud.

Overcasting Staff. Measuring scale used by shipwrights to determine the differences in timbers, or frames, from midships towards ends.

Overfalls. Violently disturbed water where a current sets over an irregularity in sea bed. Level tends to sink where bed rises, and to rise where bed sinks.

Overhand Knot. Simple knot made in end of a rope by taking end across rope and round it, and then through bight thus formed.

Overhaul. To examine with a view to repairing or refitting. 2. To overtake. 3. To extend a tackle so that distance between blocks is increased.

Overhang. Projection of upper part of stern abaft rudder-post.

Overhead. Underside of a deck that is above another deck.

Overlap. In yacht racing, exists when two yachts are on parallel courses and forward end of bowsprit of one yacht is forward of stern of another yacht.

Overlapping Rule. When two racing yachts are approaching a mark or obstruction, and an overlap has been established, the yacht further from the obstruction shall allow sufficient room for the nearer yacht to clear the obstruction.

Overload. To take excessive weight into a ship so that the appropriate load line becomes submerged.

Overlop.* Old name for 'Orlop Deck'.

Over Rake. Said of the action of heavy seas that rise up and sweep into an anchored ship lying head to wind.

Over Run. To go past or beyond an intended position or distance.

Overset. Capsize.

Overshoot. To go ahead of an intended position or line.

Overtaking. Coming up to another vessel from any point abaft the other vessel's beam. In the Rules for Preventing Collisions at Sea an overtaking vessel is one that is coming up with another vessel from any direction more than two points abaft her beam.

Over Tide. Delayed part of a tidal undulation that arrives after tide has begun to fall. May cause falling tide to rise or stop temporarily.

Owner. Registered owner of ship. In R.N. is a nickname for the Captain.

Owner's Liability. Statutory limit of liability of shipowner for losses due to the improper navigation of his vessel when occurring without his fault or privity. Limits are £15 per registered ton if there be loss of life, £8 per ton if no loss of life.

Ox Bow. Bend or reach in a river.

Ox Eye. Small cloud, or meteor, immediately preceding a violent storm off Cape of Good Hope. Mentioned by Falconer, but not by meteorologists.

Oxter Plate. Specially-shaped plate where side-plating ends in way of after deadwood.

Oya Siwo. Cold counter current setting S'ward along SE coast of Kamchatka and Kurile Islands, and along E coast of Yezo. Floating ice is carried between Kuriles and Yezo in early spring.

P

Packet. Mail vessel that may also carry passengers and cargo. Sometimes applied to a passenger vessel on a regular run.

Packet Boat. 'Packet.'

Packet Ship. 'Packet.'

Pack-Ice. Numbers of large pieces of floating ice that have come together and lie more or less in contact.

Pad. Shaped timber put on top of a wooden beam to give required camber. 2. Large and cylindrical coil of spunyarn or nettle stuff.

Paddle. To propel a boat by using a paddle. 2. To row with a short stroke and very little weight. 3. Short oar with a broad blade. Held with both hands and not shipped in crutch or rowlock. 4. Board, or float, of paddle-wheel.

Paddle-Beam. Strong thwartship beam fitted before and abaft a paddle-wheel.

Paddle-Box. Casing over upper half of a paddle-wheel.

Paddler. Vessel propelled by paddles.

Paddle Shaft. Steel shaft by which paddles are turned by engines. 2. Handle of a wooden paddle.

Paddle-Wheel. Circular skeleton framework that carries paddle-boards. Is turned by an engine, and so propels vessel.

Paddle-Wheel Effect. That effect of a screw propeller which tends to pull ship's stern to one side of her course. Due to lower part of blade working in water more unyielding than that at upper part.

Paddy's Purchase. Seaman's scornful name for any lead of a rope by which effort is lost or wasted. 'Paddy's purchase, spunyarn over a nail.'

Padeye. A ring or eye fixed to the deck to which a block may be shackled. (U.S.).

Pad Piece. Pad (timber).

Painter. Rope at stem of boat for securing it or for towing purposes. 2. Chain by which an Admiralty pattern anchor is secured in place. 'Shank Painter.'

Painter's Colic. Form of lead poisoning due to lead in paint getting into system of a painter.

Pall. Old form of 'Pawl'.

Pallium. Old name for nimbostratus cloud.

Palm. Leather or hide strip that goes round hand and has an iron disc for forcing a sailmaker's needle when sewing canvas or roping it.

Palm of Anchor. Flat face of fluke that provides a holding surface.

Palm and Needle Hitching. Series of half hitches made with sail-maker's twine and a palm and needle.

Palm and Needle Whipping. Whipping, at end of rope, that has been finished off by bringing end of whipping twine down a cantline of the rope, under the next strand, up the next cantline, behind the next strand and down the cantline. Palm and needle are necessary.

Palowa. Sailing craft of China Seas. Schooner rigged, whale-boat stern, about 70 ft. long.

Pampero. Line squall of Argentina and Uruguay. Marked by thunder, lightning and rain.

Pan. A spoken radiotelephony message prefixed with the word 'Pan' indicates that an urgent message concerning the safety of a vessel, aircraft or person is about to be made.

Panama Canal Tonnage. Computation for tonnage of ships passing through Panama Canal. Approximates nett registered tonnage, but has important differences.

Panama Lead. Circular fair leads at ends of a ship. Necessary when being towed by shore locomotives in Panama Canal.

Pancake Ice. Small, circular sheets of newly-formed ice that do not impede navigation.

Pangaia. Mozambique vessel mentioned by Hakluyt. 'Like a barge, with one matsail of coconut leaves. The hull sewed together with the rinds of trees, and pinned with wooden pins.'

Panting. A more or less rhythmic in and out movement of ship's plating due to variations in water-pressure. Particularly noticeable forward when pitching.

Panting Beam. Beam placed athwartships to support shipside plating against panting stresses.

Panting Stress. Stress, due to water pressure variations, that tends to cause an in and out movement of ship's underwater plating.

Parallactic Angle. Angle between hour circle of an observed heavenly body and the arc of a circle of altitude intercepted by the body and observer's zenith. Is angle X in PZX triangle. Also called 'Angle of Position'.

Parallactic Inequality. Variation in tidal phenomena that is due to variation in Moon's distance from Earth.

Parallax. Apparent change in position of an observed object when due to change in position of observer. 2. Parallax of sextant is equal to angle, at an observed object, between a line from centre of index glass and another line from horizon glass. Error is quite negligible unless observed object be very near.

Parallax in Altitude. Difference between altitude of heavenly body above sensible horizon and its altitude above rational horizon. Is maximum when body is in sensible horizon.

Parallel Index. Lines parallel to the bearing-marker on a radar display, useful for passing an intended distance from a point of land or vessel.

Parallel of Altitude. Small circle parallel to plane of horizon and passing through all points having the same altitude.

Parallel of Declination. Small circle of celestial sphere that passes through all points having the same declination.

Parallel of Latitude. Small circle of terrestrial sphere, parallel to Equator, passing through all positions having the same latitude.

Parallel of Position. Name sometimes given to a 'Circle of Equal Altitude'.

Parallel Ruler. Rulers used for drawing and transferring courses and bearings on a chart always moving with their edges parallel.

Parallel Sailing. The sailing of a vessel along a parallel of latitude. Course will be East or West true. Difference of longitude will be distance run, in miles × Secant of Latitude.

Parallel Sphere. Terrestrial sphere as it appears to an observer at the Poles. All heavenly bodies appear to move parallel to horizon.

Paranthelion. Mock sun occasionally seen at same altitude as Sun but more than 90° away from it in azimuth.

Paraselene. Mock moon occasionally seen 22°–25° away from Moon in azimuth.

Paravane. Torpedo-shaped body with transverse and inclined plate. Towed from stern or bows of ship as a protection aganist moored mines.

Parbuckle. Simple two-power purchase made by securing bight of a rope and pulling upwards on the two ends. Any object of circular section can be laid in bights of loops, and will roll over as it is lifted. To parbuckle is to lift with a parbuckle.

Parcel. To wrap canvas, hessian, etc., tightly around the lay of the splicing in a rope preparatory to serving. Put on in direction of lay. 2. Separated part, of cargo, which is all of one nature, or is for one consignee, or for one port.

Parcelling. Material used for parcelling a rope.

Parclose. Limber hole of a ship.

Parhelion. Mock sun frequently observable in high latitudes. One is to be seen at 22° away from either side of true Sun, and is surrounded by halo or halos.

Parliament Heel. List deliberately put on a ship for careening purposes.

Parrel. Rope or collar by which the jaws of a gaff or yard confine a mast.

Parrel Trucks. Large wooden balls threaded on a rope parrel to prevent parrel gripping mast when hoisting or lowering.

Parson's Turbine. Reaction turbine in which rings of blades on rotors are increased in size along path of steam, so allowing for expansion of steam.

Part. To separate, or to break, a rope or cable.

Part Brass Rags. R.N. term signifying to break a friendship.

Partial Awning Deck Type. Describes vessels having continuous deck and side plating from amidships to forecastle.

Particular Average. Indemnity due from a particular person or persons to make good a particular maritime loss against which insurance has been effected.

Particular Average Loss. Maritime loss that is indemnified by particular average.

Particular Charges. Expenditure incurred in averting a particular average loss; salvage and General Average charges being excepted.

Particular Lien. Legal claim upon certain property for money expended in connection with the property.
Parting Strop. Strop inserted between two hawsers, and weaker than the hawsers, so that strop, and not hawsers, will part with any excessive strain. 2. Special strop used for holding cable while parting it.
Partners. Fore and aft stiffeners on underside of deck to strengthen it in way of piercings of deck for masts, capstan spindle, etc.
Passage. Narrow channel 2. Conveyance by ship.
Passage Boat. Boat that conveys goods and passengers.
Passage Broker. Person who is licensed by Government to sell or let steerage passages from U.K. to places outside Europe and Mediterranean Sea. Is required to give a bond to Government, and may employ agents approved by Emigration Officer.
Passage Money. Money paid for conveyance by ship.
Passage Winds. Trade winds, especially the 'Westerlies'.
Passenger. Any person other than Master, owner, owner's family or owner's servants, who is carried in a ship. Used sarcastically to denote a member of crew who does not pull his weight.
Passenger Ship. Vessel carrying fare-paying passengers.
Passenger Steamer. In British law, is a steamer carrying more than 12 passengers.
Passe Volant. A 'Quaker' or dummy gun. 2. A movable gun.
Passing Ship. Said of a vessel going in a direction opposite to that of one's own ship.
Patache. French name for a small sailing vessel used as a tender.
Patent Log. Former name for a towed log. Cherub Log.
Path. That direction and route that a cyclonic depression may be expected to take.
Path Indicator. Instrument that indicates amount and direction of departure of ship's head from a set course.
Paul. Until fairly recently was the common spelling of 'Pawl'.
Paunch Mat. Protective mat made by entwining strands of rope so that a thick mat with close-laid surface results.
Pavo. 'Peacock.' Southern constellation between Fomalhaut and Antares. Has one navigational star.
Pawl. Short, pivoted bar, with shaped toe, that trails over a toothed rack while machine is in motion. Pawl drops behind tooth of rack, by gravity or operation of a spring, and prevents reverse movement when moving power ceases.
Pawl Bitt. Vertical timber opposite middle of windlass. Carries pawl engaging in ratchet wheel on barrel.
Pawl Post. 'Pawl Bitt.'
Pawl Rack. A well-secured series of standing stops against which a pawl can take.
Pawl Rim. Toothed wheel surrounding barrel of windlass, and in which a pawl engages.
Pay. To cover the caulking of a seam with pitch or marine glue.
Pay Away. To pay out a rope more quickly.
Pay Down. To pass a cable or hawser below deck.

Paying Off Pendant. Very long pendant flown by H.M. ship when proceeding home to pay off. Length may be anything up to one foot for every month in commission, plus length of ship.

Pay Off. To discharge a crew and close Articles of Agreement of a merchant ship. 2. To terminate commission of H.M. ship. 3. Said of ship's head when it moves away from wind, especially when tacking.

Pay Out. To veer a rope or cable.

Pay Round. Turn ship's head to leeward by wind and sail action.

Pazaree. Rope, from clew of foresail, rove through block of lower studdingsail boom when running free.

Pea. Extremity of arm of anchor. Bill, or peak, of anchor.

Pea Jacket. Loose jacket, of coarse woollen material, formerly used by seamen and fishermen.

Peak. After upper corner of spanker or trysail. After end of gaff. 2. Pea of anchor.

Peak Downhaul. Rope rove through block at end of gaff to steady gaff when hauling it down.

Peak Halyards. Rope or purchase used for hoisting peak of gaff. 2. Ensign halyards rove through block at peak of gaff.

Peak Purchase. Peak halyards when rove as a purchase.

Peak Tank. Ballast tank in extreme end of vessel, either forward or aft.

Peak Tye. Tye rove for hoisting peak of gaff.

Pegasus. Northern constellation on side of Pole opposite to Ursa Major. Distinctive feature is the 'Great square of Pegasus' made by Alpheratz, Scheat, Markhab and Algenib.

Peggy. Merchant Navy nickname for seaman whose turn of duty it is to keep the messing place clean.

Peg to Windward. Beat, claw or work to windward.

Pelican Hook. Name sometimes given to a slip hook.

Pelorus. Dumb compass dial, pivoted and movable by hand, which can be shipped in an appropriate position for observing bearings of objects obscured at compass. Has its own lubber line. Objects observed when pelorus is set to zero will indicate their relative bearings; when set to ship's course they will indicate compass bearings.

Pelorus Jack. A white dolphin, about 15 ft. long, that persistently accompanied steamships through French Passage in Pelorus Sound, New Zealand, from the 1870s to 1912. His age has been estimated as nearly 300 years. Was a unique specimen, and his life was protected by legislation of New Zealand Government. A report of his death resulted in flags being flown at half mast in Wellington.

Penalty Clause. Clause attached to an agreement to stipulate penalty for infringement or non-fulfilment, so making it binding.

Pencel. Very small, narrow flag.

Pendant. Length of rope or wire connecting the standing block of a purchase with a fixed point of attachment. Used in derrick guys, at booms, yardarms, etc. 2. Alternative form of 'Pennant'.

Pennant. Four-sided flag with a head deeper than the fly, the upper and lower sides sloping towards the middle line. Usually spelt 'pendant', but this is open to criticism.

Pentad. Period of 5 days. Used in meteorology as being an aliquot part ($\frac{1}{73}$) of a year.

Pentekontor. Ancient Greek vessel of about 700 B.C. propelled with 50 oars.

Penumbra. Modification of an eclipse by the formation of a partly-illuminated area, or penumbra, between the lighted and eclipsed areas. In eclipse of Moon, it is due to sunlight being refracted by Earth's atmosphere and falling on some of Moon's eclipsed part.

People. Old name for a ship's company.

Perch. Vertical pole erected as a navigational aid and carrying a distinctive topmark.

Periplus, Peripli. Voyage or voyages, or sailing directions, of the ancient Greeks.

Performance Monitor. A device for testing the performance of a radar set and indicating the result.

Perforst Men. Seamen taken out of a merchant ship for service in the Royal Navy. Corruption of 'per force'.

Perigee. That point, in orbit of a solar system body, particularly Moon, at which it comes nearest to Earth.

Perihelion. That point, in orbit of a solar system body, at which it comes nearest to Sun.

Perils of the Sea. In policies of insurance and in bills of lading it denotes fortuitous accidents and casualties due to the sea. Does not include ordinary action of winds and waves.

Periodical Comet. Comet whose orbit is around Sun, and so reappears at intervals.

Periodical Meteors. Meteor showers, that occur at more or less constant intervals. More precisely, interstellar debris lying in Earth's orbit and becoming incandescent when subjected to friction of Earth's atmosphere.

Periodical Stars. Variable stars whose magnitudes change during a certain period.

Periodical Survey. Survey of a ship every four years in accordance with international regulations.

Periodic Month. 'Tropical Month.'

Periodic Wind. 'Monsoon.'

Period of Encounter. Time interval between successive wave crests passing a given point in a vessel.

Period of Roll. Time, in seconds, taken by a vessel to roll from extreme angle on one side to extreme angle on opposite side.

Period of Wave. Time interval, in seconds, between passage of two wave crests past a stationary point. With ocean waves, this interval, in seconds, is about 2/7 speed of wave in knots.

Periscope. Long, slender prismatic telescope fitted in submarines for observing surface vessels while submarine is submerged.

Periscope Depth. That submersion of a submarine that leaves only the periscope above sea level.

Permanent Aunora. Slightly illuminated area in the night sky that is sometimes observable. Caused by ultra violet radiation of Sun in upper reaches of atmosphere.

Permanent Magnetism. That magnetism that is retained in whatever position the magnetised body occupies in a magnetic field.

Permanent Wind. Wind that blows in one direction continuously. Found between latitudes 20° and 40°N approximately.

Permeability. Property of soft iron to receive magnetism. 2. Capacity of a space to allow entry of water, having due regard to contents of the space.

Pernavigate. To sail over, or through.

Perpetual Day. Protracted interval during which Sun's diurnal movement does not effect length of day. Maximum period, at Poles, is about six months.

Perpetual Night. Protracted interval during which Sun's diurnal movement does not effect length of night. Maximum period, at Poles, is about six months.

Personal Equation. Factor or errors, more or less constant, that is to be ascribed to the personal qualities and limitations of the person responsible for an observation, deduction or result.

Personal Error. Error due to personal equation.

Personnel. Comprehensive term for all persons collectively in an undertaking, thus differentiating them from the 'material'.

Perspective Glass. Old name for telescope.

Perturbation. Irregularity or disturbance in a planet's movement when due to forces not normally affecting it. 2. Variation in magnetic phenomena when due to eruptions or atmospheric electricity.

Peruvian Current. Ocean current, about 150 miles wide, setting from Valdivia and along coast towards Panama. Divides in vicinity of Payta.

Pescod Wing Fin. Horizontal and curved fin that is fitted a little below centre line of propeller shafting to give a good direction to water flowing towards propeller.

Peter Boat. A double-ended boat.

Pett's Disengaging Gear. Boat releasing gear in which boat is held on two horizontal hooks in fore and aft line of boat and at a greater distance apart than are the falls. Wire fore and after between lifting eyes on hooks keeps eyes in position; hooks have bill uppermost, and bill has a slight upward cant. After hook is hinged and controlled by lever, which can be locked in position. When after hook is canted by lever the after block slips off, forward block then slips off. Boat drops into water slightly stern first.

Petty Average. The small expenses and charges borne by a vessel when entering a port to load or discharge. Generally referred to as 'Average Accustomed'.

I

Petty Officer. Rank intermediate between officer and rating, and in charge of ratings. Usually messed apart from ratings, and has special privileges appropriate to his position.

Phact. Star α Columbae. S.H.A. 275°; Dec. S34°; Mag. 2·8.

Phantom Ship. 'Flying Dutchman.' There are, however, other phantom ships that are reported as having been sighted.

Pharos. A lighthouse or beacon. So called from the island of Pharos, in Bay of Alexandria, on which the first lighthouse was built by Sostratus Cnidius in 3rd century B.C. Was 450 ft. high and lasted for over 1000 years.

Phase. Appearance of Moon, or inferior planet, whose illuminated surface varies with its position relative to Sun and Earth. Mars, also, has a slight phasing. 2. Particular stage in recurring sequence of movements or changes usually expressed in degrees, the complete sequence or period being 360°. 3. Changes in a navigational beacon light in one period of exhibition.

Phase Inequality. Variation in tidal interval, or amplitude, between successive high waters as Moon goes through her phases.

Phase Lag. Lag, in time or angle, between exertion of a tide producing force and the appearance of its effect.

Phosphorescence. Luminosity of sea surface due to minute animal organisms in the water.

Pick. Name sometimes given to pea of anchor. Colloquial name for an anchor.

Picket Boat. Fast, decked and mechanically-propelled boat carried in first class ships of R.N.

Picking Up Rope. Comparatively small rope carried from an arrived ship to a buoy, to hold ship while stronger moorings are attached.

Pier. Erection projected from land into water to form a landing, loading and discharging place; for a promenade or for protecting a port or harbour from effect of heavy seas. 2. Supporting member for an arch or span.

Pierhead Jump. The boarding of a vessel almost at the moment of sailing.

Pig. A piece of metal ballast.

Piggin. Very small wooden pail having one stave prolonged to form a handle. Used as a bailer in a boat.

Pile. A strong post driven into the sea- or river-bed to mark the edge of the channel or to serve as a mooring.

Pile Driving. Said of a ship when, in heavy weather, she lifts her forefoot out of the water and it falls heavily into the sea.

Pile Up. To run a vessel ashore, or aground on a reef or rock.

Pilferage. Petty theft.

Pillars. Vertical members, of a ship's construction, by which decks and beams are supported and the transverse form of vessel is maintained in the vertical plane.

Pillar Sextant. Type of sextant in which rigidity of frame is attained by having a rather massive vertical member.

Pillow. Wooden block on which inner end of bowsprit rests.

Pilot. Qualified person authorised to pilot incoming and outgoing vessels in a pilotage area. 2. One who controls a vessel. 3. Volumes of the Admiralty Sailing Directions, e.g. 'The Mediterranean Pilot'.

Pilotage. Service duties, remuneration or establishment of a pilot or pilots. 2. Navigation of ship by methods that do not require celestial observations.

Pilotage Act (1913). British Act of Parliament dealing with pilots, pilotage and pilotage authorities. Limitation of liability of pilotage authorities is dealt with in an Act of 1936. *See* 'Limitation of Liability'.

Pilotage Authority. Corporate body, approved or appointed responsible for the organisation and conduct of pilotage in a given port or area.

Pilotage District. Area controlled by a particular Pilotage Authority.

Pilotages. Fees and charges for pilotage service.

Pilot Boat. Small craft used for embarking or disembarking pilots in sheltered waters.

Pilot Cutter. Sea-going vessel that cruises in a specific area for purposes of putting pilots on board inward bound ships, and for receiving them from outward bound ships.

Pilot Fish. Fish, about a foot long, sometimes seen preceding a shark. Bluish in colour with five to seven dark bars. May sometimes attend a ship.

Pilot Flag. Distinctive flag of a pilot vessel. Small replica may be flown by a piloted vessel. British flag is square with upper half white and lower half red.

Pilot Jack. Union flag with white border. Used as request for pilot's services.

Pilot Line. Astronomical position line along which a vessel can conveniently sail in good safety.

Pilot's Fairway. Channel in which pilotage is compulsory.

Pilot Signals. Signals made by a vessel requiring a pilot. International Code flag G, or at night, a blue light, or 'G' by flashing.

Pilot Station. Position, at sea or ashore, at which pilots are stationed for embarkation on vessels requiring pilotage.

Pilots' Water. Any area, of sea or harbour, in which pilotage is compulsory.

Pin. Belaying pin. Axis of sheave or roller. Keep pin. Small and thin metal strip, or rod used for securing.

Pinch. To sail very close to the wind with some loss of speed.

Pinch Bar. Iron or steel lever with curved or inclined end and a tapered extremity, or toe. Toe forms lifting end, and curve, or angle of bevel, acts as fulcrum; thus giving considerable leverage.

Pineapple Knot. Ornamental knot that may have practical uses. Has appearance of an elongated 'turk's head'.

Pingle. Name formerly given to a small sailing craft of northern England. Probably connected with 'Pink'; a little pink.

Pink. Narrow sterned sailing craft with lateen rig. Stern projected aft considerably. Used for reconnoitring, carrying stores, and similar purposes.

Pink Stern. A high and narrow stern.

Pinnace. Formerly, small, two-masted sailing vessel sometimes with oars. Now rowing, sailing or mechanically-propelled boat of R.N. Is diagonal built; 36 ft. in length.

Pin Rack. Rack carrying belaying pins.

Pin Rail. Horizontal rail, at ship's side, carrying belaying pins.

Pintle. Vertical pin, on forward edge of rudder, that ships into gudgeon and forms a hinge.

Pinyano. Small, one-masted fishing vessel of China Sea. Fitted with outrigger.

Pioneer. Net-cutting attachment formerly fitted into nose of torpedo to cut through torpedo-nets.

Pipe. To call seamen, or to direct them, by sounds on a boatswain's call or pipe.

Pipe Down. Order to boatswain's mate to pipe hands 'down from aloft'. Now used, in R.N., to inform hands that they will not be required for work; or, at night, that hands are to turn in. 2. Be quiet.

Pipe Stool. Shaped support in which a pipe rests.

Piping the Side. Naval courtesy paid only to specified naval officers, in uniform, boarding or leaving one of H.M. ships during daylight hours. Consists of two calls on boatswain's pipe—one on approach to ship of visiting officer, the other as officer enters ship. Similarly, but in reverse order, as he leaves it.

Piracy. Robbery from a ship. The forcible taking of a ship, her cargo, apparel or furniture from the possession of the owner and for private gain. Also, the forcible entry into a ship for the purpose of damaging her.

Piragua. Large canoe of Central America.

Pirates. Robbers of a ship, not necessarily on the high seas. Includes mutinous passengers, and robbers who attack from the shore.

Pirogue. Form of 'Piragua'.

Pitch. Dark-coloured solid obtained from distillation of tar. Has a low melting point and is insoluble in water. Used for paying of deck seams and stopping of small leaks.

Pitch of Propeller. Distance vessel would advance with one turn of propeller if there were no slip. Also applied to angle that propeller blade makes with propeller shaft. It is this pitch which produces propulsion of ship.

Pitch of Rivets. Spacing between rivets measured from centre to centre of the rivets.

Pitching. Downward falling of a vessel's bows as water support leaves them.

Pitch-pole. To be overthrown in a fore-and-aft direction.

Pitometer Log. Submerged log actuated by pressure set up by ship's advancing through water. Speed is indicated directly; distance run is indirectly obtained by additional mechanism.

Pitting. Localised corrosion causing small pits to form in metal.

Pivoting Point. That point, inside a vessel, on which she turn when under helm.

P.L.A. Port of London Authority.

Plain Sail. Sail with no reef taken in it.

Plain Sailing. 'Plane Sailing'.

Plait. Yarns or small line intertwined to make sennit, gaskets or foxes.

Plan. Chart covering a small area on a very large scale. There is no distortion, relative distances and positions being maintained.

Plan Position Indicator. *See* Cathode Ray Tube.

Plane Chart. Chart constructed on a supposition that surface of Earth is flat in charted area. Except for small areas at Equator it would be erroneous. Is not used in modern chart construction. Mercator charts were, at one time, called 'plane charts'.

Plane of Ecliptic. Plane of celestial sphere passing through centres of Earth and Sun.

Plane Sailing. That method of solving certain navigational problems on assumption that Earth's surface, in the area concerned, is a plane.

Planet. Satellite of Sun that reflects Sun's light. Excluding minor planets there are eight, Earth not being reckoned. Those revolving inside Earth's orbit are termed 'minor planets', those outside Earth's orbit being 'major planets'.

Planetarium. Mechanised model of Solar System, not to scale, used for illustrating movements of planets around Sun, constellations, etc.

Planetoid. A minor planet, or asteroid.

Plank. Technically, length of timber more than 9 inches wide and from $1\frac{1}{2}$ to 4 inches in thickness.

Planking Clamp. Implement for bending a plank to rib of a wooden vessel, and holding it in place until fastened.

Plank on Edge Type. Name given to deep and narrow yachts that developed between 1852 and 1876, about. Name is often given to deep and narrow vessels in general.

Plank Sheer. Plank resting on top timbers of ribs or frames.

Plankton. Mass of minute animal and vegetable organisms that exists in the sea below the surface and above the bottom.

Planter. Tree trunk with its root in bed of a river and its top just below water level. May be a navigational hazard in some rivers of western America.

Plat. Old name for a chart. 2. Plait.

Plate. Iron or steel sheet forming part of ship's deck or hull plating. 2. Iron or steel bar or band—such as 'Chain Plate'.

Platform. Plated deck, in engine-room, from which the engines are tended and controlled. 2. Name given to 'Orlop Deck'.

Pledge. Length of oakum used when caulking a seam.

Pleiades. Cluster of seven visible stars in constellation Taurus. Name means, 'to sail the seas'; this name being given because the ancient Greek navigational season began when Sun and Pleiades rose together.

Pleion. Meteorological term for an area in which meteorological conditions and factors are above normal.

Plot. A diagram for solving navigational or tactical problems. True Plot: A plot in which own ship's movement through the water is depicted to scale and other ships' movements are found by periodically plotting their range and bearing. Relative Plot: Own ship's position remains fixed and the apparent motion of other ships is shown, i.e. their movement relative to own ship.

Plough. One of the colloquial names for constellation Ursa Major.

Plough Star. Arcturus, in constellation Bootes.

Plume. The feather-shaped echo produced on a radar display by an Echo Box.

Pluviograph. Self-recording rain gauge.

Ply. To work to windward. 2. To sail regularly between two ports. 3. A strand in cord or rope.

Pneumercator Gauge. Instrument for indicating depth of a liquid, or draught of a ship, by denoting the pressure necessary to balance the gravitational pressure of the liquid—the pressure being indicated by a gauge or a balancing column of mercury. This pressure is read off against a specially-calibrated scale.

Pocky Cloud. Name sometimes given to 'Mammatus'.

Podger. A short steel bar, pointed at both ends, used as a lever, etc.

Point. Tapered end of a rope with alternate yarns bound round it in alternate succession. Done to prevent fraying of end, and to facilitate reeving through a sheave. 2. Reef Point. 3. Point of compass$=11\frac{1}{2}°$.

Pointed Sun. Name sometimes given to actual Sun when observing it with a reflecting instrument.

Pointers. Two principal stars of Ursa Major, a line through them pointing to Polaris.

Point Line. Small rope used for reef points. Usually about inch to $1\frac{3}{4}$ inch in size. Generally referred to by the number of threads, 15 to 21, used in making it.

Point of Origin. Accurately determined position used as a point of reference when surveying.

Point of Definition. An epoch or point from which reckonings are made and measured. Particularly applied to measurements of time. First Point of Aries and mean Sun are points of definition of sidereal time and mean solar time, respectively.

Point of Tangency. Position on a gnomonic chart where the plane to which the various positions were projected was assumed to be touching surface of Earth. At this point there will be no distortion in distance or compass bearings; positions remote from this point will have errors in both distance and bearing, increasing with their distance from the point.

Polacre. Former Mediterranean sailing vessel having three pole masts. Fore and mizen masts were lateen-rigged, mainmast square-rigged.

Polar. Pertaining to poles of a sphere; to extremeties of Earth's axis; to points in celestial concave immediately above poles of Earth; to points of no magnetic dip on surface of Earth; to points of maximum force in a magnet.

Polar Air. Cold air; not necessarily of polar or even arctic origin.

Polar Angle. Angle, at pole of Equinoctial, between two hour circles or meridians.

Polar Circles. Arctic and Antarctic circles in latitudes 66° 33′ North and South respectively.

Polar Distance. Value, in arc, of that part of hour circle intercepted between elevated pole of celestial sphere and an observed heavenly body.

Polar Front. Line of demarcation that may develop between air from high latitudes and air from low latitudes.

Polaris. The Pole Star, α Ursae Minoris. R.A. 01 h 49 m; Dec. 89°; Mag. 2·1. 2. Missile which can be launched under water and aimed at a target 2500 miles distant.

Pole. Of Earth, is extremity of its axis of rotation. Of heavens, is a point 90° from every point in circumference of Equinoctial. Of a great circle, is the extremity of a diameter of the sphere passing perpendicularly through centre of the great circle. 2. That part of a mast between truck and upper eyes of rigging. 3. A pole mast. 4. Long spar used for propulsion, in shallow water, by resting end on bottom and applying power to part above water.

Pole Axe. Weapon formerly used when boarding enemy ship. Later called 'tomahawk'.

Pole Compass. Standard compass shipped on a pole to raise it above iron of ship, and so reduce effects of local attraction.

Pole Mast. Mast made from a single pole, so differentiating it from a made or built mast.

Pole Star. Polaris. Navigational star that is nearest to north pole of heavens. Principal star in Ursa Minor.

Pole Star Tables. Tables, in Nautical Almanac, by which altitude of Polaris can be used for determining latitude when local sidereal time is known.

Policy. In marine insurance is a legal contract of indemnity for a maritime loss. Principal forms are Time, Voyage, Floating and Valued. Issued by underwriters or by corporate bodies.

Policy Proof of Interest. Usually referred to as P.P.I. Term used when person insuring has not declared his interest, but it has been assumed that the policy would not have been taken out unless interest, or contingent interest existed. If no interest exists the insurance is illegal and void in law.

Polyzoa. Very minute molluscs that exist in colonies.

Pompey. Traditional nickname for Portsmouth.

Ponente. Westerly wind in Mediterranean Sea.

Pontoon. Buoyant construction used for a landing place; for providing a road over water; for raising wrecks; for giving additional buoyancy.

Pool. Enclosed, or nearly enclosed sheet of water. 2. Fluctuating congregation of men from which can be drawn hands required for manning ships, and to which can be added men available for manning.

Poop. Short deck raised above upper deck right aft.

Pooping. Said of a vessel, or of the sea, when following seas sweep inboard from astern.

Poor Jack, Poor John. Salt fish, particularly salt cod, when issued as rations.

Popham's Code. System of signals, by flags, devised by Captain Sir H. Popham, R.N., in 1800, for communication between ships of Royal Navy. Was used in making Nelson's memorable signal at Trafalgar.

Poppets. Shaped pieces of wood that close the cut away parts of wash strake through which oars project when rowing. 2. Shores on bilgeway of launching slip, and forming part of cradle.

Popple. A short, confused sea.

Porcupine. Nickname for a wire rope when broken wires stand out from it.

Port. Harbour or haven in which shipping can lie in safety. Legally: a harbour with facilities for ships to load, unload or obtain supplies, and which has been appointed for travellers to enter or to leave the country. 2. In ship construction, an opening in ship's side to allow light or air to enter; for cargo, or baggage, to be taken in or discharged; for a gun to protrude; for water on deck to flow overboard, and other similar purposes. 3. In engineering, is an opening in a valve, cock, or cylinder to allow passage of steam, liquid or gases. 4. As a direction, is equivalent to 'left hand' when facing forward.

Port Admiral. Admiral in charge of a Naval port.

Portage. Wages of seaman earned in a complete voyage. 2. Port wages of a seaman. 3. Short stretch of land that interrupts a line of water communication between two places—a boat has to be carried or transported across it. 4. Entrance or opening in side of a ship.

Portage Bill. Document showing earnings of each member of crew, during a complete voyage, together with all rightful deductions to be made. These deductions include such moneys as allotments, advances of pay, etc.

Port Authority. Corporate body, or individual, responsible for the administration of a port area and for the carrying out of statutory duties.

Port Bar. Shoal at entrance of a port. Boom protection at entrance of port during hostilities. 2. Bar by which the fitting that closes a port in ship's side is made watertight and secure.

Port Charges. Port dues. 2. Expenditure consequent on a vessel being in port.

Port Clearance. Document certifying that vessel has liberty to leave a port. Issued by appropriate authorities for the port. In British ports the authority is H.M. Customs. Name is also given to the ship's Victualling Bill with Clearance Label pinned and sealed to it.

Port Dues. Established charges, made by a port authority, payable by vessels entering or using the port.

Portfire. Casing containing an inflammable composition that burns slowly in all states of weather.

Port Flange. Small guttering above a port hole or scuttle to deflect water running down ship's side. Also called 'Rigol' or 'Eyebrow'.

Port Hole. Small aperture, usually circular, in ship's side. Used for lighting, ventilating and other purposes.

Port Lanyard. Small length of rope or chain by which a port may be opened or closed.

Portlast. Gunwale, or upper edge of bulwarks, of a ship.

Port Marking. Distinctive mark put on cargo for one particular port when carrying cargoes for more than one port.

Port of Refuge. Place or harbour, other than loading port or intended destination, to which a vessel proceeds to avoid an imminent peril.

Portoise. 'Portlast.'

Portolan Charts. Hand-drawn charts of 14th century.

Portolani. Italian sailing directions of 13th and 14th centuries.

Port Policy. Contract of marine insurance covering risks that may arise while vessel is laid up in port.

Port Riggle, Rigol. Rigol above a scuttle or port in an exposed position.

Port Sail. Old sail, used as a 'save-all', between a lighter and a ship that is loading or discharging cargo.

Port Sanitary Authority. Body appointed to carry out statutory duties of a port authority in regard to all matters concerning health and prevention of disease in connection with shipping. Responsible for inspection of ships, and deratisation.

Port Sash. Window fitted into upper half of a square port.

Port Sill. One of the four short timbers lining a square port.

Port Speed. Rate of loading or discharging at a port when considered in conjunction with the working hours of the port.

Portuguese Man of War. Jellyfish with large oblong air-bag and pendulous tentacles. Stings when touched.

Portuguese Sennit. Alternative name for 'Boatswain's Plait'.

Position Circle. 'Circle of Position.'

Position Lights.* Two all-round white lights, vertically, shown by a warship when in company.

Position Line. 'Line of Position.'

Positive Slip. Difference between theoretical advance of ship, by propeller action, and the actual advance made when it is less than theoretical advance. Due to propeller working in a yielding medium. ('Slip.')

Post Captain. Former rank in R.N. Denoted a Captain who had been in command of H.M. ship for three years.

Post Meridian. 'Post Meridiem.'

Post Meridiem. Latin for 'After noon'.

Post Ship. Former name for a first-class warship.

Pouch. Name formerly given to a 'grain feeder' or a space enclosed by shifting boards.

Pounding. The heavy falling of a ship into the sea, or on the ground, after having been lifted by wave action.

Powder Magazine. Space in which gunpowder charges are stowed.

Powder Room. Space in which bulk gunpowder is stowed.

Prahu. Malayan craft propelled by oars and sails. About 50 ft. long. Also, double-ended boat of Ladrone Islands. About 30 ft. long and fitted with outrigger. Steered with paddle.

Pram. Dinghy built with a small tramson at the bow as well as at the stern.

Pratique. Permission for a vessel to traffic or have communication with the shore. Granted after ship has been visited by medical and sanitary authorities.

Prayer Book. Seaman's nickname for a small holystone.

Precession. Movement of axis of a free gyro when subjected to an angular force that is not coincident with plane of rotation. It results in direction and plane of spin taking up a position so that each particle in gyro takes the shortest course to the new points arising from the angular movement of axis.

Precession of Earth's Axis. Slow, circular movement of Earth's poles around axis of Ecliptic at an angular distance of 23° 27'. Period of the movement is nearly 26,000 years. Caused by gravitational pull of Sun and Moon and Earth's equatorial bulge.

Precession of Equinoxes. Gradual backward movement of First Points of Aries and Libra along the Ecliptic so that their celestial longitudes are continuously decreasing.

Premium. Money paid for insurance against a marine risk.

Press Gang. Naval ratings, under an officer, who went ashore and impressed men into naval service.

Press of Canvas. All sail set and all sails drawing.

Pressure Gradient. Rate of change of barometric pressure across isobars in a synoptic chart.

Presumed Total Loss. Said of a vessel when she has not been sighted or heard of for a considerable time but there is no evidence of her having sunk or being destroyed.

Preventer. Term applied to duplicated rigging. In some cases it seems to be used with its original—and literal—meaning of 'coming before'.

Preventer Backstay. Topmast backstay that could be slacked off when on lee side and vessel close-hauled.

Preventer Bolts. Through bolts along lower edge of preventer plate. Used for backing up chain-bolts passing through upper edge of plate.

Preventer Fid. Iron bolt sometimes kept along, and secured to, eyes of topmast rigging. Directly heel of mast was clear of mast hole in trestle trees, when hoisting, fid was passed through hole in mast so that mast would not fall to deck if mast rope parted.

Preventer Main Braces. Main yard braces that led forward. Were additional to braces leading aft.

Preventer Plates. Iron plates running downwards, on sides of wooden vessels, from chains to strakes below. Purpose was to spread strain of shrouds and prevent seams of side opening.

Prick. To mark off ship's position on a chart. To draw a course on a chart. 2. To put an additional seam in middle of cloth of a sail.

Pricker. Small, thin marline spike used for stabbing holes in canvas and when splicing small rope.

Pricking Note. Customs document authorising the shipment of stated goods.

Pricking off the Ship. Marking ship's position on chart—generally at noon.

Pride of the Morning. Mist at sunrise: usually indicating a fine and sunny day.

Primage. Money paid by shipper to Master of ship for diligence in care of cargo. Not now paid to Master, but added to freight. Amount was usually about 10% of freight.

Primage and Average Accustomed. Words inserted in a Bill of Lading when an additional payment is due, at customary rate, on right delivery of cargo.

Primary Circle. That great circle that is a plane of reference for all great circles passing through its poles. Primary circle of Earth is Equator.

Primary Planet. Name sometimes given to those planets revolving around Sun, thus distinguishing them from lesser bodies revolving around a planet.

Primary Tide. That part of a tidal undulation that is the direct response to a tide-generating force. Term is used when comparing it with a composite tide.

Prime Entry. Statement made to Customs authorities, by Master of an arrived ship, declaring the nature and approximate quantity of cargo brought in. Is a pre-requisite for inward clearance.

Prime Meridian. That meridian from which longitude is reckoned. By common consent this is now the meridian of Greenwich. Originally, was that meridian on which the magnetic variation of compass was zero in a certain latitude. Has varied in longitude between Jerusalem and Brazil, but most frequently through Azores and Canary Islands. First passed through London (St. Paul's Cathedral) in 17th century. First drawn through Greenwich, 1794.

Prime Vertical. Great circle of celestial sphere, and secondary to horizon, passing through east and west points of horizon.

Priming. Of tide, is a decrease in time interval between successive high waters. Roughly speaking, it occurs as tides decrease from spring to neap. 2. Of a boiler, is the projection of minute particles of water into the steam; generally due to impurities in feed water, or to violent motion of ship. 3. Of a pump, is the insertion of water to expel air. 4. In painting, is the first coat applied to a bare surface.

Priming and Topping. Preparation of a boiler furnace before lighting fire. Priming consists of laying small coal over fire-bars. Topping is the laying of a transverse wall of coal a little distance inside furnace. Kindling wood, or fire from another furnace, is laid against topping to ignite it.

Priming Valve. Spring-loaded valve, on top of cylinder, that allows any condensed steam to escape as piston comes upward.

Prismatic Coefficient. Immersed volume of a vessel expressed as a fraction of a block whose length is that of the vessel and the shape of which is that of the immersed midship section of the vessel.

Prismatic Compass. Compass fitted with a reflecting prism and a sighting vane. Used for observing azimuths.

Prismatic Telescope. Telescope having reflecting prisms to enlarge an observed object. Periscope is a well-known example.

Privateer. Ship, other than a warship, fitted out by persons to whom letters of marque had been given. Name was also given to person commanding such a ship. To privateer is to attack enemy shipping under letter of marque.

Private Ship. Naval term for any warship that is not a flag ship.

Prize. Vessel captured in war and granted to capturers by sovereign.

Prize Court. Wartime court set up to adjudicate on naval prizes taken.

Prize List. Names, ranks and ratings of personnel in a captured ship.

Prize Master. Officer, from capturing ship, who takes charge of a captured ship.

Prize Money. Share of value of captured merchant ships, paid to crews of H.M. ships. Originally paid to personnel of capturing ship, but in war of 1914–18 was shared amongst all personnel. In war of 1939–45 was shared amongst R.N. and R.A.F. Now discontinued.

Proa. Canoe of Ladrone Islands. One side is curved, the other straight, outrigger being fitted on straight side. Has lateen sail and can be sailed either way. Usually about 30 ft. long and 3 ft. beam.

Procuration. The acting of one person on behalf of another. 2. A document authorising one person to act on behalf of another.

Procyon. Star α Canis Minoris. S.H.A. 246°; Dec. N05°; Mag. 0·5. Diameter is twice that of Sun, candlepower being 5 times greater. Distant 10 light years; temperature 6500°A. Name is Greek for 'Before the Dog', on account of it rising before Sirius.

Profile Draughts. Two sheer plans on principle of cargo plans. One gives layout of ship; the other giving layout of fittings in ship.

Pro Forma Policy. Temporary and unsigned policy issued to an insurer pending the preparation and signing of the actual policy.

Progressive Wave. Elevation of water, with its accompanying depression, that moves laterally along surface of sea. Considered in tidal investigations.

Projections. Attempts to delineate some part of curved surface of Earth on the flat surface of a map or chart. It is impossible to do this with accuracy. In the projections used by seamen the distortions are either negligible in practice or are of a known nature and value and can, therefore, be allowed for. The different projections are treated under their separate names.

Prolate Spheroid. Spheroid generated by semi-rotation of an ellipse around its major axis. Sometimes applied to a spheroid that rotates on its major axis.

Prolongation Clause. Inserted in a charter party to give charterers option of continuing a charter beyond a given date. States the conditions under which this can be done.

Prolonged Blast. Blast, of 4 to 6 seconds duration, on a whistle, foghorn, or siren.

Promenade Deck. One of the decks of a passenger steamer. Usually more or less open and free from obstructions.

Promissory Note. Written and stamped undertaking to pay a specified sum of money on or before a specified date.

Proof Load. Excessive load put on an item under test. May vary between 10% and 100% more than the load that the item is intended to take.

Proof Strain. Excessive strain put on an item under test. Always exceeds strain that the item is intended to take.

Proof Stress. Value used to indicate strength of metal when it is difficult to determine yield point. Metal is stretched and its elongation under the stated stress is expressed as a percentage, the value of the stress being stated.

Proof Timber. Vertical straight line, representing a timber, drawn on a sheer draught for checking fairness of ship's form.

Propeller. Instrument by which a vessel is propelled. Attached to after end of a shaft that is connected to engine. Usually has three or four blades, each being part of a screw thread, and is keyed and secured to after end of tailshaft.

Controlled Pitch Propeller. The blades of the propeller can be altered in position to give ahead, neutral, or astern drive, the engine turning in a constant direction.

Ducted, or Shrouded, Propeller. A propeller rotating within an open-ended cylinder sometimes called a 'Kurt Nozzle'. The duct increases significantly the bollard pull of a tug. If the duct and propeller is turned horizontally great manoeuvrability is achieved.

Propeller Post. That part of stern framing that carries after end of stern tube, and supports end of tail shaft.

Proper Motion. The actual movement of a heavenly body as distinguished from a parallactic change in its position due to Earth's movement in space. Name is given, also, to Sun's apparent movement in Ecliptic, to distinguish it from his apparent diurnal motion. 2. The movement on a true-motion radar display of the echo of another ship. It shows her course and speed. ('Course Steered and Speed.')

Proper Pilotage. That branch of navigation dealing with the conducting of a ship by methods involving astronomical observations and calculations. Now termed 'Navigation' or 'Astronomical Navigation'. In Elizabethan times it meant ocean navigation.

Proper Return Port. Port to which a seaman can claim to be returned on completion of his service to a ship.

Propogation. Movement of crest of a progressive wave.

Proportional Lengths. Relative dimensions of a ship and appropriate lengths of masts and spars. These used to be tabulated thus:—
Length of Ship=Breadth×7. Main Yard=2·3 Breadth. Depth of Hold=Length×0·09. Lower Topsail Yard=1·85 Breadth. Mainmast=Breadth×2·25. Spanker Gaff=Breadth. Foremast=Breadth×2·09. Bowsprit=0·7 Breadth. Mizen Mast=Breadth×2.

Proportional Logarithms. Used when 'Clearing a Lunar Distance'. Was the logarithm of 10,800 (the number of seconds in 3 hours) diminished by the number of seconds by which a quantity dealt with was less than 3 hours. Proportional log. of 2 hours would be log. of 10,800 minus log. of 3600. Now quite obsolete for this purpose.

Propulsion. The driving forward of a vessel.

Protection and Indemnity Association. Association of shipowners who combine to indemnify any of their members against third party claims and against risks not normally covered by marine insurance.

Protest. Statement under oath, made before a notary public, concerning an actual or anticipated loss, damage or hindrance in the carrying out of a marine adventure.

Proved. Said of anchors and chain cables when they have been tested and found to be of required quality and strength.

Proving Establishment. Establishment where anchors and chain cables are tested and proved. Those in Great Britain are controlled by Department of Trade and Industry.

Prow. Old name for stem of a vessel, or for the bows. 2. Alternative name for 'Proa'.

Proxima Centauri. Name given to α Centauri on account of it being the nearest star to Earth.

Proximate Clause. Nearest or most immediate cause of a maritime loss. Used in marine insurance when a loss is due to a sequence of events or a combination of circumstances.

Psychrometer. A hygrometer, but sometimes limited to those hygrometers in which air-flow past wet bulb is accelerated by mechanism.

Pteropod Ooze. Ooze containing small conical shells. Found in various areas at depths between 400 and 1500 fathoms.

Puddening. Rope strands when used to make a fixed fender or chafing gear. Strands are usually woven, but not always so.

Pudding Chain. Short link chain especially made for reeving through a block. Used for halyards and sheets before wire rope was introduced.

Pudding Fender. Cylindrical canvas bag containing cork or coir and covered with leather or grafted small stuff.

Pulley. Block with sheave to change direction of rope or to give mechanical advantages—in latter case is usually called a 'tackle'.

Pulling (an Oar). Propelling a boat by facing aft and pulling on an oar, or oars.

Pulling Boat. Any boat propelled by the pulling of oars.

Pulpit. Guard-rail round the bows of a yacht.

Pulse. Very short (usually less than one-millionth of 1 second) radio signals transmitted in rapid succession by a radar transmitter.

Pump Box. Casing covering top of a pump. 2. Leather piston fitted with a non-return valve.

Pump Brake. Handle by which a pump is worked.

Pump Hook. Hook, with long handle, for lifting a leather pump box.

Pumping. Of barometer: fluctuations in height of mercury column due to violent movement of ship, or of wind effect at cistern.

Pump Leather. Stout leather from which pump boxes were formerly made.

Pump Spear. Rod to which upper pump-box was attached.

Pump Well. Shaped space into which water flows, and from which it is pumped; pump suctions leading to it.

Punt. Small craft propelled by pushing on a pole whose lower end rests on the bottom of the waterway. 2. To propel a boat by resting end of a pole on bottom of waterway. 3. Copper punt.

Puoy. Spiked pole used for propelling a barge or boat by resting its outboard end on an unyielding object.

Purchase. Mechanical advantage gained by leverage, tackle or positioning. 2. Apparatus by which mechanical advantage is gained.

Purchase Blocks. Sheaved blocks used in forming a purchase.

Purchase Fall. Rope rove through blocks to obtain mechanical advantage.

Purple Light. Rather bright patch of sky sometimes observable about 25° above point at which Sun set. Maximum brightness occurs when Sun is 4° below horizon.

Purse. Bag-shaped fishing-net, the mouth of which can be drawn together and closed.

Purser. Usually pronounced 'pusser'. Officer responsible, under Captain, for ship's disbursements, money transactions and stores. In R.N. he has been displaced by accountant officers. In 17th century he was responsible to owners for all cargo and freight transactions.

Purser's Dip. A candle.

Purser's Dirk. Nickname for a midshipman's dirk, and for uniform pattern knife carried by seaman in R.N.

Purser's Eighths. Deductions from certain stores that was, formerly, retained by a purser in R.N. as an agreed payment for his services. Discontinued in 1852.

Purser's Grin. Hypocritical smile, or sneer.

Purser's Knife. Seaman's clasp-knife, of uniform pattern, in R.N.

Purser's Pound. Sixteen ounces less $\frac{1}{3}$; 14 ounces.

Pusher. After mast in a six-masted sailing vessel.

Pushpit. A guard-rail round the stern of a yacht.

Put. To change direction of a vessel: e.g. to put about.

Puttock. Corrupted form of 'Futtock'.

Pyranometer. Instrument for measuring either nocturnal radiation or sky radiation.

Pyrgeometer. Instrument for measuring nocturnal radiation.

Pyrheliometer. Instrument for measuring rate at which heat falls on earth's surface.

Pyrometer. Instrument for measuring very high temperatures. Usually based on increased electrical resistance of platinum wire when heated.

Pythagoras' Theorem. The area of a square on hypotenuse of a right-angled triangle equals sum of squares on other two sides. An important trigonometrical corollary from this is that $\text{Sin}^2 + \text{Cos}^2 = 1$.

Pyxis Nautica. Former name for a mariner's compass in a box.

Q

'Q' Ship. Merchant vessel with concealed armament, and manned by naval crew, that decoyed German submarines into gun range during 1914–18 war.

Quadrant. Quarter of a circle. 2. Nautical reflecting instrument that preceded sextant and measured angles up to 90°. Invented by Thomas Godfray of Philadelphia and John Hadley of England in 1730, each being independent of the other. 3. A 13th century instrument for measuring the altitude of a star. It was a thin plate of metal or wood, a quarter of a circle in shape, marked with degrees round the arc and with pin-hole sights on one edge. A plumb line hung from the centre. Two observers were needed, one sighting the star, the other reading the scale. 4. Horizontal fitting, that is a sector of a circle, attached to head of rudder stock to take steering chains and form leverage for controlling rudder. Sometimes carries a toothed rack into which a pinion is meshed.

Quadrantal Deviation. Compass error arising from induced magnetism in horizontal soft iron. Changes name, E or W, in successive quadrants.

Quadrantal Triangle. Spherical triangle having one side of 90°.

Quadrant Davit. Boat davit whose head can be moved through 90° in vertical plane; Welin type being, perhaps, the best known.

Quadrantids. Meteor shower visible in northern sky at beginning of January; radiant point being in constellation Quadrans Muralis.

Quadrate. Said of two heavenly bodies when 90° apart.

Quadrature. Relative position of a heavenly body when 90° from another. 2. Position of Moon when she is halfway between conjunction and opposition, thus being quadrate with Sun.

Quadrireme. Roman vessel, possibly with four banks of oars. Greek equivalent 'Tetreres'.

Quadropod Engine. Four-cylinder reciprocating engine in which steam goes to fourth expansion. Cranks in each pair are set 180° apart; one pair being at right angles to other pair.

Quality of the Bottom. Nature of the sea bed as ascertained by arming of lead.

Quant. Pole with flat disc at lower end. Used for propelling small craft by pushing on bed of river, or other shoal water.

Quarantine. Segregation and restraint of a vessel coming from an infected port, or having infections or contagious diseases on board.

Quarantine Flags. Flag Q signifies ship hoisting it is believed to be healthy and requests free pratique; QQ signifies ship is suspect; QL signifies ship has cases of infectious disease.

Quarter. That part of a vessel between the beam and the stern.

Quarter of Yard. One-third of a yard between slings and lift on either side; being named 'first', 'second' and 'third' quarters from slings.

Quarter Badges. Carved ornamental work on quarters of olden ships. When gilded, were termed 'gingerbread'.

Quarter Berth. A bunk partly under the side of the cockpit.

Quarter Bill. List of different stations manned in action, together with names of men manning each station.

Quarter Block. Wooden block, on quarter of yard, through which clewline is rove.

Quarter Boards. Additional weather boards erected above quarter rail in bad weather with following sea.

Quarter Boat. Boat carried at davits, on quarter of ship, and kept ready for immediate use when at sea.

Quarter Cask. Cask with a capacity of 28 gallons, or half a hogshead.

Quarter Cloths. Painted canvas on outboard side of hammock nettings on ship's quarter.

Quarter Deck. Upper deck from mainmast to right aft. In vessels with a poop it ends at break of poop. In Royal Navy it extends from right aft on upper deck to some line forward of after gangway.

Quarterdecker. Name given to an officer who is more conscious of his rank than of his duties. 2. Ship having a raised deck, but not a poop, aft.

Quarter Deck Type. Steam vessels in which the upper deck abaft the machinery space is raised above the level of the forward deck; thus allowing vessels with full cargoes to trim by the stern.

Quarter Diurnal. Applied to a tidal undulation, or constituent, that occurs four times in a tidal day.

Quarter Fast. Mooring rope led aft from quarter when securing a ship.

Quarter Gallery. A balcony-like projection on quarters of olden ships; usually fitted with windows.

Quarter Gasket. Short length of sennit used for securing a furled sail at quarter of a yard.

Quarter Gunner. Responsible seaman who, under Gunner of the ship, was responsible for four guns.

Quarter Hoop. Hoop, on cask, barrel, etc., that is between chime and bilge hoops.

Quartering Wind. Wind blowing from a point about four points abaft a vessel's beam.

Quarter Iron. Boom iron on yard to take heel of studdingsail boom. Fitted at $\frac{3}{16}$ length of yard from yard arm.

Quartermaster. In R.N. is a petty officer, or other responsible rating, who works under officer of the watch and is responsible that the helmsman carries out his duties correctly. He takes the wheel on important occasions. In harbour, he keeps his watch at the gangway. In M.N. a leading rating who steers the ship and keeps gangway watch.

Quarter Pieces. Carved figures at after ends of quarter gallery.

Quarter Pipe. Reinforced oval aperture in after bulwark plating. Used as fairlead for mooring ropes.

Quarter Rail. Quarter deck bulwarks in a wooden ship.

Quarters. The allotted positions, or stations, of ship's complement in specified circumstances, e.g. 'General Quarters'.

Quarter Slings. Standing lifts of a yard, made of chain or rope, used in 16th century.

Quarter Spring. Rope led forward, from quarter of a vessel, to prevent her from ranging astern; or to heave her ahead.

Quarter Timber. Frame timber in quarter of a wooden vessel.

Quartile. Quadrate.

Quartile Aspect. Quarter aspect.

Quay. Artificial erection protruding into the water to facilitate loading and discharge of cargo, landing and embarkation of passengers, repairing or refitting of ships.

Queen's Hard Bargain. R.N. nickname for an inefficient seaman.

Quick Flashing. Name given to lights, on buoys and other navigational aids, that show more than 60 flashes in one minute.

Quicksand. Sand that is permeated with water and is unable to support the weight of a man.

Quick Saver. Rope span, on fore side of sail, to prevent undue bellying of courses when sailing free.

Quicksilver Horizon. Artificial horizon, consisting of mercury in a trough, used for taking sextant altitudes ashore.

Quick Work.* Inside planking between gun ports. 2. Planking of ship's side above upper deck. 3. Sometimes applied to underwater planking.

Quid. Piece of tobacco for chewing. Variant of 'cud'.

Quilting. Sennit-plaited around a bottle, or rounded object, to protect it.

Quinquereme. Large Roman vessel with, perhaps, five banks of oars. Greek equivalent 'Penteres'.

Quintal. One hundred kilogrammes. Formerly, 100-lb. avoirdupois.

Quoin. Wedge-shaped piece of wood used for preventing rolling of casks, barrels or other rounded objects.

R

'R.' The point of definition of mean time. As it is directly opposite to mean Sun, in Equinoctial, its position is that of mean Sun plus or minus 12 hours of R.A.

Rabbet. Cut-away part in stern, sternpost or keel of a wooden vessel, for bottom planking to fit into.

Race. Strong and rapid current in a small area of the sea; more especially when accompanies with disturbed water.

Racing. Rapid revolution of propeller and engines when ship's stern lifts out of water, or when a large wave falls away from the propeller.

Rack. Wood or iron frame with belaying pins, sheaves or blocks. 2. Old form of 'wrack' or 'wreck'.

Rack Bar. Name sometimes given to the bar used in a Spanish windlass.

Rack Block. Several sheaves fitted into one block of wood and used as leads for running gear.

Racking. Binding together two ropes by passing a smaller rope alternately over and under each of them. 2. The smaller rope used when racking.

Racking. The distorting of a ship's transverse shape through undue strain.

Racking Strain. Excessive stress that alters or distorts a vessel's transverse shape.

Racon. A radar beacon which transmits a signal on receiving a radar signal from a ship and thus shows the range and bearing of the racon on the ship's display.

Radar. Electronic system by which the bearing and distance of an object are found by the emission of a radio pulse, an observation of the direction of its return and the measurement of the time elapsed between emission and return.

Radar Beacon. A radio transmitter transmitting signals at radar frequencies which can be received and identified by a ship's radar set.

Radar Reflector. Arrangement of flat metallic surfaces set at right angles to each other which reflect radar signals back from whence they came. Used to improve the reflective power of small objects.

Radar Simulator. Electronic apparatus, used in training, by which simulated echoes of ships or coastline are made to appear and move upon radar displays.

Raddle. To interlace yarns to form a gasket.

Radiant Heat. Heat transmitted in form of electro-magnetic waves, and not by conduction or convection.

Radiation. Emission of energy, such as light or heat, in the form of electro-magnetic waves that do not heat the medium through which they pass.

Radiation Pressure. Pressure of radiant energy on a unit area. The pressure of sunlight on Earth is about 2 lb. per square mile.

Radio. General name for methods of signalling or communicating through space by electro-magnetic waves.

Radio Aids. Term that includes all radio signals and emissions that can be used in navigational practice.

Radio Beacon. A radio station which sends out special signals for reception by a ship's radio direction finder, the bearing of the radio beacon being thus obtained.

Radio Compass. Directional radio receiver calibrated to indicate the direction in which a radio wave approaches.

Radio Direction Finder. Instrument for detecting a radio signal and for indicating the relative bearing on which it is received.

Radiolaria. Minute creatures having a spherical, or conical, body from which small filaments project.

Radiolarian Ooze. Deep-sea deposit containing minute skeletons of radiolaria. Forms sea bed of large areas of Pacific and Indian Oceans at depths of 2000 to 5000 fathoms.

Radiosonde. Small compact radio transmitter attached to a free balloon for the purpose of obtaining upper air observations.

Radio Time Signal. Time signal broadcast by radio.

Radius Vector. Line from a pole, or focus, that fixes position by measurement of angle between vector and a primitive. In astronomy, is a straight line connecting a planetary body with Sun.

Radome. A bun-shaped cover placed over a radar scanner to prevent risk of fouling and to protect it from the weather.

Raft. Floating structure made for life-saving purposes in shipwreck. 2. Timber or logs fastened together for transport by water.

Rafting. Overlapping of edges of two ice-floes, so that one floe is partly supported by the other.

Raft Port. Square opening, in end of ship, for loading long timber.

Rag Bolt. Bolt having jagged cuts across shank, to prevent bolt working out after being driven in.

Rail. Top of bulwarks. 2. Curved timber going from bow to support knee of head.

Rail of the Dead. Name sometimes given to 'Rail 2'.

Raise. To initiate, as 'Raise a bottomry bond'. 2. To cause to appear above horizon, as 'Raise the land' or 'light'. 3. To dispose rope and blocks in such a manner that a purchase is obtained—'Raise a purchase'. 4. To sail towards an object so that its altitude increases.

Raise a Purchase. See 'Raise'.

Raise Tacks and Sheets. Order given when tacking a square-rigged ship. As ship moves through wind, tacks and sheets are kept adjusted so that sail is kept filled and does not go aback.

Rake. Inclination, in fore and aft line, of a mast, funnel, stem, stern post, or other nearly vertical member. 2. Inclined shape of after edge of a rudder. 3. To fire projectiles fore and aft along deck of an enemy vessel.

Raker.* Gun so placed as to rake an enemy vessel.

Rakish. Said of a mast, or other member, having a rake.

Rally in. To haul in quickly.

Ram. To strike a vessel with stem of one's own ship. 2. Strengthened stem, or projecting forefoot, formerly fitted to warships for sinking enemy ship by ramming.

Ramberge.* Long and narrow war vessel, propelled by oars and specially fitted for ramming. Corruption of 'Ram Barge'.

Ram Block. Wooden deadeye.

Ram Bow. Ship's bow when fitted with a ram.

Ram Head. Special type of halyard block.

Ramark. A radar beacon which transmits continuously and thus shows its bearing on the display of a ship's radar.

Ramie. Egyptian cotton fibre used for making yacht ropes.

Ramline. Thin line, or cord, used for getting a straight line along a mast or spar.

Ramshorn Hook. Anchor-shaped hook on which two ends of a sling can be placed so that one end of sling goes not ride on other end.

Ran. Reel of 20 yards of rope. 2. Yarns coiled on a spunyarn winch.

Range. To sail parallel to a coast, shoal or other object. 2. The extreme limit at which a light will be visible to an observer with a given height of eye.

Range Alongside. To come close abeam of another vessel.

Range Finder. Instrument for indicating distance of an observed object. When the refracted images are aligned, by movement of prisms, the range is mechanically indicated.

Range Light.* Name sometimes given to an additional, and optional, masthead light of a steamship.

Range of Tide. Difference in height between any high (or low) water and either the preceding or succeeding low (or high) water.

Ranging Cable. Bringing cable on deck and laying it fore and aft in long bights. Sometimes done when preparing to anchor in deep water. Also, laying cable, in shackle lengths, on deck or dock bottom, for examination, refitting or survey.

Rank. Comparative station or rank of an officer.

Rap. Skein of yarn 20 fathoms long.

Rapaki. Masses of detached and uneven land ice met with in rivers and bays.

Raper's Code.* Signalling code, by use of flags, introduced by Admiral Raper, R.N., in 1828.

Rap Full. Said of a sail when fully distended by the wind.

Rapson's Slide. Type of steering-gear in which steering-chains are connected to a collar free to slide on tiller. Advantage is that leverage increases with angle of helm. Disadvantage is its tendency to walk back.

Ras. Arabic word, meaning 'Head', used in some star and geographical names.

Rasalhague. Star α Ophiuchi. S.H.A. 97°; Dec. N13°; Mag. 2·1.

Rasin.* Doubling piece on inner side of wale of wooden ship. Was cut away to form socket for deck carline.

Rasing Iron. Iron tool used for tearing out of old caulking.

Rate. Old scale for classing of warships. Based on number of guns carried; first rate carried 100 or more guns; fifth rate carried 32 to 40. Lowest rate was 'sixth'. 2. Rate of a chronometer is the amount it gains or loses in 24 hours.

Rateau Turbine. High-speed turbine of impulse type, and compounded for pressure.

Rating. Seaman other than an officer.

Rating a Chronometer. Determining its losing or gaining rate.

Ration. Stipulated amount of provisions for a specified period.

Rational Horizon. Great circle of celestial sphere, its poles being the zenith and nadir of observer. It follows that this plane passes through centre of Earth, and parallel to visible and sensible horizons.

Ratio of Range. Factor expressing range of tide, at a given place, in arithmetical proportion to the range at a specified position.

Ratio of Rise. Factor expressing rise of tide at one position as compared with rise of tide at another position.

Ratlines. Small ropes stretched horizontally between shrouds to form foot and hand holds when going aloft. Seized to forward and after shrouds, clove-hitched around intermediate shrouds.

Ratline Stuff. Soft laid, tarred hemp, three-stranded with rather long jaw, and from one to one and three-quarters of an inch in size. Used for ratlines.

Rattle Down. To fit ratlines to shrouds.

Razee. To cut down an upper deck of a vessel so that her depth is decreased. 2. A vessel that has had an upper deck cut down.

Reach. Straight stretch of water between two bends in a river or channel.

Reaching. Sailing with wind on beam or before it. Sailing closehauled on alternate tacks.

Reaction Rudder. Rudder so designed and shaped that effective use is made of the screw race.

'Ready About.' Cautionary order given preparatory to tacking under sail.

Ready to Load. State of a vessel when she is in a loading berth and is, in all respects, ready to load in all holds.

Rear Admiral. Flag officer in Royal Navy. Junior rank of admiral, being intermediate between Commodore and vice-admiral.

Rebate. Alternative form of 'Rabbet'.

Receivers of Wreck. Officers appointed by Board of Trade to take charge of wrecks and wreckage on British coasts and to take necessary steps for the saving of life and property in peril.

Reciprocal Bearings. Compass bearings taken simultaneously at two different stations, the bearing of one station being the reciprocal of the bearing of the other. Frequently used in compass adjustment.

Reckoning. Computation by which the position of a ship is found.

Recognition Signal. System of lights, or pyrotechnic signals, by which a vessel can indicate her ownership and identity.

Reconcile. Shipbuilding term meaning to join one member fairly with another so that the sweep is smooth. Especially applied to curves that reverse.

Rectilinear Stream. Tidal stream that runs alternately in approximately opposite directions.

Rector. Name given to Master of a ship in 11th and 12 centuries.

Recurvature. Meteorological term for the change in direction of travel of a cyclonic storm. First direction is westerly, then towards elevated pole, finally easterly.

Red Duster. A somewhat affectionate nickname for the Red Ensign.

Redelivery Clause. Inserted in a time charter to specify time, place and circumstances of redelivery of a vessel on termination of a time charter; also defines compensation for non-fulfilment.

Red End. Of magnet, is the north-seeking end.

Red Ensign. Red flag having Union flag at upper inner canton. is the proper ensign of British Merchant Navy.

Red Pole. Of magnet, is that end having same polarity as Earth's south magnetic pole. It is usual to make an arbitrary assumption that lines of magnetic force emerge from this pole.

Red Squadron. Former division of a fleet of warships. Occupied the van of the line and flew a red pendant. Was commanded by the admiral. Discontinued 1864.

Reduced Chart. Old name for a chart constructed on a recognised projection, as distinguished from a plane chart.

Reduced Latitude. Angle between radius of Earth, at a given point, and plane of Equator. Spheroidal shape of Earth causes this to be less than the geographical latitude, except at poles and Equator.

Reduced Zenith. Point at which a line passing from centre of Earth, and through an observer, would meet celestial concave. The declination of this point would be less than declination of observer's zenith.

Reduction. A 'leading back'. Correction of an apparent position or value, to give a true position, or value.

Reduction Gearing. Mechanism by which a high-speed of rotation, in one unit, is converted to a lower speed, but greater power, in another unit.

Reduction of Latitude. Angular difference between the geocentric and geographical latitudes at any given point on Earth's surface. Is maximum (11′ 44″) in lat 45°. It is subtractive from geographical latitude, or additive to geocentric latitude. Reduction may be looked upon as angle, at Earth's surface, between a downward perpendicular and an extended radius of Earth at that point.

Reduction to Soundings. Calculation of the correction to be applied to a sounding taken in tidal waters so that it can be compared with soundings referred to a standard level of chart datum.

Reduction to the Meridian. The application of corrections to altitude of a heavenly body, observed when near meridian, so that its meridian altitude may be deduced.

Reed Boiler. Water tube boiler of Thornycroft type, but having tubes more curved.

Reef. Ridge, or chain, of rocks near surface of the sea.

Reef. That part of sail between head in square sails, and foot in fore and aft sails, and the first line of reef points. Also, part of sail between any two lines of reef points.

Reef Band. Strip of canvas stitched to sail in way of reef points, for strengthening.

Reef Cringle. Cringle inserted in leech of sail to take block of reef tackle.

Reef Earing. Rope that secures upper corner of a reefed square sail to yard, or lower inner corner of reefed fore and aft sail to boom.

Reefer. One who reefs a sail. As midshipmen were stationed in tops during reefing the name was applied to them. 2. Short, double-breasted jacket, as worn by midshipmen. 3. Cargo ship fitted with refrigerating apparatus but capable also of carrying cargo other than refrigerated.

Reefing. Reducing effective area of sail by gathering in a certain amount of it—at the head in square sails, at foot in fore and aft sails—and securing it by tieing reef points around.

Reefing Halyards. Rope round the rolling spar of a patent reefing topsail.

Reefing Jackstay. Additional jackstay about five inches abaft proper jackstay of a yard.

Reef Knot. Made with two rope ends so that bight of each part lies either over or under both parts of other rope.

Reef Line. Small ropes rove through holes in reef band of a square sail and having ends on yards. Used for tricing up head of sail when reefing.

Reef Pendant. Tackle for hauling down leech of a fore and aft sail to the boom when reefing.

Reef Points. Lengths of small line secured to reef band of sail and passing through it. Used for confining reefed area of sail,and for securing reefed part of square sail to yard.

Reef Tackle. Small purchase for heaving reef cringle of square sail to the yard when reefing.

Reel. Horizontal drum, with circular side plates, around which ropes and wires are wound for compact stowage, and for ready use. 2. Small wooden framework on which log line is reeled. Has an axle that extends on either side, for reelman to hold when the log is streamed.

Reeler. Man whose duty is to reel up line of ship log as it is hauled in. Name also given to man who holds the reel.

Reeve. To pass end of a rope through a block, thimble or other opening.

Reeving.* Forcing open seams inside of a wooden ship so that caulking can be inserted.

Reeving Beetle. Heaviest mallet used by caulkers.

Reeving Iron. Wedge-shaped tool, of steel or iron, used when reeving.

Refit. Removal of worn or damaged gear and fitting of new gear in replacement.

Reflecting Circle. Instrument of the sextant type but having a limb graduated through 360°. Besides being able to measure large angles it has the further advantage that, by reversing the instrument, two observations can be taken—in opposite directions—and any error of the instrument will cancel out when the mean of the two values is taken. Invented by Mayer in 1744. Improved by both Troughton and Borda.

Reflecting Sector.* Name given to a sextant, quadrant or octant to differentiate it from a reflecting circle.

Reflecting Telescope. Telescope in which the image is enlarged by increasing the angle of the rays from it by the use of paraboidal mirrors.

Reflection. A throwing back of light rays, or heat rays. Sometimes applied to sound waves. 2. An image that is observed through reflection.

Refloat. To float again. In Elizabethan days it often meant a 'flowing back'.

Refracting Telescope. One in which the enlargement of the image is obtained by the use of lenses that refract rays from an observed body through an angle larger than that subtended at the naked eye.

Refraction. Deflection, or bending, of a ray of light, heat or radiant energy, as it passes from surface of one medium into another medium of different density.

Regatta. Originally, a gondola race; now, a gathering of yachts or boats for racing.

Register. Written document or book in which specific information is entered. Specifically applied to a ship's 'Certificate of Registry'.

Register Tonnage. Measurement of a ship, based on internal capacity, as entered in her Certificate of Registry. Can be 'Nett' or 'Gross'.

Registrar. One whose duty is to keep a register or record. Chief Officers of Customs are usually registrars of shipping.

Registrar General of Shipping and Seamen. Official of Department of Trade. He is responsible for keeping records of British ships, and of the men serving in them.

Registration of Ship. Legal procedure by which a vessel acquires British nationality on building, or by transfer.

Regression. Backward movement of Moon's nodes around Ecliptic. Amount is nearly 19° 20' each year, so that this backward circle repeats every 18·6 years. This is considered in tidal prediction.

Regulus. Star α Leonis. S.H.A. 208°; Dec. N12N°; Mag. 1·3. Name is Latin for 'Petty King'.

Relative Bearing. Direction of an observed object when expressed as an angle with ship's fore and aft line.

Relative Course. Course steered by another ship when expressed as the angle that course makes with course of one's own ship.

Relative Humidity. Humidity of atmosphere when expressed as a percentage of the humidity of saturated air.

Relative Magnitude of Star or Planet. Classification of its brightness compared with other stars as viewed from Earth, thus differing from 'absolute' magnitude. Is expressed as a number, which increases as brightness decreases. Stars of 6th magnitude and below can be seen with naked eye. Luminosity of any star is 2·512 times that of a star one above it in relative magnitude.

Release. To set free. In engineering, is applied to the moment when steam is first allowed to escape from cylinder. In ship's business, means a discharge from a contracted undertaking. To release a ship is to withdraw all opposition to her sailing or movement. To release cargo is to authorise its removal from ship.

Release Note. Document authorising Master to deliver cargo to holder of the note.

Relieving Gear. Any attachment to a rudder, tiller or quadrant, that damps and minimises the variations in stresses on tiller connections when a vessel is in a seaway and, particularly, when stern and rudder are rising and falling in the sea.

Relieving Tackle. Relieving gear consisting of two tackles, one on either side of tiller, having a continuous rope rove through both tackles; standing blocks of each tackle being attached to ship. Any effect of sea on rudder causes one tackle to render, and the other to heave. Friction of fall through sheaves damps shock on steering connections.

Remberge.* 'Ramberge.'

Remora. Fish, about 8 inches long, that attaches itself, by suction, to a ship's underwater body for transport. Fairly common in Mediterranean Sea.

Render. Said of rope when it yields to excessive stress by surging or slipping. Also said when it passes freely through a block or opening.

Repatriation of Seaman. The sending of a seaman to a proper return port in his own country.

Repeater. A 'Repeating ship'.

Repeating Circle. Reflecting instrument, on sextant principle, for measuring angles. As graduations extend to 180° on either side a succession of angles can be taken, and the mean value taken, thus reducing any error due to graduation.

Repeating Ship. Frigate, or small craft, formerly detached from the battle line to repeat admiral's signals from a position in view of all ships.

Replacement Clause. Inserted in a policy of marine insurance to limit liability of insurers to the replacement of a damaged part of machinery, and not the whole machine.

Reporting Day. Day on which a vessel reports her readiness to load or unload cargo. May, or may not count as a lay day.

Report List. Document describing ship and cargo, list of passengers and stores, together with particulars of any navigational danger sighted during voyage. Signed, in duplicate, by Master and presented to Customs authorities when entering inwards.

Reprize.* Vessel recaptured after being taken by enemy. If recapture within 24 hours of capture was returned to former owner; if after 24 hours of capture, was property of ship recapturing.

Request Note. Application to Customs authorities for permission to remove goods liable to duty.

Resaca. Alternative name for 'Underset'.

Reserve Buoyancy. That part of a vessel's buoyancy that keeps her watertight deck above the level of the load line.

Respondentia. Contract in which a master of a ship pledges freight and cargo as security for a loan of money necessary to enable vessel to reach her discharging port.

Respondentia Bond. Legal document whereby Master pledges freight and cargo when raising respondentia.

Restraint of Princes. Commands of a sovereign state, whether friendly, nautral or enemy—that result in the non-fulfilment of an intended voyage.

Restrictive Endorsement. Endorsement of a bill of exchange so that its negotiation is limited and circumscribed.

Retardation. A slowing up. A lateness of arrival. Opposite to acceleration.

Retard of Tide. Interval between conjunction, or opposition, of Sun and Moon and the appearance of the resultant spring tide at a place.

Retentivity. The power of steel or iron to retain magnetism. This power is more or less proportional to their resistance to being magnetised.

Retrograde Motion. Movement of a heavenly body in a direction opposite to that of Earth's rotation and Sun's annual revolution; the Right Ascension and celestial longitude of the body will then decrease. A few solar system bodies—comets and some satellites—have this motion. Retrograde movement of a planet is an optical illusion arising from Earth's orbital movement.

Return List. D.T.I. form, Eng. 2 or Eng. 2a, for reporting particulars of members of crew engaged after Articles have been opened.

Return Port. The proper return port of a discharged seaman.

Return Tubes. Those fire tubes, in a marine boiler, that return the fuel gases from the combustion chamber to the front of boiler.

Revenue Cutter. Small sailing vessel, cutter rigged and armed, manned by Royal Navy and used for prevention of smuggling and for maintaining order on the fishing grounds. Superseded by mechanically-propelled fishery protection vessels.

Reversal. Difference in directions of surface and upper winds when exceeding 90°.

Reversed Frame. Angle bar riveted to inboard edge of a frame so that its flange is in a direction opposite to that of the frame.

Reverse Laid. Said of ropes having yarns and strands laid up in the same direction. Sometimes called 'unkinkable' lay.

Revolving Storm. High wind flowing around an area of low pressure. Also called a 'cyclone'.

Rhodings. Brass bearings for axle of a pump wheel.

Rhumb. Line on surface of Earth, that cuts all meridians at a constant angle that is other than a right angle. A loxodromic curve. 2. One of the points of the compass other than a cardinal point.

Rhumb Line. Any part of a rhumb as projected on a chart.

Rhumb Sailing. Method by which a course and distance along a rhumb is converted into the resultant change in latitude and longitude.

Rib. Curved, transverse member, made of timber, going outwards from keel of a wooden vessel. Controls shape of the vessel and forms means of attachment of outside planking. In iron and steel shipbuilding it is replaced by 'frame'.

Riband. 'Ribband.'

Rib and Truck. Name given to a parrel made up of large, spherical wooden spheres threaded on rope. Three to five of these are usual, being separated by thin wooden 'ribs'.

Ribband. One of the horizontal strips of fir nailed to ribs of a wooden vessel, when being built, to maintain the ribs in their place while planking is fastened.

Ribband Carvel. Carvel build, but with wooden strips covering seams on inner side of the vessel.

Ribband Lines. Oblique fore and aft sections of a vessel.

Ribband Shore. Supporting strut from building slip to rib of a vessel under construction.

Ribbing Nail. Large round-headed nail used for fastening ribbands.

Ricker. Stem of a young tree. Used for making shaft of boathook, mast or spar in boat, or for dunnage.

Ride. To yield to a sea or swell. 2. To bear down with full weight of the body.

Rider. An additional rib on inside of sheathing of hold of a wooden vessel. 2. A second tier of casks or barrels. 3. A riding turn of rope.

Ridge. Longitudinal area of high barometric pressure. 2. Longitudinal extent of a raised part of sea bed.

Ridge Rope. Centre-line rope over which an awning is spread.

Riding a Try. Heaving to, in bad weather, and lying to the wind with no sail set.

Riding Bitts. Two strong bitts, in fore part of vessel, around which turns of cable can be taken.

Riding Light. White all round light hoisted forward, by a vessel at anchor, from sunset to sunrise.

Riding Sail. Storm canvas set by ship when riding to a sea anchor.

Riding Slip. Short length of chain, attached to forecastle deck, having a slip shaped to clamp a link of chain cable. Generally used as a precautionary measure when riding at anchor.

Riding the Rigging. Coming down a stay or backstay in a boatswain's chair that has a shackle around the stay or backstay. Usual when blacking down the rigging, or when working on it.

Riding Turn. Turn of a rope that rides over or across another turn or turns.

Rig. Manner or fashion in which a vessel's masts, sails, and spars are fitted and arranged. 2. Type of a sailing vessel. 3. To fit out a vessel with necessary rigging. 4. To prepare or assemble an apparatus or gear. 5. The dress of a man.

Rig/Drilling, Rig/Oil Rig. A construction standing upon the seabed, but capable of being floated into position, used for drilling for, or extracting oil or gas.

Rigel. Star β Orionis. S.H.A. 282°; Dec. S8°; Mag. 0·3. Diameter is 38 times that of Sun; candlepower is 18,000 times greater; distant 540 light years.

Rigger. Man who makes or fits rigging, or who assists in doing so.

Rigging. The ropes, wires, tackling and other furniture necessary for the working of a ship. 2. Shrouds and their ratlines. 3. The fitting and placing of rigging.

Rigging Screw. Bottle screw used for setting up wire rigging. A Warwick screw. 2. Steel screw clamp used for turning in end of wire ropes when splicing around a thimble.

Right Ascension. Measurement of a heavenly body's distance from from First Point of Aries, and expressed in terms of sidereal time. Is the angle at the Pole between a circle of Right Ascension passing through the body and a circle passing through First Point of Aries. Can be measured by arc of Equinoctial intercepted by the foregoing circles.

Right a Ship. To bring a vessel upright after she has been listed or careened.

Right-Handed. Said of a rope when strands trend to the right as one looks along it. Said of a propeller when upper edge of blade turns to starboard when going ahead.

Righting Lever. Leverage by which the force of buoyancy, acting on the metacentre of an inclined floating body, causes the body to turn until centre of buoyancy and centre of gravity are in same vertical line. Length of lever is the horizontal distance between perpendiculars passing through centre of gravity and centre of buoyancy.

Right Knot. A reef knot.

Right of Search. Authority to search a vessel at sea.

Right of Way. Legal right of a vessel to maintain her course and speed when in the vicinity of another vessel.

Right Sphere. Terrestrial sphere as it appears to an observer at Equator. Circles of revolution of heavenly bodies are perpendicular to the horizon.

Right the Helm. To put the rudder amidships.

Right Whale. The Greenland whale.

Rigil Kentaurus. Star α Centauri. S.H.A. 141°; Dec. S61°; Mag. 0·1. It is, excepting Sun, the star nearest to Earth. Its diameter is about that of the Sun, but its candle power is 1·2 times greater. Distance is 4·3 light years. Also called 'Proxima Centauri', 'Alpha Centaurus', 'Rikent'.

Rigol. Small, curved angle bar over a scuttle in ship's side. Placed to prevent entry of water when scuttle is open and water is running down side. Sometimes called 'Eyebrow'.

Rim. Notched plate, of capstan or windlass, in which a pawl can engage. 2. 'Top Rim.'

Rime. Rung of a ladder. 2. Hoar frost or frozen dew.

Ring. Ring or shackle in inboard end of anchor shank for attachment of cable.

Ringbolt. Bolt secured to vessel and carrying a loose ring to which a block, tackle or rope can be attached.

Ring Compressor. *See* 'Compressor'.

Ring Rope. Rope with one end made fast to a ring bolt; used for backing up another rope that is under heavy stress.

Ring Sail. Small sail set on a short mast, at taffrail, in fair weather.

Ring Stopper. Used for maintaining control of a wire rope that is being run out. Length of small chain has one end made fast to a ring bolt, the other end being led over the wire and back through the ring. By hauling on end of chain, wire is nipped.

Ring Tail. Small sail set abaft leech of spanker in the same manner as a studding sail is set on a square sail.

Riots and Civil Commotion Clause. Included in a policy of marine insurance to relieve insurers of liablity for loss due to strikes, labour disturbances, riots and suchlike.

Rip. To tear old caulking out of a deck seam.

Ripping Iron. Tool used for tearing old caulking out of a seam. 2. Tool for removing sheathing boards and copper sheathing from a ship's bottom.

Ripple. Small curling wave, or ruffling of surface of water.

Rise. To come above the horizon.

Rise of Tide. Height of sea level above chart datum when due to tide-raising forces.

Rising. Stringer, in a boat, on which thwarts rest.

Rising Floor. Floor timber, that rises, fore and aft, above plane of midship floor.

Rising Glass. Said of barometric pressure when indicated by rise of mercury in a barometer.

Rising Line. Curved line, on draughts of a ship, showing heights of floor timbers throughout the vessel.

Rising Square. Square marked with height of rising line at any part of the ship.

Rising Wood. Timber worked into seat of a floor and into keel, for steadying the keel.

Risk of Collision. Exists when two vessels are so situated that a collision will be inevitable unless one vessel, at least, takes avoiding action.

Risk the Run. To sail without convoy, or to break away from a convoy, in time of war.

River Gunboat. Small warship, carrying a fairly large gun, having a broad underwater body and a shallow draught. Formerly used in Chinese rivers and other inland waters.

Rivet Spacing. Pitch of rivets.

Roach. Curvature of foot of a square sail, to clear stays, etc.

Roadstead/Roads. Sheltered water with good holding ground, in which ships may anchor and ride safely.

Roaring Forties. Strong westerly winds prevailing south of latitude 40°S. Sometimes applied to the latitudes in which the winds prevail.

Robands. Short lengths of sennit plaited round head rope of square sail for securing sail to the jackstay.

Robins. Variant of 'Robands'.

Robinson's Disengaging Gear. Releasing gear for ship's boats. Boat's falls are held by hinged hooks fitted in the slings. On release of a tackle these hooks are free to open upwards and allow boat to drop into the water.

Rockered. Said of a keel whose lower edge sweeps downward as it goes aft.

Rocket. Pyrotechnic projectile used for signalling, or for life-saving purposes. Sometimes used for establishing connection with another vessel.

Rocket Apparatus. Line-carrying rockets and apparatus for firing them and aligning them so that a line can be carried to a wrecked vessel in the vicinity of the shore. Breeches buoy can be used for removing persons from wreck. Provided at all critical points around coasts of British Isles.

Rogue's Yarn. Coloured thread inserted in each strand of a rope issued by H.M. Dockyards. Colour varies according to the dockyard issuing the rope. Indicates that the rope is Admiralty property.

Roll. Rhythmic inclination of a vessel from side to side when in a seaway.

Roll Cumulus. Name given to cloud when disposed in long parallel rolls.

Rolled Section. Sectional shape of a steel bar or girder when the shape was imparted as the bar passed through the rolling mill.

Roller. Long, smooth, swelling wave, often without crest, not generated by a prevailing wind.

Roller Jib. *See* 'Du Boulay Roller Jib'.

Roller Reef. A reef made by rotating the boom to which the foot of a sail is attached. This winds the sail round the boom like a roller blind.

Roller Sheave. Sheave of a block when steel rollers have been placed round the pin to reduce friction.

Rolling. Thwartship swinging of a vessel when in a seaway.
Rolling Chock. A bilge keel. 2. Jaw of a yard, which steadies the yard as the ship rolls.
Rolling Hitch. Manipulation of end of a rope when attaching it to a spar or another rope. Round turn is taken and then passed over first turn; second turn is made alongside first turn and end brought up through this second turn. Name was given because this is appropriate hitch to put on a spar or cask that is required to be rolled.
Rolling Period. Period of roll. Time, in seconds, taken by a vessel to roll from one side to the other.
Rolling Tackle. Extra tackle extending from near slings on masts to weather quarter of a yard. Holds yard to mast when rolling to windward.
Roman Indiction. Number that denotes the position of a year in a system of 15-year periods, beginning 3 B.C.
Ron Finish. Finishing off of a 'point' in end of rope by forming a footrope knot over the heart.
Roof Error. Error in sextant indication that is caused by refractive effect of glass roof of a mercury trough when using it as an artificial horizon.
Room and Space. Longitudinal distance between centre lines of ribs of wooden vessels; 'room' being width of rib, 'space' being distance between ribs.
Roomer.* Elizabethan name for putting about before the wind. To 'put roomer' means 'to wear'.
Rooming. The navigable water to leeward of a vessel.
Roost. Strong and turbulent current between Orkney and Shetland Islands.
Rooves. Small, annular pieces of copper that fit over nail ends in clincher-built craft; over them the nail end is flattened to form clinch.
Rooving Iron. Small implement for holding a roove over end of a clinch nail. Has a hole in centre so that nail can be driven through roove.
Rope. Long and flexible lengths of wire, hemp, cotton, coir, leather and other materials laid up for the transmission of power and resistance, while maintaining form at any angle of bending. Size is expressed by the circumference of the rope. By convention, ropes have a minimum circumference of one inch; smaller cordage being 'lines'.
Rope Jack. Machine for laying up yarns and strands. Has circular framing with rotating hooks worked by a handle.
Ropemaker's Eye.* Eye formed in end of hemp cable. End of cable was unlaid and two strands turned over to make the eye by splicing. Third end was turned over, and its ends wormed round cable. Eye was then marled and served.
Ropery. Establishment in which ropes are made. 2. A ropewalk.
Rope's End. End of a rope, or a short length of rope.
K

Ropewalk. Covered walk, 100 to 200 fathoms in length, in which ropes are laid up. Formerly, men walked backward while paying out hemp fibres whose ends were attached to rotating hooks at end of the ropewalk. This method has been superseded by the use of machinery.

Rope Winch. Machine having three, or more, rotating 'whirlers' used for laying up the strands of a rope.

Rope Yarn. Single yarn laid up in same direction as that of the strands of a rope.

Rope Yarn Knot. Correct way of joining two yarns. Yarns are split and married; two opposite foxes, one from each yarn, are led round to form a reef knot.

Roping Needle. Stout needle used when sewing canvas to rope. Has a pointed end that curves upward from line of needle.

Roping Palm. Used when sewing canvas to roping. Indentations in the 'iron' are larger, and fewer, than those in a sailmaker's palm.

Ro-Ro Ship. A 'roll-on, roll-off' vessel built with doors in her ends or slides to allow, when berthed, vehicles to drive on or off.

Rorqual. Type of whale that raids fishing-grounds in practically all seas. It is not hunted, because its blubber yield is small.

Rose. Name given to a compass card, or other diagram, having radiating lines. 2. Strum.

Rose Box. Strum Box.

Rosebur. Roove, or washer, over end of a clinched nail or fastening.

Rose Knot. Wall knot followed by crown knot, and each knot followed round; finished with a diamond knot, and ends tucked through centre.

Rose Lashing. Under and over lashing finished off with concentric turns around the crossings and between the turns.

Rotator. Log unit having inclined vanes that cause it to rotate as it is drawn through the water.

Rotary Stream. Tidal stream that changes its direction through 360° in one cycle.

Rotor Ship. Experimental ship of the 1920s. Propelled by wind-pressure acting on rotating towers.

Rotten Ice. Floes that have become honeycombed through melting.

Rough Log. Log-book kept, on deck, by officer of the watch.

Rough Tree. Shaped, but unfinished, mast or spar.

Rough Tree Rail. Timber resting on tops of frames and forming the upper part of a bulwark.

Round. To sail round a buoy, promontory or other fixed point, at a uniform distance, when changing direction.

Round House. Originally, the poop. Later, a square cabin amidships and abaft mainmast of a sailing ship.

Round In. To haul the fall of a tackle and close the distance between its blocks.

Rounding. Altering course around a position and maintaining a pre-arranged distance from it. 2. Rope used for serving a larger rope. 3. Formerly, condemned running rigging less than four inches.

Roundly. Quickly and smartly.

Round Ribbed. Said of a vessel with curved tumble home.

Rounds. Wooden rungs of a rope ladder.

Round Seam. Single seam used for joining two edges of canvas. Stitches are passed through at right angles to both surfaces, with 35 to 40 stitches to the foot.

Round Seizing. Put around two ropes when the strain is in the same direction on each. Seizing is secured to one rope, and seven round turns passed round both parts. End of seizing then passed up through these turns, and out under first turn. Six round turns then passed in cantlines of first turns, end passed between sixth and seventh lower turns. Round turn then taken across all turns, finishing off with a clove hitch, having first round turn inside the hitch.

Round Spliced. Splice made with flattened strands, so that splice will be circular in section.

Round To. To bring ship's head to the wind.

Round Top. Circular platform near mast head.

Round Turn. Complete turn of rope around a bollard, bitt, etc. 2. Complete turn of one cable around another when riding to two anchors.

Round Up. To close the space between the two blocks of an extended tackle by hauling on the fall when there is no weight on the tackle.

Rouse. To haul on a rope or cable without any mechanical advantage.

Rouse about Block. A large snatch block.

Routier. French name for an early book of sailing directions.

Rove. Past participle of 'Reeve'. 2. Alternative form of 'Roove'.

Rover. Pirate. Freebooter.

Rovings. Robands.

Row. To impel a boat by pulling on oars.

Row Boat, Rowing Boat. Boat propelled by oars alone.

Rowl. Sheave of a single block. 2. Light crane for discharging cargo.

Rowlock. Opening in which an oar is pivoted when rowing. May be a cut away part in wash strake, or space between two thole pins.

Row Ports.* Small ports, near waterline, used when propelling vessels by oars pulled between decks.

Rowse. 'Rouse.'

Royal. Mast or sail next above topgallant.

Royal Mail Pendant. White pendant with a red crown over a post horn and the words 'Royal Mail' in red. Worn by vessels carrying Royal Mail under contract.

Royal Marines. The corp of soldiers who chiefly serve on board H.M. ships.

Royal Mast. Mast immediately above topgallant mast, being an extension of the topgallant mast.

Royal National Lifeboat Institution. Voluntary society that maintains lifeboats and life-saving apparatus around coasts of the British Isles.

Royal Observatory. Establishment in which time is ascertained and celestial movements and phenomena are observed and noted. At Greenwich from 1675 to 1943. Now at Herstmonceux Castle.

Royal (Sail). Sail next above topgallant sail. Generally the upper sail on mast of a square-rigged ship.

Royal Yacht Squadron. Premier yacht club of the British Empire. Founded at Cowes in 1812; given title 'Royal' in 1820.

Royal Yard. Yard next above topgallant yard: carries royal sail.

R/T. Radio telephone.

Rubber. Steel block with rounded face and wooden handle. Used for rubbing down seams in canvas after they have been sewn. 2. 'Rubbing Piece.'

Rubbing Paunch. Batten secured vertically on fore side of mast and over the hoops of a built mast. Prevents damage to yards by hoops, when yards are sent up or down.

Rubbing Piece. Raised wooden beading fitted horizontally around outside of boat. Takes chafe when boat is alongside.

Rubbing Strake. Doubled strake on outside of a boat. Acts as a rubbing piece, and can be renewed when worn.

Rubbing Wale. Alternative name for 'Rubbing Piece'.

Rudder. That implement or fitting by which the direction of a vessel is controlled by steering. Almost invariably fitted at stern, and free to move through about 35° on either side. Hinged to stern post or rudder post—but occasionally balanced. *See* 'Balanced Rudder'. 2. A paddle used for steering.

Rudder Band. Alternative name for 'Rudder Brace'.

Rudder Brace. Horizontal attachment to a rudder, carrying either a pintle or brace.

Rudder Breeching. Rope, more or less vertical, that takes part of weight of rudder off the gudgeons.

Rudder Case. 'Rudder Trunk.'

Rudder Chains. Small chains shackled to rudder and led inboard and secured. Hold rudder should it become unshipped. Also, form alternative steering connections if steering chains part.

Rudder Chock. Wooden support for rudder when in dry dock.

Rudder Coat. Canvas cover attached to rudder stock where it emerges from a trunk. Prevents sea entering ship in heavy weather.

Rudder Frame. Streamlined frame to which plates of a double-plate rudder are fastened.

Rudder Head. Upper end of rudder stock, to which tiller is attached.

Rudder Hole. Opening in deck through which rudder head protrudes.

Rudder Iron. Brace or pintle of a rudder.

Rudder Pendants. Lengths of rope or wire measured and fitted so that rudder chains can be connected to tackles in an emergency.

Rudder Port. Casing, above helm port, through which rudder stock enters ship.

Rudder Post. Name sometimes given to stern post when rudder is attached to it.

Rudder Stock. Vertical member of rudder, to which rudder blade is attached.

Rudder Stops. Projections on rudder, and, or, rudder post that prevent rudder being angled more than 38° (about).

Rudder Tackles. Tackles used for controlling rudder or tiller. Are connected to rudder chains, and used when steering connections to wheel break down.

Rudder Trunk. Casing extending from helm port to the deck on which the tiller or quadrant is situated.

Rule of the Road. Seaman's usual name for the 'Regulations for Preventing Collision at Sea'.

Rumb. Old form of 'Rhumb'.

Rumbo, Rumbowline. Outside yarns of old rope laid up again for use as lashings, and other purposes not demanding much strength.

Rummage. Originally meant 'to stow cargo'. Now means 'to search a ship carefully and thoroughly'.

Rummager. Originally, 'one who stowed cargo'. Now, one who searches a vessel for undeclared goods and articles.

Run. Voyage between two ports, especially when regular. 2. Distance sailed between two observations, or epochs. 3. After part of ship's underwater body where it rises and sweeps towards stern post. 4. To sail with wind astern—or nearly so.

Rundle. Drum of a capstan. 2. Round rung of a rope ladder.

Run Down. To collide with a vessel that is directly ahead. 2. To run north or south into a desired latitude; to run east or west into a desired longitude: in both the foregoing, is more applicable when numerical value of latitude or longitude is decreasing.

Rung. Ground timber of frame of a wooden vessel.

Rung Head. Upper end of a ground timber.

Runlet. Small barrel usually containing 15 gallons, but may vary between 5 and 20 gallons.

Runner. Person whose duty is to take messages. 2. A smuggler. 3. A person who solicits business on behalf of another. 4. Vessel that runs a blockade. 5. Tackle in which one end of rope is made fast and block runs on bight: nominal advantage being twofold. 6. Backstay which can be slackened or detached to avoid fouling the boom. Running Backstay.

Runner Tackle. Luff tackle attached to hauling end of a runner purchase.

Running. Sailing with wind astern, or nearly so.

Running Agreement. Made between Master and crew to allow more than one foreign voyage to be made without paying off. Expires at end of six months, or on vessel's first arrival in United Kingdom after that period, with maximum period of two years.

Running Block. That block, of a purchase, that moves in position as fall is veered or hauled. Usually called 'Moving Block'.

Running Bowline. A bowline (loop) made in the end of a rope and around its own standing part.

Running by the Lee. Running under sail with the main boom on the weather side.

Running Days. Days that are counted successively and without any exception or interruption.

Running Down. Striking a vessel that is at anchor, or that has the right of way.

Running Down Clause. Institute Time Clause that defines liability of underwriters to owner of a ship that runs down another. Liability does not exceed three-quarters value of ship that runs down.

Running Fix. Determination of a ship's position by taking a line of bearing, running a known distance, transferring first line to new position and crossing it with another position line.

Running Free. Sometimes defined as sailing with wind abaft the beam, but not right aft. As far as the 'Rule of the Road' is concerned, a vessel is runnnig free when she has the wind more than one point abaft that point at which she would be close hauled.

Running Gear. All rigging, ropes and tackles that move, or are movable.

Running High. Said of a sea when waves are high. Said of a gyro compass when its indication is numerically higher than it should be.

Running Hook. One of the tack hooks a little off centre line of boat at stem. Tack of sail is put on it when running before wind.

Running Lights. Statutory navigational lights shown by a vessel when under way.

Running Moor. Anchoring by dropping first anchor while ship has headway, and letting go second anchor after she has gone farther ahead.

Running Part. Any part of a tackle that moves when worked—as distinguished from the standing part.

Running Rigging. All ropes rove through blocks and worked as may be necessary, as distinguished from standing rigging.

Running the Easting Down. Making easterly departure by running before a westerly wind.

Running Voyage. Old name for a wartime voyage when made independently and not in convoy.

Run Out. To put out a mooring, hawser or line from a ship to a point of attachment outside her.

Run the Longitude. To sail along a meridian.

Russell's Log. Early 19th-century towed log, of spiral type and made of copper.

Russian Sennit. Loose matting made by weaving several stands—or lengths of small rope—athwart and over and under their own parts.

Rutter. Common, but corrupted, form of 'Routier'.

S

Sabik. Star η Ophiuchi. S.H.A. 103°; Dec. S16°; Mag. 2·6.
Saccade. The slatting of sails in slight airs and with heavy swells.
'Sack of Coals.' Old name for 'Coal Sack'.
Sacred Anchor.* Anchor, in ancient Greek vessels, that was not let
go except when in imminent danger.
Sacred Knot. Old name for 'Brahmin Knot', or 'Triangle Knot'.
Saddle. Shaped piece of wood attached to a mast or spar to form
a rest for another spar. One on bowsprit takes heel of jib
boom; those on yards take studdingsail yards; those on mast
form a rest for jaws of gaff or boom.
Safe Port. Port in which a vessel can lie at all times in good safety
and free from perils of political, natural, hygienic, or other nature.
Safety Certificate. International certificate compulsorily carried by
every passenger steamer of 1600 tons and upward when proceeding on an international voyage. Modified certificate is given
to a passenger vessel on a voyage not exceeding 200 miles from
land.
Safety Hook. Cargo hook fitted with a self-mousing device.
Safe Working Load. The stress that a rope, chain, hook, or appliance can safely carry without risk of deformation or fracture.
Sag. To droop in the middle. 2. To drift to leeward.
Sagging Strain. Excessive stress causing a sagging to develop.
Sagittarius. Constellation situated between R.A. 18 h and 20 h,
Dec. 16°–20° S. Has no star brighter than magnitude 3.
2. Ninth sign of Zodiac, extending from 240° to 270° celestial
longitude. Sun is in this sign from November 23 to December 22
(about).
Sag to Leeward. To make excessive leeway.
Sail. Shaped and fitted canvas, or other material, used for moving
a vessel by force of the wind. 2. A sailing vessel when under
sail. 3. A short voyage in a vessel under sail.
Sailboard. A buoyant plank, fitted with mast, sail and wish-bone
boom, upon which the sailor stands while sailing.
Sail Burton. Whip rove for sending a sail aloft for bending.
Sailcloth. Light grade canvas used for sails of boats. Supplied in
12-, 15-, and 18-inch widths.
Sail Clutch. Iron band used, instead of hoop or lashing, to attach
a sail to a mast or boom.
Sail Cover. Canvas covering put over sail when not in use.
'Sail Ho.' Report of a look-out man who has sighted a sailing
vessel.
Sail Hook. Small hook for holding canvas while it is being stitched.
Sail Hoops. Rings encircling a mast and attached to luff of a fore
and aft sail.
Sailing. Proceeding under sail. 2. Departing from a port or
harbour.
Sailing Boat. Small boat propelled by sails.

Sailing Directions. Books dealing with winds, weather, currents, and other circumstances prevailing in a given area. Compiled to give the navigator all helpful and relevant information available. Name was given formerly to 'Sailing Instructions', and to 'Sailing Orders'.

Sailing Free. Sailing with wind between right aft and that direction in which vessel would be close-hauled.

Sailing Ice. Small masses of drift ice with waterways in which a vessel can sail.

Sailing Instructions. Orders given by officer commanding a convoy to commanders of ships under convoy; detailing action to be taken in particular circumstances, code of signalling and special signals, position of rendezvous and other necessary orders and instructions. 2. Orders given relative to a particular voyage.

Sailing Master. Formerly, an officer in Royal Navy responsible to the captain for the correct navigation of the ship.

Sailing Orders. Final orders given to a warship. 2. Orders specifying time of sailing.

Sailings. Methods by which the course and distances sailed by a ship, and the set of tidal streams and currents, are related to the change in her geographical position.

Sailing Thwart. That thwart, in a boat, at which a mast is clamped or shipped.

Sail Loft. Large covered space in which ships' sails are cut, measured and made.

Sailmaker. Man whose occupation is to make and repair sails, together with other canvas work.

Sailmaker's Eye Splice. Used only in ropes stitched to canvas. Strands are tucked with the lay, for neatness.

Sailmaker's Whipping. The most efficient of the whippings, particularly suitable when end of rope is exposed to wind. In addition to the turns of whipping passed round the end of rope, frapping turns are passed round whipping in each cantline of the rope.

Sail Needle. Special needle used when sewing canvas. Pointed end is triangular in section. Made in four sizes, 14, 14½, 15, 16, the higher numbers being less substantial than the lower.

Sail Numbers. Letters and numbers on sails of racing yachts. Upper number indicates length of yachts in metres; lower number is a private number; letter(s) indicate nationality.

Sailor. Man or boy employed in sailing deep-water craft. Word is sometimes loosely used to include men who go to sea. Used officially to denote a seaman serving on deck. At one time was a man with previous sea experience, but who was not rated able seaman.

Sailor's Disgrace. Nickname for the 'foul anchor' badge of the Lords of the Admiralty. Was the badge of Lord Howard of Effingham, who commanded the English Fleet against the Armada.

Sailors' Home. Establishment or hostel, in a seaport, for the reception, accommodation, and entertainment of seamen temporarily on leave, or awaiting a ship.

Sail Room. Compartment in which sails are stowed in ship.

Sail Twine. Medium-weight flax twine used for general sewing of sails and canvas by hand.

Saint Elmo's Fire. Discharge of atmospheric electricity sometimes observable on masts and yards in certain states of stormy weather. Positive discharge gives the appearance of streamers; negative discharge has the appearance of a luminous coating.

Saint Nicholas. The patron saint of seamen; which accounts for the number of seaports having churches dedicated to him.

Saker. Olden gun that threw a ball weighing five to seven pounds.

Salamba. Bamboo fishing raft, with mast and sail, used in sea around Manila.

Salinity. Saltness. The amount of dissolved salt in water. Usually expressed as a ratio as compared with fresh water—fresh water being 1000 and sea water about 1026 but varying, in ports and harbours, between 1000 and 1031 (Port Said). Also known as the specific gravity of sea water.

Salinometer. Instrument for indicating the proportion of salt in a given quantity of water.

Salinometer Cock. Small cock, on a marine boiler, by which water may be drawn for test purposes.

Sallee Man. Old name for the 'Portuguese Man o' War'.

Sallee Rovers. Moroccan pirates, from the port of Sallee, who preyed on Mediterranean shipping in the 16th, 17th and 18th centuries. Their galleys were neither large nor formidable, and the prowess of the rovers has been greatly exaggerated.

Sallying. Rolling a vessel, that is slightly ice-bound, so as to break the surface ice around her. May sometimes be done when a vessel is lightly aground, but not ice-bound.

Sally Port. Aperture, in quarter of a fire ship, for escape of crew after she has been ignited.

Salmiel Wind. 'Simoon.'

Saloon. Mess room for deck officers in a merchant ship. 2. Main cabin in a passenger ship.

Salt. Landsman's nickname for a seaman.

Salt Beef Squire. Naval nickname for an officer promoted from the lower deck.

Salt Horse. Salt beef. In R.N. the name is jocularly applied to an officer who has not specialised in any subject.

Saltings. Low-lying land made marshy by salt water.

Saltire. Diagonal cross, of any colour, in a flag or ensign.

Salt Junk. Salt beef.

Salute. A mutual gesture of respect and greeting. Initiated by the inferior in rank, and returned by the superior. Made by hand, the firing of guns, the letting fly of sheets, the veiling of topsails and the dipping of ensigns.

Salvage. The saving of a vessel, or cargo, from extraordinary peril or danger. 2. Compensation or reward given for the salving of property in peril. 3. Rope made of yarns laid parallel and bound together.

Salvage Agreement. Document, or undertaking, by which recompense for salvage services is agreed and promised under specified conditions.

Salvage Association. A corporate body that deals with salvage but does not actually carry it out. Incorporated, by Royal Charter, 1856. Governed by Lloyd's and company underwriters. 2. Company specialising in marine salvage, and owning ships and plant designed and fitted for the purpose.

Salvage Award. Sum of money awarded by Admiralty Court, or arbitrators, as recompense for salvage services rendered.

Salvage Clause. Inserted in charter party to allow vessel to attempt or render salvage services for the preservation of property in peril at sea.

Sambuk. Arab dhow with a low-curved stem and a high stern that is often lavishly decorated.

Sampan. Punt-like boat used in Chinese waters, Java, and Madagascar for fishing, carriage and merchandise, and other purposes.

Samping. When applied to wind, means 'easing' or 'dropping'.

Samson Line. Small line supplied in 30-fathom hanks weighing from one to one and a quarter pounds.

Samson Post. Stump mast for a derrick. 2. Strong oak post on fore deck of a yacht; used as a mooring-post. 3. A cable bitt. 4. A towing bollard.

Sand Strake. Garboard strake of a boat.

Sand-Warped. Left on a sand bank at ebb tide. 2. A temporary stranding at half flood of tide.

'Santa Clara.' Ship named in the earliest marine insurance policy still existing—which is dated October 23, 1347, and covers her voyage from Genoa to Majorca.

Sargasso Sea. Area of Atlantic in which surface is extensively covered by 'gulf weed'. Approximate extent is from 19° W to 47°W, and from 20° N to 25° N.

Saros. Period of 18·03 years, which is the interval at which lunar and solar eclipses repeat themselves in approximately similar circumstances.

Satellite. A secondary planet that revolves around a primary planet. Is often, but erroneously, called a 'moon'. Name is sometimes given to the fictitious bodies assumed in the harmonic analysis of tides.

Satellite Navigation. Navigation, and the instruments for it, by receiving and measuring signals from artificial satellites orbiting the earth.

Saturated Steam. Steam that has the same temperature as the water from which it is generated—as distinguished from superheated steam.

Saturation. The carrying of the maximum amount of water vapour by the atmosphere in a given state. Amount that can be carried increases and decreases with air temperature.

Saturation Deficit. Difference between vapour pressure in a given state of the atmosphere and the maximum pressure it could carry.

Saturn. Sixth major planet from Sun. Diameter is about nine times that of Earth; distance from Sun is about 10 times that of Earth. Has nine satellites and a system of broad, flat rings around its equator.

Saucer. Iron or steel bearing, shaped like a saucer, on which vertical spindle of a capstan rests on deck below.

Save All. Strip of canvas laced to roach of a square sail to get additional wind effort. 2. Alternative name for 'Water sail'.

Saxboard. Uppermost strake of an open boat.

Scale. Numerical relationship between distance on chart and actual distance between any positions. 2. Measure, or diagram, that converts charted distance to actual distance. 3. Hard deposit that forms on inside of boilers, or on exposed ferrous metals.

Scaling. Removing scale from a surface on which it has formed. 2. Adjustment and graduation of gun sights. 3.* Cleaning the bore of a gun by firing a small powder charge.

Scampavia. Neapolitan rowing vessel, about 150 ft. long, having a 6-pounder gun forward. Had lateen main and mizen sails. Was discontinued in first half of 19th century.

Scandalize. To top yards by alternately opposite lifts, brace them on opposite tacks, loose sails in the buntlines and, in general, give the ship as untidy an appearance as possible. Was the orthodox method—especially in ships of Latin countries—of showing grief or mourning.

Scanner. The rotating or oscillating aerial of a radar set.

Scanting. Said of a wind when it draws ahead.

Scantlings. Lengths of timber having a square section not more than 5 in. by 5 in. 2. Measurements of members used in construction of either wood or steel ships. 3. Transverse measurements of a piece of timber.

Scarf. Alternative form of 'Scarph'.

Scarph. Joint used when uniting ends of two strakes or planks. Ends are bevelled, and shoulders may be cut, so that there is no increase of thickness at the doubling. With iron and steel members, bevelling increases area of weld.

Scend. Upward rising of a vessel's fore end when her stern falls into trough of sea.

Schafer Method. Procedure for restoring a person apparently drowned. Expirational movements are slow and deliberate, inspirational movements being as quick as possible. This method has less initial delay than the Silvester method.

Scheat. Star β Pegasi. S.H.A. 15°; Dec. 28°N; Mag. 2·6. Name is corrupted Arabic for 'Fore Arm'.

Schedar. Star α Cassiopeiae. S.H.A. 350°; Dec. N56°; Mag. 2·5.

Schermuly Pistol. Firearm that ignites and aligns a line-carrying rocket.

School. Shoal of fish, or whales.

School Ship. Instructional ship permanently moored in harbour.

Schooner. Fore and aft rigged vessel having two or more masts. First built Gloucester, Mass., about 1713.

Schottel. Propulsion and steering unit, a propeller-rudder. The horizontal propeller is driven by a vertical shaft and pivots like a rudder-blade.

Schuyt. Fore and aft rigged Dutch fishing-boat, having one or two masts.

Scirocco. Warm wind blowing from South to SE, in Mediterranean Sea, and preceding a depression moving E'ly. Name is loosely given to any warm S'ly wind in this area.

Scope. The amount of cable by which a ship rides to an anchor.

Scorbutic. Pertaining to scurvy; giving rise to scurvy.

Score. Cut-out part, of shell of a wooden block, that receives and confines the strop.

Scoriae. Reddish-brown, or black cinders of volcanic eruption.

Scorpio (Lat.=Scorpion). Constellation situated between R.A.'s 15 h 50 m and 17 h 50 m, and Dec. 20° to 43° S. Contains three bright stars, the principal being Antares.

Scotch Boiler. Cylindrical boiler with combustion chamber furnaces and smoke tubes fitted in water space. Can be single or double ended. Usually has three furnaces.

Scotched Up. Shored up.

Scotchman. Any wood batten, hide, or metal put on rigging to take a chafe. Any wooden construction placed for protective purposes.

Scotch Mist. Combination of drizzle and thick mist.

Scott-Still Engine. Small engine using steam generated by the gases exhausted by a diesel engine.

Scoute. Manx sailing craft, formerly used in herring fishery.

Scow. Flat-bottomed, square-ended craft used for transport of cargo.

Scowing. Name sometimes used for 'Becueing'.

Scran Bag. Bag, or compartment, in which articles of clothing, left lying about by naval ratings, are stowed. The articles are redeemed by payment of a small piece of soap. 2. Bread bag.

Scrap Log. Alternative name for 'Deck Log'.

Screen. Canvas partition or protection. 2. Thwartship plating of an erection on upper deck. 3. Wood or metal fixture that limits arc of visibility of a navigational light.

Screen Bulkhead. Thwartship bulkhead on upper deck at forward or after end of midships accommodation.

Screw. Screw propeller. 2. Steamer having screw propulsion.

Screw Alley. Enclosed space with a gangway alongside propeller shaft. Used when examining, lubricating, or refitting bearings of propeller shaft, or when withdrawing tail-end shaft.

Screw Aperture. Opening, in after deadwood, in which propeller revolves.

Screw Coupling. Joining piece in which a screw thread is fitted for adjusting distance or tension.

Screw Current. Moving water of the sea that flows along ship's side into the propeller, and then is driven aft and quarterly by the propeller blades.

Screw Effect. Deviation of a steamship's head from a prolongation of her fore and aft line when caused by transverse thrust—or paddle-wheel effect—of her propeller. Corrected by rudder.

Screw Log. Any log that indicates distance or speed by the screw effect of water acting on inclined planes of the log rotator.

Screw Post. 'Propeller Post.'

Screw Propeller. Immersed system of inclined planes that is revolved by an engine and forces ship in a fore and aft direction. Usually called 'propeller' or 'screw'.

Screw Race. Turbulent water thrown astern of ship by a revolving propeller.

Screw Rudder. Small screw propeller fitted at angle to fore and aft line of ship. Used for altering ship's heading, particularly when stopped. Now obsolete.

Screw Stopper. Cable stopper fitted with a bottle screw for tautening.

Screw Well. Vertical trunk into which a propeller could be lifted after being slung in tackles and tail-end shaft withdrawn. Was used, with more or less success, in old warships having sail and screw propulsion.

Scroll, Scroll Head. Decorative work at stem head of a ship—as differentiated from a 'figure' head.

Scrowl. 'Scroll.'

Scud. Fractonimbus cloud driven, by the wind, under cumulonimbus.

Scudding. Running before a gale with minimum canvas set.

Scull. Short oar, usually with spoon blade, rowed with one hand. 2. Small boat rowed by one man.

Sculler. Man who sculls a boat. 2. Boat propelled or impelled by sculling.

Sculling. Propelling or impelling a boat by sculling. 2. Impelling a boat by putting a scull over the stern, inclining the blade and moving it transversely.

Scupper. Hole in waterways, or bulwarks, for allowing water on deck to flow outboard.

Scuppered. Slang term for frustrated, knocked out, or killed.

Scupper Hole. The hole in a scupper.

Scupper Hose. Short length of pipe to lead scupper water clear of ship's side.

Scupper Leather. Piece of leather used to form a non-return valve in a scupper.

Scupper Lip. Projection on outboard end of a scupper discharge. Ensures water being thrown clear of ship's side.

Scupper Nail. Short nail having a large flat head.

Scupper Plate. Longitudinal plate under a waterway.

Scupper Shoot. Semi-circular spout projecting outboard, to lead scupper water clear of ship's side.

Scurvy. Form of anaemia caused by a deficiency of vitamin C. Marked by ulceration of mouth, debility, lassitude, haemorrhage, and other symptoms.

Scuttle. Small opening—in a deck, side of a ship, or compartment—that can be closed as required. Literally means a 'shutter'.

Scuttle Butt. Covered cask, having lid in head, in which fresh water for current use was formerly carried.

Scuttling. Deliberately making, or uncovering, any opening in a vessel so that sea can enter. Sometimes done to allow water to enter a stranded ship to prevent her bumping on the ground.

Scylla. One of the whirlpools (garofali) in Straits of Messina, named after a fabulous monster.

Sea. Large expanse of water forming part of an ocean, or connected with it. 2. Waves or swell. 3. The movement and direction of waves. 4. Large inland lake.

Sea Acorn. A barnacle.

Sea Anchor. Floating construction, either temporary or permanent, so shaped that it offers minimum area to the wind, and gives maximum resistance to translation through the sea. Used when it is necessary to keep a vessel head to sea and anchoring is impossible. Sea anchor is streamed by a line connecting sea anchor with ship. A drogue, as used in boats, is the simplest form.

Sea Battery. Assault upon a seaman, by Master, while at sea.

Sea Bed. Ground at the bottom of a sea or ocean.

Sea Belch. Breakers, particularly a line of breakers.

Sea Birds. Birds that live on, by, and from, the sea. Two chief classes are Laridae and Larinae (gulls) and Tubinares (petrels). In general, they have webbed feet, and beaks adapted for seizing fish.

Sea Blubber. Nickname for jelly fish.

Seaboard. Coast, or land, continuous to a coast. Sometimes used as meaning 'seaward'.

Sea Boat. Ship's boat kept ready for immediate lowering while at sea: sometimes called 'accident boat'. 2. Applied to a ship when assessing her behaviour in a seaway.

Sea Borne. Carried by the sea. 2. Carried over the sea in a ship.

Sea Bound. Encircled by the sea.

Sea Boy. Young lad, less than 18 years of age, employed in a ship.

Sea Breeze. Wind from the sea that blows across land.

Sea Brief. 'Sea Letter.'

Sea Captain. Master of a sea-going vessel. Certificated officer competent and qualified to be master of a sea-going vessel.

Sea Cock. Screw-down valve, in bottom of a ship, by which sea water can be allowed to enter a pipe system.

Sea Craft.* Timber supporting lower deck beams of a wooden vessel.

Sea Disturbance. State of sea surface as compared with its mean level. Generally expressed by a number in a scale in which 0 represents perfect smoothness, and 10 is the maximum disturbance known to seamen.

Sea Dog. Old and experienced seaman. 2. Dog fish. 3. Elizabethan privateer.

Sea Eagle. Bald-headed eagle (adopted as emblem by U.S.A.). 2. Sting-ray fish.

Sea Eggs. Echinoidiae that are usually called 'Sea Urchins'.

Sea Fardinger.* A seaman.

Seafarer. One who earns his living by service at sea.

Seafaring. Serving at sea for a livelihood.

Sea Fire. Phosphorescence of the sea surface.

Sea Fret. Dawn mist at sea.

Sea Gait. Rolling swell. 2. Position of two ships when alongside one another in a swell.

Sea Gates. Pair of gates that close entrance to a dock, tidal basin, or harbour against the action of storm waves.

Sea Gauge.* Former deep-sea sounding appliance in which a column of mercury was acted upon by water pressure, the mercury compressing trapped air. A viscous substance, on top of mercury column, denoted height to which mercury rose.

Sea-Going. Applied to men, or craft, when differentiating between sea service and service in sheltered waters.

Sea Gull. Name that includes all birds of the gull family that fly mostly above the sea.

Sea Hog. Porpoise.

Sea Horizon. The line in which sea and sky appear to meet.

Sea Horse. Name given to walrus, hippopotamus, and hippocampus; the last being a small fish with a head resembling that of a horse.

Sea Kindliness. That characteristic of a ship by which she behaves well in heavy weather, and adapts herself to varying states of the sea.

Seal. Warm-blooded carnivorous animal found in arctic and antarctic regions and in lower latitudes. Limbs have developed into flippers.

Sealer. Man who hunts seals. 2. Vessel used in seal hunting.

Sea Lawyer. Nautical name for an argumentative person.

Sea Legs. Ability to walk fairly steadily when a vessel is labouring in a seaway.

Sea Letter. Custom house document carried by a neutral vessel on a foreign voyage in wartime. Gives port of departure, destination, nature of cargo, and other relevant particulars required by a boarding officer.

Sea Level. A more or less theoretical level based on that which the sea surface would have if there were no tide, swell or wave. It thus approximates half tide level. Datum for British surveying is the mean level at Newlyn, Cornwall.

Sea Lion. Name given to a seal found in Pacific Ocean. Male is about 12 ft. long, weighs about half a ton, and has golden-brown hair.

Seam. Joining of edges of canvas, or other fabric, made by stitching. 2. Longitudinal meeting of edges of planks, strakes, or plates.

Seaman. Generally, one who follows the sea as a profession. This meaning is often limited. Merchant Shipping Acts define him as any person serving in a ship, other than the Master. In the Royal Navy, is a man who works on deck. 2. A merman.

Seamanlike. In a manner, or fashion, befitting a seaman.

Seaman's Disgrace. 'Sailor's Disgrace.'

Seamanship. The professional skill of a seaman. The art of working, managing, and handling a vessel, in a seaway, in a seaman-like manner.

Seamark. Erection, in shoal water, elevated above sea level to act as a beacon, navigational aid or warning.

Sea Mew. 'Sea Gull.'

Sea Mile/Nautical Mile. Distance equivalent to length of one minute of latitude at the position concerned. Varies between, approximately, 6045 ft. at Equator and 6081 ft. at Poles. Standardised, for log purposes, as 6080 ft.

Seaming Palm. Sailmaker's palm used when sewing seams. Indentations in iron are smaller than those in roping palm, and it has no leather thumb guard.

Seaming Twine. Flax twine, 2-ply, used for sewing canvas. Supplied in hanks up to 1 lb., which equals one mile of twine.

Sea Otter. Fur-bearing animal of Behring Straits and Kamchatka.

Sea Parrot. Seaman's name for the puffin.

Sea Pass. Duly attested document given to a neutral vessel, during war, by a belligerent power. Exempts her from search or seizure by vessels of that power.

Sea-Pie. Seaman's dish made with alternate layers of pastry and meat; usually two of meat and three of pastry.

Sea Plats.* Old name for charts.

Sea Rate. Average gaining or losing rate of a particular chronometer while at sea.

Searcher. Customs officer who searches a vessel for undeclared goods or stores.

Search(ing) Note. Document given to Master by Customs officer, when ship has been searched for unentered goods.

Sea Reach. Length of a river between its discharge into the sea and its first bend inland.

Sea Reeve.* Former official who kept watch on seaward borders of estate of a lord of the manor. He took charge of wrecks, and prevented smuggling.

Sea-Risks. Special risks, incidental to a sea voyage, that may affect persons or goods.

Sea-Room. Sufficient expanse of sea for a vessel to manoeuvre without risk of grounding, or collision with other vessels.

Sea Rover. Pirate, or a pirate vessel. 2. One who travels by sea with no fixed destination.

Sea Scarph. 'Sea Craft.'

Sea-Serpent. Animal of serpentine form, and immense size, credibly reported to have been sighted at sea. No final proof of its existence has yet been established.

Sea-Service. Service rendered, as one of the crew or complement, in a sea-going ship.

Seasickness. Disorder of the nervous system brought about by ship's movement in a seaway.

Sea-Slug/Sea-Cat/Sea-Dart. Types of ship-to-aircraft guided missiles.

Sea Smoke. Vapour rising like steam or smoke from the sea caused by very cold air blowing over it. Frost-smoke, steam-fog, warm water fog, water smoke.

Sea-Snake. Venomous snake found swimming, near land, in waters of Indian and Pacific Oceans. Is eaten by natives of Tahiti.

Seasonal Area. Part of a seasonal zone, but having a load line period that differs somewhat from the load line period of the zone.

Seasonal Correction to Mean Sea Level. Correction to be applied to mean sea level, at a place, to find the sea level in a given season.

Seasonal Zone. Area of an ocean or sea, in which different load lines are in force in different seasons.

Sea Suction. Underwater opening in a ship, through which sea-water is pumped for wash deck, fire, ballast, sanitary, or other uses.

Seat. Any part, or member, on which another part, or member, rests.

Sea-Term. Word, phrase, or name particularly used by seamen.

Sea Thermometer. An ordinary thermometer, but with a cup round the bulb so that some water is retanied when taking temperature of surface water of the sea.

Sea-Urchin. Sea creature having a bony casing, rather like an orange, with numerous small spikes. Starts as a free-swimming creature, the bony covering developing later.

Sea-Wall. Embankment, or masonry, erected to protect land from damage by sea action.

Seaward. Towards the sea.

Sea-Water. Water comprising the salt-water seas and oceans. Contains chlorides, sulphates, bromides, carbonates, etc. Specific gravity is about 1025—but varies between 1001 and 1031 (Suez).

Seaway. Expanse of water with definite wave motion.

Seaweed. Weed growing in sea-water, technically known as 'fucaceæ'. Has simple spores, and is world-wide in extent. Some seaweed is edible; most is good for manuring land. Nearly 500 known species.

Seaworthy. Said of a vessel when in all respects fit to carry a proposed cargo, or passengers. 2. Capable of withstanding risks incidental to the sea.

Seaworthiness. In a limited sense, is a vessel's fitness to withstand the action of the sea, wind, and weather. In a broader, and legal, sense, it requires that the vessel must be handled and navigated competently, fully manned, adequately stored, and in all respects fit to carry the cargo loaded.

Second. Sixtieth part of a minute of time. 2. Sixtieth part of a minute of arc.

Secondary. Applied to a circle, cold front, depression, meridian, or port, to distinguish it from a primary. Often used to denote a secondary depression.

Secondary Circle. Any great circle whose plane is perpendicular to a primary circle. It follows that a secondary circle will contain the axis and poles of the primary; and that the primary will contain the axes and poles of all its secondaries.

Secondary Cold Front. Front of polar air following first cold front.

Secondary Depression. Second area of low pressure formed inside a meteorological depression. Generally moves round primary depression, and may combine with it.

Secondary Meridian. Meridian whose position has been determined absolutely or astronomically, and not by reference to a prime meridian.

Secondary Port. Port, or position, whose tidal phenomena are deduced by reference to tides at an appropriate standard port.

Second Class Paper. Written undertakings to pay, whose financial value is open to doubt.

Second Differences. Differences that affect a primary difference when the variation in value of a quantity is not uniform.

Second Futtock. Second portion of rib of a wooden vessel, counting from keel.

Second Greaser. Old nickname for a second mate.

Second Hand. Person next below Skipper of a fishing-vessel, usually certificated.

Second Rate. Former classification of a warship carrying 90 to 100 guns. In U.S.N., was a vessel of 2000 to 3000 tons.

Secret Block. Block in which sheave is completely covered except for a small lead to swallow of block.

Sector. Arc between two radii, or two lines of bearing.

Secular. Pertaining to, or connected with, the passing of time.

Secure. To make fast so that displacement cannot occur.

Securite (Safety). A radiotelephone message prefixed by the spoken word, 'say-cur-ee-tay', indicates that a message concerning the safety of navigation or giving important meteorological warning is about to be made.

Seel. The roll of a vessel at sea.

Segmental Bar. Rolled steel having section that is semi-circular, or nearly so.

Segmental Strip. Rolled steel section with lower side a chord of a circle, the upper side being an arc appreciably less than a semicircle.

Seiche. Short period oscillation in level of enclosed, or partly enclosed, area of water when not due to the action of tide-raising forces.

Seine. Long fishing-net, 60 fathoms or more, in the form of a bag. About 8 to 16 ft. deep. Upper end is buoyed, lower end is weighted.

Seine Boat. Craft for fishing with seine net.

Seine Fishing. Catching fish with a seine net.

Seize. To bind together two ropes, or two parts of the same rope, with small stuff tightly turned around them.

Seizing. The turns of small stuff with which two parts of rope are seized. Principal forms are Flat, Round, and Racking seizings.

Seizing Wire. Seven wires, of galvanised iron or mild steel, with six of the wires laid up around a central wire. Used when seizing wire ropes.

Seizure. Taking of a ship by overpowering force, or by lawful authority.

Selene. Greek word for 'Moon'.

Selenography. The delineation of Moon's face.

Selenology. Branch of astronomy dealing with Moon.

Self-Mousing Hook. Hook having a spring mousing that allows easy hooking on, but prevents accidental unhooking.

Self-Trimmer. Vessel with large hatches and clear holds that allow coal, grain and similar cargoes to be teemed into any part of a hold.

Selvagee. Rope made by spunyarn being laid in parallel lengths, and bound together with marline-hitched spunyarn passed around all parts. Has great flexibility and grip.

Selvagee Strop. Strop made by laying spunyarn in coils and binding it with marline-hitched spunyarn.

Selvedge. Normal edge of woven material, such as canvas. 2. An alternative form of 'Selvagee'.

Semaphore. Method, or apparatus, for signalling alphabetical letters, numbers or code signs, by visible movements and changes of position. In nautical signalling, hand flags, or apparatus having movable arms, is used.

Semi-Diameter. Half diameter of disc of Sun or Moon. As this is the distance of the centre from the limb it is of great importance when measuring sextant altitudes.

Semi-Diesel Engine. Internal combustion engine in which injected fuel is vaporised by a hot bulb and compression. Used for working auxiliary machinery, and for propulsion of small vessels.

Semi-diurnal. Pertaining to, or recurring at, periods of half a day, approximately.

Semi-diurnal Tides. Tides occurring twice in a lunar day.

Semi-menstrual Inequality. Tidal inequality that goes through all its variations in half a lunar month.

Sennit. Plaited yarns, strands, or ropes.

Senhouse Slip. Strong slip, secured to framing of ship in chain locker, to hold inboard end of cable. Tumbler is shaped to pass through open link of cable and form a snug fitting for link. Gives maximum strength when cable is veered to a clinch. Allows instant release when required. Connection between ship and slip is by chain of such length that cable can be slipped from deck immediately above chain locker.

Sensible Horizon. Plane of celestial sphere that is tangent to Earth at position of an observer: is parallel to his rational horizon, and 4000 miles above it.

Sentinel. Electric apparatus in circuit of a navigation light, and causes a bell to ring if filament of lamp fuses. 2. Apparatus formerly used in surveying vessels. Specially shaped weight was towed over sea-bed by a wire from the stern. When depth varied, angle of wire increased or decreased, and caused the bell to ring.

Separation. The means, or material, by which one parcel of a ship's cargo is separated from another.

Separation Cloths. Large cloths used for separating different parcels of bulk cargoes such as grain.

Separation Error. Error in the collimation of a sextant, or optical instrument.

Septentrional. Pertaining to the North. From the Greek for 'Seven ploughing oxen' (Ursa Major).

Serein. Rain falling from a cloudless sky. Very abnormal.

Service. Serving put on a rope. 2. Duty performed. 3. Group of persons performing and sharing the same duties.

Services. Royal Navy, Army, Royal Air Force.

Serving. Rendering service. 2. Small stuff tightly wound around a splice or rope to protect it. 3. Act of putting on a serving.

Serving Board. Flat wooden tool used for serving a rope tightly and neatly.

Serving Mallet. Wooden mallet with a semi-circular groove along its cylindrically-shaped head. Used for serving when considerable tension is desired.

Set. Direction in which a current flows.

Set and Drift. Direction and distance that a current travels in a given time.

Set Bolt. Bolt used for forcing another bolt out of its hole.

Set Flying. A sail set attached only by its halyard, sheet and tack but not by hanks to a stay.

Set Sail. To make sail. To loose sail and sheet home. 2. To sail away from a place.

Settee Rig. Boat rig having two masts, each carrying a four-sided fore and aft sail in which the luff is much shorter than the leech.

Set the Watch. To name a watch and detail it for duty on deck.

Setting. Said of a heavenly body when it moves down to western horizon. 2. Setting a course is putting ship's head in a desired direction. 3. Setting an observed object is ascertaining its compass bearing.*

Setting Pole. A quant. Long pole by which a craft is propelled by putting pole on bed of the waterway, and bearing on it.

Settle. To ease a halyard, or other rope used for hoisting, by a small amount. 2. To cause the land, or a light, to go below horizon by sailing away from it.

Settling Tank. Stokehold tank into which fuel oil is pumped and allowed to settle before being used. Oil is drawn through a filter so that solid contents, usually sand, are left behind.

Set Up. To tauten standing rigging with lanyards, tackles, or screws.

Sewed. Said of a vessel when water level has fallen from the level at which she would float. Also said of the water that has receded and caused a vessel to take the ground.

Sewn Boat. Boat made with a double skin of Honduras mahogany. Inside planking is at right angles to keel, and $\frac{5}{32}$-inch thick. Outer skin goes horizontally, and is $\frac{1}{4}$-inch to $\frac{3}{8}$-inch thick. These two skins are sewed together with copper wire.

Sewing. Said of water level when it is falling away from a minimum height necessary to float a particular vessel.

Sextant. Reflecting instrument used for measuring altitudes and other angles not exceeding 120°.

Shackle. Somewhat semi-circular bar of metal having an eye in each end to take a pin. Used for connecting purposes. 2. Length of chain cable measuring $12\frac{1}{2}$ fathoms in Royal Navy, 15 fathoms in Merchant Navy.

Shackle Bolt. Bolt having a shackle at its end.

Shackle Crow. Tool for withdrawing a bolt. Somewhat similar to a crowbar, but having a shackle at toe.

Shackle Key. T-shaped key having a square section end. Used for unscrewing flush-headed shackle pins that have a square countersunk recess in head.

Shades (of Sextant). Coloured glasses by which excessive light is excluded.

Shaffle. Lug that takes the pivot pin of a gooseneck.

Shaft. Propeller shafting. 2. That part of an oar that lies between blade and loom.

Shaft Alley. Footway alongside propeller shafting, extending from engine-room to stern gland.

Shaft Coupling. Flange and bolt connection of two lengths of propeller shafting.

Shaft Pipe. Old name for 'Shaft Tube'. Especially applied to a tube in stern frame of wooden vessel, through which shaft passes.

Shaft Tube. Circular casing through which propeller shaft passes to propeller.

Shaft Tunnel. Enclosed space, between engine-room and stern gland, through which propeller shaft extends and in which are the shaft bearings.

Shake. Crack in timber due to faulty seasoning or drying. 2. To take hoops off a cask, barrel, etc., and reduce it to its original parts.

Shakedown Cruise. Voyage of a newly-commissioned warship in which frequent drills are carried out to familiarise the crew with their various stations and duties.

Shake Out a Reef. To loose a reef in a sail, adjust the sail and sheet home.

Shakes. Staves and headings of casks and barrels when dismantled and bundled together.

Shakings. Hoops, staves, and headings of a cask or barrel when dismantled. 2. Cuttings of canvas, rope, etc., that accrue after fitting or refitting work. Termed 'arisings' in Royal Navy.

Shallop. Small boat for one or two rowers. 2. Small fishing vessel with foresail, boom mainsail, and mizen trysail. 3. A sloop.

Shallow. Area where depth of water is small. A shoal.

Shallow Water Constituent. Quarter diurnal effect on a tidal undulation that is retarded in its translation by shoaling of ground or constriction of its path.

Shallow Water Tide. That tidal component which, due to shoaling or constriction, is separated from the main undulation, and arrives later.

Shamal. A north-west wind in Persian Gulf.

Shamrock Knot. Manipulation of bight of a rope so that three loops are formed round a central ring. Also called 'Jury Mast Knot'.

Shanghaied. Forcibly put aboard a vessel other than one's own ship. Practically impossible nowadays, but was formerly common in certain American ports when crews deserted on arrival and bounties were paid to those providing a crew.

Shank. That part of an anchor between the ring and the arms.

Shank Painter. Chain by which shank of anchor is held when stowed on a billboard.

Shanty. Alternative name for 'Chanty'.

Shaping a Course. Laying off the course a vessel is to steer. Also used as meaning the steering of the course.

Shark. Large carnivorous fish found in tropical and sub-tropical waters. Principal types are the Basking, Dogfish, Hammer-headed, Tiger and White sharks.

'Shark Flies the Feather.' Nautical saying embodying the strange fact that a shark will attack and devour any creature but a bird.

Sharkskin. Dried skin of the shark. Is rough, but free from scales. Used for smoothing wood, and for handgrips of swords.

Shark's Mouth. Deep and narrow indentation in canvas of an awning when in the way of a stay or other permanent rigging.

Sharpie. Long, narrow, flat-bottomed sailing boat.

Sharp Up. Said of yards when braced as far forward as possible.

Shaula. Star λ Scorpii. S.H.A. 97°; Dec. S37°; Mag. 1·7.

Shear Hook.* Barbed hook that was fitted to yard arm of fireship to hook into rigging of any enemy vessel it collided with.

Shearing Stress/Strain. Force that is exerted so that it tends to make one part of a member slide over the other part; so exerting a scissors-like action on fastenings passing perpendicularly through both parts.

Sheathed. Said of a steel vessel when her underwater surface has been covered with wood to which copper sheathing has been fastened.

Sheathing. Protective covering. Particularly applied to copper placed on underwater surface of ships to prevent fouling and attacks of marine animal life. Also applied to wooden linings in holds, etc.

Sheathing Nail. Flat-headed cast nail of tin and copper alloy. Used for nailing copper sheathing on underwater surface of a wooden or sheathed vessel.

Sheave. Grooved wheel in which a rope runs and alters its direction. May be of metal or wood; lignum vitae being usual in the latter.

Sheave Hole. Aperture in which a sheave is fitted.

Sheepshank. Manipulation of a rope by which its effective length is reduced, and can be restored quickly. Rope is bighted so that three parts lie alongisde and a bight is at each end; half hitch, in same rope, being passed over each bight.

Sheer. The upward sweep, from amidships to forward and aft of a vessel's freeboard deck. Also, the amount that the forward of after end of a deck is higher than midship part when keel is horizontal. Standard sheer, in inches, is 0·2 of vessel's length in feet+20 inches, for forward sheer; half this amount for after sheer.

Sheer Batten. Wooden batten used for same purpose as sheerpole.

Sheer Draught. 'Sheer Plan.'

Sheer Head Lashing. Used when rigging sheer legs. Heads are crossed and end of lashing is timber hitched to one leg, above the crutch. Taut turns are then passed, working downward. Finished off with three or four frapping turns around all parts, end being clove hitched to sheer head above the crutch.

Sheer Hulk. Old vessel fitted with sheers for stepping, or removing masts of ships.

Sheer Lashing. Variation of sheer head lashing. Rope is middled and passed round cross of legs. Turns are taken upwards with one part, downward with the other. When sufficient turns, ends are brought to centre and lashed.

Sheer Legs. Two splayed legs forming sheers.

Sheer Line. Line of main deck at its junction with ship's side.

Sheer Mast. One leg of a pair of sheers.

Sheer Mould. Thin wood template with one edge shaped to indicate sweep of deck sheer; used for transferring sheer line to side of plating.

Sheer off. To move away obliquely.

Sheer Plan. Drawing in which are delineated longitudinal, vertical, and horizontal sections, and transverse vertical sections, of a vessel or proposed vessel.

Sheerpole. Iron bar lashed to lower eyes of lower rigging to prevent shrouds, and deadeyes or screws, from turning.

Sheer Rail. Lower strake of bulwark planking in a wooden vessel.

Sheers. Splayed legs erected more or less vertically and meeting— or crossed—near top, where upper end of a purchase is attached for lifting purposes. Inclination of plane of these legs is controlled by tackles—or by a third, and longer, leg at right angles to the other pair. Used when masting ships and for other purposes requiring a high lift of a heavy weight.

Sheer Strake. Main strake in a vessel's side plating, being that to which main deck beams are fastened. In a boat, is the strake to which upper ends of ribs are fastened—sometimes called 'top strake'.

Sheet. Rope or purchase by which clew of a sail is adjusted and controlled when sailing.

Sheet Anchor. A third bower anchor. Originally, was heaviest anchor in ship, and used in heavy weather. Formerly called 'waist' anchor, on account of its being stowed abaft fore shrouds. Rarely carried nowadays, except in H.M. ships—where it is a spare, or additional, starboard bower anchor.

Sheet Bend. Simple and secure method of attaching a rope to an eye or loop. End of rope is passed through eye, over one side of it, behind the eye and then under its own standing part. Double sheet bend is made by putting a round turn below, and following, the first turn.

Sheet Cable. Cable attached to a sheet anchor.

Sheet Home. To haul on a sheet until it is taut and sail is fully extended.

Sheets. After space, in a boat, that is abaft thwarts. Sheets of sails are tended there when under sail. 2. Cockpit of a yacht.

Shelf. Strong timber bolted to inner sides of ribs of a wooden vessel, to form housing for deck beams. In a boat, it carries the thwarts. 2. Rather abrupt rising of sea-bed from deep water to shallower water.

Shelf Ice. Land ice, either afloat or on ground, that is composed of layers of snow that have become firm but have not turned to glacier ice.

Shelf Piece. Shelf that houses deck beams.

Shell. Outside plating, or strakes, of a vessel. 2. That part of a block in which a sheave revolves, and to which the hook or shackle is attached.

Shellback. An old and experienced seaman.

Shell Plating. Steel or iron plating that forms shell of a vessel.

Shelter Deck. Deck above main deck when it is not permanently closed against wind and weather. It is thus exempted from certain tonnage dues.

Shelter Deck Type. Type of vessel having a continuous shelter deck above main deck.

Shelving. Said of sea-bed when it slopes from shoal water to deep water with comparatively small inclinations.

Sheratan. Star β Arietis. S.H.A. 332°; Dec. N21°; Mag. 2·7.

Shield Ship.* Warship having movable shield around each gun until moment of firing.

Shift. Of wind, is a change in its direction. 2. To shift a vessel is to move her from one berth to another.

Shifting. Moving a vessel from one berth to another. 2. Movement of stowed cargo by movement of ship in a seaway. 3. Changing of wind's direction. 4. Separation of blocks of a tackle when they have been hauled 'two blocks'.

Shifting Backstay. Backstay that was let go, when tacking, and shifted to the new weather side. Is a seaman's name for a man who has no standing job, but is put to any work that may require doing at the time.

Shifting Boards. Planks and boards erected in a hold to prevent a cargo from shifting. Particularly necessary with bulk grain and similar cargoes. Also used for preventing shift of solid ballast.

Shifting Centre.* Former name for 'Metacentre'.

Shifting Sands. Quicksands. Sands that are loose and fluid when wet, and cannot support weight.

Shift of Butts. Arrangement of a series of butted joints so that they do not lie in a line, or approximation of a line.

Shift of Wind. A definite change in wind direction.

Shingle. Coarse gravel that has been partially rounded by sea action.

Ship. A sea-going vessel. 2. Vessel having a certificate of registry. Technically, a sailing vessel having three or more masts with yards crossed on all of them. In Victorian times, any vessel with yards on three masts was termed a 'ship' even if other masts were fore and aft rigged. To ship, is to put on or into a vessel; to put any implement or fitting into its appropriate holder.

Shipbreach. Shipwreck.

Shipbreaker. One who breaks up old and unserviceable vessels.

Shipbroker. One whose business is the buying and selling of vessels. 2. One who acts as an intermediary between a shipowner and a shipper. 3. One who acts as a ship's agent.

Shipbuilder. One whose business is the building of ships.

Ship Building. The construction of ships.

Ship Canal. Canal connected with sea and of such size that sea-going vessels can safely navigate it.

Ship Chandler. Tradesman who deals in cordage, canvas, and other commodities required when fitting out or storing a ship.

Ship Construction. Ship building, more especially as applied to steel ships.

Ship Fever. Typhus. In 18th century was the name given to typhus when caused by insanitary conditions in overcrowded ships.

Ship Handling. Manoeuvring of a vessel in circumstances requiring precise and skilful movements of rudder, engines, or sails.

Shiplet.* Old name for a small ship.

Shipman.* Old name for a mariner of any rank or rating.

Shipmaster. A person in command of a ship. A person certified as competent to command a ship. A master mariner.

Shipmate. One who serves, or served, in the same ship as another.

Shipment. The putting of cargo into a vessel. Goods, or parcel of goods, put into a vessel for carriage.

Ship Money. General levy formerly made on all counties, boroughs, cities, towns, and ports of England for upkeep of Royal Navy. Usually made in time of war. When Charles I called for it in time of peace it aroused opposition that culminated in the Civil War.

Ship of the Line.* Ship having at least two decks and an armament sufficient for her to take a place in the battle line.

Shipowner. One who owns a ship, or who owns one or more $\frac{1}{64}$ parts of a ship.

Shipper. One who puts goods into a ship for carriage. At one time the name was applied to a seaman.

Shipping Articles. Articles of Agreement entered into by the Master and crew of a ship before commencement of a voyage. Articles of British ships are opened in presence of the Superintendent of a Merchant Shipping Office.

Shipping Federation. Association of shipowners that watches their interests, maintains agreed standards and represents owners in conferences and discussions with representatives of ships' personnel.

Shipping the Swab. Old Royal Navy colloquialism for promotion to rank of lieutenant. Relic of the time when lieutenants had one epaulette.

Ship-Rigged. Square rigged on all of three or more masts.

Shipshape. Arranged neatly and compactly.

Ship's Husband. Person formerly carried in a merchant ship to transact ship's business and purchase stores. In earlier times, was the boatswain, and was in charge of the crew and of the fabric of the ship.

Ship's Papers. Books and documents required to be held by a ship. Include Certificate of Registry, Articles of Agreement, official log-book, bill of health, free-board certificate, radio certificate, and documents relating to cargo.

Ship Time. Time kept by a ship in a given longitude. May be Zone Time, but is frequently Local Mean Time at last noon position. To avoid large time corrections the time may be corrected frequently when making large differences in longitude.

Ship Worm. The mollusc, *teredo navalis* which attaches itself to the underwater surface of ships.

Shipwreck. Destruction or loss of a ship at sea. To cause the loss of a ship. Name is sometimes given to wreckage.

Shipwright. Man skilled in the building and repairing of ships.

Shipyard. Yard or ground, near water, in which ships are built.

Shirt in Rigging.* Signal formerly made by a merchant vessel when asking for a boat to be sent to her by a warship.

Shiver. Old name for 'Sheave'. 2. To put luff of a sail into the wind so that the wind is spilled out of it.

Shoal. Ground with its upper surface a little below surface of the water. 2. Water shoals when its depth decreases.

Shoe. Board or block in which heel of a derrick or sheer leg is housed. 2. Step of a mast.

Shoe an Anchor. To lash a board, or plate, to fluke of anchor to increase its grip in the ground. Sometimes put on Admiralty pattern anchor to prevent bill catching on edge of side plating when fishing the anchor.

Shoe Block. Block with two sheaves, one above the other, and the pin of one sheave athwart line of pin of the other sheave.

Shole. Flat timber, or plate, put under heel of a derrick or sheer leg to spread the thrust. 2. Piece of wood attached to lower edge of rudder to protect it when ship takes the ground. 3. Old form of 'Shoal'.

Shoot Ahead. To move ahead swiftly. To move ahead of another vessel quickly when underway.

Shoot Anchor.* Sheet Anchor.

Shooting in Stays. Carrying a good amount of way when going from one tack to the other under sail.

Shooting Stars. Meteors.

'Shoot the Sun.' To take Sun's altitude with sextant or quadrant.

Shore. Legally, area between high and low water marks on the coast. Commonly, the land immediately inshore of the sea.

Shore. Strong prop that supports or steadies a vessel's hull while building or in dock. Applied in line of a floor, frame, or rib. To shore is to place shores so that they steady or support.

Shore Floe. Field or floe ice that has become joined to shore, and does not rise and fall with tide.

Shore Horizon. Line made by sea surface along the shore, as viewed from ship.

Shoring. Supporting with shores. 2. All the shores used when shoring.

Short Bills. Bills of Exchange that become payable within 10 days of sighting.

Short Delivery. Delivery of cargo when short of bill of lading amount.

Shorten In. To decrease the amount of cable by which a vessel is riding.

Short Exchange. Rate of exchange for 'Short Bills'.

Shorten Sail. To reduce effective sail area of a ship under sail by furling or reefing.

Short Glass. Sand glass used in connection with ship log when speed exceeds five knots. Empties in 14 seconds; log indication being doubled to find speed.

Short-Handed. Not having full crew. Undermanned.

Short Jaw. Said of a rope when lay of strand is appreciably more than 45° from the run of the rope.

Short Shipped. Amount of cargo not loaded because of non-arrival at ship, or because ship had no space available.

Short Splice. Joining of ends of two ropes by unlaying an end of each, marrying them and tucking each strand over and under strands in other rope.

Short's Ship Clinometer. Instrument for measuring angle of heel, or roll, by the movement of mercury in a tubular glass arc.

Short Stay. Said of a vessel's anchor, or cable, when the amount of cable out is not more than one-and-a-half times the depth of water.

Shot. Projectile that has no explosive burster and is fired from a gun. 2. In fishing: the nets that are put out at one time; also, the catch that is hauled in. 3. Two hemp cables spliced together; also, the name given to the splice.

Shot Anchor. Sheet anchor.

Shot Box. Wooden box containing shot. Formerly, box in which canister and grape shot were kept alongside a gun.

Shot Garland.* Framework attached to a hatchway coaming to take cannon-balls.

Shot Hole Stopper. Two-hinged semi-circles of steel, on end of a threaded shaft having a crosspiece and butterfly nut. Was passed outboard through a shot hole, in semi-circular form, and then opened out and clamped to ship's side.

Shot Plug. Conical piece of timber used for plugging shot holes.

Shoulder Block. Block having a projecting piece just above swallow of sheave. Used on masts and yards in places where block might lie too close to mast or spar, and so jam rope.

Shoulder of Mutton Sail. Triangular sail sometimes used in boats. Apex is at mast head, foot is stretched along a boom.

Shoulder Pipe. Reinforced oval aperture in forward bulwark plating just abaft break of forecastle. Used as a fairlead for spring, mooring rope, boat rope, etc.

'Shove Off Forward.' Order given to bowman of a boat when he is to bear boat's head away from the ship or structure that she is alongside.

'Show a Leg.' Phrase used in Royal Navy when calling hands from their hammocks. Said to be a survival from days when women were allowed to sleep aboard warships. More likely to mean, 'Show some intention of turning out.'

Shroud. Rope or wire rigging that supports a mast or bowsprit in a thwartship direction.

Shroud Bridle. Bridle used to confine running rigging to a shroud.

Shroud Hoop. Band attached to mast near head, having lugs to which upper eyes of shrouds are attached.

Shroud Knot. Knot for temporarily reuniting a shroud that has parted. Ends are unlaid, married, and a wall knot made in each three strands.

Shroud-Laid. Said of ropes consisting of four strands laid up around a central heart.

Shroud Plate. Iron plate, on side of ship or boat, to take lower ends of shrouds. 2. Iron band at head of lower-mast to take lower eyes of futtock shrouds.

Shroud Stopper. Short length of rope used for securing to a shroud above and below a part that had become stranded.

Shroud Truck. Wooden thimble seized to a shroud to form a fairleader for a rope of running rigging.

Shuga. Slush when in Russian rivers.

Shutter. Poppet closing rowlock of a boat.

Sibidsibiran. Small, one-masted fishing vessel of China seas. Is fitted with an outrigger.

Sick Bay. Space, in a warship, reserved for the treatment of the sick and injured.

Sick Berth. Alternative name for 'Sick Bay'.

Side Benches. Fore and aft benches in lifeboat, lying above thwarts and tops of air tanks.

Side Boy. Boy, or ordinary seaman—in Royal Navy—whose duties are to work under quartermaster of the watch and keep the gangway clean, man the side when required, pass end of man-ropes to passengers in a boat, carry messages from officer of the watch. At sea, he is bridge messenger.

Side Error. Sextant error due to horizon glass not being perpendicular to plane of instrument. Ascertained by clamping index bar to zero and observing whether direct and reflected images are coincident. Corrected by adjustment of screw in back of mirror frame.

Side Fishes. Rounded pieces, on outside of a made mast, that give mast its circular form.

Side Girder. Longitudinal member going fore and aft parallel to centre girder. It may be continuous, in which case floors are not continuous; or it may be intercostal between continuous floors.

Side Keelsons. Two small keelsons lying on either side of main keelson to give increased longitudinal strength.

Side Ladder. Rope ladder put over ship's side for manning or disembarking from boats.

Side Lights. Red and green screened lights compulsorily shown by vessels underway between sunrise and sunset.

Side Party. Men detailed for upkeep and patching of ship's side paintwork.

Sidereal. Pertaining to, or measured by, the fixed stars.

Sidereal Clock. Timepiece regulated to keep sidereal time. It gains 24 hours a year on a clock keeping mean solar time.

Sidereal Day. Interval between successive transits of First Point of Aries across a meridian. Is 3 minutes 55·91 seconds shorter than a mean solar day.

Sidereal Hour Angle (S.H.A.). The westerly hour angle of a fixed star from the First Point of Aries.

Sidereal Month. Interval between two successive transits of Moon across the same star. Value is 27 days 7 hours 43·2 minutes.

Sidereal Period. Time taken by a planet to make one revolution of its orbit.

Sidereal Time. Time based on hour angle of First Point of Aries.

Sidereal Year. Time taken by Earth to go round its orbit when a fixed star is taken as a point of definition. Length is 365 days 06 hours 09 minutes 10 seconds.

Side Skids. Vertical timbers suspended over ship's side to keep cargo clear of side when loading or discharging.

Side Stitch. Running seam put in alongside seam of a sail to give additional strength.

Sighting. Observing with the eye. Applied to document, means examining and signing as evidence of satisfaction as to its authenticity.

Sighting the Bottom. Drydocking, beaching, or careening a vessel and carefully examining the bottom with a view to ascertaining any damage it may have.

Sight Test. Examination of eyesight to discover any defect in it. Includes Distance, Form, and Colour tests.

Sign. Formerly meant a 'constellation'. Now means a constellation in the Zodiac and, more generally, the twelfth of the Zodiac in which a certain constellation is.

Signal. A pre-arranged act or exhibition that has a specific meaning.

Signal Halyards. Ropes by which flag signals are hoisted. Vary in size from ¾ inch to 1¼ inch. Usually have a proportion of reverse-laid yarns, to prevent torsion causing flag to coil up around its halyard.

Signal Letters. Four letters allotted to a vessel for indicating her name and port of registry by International Code. The first letter indicates nationality.

Signalling. Communicating by means of sounds, signs, shapes, flags, or lights.

Signalling Lamp. Lamp constructed and fitted for signalling by Morse code. Compulsorily carried by vessels on international voyages.

Signalman. Trained man whose duty is concerned with the making and receiving of signals.

Signals. Communications made by signalling.

Signed Under Protest. Words incorporated when signing under duress and not concurring entirely with import of document signed, and after stating grounds of non-concurrence.

Signs of Ecliptic. 'Signs of Zodiac.'

Signs of Zodiac. Twelve portions of Zodiac, each 30° in celestial longitude. They divide Sun's annual path into sectors, and are named after the principal constellation that was in each sector when division was introduced. Due to precession of equinoxes, the signs move backwards from their constellations at a rate of about one 'sign' in 2100 years.

Sill. Lower horizontal member of a port of opening. 2. Upper edge of bottom of an opening into a dock.

Silometer.* Name formerly given to instruments measuring distance run by a ship, and not requiring the consideration of a time interval. Walker and Chernikeef logs are of this type; the Pitometer is not.

Silvester Method. Method for restoring the apparently drowned. Arms of rescued man are used for exciting respiratory action.

Simoon. Whirlwind that generally carries sand from Arabian and African deserts. Occurs in spring and summer, usually lasting from 10 to 20 minutes.

Simpson's First Rule. Area of a plane figure bounded by a straight line, two perpendiculars and a parabolic curve can be calculated from formula $x(a+4b+2c+d)$ when figure is divided into an even number of parts by perpendiculars at constant intervals, along base line; a being first ordinate, b the even numbered ordinates, c the odd numbered ordinates, d the last ordinate, x the common interval between ordinates.

Simpson's Rules. Rules for finding areas of plane figures bounded by a straight line, two perpendiculars and a parabolic curve. They include Simpson's First and Second Rules and the 'Five-Eight' Rule.

Simpson's Second Rule. Base line is divided into equal parts that are a multiple of 3, the number of ordinates being $3x+1$. Assuming 9 equal parts (10 ordinates), area will be found by the sum of end ordinates, plus twice 4th and 7th ordinates, plus three times all other ordinates, multiplying the sum by $\frac{3}{8}$ of the common interval.

Simultaneous Altitudes. Altitudes of different heavenly bodies taken at the same time, approximately.

Singing Propeller. Propeller that gives a more or less musical note while revolving under water. Due to variations in flow of water to the propeller, and other possible causes.

Single-Banked. Said of boats that pull one oar at each thwart. Said of an oar when pulled by one man.

Single-Day Tide. Tide going through its cycle once in a tidal day. More usually called a 'diurnal' tide.

Single-Deck Type. Name given to vessels having no deck below upper deck.

Single-Plate Centre Keelson. Vertical plate going fore and aft, on top of floors and riveted to a lug and reverse bar at each floor.

Single Whip. Rope rove through a standing block for hoisting purposes.

Singling Up. Taking in all ropes not wanted, so that only a minimum number of ropes will require casting off when leaving a berth or buoy.

Sink. To become submerged. To move downwards. To go down to bottom of the sea. To go below the horizon.

Sinking a Strand. Procedure followed when long splicing 4-stranded rope to 3-stranded rope. After splicing three strands, fourth strand is tucked under nearest strands as most convenient for making a neat finish.

Siren. Fitting that gives a powerful and penetrating sound that is caused by passage of steam, or air, through a rotating disc with numerous perforations. Can be trained horizontally so that maximum volume of sound can be emitted in any required direction. 2. Mermaid. In Greek mythology these were supposed to lure ships to destruction by resting on a rock and singing sweetly.

Sirenia. Marine mammals that feed on aquatic vegetation.

Sirius. Star α Canis Majoris. S.H.A. 259°; Dec. S17°; Mag. 1·6. Has a small companion, Sirius B. Sirius A has diameter about 1·8 that of Sun, but candlepower is 26 times greater. Distant about nine light years; temperature 11,200° A. Is the brightest star in the sky. Name is Greek for 'Scorcher'.

Sirocco. 'Scirocco.'

Sisal. Fibre obtained from the agave plant of Mexico, Yucatan, and British East Africa. Used for ropemaking.

Sister Block. Two sheaves, one above the other, in same shell. Shell is shaped with flat, circular ends and a short circular shaft between the two sheaves.

Sister Keelson. An internal keelson running along either bilge.

Sister Ship. Ship built to same design and dimensions as another. 2. Ship belonging to same owner as another.

Sister Ship Clause. An Institute Time Clause that refers collisions between ships of the same ownership to the judgment of an arbitrator agreed upon by insurers and owner.

Sixern. Shetland Isles fishing boat. Double-ended, about 22 ft. long.

Sixteen Bells. Eight double strokes on ship's bell; customarily struck at midnight when new year commences. Eight bells are for 24 hours of passing year, eight bells for 00 hours of New Year.

Sixty-fourth. Minimum legal share in a registered ship. One share constitutes part ownership: there can thus be up to 64-registered owners of a ship.

Skeg. Angular member, or knee, connecting and bracing keel and stern post of a wooden vessel.

Skeg Shore. Shore put under skeg of a vessel to steady her at the moment of launching.

Skerry. Reefs or rocky islets.

Skid. Thwartship beam or girder on which a boat is stowed. 2. Timber placed horizontally to facilitate the sliding of heavy weights. 3. Wooden fender placed vertically on ship's side to keep cargo clear when loading or discharging.

Skid Beam. One of the beams supporting a light deck on which boats are stowed.

Skiff. Small, lightly-built boat used in sheltered waters. May be propelled by oars or sail.

Skimming Dish. Small sailing craft having broad beam and fairly flat bottom.

Skin. Outside plating, or timbers, of a vessel. If there are two skins, it is the inner one. 2. That part of a sail that is outside when it is furled.

Skinning a Sail. Making a smooth skin, with taut canvas, when furling a sail.

Skipper. Master of a fishing vessel. Colloquial name for any Master or commanding officer.

Skylight. Glazed opening in deck that allows light to pass to deck below. Glazed covering is usually hinged, to allow air to pass in fine weather.

Sky Pilot. Ship's chaplain. Often applied to any clergyman.

Skysail. Square sail set above royal yard.

Skyscraper. Triangular sail set above royal yard.

Slab. That part of a reefed square sail that hangs downwards.

Slabbed Knee. Beam knee made by removing bulb of beam and welding a triangular plate to it.

Slab Hatch Covers. Several hatch covering planks held in a steel frame that can be lifted by a derrick, thus speeding the uncovering and covering of hatches. First introduced by Captain R. E. Thomas, 1909.

Slab Ice. Slob.

Slab Lines. Vertical ropes on fore side of square sail, from head to foot. Fastened to roping at each end, and at intervals between. Used for hauling up sail when reefing.

Slab Reefing. Reefing with reef-points or ties, as opposed to roller-reefing.

Slack in Stays. Slow in going from one tack to the other when under sail.

Slack Water. State of a tidal stream when there is no lateral movement of the water.

Slamming. The striking of the sea surface, by the forward flat bottom, when a vessel is pitching in a head sea and lifts her forepart out of the water.

Slant (of Wind). Favourable wind for sailing a desired course. 2. A temporary breeze during a calm or period of light airs.

Slatting. The beating of a loose sail against a mast. 2. Slackening and tautening of luff of a sail when too close to wind.

Slaver. Vessel engaged in transporting slaves.

Slave Ship. 'Slaver.' Colloquially used to denote a vessel in which the crew have to work unusually hard.

Sleepers. Knees connecting transom to after timbers of a wooden ship. 2. Thwartship timbers that rest on trestle trees to support a top.

Sleet. Precipitation of rain and snow, or snow and hail.

Slew. To turn on a pivot, and in a horizontal plane.

Slice. Wedge piece inserted between bilgeway and keel to lift a vessel ready for launching. 2. Long iron bar used for stirring up fires in furnaces of boilers, and for clearing spaces between furnace bars. 3. Lever, with chisel end, used for removing planking or copper sheathing.

L

Slide Valve. Mechanism that admits steam on alternate sides of piston of reciprocating engine. Operated by the engine. Two commonest are 'Piston' and 'D' types.

Sliding Baulk. Substantial flat timber put under bilges of a vessel being launched, and resting on bilgeways of launching slip. Travels with ship when launching.

Sliding Gunter. Nearly vertical yard carrying a small sail that was set (1) above royal or skysail, (2) carries the main sail of a boat.

Sliding Keel. 'Drop Keel.'

Sliding Ways. Inclined ways on which a vessel is built, and down which she slides when launched.

Sling. A rope with its ends short-spliced together used to lift cargo.

Slings. Chains or ropes by which a yard is suspended from a mast. 2. The middle part of a yard. 3. Chains or wires by which ships' boats are hoisted; specifically those attached to the boat.

Slip. Of propeller, is the difference between theoretical advance of ship by propeller action and the actual advance. Mainly due to propeller acting in a yielding medium. *See* 'Positive slip', 'Negative slip'.

Slip. Particulars of a maritime risk against which insurance is required. Made out by broker and offered to underwriters. When initialed by insurer it is treated as an acceptance of risk, and is exchanged for signed policy.

Slip. Inclined bed of masonry, sloping towards water, on which ships are built. 2. Inclined bed, often fitted with rollers, on to which vessels can be hauled for examination of underwater body, for painting and for repairing. 3. Hinged tongue of metal, fitted with a securing link, used for holding a rope or cable that may require instant release. 4. To slip is to let go inboard end of cable or rope, and get underway.

Slip Hook. Hook fitted with a hinged portion that can be slipped, so that a weight carried by it can be disengaged and allowed to fall off.

Slip Knot. Knot that is free to run along the rope around which is is made. 2. Knot made with bighted end of rope so that, by pulling on the rope, the knot falls apart.

Slippery Hitch. Derisive name for a bend, or hitch that does not hold. Name is sometimes given to a 'Slip Knot'.

Slip Rope. Rope whose end is passed outboard through forward fairlead, through ring of a buoy and brought inboard. When moorings are taken in, the inboard end of rope can be released to free the ship.

Slip Stopper. Chain that confines a stowed anchor to the billboard By releasing a slip, in end of chain, anchor is freed.

Slipstream. Current of water projected on rudder by propeller action.

Slipway. One of the inclined longitudinal timbers supporting a vessel on a building or repairing slip. Inclination varies between one in 12 to one in 24, according to size of vessel it is designed to take.

Slob. Loose and broken ice in bays, or along exposed edges of floes.

Sloop. One-masted sailing vessel having fore and aft rig, bowsprit, and jib stay. Name is often given to any such vessel having a single-head sail. 2. Small vessel, mechanically-propelled and used for patrol, escort, and other duties in time of war, formerly ship-rigged.

Slop Chest. Chest, or compartment, in which is stowed clothing for issue to crew.

Slop Room. Compartment in which clothing for issue to crew is stowed.

Slops. Clothing that is slipped on. Formerly, name was given to all clothing carried for issue to crew.

Slop Tank. Tank in an oil-tanker used to receive the washings from other tanks when these are being cleaned, the contents of the slop tank later being discharged ashore.

Slot Ice. Ice-carrying slots caused by erosion, and other action.

Sludge. Collection, on surface of water, of ice crystals that are not welded together. Does not prevent navigation. Name is sometimes given to 'Brash'. 2. Mud brought up by a dredger.

Slug. Slugg. Seventeenth-century term for a slow-sailing vessel.

Sluice. Valve, in form of a door, that moves perpendicularly to the direction of the flow it controls. Found in bilges, tanks, and flooding openings of dry docks.

Slush. Sludge ice. 2. Fat skimmed off galley coppers when boiling meat. Formerly used for lubricating and preservative purposes.

Slush Bucket. Grease bucket. Was formerly kept in tops of sailing ships, being used for greasing masts, blocks, and running gear.

Smack. Small vessel having one mast and sloop, or cutter, rig. Formerly used in near-European trade, and, until recently, in fishing trade. Tonnage did not exceed 200 tons (about).

Small (of Anchor). That part of shank immediately below the stock.

Small Bower. Name formerly given to port bower anchor—which was used for holding ship in calm weather with no strong wind.

Small Circle. Circle, of a sphere, whose plane does not pass through centre of the sphere.

Small Craft. Comprehensive term for vessels of small size. As it is used in a relative sense, no tonnage value is applicable.

Small Damage Club. Mutual indemnity society, of shipowners, that covers damage to vessels of members when amount of damage does not exceed 6% of the insured value of the vessel concerned, and is, therefore, excluded from usual policy of insurance.

Small Stuff. Yarns, marlines, and lines below one inch in circumference.

Smelling the Ground. Said of a vessel when her keel is close to the bottom and all but touching it.

Smiting Line. Rope attached to a number of rope yarn stops that were around a furled sail. By pulling on this line the whole of the sail was instantly released, and could be sheeted home.

Smoke Fog. Off-shore fog generated, mainly, by smoke particles.

Smoke Helmet. A head covering to which fresh air is supplied through a tube and pump, for use in fighting fires.

Smoke Sail. Canvas screen placed abaft galley funnel to keep smoke soot particles from falling on quarter deck or poop.

Smoke Stack. U.S.A. name for a steamship's funnel.

Smooth. Comparatively smooth area of sea surface in a stormy sea.

Smuggler. Man or vessel engaged in smuggling.

Smuggling. Importing or exporting dutiable goods without paying the appropriate Customs duties.

Snaffle. Lug that takes pivoting pin of a gooseneck.

Snake. To worm. To lay yarn or small rope in cantlines of a larger rope.

Snap Hook. Self-mousing hook having a spring strip across mouth.

Snatch. Fairlead or thumb cleat having a spring strip across the mouth.

Snatch Block. Block having a hinged part, in line of swallow, which can be opened to allow bight of a rope to be laid on the sheave.

Snekkja. Norse longship of 50 to 60 oars, c. 900 A.D.

Snorkel/Snort. A large vertical tube extending above a submarine's conning-tower to enable fresh air to be obtained when the submarine is just submerged. 2. A short tube with a face-mask worn by a swimmer for a similar purpose.

Snorter. Alternative name for 'Snotter'. 2. A very high wind.

Snotter. Rope strop, or metal ring, holding heel of a sprit or gaff to the mast. 2. Grommet strop used for passing over a yard arm and around tripping rope when sending a yard aloft, or on deck, so keeping mast alongside the rope. 3. Canvas strop through which bags are slung. 4. A length of rope or wire with an eye spliced in each end, used for slinging bales, etc.

Snotty. Nickname for a midshipman in Royal Navy.

Snow. Brig-rigged vessel whose main trysail, or 'driver', is carried by encircling rings, on a small mast immediately abaft main mast.

Snowberg. Tabular berg.

Snow Box. Compartment, in a refrigerating machine, having baffle plates on which the moisture in expanded cold air is converted into ice particles.

Snub. To stop suddenly a rope or cable that is running.

Snubber. A cable stopper.

Snubbing Line. Rope used for checking a vessel's way when warping her into a dock or basin.

Snug Down. Reduce sail in anticipation of increased wind.

Sny. Boatbuilding term used when referring to the upward sweep of a boat's strake before attachment to the ribs. The strake has a horned, or crescent, shape; the upward sweep from middle to ends being the sny.

Soft Iron. Iron, or ferrous alloy, that becomes magnetic when in a magnetic field but loses its magnetism when removed from the field.

Soft Laid. Said of rope or yarn that has been rather loosely laid up to gain flexibility and grip.

Soft Tack. Fresh bread.

Solan Goose. Solent Goose. Gannet. Sea bird with blue face, greyish-white bill, white plumage with some black in it. Head and neck are buff. Overall length is about three feet. Large numbers are to be seen in Firth of Forth—especially Bass Rock— and in Baltic.

Solano. Easterly rain-wind in Straits of Gibraltar and on SE coast of Spain.

Solar. Pertaining to the Sun.

Solar Constant. Deduced value of Sun's radiation at upper boundary of Earth's atmosphere. Is expressed as 1·94 calories per square centimetre per second.

Solar Constituent. That part of a tidal undulation that is due to the tractive effort of the Sun.

Solar Cycle. Period of 28 years, after which days of the week fall on same dates in the month.

Solar Day. Interval between successive transits of Sun (true or mean) across a particular meridian.

Solar Eclipse. Eclipse of Sun.

Solar Month. Interval in which Sun passes through a sign of the Zodiac.

Solar System. Sun, nine planets with their satellites, the asteroids, periodic comets, and meteors.

Solar Time. Time measured by hour angle of either the Mean or True Sun.

Solar Year. 'Tropical Year.'

Soldier's Wind. Wind with a direction that allows a vessel to sail out and return on one tack each way. 2. Sometimes said of a wind that allows a vessel to go from one point to another on one tack—but this is a 'fair' wind.

Sole. Piece attached to lower edge of a rudder to bring it to level of a false keel. 2. Bottom part of a launching cradle.

Solid Thimble. Metal block, with small circular hole, inserted in eye of a wire rope when maximum strength is required.

Solitary Wave. High and lone wave that is out of all proportion to the prevailing sea. Generally produced by a wave that has moved fast before a wind, and overtaken smaller waves under its lee. By absorbing these, its size increases rapidly.

Solstice. Either of the two points in Ecliptic that are most remote from plane of Equinoctial. At these points Sun appears to stand still in declination for an appreciable time.

Solstitial Colure. Hour circle passing through solstitial points. Contains poles of Equinoctial and Ecliptic.

Solstitial Points. The two points in Ecliptic that are most remote from Equinoctial. When Sun is in either of these points his declination stands still for two or three days.

Solstitial Tides. Tides occurring about the period of the solstice. Diurnal inequalities of tropic tides may be unusually large.

Somerville Sounding Gear. Used in surveying vessels. Weight is towed along sea-bed by a line from forward so adjusted that weight is just forward of propellers. An up and down line from weight is rove through a block with a small weight in inboard end, so keeping line taut: this line is marked so that depth can be read.

Sonic Sounder. Instrument that measures sea depths by measuring time interval between emission of an audible sound and the return of its echo from sea-bed.

Son of a Gun. Seaman who was born aboard a warship. As this was once considered to be one of the essentials of the perfect seaman it has long been a complimentary term.

Sonor. *See* Asdic.

Soogee Moogee/Sujee-mujee. Cleansing powder used for cleaning wood and paintwork.

SOS. Morse symbols of 3 shorts, 3 longs, 3 shorts, made by any signalling method. The international signal, 'I am in distress and require assistance.'

Sothis. Egyptian name for the star Sirius.

Souillagouet Method. Solution of the *PZX* triangle by dropping a perpendicular from *X* to observer's meridian, and so making two right-angled triangles.

Soul and Body Lashing. Spun yarn passed around open parts of oilskin clothing to exclude water and wind.

Sound. Narrow expanse of water between two land masses. 2. Sound waves of a frequency (less than 3800 per second) that can be detected by the human ear. 3. To ascertain depth of Water by measuring distance from surface to bottom. 4. Whaling term used to denote the quick descent of a whale in the sea, particularly after being harpooned.

Sounding Bottle. Small container, or bottle, lowered into the sea to bring up a sample of sea-water from a desired depth.

Sounding Machine. Apparatus for dropping a line and sinker to sea-bed, measuring the amount of line out, heaving in the sinker and indicating the actual depth of water.

Sounding Pipe. Tube leading from a deck to any place or compartment containing water or liquid. Forms a lead for a graduated rod, to which is attached a line.

Sounding Rod. Graduated rod, attached to a line, used for measuring depth of liquid in a space.

Sound Signal. Any signal transmitted by a system of sounds.

South. Point or direction opposite to North. For a heavenly body to 'South' is for it to come to the meridian south of observer.

South-East Trade Drifts. Surface currents set up in nearly all oceans by SE trade winds. In general, they merge into the Equatorial Current; in Indian Ocean the drift originates the current.

South Equatorial Current. A term often used to denote the Equatorial Current by those who consider the North-East Trade Drift to be the North Equatorial Current.

Southerly Burster (Buster). Wind off S and SE coasts of Australia during summer and autumn. Usually develops from a wind between North and West, which chops round and brings cold and stormy conditions.

Southern Cross. The conspicuous constellation Crux.

Southing. Distance, or difference of latitude, made good in a direction due south. Of a heavenly body, is its meridian transit south of observer.

South Seas. Former name for South Pacific Ocean.

South-West Monsoon Currents. Drift currents set up in China Sea, Arabian Sea, Bay of Bengal, off coasts of Burma and west India by South-West Monsoon.

Sou'wester. Oilskin headgear having projections to protect back of neck, ears, and eyes. 2. South-westerly gale.

Span. Length of rope, with eye in each end, stretched between two points of attachment.

Span Block. Block hooked or shackled into eyes of a span lying across a mast cap and around mast.

Spanish Burton. Purchase made with two single blocks. Rope spliced in head of moving block, rove through standing block, then through moving block. Hook inserted in second drift between standing and moving block. Gives power of three, but only a short lift.

Spanish Fox. Made by unlaying a yarn, smoothing it down, and laying it up in the opposite direction.

Spanish Bowline. Rather complicated manipulations of a bighted rope to form two separate and permanent loops in the bight. Rarely, if ever, used nowadays, but was formerly used in jury rigging.

Spanish Reef. A lubberly reef. Made by settling yard of a square sail, or knotting the head of a jib.

Spanish Windlass. Simple and powerful mechanism for heaving together two parts of rope. Short round bar is laid across two parts of rope and a small line is passed round the two parts. Ends of small line are passed over cross bar, and marline spikes inserted into ends by marline spike hitches. By using cross bar as fulcrum the two ropes are drawn together.

Spanker. Fore and aft sail, spread to a gaff and boom, on after side of after mast of a ship or barque. Sometimes called 'Driver'. Name was given to after mast of a five-masted ship.

Spanker Boom. Boom on after side of after mast of a ship or barque, to which the foot of spanker was stretched.

Spanker Gaff. Spar to which head of a spanker is stretched.

Spanking. Applied to a wind, or movement of a vessel, to denote brisk and lively.

Span Shackle. Large steel bolt, secured below forecastle deck beams and above topgallant forecastle deck, with a strengthened socket into which cat davit was shipped.

Spar. Long and rounded piece of timber. General name for any yard, gaff, or boom.

Spar Buoy. Long spar, moored more or less vertically, that acts as a navigational aid.

Spar Ceiling. Removable side battens fitted in a hold to keep cargo off ship's side, and to provide for through ventilation of cargo.

Spar Deck. Originally, a deck formed by spars resting on beams. Later, name was given to vessels of somewhat light construction above main deck, and intended to carry both cargo and passengers.

Speak. To communicate with another vessel, or with a shore station.

Speaking Trumpet. Trumpet-shaped instrument that preceded the megaphone at sea.

Special(ly) Flexible Steel Wire Rope. Name given to steel wire ropes having 37 wires around a fibre heart in each of six strands.

Special Surveys. Examination and inspection of registered ships at intervals of 4, 8, and 12 years from date of building. They are termed No. 1, 2, and 3 respectively—No. 3 being the most rigorous. After No. 3 survey the next is '2nd No. 1', and so on.

Specific Heat. Amount of heat required to raise temperature of a given mass through a given range when defined as a ratio of the amount of heat required to raise heat of a similar mass of water through a similar range. Sometimes defined as the amount of heat required to raise temperature of one pound of substance from 39° to 40° F.

Specific Gravity. Weight of any given volume of a substance expressed as ratio to weight of an equivalent volume of fresh water at temperature of 4° C.

Specific Volume. Amount of space occupied by a unit of mass. Of steam, is the space, in cubic feet, occupied by 1 lb. at a given pressure.

Specksynder. Chief harpooner in a whaler; formerly in charge of whale-catching operations when on whaling ground.

Spectacle Eye. Flat plate with two eyes, pivoted at davit head to form attachment for guy and jackstay.

Spectacles. Figure-of-eight clew irons put in a sail for attachment of chain sheets.

Spectioneer, Spectioner. 'Specksynder.'

Speculum. Concave metal mirror in a reflecting telescope.

Speed. Of a ship, is her velocity through the water in a given condition. Of a piston, is the number of feet it travels in one minute. Of crank pin, is distance centre travels in one minute.

Speed Error. Error of indication, by a gyro compass, due to torque set up by speed of ship.

Speed of Wave. Rate at which successive crests pass a fixed point. In ocean waters, speed in knots is approximately 0·8 speed of wind.

Speed Trial. The running of a vessel on a measured distance to ascertain her exact speed.

Spell. Time spent on a particular duty, or when relieved from duty.

Spencer. Loose-footed trysail set abaft mast and with head extended along a gaff.

Spencer Mast. Small mast, immediately abaft a principal mast, for carrying a trysail.

Spend. To spend a mast, spar, or sail is to cause it to be carried away in bad weather.

Sperm Whale. Alternative name for 'Cachalot'.

Sperry Gyro Compass. Electrically-driven gyroscope, revolving at about 9000 revolutions per minute, that carries corrector devices for precessing it into the meridian and maintaining it there. A 'phantom' follows all movements of axle relative to vessel's fore and aft line.

Sphere. Solid figure generated by half revolution of a circle about one of its diameters.

Spherical Aberration. Deviation of light rays from a focus after passing through curved lens. Results in a coloured fringe caused by unequal refraction of lenses breaking up the light into its constituent colours.

Spherical Angle. The inclination of one great circle to another. Can be measured by intercepted arc of a great circle to which they are both secondaries, or by angle between lines tangent to the circles at their point of intersection.

Spherical Sailing.* Methods of navigation that take into account the spherical shape of Earth—instead of assuming a plane surface. Term is obsolete; methods are comprised in great circle sailing.

Spherical Triangle. Area, on surface of sphere, bounded by arcs of three great circles.

Spheroid. Solid that is almost, but not quite, a sphere. Its section is an ellipse, and not a great circle.

Sphinxer. Original name of a 'Spinnaker'.

Spica. Star α Virginis. S.H.A. 159°; Dec. S11°; Mag. 1·2. Name is Latin for 'Ear of Corn'.

Spica's Spanker. Four stars, in constellation Corvus, forming an irregular quadrilateral resembling a spanker; the gaff pointing to Spica.

Spider. Iron band, around a mast, to take lower end of futtock rigging.

Spider Band. Iron band, around mast, for carrying belaying pins.

Spidereen Frigate. Fictitious vessel. A seaman who did not wish to give the name of his ship used to say, 'The spidereen frigate with nine decks.'

Spider Hoop. Spider band.

Spider's Web. Spiders were formerly carried in surveying ships of

Royal Navy as store articles. Their purpose was to produce cross 'wires' for theodolites. Spider's Web Diagram, a diagram consisting of a number of concentric circles and radii used for plotting radar and tactical diagrams.

Spike Bowsprit. Single bowsprit combining duties of bowsprit and jib boom.

Spike Plank. Plank running from bulwark to bulwark before mizen mast of arctic whalers. Allowed ice master to cross quickly from side to side when navigating ice-lanes.

Spike Tackle. Purchase used by whalers to hold carcase alongside while blubber was removed.

Spile. A small tapered wooden pin.

Spile Hole. Small hole bored in cask or barrel to allow air to enter when emptying.

Spiling. Curved edge of a shaped strake when laid flat.

Spilings. Perpendicular distances from a line that joins two ends, of a spiling, to points of the spiling.

Spill. To take wind out of a sail by putting its leech into the wind.

Spilling Line. Rope put on sail, in bad weather, for spilling wind out of sail when clewing uo.

Spinaker, Spinnaker. Large sail put on side of mast opposite to mainsail when running. First used, 1886, in H. C. Maudslay's 'Sphinx'. For this reason, was called 'Sphinxer'; later became 'spinaker'.

Spindle. Strong and firmly supported steel shaft around which a capstan revolves; or which, when keyed to capstan, will revolve the capstan.

Spindle.* Timber forming the diameter of a 'made' wooden mast.

Spindle Eye. 'Flemish Eye'.

Spindrift. Finely-divided water swept from crest of waves by strong winds.

Spinnaker Boom. Spar that extends the foot of a spinnaker.

Spinning Jenny. Formerly, winch for making rope yarn. Now, platform, suspended from a swivel and used for uncoiling wire rope.

Spirket. Space between floor timbers of a wooden ship. 2. A large wooden peg.

Spirketing. Inside strake between waterways and the port sills of old wooden ships.

Spit. A projecting shoal.

Spitfire. Name sometimes given to a small jib used as a storm sail in a boat.

Splay Tackle. Purchase extended between heels of sheer legs, to adjust and maintain their distance apart.

Splice. Join in rope made by intertwining ends of strands. 2. To join ropes by splicing.

Splice Main Brace. To issue an extra ration of rum. The main brace, often a tapered rope, was spliced only in the most exceptional circumstances.

Splicing Hammer. Hammer with a head having a flat face at end and a tapered part at the other end.
Splicing Shackle.* Formerly used for joining hemp to chain cable. Hemp cable was spliced round a solid heart thimble that was pierced to take pin of chain cable.
Spline. Piece of thin, flexible, straight-grained wood, about 6 ft. long, used for setting off curves of boats and yachts.
Split Knee. Steel beam knee made by cutting horizontally into end of beam and turning down the lower section.
Splitting Tacks. Yacht racing term for going about when 'lee bowed'.
Spoke. One of the hand-grips of a steering-wheel.
Sponson. Outboard decking before or abaft a paddle-box. 2. Projection of upper deck outboard of ship's side for carrying a gun, searchlight, or other fitting.
Sponson Beam. Strong athwartship beam that supports lower end of a paddle-box.
Sponson Rim. Timber connecting paddle-beam to side of vessel.
Spontaneous Combustion. Burning of a substance by the generation of heat consequent on a chemical change taking place inside the substance.
Spooning. Running directly before wind and sea.
Spoondrift. 'Spindrift'.
Spouter. A whale when spouting.
Sprag. A bolt inserted in the spur wheel of a towing winch to prevent the winch from turning.
Spray. Water blown, or thrown, into the air in particles.
Spreaders. Spars, or irons, put on a mast to increase the interior angle that a shroud or backstay makes with the mast.
Spreading. Distributing a fire over the firebars in a boiler furnace when the fire is lit, or after it has been banked.
Spring. Rope from after part of a vessel led outside and forward to a point of attachment outside vessel. By heaving on it ship can be moved ahead. Sometimes led to anchor cable, for casting ship's head. 2. Tendency of a vessel's head to come nearer to wind. 3. The opening of a seam. 4. Partial fracture in a mast or spar.
Spring a Leak. To start leaking, possibly through straining.
Spring a Luff. To come closer to the wind when close-hauled. 2. To come into the wind and set to leeward.
Spring Beam. Strong fore and aft timber connecting the outboard ends of a paddle-box.
Spring Block. Pulley block having a spring connection to ring-bolt. Formerly used for sheet blocks, and others, so that they yielded slightly to sudden gusts of wind.
Springing. Moving a vessel ahead by means of a spring. 2. Loosening the butt of a plank in a vessel's bottom.
Spring Range. Difference between heights of high and low water of a spring tide.

Spring Stays. Additional mast stays set up in warships before action.

Spring Tides. Tides occurring about New and Full Moon; rising farthest above mean level, and falling farthest below it.

Sprit. Spar going diagonally from tack to peak of a four-sided fore and aft sail, to spread it. Lower end usually rests in a snotter.

Spritsail. Fore and aft sail spread by a sprit between tack and peak. 2. Square sail spread by gaffs on either side of bowsprit and just abaft the dolphin striker.

Spritsail Gaff. One of the gaffs on either side of bowsprit for carrying a spritsail. Also called 'Whisker Gaff'.

Spritsail Sheet Knot. Knot used for joining ends of a piece of rope when making a strop for a spritsail sheet block. Rope was rove through longitudinal holes in sheet block and both ends were passed through thimble in clew of spritsail, the knot being made to secure it. Seizing was then put on close to block.

Spritsail Yard. Yard, across bowsprit, for spreading guys of jib boom and flying jib boom. Sometimes carried a spritsail.

Sprockets. Recesses in rim of a wheel, or drum, around which chain is passed; being shaped so that link of chain lies snugly. more particularly applied to those on capstans and windlasses for taking links of chain cable.

Sprung. Said of a wooden mast or spar when it is strained, or partly fractured, by excessive stress.

Spume. Froth of foam of the sea.

Spunyarn. Two or more yarns twisted together but not laid up; usual numbers being 2, 3, 4, 6 and 12 yarns. Usually supplied in coils, or 'pads', of 14 or 56 lb.

Spur. A projection. 2. Curved timber used as a bracket. 3. Timber attached to bilge of wooden vessel while building—for protective purposes. 4. Projecting piece on certain old types of anchor. 5. Spiked sole of a whaleman's boot, used when flensing.

Spurling Line. Small line that, formerly, led from a tiller or wheel to a tell-tale in cabin, to indicate amount of helm being used.

Spurling Pipe. Tube leading from forecastle to cable locker and enclosing the cable. 'Navel Pipe.'

Spurnwater. Eyebrow, or rigol, fitted above a port hole or scuttle to deflect water which may run down.

Spy Glass. Short telescope, with large object glass, that preceded binoculars at sea.

Squall. High wind that arrives suddenly and ceases suddenly. May, or may not, blow in direction of the prevalent wind.

Square.* That part of the shank, of old type of anchor, to which the stock and shackle were attached.

Square Knot. Interlacing and securing of two ropes crossing at right angles. An 'S'-shaped bight is put in one rope; second rope interlaces the 'S' at right angles.

Square Rig. That rig in which the principal sails are bent to yards across the masts. 2. In Royal Navy, the name is colloquially given to the bluejackets' uniform—to distinguish it from the 'fore and aft' rig of petty officers.

Square Sail. Four-sided sail bent to a yard; particularly one carried by schooners when running.

Square Yards. To brace the yards at right angles to fore and aft line, and to adjust lifts so that yards are horizontal.

Squat. The increase of a vessel's draft caused by her movement through the water. In shallow water with high speed squat may amount to one metre.

Squeegee. Flat piece of wood with vertical rubber strip in lower end. Shipped on a handle and used for removing water from deck.

Squilgee. American form of 'Squeegee'. 2. (U.S.N.) Toggle used when setting lower studdingsail. It held a strop that passed around sail and yard, and was withdrawn immediately before sheeting home.

Stabber. Thin, tapered marline spike.

Stability. That property of a ship, or body, by which it maintains a position of equilibrium, or returns to that position when a force that has displaced it ceases to act.

Stable Equilibrium. A ship which, when forcibly inclined, returns to her original upright position is in stable equilibrium.

Stack. Ship's funnel. (U.S.).

Staff.* Prefix formerly applied to officers of Royal Navy, other than executive officers, who were of rank equivalent to lieutenant-commander.

Stage. Plank, or planks, fitted with transverse bearers, slung by ropes and put over ship's side, or in holds, for men to work on.

Stage Lashing. New, soft-laid, hemp rope used for lashing stages, and other purposes. Is pliable and grips well.

Stakes.* Former name for 'Strakes'.

Staith. Elevated structure from which coal and other cargoes can be loaded into a vessel. Name is also given to a landing-place, or loading-place.

Stamukha. Ice masses grounded in shoal water.

Stanchion. Vertical member, usually metal, carrying ridge rope, guard rails, or manropes. 2. Vertical members that support deck beams.

Stand. A sail is said to 'stand' when it is drawing. 2. Of tide, is the time interval between instant of high, or low, water, and the commencement of fall or rise, respectively.

Standard. Short name for 'Royal Standard'. 2. That which acts as a criterion, to which others are compared or referred.

Standard Compass. Magnetic compass placed in a selected position, carefully adjusted and checked, and used as the principal compass for navigational purposes.

Standard Knee. Timber knee so placed that one arm is horizontal and the other is vertical.

Standard Nautical Mile. An invariable unit of length on which speeds and log registrations are based. Usual value, for British shipping, is 6080 ft. This is equal to length of one minute of the meridian in Lat. 54° 05′.

Standard Port. A port, or place, for which daily predictions of times and heights of tides have been calculated, so that tidal times and heights at certain other ports can be deduced from those at the standard port.

Standard Rudder. Pre-arranged angle of helm used by ships in formation when turning together, or manoeuvring.

Standard Salvage Agreement. Standardised form of salvage agreement recognised by Lloyds Corporation and practically all insurance and salvage corporations.

Standard Sheer. *See* 'Sheer'.

Standard Time. Official and authoritative time kept in a country or place. It is usually, but not always, a complete number of hours different from Greenwich Time. Also called 'Civil Time'.

Stand By. To remain in the vicinity of a vessel to render assistance necessary. 2. Cautionary order to be in readiness.

Stand In. To steer or sail towards the land.

Standing Block. Block that is fixed in position, particularly that block, of a tackle, that does not move in position when the fall is hauled upon.

Standing Lug. Lugsail in which the tack is made fast near the mast. Yard projects about a quarter of its length before mast, and remains on the same side of mast on either tack.

Standing Part. That part of a tackle fall that is made fast to a block and extends to the moving block.

Standing Rigging. Shrouds, stays, trusses, pendants, etc., that support masts, yards, booms, and gaffs by being fixed and immovable.

Stand Off and On. To sail, alternately, towards the land and away from it.

Stand On. Maintain course and speed.

Stand Out. To sail away from a port, or the land.

Stand Up. To keep close to the wind or come closer to it.

Starboard. Direction equivalent to 'right hand' when facing forward.

'Starboard,' Order to helmsman to turn wheel to starboard—tiller to port—so that ship's head turns to starboard. Previous to 30th June, 1931, the word signified the opposite directions.

Starboard Tack. Having the wind on the starboard side when under sail. Having starboard tacks boarded, and port sheets taut.

Starbowlines. Name familiarly given to the starboard watch.

Star Chart. Projection of celestial concave to a plane surface for showing relative positions of fixed stars. Various projections are used, according to purpose of chart.

Star Contra Propeller. *See* 'Contra Propeller'.

Star Globe. Small globe on which are depicted the fixed stars of lower magnitude, circles of right ascension, parallels of declination, and the Ecliptic. As these are depicted on a convex surface we have a 'looking glass' effect, but star indentification is much-simplified by use of the globe.

Star Knot. Ornamental knot put in end of six-stranded rope. End is unlaid to a whipping, 'half crown' is put in each strand—the standing part on top and in direction of lay of rope. End of each strand is passed through 'half crown' of next strand, then passed under its own part and brought to centre. Finished off as wall knot, or crowned.

Star Magnitudes. *See* 'Magnitude of Star'.

Stars. Self-luminous heavenly bodies, outside solar system, whose apparent positions relative to other stars do not change. Nearest star is about $4\frac{1}{4}$ light years distant; Canopus is more than 150 times this distance away. About 7000 stars—down to magnitude 6—are visible to the naked eye; 2,000,000,000 have been photographed or observed telescopically. Starlight in any hemisphere does not exceed $\frac{1}{400}$th of full moonlight.

Start. To commence to pour liquid from a cask. To break an anchor out of the ground. To slightly ease a tackle, fall, or sheet. 2. Short length of rope sometimes used to hasten a laggard youngster.

Statics. 'Atmospherics.'

Station Bill. List of ship's company giving the stations of each individual in various drills and emergencies.

Station Keeping. Maintaining a prescribed distance and bearing from a specified ship.

Station Pointer. Instrument for determining position of observer from observations of two horizontal angles between three distant objects whose positions are charted. Consists of a graduated circle having one arm fixed and two arms movable, all radiating from centre. Invented by J. Hubbard, F.R.S., b. 1753, d. 1815.

Statute Mile. Arbitrary unit of length with value of 5280 ft. Adopted as legal unit of distance in reign of Queen Elizabeth I. Rarely considered in nautical work.

Staunch. Said of a vessel that is firm, strong, and unlikely to develop leaks.

Staunching. Putting water in a boat, cask, or wooden bucket, to close the seams by wetting the wood.

Stave. Strip of wood shaped when making a cask, tub, or bucket.

Stave In. To break or displace a stave.

Stave off. To bear off with a staff, boathook, long spar, etc.

Stay. A rope that steadies a mast in a fore and aft direction, more particularly when on fore side of mast. To 'stay' is: (1) to incline a mast correctly by adjustment of stays; (2) to go about under sail.

Stay Holes. Holes, in luff of a staysail, that takes the hanks which ride along the stay.

Staying. 'Tacking'.

Staysail. Sail whose luff is attached to a stay.

Stay Tackle. Purchase suspended from triatic stay for working cargo, or lifting weights.

Stay Tube. One of the smoke tubes of a cylindrical marine boiler. Is of thicker metal than ordinary tubes and is held to tube plates by nuts on end of tube, instead of by expansion of end; thus giving extra support to tube plates. About one-quarter of smoke tubes are stay tubes.

'Steady.' Order given to helmsman when ship's head is on a desired course, and he is required to keep vessel on that course.

Stealer. Single plate, or strake, that is joined to two strakes of plating that have narrowed—owing to the form of the vessel.

Steam Cornet. Swallow-tailed pendant formerly flown above house flag by a vessel having steam propulsion in addition to sails. Name was sometimes given to 'A' flag when hoisted by a steam vessel on steaming or engine trials.

Steamer. A vessel propelled by steam.

Steamer Lanes. Ocean tracks usually followed by mechanically-propelled vessels.

Steamer Tracks. 'Steamer Lanes.'

Steaming Covers. Canvas covers put on masts, and yards of a steam vessel when underway. They protect these from smoke and sparks from funnel. Rarely seen nowadays; formerly, quite usual.

Steaming Fog. Name sometimes given to 'Arctic Sea Smoke'.

Steaming Light. The masthead light shown by a mechanically-propelled vessel in accordance with Rule of the International Regulations for preventing collision at sea.

Steam Metal. Brass used in steam engines. Is alloy of copper (87%), zinc (3%), tin (7%), lead (3%).

Steamship. Vessel propelled by steam and capable of being navigated on the high seas.

Steam Tiller. Steam engine mounted on a tiller, and controlled by steering-wheel and its own hunting gear.

Steam Trawler. Trawl-fishing vessel propelled by steam.

Steam Trials. Tests put on boilers and engines of a vessel, particularly when new or refitted, to ascertain their effectiveness and seaworthiness.

Steam Whistle. Whistle whose sound is produced by the passage of steam. When fitted in steam vessels it must be at least 30 inches in height and five inches in diameter. Diameter of steam pipe is not less than two inches, and pipe must be lagged. Audibility must be two miles at least.

Steeler. 'Stealer.'

Steer. To govern the course of a vessel by controlling, directly or indirectly, the helm or rudder. To steer a course is to keep ship's head in a given direction. A vessel is said to steer when she answers the helm.

Steerage. Accommodation that was, originally, in the vicinity of the rudder; later, it was forward of the main cabin. In both cases it was inferior to the cabin. Nowadays, is applied to accommodation for passengers other than cabin passengers.

Steerage Passenger. Passenger who is allotted less than 36 superficial feet of space for his, or her, exclusive use.

Steerage Way. Sufficient speed through the water for a vessel to answer her helm.

Steering Chains. Chains by which the wheel operates the rudder, directly or indirectly.

Steering Compass. Compass fitted with a lubber line, and mounted forward of wheel, or tiller, so that it can easily be seen by helmsman.

Steering Crutch. Crutch shipped near sternpost of a boat to take a steering oar.

Steering Engine. Steam, electric, or hydraulic engine that is controlled by a steering-wheel, and moves tiller and rudder in response to movements of the wheel.

Steering Gear. All connection and mechanisms between the steering-wheel and the rudder, by the working of which the vessel is steered.

Steering-Oar. Oar used, over the stern, for steering a boat.

Steering Rules. Rules of the 'Regulation for Preventing Collisions at Sea'.

Steering Sail. Canvas set to assist steering, rather than to aid propulsion.

Steering Wheel. Wheel, with spokes projecting beyond its outer circumference, by which the rudder is controlled directly or indirectly. Commonly called 'the wheel'.

Steeve. Angle above the horizontal made by a bowsprit, cat davit, or other outboard spar. 2. Long spar having one end fitted for taking hook of a tackle, the other end being fitted for forcing items of cargo into place.

Steeving. The steeve of a bowsprit. 2. Adjusting the steeve of a bowsprit. 3. Forcing cargo into position with a steeve.

Stem. Vertical member rising upwards from fore end of keel, to which it is scarphed or connected. Fore ends of strakes are fastened to it.

Stem Band. Metal strip fastened to fore edge of a boat's stem.

Stem Fender. Fender put athwart stem of a vessel to prevent damage by, or to, the stem.

Stem Head. Upper extremity of a stem.

Stem Jack. Small national flag hoisted at jackstaff at stem.

Stem Knee. Curved member connecting stem and keel.

Stemming. Maintaining position over the ground when underway in a river or tidal stream. 2. Reporting a vessel's arrival in dock to the dock authority, or Customs.

Stem Piece. Bracket-shaped piece, on stem, for supporting a bowsprit. 'Independent Piece.'

Stem Post. Stem bar. Foremost member of a vessel's construction, rising vertically from fore end of keel.

Stemson. Internal compass timber, connecting apron and keelson, in wake of scarph of stem of a wooden vessel.

Step. The fitting in which the lower end of a mast is placed. To step a mast is to upright it, and ship the heel in the step.

Stepney. For generations has been considered the parish of British seamen. It was customary, until recently, to inform rector of the parish church of all births and baptisms at sea. Births now are notified to Somerset House from official logs, when rendered.

Stereographic Projection. Representation of concave surface of a hemisphere to a plane that is a great circle of the sphere; the observer being considered as being at inferior pole of the great circle.

Stern. After end of a vessel. Originally, the word meant 'steering part'—and was applied to tiller and rudder.

Stern Anchor. Anchor carried aft for anchoring by the stern.

Sternboard. Track of a vessel when going astern. 2. To make a sternboard; to force a vessel astern under sail.

Stern Chase. Pursuit of one vessel by another vessel astern of her.

Stern Chaser. Gun capable of firing directly astern.

Stern Fast. Mooring-rope leading, approximately, astern.

Stern Frame. Substantial member often combining rudder-post, propeller post, and their extensions. After ends of plating are secured to it. It frequently carries rudder and propeller.

Stern Knee. Extension of keelson to take heel of stern post.

Stern Light. White light shown astern by all vessels when being overtaken. Usually fixed, and shown from sunset to sunrise.

Sternmost. Farthest astern.

Stern Port. Opening in stern of ship for gun, ventilation, admission of light, or for loading cargo.

Stern Post. Vertical member at after end of hull. In single-screw vessels it usually carries rudder and forms part of stern frame. In wooden vessels, is a vertical timber resting on after end of keel.

Stern Sheets. That space, in a boat, abaft after thwart; or between after thwart and backboard.

Sternson. Stern knees.

Stern Tube. Watertight cast-iron tube through which propeller shaft is passed for attachment of propeller.

Stern Walk. Kind of balcony that, until recent years, was fitted on the sterns of larger warships.

Sternway. Astern motion of a vessel through the water.

Sternwheeler. Shallow draught steam vessel propelled by a wide paddle-wheel at stern. Formerly used on Nile, Mississippi, and other rivers.

Stevedore. Man who stows or unloads cargo in a hold.

Steward. Man concerned with the feeding of officers, crew, and passengers in a ship, and with the cleanliness and upkeep of living accommodation.

Stick a Cringle. To insert a thimble in a rope loop worked in a bolt-rope or awning roping.

Sticks. Nautical nickname for masts.

Stiff. Said of a vessel when she offers exceptional resistance to forces tending to list her, especially when under sail.

Stiffening. Ballast put in a vessel to increase her stability.

Stiffening Order. Permit, by shore authorities, for a vessel to load some of next cargo before completing discharge of present cargo. It is done to maintain stability of vessel without taking in water ballast.

'Still'. Spoken when it is necessary to stop some previous order from being carried out. Operations are resumed at the order 'Carry on'.

Sting Ray. Target-seeking torpedo which can be launched from the air.

Stink Pot.* An earthenware container holding an inflammable and foul-smelling composition. Formerly used as a projectile in naval warfare. Was an early forerunner of gas warfare.

Stirrup. One of a series of short pendants on a yard. Lower end has a thimble through which the footrope passes. 2.* Plates, on each side after deadwood, that were through-fastened.

Stock. Of anchor, is the cross-piece just below ring of anchor. Being at right angles to line of flukes it ensures fluke biting, and resists shank turning, and so releasing fluke from ground.

Stockholm Tar. Vegetable tar used for preservation of ropes and, sometimes, canvas from the effects of water. Extracted from pine tree (*pinus sylvestris*). Produced by Sweden, Norway, Germany, and Russia. An inferior type is produced in America.

Stocks. Erection on which a vessel is built, and which supports both ship and cradle.

Stock Tackle. Purchase used for bringing stock, of a stocked anchor, vertical when stowing.

Stokehold. Compartment in which ship's boilers are situated, and in which they are tended and fired.

Stokehole. Hatch, or scuttle, in a deck through which coal is passed to bunkers. Now called 'bunker hatch' and 'bunker plate', respectively.

Stoker. Man who feeds and attends a boiler furnace.

Stomach Piece. Name sometimes given to 'Apron' or 'Breast Hook'.

Stools. Shaped bearers on which a cylindrical boiler rests. 2. Name sometimes given to the chains, or channels, in which lower ends of backstays are set up.

Stopper. Short length of rope, one end of which is firmly secured, used for temporarily holding a rope under tension, so allowing part not under tension to be manipulated as required.

Stoppering. Holding a rope under stress by means of a stopper.

Stopper Knot. Formerly made in end of a stopper for holding hemp cable. Now used in end of a rope stopper, or when a neat knot is desired in end of a rope. Made by forming a wall knot and passing each end through next loop before heaving taut.

Stopping. Preventing leakage by inserting suitable material in a seam or opening.

Stopping a Flag. Making a wheft of it by passing a stop around its middle depth. Preparing a flag for breaking out.

Stops. Small lengths of rope, line, sennit, yarns, etc., that are used for tying; particularly for tying a sail when furled.

Stop Valve. Any valve that can close a pipe against the passage of a fluid.

Store Ship. Vessel employed in carrying stores for a fleet or squadron.

Storis. Large drift ice, more than two years old, that passes down the south-east coast of Greenland.

Storm. Violent disturbance of atmosphere that produces winds of Force 10 Beaufort scale (48–55 knots).

Storm Bound. Confined to an anchorage or haven through being unable to proceed because of stormy weather.

Storm Canvas. 'Storm Sails.'

Storm Cone. Black cone hoisted at various points on coasts of British Isles when a gale is expected. Hoisted point upwards when gale is expected to commence from N'ly point, point down when from a S'ly point.

Storm-Modifying Oil. Fish or vegetable oil carried for distribution on surface of stormy seas. Its action is purely mechanical; friction of air being greatly reduced.

Storm Plates. General name given to hinged plates of sheet iron that can cover up a ventilation hatch, or grating, in stormy weather.

Storm Sails. Sails made of particularly heavy canvas, and of reduced dimensions, for use in heavy weather.

Storm Signals. Visual signals by means of flags, shapes, and lights that are exhibited on coasts of most maritime countries. By means of an appropriate code they give warning of approaching bad weather to vessels in the vicinity.

Stove In. Said of a boat when one or more of the strakes has been forced in, thus causing a leak. Also applied to a cask, barrel, etc., when a stave or heading has been forced in.

Stow. To pack compactly and safely.

Stowage. The compact, safe, and appropriate placing of cargo in a hold. 2. Place or compartment in which goods can be stowed. 3. The act of placing cargo in a hold.

Stowage Factor. The number of cubic feet required for stowing one ton—or unit quantity—of a named commodity. It includes space necessary for appropriate dunnage and packing, and allows for unavoidable broken stowage.

Stowaway. One who conceals himself on a ship about to sail, with an intention of being taken to sea.

Strain. Permanent deformation, or weakening, caused by excessive stress.

Strain Bands. Doubling strips of canvas going vertically down the middle of a square sail to strengthen it.

Straining Screw. Type of bottle screw which has a swivel hook at one end and an eye, on threaded screw, at the other end. Used for setting up guard chains, awning ridge ropes, and other purposes.

Strand. A number of fibre yarns, or wires, twisted together. Three or more strands twisted together form a rope. 2. The edge of the land. A beach.

Strake. A continuous line of plating, or planking, extending along ship's side from forward to aft.

Strait/s. A narrow stretch of water joining to larger areas.

Stranding. Accidentally running aground, or being forced aground, by extraordinary circumstances outside the usual course of navigation. In marine insurance, it must be of such a nature that the voyage is brought to an end.

Strange Sail. An unidentified vessel that appears above the horizon.

Strap. Plate covering a joint, in wood or metal, and securely fastened to each of the joined pieces to regain strength lost by joining.

Stratocumulus. Cloud form intermediate between stratus and cumulus. May be closely packed, or separated by more or less horizontal streaks of sky.

Stratosphere. The upper shell of atmosphere. In it there is little change of temperature with height. It is cloudless, and contains two regions of high ionisation—the Kenelly-Heaviside and Appleton layers.

Stratus. Uniform layer of cloud very much like elevated fog. Height may be anything less than a mile.

Stray Line. That part of a hand log-line that extends between the log chip and the bunting mark at which timing commences.

Strays. Atmospherics.

Streak.* Old form of 'Strake'.

Stream. A course of running water, whether between banks or through the sea.

Stream a Buoy. To put an anchor buoy into the water just before letting anchor go.

Stream Anchor. An anchor whose weight is about ⅓ that of the bower anchors. Carried aft to act as stern anchor when required, or for kedging purposes.

Stream Current. Ocean current that flows in a definite direction—so differing from a 'drift' current—that always sets to leeward. They are the result of drift currents that have been arrested by some obstructions in their paths.

Stream the Log. To put the rotator in the water and pay out the log line. The reverse operation is to 'Hand the Log'.

Stress. The effect of an applied force that does not cause permanent deformation.

Stretcher. Small piece of timber athwart a boat propelled by oars, and against which the rower braces his feet.

Stretch Off the Land. Old sailing ship term for taking 'forty winks'.

Strike. To lower sail or ensign as a mark of respect. 2. To haul down an ensign as token of surrender. 3. To 'strike soundings' is to pick up soundings with the lead, or sounding machine. 4. To lower an upper mast.

Strike Clause. Inserted in shipping documents to relieve ship of liability for loss caused by strikes and other labour disputes.

Striker. Paint brush, usually round, with long handle that is nearly at right angles to bristles. Used for extending reach of man when painting—especially when painting ship's side from a boat. Also called 'man helper'.

Striking Topsail. Salute, by a sailing vessel, that goes back to Saxon days at least. Made by letting go topsail halliards and re-hoisting. Also called 'Veiling Topsail'.

String.* Inboard side of a vessel's topmast strake.

Stringer Plates. Plate stringers in iron and steel vessels.

Stringers. Longitudinal members that, in conjunction with frames, give girder strength to a vessel. Name is sometimes given to battens that go fore and aft along ship's side in holds.

Strip to a Gantline. To send down all yards, unreeve all running rigging, send down all upper masts and leave only gantlines rove on lower masts.

Stroke. Distance an oar is pulled through the water in the action of rowing. 2. The rate at which oars are pulled. 3. Man who rows the after oar in a boat, and so sets the time and distance that oars are pulled. 4. One complete pulling of an oar. 5. Stroke of a reciprocating engine is the distance travelled by the piston when moving from one end of cylinder to the other.

Stroke Oar. *See* 'Stroke (3)'. Name may be given to man or oar.

Strongback. Fore and aft beam over a boat when in the crutches and covered. It supports cover and gives it sufficient slope to shed any water that may fall on it.

Strong Breeze. Wind blowing between 22 and 27 knots. Is Force 6 in Beaufort scale.

Strop. Short length of rope with ends spliced together to make a loop; or with ends eye-spliced. Used for making a sling, or an attachment for hook, shackle, or rope.

Strop and Toggle. Method of securing when quick release may be required. A bale sling strop has a toggle in one end, this being passed through and across the other bight.

Strop Knot. Made with looped lines or cords. Crown knot is made, followed by wall knot; loops then projecting from knot.

Structural Stress. Stress that tends to deform the whole structure.

Strum Box. Metal box having perforated circular holes in sides. Is put round end of a suction pipe to prevent entry of any material that may choke the pump. When fitted in bilges of hold spaces the perforations must not exceed $\frac{3}{8}$ inch in diameter; total area of all perforations must be, at least, twice the sectional area of suction pipe.

Strut. Diagonal member that supports or braces another member.

Stud. The strengthening piece across a link of chain cable.

Studded Links. Those links, of chain cable, that are strengthened and supported by a transverse stud across their widest part.

Studdingsail. Fine weather sails set on either side of square sails, their heads and tacks being stretched to studdingsail booms.
Studdingsail Booms. Sliding booms projecting from yards to take studdingsails.
Studsail.* Contraction of 'studdingsail'.
Stuffing-Box. Short sleeve of metal, at end of cylinder, through which a piston rod passes. Is made tight by fibrous material (packing) that is compressed by screwing up a retaining gland.
Stump Mast. Lower mast with no tops and with no mast above it.
Stump Topgallant Mast. Topgallant mast with no royal mast above it.
Stuns'l, Stons'l. Usual pronunciation of 'Studdingsail'.
Stuns'l Halliard Bend. Made by passing two round turns around spar, passing end around standing part, under both round turns, back over last round turn and under first round turn.
Stylus. Alternative name for 'gnomon'.
Submarine. Beneath the sea surface, or beneath the sea. 2. War vessel designed for travelling below surface of sea.
Submarine Cable. Telegraphic or telephonic cable laid on sea bed.
Submarine Escort. War vessel that remains in a sea area in which submarines are exercising in peacetime. Its duty is to see that passing ships keep clear of the area.
Submarine Sentry.* Wooden hydroplane, or 'kite', formerly used for indicating when a vessel entered water with less than a specified depth. While vessel was making way—at a specified speed—the kite kept to the specified depth. If vessel went into water less than the specified depth a projection below the kite struck the ground and caused the kite to surface. Change in lead of wire usually operated an alarm bell.
Submarine Sound Signal. Navigational warning made by light vessel or other craft, that is transmitted through water instead of air; thus greatly increasing range and audibility. Two types in common use are submarine bells and oscillators, ranges being 15 and 50 miles respectively.
Submerged Log. Speed and distance log that protrudes from bottom of ship. The Chernikeef and Pitometer logs are examples.
Subsolar Point. That point on Earth that is vertically beneath Sun. Sun's geographical position.
Subrogation. The transfer of all rights and remedies of an assured party, who has suffered a loss, to a party who has indemnified him for the loss. The indemnifier then has all rights and remedies that were previously held by the assured party.
Suck the Monkey. Originally, to suck rum from a coconut—into which it had been (illicitly) inserted, the end of the nut resembling a monkey's face. Later, illicitly to suck spirit from a cask, usually through a straw.
Suction. The drawing of a fluid by formation of a vacuum that the fluid is free to occupy. Technically applied to the effect of

a large vessel passing a small vessel in confined waters; which may cause the smaller vessel to sheer towards the larger.

Sue. To require more water for flotation. Word is loosely applied and is sometimes referred to the vessel, and sometimes referred to the water—'Vessel sues six feet' or 'Tide sued six feet'. In either case the vessel requires a further six feet of water to float. Often spelt 'sew, sewed'.

Sue and Labour Clause. Included in a policy of marine insurance to authorise and encourage action for the prevention or mitigation of a marine loss, and to reimburse the expenses of those who sue and labour to these ends.

Suez Canal Tonnage. Computation of tonnage for vessels passing through Suez Canal. Approximates nett registered tonnage, but has important modifications of it. Is never less than half gross tonnage.

Sufferance Wharf. Wharf at which goods liable to duty may be discharged before duty is paid.

Suhail. Star λ Velorum. S.H.A. 223°; Dec. S43°; Mag. 2·2.

Suit of Sails. Complete set of sails, either for a mast or a vessel.

Sujee; Suji-muji (spelling various). Soap or cleaning-powder mixed with fresh water. To wash paint with sujee.

Sumatras. Violent thundery squalls in the Malacca Strait, usually at night, during the S.W. Monsoon.

Summer Solstice. That point of time at which Sun reaches his highest declination and noon altitude. At this point his declination is more or less constant for an appreciable time. Occurs about June 21 in northern hemisphere, about December 21 in the southern. By convention, the former is generally accepted.

Summer Tanks. Comparatively small tanks on outboard sides of expansion trunks of an oil tanker. Are reserve spaces that may be filled with oil to bring vessel to her marks, particularly in summer.

Summer Time. Advancement of mean time indications of clock by one hour (usually) during and around summer months. Dates of adoption and cessation of British Summer Time are decreed by Order in Council.

Sumner's Method. The finding of ship's position by two successive altitudes of one heavenly body, or by more or less simultaneous altitudes of two heavenly bodies. From these altitudes are calculated the position of the intersection of the two circles of equal altitude. One of these intersections is the ship's position. First used by Captain Thomas H. Sumner (U.S.A.) on 17th December, 1837. He published a book on the method in 1843.

Sun. Star around which Earth, planets, and other solar system bodies revolve. Distance from Earth is 93,005,000 miles; weight is $1,842 \times 1,000,000^{24}$ tons; diameter 864,392 miles. Apparent diameter 31′ 32″ to 32′ 36″. Horizontal Parallax 8·8″. Volume is about 330,000 times that of Earth.

Sunday Letter. Letter that will represent Sundays of a year if we letter the days in a recurring sequence from A to G. The letter drops back one in each successive year, and drops back one letter on February 29.

Sun Dog. Name often given to a refracted image of Sun occasionally seen about 20° to 30° away from Sun, but at same altitude.

Sunfish. Common name for the basking shark.

Sun over Foreyard. Nautical equivalent to 'Time we had a drink.'

Sun Pillar. Vertical shaft of light, above or below Sun, caused by reflection of sunlight from small snow crystals.

Sunrise. For nautical purposes is when Sun's upper limb is in eastern horizon. Zenith distance is then 90° 50'. (Refr. 34', S.D. 16'.)

Sunset. For nautical purposes is when Sun's upper limb is in western horizon. Zenith distance is then 90° 50'.

Sun Sights. Altitudes of Sun taken to fix ship's position by position lines.

Sunspot Numbers. Used for indicating amount of Sun's disc covered by spots; 100 represents 0·2 of disc covered. In last 190 years the sunspot number has not exceeded 139.

Sunspots. Dark areas observable on Sun's disc, and due to vortices in its incandescent envelope. Though coincident with magnetic fluctuations and meteorological phenomena they are not necessarily responsible for them.

Super. Colloquial name for a marine superintendent.

Supercargo. Man formerly carried in a ship to supervise the loading and discharge of cargo, and to transact business concerning it.

Supercooled Water. Water that is liquid at temperatures below 0°C. Small water-drops in atmosphere can remain liquid at −40°C.

Superheat. Additional heat given to steam to increase temperature without increasing volume and pressure. Allows for a certain amount of cooling without causing condensation, so giving increased efficiency.

Superheated Steam. Steam that has been given increased heat after leaving boiler, pressure remaining constant. Has greatly increased efficiency as compared with saturated steam. In marine boilers, superheat is not carried beyond 750°F.

Superheater. Arrangement of small steam pipes in exhaust gases of furnaces. Used for increasing temperature of the steam.

Superior. Word used for denoting one of two similar occurrences or positions, differentiating it from the other—which is termed the 'inferior' position or occurrence. A signal is said to be superior to another when hoisted before, either in regards time or hoist. It is said to be inferior when it is after either in time or hoist.

Superior Conjunction. Position of an inferior planet when it is in conjunction with Sun and 180° away from Earth.

Superior Planet. Planet whose orbit around Sun lies outside that of Earth.

Superior Transit. That passage across the meridian, of a circumpolar body, at which it attains its greater altitude.

Super-Pressure Boiler. Steam boiler working at pressure exceeding 650 lb. per square inch.

Superstructure. Loosely applied to permanent erections above upper deck. For load-line purposes, is a decked structure above the freeboard deck and extending from side to side of the vessel. Raised quarter deck is a superstructure.

Supporters. Strong knees immediately beneath catheads of wooden vessels.

Surf. Broken and tumultuous sea caused by waves breaking on a lee shore.

Surface Condenser. Condenser in which exhaust steam is condensed to water by coming into contact with outer surfaces of numerous small pipes through which cold sea water is pumped.

Surf Boat. Craft especially designed for working in surf. Is usually high at ends, broad-beamed, and steered with an oar—to which it is very responsive.

Surge. Name given to the so-called 'tidal wave', which is not due to tidal forces. Investigation of its behaviour is still proceeding, but it is accepted that it may arise from meteorological causes, or from seismic disturbances. It may travel hundreds of miles an hour. 2. To allow a rope to render or run out while being hauled on a drum or capstan. 3. To fail to grip a drum or capstan when heaving. 4. The swell of a drum or capstan. 5. Change of barometric pressure additional to those due to movements of depressions or anticyclones.

Survey. To examine and inspect visually. 2. Visual examination or inspection. 3. Periodical examination of a vessel, her fittings, machinery, accommodation, etc. 4. Particular, but casual, inspection of stowage, hatches, cargo, etc. 5. To ascertain the depths, nature, and contours of the sea-bed and the heights, nature, and contours of the adjacent land.

Surveyor. One who examines and surveys for the purpose of ascertaining and reporting condition, state, quantity, quality, strength, etc., relative to standard requirements.

Swab. Seaman's mop for drying decks. Made of old rope unlaid and seized on the bight; about four feet in length. Sometimes made smaller and seized to a wooden handle for putting highly-alkaline solutions on deck for cleansing purposes.

Swabber. One who swabs a deck. Anciently, an inferior officer who was responsible for the cleanliness of the decks.

Swab Hitch. Name often given to a single sheet bend.

Swallow. That opening, in a block, through which the rope is rove.

Swallow Tail. Flag or pendant having a V-shaped indentation in the fly.

Swallow the Anchor. To leave the sea and settle ashore.

Swamp. To overwhelm with water; not necessarily to sink.

Swash, Swatch. Narrow channel, or indentation in a sandbank, or between a sandbank and the shore.

Swashway, Swatchway. Swash, Swatch.

Sway. To hoist an upper mast or yard.

Sway Away. Order to hoist a yard, or upper mast.

Sweat Up. To haul on a rope to hoist the last possible inch or so.

Sweep. Long oar used in barges and lighters for turning them. Only used rarely for propulsion. Formerly used in small sailing vessels. 2. To propel with sweeps. 3. To search for a sunken object by towing a bight of wire until it is brought up by the object. 3. To search an area of the sea with two or more ships working in concert. 4. The harmonious curve of a vessel's line or plating. 5. Circular frame on which tiller moved in certain olden ships.

Sweeping and Creeping. Searching an area of the sea-bed with a sweep wire and a grapnel.

Sweepings. Cargo, such as grain, that has escaped from its bags and has been swept up in the hold. Is delivered to consignee as 'sweepings'.

Swell. Succession of long and unbroken waves that are not due to meteorological conditions in the vicinity. Generally due to wind at a distance from the position.

Swifter. Extra stay or backstay. 2. Foremost shroud of lower rigging. 3. Rope secured in slots at end of capstan bars, to prevent bars from coming out of poppets of capstan while heaving.

Swifting. Tautening up by passing frapping turns. So applied to 'undergirding'. Swifting in of shrouds is done when refitting ratlines. Middle shroud is tautened and those on either side of it are slightly slackened. Ratlines are then fitted. When swifting turns are taken off, the shrouds are set up—so tautening the ratlines.

Swig. To get maximum pull on a rope by pulling on it, at right angles to its direction, after it has been hauled taut and turned up.

Swim. Overhanging portion of bow or stern below maximum load line. It increases a vessel's flotation as she sinks deeper in the water.

Swim-Headed. Said of barges with bows, or ends, that are flat and inclined upwards and outwards from the bottom.

Swing. To move sideways at a constant distance from a point ahead such as swinging to an anchor. 2. To put ship's head through all points of the compass to ascertain compass errors on all directions of ship's head.

Swinging Boom. Boom pivoted on ship's side and secured at right angles to fore and aft line, and horizontal, when in harbour. Used for the securing of duty boats not immediately needed. Originally, was the lower studdingsail boom.

Swinging Ship. Putting ship's head through all points of compass to determine compass error and, thence, deviation on different headings.

Switchboard. Panel fitted with switches and inserted between dynamo and outside electrical circuits. Used for controlling electrical supply.

Swivel. Formerly gun mounting that allowed gun to be trained through a lateral arc. 2. A gun on a swivel mounting. 3. A pivot free to move in an immovable part.

Swivel Block. Pulley block that is pivoted in the lug or hook by which it is attached.

Swivel Piece. Small length of cable, consisting of a swivel with a studded and an open link on each side of it. Often put between outboard end of cable and anchor; also between inboard end of cable and its attachment in chain locker. 2. Swivel and link connecting the two 'monkey faces' of mooring swivel.

Sword. Long and fairly thin piece of wood used for beating down the crossed strands when making sword matting.

Swordfish. Powerful and swift fish with a swordlike projection from lower jaw. Found in tropical and subtropical seas. Are inveterate enemies of whales and other cetacea. Length is from 12 to 15 ft., including sword (three feet). Young swordfish have both jaws prolonged.

Sword Matting. Woven rope made by stretching four to eight strands and then lifting alternate strands and passing small rope, or strand, across jaw thus formed. This crossing 'wheft' is then beaten in with a wooden 'sword'. Strands previously up are now put down, and wheft is again passed, this process being repeated until required length is made. It makes excellent gripes for boats.

Symbol. Letter, character, or device that has a special signification.

Sympathetic Damage. Loss in value of an item of cargo due to its contact with, or proximity to, other articles or cargo that affect it adversely without damaging it physically.

Synchronism. Coincidence in time. Occurring at the same instant. Particularly applied to coincidence of a vessel's roll with the period of a wave motion acting transversely.

Synodical Month. Interval between two successive conjunctions of Sun and Moon. Also called a 'Lunation'. Value is 29 days 12 h 44·05 m mean solar time.

Synodical Revolution. 'Synodic Period.'

Synodical Year. Equals 12 synodical months. Length 354 days 08 h 48 m 36 s mean solar time.

Synodic Period. Of Moon or a planet, is the interval between any two consecutive conjunctions. With inferior planets, the conjunctions must be of same type—inferior or superior.

Synoptic Chart. Chart in which weather conditions, at a given time, are expressed by a system of letters, numbers, and symbols.

Syphering. Lapping the chamfered edge of one plank, over the chamfered edge of another, so that there is a smooth surface at the lap.

Syren. 'Siren.'

System Internationale. The metric units and their abbreviations are:

length: metre m
mass: kilogram kg
time: second s
current: ampere A
luminosity: candela cd

angle: radian
area: square metre
volume: cubic metre
frequency: hertz
(cycles/sec.)
speed: metre/sec.

force: newton
couple: newton-metre
pressure: newton/sq. metre
(pascal)
work, energy: joule
power: watt W

Syzygy. That position of Moon, or a planet, when it is in opposition or conjunction.

Syzygy Tide. Afternoon tide, at a place, when Moon is in syzygy.

Tab   344   Tack Tricing Line

T

Tab. Name sometimes given to tabling on a sail.

Tabernacle. Vertical casing, having three sides at right angles, into which a mast is stepped and clamped.

Table. To strengthen foot of a sail by stitching an additional strip of canvas along it. 2. Flat-topped projection on either side of mast and in same thwartship line. Takes heels of cargo derricks. 3. Pre-computed values set out for ready reference.

Table Shore. Low, flat shore of sea.

Tabling. Broad hem at foot of sail that is sewn to a boltrope.

Tabular. Said of values that have been obtained from tables.

Tabular Log. Logarithm whose index has been increased by 10 to avoid having minus values.

Tachometer. Instrument for indicating velocity. Name is given to a 'counter' indicating number of propeller revolutions per minute.

Tack. Lower foremost corner of a fore and aft sail. 2. Rope by which the weather lower corner of a course is hauled down. 3. Direction of a vessel's fore and aft line relative to the wind when under sail; being starboard or port tack according to whether wind is on starboard or port side respectively. 4. Distance sailed on one tack. 5. Lower corner in head of flag or pendant.

Tack Block. Standing block through which tack (rope) of a sail is rove.

Tacking. Putting ship's head through the wind, and so bringing wind on the other bow. 2. Working to windward, under sail, by sailing alternately on different tacks.

Tack Knot. Double wall and crown knot worked in standing end of a tack (rope).

Tackle. The running gear of a ship. 2. Purchase made by reeving rope or chain through one or more blocks.

Tackle Boards. Frame, at end of a ropewalk, having attachments for yarns that are to be twisted into strands.

Tackle Post. Fitting, in a ropewalk, having attachments for laying-up strands of a rope.

Tack Line. Length of signal halliard inserted between two groups of signal flags when hoisted at the same halliard.

Tackling. Sails and all running rigging of a vessel.

Tack Purchase. Gun tackle purchase in tack of a fore and aft mainsail.

Tack Rivet. Temporary rivet put in to hold a plate in position while being erected and faired. It is then punched out and the permanent rivet inserted.

Tack Pins.* Old name for 'belaying pins'.

Tack Tackle. Small tackle used for sweating down tacks of courses.

Tack Tricing Line. Line fitted with a thimble and used for tricing tack clear of the water when vessel is lying over.

Taffrail. Originally, upper edge of stern. Later, an ornamental rail going around stern and above the original taffrail. Now, upper edge of bulwark around the stern.

Taffrail Log. Name given to a patent log towed from aft.

Tail Board. Carved work under bowsprits of old ships.

Tail Block. Block having a short rope tail spliced around strop at head, for attachment by hitching.

Tail-end Shaft. 'Tail Shaft.'

Tail Jigger. Jigger with a selvagee tail, instead of a hook, in the double block.

Tail of Bank. Seaward end of a longitudinal shoal in an estuary.

'Tail On.' Order to assist in manning the fall of a tackle.

Tail Shaft. That part of a propeller shaft shaft that passes through the stern tube and is fitted to take attachment of the propeller.

Tail Splice. The joining of one rope to another rope that differs in size, or in material.

Tail Tackle. Luff tackle, or watch tackle, with rope or selvagee tail in head of double block, and hook in single block.

Take a Turn. To take a temporary turn with a rope preparatory to taking in some more of it.

Take Charge. To break away from control.

Take In. To furl, or to lower, sails. 2. To load. 3. To haul in. 4. To receive.

Taken by the Lee. Said of a sailing vessel when her sails are thrown aback by a sudden shift of wind.

Take Up. Said of seams of a boat when they tighten up and cease to leak.

Taking Off. Said of tide or wind when it is getting less.

Tallant.* Rounded upper part of a rudder.

Tally. To count. Particularly applied to the count of items loaded or discharged by a vessel. 2. The count obtained from tallying. 3. Agreement in numbers or quantities.

Tally Board. Board, bearing instructions, that comes to a wrecked ship with a life-saving rocket line.

Tally Book. Book in which is kept a reckoning of items of cargo received or discharged from a hatch or vessel.

Tan. Solution of gum and dark red dye. Used for preserving sails.

Tandem Block. Block having two sheaves in the same plane.

Tangent. Line that touches circumference of a circle but will not cut the circumference if produced in either direction. More precisely, a line that is perpendicular to the radius of circle at the point of contact with the circumference.

Tangent Circle. Circle at which the surface of a conical or cylindrical projection touches the sphere. In cylindrical projections it is a great circle; in conical projections it is a small circle.

Tangent Point. That point, on a sphere, at which the plane of the projection touches it.

Tangent Sailing. Name formerly given to 'Middle Latitude Sailing'.

Tank. In general, any cistern or reservoir in which liquids are stowed. Particularly applied to one containing water ballast, fresh water, oil-fuel, etc.

Tanker. Vessel specially constructed for carrying liquids in bulk. Vessel constructed for carrying oil in bulk.

'Tanky.' Petty officer in R.N. whose duty is to look after fresh-water tanks. At one time these tanks were under the charge of the navigating officer, who shared the nickname.

Tapered Ropes. Ropes whose circumference gradually diminished towards one end. Formerly used for sheets and tacks in Royal Navy. While having full circumference at working part, the rope rendered easily through a sheave or block when veered or slackened.

Tapering. Gradually reducing diameter of extreme end of rope so that end is easily passed through a block or thimble.

Tap Rivet. Rivet substitute having thread on shank and a head shaped to take a spanner. Used in places where riveting is impossible. Holes are threaded, tap rivet is screwed home, head is then cut off.

Tar. In nautical work, usually means Stockholm tar. Coal tar, however, is often used for preservation of steel decks, particularly the refined tars. Black tar varnish is often used for coating outside of underwater steel plating. 2. Colloquial name for a blue-jacket; rarely applied to a Merchant Navy seaman.

Tare. Amount to be deducted from gross weight to ascertain nett weight of a commodity that is packed.

Tarpaulin. Originally, canvas dressed with tar, or a substitute for tar. Now applied to canvas treated with a waterproofing and preservative dressings. Used for covering hatches, and for protective purposes. 2. Old name for a seaman. 3. Old name for a seaman's waterproof hat.

Tarpaulin Canvas. Rather coarse but flexible canvas. Made from second quality yarns, but not lacking in strength, and free from jute.

Tarpaulin Muster. Old name for a general collection for a charitable purpose. Name probably arose from the passing round of a tarpaulin hat.

Tartane.* Small coasting vessel of the Mediterranean Sea of about 40 tons. Has a clipper bow, pointed stern, one mast, lateen sail and jib.

Taunt, Taunto. High, or tall. Said of masts that are unusually high, or of a vessel having high masts.

Taurus. (Lat.='Bull'.) Constellation situated between R.A. 03 h 20 m and 04 h 40 m and Dec. 8° to 27°N. Has two navigational stars (Aldebaran and Nath). Also, second sign of Zodiac, extending from 30° to 60° celestial longitude. Due to precession of equinoxes, constellation Aries is now in sign Taurus, and constellation Taurus is mainly in sign Gemini. Sun is in Taurus from April 21 to May 20 (about).

Taut. Tight or well stretched. Neat.

LAUNCHED IN 1832

AND STILL WELL AHEAD

WRITTEN by men who know the ropes and read all round the globe between Greenland and the Antarctic, the *Nautical Magazine* needs no introduction to seafarers, shipping people and marine enthusiasts of any nationality. Its subscribers, some of whom were avid readers long before many modern countries were on the map, are found under every flag, afloat and ashore. If you are not yet one of them, now is the time to sign on. The first issue came out over 149 years ago, and there is still no better bargain anywhere for only 80p a month; or £12·84 (U.K.), £13·20 (Overseas) a year, mailed, free to any address on earth, even to the South Pole.

Right from the windjammer reign of Britain's sailor-king William IV, through the succeeding steam age of Queen Victoria, and into our own era of atomic ships, the *Nautical Magazine* has been the voice of the experienced navigator. It still is, more than ever. And not only of masters, mates, apprentices and pilots, but engineers, radio officers, pursers, stewards, the deck crowd and the black gang. The independent voice of all those whose life is the sea and whose know-how is the key to the world's commerce. So you are welcome to write letters to the Editor—who will print them gladly—on any apt subject under the sun, moon and stars, provided you keep your temper. Your views will be read by owners, builders, marine superintendents, examiners and navigation teachers, for they are all among our subscribers, as well as old-timers who have swallowed the anchor but keep abreast in our correspondence columns. Regular letter-writers and readers prefer the three-year subscription for only £37·50 (U.K.), £38·50 (Overseas), which saves money and time. Many much-needed reforms in the Merchant Service stem from the pages of the *Nautical Magazine*, which was founded by Rear-Admiral A. B. Becher, the foremost hydrographer of his day, and who was also its first editor for 39 years until he retired in 1871. And the Admiralty got so much information out of the *Nautical Magazine* for its own early survey records that it used to grant the editor £100 a year, that is, £50 from Naval Funds and £50 from the Mercantile Marine Fund. Today our sheet-anchor is the subscription at £12·84 (U.K.), £13·20 (Overseas) a year from men—and women, too—who know a good thing when they see it.

So the *Nautical Magazine* started serving the Merchant Marine eight years before the very first Cunard liner *Britannia* left Liverpool on her maiden voyage to Halifax and Boston. And since that time it has had only six editors before the present one, who is the son of the fifth editor.

It was in the editorial epoch of the founder, Rear-Admiral Becher, that the *Nautical Magazine* brought new ideas to the shipyards and was active in exposing a lot of dirty work, not least in marine insurance, thanks to its alert readers and writers. Among these we find James Ballingall, a Scottish shipping surveyor who ended in Australia and who was the first witness called upon to give evidence before the House of Commons 'Shipwreck Committee' of 1836, which made life at sea last longer. As a source of maritime history, the *Nautical Magazine* has no equal. Indeed, it is not only the second-oldest monthly in the world, but also the oldest reviewer of books in the English language. The Editor is always ready to obtain for *Nautical* readers any British books that are in print, on any subject, upon receipt of the published price, plus postage.

Expert book reviews; salty letters to the Editor; shipping news from all over the world; examination results for named Extra Masters, Masters, Mates and Engineers; the new ships ordered, launched and tried for British owners; monthly list of recent casualties from the Liverpool Underwriters' Association; the movements of Merchant Navy men, a personnel section where one often finds old shipmates mentioned; a dozen feature articles by well-known and unknown writers—scientific, technical, professional, dead serious or dead-pan funny. These are only a few of the items you get for 80p a month. The *Nautical Magazine* is loaded down to the marks with worthwhile reading material. Yarns to while away a watch below; problems to ponder over a whole voyage. Do you collect stamps? Want to start an argument around the globe? It's all yours, for only 80p a month; £12·84 (U.K.), £13·20 (Overseas) a year, or £37·50 (U.K.), £38·50 (Overseas) for three years. Just sign the subscription order form and send it with your remittance to Brown, Son & Ferguson, Ltd., 52 Darnley Street, Glasgow, G41 2SG, Scotland.

And remember, the *Nautical Magazine* is absolutely independent, so you are at liberty to express your opinion freely on anything and everything of interest to men of the Merchant Service.

Taut Bowline. Said of a bowline when it is fully stretched with ship sailing closed hauled. 'On a taut bowline' denotes a vessel sailing close hauled and as near to wind as possible.

Taut Leech. Said of a sail when well hoisted and having no tendency to 'bag'.

Taut Wire Measuring Gear. Used in surveying ships to indicate an exact distance run. About 140 miles of pianoforte wire is carried on a drum, one turn being led round a 'counter' wheel having a circumference of ·01 of a cable, 0·001 of a mile. End of wire is weighted and lowered to sea-bed. As ship goes ahead, the wire is allowed to go out. Number of revolutions of 'counter' wheel is registered, thus giving a distance. Accuracy is within 0·2 per cent.

Tavistock Theodolite. Instrument used for precise measurement of angles in marine surveys.

T-Bar. Rolled steel section of T-shape.

Tchebycheff's Rule. For finding area of a figure bounded by straight lines and a curve. Ordinates are drawn to suit shape or curve, their mean value being multiplied by length of base line. Used as an alternative to 'Simpson's Rules'.

Teak. Valuable and important wood grown in India and Burma. When seasoned, will not warp, split, crack, or alter shape. Is not injured by contact with iron, is easily worked and is not attacked by ants or other insects. Specific gravity, 0·64.

Team Boat.* Ferry boat having paddles worked by a team of horses.

Tee Bar Bulbed. Tee bar with bulb along lower edge.

Teem. To pour. To empty.

Telegraph: Engine-room or Docking Telegraph. A mechanical or electrical device which, on a lever being moved, transmits or acknowledges orders for engine movements or handling of ropes.

elegraph Men. Hands stationed on bridge of a steam, or motor, vessel to work engine-room telegraphs as ordered.

Telegraph Ship. Vessel specially constructed for laying, picking up, or working on, a submarine telegraph cable.

Telemotor. Steering-gear which controls a steering engine by hydraulic pressures set up by movements of the steering-wheel.

Telescope. Optical instrument for magnifying image of distant objects, so making them to appear nearer. Crude form was in use before 1570. In 1608, two Dutch spectacle makers, Jansen and Lippershey, made three instruments 'for seeing at a distance'. Galileo improved on these by using double concave eyepieces. Kepler introduced convex eyepiece. Light-collecting power depends entirely on area of object glass. Different types include terrestrial, refracting, reflecting, and prismatic telescopes—and the periscope.

Telescopic Funnel. Funnel that can be lowered vertically, either entirely or in sections. Originally used in vessels having sails and engines. Now confined to small craft that pass under bridges.

M

Telescopic Topmast. Topmast that can be lowered inside a tubular lower mast when required.

Telltale. General name for a mechanical indicator—such as the pointer on a helm indicator, or the repeating pointer from engine room. Formerly, was an indicator on beam of cabin—showing position of helm or rudder.

Tell-Tale Compass. Inverted compass formerly attached to beams of cabin so that direction of ship's head could be ascertained at any moment by the Master.

Tell-Tale Shake. The shaking of a rope, by a man working aloft, to indicate that he wishes it to be slacked or let go.

Temperature Gradient. Rise or fall in temperature of a mass as registered in a horizontal direction through the mass.

Temperate Zones. Those areas of Earth's surface lying between the Arctic and Antarctic Circles and the Tropics.

Temperly Transporter. Substantial beam, of I-section, having a carriage on lower flange and fitted with slings and guys. When slung from a derrick it permits hoisting from points approximately below beam, hauling of carriage to a point in beam above lowering position, and lowering—all with one winch. Requires adjustment of guys, possibly of toppinglift, when loading or discharging points are changed.

Tempest. Violent wind storm.

Template, Templet. Piece of thin wood, or metal, cut to shape of a required fitting or member, and so acting as a pattern. 2. Perforated strip of metal used as a guide for siting rivet holes.

Tend. To attend. Formerly said of a vessel at anchor when she swung to the prevailing tidal stream.

Tendency. Inclination to change. Particularly applied to changing of barometric pressures. 'Barometric Tendency.'

Tender. Said of a vessel having a small righting moment; so being easily moved from her position of equilibrium, and slow in returning to it. 2. Small vessel employed in attending a larger vessel, or vessels. 3. To offer for acceptance, or consideration. The act of offering for acceptance or consideration.

Tenor. General meaning, or purport, of a document or statement.

Tensile Strength. Amount of tension that can be put on a member or fitting without rupturing it.

Tensile Stresses. Of a ship, are those components of hogging and sagging stresses that tend to rupture the fore and aft members of her construction.

Tension. State of being stretched or strained so that rigidity is generated. 2. Name sometimes given to 'voltage'.

Tenth Wave. Commonly believed to be higher than preceding nine waves. Although it is true that wind effect causes one wave to override another, and so make a larger wave, it is not established that the eleventh wave will do this—so making a larger tenth wave. In some places the fifth wave is consistently larger.

Tephigram. Diagram showing atmospheric conditions at various levels of altitude.

Terce. Cask holding 42 gallons, $\frac{1}{3}$ of a pipe or butt. Tierce.
Tercentesimal Scale. Temperature scale in Absolute units, so going into the third 'hundreds'.
Teredo navalis. Soft, cylindrical mollusc, about 24 to 30 inches long, that bores into timbers of wooden ships. Has small shells attaches to tail, and used these for lining the hole made.
Teredo Worm. Common name for 'Teredo navalis'.
Term. Short name for 'Term Piece'.
Terminator. Line dividing illuminated surface of Moon from surface not illuminated. Sometimes applied to same line on planets, including Earth.
Term Piece.* Carved work, on olden ships extending from the taffrail to foot rail of balcony, and then going down the side timbers of stern.
Terrada. Oriental sailing vessel of 16th century, usually having one or two masts.
Territorial Waters. Water adjacent to a coast and over which the sovereign power of the country claims control. Usually taken as being within three miles off the coast, but this is not universally accepted. There is no hard and fast international agreement on the application of this rule to wide estuaries, gulfs, bays, etc.
Terrestrial. Pertaining to Earth. Used generally to differentiate points, lines, and circles of terrestrial sphere from similar points, lines, and circles of celestial sphere.
Terrestrial Magnetism. Natural magnetism of Earth.
Terrestrial Radiation. Emission of heat by land during night.
Terrestrial Telescope. The telescope generally used at sea. Object viewed is observed correctly, and not inverted. This rectification causes a certain amount of light to be lost.
Tethys. Greatest of the sea deities of Greek mythology. Wife of Oceanus and mother of all great rivers, and of 3000 Oceanides.
Tew. Chain or rope used for towing. 2. To beat hemp for rope-making.
Tewing Beetle. Flat piece of wood formerly used for beating hemp.
Thalamites. The oarsmen in ancient Greek triremes, who sat lowest, or next to the vessel's sides.
Thames Measurement. Yacht measurement by 'Thames Tonnage'.
Thames Tonnage. Yacht measurement introduced 1855 by Royal Thames Yacht Club. Calculated by $\dfrac{B^2\,(L-B)}{188}$ when B is beam and L is extreme length in feet.
Theoretical Navigation.* Old name for all calculations made for fixing ship's position. It thus included Common and Proper Pilotage—or Pilotage and Navigation.
Thermal Conductivity. Efficiency, of a substance, to conduct heat; silver having the greatest thermal conductivity.
Thermal Efficiency. Work done by an engine when expressed as a ratio of the heat energy in the fuel consumed. Due to funnel emissions, radiation, and other losses, maximum thermal effic-

iency of boilers and engines combined is about 0·3; of turbines is about 0·2, reciprocating engines about 0·17.

Thermogram. Recording made by a thermograph.

Thermograph. A recording thermometer.

Thermometer. Instrument for measuring temperature, usually by the expansion or contraction of a column of mercury or alcohol. As the range of these two substances is somewhat limited, it is necessary to use other means for measuring high temperatures. Instruments for measuring furnace temperatures are 'pyrometers'.

Thermometrograph. Self-registering thermometer made by Cavendish, 1752.

Thermotank. Casing containing pipes through which steam, cold water, or brine may be passed. Air for ventilation can be drawn round these pipes. and so brought to any required temperature.

Thick and Thin Block. Block having two sheaves, of different sizes, through which two different ropes were rove. They were fitted, for example, on quarters of a yard to take sheet and clewline.

Thieves. In marine insurance are persons, not belonging to the ship, who commit robbery with studied intent.

Thimble. Metal ring, with concave side into which a rope may be spliced, or seized; thimble can then take shackle pin, hook, or rope without chafing rope into which thimble is fitted. Made in various shapes. Usually of galvanised iron, steel, brass, or gunmetal.

Thimble Eye. Round hole, in steel or iron plate, with edge rounded or built up so that a rope can be rove through it instead of through a sheave.

Thirty-day Returns. Proportional repayment of insurance premiums for each 30 days an insured vessel is laid up, or taken off insurance.

Thofts.* Old name for thwarts of a boat.

Thole, Thole Pin. Metal or wooden peg inserted in gunwale of a boat for oar to heave against when rowing without crutch or rowlock.

Thomson Deflector. *See* 'Deflector'.

Thomson's Sounding Machine. The earlier type of the Kelvin Sounding Machine. Line used was two pianoforte steel wires twined round one another.

Thornycroft Boiler. Water-tube boiler consisting of two lower water drums and an upper steam drum, connected by curved tubes, and all mounted in the heating space.

Thoroughfoot. The fouling of a tackle by one of its blocks being passed through the running parts of the tackle. Probably a corruption of 'through put'.

Thorough Put. Thoroughfoot.

Thranites. The uppermost oarsmen of the three tiers of a Greek trireme.

Thrapping.* Frapping.

Thrashing. Said of a vessel under sail when she is sailing fast on a wind.

Thread. Two or more single yarns twisted together.

Threatening. Term applied to weather when the indications are that it will become bad, or worse.

Three-Circle Type. Name given to a sextant in which strength and rigidity of frame are obtained by having three open circles, in form of a trefoil, incorporated in the frame.

Three-Decker. Ship having three gun decks below the upper deck; thus having five decks in all. Name is sometimes given to a sea pie made of layers of meat, vegetables, and pastry.

Threefold Purchase. Purchase rove through two treble blocks, so gaining a power of six or seven—depending on which block moves.

Three Half Hitches (are more than the King's yacht wants). Rebuke to those who make excessive and unnecessary fastenings of ropes.

Three-Island Type. Name given to cargo vessels having raised forecastle, midship houses, and poop, and rather low freeboard elsewhere. Distinguishes them from flush deck vessels, and others.

Three L's. Lead, latitude and look-out. First used by Sir John Norris (1660–1749) as being the best guide for 'Coming up the Channel'.

Three-Point Problem. Name given to problem of fixing position by measurement of horizontal angles between three identified and charted objects. Now solved by the Station Pointer.

Three Sheets in the Wind. Said of a man under the influence of drink. A ship with three sheets in the wind would 'stagger to and fro like a drunken man'. Conversely, a drunken man staggers to and fro like a ship with three sheets in the wind.

Three-Stranded. Defines all ropes having three strands.

Throat. The part of a gaff that rests against a mast, and from which the jaws spring. 2. Fore upper corner of a fore and aft sail. 3. Angle at junction of arm and shank of an Admiralty pattern anchor. 4. Interior angle of knee or compass timber.

Throat Bolts. Eye bolts in jaw end of gaff and in lower part of a top. They take hooks of throat halliards.

Throat Brails. Brails that lead through blocks below jaws of a gaff.

Throat Downhaul. Rope for bousing down the throat of a gaff.

Throat Halliard. Rope or purchase for hoisting throat of a gaff.

Throat Seizing. Put round two parts of a rope that has a circular bight and the parts going in opposite directions. Similar to a round seizing but without the frapping turns.

Through Bill of Lading. Bill that covers transit of goods from consignor to consignee when more than one means of transport is employed.

Through Fastenings. Nails, screws, bolts, rivets, etc., that go through all parts they join together, the outer ends being so secured that accidental withdrawal is precluded.

Thrum. To pass small tufts of rope yarns through canvas to make a mat. 2. The small tuft so used.

Thrum Mat. Mat made by thrumming rope yarns, or other fibres, into a textile backing.

Thrust. A pushing force exerted along a line.

Thrust Block. Substantial fitting secured to a vessel to take the thrust of screw propeller, and so cause vessel to move ahead or astern. In simpler forms, webs on thrust shaft work in grooves in thrust block. *See* 'Mitchell Thrust'.

Thrust Shaft. That section or propeller shafting which transmits propeller thrust to thrust block, and so to ship.

Thuban. Star α Draconis. R.A. 14 h (approx.); Dec. 64½°N; Mag. 3 (var.). When Great Pyramid was built it was the pole star.

Thumb Cleat. Small cleat having only one horn. Generally used as a fairlead.

Thumb Knot. Name sometimes given to the 'overhand' knot.

Thunder. Noise made when lightning flash passes through atmosphere and causes rapid expansion and contraction of air. As flash is comparatively long, the noise from each point in path arrives later as its distance from observer increases, thus giving a continuous sound.

Thunderbolt. Lightning flash that touches surface of Earth and causes damage. Name is sometimes given to a meteorite that strikes Earth.

Thunder Cloud. Unusually dark nimbus cloud from which lightning flashes emanate.

Thunderstorm. Storm in which thunder is heard; caused by decreases in upper air temperatures being abnormal. This vertical instability causes large cloud formations, with correspondingly large electrical charges.

Thurrock.* Old name for the hold of a ship.

Thwart. Transverse seat in a boat, for rowers to sit on.

Thwart Hawse. Forward of and across the fore and aft line of another vessel.

Thwart Marks.* Old name for 'leading marks'.

Thwartships. Usual contraction of 'athwartships'.

Ticket. Colloquial name for a 'Certificate of Competency'. Generally looked upon as a disparaging name but, etymologically speaking, is perfectly appropriate.

Tidal. Pertaining to tides.

Tidal Basin. An area of water that is partly enclosed, but is subject to fluctuations due to rise and fall of tides.

Tidal Constants. Amounts by which the tide, at a particular place, differs from tide at a port of reference. They may be 'time' or 'height' constants. Time constant applied to time of high or low water at port of reference will give approximate time of high or low water at that particular place. Similarly, height constants will give heights of high and low water.

Tidal Current. Name sometimes given to 'tidal stream'.

Tidal Friction. Retardation of Earth's rotation by Moon's tractive effort on atmosphere and waters of Earth; so causing day to be lengthened by about 0·002 of a second in 100 years. In about 50,000,000,000 years the day and month will be of equal length (about 47 × 24 hours).

Tidal Harbour. Harbour whose depth of water depends on state of tide.

Tidal Paradox. Applied to the phenomenon of a fall in surface level of water when a tidal current flows over a submerged shoal.

Tidal Prediction. Forecasting of times and heights of tidal undulation at a given place; or of the rise or fall in sea level at a given place at a given time.

Tidal River. River whose depth and rate of flow are affected by tides of the sea.

Tidal Species. The different categories into which tides and component tides can be placed. Principal are Diurnal, Semidiurnal, Quarter Diurnal, and Long Period. Mixed tides result from combination of two or more of these.

Tidal Stream. Periodical horizontal movement of water, in seas and oceans, caused by tide-producing forces.

Tidal Types. 'Tidal species.'

Tidal Undulation. The rhythmic rise and fall of sea level due to tide-producing forces. A bore, or aeger, is not an undulation.

Tidal Waters. Waters affected by rise and fall of tide, or by tidal currents.

Tidal Wave. Name given, erroneously, to an unusually large wave—that is generally due to anything but tidal action. A tsunami.

Tide. Periodic rise and fall of sea surface, at any given point, due to tractive and gravitational effects of Sun and Moon, together with centrifugal effect of Earth's gyrational movement.

Tide and Half Tide. Said of tidal streams when their directions are reversed at half flood and half ebb.

Tide and Quarter Tide. Said of tidal streams when their directions are reversed at quarter flood and quarter ebb.

Tide Day. Lunar day. 2. Interval between successive high waters of a diurnal tide; between high water of one semidiurnal tide and the second following high water.

Tide Gauge. Instrument for measuring height of tide, or for indicating it. Usually automatic in action.

Tide Pole. Iron tube, or rectangular wooden spar, used for observing tidal rises during marine surveys. Usually painted black and white—in alternate feet—with graduations that can be read from a distance.

Tide Rip. Disturbed water due to tidal current passing over marked inequalities in the bottom.

Tide Rode. Said of an anchored vessel when her head is pointing in direction from which a tidal current is flowing.

Tidesman. Customs officer who boards a vessel on arrival, and remains on board during discharge of cargo. 2. Man employed during certain states of tide.

Tide Tables. Pre-computed tables giving daily predictions of times and heights of high water—often, of low water—at selected ports and positions. 2. Ancillary tables for deriving times and heights of tide at selected secondary ports, from tabulated tides. Also, tables for finding heights of tide at a port at times intermediate between high and low waters.

Tide Waiter. Alternative name for 'Tidesman'.

Tide Water. Navigable water affected by rise and fall of tide, or by tidal currents.

Tideway. Channel through which a tidal current runs, particularly that part in which current has its maximum rate.

Tie. Short rope, other than a gasket, used for securing a sail when furled.

Tieplate. Plate fitted between, and attached to, two members to maintain their distance apart, or relative positions.

Tier. Mooring buoys at which several vessels lie alongside each other. 2. Hemp cable when flaked down for running. 3. Grating or spar shelf on which hemp cable was flaked for running. 4. A range of casks. 5. Row of vessels moored alongside one another.

Tierce. Cask holding 42 gallons. When used for salt provisions were in two sizes; one contained about 304 lb., the other about 336 lb.

Tight. Said of a ship when she does not leak.

Tiller. Lever, in head of rudder, by which steering is effected by government of the rudder.

Tiller Chain. Chain going between tiller and the machinery by which rudder is governed.

Tiller Head. The inboard end of tiller, at which it is actuated.

Tiller Rope. Rope connecting drum of steering-wheel with tiller.

Tilt.* Canvas awning over stern sheets of a boat.

Tilt Boat.* Small rowing boat having an awning, or tilt, for the protection of passengers.

Timber. Wood that has been dressed, or partially dressed. 2. Frame of a wooden vessel or boat. 3. Large piece of wood used in the construction of a wooden vessel.

Timber and Room. Horizontal distance from one frame of a wooden vessel to the next frame. Measured by width of the timber, plus space between frames.

Timber Dogs. Two claws riding on a single ring. Used for gripping timber logs for lifting.

Timber Head. Projection of rib of a wooden ship above the deck, for use as a bollard. Name now given to wooden bollards on piers and wharves when they are heads of vertical timbers.

Timber Hitch. Made by passing rope round a spar and then taking end round standing part and dogging it round its own part. With an additional half-hitch it is the appropriate method for towing a spar or piece of timber.

Timber Load Line. Special load line used only when carrying a timber deck cargo.

Timber Spacing. Alternative name for 'Timber and room'.

Time. Mode by which is measured the passage of events. A measure of duration. In navigation, all time is measured by hour angle of a specific body or point, and is based on diurnal rotation of Earth, monthly revolution of Moon around Earth, the annual revolution of Earth round Sun.

Time Azimuth. Bearing, of a heavenly body, derived from latitude of observer, declination and hour angle of the body observed.

Time Charter. Agreement whereby a shipowner leases his vessel to a charterer, for a specified period and under conditions agreed.

Time Clauses. Institute clauses applicable to a 'Time' policy of insurance.

Timeneoguy. Small rope tautly stretched to prevent sheets and tacks fouling when working ship. Originally, was a tack tricing line that kept sail from obscuring view of helmsman, or 'timoneer'.

Time Penalty Clause. Inserted in a policy of marine insurance to free insurer from all claims for loss consequent on loss of time.

Time of Origin. Time at which a signal is ordered to be sent. Serves as a reference number identifying the signal.

Time Policy. Contract of insurance covering a risk for a specified period, not exceeding one year for marine insurance policies.

Time Signal. Visual, radio, or telegraphic signal made to indicate an exact instant of time.

Time Zones. Sectors of Earth's surface bounded by meridians 15° apart, zero zone being $7\frac{1}{2}°$ on either side of prime meridian. Times kept in these zones vary from Greenwich in complete hours. Each zone is identified by a figure denoting the number of hours that its time differs from G.M.T., and a sign, $+$ or $-$, indicating how the difference is to be applied to Zone Time to get G.M.T.

Tingle. Sheet of lead or copper that has been tacked on outside of a boat to stop a leak. Usually put over canvas, fearnought, or other fabric that has been soaked in tallow or oil. A pad of oakum is often used.

Tipping Centre. That point, in fore and aft line of a vessel, that does not rise or fall with change of trim. It is the point at which the tipping change appears to be hinged.

Tireplate. Iron plate extending athwartships, on under side of deck, in way of mast of a sailing vessel. Placed to prevent mast wedges distorting deck planking in way of mast.

Title of Chart. Includes particulars regarding date of survey, names of ship and officers engaged in survey, compass variation at a given date, secular change in variation, geographical position of a named point, units used for denoting soundings, tidal data, conspicuous objects, natural scale of chart, abbreviations used.

Toggle. Piece of wood, or other material, used in conjunction with a becket when quick attachment or release is required. Any small spar passed through eye of rope, that has been rove through an aperture or ringbolt, is a toggle.

Toleration. Amount of inaccuracy that can be accepted in any item that is made to specified dimensions.

Tom, Tomm. To shore up. 2. A shore, or support.

Tomahawk. Small pole axe used for fire-fighting, and other purposes.

Tom Bowling. The ideal seaman. Immortalised in Dibden's song, and in Smollett's 'Roderick Random'.

Tom Cox's Traverse. Work done by a man who bustles about doing nothing. Usually amplified by adding 'running twice round the scuttle butt and once round the longboat'.

Tompion. Plug put in muzzle of gun to keep bore clean and water-tight.

Tongue. Upper main piece of a built mast. 2. Rope spliced into upper part of a standing backstay. 3. Clapper of a bell.

Tonnage. Expression of a ship measurement that is not necessarily based on weight. In some cases it is derived from cubic capacity —this usage being ascribed to the number of 'tuns' that would stow in the space. The principal ship tonnages are Gross, Net, Displacement, Deadweight, and Under Deck tonnages.

Tonnage Deck. That deck that forms the upper boundary of the space measured when assessing tonnage. In vessels having less than three complete decks it is the upper deck. In all other cases it is the second deck from below.

Tonne. Metric unit of weight. Equals 0·9842 avoirdupois ton and 1000 kilo.

Tons Burden. Carrying capacity of a vessel expressed in tons. In Section 3 of Merchant Shipping Act it means 'net registered tonnage'.

Tons per Inch. Number of tons required to increase a vessel's draught by one inch at a given draught.

Top. Platform at head of lower mast. Rests on trestle trees and thwartship bearers. Gives a good spread to upper rigging. 2. Division of the watch in Royal Navy.

Top Block. Iron-bound block, connected to eyebolt under lower cap, to take the top rope when sending topmast up or down.

Top Brim. Top rim.

Top Button. Truck at a mast head.

Top Chains. Preventers, in sailing warships, that took weight of the lower yard if slings were shot away.

Top End. Rectangular block at lower end of piston of a marine reciprocating engine. Upper end of connecting rod is hinged into it.

Topgallant Bulwarks. 'Quarter boards.'

Topgallant Forecastle. Short deck right forward, and raised above the upper deck, to carry machinery for working cable.

Topgallant Mast. Mast above topmast. When royal yards are crossed the mast is longer: the upper part being the royal mast, the lower part being the topgallant mast.

Topgallant Yard. Yard next above topsail yards. Topgallant sail is bent to it.

Top Hamper. The fittings, furniture, and tackles that are above the upper deck of a vessel; more especially those that are aloft.

Top Lantern. Lantern from which a 'top light' is shown.

Top Light. Light shown from a main or mizen top as a guide to following warships when in line ahead.

Top Lining. Doubling piece of canvas, on after side of topsail, to take any chafe against the top rim. 2. Platform of thin wood fastened on after side of crosstrees.

Topman. Seaman whose duties are in the top when under sail. 2. In Royal Navy, is a rating in the 'foretop' or 'maintop' division of a watch.

Topmast. Mast immediately above a lowermast—into which it may be telescoped, or to which it may be fitted.

Topmast Backstays. Two stays leading aft, one on either side, to stay a topmast against forward acting forces.

Topmast Stay. Standing rigging that stays a topmast in a forward direction. That on fore topmast is set up well forward on deck. Main and mizen topmast stays are set up in fore and main tops, respectively. Alternatively, they may be doubled in number and led to either side of ship forward of the mast.

Top Maul. Maul kept in fore and main tops for removing topmast fid when required.

Top Minor. Hole through which a strand is drawn to twisting machine when making rope by hand.

Topping. Raising one end of a yard or boom higher than the other end.

Topping a Furnace. *See* 'Priming and Topping'.

Toppinglift. Rope or tackle for lifting the head of a derrick or boom.

Topping Maul. Carpenter's hammer having a conical point and large, flat, circular head.

Toprail. Rail, supported by stanchions, along after edge of a lower top.

Top Rim. Edge of the top on lower masts of sailing ships. After side was often fitted to take stanchions. Usually divided into 'fore', and 'after', and 'side' rims. Name was given, also, to a curved beading, on fore side of rim, to reduce chafing of topsail.

Top Rope. Rope by which a topmast is hoisted or swayed up.

Topsail. Sail next above course in square-rigged vessels, and above mainsails in fore and aft rigged vessels. Those in square-rigged vessels originally carried three reefs. In merchant vessels, the sail was, later, divided into an upper and a lower topsail, both without reefs.

Topsail Breeze. Fresh breeze in which a yacht can carry topsails.

Topsail Halliard Bend. Made by taking three turns around a spar, then end around standing part and under all three turns, then back over two turns and under the last turn. Allows spar to be hoisted close to block.

Topsail Schooner. Schooner, usually two-masted, having square topsails on fore mast.

Topsail Sheet. Rope by which clew of a topsail is hauled out. To 'pay a debt with a topsail sheet' is to sail without paying the debt.

Topsail Yard. Yard to which head of a topsail is bent.

Topside Line. Sheer line drawn above top timber at upper edge of gunwale.

Topsides. That part of ship's side that is above waterline. Used colloquially for 'on deck'.

Top Tackle. Purchase used for swaying a topmast.

Top Timber. Timber immediately above the futtocks in ribs of ship's side.

Tormentor. Large fork used for lifting boiled salt meat out of a galley copper.

Tornado. Whirlwind having a diameter of less than a quarter of a mile, and a speed of travel of about 30 knots. Wind velocity may exceed 200 knots. Local effects may be disastrous.

Torpedo. Fish that kills its prey by making physical contact and discharging electricity. Varies in weight between 20 and 100 lb. Its electrical shock can kill a human being. 2. Name formerly given to a submarine mine or any container of explosive fired, above or below water, when alongside an enemy vessel. 3. Locomotive container of explosive that can be adjusted to travel at a desired depth, along a pre-arranged course or courses—and to explode on graze or impact.

Torpedo Boat. Small, fast craft introduced for attacking large warships with torpedo. First in Royal Navy (1877) was H.M.S. 'Lightning', 27 tons, 19 knots. Modern torpedo-boats are motor-propelled.

Torpedo Booms. Steel booms hinged near waterline and with heads attached to a steel ridge rope to which a torpedo net was laced. Netting was normally carried on shelf along ship's side. When torpedo attack was expected, nets were dropped and booms hauled perpendicular to ship's fore and line; thus forming a net screen against torpedoes.

Torpedo Catcher. Fast craft designed for attacking and destroying torpedo boats. First in Royal Navy was H.M.S. 'Rattlesnake' (1886).

Torpedo Gunboat. Gunboat fitted with torpedo tubes.

Torpedo Net. Netting made of interwoven steel wire rings and used as defence against torpedo. Extended almost full length of ship, on both sides, and to a depth of about 20 ft. Disadvantages outweighed advantages when torpedo was fitted with pioneer. Nets were discontinued after 1914–1918 war.

Torpedo Ram.* War vessel fitted with a ram, and with torpedo tubes that fired directly forward.

Torricelli's Theorem. Refers to velocity of water through an orifice. Usually given as $\sqrt{2gh}$ when h is difference of levels on either side of orifice, g being coefficient of gravitational force. Due to frictional and other factors, the practical velocity is about 0·6 of theoretical velocity.

Torrid Zone. That area of Earth's surface that lies between the Tropics of Cancer and Capricorn.

Torse. A coarse kind of hemp.

Torsion Meter. Instrument for measuring amount of torque in a shaft. Used for measuring torque in propeller shaft turned by a turbine; thus arriving at horsepower of engine.

Total Eclipse. Eclipse of Sun, or Moon, in which no part of the disc is illuminated.

Total Loss. Used in marine insurance to denote that the subject of insurance has been completely lost, or has been so damaged that it is valueless.

Touch. To make a brief call at a port or place. 2. To touch the bottom without grounding. 3. Said of a sail when its luff comes into the wind. 4. Tinder or match used for firing muzzle-loading guns. 5. The broad end of a tapered plank when in contact with narrow end of another tapered plank.

Touch and Go. To touch the ground, with the keel, for a minute or so and then proceed again.

'Touch and Stay.' Inserted in a marine insurance policy to permit vessel to call at a customary port for purposes connected with the voyage. Does not give liberty to deviate.

Touch Hole. Priming hole of a muzzle-loading gun, to which tinder or match was applied for igniting charge.

Touch Off. To fire a muzzle-loading gun by touching the priming with a match or tinder.

Touch the Ground. Temporarily and lightly to make contact with bottom when in shoal water.

Tow. Coarse fibres of hemp that have been separated from the finer fibres.

Tow. To draw through the water by means of a rope, hawser, or cable. 2. Vessel or craft being towed.

Towage. The act of towing. 2. Service rendered by towing.

Towage Clause. Clause in a charter party, and repeated in a bill of lading, giving a vessel permission to tow, or to be towed, in stated circumstances.

Towing Bridle. Length of chain, or rope, having a hook in each end and carried by towing vessel. End of tow rope is attached to the hooks.

Towing Horse. An arched transverse beam from bulwark to bulwark in a tug to keep the towrope clear of the deck.

Towing Light. The additional white light shown on foremast of a steam vessel when towing.

Tow Line, Tow Rope. Rope or hawser by which a vessel is towed.

Trabaccolo. Adriatic cargo vessel or trawler of about 60 tons. Original rig: two masts, lugsails, bowsprit and jibs.

Track. Route, in sea or ocean, along which vessels customarily travel. 2. That part of a line of advance that has already been travelled; particularly applied to storms. 3. Disturbed water astern of a vessel. 4. To tow a boat from a tow path.

Trackage. Towage, particularly from a tow path.

Tracking. Towing, particularly from a tow path.

Tractive Force. That part of Moon's gravitational pull that causes the water of Earth to move horizontally towards Moon.

Trades. Short name for 'trade winds'. Also used as denoting the cargo usually carried by a vessel or vessels; e.g. 'grain trade', 'timber trade'—or the areas traded in, such as 'Baltic trade', 'short sea trade'.

Trade Winds. More or less constant winds that 'tread' the same path for long periods. They blow from tropical high pressure areas towards the equatorial low-pressure area.

Trading Flag. Ensign of the country in which a vessel is at that time. Usually hoisted at foremast head in merchant vessels. Also called 'complimentary ensign'.

Trail Boards. Carved boards on either side of a figure head.

Training Ship. Ship carrying instructors and fitted out for training purposes. The training may be specialised, or general.

Training Wall. Wall, or embankment, erected at sides of a harbour or river to keep the water in predetermined bounds, or to deflect the water into a desired direction.

Train Tackle. Purchase, from ringbolt in deck to rear end of gun carriage, for holding a broadside muzzle-loading gun while back for loading.

Trajectory. Used in meteorology to denote the path taken by any particular particle of air when moving over Earth's surface. In gunnery, is the path of the projectile from gun muzzle to the surface of Earth, or to its bursting position.

Trammel. Fishing net made up of a 40-fathom length of small mesh net between two 40-fathom lengths of large mesh net. Extended between two ropes moored in line of tide.

Tramontana. North wind in Mediterranean Sea.

Tramp. Cargo steamer that is not confined to any particular run or to any particular cargo, but carries any cargo that is profitable and convenient.

Transfer. Distance a vessel moves away from her original line of advance when altering course under helm. Is measured along a line perpendicular to her original course, and to the point where she is on her new course.

Transient Ship. Name formerly given to a 'Tramp'.

Transire. The 'outward clearance' document of a vessel going from one United Kingdom port to another. Issued by Collector of Customs to Master at loading port. Delivered before discharging, to Collector of Customs at discharging port.

Transit. Passage of a heavenly body across meridian of observer. 2. Passage of an inferior planet across Sun's disc. 3. In pilotage, the position of two distant, fixed objects when they are in line to an observer; the line passing through them and observer being a position line.

Transom. Name sometimes given to 'Transom Frame'. 2. One of the thwartship beams bolted to stern post of a wooden vessel. Carries after ends of deck planking and helps to preserve shape of after body. 3. The stern timbers, or plating, of a vessel with a flat stern. As this stern formed the after side of the cabin, the name was sometimes applied to the cabin itself.

Transom Floors. Triangular steel plates rising vertically from upper arch above screw aperture of a single screw ship.

Transom Frame. Strong horizontal girder with its vertical centre line secured to stern post. It takes the cant frames of an elliptical stern and supports the quarters and overhanging stern.

Transom Knee. Knee bolted to transom and after timber.

Transom Stern. Stern consisting of a flat thwartship plate that is approximately vertical.

Transport. To carry from one place to another. Particularly applied to a vessel carrying troops or government stores.

Transporting Line. Rope led from ship to an appropriate place on shore, particularly in a dock or basin, for moving a ship by warping.

Trans-Ship. To put out of one ship into another. Often written 'tranship'.

Transverse Member. Shipbuilding term for a beam, the two frames to which it is attached and the floors at lower ends of frames. If the beam is pillared, the pillar is included.

Transverse Stress. A stress that tends to deform the transverse shape of a vessel or member.

Transverse Thrust. Any thrust that is perpendicular to the normal. Particularly applied to that component of the force exerted by a screw propeller which tends to move the stern side-wise. Its effect is frequently termed 'paddle-wheel effect'.

Traveller. Hoop, ring, or cylinder that can travel freely when encircling a mast, spar, horse, rope, or bar.

Traverse. Zig-zag track of a sailing vessel when plying to windward. 2. A term used in surveying to describe a series of connected lines, of known length and direction, on surface of Earth. If the last line of the series joins the first line, and so encloses a figure, the traverse is termed a 'closed traverse'. 3. To traverse a yard is to brace it as far aft as possible.

Traverse Board. Circular board marked with points of compass and having holes radiating from centre and towards each compass point. In these holes pegs were inserted, at an appropriate distance from centre, to indicate direction and distance run on the different tacks during a watch, 16th century.

Traverse Sailing. Sailing towards a position by a succession of alternate tacks.

Traverse Table. Table giving lengths of sides of all right-angled triangles when one angle, other than right angle, and one side are given. Included in all nautical tables for determining departure and difference of latitude made good when sailing obliquely to the meridian and distance run is known.

Traverse Wind. Head wind.

Trawler. Vessel fitted for catching fish by trawling.

Trawling. Dragging a trawl net along the sea bed for the purpose of catching fish. Can only be done in areas where sea bed is fairly smooth and free from obstructions.

Trawl Warp. Wire rope, leading through a block in gallows, by which a trawl net is towed.

Tread. The length of vessel's keel.

Treble Block. Block having three sheaves on the same pin.

Tree. Wooden beam, or bar, used in the furniture of a ship. Usually qualified by a word giving its particular function or description; e.g. crosstree, rough tree, chess tree, trestle tree, waist tree, etc.

Treenail. Cylindrical length of wood, from one to two inches in diameter, used for securing planking to frames, and other purposes, in wood-built vessels.

Trekschuyt. Covered boat formerly used in Holland and Flanders for transporting goods and passengers. Was towed by horses or oxen.

Trend. The increase in girth of an Admiralty pattern anchor shank as it approaches the arms. Extends for a distance equal to that of arms. 2. Angle between a vessel's fore and aft line and the cable to which she is riding.

Trennels. Tree-nails.

Tressle Trees.* Trestle trees.

Trestle Trees. Brackets, of wood or steel, on either side of lower mast, to support a top. With wooden masts, they rest on hounds. In modern ships they are riveted to steel mast, and support the fid on which heel of topmast rests.

Trial Trip. Short voyage of a newly-built, or repaired, vessel to test engines, steering, and other machinery, and to ascertain ship's capabilities and deficiencies.

Triangle Knot. Made in bight of rope so that two firm loops are formed. Not used in practical work, but is of interest as being a ceremonial knot of Brahmins.

Triangulation. Method used in surveys. Distance between two stations being known accurately, the distance of another station can be computed trigonometrically from the angles between it and each of the other stations.

Triangulum Australe. 'Southern triangle.' Well-marked stellar triangle about halfway between Scorpio and south pole. R.A. 16 h; Dec. 69°S (approx.).

Triatic Stay. Stay going horizontally from cap of one mast to cap of next mast. Common in vessels fore and aft rigged. Sometimes called 'jumper stay'.

Trice. To haul up by pulling downwards on a rope that is led through a block or sheave.

Tricing Line. Any small rope used for tricing; particularly that led through block at jaws of gaff to tack of a gaffsail.

Trick. A spell of duty connected with the navigation of a vessel; more particularly, at the wheel or look-out.

Trident Log. Towed log, on 'Cherub' principle, that has an electrical unit for repeating the indications at a point distant from log.

Triemiolio. Light, fast vessel of Rhodes in classic times.

Trim. Difference, or relationship, between the forward and after draughts of a floating vessel. Ship is said to be trimmed by the head or stern according to which end is deeper in the water.

Trimaran. A vessel having three hulls, the central one usually being the largest.

Trim Indicator. Instrument for measuring and indicating the longitudinal inclination of a vessel.

Trimmer. Man who shovels bulk cargo, particularly coal, from hatchway to the wings and under deck spaces in a hold. 2. Fireman who shovels coal from bunker to a position nearer to stokehold.

Trimming. Adjusting. Applied to cargo, denotes placing it in its proper position and, if necessary, winging it out. Applied to a vessel, denotes placing and arranging cargo so that there is a desired relationship between the forward and after draughts. Trimming a bunker is passing the coal in it to another bunker, or to a position where it will be handy for feeding fires. Trimming yards and sails is carefully adjusting them so that the maximum wind effect is obtained.

Trinity House. Short name for the 'Guild or fraternity of the most glorious and undivided Trinity and of St. Clements', chartered by Henry VIII and established at Deptford—where pilots boarded outgoing vessels. Its first duties embraced the supervision of construction of ships for the Royal Navy. In 1604 it divided into Elder Brethren and Younger Brethren, the latter being an honorary rank. Was dissolved by Parliament in 1647, but reconstructed in 1660. Now mainly concerned with lights, buoyage, and other navigational aids, and as nautical advisers in the Admiralty Division of the High Courts of Justice.

Trinity Masters. Elder Brethren of Trinity House.

Trinkets.* Long strips of canvas stretched along seams of hatch planks before putting on tarpaulins.

Trip. Voyage. 2. Distance run by a sailing vessel on one tack.

Tripod Mast. Steel mast consisting of three members whose heels are spaced as a triangle, and whose heads meet and are secured together. No stay or shrouds are required. First used in H.M.S. 'Captain' (1870); but the idea is much older, and is to be noted in many small craft all over the world.

Tripping. Breaking an anchor out of the ground. 2. Said of a boom when its outboard end skims the water. 3. Raising the heel of an upper mast.

Tripping Line. In general, a line that stops a particular item from doing its work. On a sea anchor, it capsizes the anchor and is used for hauling it in; on the clew of a sail, it hauls it up and spills the wind out of the sail. On heel of an upper mast, it lifts the mast and takes the weight off the pin or pawl.

Tripping Palm. More or less flat projection on arm of a self-canting anchor. Its duty is to bite into the ground and ensure that the flukes turn downward to bite into the ground.

Triquetrum.* Ancient navigational instrument for measuring altitude of Sun. Consisted of two pieces of timber hinged at ends. One leg was kept in horizontal plane, the other was pointed to Sun.

Trireme. Ancient war vessel of Carthaginians, Greeks, and Romans. Had three tiers, or banks, of oars.

Triton. Greek sea god, son of Neptune.

Trochoid. Curve that would be made in the vertical plane of a point in a circle that is rolling on a horizontal plane. Is of much importance when considering motions of free waves of the sea.

Troll. To fish by drawing bait through the water.

Trooper. Troop ship. Transport.

Trooping. Royal Naval term for carrying relief crews for vessels on foreign stations, and for bringing back the crews relieved. 2. Carrying troops by sea.

Troop Ship. Vessel fitted for carrying troops and their equipment. A transport.

Tropical Air. Air that has travelled from low latitudes to high latitudes.

Tropical Cyclone. Meteorological depression originating in low latitudes.

Tropical Month. Interval between successive transits of Moon through the same point in Ecliptic. Value is 29 d 12h 43·075 m.

Tropical Year. Time taken by Earth to go round Ecliptic from First Point of Aries. As First Point of Aries has a variable retrograde motion (about 50·26″ annually), Earth does not complete a sidereal revolution. Length is about 365 d 05 h 48 m 48 s, but this varies slightly.

Tropic of Cancer. Parallel of latitude, or declination, 23° 27′ N, being the highest parallel reached by Sun in his northerly motion. Reached about June 21.

Tropic of Capricorn. Parallel of latitude, or declination, 23° 27′S, being the highest parallel reached by Sun in his southern motion. Reached about December 21.

Tropics. The tropics of Cancer and Capricorn. The area of Earth between the tropics.

Tropic Tides. Diurnal tides whose amplitudes vary with the declinational values of the tide-raising bodies—Sun and Moon.

Tropopause. Boundary between the troposphere and stratosphere.

Troposphere. The atmospheric shell in which we live. Extends upwards to a height of about 10 miles in the tropics, about seven miles in temperate latitudes, perhaps, five miles at poles. Temperature decreases, more or less uniformly, with heights. Winds are not constant, rain can be precipitated.

Trot. Line of mooring buoys laid out at regular intervals. 2. Line of fishing hooks laid out at regular intervals when 'bottom fishing'.

Trough. Hollow between two waves in water. 2. Area of lowest barometric pressure in a cylonic storm, lying perpendicularly—more or less—to direction of travel of the storm.

Truck. Circular piece of wood fitted on head of an uppermost mast. Generally carries flag halliards, sometimes a wind vane.

Truckle.* To lower a sail slightly.

Trucks. Large wooden beads through which jaw rope of a gaff is rove. They reduce friction on mast when gaff is lowered or hoisted. 2. The small wheels of a wooden gun-carriage.

True. Word used when denoting values from which known errors have been eliminated. Used in this sense we have 'true altitude', 'true course', 'true azimuth', etc. Also used when differentiating between similar entities in different forms, such as 'true', and 'mean' Suns, 'true' and 'magnetic' north, etc.

True Altitude. Angular value of arc of vertical circle intercepted between a heavenly body and rational horizon. Deduced from apparent altitude by application of corrections for refraction, parallax and dip.

True Azimuth. Angular distance of a heavenly body from observer's meridian. Measured from the elevated pole.

True Bearing. Angle between observer's meridian and the great circle passing through observer and object observed. Expressed in three-figure notation, or quadrantally.

True Distance. Length of arc of great circle intercepted between two points on Earth.

True Lay Wire. Wire rope in which each wire is shaped in the spiral form it must have in the rope—and is not twisted into this shape.

True Sun. The apparent, or actual, Sun as distinguished from mean, and other, suns.

Trundle Head. That upper part of a capstan which contains the sockets into which the capstan bars are shipped.

Trunk. Rectangular space bounded by vertical plating and capable of being closed on upper side. Lower side is generally open to a larger enclosed space.

Trunk Ship. Vessel having trunks at deck level to act as feeders to holds.

Trunnels.* Treenails.

Truss. Chain confining lower yard to mast. Sometimes is an iron fitting for same purpose, and may be on yard, mast, or both.

Truss Hoop. Iron band, around mast or yard, that is attached to truss.

Try. To lie to under storm canvas, reduced sail, or even, bare poles.

Try Back. Veer a little.

Trysail. Fore and aft sail, set to a gaff, used when lying to in heavy weather, or when sailing on a wind.

Trysail Gaff. Gaff to which head of trysail is extended.

Trysail Mast. Small mast formerly carried slightly abaft principal mast, to take a trysail.

Tsunami. Wave generated by an under-water upheaval of the earth's crust. Can travel great distances and cause destruction on arrival at a coast. Improperly called a tidal wave.

Tube Plates. Perforated plates in combustion chamber and front end of marine boiler. They take front ends of smoke return tubes, which are fitted between them.

Tubinares. Means 'Tubular nostrils.' Applied to petrels, in which this characteristic is pronounced.

Tuck. After part of vessel, where bottom planking comes to the counter.

Tuck a Strand. To pass end of one strand under an unlaid strand when splicing. Colloquially: to gain an advantage, or favourable notice.

Tuck Rail. Lower strake of horizontal timber in counter of a wooden vessel.

Tufa. Light porous stone, rather like sandstone, that sometimes contains vegetable matter.

Tug. Strongly-built and fully-engined vessel especially designed for towing.

Tugboat. A small tug.

Tumble Home. The inward inclination of a vessel's sides due to her breadth at upper deck being less than her maximum breadth.

Tumbler. Hinged pin on which end link of chain holding an anchor is placed. When shaft—on which pin is fixed—rotates, the link falls off and anchor is released.

Tumbler Bolt. Device used for making good a missing rivet, and other purposes, when outside of plating is inaccessible. Works on the principle of a toggle. Consists of a circular rod having a slot in which a piece of steel, of same size as slot, is pivoted off centre. Inboard end of rod is threaded. When passed through hole the hinged part falls at right angles to bolt; nut on inboard end is screwed up to clamp leak-stopping unit in place.

Tun. Large cask holding 252 gallons (four hogsheads) of wine. 2. Wine measure of same quantity.

Tunnage. Duties levied on every tun of wine, and pound of goods, shipped from or to England. Introduced about 1348. Was the beginning of the present Customs duties.

Tunnel. Arched casing around propeller shafting. Extends upwards in after holds of cargo vessels with engines amidships. Goes to stern gland and allows access to propeller shaft bearings.

Turbine. Machine in which rotary motion is produced by high velocity of a fluid acting on blades appropriately mounted in its path. Can be divided into two types, 'impulse' and 'reaction'. Broadly stated, an impulse turbine is turned in same manner as an undershot water mill; reaction turbine being turned on same principle as a windmill. Marine turbines are steam or (petroleum) gas-driven. The latter needing no boilers.

Turbulence. Disturbed, or eddying, movement of any fluid when passing over any obstruction—solid, liquid, or gaseous—in its path. Is of importance in meteorology.

Turk's Head. Knot put in end of rope by unlaying strands, making a 'wall' and crowning it, then following through twice. Can be made with a single line. Resembles a turban in appearance.

Turn. Complete encirclement of a cleat, bollard, or pin by a rope.

'Turn.' Order given to man holding sand-glass when heaving the (hand) log and stray line is out. He then turns glass so that sand runs down, and reports, 'Done'.

Turn Buckle. Stretching screw; bottle screw.

Turned Knee. Beam knee made by curving bar to shape required.

Turner's Reefing Gear. Single-handed gear for yachts. Main boom is on an axis, and can be rotated by a lever and pawl acting on a ratchet wheel near heel of boom. Thus causes sail to be rolled up around the boom.

Turning Centre. That point on which a vessel turns when under helm. Any point forward of this will turn in a direction opposite to that of any point abaft it. In most vessels of normal form this point lies between 0·3 and 0·4 of vessel's length from forward—but much depends on trim.

Turning Circle. Circle whose diameter is the distance from the point at which helm is put over and the point where direction of ship's head has changed 180°, or 16 points. It varies with speed, draught, trim, and amount of helm.

Turn Turtle. To turn over completely, with keel uppermost.

Turn Up. To fasten a rope securely by taking turns around a cleat or bollard.

Turret Deck Type. Applied to a vessel constructed on a principle introduced by Doxford, of Sunderland. Side plating curves over to form a harbour deck, and then upwards again to form a 'trunk' or 'turret'. Ships of this type are practically self-trimming. Hold pillaring is either very small, or entirely absent. Web frames are used for maintaining strength and form.

Turret Ship. Warship carrying main armament in a turret or turrets. 2. Vessel of turret deck type.

Twelfths Rule. For finding the approximate amount the tide will fall in a certain time.

1st hour's rise or fall $= \frac{1}{12}$ of tide's range
2nd   ,,   ,, ,, ,, $= \frac{2}{12}$,,   ,,   ,,
3rd   ,,   ,, ,, ,, $= \frac{3}{12}$,,   ,,   ,,
4th   ,,   ,, ,, ,, $= \frac{3}{12}$,,   ,,   ,,
5th   ,,   ,, ,, ,, $= \frac{2}{12}$,,   ,,   ,,
6th   ,,   ,, ,, ,, $= \frac{1}{12}$,,   ,,   ,,

Twice Laid. Rope made from good yarns taken from old ropes.

Twiddling Line. Small line made fast near hand wheel of a sailing vessel and passed round a spoke of the wheel to ease strain on arms of helmsman. Particularly useful when vessel makes sternway. 2. Small line rove through sheaves of a yoke, the end being made fast in boat, to form a purchase for yoke lines when steering. 3. Name given to the 'twitching line' of old magnetic compasses of large diameter. These cards were sluggish in action. A small piece of sail-maker's twine was made fast to card, usually with beeswax, so that helmsman could give card a twitch if it appeared to be dead.

Twig.* To swig. To sweat up on a rope.

Twilight. Partial illumination by sunlight during interval between Sun's upper limb being on horizon and his centre being 18° below it. Caused by the scattering, refraction, and reflection of light by Earth's atmosphere. *See* 'Civil', 'Nautical', and 'Astronomical' twilights.

Twilight Arch. Upper boundary of a slightly illuminated tract of sky when Sun is below visible horizon.

Twilight Stars. Stars suitably placed for observation during morning or evening twilight.

Twine. Two or more threads twisted together to make a small line. 2. The linen thread with which canvas is sewn.

Twin Propellers. Twin screws.

Twin Screw. Said of a vessel having two propellers.

Twin Screws. Pair of screw propellers, one on either side, which rotate in opposite directions when propelling a vessel. Introduced in 1888.

Twist Knot. Plait knot.

Twitching Line. *See* 'Twiddling Line'.

Two Blocks. Said of a purchase or tackle when it has been hauled upon until its two blocks are touching one another.

Two-Stroke Cycle. Charging and compression on one stroke, ignition and scavenging on second stroke, of an internal combustion engine.

Two-Stroke Engine. Internal combustion engine having a power impulse on alternate strokes.

Tye. Rope by which a yard is hoisted. Usually rove through a sheave on mast.

Tye Block. Special iron-bound block shackled to a yard. Tye is rove through it to obtain extra purchase.

Typhoon. Violent cyclonic storm prevalent in seas around China, Japan, and the Philippine Islands.

Tyzack Rail Bar. Rolled section used as gunwale capping. Comprises a flat rail with bulb on lower side of one edge, other edge having flat strip at right angles to bar—this strip being drilled with holes for riveting to bulwark plating at upper edge.

U

Ullage. The amount by which a container or package is short of its standard content. Also applied to a container or package short of its standard content.

Ulloa's Circle. White 'rainbow' seen in fog, or at night.

Ultimate Strength. The stress, usually expressed in tons per square inch, that exactly balances the resistance to fracture, or rupture, of a member or material under stress. Sometimes defined as the minimum load that will cause fracture or rupture.

Umbra. The conical shadow that an eclipsing heavenly body has on that side of it that is remote from the light source. Occasionally applied to the dark area of a sunspot.

Una Rig. Single sail spread to a yard or gaff and set on a mast stepped well forward. Used for small craft, and in Norfolk wherries.

Unbend. Untie. Cast loose.

Unbit. To cast off the upper securing turns of the cable from the bits, leaving the riding turn on.

Under Bare Poles. Said of a vessel running before the wind with no sail set; the motion of the vessel being due to wind pressure on her stern and upper works.

Under Canvas. Under sail.

Undercurrent. Moving water that is below the surface and having a direction and/or rate that differs from that of surface water.

Under Deck Tonnage. Tonnage based on space below tonnage deck, each 100 cu. ft. counting as one ton. Measured from top of floors—or ceiling, if any—to underside of tonnage deck.

Under Foot. Said of anchor when it is under ship's forefoot, and cable is nearly up and down.

Undergrid. To pass hawsers under a vessel and heave them taut across the upper deck. Done when seams show signs of opening through strains on mast, or through heavy weather. Also called 'frapping'.

Undermanned. Said of a vessel when she is short of personnel she should have in the prevailing circumstances.

Under Power. The condition of a vessel when mechanical power is being used to propel her through the water.

Under Protest. Applied to an action, payment, or signature when it is not freely rendered but is qualified by a statement made before the rendering. It thus leaves the matter open to dispute.

Underrun. To follow up the lead of a submerged rope or wire by putting rope over a boat, and hauling the boat along it.

Under Sail. Having sail set. Making way through the water by action of wind on the sails.

Undersail.* To sail in the lee of a shore or headland.

Underset. The seaward setting current that moves under the surface water that is being driven shoreward by wind. Undertow.

Under the Lee. Under the shelter of an object to windward.

Undertow. Water flowing to seaward under surf.

Underwater Body. That volume of a vessel's hull that is immersed at a given draught.

Under Way. Not attached to the shore or the ground in any manner. Usually, but not necessarily, moving through or making way through the water.

Under Weigh. Under way.

Underwriter. A person who insures, wholly or in part, a marine risk by stating the amount for which he is liable in the policy, and then signing the policy. Underwriters at Lloyd's are required to deposit, with Lloyd's, securities to the value of, at least, £5000.

Underwriting. Contracting to make good, wholly or in part, a marine loss; signing to this effect at the foot of a policy of marine insurance.

Undulation. A rising above and a falling below a mean level in the manner of a smooth wave, or ripple.

Undulatory. Having an up and down movement, together with a sidewise movement, but without any translation of the particles of the fluid.

Unfurl. Cast loose a sail by letting go the gaskets.

Uniform System of Buoyage. Buoyage system in which the shape and/or colour of any buoy or beacon has a definite significance. Most maritime nations have a uniform system of their own. International system introduced in 1977.

Union. The device in the upper canton of an ensign or flag. Short name for the Union Jack, or the stars device of U.S.A. ensign.

Union Flag. Union of an ensign when flown by itself.

Union Hook. Swivelled cargo hook with ring carrying two swivels for connection to the two runners of a union purchase.

Union Jack. Device for a flag that forms the inner upper canton of a national ensign, or is used separately. Particularly applied to the British jack, which contains the crosses of Saints George, Andrew, and Patrick.

Union Purchase. Method of rigging cargo derricks so that they need not be moved while loading or discharging a hatch. One derrick plumbs the hatch, the other derrick plumbing the loading or discharging point overside. Runner of each derrick is shackled to the same cargo hook. Precision in plumbing results.

Universal Rating Rules. Measurements of yachts over 15 metres (49·2 ft.) L.W.L. Adopted in United Kingdom, 1931.

Universal Yacht Signals. Code of signals for yachts, produced by G. H. Ackers, 1847. Revised 1851 and 1859. Fell into disuse soon after the introduction of the 'Commercial Code' of 1857.

Universal Time. Alternative name for 'Greenwich Mean Time'.

Unload. To discharge, or remove, cargo.

Unmoor. To cast off hawsers by which a vessel is attached to a buoy or wharf. To weigh one anchor when riding to two anchors. To remove a mooring swivel when moored to two cables.

Unrig. To remove rigging. To take off tackling or fittings.

Unseaworthy. Said of a vessel when she is not in all respects fitted to perform her contracted tasks. In a limited sense it is used to denote a vessel not fit to face the hazards of the sea; in a larger sense, particularly as regards insurance interests, it includes her incapability of carrying cargo properly, her failure to have officers that are properly qualified, her lack of navigational aids, and other similar negligences.

Unship. To remove from a ship. To remove an item from its place.

Unstable Equilibrium. A ship which, when forcibly inclined, heels still further, and may capsize, is in unstable equilibrium.

Unukalkay. Name of star 'Cor Serpentis', or α Serpentis.

Unwatched. Said of a navigational beacon light that is shown from a position at which there is no permanent attendant.

Up. To put the helm up is to move tiller to windward. Applied to sails, means to hoist the sail.

Up Anchor. Weigh anchor.

Up and Down. Said of cable when it extends vertically and taut from anchor to hawsepipe.

Upper Deck. In ships with more than one continuous deck, is the highest continuous deck.

Upper Transit. Passage of a heavenly body across observer's meridian.

Upper Works. All erections above the freeboard deck.

'Up Right and Down Straight—Like a Yankee Main Tack.' Old phrase of a seaman when boasting of his candour. American ships, at one time, had comparatively short main tacks.

Upside Down Ensign. Old signal of distress.

Uptake. Enclosed casing that takes furnace gases from ends of boiler tubes to base of funnel.

Up Together. Order to the oars, on both sides of a boat, to give way together.

Uranography. The mapping of heavenly bodies on a chart or star globe.

Uranus. Planet between Saturn and Neptune. Not used in navigation. Discovered by Herschel, 1871. Has five small satellites.

Ursa Major. 'The Great Bear.' Most brilliant of the northern constellations. Contains seven bright stars: Dubhe, Merak, Phecda, Megrez, Alioth, Mizar, and Alkaid; the first two point to Polaris. This constellation is also called the 'Plough', 'Dipper', 'Charles Wain', and 'Waggon and Horses'. It has been called the 'Corn Measurer' by the Chinese, and considered as a hippopotamus by the Egyptians.

Ursa Minor. 'The Lesser Bear.' Northern constellation containing Polaris, α Ursae Minor.

Uvroe, Uvrou. Euphroe.

V

Vailing Topsail. Letting go topsail halyards as a salute.

Valuation Clause. Inserted in a policy of marine insurance to cover cases when ship becomes a constructive total loss. Stipulates that insured value of ship shall be considered to be her value if repaired. If cost of repairing exceeded insured value the latter would be paid by insurers.

Valve. Mechanism that controls rate and amount of flow through an aperture.

Valve Metal. Red brass consisting of 80% copper, 8% zinc, $3\frac{1}{2}$% tin, and $2\frac{1}{2}$% lead.

Van. The leading ship, or ships, in a fleet or squadron.

Vane. Contrivance for indicating direction of wind. 2. Blade of a towed or submerged log. 3. Small flat plate used when sighting.

Vangs. Ropes, one on either side of a gaff, by which the gaff is hauled into a desired direction, and held there.

Variables. Airs and inconstant winds in sea area between N.E. and S.E. trades. Area is about 500 miles wide in September, decreasing to about 150 miles at end of year. Also 'Variables of Cancer and Capricorn'.

Variable Stars. Stars whose apparent magnitudes vary periodically. Algol is an example, its magnitude changing from 2nd to 5th magnitude in less than three days. Some of them are binary stars in which one star passes in front of the other; others are giant stars that undergo some internal change.

Variation. Angle between magnetic and true meridians at any given position. 2. Change in orbital speed of Moon between syzygy and quadrature.

Vast. Usual contraction of 'Avast'.

Veer and Haul. To pay out cable and then immediately to haul on it. Slack made by veering allows hauling machinery to pick up speed.

Veering. Applied to cable or hawser, means paying out. Applied to wind, means altering direction clockwise.

Vega. Star α Lyrae. S.H.A. 81°; Dec. N39°; Mag. 0·1. One of the 'hydrogen' stars, or A stars. Its diameter is $2\frac{1}{2}$ times that of Sun, its candlepower being 50 times greater. Is 26 light-years distant from Earth.

Vehicle. That liquid which carries the base and pigment of a paint.

Veiling Topsail. Vailing topsail.

Velocity. Speed. Usually expressed by units of distance travelled in a specified unit of time. The 'knot' is an unit of velocity, and does not require a time value.

Velocity of Light and Radio Waves. 186,285 statute miles per second. Is about 43 miles per second less in air. Approximately 11 million miles a minute. 161,800 sea miles per second. 328 yards per microsecond. 300 million metres per second.

Velocity of Sound. In air is about 1090 ft. per second at 32°F. (0°C.) and increases 1·14 ft. per second for each degree F. (2·05 for degree C.) above. In water, velocity varies with salinity, temperature, and pressure (depth), but lies between 785 and 845 fathoms per second for small and great depths respectively.

Velocity of Translation. Speed of movement of a storm centre.

Velocity of Wave. Speed at which crest moves.

Vendavales. Squally SW winds in vicinity of Straits of Gibraltar between September and March.

Ventilator. Any arrangement that removes foul air from a space and supplies fresh air to it.

Vent Pipe. Pipe placed to facilitate escape of air or vapour.

Venture. An enterprise in which there is a risk of loss.

Venus. Second planet from Sun, mean distance from him being 67,200,000 miles. Being an inferior planet it phases, and has a limited elongation of 48°. Distance from Earth varies between 26 and 160 million miles. May be observed in daytime occasionally.

Ventilation. The provision of an air current, or of a free passage of air.

Verano. Dry weather spell during winter in Central America.

Veranillo. A spell of fine weather, for about three weeks, during the summer rainy season in Central America.

Vernal Equinox. Spring equinox. The date, about March 21, when Sun crosses Equinoctial from south to north declination. Although this corresponds with autumn in the southern hemisphere, the name is fairly universal.

Vernier. Auxiliary scale, close alongside principal scale, for reading fractional values of main scale by noting coincidence in alignment of graduations on vernier and main scale; the vernier graduation indicating the fractional value.

Vertex. The highest point in a curve. The zenith. That point at which a great circle track reaches its highest latitude. That point in any geometrical figure that is farthest from the base.

Vertical Circle. Any great circle, of the terrestrial sphere, whose plane is perpendicular to the horizon. It follows that all vertical circles will pass through the zenith.

Vertical Keel. Continuous fore and aft plating resting vertically on a flat plate keel.

Verticals. Short name for vertical circles of the celestial sphere.

Very's Lights. Pyrotechnic signals, fired from a pistol, showing red, white, or green stars for signalling purposes.

Very's Pistol. Pistol-type implement for igniting and holding a Very's light.

'Very Well Dice.' Until comparatively recently was an order to helmsman to keep her head in the direction she then had. Now replaced by order 'Steady', or 'Keep her so'.

Vesper. Name given to Venus when an evening star.

Vessel. Defined by Merchant Shipping Act as 'any ship or boat, or other description of vessel, used in navigation'.

Vice-Admiral. Flag officer next in rank above rear-admiral, and next below admiral.

Victualler.* Small vessel employed in keeping a fleet of warships supplied with provisions.

Victualling Bill. Customs document allowing shipment of bonded victualling stores to an outward-bound vessel.

Victualling Yard. Naval storehouse that supplies provisions and other paymasters' stores to ships of Royal Navy.

Vigia. Uncharted navigational danger that has been reported but has not been verified by survey.

Viol. Voyal.

Viol Block. Block having a cut-away part in shell so that a rope can be put over sheave. Similar to a snatch block but not having the hinged keeper.

Virazon. Spanish name for a sea breeze.

Virgo. Constellation situated between R.A. 11 h 45 m and 14 h 10m, and Dec. 11° S and 12° N, approx. Contains bright star Spica, α Virginis. Also, sixth sign of Zodiac, extending from 150° to 180° celestial longitude. Sun is in this sign from August 23 to September 22 (about).

Vise. Endorsement on a document as evidence that it has been sighted, examined, and found correct by a proper authority.

Visitation and Search. The right of warships of a belligerent power to stop shipping, on the high seas or territorial waters of an enemy, for the purpose of searching them for contraband. No claim for loss or expense incurred by the searched ship can be made against the belligerent power for the reasonable exercise of this right.

Visibility. Term used to express the clearness of the atmosphere and the maximum range at which objects and lights can be clearly sighted. Thirty-one miles is 'excellent visibility'.

Visibility. Of a light, given on charts, is the distance at which it can be seen on a dark night, with clear atmosphere, by an observer whose height if eye is 15 ft. above level of high water.

Visible Horizon. The boundary of Earth's visible surface at the position of an observer. The circle in which it appears to meet the sky is below the sensible and rational horizons by an amount depending on height of observer's eye above sea level.

Voith Schneider Propulsion. The engine shaft passes vertically through the bottom of the hull and rotates a wheel to which paddles or blades are attached at right angles to the wheel. The attitude of the paddles, controlled from the bridge, can be changed to direct their thrust and the vessel is highly manoeuvrable.

Voltmeter. Instrument for measuring and indicating the voltage, or electro-motive force, of an electrical current.

Volume of Displacement. Displacement of a vessel when expressed in cubic measurement.

Voluntary Stranding. Intentional and deliberate stranding of a vessel for the greater safety of ship and contents.

Votive Ship. Model ship placed in a church or chapel as a thanksgiving for some danger escaped or as the fulfilment of a vow.

Voyage. In general, a journey by sea from one place to another, or to other places. In certain cases the voyage is considered as beginning when vessel arrives at her loading port, and ending when she has been moored in good safety at her discharging port for 24 hours.

Voyage Policy. Contract of marine insurance covering a voyage from one port to another, or others.

Voyal.* Endless rope that was led round a capstan and through leading blocks to allow cable to be hauled by lashing the cable to the rope. Commonly used for hauling cable to locker when locker was some distance from capstan.

V-Shaped Depression. Depression in which the isobars form a series of parallel Vs with line of low pressure passing through the angles. Low pressure area is in direction of open ends of Vs.

V-Shaped Trough. V-shaped depression.

V-Stern. A stern that has a more or less vertical, triangular transom plate.

Vulgar Establishment of Port. Interval between time of Moon's transit at a place, at Full or Change, and the occurrence of the following high water at the place.

W

Waft. To convoy or escort, a vessel (16th century), 2 Weft.

Wager Policy. Policy of marine insurance issued to an insurer who has not declared his interest in matter insured. If he has no interest, policy is void in law. Is usually honest, and is honoured by the insurers unless suspicious features are evident.

Waggoner. Name formerly given to Ursa Major, Auriga, or Bootes.

Waggoner.* Chart atlas of 17th century. Corrupted form of Wagenhaer, a Dutch cartographer.

Wails.* Wales.

Waist. Upper deck between forecastle and poop, or quarter deck. In sailing ships might be between fore ends of fore and main hatches, or between fore and main masts.

Waist Anchor. Spare bower anchor stowed at fore end of waist.

Waist Block. Sheave in midship bulwarks of a sailing vessel.

Waist Cloth. Canvas cloth covering hammock nettings in waist of a warship.

Waister.* Inexperienced or partially incapacitated seaman who was given duties in the waist of a warship, instead of working aloft.

Waist Pipe. Strengthened aperture in midship bulwarks, through which mooring hawsers are led.

Waiver Clause. Inserted in a policy of marine insurance to safeguard insured and insurers when vessel appears to be a constructive total loss. It allows either party to take steps to recover, save, or preserve the property in peril without prejudicing any right regarding abandonment.

Wake. The water immediately astern of a moving vessel. It is disturbed by vessel's motion through it and by the subsequent filling up of the cavity made.

Wake Current. That stream of water that flows to fill in the cavity left by a vessel moving through water.

Wale Knot. Wall knot.

Wales. The strongest strakes in hull of a wooden vessel.

'Walk Away.' Order to haul on a rope by taking it in hand and walking.

'Walk Back.' Order to keep a fall in hand but walk back so that the purchase will overhaul by virtue of its load.

Wallings. The two large mesh nets of a trammel.

Wall Knot. Made in end of a rope by unlaying strands, and passing each strand up and through bight of next strand, working in direction of lay of rope.

Wall-Sided. Said of a vessel having perpendicular sides.

Walt, Walty. Crank, cranky.

Walrus. Carnivorous sea mammal, about 10 to 12 ft. long, found in arctic regions. Name means 'whale horse'.

Wane. Decrease of Moon's illuminated area, as viewed from Earth.

Waning. Said of Moon when she is in her third and fourth quarters, and her illuminated area is decreasing. Also applied to inferior planets when phasing.

Wapp.* Small sheave, or thimble, in end of a pendant for use as a fair leader.

Ward Robe. Space in olden ships for stowage of valuables taken out of enemy vessels. Being empty when leaving home ports, it was used as a mess room for officers of lieutenant's rank—for whom no mess was then provided.

Ward Room. General mess room and meeting place, in H.M. ships, for officers of lieutenant's rank and above, but excluding flag officers and commanding officer.

Ward Rope.* Early 17th-century spelling of 'ward robe'.

Warkamoowee. Cingalese canoe with outriggers and sail. Manned by about five men.

Warm Front. A indeterminate line on which a mass of warm air meets and rises over a mass of colder air. Its approach is usually accompanied by rain.

'Warming the Bell.' Striking 'eight bells' a little before time at the end of a watch.

Warm Sector. Mass of comparatively warm air between colder air masses.

Warp. The longitudinal threads in canvas and other textiles. 2. Hawser used when warping. Originally, was a rope smaller than a cable. 3. The line by which a boat rides to a sea anchor. 4. Mooring ropes.

Warpage. The act of warping. 2. A charge made for warping a vessel in harbour.

Warped Strop.* Selvagee strop.

Warping. Moving a vessel by running out a hawser to a fixed point, securing the end at that point, and then heaving on the rope.

Warping Chock. Chock on side of dock, used when warping vessels.

Warping Hook. Brace used for twisting a yarn when ropemaking.

Warranted Free Of. Firm statement and guarantee that an insurer is not liable for losses in connection with risks specified. 2. Firm statement and guarantee that a specified substance or article is not adulterated or contaminated with, or by, a specified factor.

Warrant Officer. Naval officer whose authority derived from a warrant issued either by or on behalf of the Lord High Admiral of Great Britain and Ireland. Rank was junior to commissioned officer, but senior to all subordinate officers. This rank is now obsolete in Royal Navy.

Warrant Shipwright. Warrant officer of Royal Navy who was responsible for control of ship's carpenters and other duties connected with the efficiency of ship's structure. Now 'Commissioned Shipwright'.

Warranty. Emphasised statement and undertaking that certain conditions exist or shall exist; or that certain things have been done or shall be done. The warranty may be specifically stated, or it may be implied by some act or statement.

Warranty of Seaworthiness. One of the 'Implied warranties' in marine insurance. The mere fact of applying for an insurance policy implies a warranty, by the applicant, that the ship is seaworthy in all respects.

Warwick Screw. Rigging screw with sides of shroud cut away to allow the placing of locking blocks on square ends of screws when set up; thus preventing any slacking back.

Wash. Broken water at bow of a vessel making way. 2. Disturbed water made by a propeller or paddle wheel. 3. Blade of an oar.

Wash Board. Wash strake.

Washing Down. Said of a vessel when she is shipping water on deck and it is running off through scuppers and freeing ports.

Washington Conferences. International marine conferences held in Washington, U.S.A., between October and December, 1889. Largely concerned with regulations for preventing collision at sea.

Wash Port. Aperture, in the bulwarks of a vessel, that allows water on deck to flow outboard.

Wash Strake. Upper strake of a boat's side planking. 2. Special lengths of wood fitted longitudinally above gunwale of a boat to give more freeboard when under sail.

Watch. Period of time, normally four hours, into which an nautical day is divided. The period between 16 hrs. and 20 hrs.—4 p.m. to 8 p.m.—is divided into two 'dog' (docked) watches, so that similar watches are not kept on consecutive days. 2. Group into which crew is divided for duty; port or starboard watch if into two watches. To keep, or stand, a watch is to be on duty for a watch.

Watch and Watch. Keeping alternate watches throughout.

Watch Bell. Bell used for striking the half hours of each watch.

Watch Bill. Nominal list of men in a watch, together with their special duties and other relevant particulars.

Watch Buoy. Buoy moored in vicinity of a light-vessel to mark her position, and to give warning if she should drag her moorings.

Watching. Said of a mark buoy when it is fully floating.

Watch Tackle. Small tackle consisting of one single block, one double block, and a rather short fall. Used for general purposes on deck. Formerly used for getting a small but strong pull on running rigging. Also called 'Handy Billy'.

'Watch, There, Watch.' Call made when using a deep-sea lead and line. Is called when the last bights of line are going out of one man's hand, and warns next man that his bights will run out.

Water. To take in water for drinking or boiler purposes. To pump fresh water into a ship.

Water Anchor. Sea anchor. Drogue.

Water Bailiff. Name sometimes given to the Customs Officer of a port.

Water Ballast. Water carried by an unloaded vessel to increase her stability and give greater submersion to her propeller. Usually carried in double bottom, deep, and peak tanks.

Waterborne. Floating. 2. Carried by water.

Water Breaker. Small cask used for carrying drinking water in a boat.

Water Laid. Said of rope laid up left-handed. Sometimes applied to cable-laid rope.

Waterline. That line in which the surface of the water meets the ship's side at a specific draught. 2. Line painted round ship's side at approximate position of her load waterline.

Waterlogged. State of a vessel that has taken in so much water that she floats by the buoyancy of her fabric and her contents.

Waterplane. That horizontal section of a ship's hull which represents her shape in the water in that particular horizontal plane.

Water Sail.* Fine weather sail that was formerly set beneath a lower studdingsail in fine weather.

Water Splice. Cut splice in which the two parts between the splices are twined round each other before tucking the second splice.

Waterspout. A whirling up-current of warm, moist air, the outside of which is cooled and cloudlike. Height may be anything between 20 and some thousand of feet, width being from 20 to 500 ft. Caused by instability in atmosphere. Occurs in temperate zone, but mostly in tropical zones. They last for 10 to 30 minutes. When they break they may throw down heavy masses of water and, perhaps, ice. Gunfire does not affect them.

Watertight. Impervious to water.

Watertight Doors. Steel door so fitted and strengthened that it will prevent water passing when door is sealed.

Watertight Hatch. Hatch so fitted and strengthened that it will prevent water passing when hatch is closed and secured.

Watertight Sub-division. The dividing of a vessel into small compartments fitted with watertight doors and hatches so that, in case of damage, the inflow of water will be arrested and localised.

Water-tube Boiler. One in which the water is confined to numerous small tubes that pass through the heat from the furnaces. Its great advantage lies in these tubes being able to support pressures far above those possible in Scotch and other cylindrical boilers. A further advantage is that considerable less weight of water is necessary. They require very careful tending. There are numerous types, some working at extremely high pressures.

Waterways. Channels along ship's sides on deck, into which water runs and is carried to scuppers.

Watt. Electrical unit of power, equivalent to one ampere at one volt. 746 watts per minute is equivalent to one horsepower.

Wave. A perpendicular oscillation in the surface of a liquid. An undulation, of surface of a liquid, that appears to be progressive but, actually, is not.

Wave Guide. A copper tube of rectangular section which conveys signals between a radar transmitter-receiver and scanner.

N

Wave Length. Distance between successive crests, or troughs, of radiant energy. Usually defined as distance travelled by the energy in one cycle. Violet light ray has a wave length of one 70,000th of an inch; red light ray is twice this length.

Waveson. Goods floating on surface of sea after a wreck.

Wave Velocity. *See* 'Velocity of wave'.

Waxing. Said of Moon when she is in her first and second quarters and her illuminated area is increasing. Sometimes said of inferior planets.

Way. Vessel's inertia of motion through the water.

'Way Aloft.' An order to go aloft on a mast. Contraction of 'Away aloft'.

Way Bill. Document signed in triplicate, accompanying mails carried in a ship. Gives details of mails and number of bags and sealed packets. At destination, one receipted way bill is returned to sending office, one is given to receiving office, third is retained in ship. 2. Document accompanying goods carried by a common carrier.

'Way Enough.' Order given to a boat's crew when going alongside under oars. Denotes that boat has sufficient way, and that oars are to be placed inside the boat.

Ways. Baulks or skids along which vessels are launched after building.

'Way Wiser.'* Alternative name for the 'Nautical Dromometer'.

Wearing. Going from one tack to the other, under sail, by putting ship's stern through the wind. 2. 'Wearing colours' is flying the ship's national ensign. Wearing a flag is flying it.

Weather. Phenomena of the atmosphere that affect mankind. These include wind, visibility, temperature, air pressure, precipitations, and electrical discharges. 2. To pass to windward of a point or object. 3. Windward, or nearer to the wind.

Weather Anchor. Anchor on the weather bow of a ship coming to anchor. 2. Anchor that lies to windward of any other anchor.

Weather Board. Windward side of a vessel.

Weather Bound. Said of a vessel unable to sail, or confined to a port of anchorage, by stress of weather.

Weather Bow. That bow, of a vessel, that is on her windward side.

Weather Cloth. Canvas screen temporarily placed for protection of helmsman, or officer of watch, against wind and spray. 2. Formerly, canvas covering for an exposed hammock netting.

Weather Deck. Deck that is open to weather and sea.

Weather Eye Open. To keep a good look out to windward.

Weather Gage, Gauge. The advantage of position due to being to windward of a vessel, or hazard.

Weather Glass. Popular name for a barometer in which the various barometric pressures are accompanied by words indicating the probable weather.

Weather Gleam. Unusual gleam in horizon dead to windward. Usually foretells an abatement in wind force.

Weather Helm. Amount the tiller is moved to windward to keep a vessel under sail on her course, and to prevent her from coming to the wind.

Weathering. Passing to windward.

Weather Lurch. A rather quick roll to windward.

Weatherly. Said of a sailing vessel that points well up to the wind and makes less than average leeway. Said of a steam vessel that is comfortable in a seaway.

Weather Map. Map of chart that shows weather conditions at a certain position, or in a certain area. It may give the conditions prevailing, or the conditions to be expected. It may be based on present information, or on past records.

Weather Notation. System of letters and figures and symbols for recording or reporting weather conditions.

Weather Quarter. That quarter of a vessel, or the sea area in its arc, that is on the windward side of the vessel.

Weather Roll. A roll to windward by a vessel.

Weather Ropes. Old name for tarred ropes.

Weather Shore. A shore that is to windward of a vessel.

Weather Side. That side which is toward the direction from which wind is blowing.

Weather Tide. A tidal current that sets to windward.

Weather Working Days. Those working days in which the loading or unloading of cargo is not held up by weather conditions.

Web Frame. A specially deep transverse frame in the form of a built girder.

Wedge. V-shaped area of high barometric pressure between two depressions.

Weeding. Clearing rigging of stops, yarns, etc., that have been attached to it.

Weekly Articles. Common name for Home Trade Agreement, under which men are paid on a weekly basis.

Weekly Boats. Common name for vessels in the Home Trade, in which crew are paid on a weekly basis.

Weeping. Said of a small leak in which water flows very slowly.

Weeping Butts. Butted joints through which water seeps slowly. Sometimes applied to similar weepings at landings of plates.

Weevil. Small beetle which, with its larvae, attacks ship's biscuit and all grain.

Weft. The short thwartship thread in canvas, bunting, and other woven material. 2. Wheft.

Weigh. To lift. Now applied to anchor only: formerly applied to the lifting of a mast.

Weir's Azimuth Diagram. *See* 'Azimuth Diagram'.

Welded Knee. Beam knee made by turning down outboard end of beam and welding it to a small plate to fit ship's side in way of bend. Name is also given to a slabbed knee.

Welding. The uniting of two pieces of metal by fusion, or by pressure or hammering after softening by heat.

N*

Welin Davits. Boat davits with a toothed quadrant at lower end, this quadrant engaging in a toothed rack fitted to deck. By means of a worm shaft, engaging in a collar on davit, the davit can be moved transversely inboard and outboard.

Welin-MacLachlan Davits. Boat's davits that move outboard transversely when the boat's gripes are released; the speed being controlled by a brake. Falls are reeled on drums, which also are controlled by brakes.

Well. Partitioned space, in bottom of a vessel, into which water runs and in which are pump suctions. 2. Compartment formerly found in some fishing boats. Water was kept in it, and fish were placed in this water when caught.

Well Deck. That part of an upper deck that is bounded, at forward and after ends, by bulkheads supporting higher decks.

Well Found. Said of a vessel that is adequately fitted, stored, and furnished.

Wending. Going from one tack to the other under sail.

Wentle.* To roll over.

West. Cardinal point of compass, halfway between North and South, and opposite to East. The intersection of horizon and prime vertical in that direction in which heavenly bodies set.

West Country Whipping. Method of whipping end of rope by middling the twine, half-knotting it on either side alternately, and finishing off by reef knotting.

Westerlies. Prevailing winds between 40° and 60° latitudes North and South.

Westing. The distance, expressed in nautical miles, that a vessel makes good in a direction due west.

Weston Purchase. Differential purchase consisting of two sprocket wheels around which is a continuous chain having one of the wheels in the bight. Fixed wheel has 18 sprockets, moving wheel has 17. One turn of fixed wheel lifts lower wheel one link, thus giving a power of 35. This purchase will not walk back.

Wet. Said of a vessel that ships seas frequently.

Wet Air. Atmospheric air when cold surfaces become damp or wet although no rain is falling. Due to condensation caused by warm, saturated air replacing cold, dry air.

Wet Bulb Thermometer. Thermometer fitted with a wick from bulb to a cistern of water so that evaporation takes place at bulb, so extracting heat. This causes a lower temperature reading. Amount by which temperature is lowered depends on rate of evaporation at bulb, which, in turn, depends on moisture content of atmosphere.

Wet Dock. In contradistinction from dry dock, is a dock in which vessels are always afloat and water level is maintained by gates that are closed before fall of tide.

Wet Fog. Fog in which moisture forms rapidly and freely on exposed conducting surfaces.

Wet Spell. Name given to a period of 15 days, or more, in which the daily rainfall has been at least 0·04 inch.

Wetted Surface. The whole of the external surface of a vessel's outer plating that is in contact with the water in which she is floating.

Whack. Colloquial name for the statutory allowance of provisions and water.

Whale. Marine mammal having warm blood, lungs, and bearing its young. Is the largest animal. Length up to 80 ft. Various types are Right (or Greenland), Rorqual, Sperm, Cachalot, Cape or Southern, Humpback, Baleen.

Whaleback. Name given to a vessel having deck with excessive camber. Formerly applied to a poop having rounded side plating at its junction with the deck.

Whaleback Cloud. Common name for Strato-cumulus lenticularis cloud.

Whale Boat. Double-ended clinker-built boat formerly used in whaling. Length was usually 20–28 ft., occasionally longer.

Whale Catcher, Whale Chaser. Small ships, of steam trawler type, used for hunting whales. Fitted with harpoon gun forward. Work in conjunction with a whale factory.

Whaler. Vessel engaged in whale catching. 2. Person employed in whale catching. 3. Ship's boat of whale boat type.

Whale Factory. Large steam vessel, specially constructed and fitted in which captured whales are hauled aboard—along a special slipway at stern—and rendered into oil and meat.

Whaleman. Man engaged in the whaling industry.

Wharf. Erection in harbour, or on banks of inland waters, for the berthing of ships for loading and discharging of cargo, fitting, or refitting. 2.* Shore of the sea. Bank of a river. 3. To place on a wharf. 4. To protect by erecting a wharf.

Wharfage. Money paid for use of a wharf, or services of it. 2. The wharf accommodation, or facilities, at a port.

Wharfinger. One who owns or manages a wharf.

Wheatstone Gyroscope. Small gyroscope for demonstration purposes. Has a 4-inch wheel and attachments for suppressing freedom and for introducing precession.

Wheel. Usual name for the steering wheel by which a rudder is moved, or a steering engine actuated. In U.S.A. the name is given to a screw propeller.

Wheel Chains. Chains by which a wheel actuates a steering engine or a rudder.

Wheel House. An erection around a steering wheel for the protection of helmsman. Usually utilised for other purposes connected with the navigation of a vessel.

Wheel Ropes. Ropes by which a wheel actuates a rudder.

Wheft. Any flag that has had a stop passed around it halfway along the fly. It then has some special significance.

Whelps. Metal strips fixed vertically on barrel of capstan—or horizontally on warping end of winch—to increase grip of rope by making the turn a polygon instead of a circle.

Where Away? Enquiry addressed to a look-out man, demanding precise direction of an object he has sighted and reported.

Wherry. Small but roomy boat used for carrying goods or ferrying passengers in sheltered waters. Compare 'Norfolk Wherry'.

Whether in Berth or Not. Term used in charter party, or other document, to stipulate that lay days shall commence when ship is ready to load, or unload, irrespective of whether ship is in the appropriate berth or not.

Whip. Rope rove through a standing block for hoisting. A double whip consists of a rope rove through two single blocks with end made fast to one of them. Gives advantage of two or three, according to which block moves. 2. To pass a whipping around end of a rope.

Whipping. Twine or small stuff passed round end of a rope to prevent it unlaying. 2. Passing a whipping around a rope.

Whip Staff. Vertical handle on end of a hand-worked tiller.

Whirling Psychrometer. Wet and dry thermometers mounted in a frame hinged on a handle. Is whirled to increase evaporation at bulb of wet thermometer.

Whirlpool. Current that has a rotatory motion over a comparatively small area. Is troublesome in that it may turn ship's head against maximum rudder at maximum speed. Its suctional effect is largely mythical.

Whirlwind. Small but very intense revolving storm, the wind circulating very rapidly around a low-pressure centre-line.

Whisker Booms. Spritsail gaffs; whiskers.

Whisker Gaff. Whisker boom.

Whiskers. Spars projecting transversely from just forward of catheads and approximately horizontally. Purpose is to give adequate spread of guys of jib boom. Sometimes called 'spritsail gaffs'.

Whistle. Sound-producing instrument that is required to be fitted on any power-propelled vessel unless a siren is fitted.

Whistle Buoy. Navigational aid buoy that emits a whistling sound through mechanism actuated by wave movement.

Whistling for Wind. Based on a very old tradition that whistling at sea will cause a wind to rise.

Whistling Psalms to the Taffrail. Nautical phrase that means giving good advice that will not be taken.

White Caps. Foam on crests of waves.

White Combination Engine. Propelling engine combining a high-speed triple-expansion engine and a Parson's reaction turbine.

White Ensign. Ensign having a white ground with a red St. George's cross, and Union in inner upper canton. Is the proper ensign of Her Majesty's ships, and shore establishments under naval command, and yachts of the Royal Yacht Squadron.

White Forster Boiler. Water-tube boiler of Jarrow type, but with a larger steam drum—that allows for removal and replacement of tubes.

White Horses. Fast-running waves with white foam crests.

White Rope. Rope and cordage made of untarred hemp.

White Squadron. Former division of a fleet of warships. From 1625 to 1653 was the rear division, under a rear-admiral. After this it was the centre division under a vice-admiral. Discontinued 1864.

White Squall. Sudden squall that causes white foam, or froth, to form on surface of sea. Sometimes applied to a squall in which there is no reduction of light.

Whole Gale.* Wind having a velocity of 48 to 55 knots.

Wholesome. Said of craft that behave well in bad weather.

Widow's Men.* Fictitious names, up to 2 per cent of a crew, that were entered in ship's books of H.M. ships. Their pay and victualling allowances were credited to the 'Widows' Fund'. Commenced 1763, abolished about 1831.

Wildcat. Cable holder, or sprocket wheel, of windlass.

Wildfire.* Inflammable composition anciently used in naval warfare. Composed of pitch, sulphur, naphtha, etc.

Willesden Canvas. Treated canvas, green in colour, often used for tarpaulins.

Williamson Turn. Used to turn a vessel 180° and bring on to her original track. The wheel is put hard over until the heading has altered about 60°. The wheel is then put hard over in the opposite direction until the heading is approaching the reciprocal of the original course and the vessel is steaming into her wake.

Willis Altitude Azimuth Instrument. Small instrument for obtaining, mechanically, altitude and azimuth of a heavenly body from its declination and hour angle, and latitude of observer.

Willis Navigating Machine. Invented by E. J. Willis (U.S.A.) for the mechanical solution of navigational problems involving latitude, altitude, declination, hour angle. Weight 47 lb.

Williwaws. Sudden and violent squalls met with in Straits of Magellan.

Willy Willy. Local name for a severe cyclone off coast of north-western Australia, and in Arafura Sea.

Winch. Machine consisting of a horizontal barrel revolving on an axis and operated by hand or power. Geared to give mechanical advantage. Used for lifting and lowering cargo, and for other purposes that require more power than can be supplied by crew.

Wind. Air that is perceptibly in motion. *See* Beaufort Scale.

Wind Bound. Confined to a port or anchorage by adversity of wind.

Wind Chute. Metal scoop that fits in a port or scuttle and projects outboard, thus deflecting air into a compartment when ship or air is moving.

Wind Dog. An incomplete rainbow, or part of a rainbow. Some times seen in English Channel, where it is supposed to indicate approach of a storm.

Wind Force. Velocity of wind as indicated by Beaufort Scale, in which 1 is a light air, and 12 is a hurricane; intermediate velocities having appropriate intermediate numbers.

Wind Gall. Luminous edge of a cloud to windward, Supposed to indicate approach of a storm.

Winding. Turning a vessel end for end between buoys, or alongside a wharf or pier.

Winding Tackle. Large purchase, comprising three-fold block aloft and double block in lower end. Secured at lower masthead and used for lifting heavy weights.

Windjammer. Colloquial name for a sailing vessel.

Windlass. Machine working on a horizontal axis and used for working cable. Usually has two sprocket wheels for holding cables, and warping drums at extremities of shaft. Actuated by steam or electricity. Gearing is provided so that one or both sprocket wheels can be meshed with engine shaft. Brakes are provided for holding cable holders when disconnected from shaft. Old types were hand-worked.

Windlass Bitts. Vertical timbers in which hand-worked windlasses were formerly mounted.

Wind Lipper. Slight disturbance of sea surface by a wind that has just arisen.

Windmill. Formerly carried by Scandinavian sailing vessels for actuating bilge pumps.

Wind Rode. Said of a vessel at anchor when the directions of her head and cable are to windward.

Wind Rose. Intersecting lines, on a weather chart, showing directions, frequencies, and strengths of wind in that locality over a certain time.

Wind Sail. Large tube of canvas with a shaped mouth that can be trimmed to the wind by lines. Used for conveying air to spaces below upper deck.

Wind Scoop. Wind chute.

Wind Taut. Said of an anchored vessel when straining at her cable and heeled by force of wind.

Wind Wale. Sponson rim of paddle steamer; connecting paddle beam to sides of vessel.

Wind Vane. Any streamer or device used for indicating direction of wind.

Windward. Towards the wind. Nearer to the wind. The direction from which the wind blows.

Windward Sailing. Sailing against wind on alternate tacks, but sailing a longer leg on that tack which is in the approximate direction of the position it is desired to reach.

Wing. That part of a hold, or 'tween deck, that lies along the side. 2. To stow cargo in wing of hold. 3.* Occasionally applied to the sponson of a paddle steamer.

Wing and Wing. Said of a fore and aft rigged vessel when she is running with sails out on both sides.

Winger.* Small water cask stowed in wings of holds in old sailing ships.

Wing Boards. Sloping boards permanently fitted in self-trimming colliers. They are inclined at angle of repose of coal, and extend to ship's side from underside of deck.

Winging Out. Putting cargo in wing of a hold, or towards ship's side.

Wing Transom. Thwartship timber in lower part of stern of old wooden ships. In warships, it formed sill of gun-room windows.

Winter Load Line. Statutory load line mark indicating depth to which vessel may be loaded in seasonal winter.

Winter Solstice. That point of time at which Sun obtains his maximum declination and minimum noon altitude, and appears to stand still in declination for an appreciable time. Occurs about December 21 in northern latitudes, June 21 in southern latitudes. By convention, the former is generally accepted.

Wireless Bearing. Radio bearing.

Wireless Telegraphy Acts. 1919–27–32. Lay down rules for the equipment, fitting, and use of radio equipment in sea-going ships.

Wireless Time Signals. Radio time signals.

Wire Rope. Rope made of wires, those used in ships being of iron or steel. Three main types used are flexible steel wires, steel rigging wires, and iron rigging wires.

Wire Rope Gauge. Small instrument, with adjustable jaws, used for measuring diameter of a rope—but graduated to indicate the corresponding circumference.

Wire Rope Grip. Bull-dog grip.

Wiring.* The rising in a boat. The fore and aft internal strip on which the thwarts rest.

Wiring Clamp. Doubling piece of wood clamped to rising of a boat to take fastening of a thwart.

Wishbone Gaff or Boom. A double gaff or boom which allows the sail to take an aeroform shape.

Withe. Ring, or boom iron, through which a secondary spar is held to a mast or principal boom.

Without Prejudice. Words used when a statement, comment, or action is not to be taken as implying agreement or disagreement, or affecting in any way a matter in dispute, or under consideration.

Wooden Walls. Name given to warships, in the days of wooden ships, in recognition of the fact that they were the outer defence of the Realm.

Woolaston Current Meter. Stationary instrument lowered into the water for measuring and indicating rate and direction of current. Has a timekeeping unit so that variations in rate and direction are shown graphically against a time scale. Measures rates up to 6 knots.

Woold/ing. Bind/ing rope tautly around a spar, particularly after fishing it.

Woolder. Strong wooden rod used for heaving rope taut when woolding.

Work. Said of parts of a ship that move through action of wind or sea. 2. To work a sight is to reduce its data to a desired value. 3. Work to windward is to ply to windward.

Work a Traverse. To reduce the various courses and distances sailed to the resultant changes in latitude and longitude.

Working Days. Those days on which it is customary to work in the given port, the length of the day being the customary number of hours. A 'working day of 24 hours' would be three working days in a port at which it was customary to work eight hours a day.

Working Foresail. Fore and aft foresail whose sheet rides on a horse.

Working Gear. Gear or clothing in general use. Sails used when working to windward.

Working Strain. Maximum stress a rope, member, or fitting will bear.

Working Up. Increasing in speed, force, or efficiency.

Worm. To put yarn, or small stuff, in cantlines of a rope that is to be parcelled and served. 2. Spiral thread, on a shaft, that engages in appropriately cut teeth on a wheel or drum. Has a large ratio of purchase and rarely 'walks back'.

Wrack. Thin, ragged, fast-moving clouds. 2. Seaweed thrown ashore by sea. 3. To destroy by wave action. 4. Old form of 'wreck'.

Wreck. Vessel so damaged as to be unseaworthy and incapable of being navigated. Legally, includes 'jetsam, flotsam, lagan, and derelict found in or on shores of sea or tidal water'.

Wreckage. Fragments of a wrecked vessel. 2. The remains of a wrecked vessel. 3. The act of wrecking. 4. Goods washed ashore from a wrecked vessel.

Wreck Buoy. Buoy marking the position of a wrecked ship.

Wreck Commission. Court that investigates the causes and circumstances of a wreck. First sat in 1876.

Wrecker. One who deliberately causes a vessel to be wrecked. 2. One who plunders a wrecked vessel. 3. One whose duty is to remove cargo from a wrecked vessel on behalf of owners.

Wriggle. Rigol.

Wring. To strain and deform by excessive stress.

Wring Bolt. Bolt used, in wooden ship building, to bend a strake into position and hold it so until fastened.

Wring Staff. Wooden handspike used for setting up wring bolts.

Wrinkle. Small protruding bight in skin of a furled sail. 2. Short and pithy piece of helpful advice.

Wrought Mat. Paunch mat.

Wrung. Said of a mast or spar that has been strained or twisted.

'Wry-necked Ned.' Nickname given to Admiral Boscawen after a wound in neck caused him to carry his head on one side.

W/T. Radio telegraph.

W.T. Water-tight.

Wythe. Alternative form of 'withe'.

X

Xebec. Small three-masted, lateen-rigged trading vessel of Mediterranean Sea and Iberian coast. Differs from a felucca by having a square sail for running.

Xiphias. The common swordfish of the Mediterranean. Has no central fin.

SHIPPING AND BUSINESS ABBREVIATIONS

a.a.	Always afloat.	c.i.f.c.i.	Cost, insurance, freight, commission and interest.
a.a.r.	Against all risks.	c.i.f.L.t.	Cost, insurance and freight, London terms.
A. & C.P.	Anchors and chains proved.	Ck.	Cask.
abt.	About.	c/l.	Craft loss.
a/c	Account. Altered course.	Cld.	Cleared.
Acc.	Accepted; acceptance.	C/N.	Cover note. Credit note. Consignment note.
A.C.	Account current.	C/O.	Case oil. Certificate of Origin. Cash order.
A/d	After date.	C.O.D.	Cash on delivery.
Add.	Addressed.	Cont.	Continent of Europe.
Ad. val.	Ad valorem.	Cont.(A.H.)	Continent of Europe, Antwerp–Hamburg range.
A.F.	Advanced freight.		
Agt.	Agent. Against.	Cont. (B.H.)	Continent of Europe, Bordeaux–Hamburg range.
A.H.	Anno Hegirae. (Epoch of Mohammedan calendar.)		
		Cont. (H.H.)	Continent of Europe, Havre–Hamburg range.
a.h.	After hatch.		
a.m.	ante meridiem.	C/P.	Charter Party. Custom of Port (Grain trade).
A.M.C.	Armed Merchant Cruiser.	C.P.D.	Charterers pay dues.
A/or	And/or.	C.R.	Current rate. Carriers' risk.
A/P.	Additional premium.		
A.R.	All risks.	C.S.	Cotton seed. Colliery screened (coal).
A/S.	After sight. Alongside.		
A.T.	American Terms (grain).	C.T.	Californian terms (grain trade).
Av.	Average.	C.T.C.	Corn Trade Clauses.
A.V.	Ad valorem.	c.t.l.o.	Constructive total loss only.
B.	Bale. Bag.	C.W.	Commercial weight.
b.	Blue sky.	d.	Drizzling rain.
B. & D.1.	Births & Deaths, Form 1.	D/A.	Discharge afloat. Days after acceptance. Documents against acceptance. Deposit account.
B.A.	Buenos Aires.		
B.B.	Bill book. Below bridges.		
B.C.	British Corporation. Bristol Channel.	D.B.	Double bottom/s/ed. Deals and battens. Donkey boiler.
B/L.	Bill of Lading.		
B.O.	Buyers' Option. Branch Office.	D.B.B.	Deals, battens and boards.
B.P.B.	Bank Post Bill.	D.B.S.	Distressed British seaman.
Brl.	Barrel.		
B.S.	British Survey. Balance Sheet.	D/C.	Deviation Clause.
		D.D.	Damage done.
B/S	Bill of Sale. Bill of Store.	D/D	Days after date. Demand draft. Delivered at docks.
B/s	Bags. Bales.		
Bs/L.	Bills of Lading.	d.d.	Delivered.
B/St.	Bill of Sight.	dd/s	Delivered sound (grain).
B.S.T.	British Summer Time.	d.f.	Dead freight.
b.t.	Berth Terms.	d.l.o.	Dispatch loading only.
B.T.U.	Board of Trade Unit.	D/N.	Debit note.
		D/O.	Delivery order.
c.	Detached clouds.	D.O.T.	Department of Overseas Trade.
C/-	Case.		
c.a.	Current account.	D/P.	Documents against payment.
C. & D.	Collected and delivered.		
C.B. & H.	Continent, Bordeaux to Hamburg.	D/R.	Deposit receipt.
		D/S.	Days after sight.
C.C.	Civil commotions. Continuation Clause.	D.T.	Deep tank.
		D.T.I.	Department of Trade and Industry.
C/D.	Commercial dock. Consular declaration.		
		D.W., d.w.	Deadweight. Dock warrant.
c. & f.	Cost and freight.		
c.f.	Carried forward. Cubic feet.	dwc.	Deadweight capacity.
		E.C.C.P.	East coast (Great Britain) coal port.
c.f.i.	Cost, freight and insurance.		
C.F.	Copper fastened.	E.C.G.B.	East coast of Great Britain.
C.f.o.	Coast for orders. Channel for orders.		
		E.C.I.	East coast of Ireland.
C.G.A.	Cargo's proportion of General Average.	E.C.U.K.	East coast of United Kingdom.
C.H. & H.	Continent between Havre and Hamburg.		
c. & i.	Cost and insurance.		
C.I.	Consular Invoice.		
C.I.E.	Captain's imperfect entry.		
c.i.f.	Cost, insurance and freight.		
c.i.f. & e.	Cost, insurance, freight and exchange.		

E. & O.E.	Errors and omissions excepted.		
E.D.	Existence doubtful (chart).		
E.E.	Errors excepted.		
e.g.	Ejusdem generis (of the same kind).		
e.o.h.p.	Except otherwise herein provided.		
E.P.	Estimated position.		
Eq. T.	Equation of time.		
est.	Estimated.		
E.T.A.	Estimated time of arrival.		
Ex.	Excluding. Out of. Without. Examined. Exchange. Executed.		
Exd.	Examined.		
f.	Fog.		
f.a.	Free alongside.		
f.a.a.	Free of all average.		
f.a.q.	Fair average quantity.		
f.a.s.	Free alongside ship. Firsts and seconds (American lumber trade).		
F.B.I.	Federation of British Industries.		
f.c. & s.	Free of capture and seizure.		
f.c.s.r.c.c.	Free of capture, seizure, riots and civil commotions.		
F.D.	Forced draught.		
f.d.	Free discharge. Free delivery. Free dispatch. Free docks.		
F. & D.	Freight and demurrage.		
f.f.a.	Free from alongside. Free foreign agency.		
F.G.A.	Foreign General Average.		
f.h.	Fore hatch.		
f.i.a.	Full interest admitted.		
f.i.b.	Free into barge. Free into bunkers.		
f.i.o.	Free in and out.		
f.i.t.	Free of income tax.		
f.i.w.	Free into wagon.		
F.L.N.	Following landing numbers.		
f.o.	For orders. Full out terms (grain). Firm offer.		
f.o.b.	Free on board.		
f.o.c.	Free of charge. Free on car.		
f.o.d.	Free of damage.		
f.o.q.	Free on quay.		
f.o.r.	Free on rail.		
f.o.r.t.	Full out rye terms.		
f.o.s.	Free on steamer.		
f.o.t.	Free on truck.		
f.o.w.	First open water. Free on wagon.		
F.P.	Floating policy.		
F.P.A.	Free of Particular Average.		
F.P.T.	Fore peak tank.		
F/R	Freight release.		
f.r. & c.c.	Free of riots and civil commotions.		
f.r.o.	Fire risk on freight.		
Frt.	Freight.		
f.t.	Full terms.		
F.T.W.	Free Trade Wharf.		
fwd.	Forward.		
f.w.d.	Fresh water damage.		
F.X.	Forecastle.		

SHIPPING AND BUSINESS ABBREVIATIONS

G/A. General Average.
G/A con. General Average contribution.
G/A dep. General Average deposit.
G.C.T. Greenwich Civil Time.
G.F. Government Form (charter).
g.f.a. Good fair average.
G.I., g.i. Galvanized iron.
G.M.A.T. Greenwich Mean Astronomical Time.
g.m.b. Good merchantable brand.
g.m.q. Good merchantable quality.
G.M.T. Greenwich Mean Time.
g.o.b. Good ordinary brand.
gr. Grain. Gross.
g.s.m. Good, sound and merchantable.
guar. Guaranteed.
G.V. Grande Vitesse (express train).

H.A. or D. Havre, Antwerp or Dunkirk.
H.C. Held covered.
H.H. Havre to Hamburg range.
hhd. Hogshead.
H.L., h.l. Hawser-laid.
H.M.S. Her Majesty's ship.
H.P. Horse Power. High Pressure. Horizontal Parallax.
H.P.N. Horse Power, nominal.
H.T. Home trade. Half-time survey.
H.W. High water.
H.W.F.&C. High Water at Full and Change of Moon.
H.W.M. High water mark.
H.W.O.S.T. High water ordinary spring tides.

I.A.L.A. International Assoc. of Lighthouse Authorities.
I.B. In bond. Invoice Book.
I.C. & C. Invoice cost and charges.
I.H.B. International Hydrographical Bureau.
I.H.P. Indicated Horse Power.
I.M.C.O. Inter-governmental Maritime Consultative Organization.
Ince Insurance.
I.R. Inland Revenue.
i.v. Invoice value. Increased value.

J/A. Joint account.
j. & w.o. Jettison and washing overboard.

K.D. Knocked down.
kg. kilogram/s.
K.I.D. Key industry duty.

l. Lightning.
L/A. Lloyd's agent. Landing Account. Letter of Authority.
L.A.T. Linseed Association Terms.
Lat., lat. Latitude.
L.C. London clause. Label clause. Landing craft.
LASH Lighter-aboard-ship.
L/C. Letter of Credit.

L.C.T.A. London Corn Trade Association.
ldg. Loading.
Ldg.&Dely. Loading and Delivery.
lds. Loads.
L.H.A.R. London, Hull, Rotterdam or Antwerp.
Lkg.&bkg. Leakage and breakage.
Ll.&Cos. Lloyd's and Companies.
L.L.T. London Landed terms.
L.M.C. Lloyd's Machinery Certificate.
l.m.c. Low middling clause (cotton).
L.O.A. Length over all.
L.Q.T. Liverpool Quay Terms.
L.R.M.C. Lloyd's Refrigerating Machinery Certificate.
L.S. Lump sum. Locus sigilli=Place of the seal.
L.V. Lightvessel.
L.W. Low water.
L.W.O.S.T. Low water ordinary spring tides.

M Mile/s (nautical)
m metre/s
M.B. Motor boat.
M.C. Machinery Certificate. Metalling Clause.
M.C.I. Malleable cast iron.
M.D. Memorandum of deposit. Months after date.
M/d. Months after date.
M.D.H.B. Mersey Docks & Harbour Board.
M.H., m.h. Main hatch.
M.H.H.W. Mean higher high water.
M.H.W.I. Mean High Water interval.
M.H.W.N. Mean High Water Neaps.
M.H.W.S. Mean High Water Springs.
M.L. Mean level. Motor launch.
M.L.L.W. Mean lower low water.
M.L.W.I. Mean low water interval.
M.M. Mercantile Marine.
m.m. Made merchantable.
M.M.A. Merchandise Marks Act.
L.W.L. Length of waterline.
M.M.S.A. Mercantile Marine Service Association.
M.N. Merchant Navy.
M.N.I. Member of the Nautical Institute.
M.N.A.O.A. Merchant Navy and Airline Officers Association.
M.N.R. Mean neap rise.
M.O.T. Ministry of Transport.
M.R. Mate's receipt.
M.R.I.N. Member of the Royal Institute of Navigation.
M.R.I.N.A. Member of the Royal Institute of Naval Architects.
M.S. Motor ship. Machinery survey. Merchant shipping. Months after sight.
M.S.A. Merchant Shipping Act.
M.S.L. Mean sea level.
M.S.R. Mean spring rise (tide).
M.T. Mean time. Empty.
M.T.B. Motor torpedo boat.
M.T.L. Mean tide level.
M.V. Motor vessel.

N/a. No advice. No account.
n.a.a. Not always afloat.
N/C. New charter.
N.C.V. No commercial value.
n.e. Not excluding.
n.e.p./s. Not elsewhere provided/stated.
N/f. No funds.
N.H.P. Nominal Horse Power.
N/m. No mark/s.
nom. std. Nominal standard.
n.o.p. Not otherwise provided.
N.P.L. National Physical Laboratory.
n.r. No risk. Nett register (tonnage).
n.r.a.d. No risk after discharge.
n/s. Not sufficient.
n.s.p.f. Not specially provided for.
N/t. New terms.

o.a. Over all.
O/C. Open charter. Old charter. Open cover. Old crop.
O/c Overcharge.
O/d On demand.
O/o. Order of.
O.P. Open policy.
O.R. Owner's risk.
O/t Old terms. On truck.

P.A. Particular Average. Power of Attorney.
P. & I. Protection and indemnity.
P/C. Petty cash. Price current. Per cent.
Pkge. Package.
P/L. Partial loss. Position Line.
P. & L. Profit and loss.
pm. Premium.
P.N. P/N. Promissory Note.
P.O.D. Pay on Delivery.
p.p. Picked ports. Per pro (on behalf of).
P.P.I., p.p.i. Policy proof of interest.
ppt. Prompt (loading).
p.t. Private terms.
Ptg. Std. Petrograd standard (timber).
P.V. Petite vitesse (Slow train).

R.A.T. Rapeseed Assoc. terms.
R. & C.C. Riots and civil commotions and strikes.
R.C.C. Royal Cruising Club.
R.C.C. & S. Riots, civil commotions and strikes.
r.d. Running days.
R.D. Reserve Decoration.
R.D.C. Running Down Clause.
R.I. Re-insurance.
R.N. Royal Navy.
R.N.L.I. Royal National Life-boat Institution.
R.N.R. Royal Naval Reserve.
R.N.V.R. Royal Naval Volunteer Reserve.
r.o.b. Remaining on board.
R.O.R.C. Royal Ocean Racing Club.
Rotn. No. Rotation number.
R/p. Return of post for orders.
R.P. Return premium.
R.S. Revised Statutes (U.S.A.).
R.T. Rye terms.

SHIPPING AND BUSINESS ABBREVIATIONS

R.T.Y.C.	Royal Thames Yacht Club.	s.p.d.	Steamer pays dues.	U.S.S.	United States ship.
R.Y.A.	Royal Yachting Assoc.	S.R. & C.C.	Strikes, riots and civil commotions.		
R.T.	Radio Telephone.	S.S., s.s.	Steamship.	V.C.	Valuation Clause.
R.C.Y.C.	Royal Clyde Yacht Club.	Std.	Standard (of timber).	v.o.p.	Valuation as in original policy.
R.F.A.	Royal Fleet Auxiliary.	Str.	Steamer.		
R.Y.S.	Royal Yacht Squadron.	S. to S.	Station to station.	V.R.D.	Volunteer Reserve Decoration.
		S.V.	Sailing vessel.		
s.	Snow.	S.W.L.	Safe working load.		
s/a.	Safe arrival.				
S. & F.A.	Shipping and Forwarding Agents.	T. & G.	Tongued and grooved.	W.A.	With average.
		T/C.	Until countermanded.	W. & E.I.	Wages and Effects Form I.
S. & H. exct.	Sundays and holidays excepted.	T.G.B.	Tongued, grooved and beaded.	W.B.	Way Bill.
s.a.n.r.	Subject to approval no risk.	T/L.	Total loss.	w.b.s.	Without benefit of salvage.
		T.L.O.	Total loss only.		
S.C.	Salvaged Charges.	T.P.I.	Tons per inch (immersion).	w/d.	Warranted.
S.D.	Sea Damaged.			w.g.	Weight guaranteed.
S.d.	Short delivery.			W/M.	Weight and/or measurement.
S.G.	Salutis gratia = Given for safety. (Lloyd's policy.)	T.Q.	Tale quale = Having such a quantity.		
		T.R.	Tons registered.	w.o.b.	Washed overboard.
S.H.P.	Shaft horse power.			w.o.l.	Wharf owners' liability.
Sk.	Sack.	u.	Ugly and threatening weather.	w/p	Without prejudice. Weather permitting.
s.l.	Salvage loss.	U.D.	Upper deck.	W.P.A.	With Particular Average.
S.L. & C.	Shipper's load and count.	U.K.f.o.	United Kingdom for orders.	w.r.o.	War risk only.
S/L.C.	Sue and Labour Clause.			W/T.	Wireless Telegraphy.
S/N.	Shipping Note.	U.S.C.G.	United States Coastguard.	W/W.	Warehouse warrant.
S.N.R.	Member of the Society for Nautical Research.			W.W.D.	Weather working days.
		U.S.N.	United States Navy.		
S.O.	Seller's option.	U.S.N.R.	United States Naval Reserve.	Y.A.R.	York–Antwerp Rules 1924.
S.O.L.	Shipowner's liability.				